T0314267

GLOBAL CALVINISM

GLOBAL CALVINISM

Conversion and Commerce in the Dutch Empire,
1600–1800

Charles H. Parker

Yale

UNIVERSITY

PRESS

New Haven & London

Published with assistance from the foundation established in memory of
Calvin Chapin of the Class of 1788, Yale College.

Yale University Press books may be purchased in quantity for educational,
business, or promotional use. For information, please email sales.press@yale.edu
(U.S. office) or sales@yaleup.co.uk (U.K. office).

Set in PostScript Electra and Trajan types by Westchester Publishing Services.
Printed in the United States of America.

Library of Congress Control Number: 2021944013
ISBN 978-0-300-23605-7 (hardcover : alk. paper)

A catalogue record for this book is available from the British Library.

This paper meets the requirements of ANSI/NISO Z39.48-1992 (Permanence of Paper).

10   9   8   7   6   5   4   3   2   1

To Jim Tracy

CONTENTS

Preface and Acknowledgments

This book weds two research themes that have animated my academic work throughout my career thus far: the Reformation in Europe and global interconnections in the early modern period. As a graduate student, I wrote a master's thesis and doctoral dissertation on topics pertaining to the social, cultural, and intellectual history of Calvinism. When, in the 1980s, I matriculated into the graduate program at the University of Minnesota to study the Reformation, I also happened to stumble quite accidentally into comparative early modern history just as the discipline of world history was taking off. The Center for Early Modern History sponsored exciting conferences on merchant empires, implicit ethnographies, religious conflict and accommodation, as well as other global topics that captivated my imagination. But at the time, I could not imagine how to study the Reformation from a world history perspective. After much reading, listening, and talking with colleagues in the field, it occurred to me about fifteen years later that I could study Protestants and world history by following Dutch Calvinists as they went out in the global sea lanes into Asia, Africa, and America to convert "pagans," "Moors," Jews, and Catholics. Many mentors, colleagues, and friends whom I am pleased to acknowledge taught me a great deal in conceptualizing, researching, and writing this book, but none more so than my PhD adviser, Jim Tracy. His own work connects early modern European history to global interactions. But more importantly, Jim's boundless curiosity, intellectual breadth, kind demeanor, and academic integrity have inspired me since I first met him in August 1987. *Global Calvinism* is dedicated to him.

The intellectual labor for this project was enveloped within deep folds of kindness, generosity, and erudition from many scholars and friends. I am deeply grateful for their contributions, though they have given far more than I can describe here. Joke Spaans and Henk Niemeijer have made numerous astute suggestions in conversations and correspondence over the last four years, and more recently they read the entire manuscript, offering a marvelously rich critique based on their profound expertise in early modern Dutch and colonial history. I am immensely appreciative of Simon Ditchfield, whose work on global Catholicism provided a way for me to think about a global Calvinism, and of Merry Wiesner-Hanks, who insisted that I had to write this book. Francesca Trivellato and Laurie Benton furnished excellent guidance in relating my interpretations to broader early modern patterns of empire building and proselytizing. Ulrike Strasser, Julia Schleck, Kaya Şahin, and Ahmet Karamustafa, along with a number of scholars at Summer Institutes sponsored by the National Endowment for the Humanities in 2013 and 2017, helped me understand more perceptively how global patterns of change enveloped Europe in the early modern period.

I am fortunate to work among an ambitious, learned, and warmly supportive community of scholars in St. Louis and at Saint Louis University. Many dear friends and colleagues gave me the benefit of their learning at critical times. Matthew Mancini, Lorri Glover, Damian Smith, Jen Popiel, and Silvana Siddali provided critical readings and feedback on early formulations of the project and on the book proposal to Yale University Press. My stalwart collaborators Claire Gilbert, Fabien Montcher, and Patrick O'Banion improved chapters and grant applications and, more importantly, engaged in ongoing conversations that have influenced my thinking on different levels. I am very fortunate to have them as colleagues and friends. Gretchen Starr-Lebeau, Nick Lewis, Annie Smart, David Hilditch, Colleen McCluskey, Toby Benis, and Sherry Lindquist have enriched my life and work in many ways. I regret that recently deceased friends Georgia Johnston, Michal Rozbicki, and Phil Gavitt did not see this book come to fruition. Participants in the early modern reading group at Washington University in St. Louis raised timely and important questions for me to think about in the book's early stages.

Other colleagues in the field of early modern history have figured significantly into this project. I am thankful to Ray Mentzer, Nick Terpstra, Ulinka Rublack, Julia Schleck, Simon Ditchfield, Mack Holt, Lee Wandel, Merry Wiesner-Hanks, and Joel Harrington for writing letters of recommendation for grants and fellowships that made research and writing of the book possible. Yudha Thianto, Henk van Nierop, Andrew Spicer, Paul Shore, and Leonard Blussé provided significant encouragement and counsel. Timo McGregor, Jim Tracy, Ulrike Strasser, Joke Spaans, and Henk Niemeijer corrected a number of my translations from Latin, Dutch, and German. Ahmad (Tommy) Pratomo gave both much-needed research assistance and invaluable orientation through the cumbersome visa bureaucracy in Jakarta.

A number of research institutions and funding agencies provided access to resources and afforded time to write. The National Endowment for the Humanities awarded me a yearlong fellowship in 2010–2011 that sponsored the initial foray into the Stadsarchief in Amsterdam, the Nationaal Archief in The Hague, the Zeeuwse Archief in Middelburg, Het Utrechts Archief in Utrecht, and the Special Collections at Leiden University's library. A short-term residential fellowship at the James Ford Bell Library at the University of Minnesota in the summer of 2012 opened the abundant collection of rare books there to me. Many thanks to the librarians, archivists, and staff members of these institutions— especially to Marguerite Ragnow at the Bell Library—for their extremely helpful and courteous service.

The College of Arts and Sciences and the Office of Vice President for Research at Saint Louis University contributed enormously to the production of *Global Calvinism*. The College bestowed on me the Eugene A. Hotfelder Professorship of Humanities from 2010 to 2016, which reduced teaching responsibilities and funded travel to conduct research at the Arsip Nasional Republik Indonesia in spring 2016. The Research Office helped significantly with financial support for a residential stay at the Institute for Advanced Study in 2019– 2020 as well as funding for the maps and final formatting. Deans (Michael Barber, SJ, Chris Duncan, Mike Lewis, Donna Lavoie), department chairs (Phil Gavitt, Michal Rozbicki, Tom Finan), research officers (Ken Olliff, Matthew Christian, David Borgmeyer, and Ann Scales), department administrators (Kelly Goersch, Chris Pudlowski), and librarians (Martha Allen, Dave Cassens, Jamie Emery, Jenny Lowe) gave unstinting and enthusiastic support for which I am extremely grateful.

A fellowship as the Felix M. Gilbert member in the School for Historical Studies at the Institute for Advanced Study provided an exceptionally stimulating and supportive environment to complete the writing and final revisions of the book. I am truly indebted to Francesca Trivellato for organizing the early modern seminar and giving amazing intellectual leadership. The final drafts of several chapters benefited immensely from the comments, critiques, and questions of Suzanne Akbari, Laurie Benton, Nicola di Cosmo, Matt Kadane, Daniel Hershenzon, Eleanor Hubbard, Jonathan Israel, Deirdre Loughridge, Beth Plummer, Lisa Regazzoni, Andrew Sartori, Gabriela Soto Laveaga, Justin Stearns, Daniel Strum, and Cordell Whitaker. Thanks also to the extremely supportive staff and librarians who took on my challenges as their own.

The editorial leadership of Jaya Chatterjee, acquisitions editor at Yale University Press, greatly enhanced the scope and quality of this book. She encouraged me to develop this project, gave me the opportunity to pose it to the press, and lent guidance at important points in the writing and review processes. I am gratified to have had the opportunity to work with her and honored to have my work published by Yale University Press. My thanks also extend to external reviewers who made a number of important suggestions and pointed out needed corrections. Eva Skewes proved to be extremely valuable in leading me through the final process of formatting the manuscript according to the press's guidelines. Gerry Krieg of Krieg Mapping gained my sincere appreciation for drawing the maps expertly and efficiently. Rachel E. Martens was invaluable in undertaking the final formatting and proofreading of the manuscript, and Anne Canright was simply amazing with the copy editing.

Vandenhoeck & Ruprecht kindly gave me permission to publish excerpts of "The Seduction of Idols: Dutch Calvinist Readings of Worship and Society in Seventeenth-Century Asia," in *Semper Reformanda: John Calvin, Worship, and Reformed Traditions*, ed. Barbara Pitkin (Amsterdam: Vandenhoeck & Ruprecht, 2018), 163–84, in chapter 3. De Gruyter permitted the use of material in "Languages of Salvation: Translating Christianity in the Global Reformation," *Archiv für Reformationsgeschichte* 108 (2017): 202–11. Extracts from the following works were reprinted with permission by Cambridge University Press: "In Dialogue with the World: Hugo Grotius' Vision of Global Citizenship and Christian Unity," *Journal of Policy History* 27, no. 2 (2015): 364–81, in chapter 2; "Converting Souls across Cultural Borders: Dutch Calvinism and Early Modern Missionary Enterprises," *Journal of Global History* 8 (2013): 50–71, in chapter 3; and "'Better the Turk than the Pope': Calvinist Engagement with Islam in Southeast Asia," in *Protestant Empires: Globalizing the Reformations*, ed. Ulinka Rublack (Cambridge: Cambridge University Press, 2020), 177–95, in chapters 3 and 6.

Finally, works of scholarship are undertaken amid the ups and downs of one's own personal life. My family has given me the unsparing support, patience, and joy necessary for sustaining and completing such a protracted project. I am deeply thankful for the love and affection of my parents, Charles and Dolores Parker; my sister, Mandy; and especially my wife, Jean, my son, Drew, and my daughter-in law, Sandra. Their presence has blessed me immensely.

I should mention two choices of terminology used in the text. First, the overseas ministers that accompanied the Dutch East and West India companies acted as pastors and missionaries, who continually expressed their intention to convert non-Christian peoples. But they did not refer to themselves as *zendelingen* (missionaries), and they remained distinct from modern-day missionaries. *Predikanten* (ministers or preachers) in overseas Calvinist congregations conceived of missions with the state-sponsored churches of the post-Reformation period. In an effort to keep their efforts securely within the appropriate historical contexts, I use "missionary" in relation to them only when referring to their work or ambitions.

Second, I use "pagan" and "paganism" (without quotation marks hereafter) to refer to the Calvinist classification of non-Abrahamic religious traditions, practices, or elements thereof, including what we know today as Hinduism and Buddhism. "Heathen" seemed excessively pejorative and "gentile" overly vague, so I have avoided those terms unless quoting a source. Similarly, I have used "Moor" and "Moors" without quotation marks. In these cases, I certainly do not intend to revive condescending orientalist tropes; rather, my aim is to historicize the constructions Calvinists employed about non-Christian peoples in the Dutch commercial empire.

Finally, I have employed then-contemporary place names, such as Ceylon for Sri Lanka and Formosa for Taiwan, with the exception of villages and towns across the East Indies. The varied orthography for these locations necessitated a standard and modern nomenclature to enable readers to identify them. Alas, there is an exception to the exception, as I retained the then-current Amboina for Ambon Island.

GLOBAL CALVINISM

Introduction: Calvinism in the Dutch Empire

At the very end of the sixteenth century, Dutch merchants embarked on a commercial enterprise to Asia that transformed an unlikely confederation of towns and provinces into a cosmopolitan center of finance and international trade for over a hundred years. After several tragic missteps in the effort to find a mythic Arctic route, an expedition led by Cornelis de Houtman in April 1595 sailed around the Cape of Good Hope and into the Orient. In search of spices and outfitted with four ships and 240 crew members, the voyage was badly bungled, largely because of de Houtman's zeal and arrogance; most of the crew died of disease. For his part, de Houtman managed to alienate most of his men along the way, antagonize merchants and rulers in the East Indies, and underwhelm his investors in the Netherlands upon his return in 1597.[1] From this clumsy venture, however, other merchants, financiers, and overseas enthusiasts concluded that they could reach the East Indies, find their way home, and turn handsome profits. Within five years, syndicates merged to form the United East India Company in 1602 (*Vereenigde Oostindische Compagnie*, hereafter VOC) and just over twenty years later the West India Company in 1621 (*Geoctrooieerde Westindische Compagnie*, hereafter WIC). By midcentury the Dutch boasted a commercial empire stretching from Formosa to Brazil, which both reflected and enlivened the Dutch Republic in the 1600s. Despite an inauspicious beginning, overseas commerce enabled the Dutch to reap the world in the seventeenth and eighteenth centuries.

The fruits of this global odyssey were on display in the markets, shops, and neighborhoods of Dutch cities and towns. No European city epitomized this global, cosmopolitan ethos in the seventeenth century more than Amsterdam. On the south side of the harbor, just north of Dam Square, stood the large

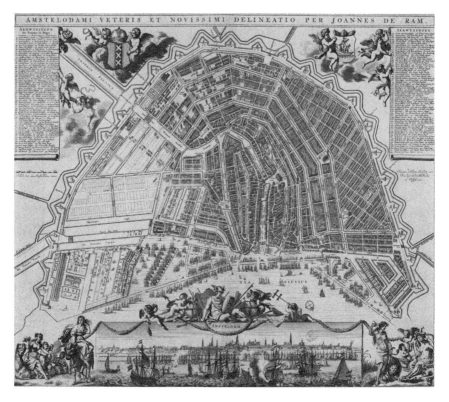

Fig. 1. Map of Amsterdam, possibly by Johannes de Ram (1683–1684);
Rijksmuseum Amsterdam

commodity exchange (*koopmansbeurs*) designed by Hendrik de Keyser that bore witness to the city's role in international finance and trade. In the interior court-yard merchants hawked tobacco, sugar, spices, silk, and beaver pelts, as European and Asian buyers from Spain, France, Persia, Anatolia, and other places haggled noisily over prices. In the industrial quarters eastward, the smell of nut-meg and pepper wafted across streets and canals from the East India House on Oude Hoogstraat near Dam Square. To the south at the site of a former convent lay the *Hortus Botanicus*, a medicinal herb garden created to cultivate plants with pharmacological properties collected from Asia and brought back on VOC ships. The great canal district in the heart of Amsterdam, including the Heren-gracht (Gentlemen's canal), Keizersgracht (Emperor's canal), and Prinsengracht (Prince's canal), showcased the fabulous homes of merchants and financiers such as Cornelis de Graeff, Jacob Cromhout, Cornelis Bicker, and Lodewijk and

Hendrik Trip, whose wealth derived from international finance, overseas trade, and war.[2]

Manifestations of global engagement in the Netherlands were not limited to Amsterdam. Both trading companies had directors who oversaw offices, known as chambers, outside Amsterdam: in Middelburg, Delft, Hoorn, Rotterdam, and Enkhuizen for the VOC and in Groningen, Middelburg, Hoorn, and Rotterdam for the WIC. Company warehouses dotted the outskirts of town, just as offices stood prominently in city centers displaying company flags. In Leiden, the botanist Carolus Clusius cleared space for a botanical garden long before the one in Amsterdam, and he worked with VOC officials to obtain plants from Asia and Africa. In Delft, artisans fashioned the famous blue Delftware after the style of Chinese porcelain imported into the Netherlands in the seventeenth century. Private collectors throughout the Netherlands assembled "cabinets of curiosities" filled with flora and natural objects they obtained from VOC and WIC personnel returning home.[3] Markets throughout Dutch cities lured townsfolk with goods from all over the world in the city squares of Middelburg, Delft, Haarlem, Utrecht, Groningen, and elsewhere. Consequently, Netherlanders could wear silk from China, plant tulip bulbs and drink coffee from Anatolia, smoke tobacco from Surinam, display tea services decorated with silver mined from Mexico, and flavor their food and drink with sugar, pepper, cinnamon, nutmeg, and cloves from Brazil, the East Indies, and Ceylon.

Just as importantly, the Dutch consumed news about peoples, landscapes, societies, and customs from around the world. Jan Huygen van Linschoten, who sailed to Asia in the service of the Portuguese, stirred the imaginations of readers in the Netherlands with his detailed maps and descriptions of sea routes, shorelines, and sandbanks in his famous travel account, *Itinerario* (1596). De Houtman himself, along with one of his captains, sought to publicize the exploits of the initial expedition and produced an account of strange peoples, animals, and landscapes in the Indies, which was published in Dutch, English, Latin, and German.[4] Writing the true untold story of exotic peoples, places, and things became a major literary genre for merchants, ministers, and mariners across the Dutch empire. Writers scrutinizing and describing the wider world took advantage of the booming market for books in the highly urbanized Dutch Republic. In 1600, approximately 68 publishers/printers were scattered across twenty cities in the Netherlands, ballooning to 247 operations in thirty-four cities by 1650. With 91 publishing firms, Amsterdam ranked as the leading hub of book production throughout Europe well into the eighteenth century. Dutch publishers churned out over 100,000 titles in the 1600s. Among this large corpus, Francisco Pelsaert, Wollebrant Geleynsen de Jongh, and Johan van Twist

Fig. 2. Nicolaes Maes (Dutch, 1634–1693), *The Account Keeper*, 1656;
oil on canvas, 26 × 21⅛ inches; Saint Louis Art Museum,
Museum Purchase 72:1950

wrote about India, Abraham Rogerius and Philip Baldaeus described paganism, Rijklof van Goens and Abel Tasman narrated their travels in the East Indies and Australia, and Willem Piso wrote about plants, animals, and disease in Brazil. Travel accounts and stories about Africa, Asia, and America proliferated in the Netherlands in the seventeenth century.[5]

In addition to the vast textual media, cartographers, printmakers, and painters created countless visual images of the world. Mapmakers and booksellers offered atlases, cartographic plates, woodcuts, and volume after volume of scenes, depictions, and descriptions of land and seascapes, animals, fish, plants, and people from around the world. In Amsterdam, a wealthy patron could purchase Abraham Ortelius's *Theater of the World* (*Theatrum orbis terrarum*, 1570) in the shop of Judocus Hondius, one of the most important cartographers of the late sixteenth and early seventeenth centuries. Similarly, the renowned Willem Janszoon Blaeu became the cartographer for the VOC and produced thousands of maps, which culminated in the massive *Atlas maior* between 1662 and 1672.[6] Even middling-rank families purchased paintings with global themes from the wide selection of artist workshops throughout the Netherlands. Hanging on the wall of Dutch homes were maps and visual accounts of people and animals from Brazil, India, Africa, and the East Indies. Nicolaes Maes's *The Account Keeper* (1656) evokes local Dutch commercial connections to the wider world. In this painting, a woman dozes while working on an account book; the chair in which she rests sits against a wood-paneled and white wall where a three-projection map of the world hangs. The goods of the world trickled back, down, and through the local shopkeeper in the Netherlands.

Netherlanders not only took in the world, but they went out into it as well. During the two-hundred-year lifespan of the East and West India Companies, thousands of personnel and settlers ventured into the global sea lanes. Dutch administrators, mariners, merchants, soldiers, ministers, workers, and settlers roamed the world, ranging from the East Indies to Formosa, Ceylon, the Malabar and Coromandel coasts, the Cape of Good Hope, Brazil, New Netherland, and Surinam, along with many other locales. The Dutch encountered the world, brought it back, and consumed it in the seventeenth and eighteenth centuries. In the process, the world transformed Dutch society.

PROTESTANTISM AND EUROPEAN EXPANSION

This book focuses on the mutual exchanges and influences resulting from Dutch participation in the global orbit of goods, peoples, and texts in the early modern period. Personnel employed by the trading companies and a number of settlers interacted directly with a wide range of peoples in Asia, Africa, and America in many different ways: economically through violent conflict, trade, and partnership; socially through coercion, enslavement, and accommodation; sexually through marriage, cohabitation, and predation; religiously through proselytization, pressure, and dialogue. These interactions not only left cultural footprints in colonial societies, but they also left their imprint on Dutch intellectual and religious currents in the early eighteenth century. This study explores these reciprocities by examining the intersection of religion and empire in the early modern period. For the Dutch, this inquiry means attending to the overlooked place of Calvinism in a paramount age of empire building, long-distance trade, migration, and proselytization. Reformed Protestants (Calvinists) occupied a central place in the increasingly globalized Dutch societies of the seventeenth and eighteenth centuries. In fact, the Netherlands emerged as the intellectual heartland of European Calvinism in the seventeenth century.

From the early 1600s to 1800—the period of the Dutch trading companies in Asia and the Americas—Calvinism also went global, as perhaps somewhere between eight hundred and a thousand *predikanten* (ministers or clergymen), abetted by hundreds of lay *ziekentroosteren* (also known as *krankbezoekeren* or visitors of the sick), and native proponents (nonordained, apprentice clergy) set up churches and schools seeking to convert pagans, Moors, Jews, and Catholics.[7] Dutch ministers traveling into overseas territories were first and foremost pastors sponsored by the companies to provide spiritual oversight to employees and their families. As the Dutch displaced the Portuguese in the East Indies, Ceylon, Brazil, and other locations, company officers sought to cultivate loyalty among natives, many of whom had undergone baptism at the hands of Jesuits and Franciscans, by bringing them over to the Reformed faith. Many ministers even went further to proselytize among pagans and Moors who had little exposure to Christianity. Dutch evangelizing efforts represented the first and most sustained endeavor by Protestants to convert peoples outside of Europe in the early modern period.

The Dutch East India Company pushed into the Moluccan Islands in the first decade of the 1600s and subsequently subdued the local principality of Jakarta on the island of Java in May 1619. Company directors in the Netherlands renamed the port city Batavia and made it the headquarters of their Asian operations. Governors allied with native forces to dislodge the Portuguese and British from a number of locations, setting up outposts across the shorelines of the Indian Ocean. The most substantial settlements included those in the East Indies (Java and the Moluccan Islands), Melaka (1641), Formosa (1624), Coromandel and Malabar coasts (1605–1650s), Ceylon (1638), and the Cape of Good Hope (1652). In the Atlantic, the West India Company established bases in New Netherland (1624), Brazil (1630), Curaçao (1634), Elmina (1637), Surinam (1667), and other stations in South America, the Caribbean, and West Africa.[8]

Calvinist congregations usually sprouted in due course after the companies planted a colonial outpost. Wherever possible, these congregations set up the basic offices and ministries of the Dutch Reformed Church. Consistories (the board of clergy and lay elders) governed the congregation, and diaconates (composed of deacons) distributed charity to the poor. Under the supervision of consistories, ministers preached the gospel, administered the sacraments, and exercised moral discipline over members. Schoolmasters, comprising *zieken-troosteren* from the Netherlands and indigenous teachers, taught catechism classes several times a week, and operated schools. *Predikanten* oversaw a considerable network of schools across the Dutch empire.[9]

The "Indies Zion" (*Indisch Sion*) became the commonplace moniker for the Dutch overseas churches in Asia, an appellation that signified an intent to construct a spiritual Jerusalem as a religious beacon to nonbelievers in non-Christian domains.[10] The Reformed Church in Batavia experienced significant growth among Asians and Eurasians, claiming a church membership of 2,300 by 1674.[11] In 1706, Batavia maintained 34 teachers for 4,873 children, Ceylon supported approximately 30 schools with 18,000 children in the late 1600s, and the company in Formosa also opened numerous schools.[12] By 1770, 240 churches, 300 indigenous teachers, and 15,000 church members were scattered across the East Indies, with several thousand more in Ceylon. The churches in South Africa were much smaller in the early eighteenth century, numbering several hundred congregants.[13] The most extensive proselytizing activity in the western sphere occurred in Brazil, which the Dutch took from the Portuguese in 1630, but lost back to them in 1654. In New Netherland, ministers spent most of their time waging campaigns against other Protestant groups, and significant evangelism never got off the ground in Surinam, Curaçao, or Elmina.[14]

Yet Calvinist missionary activity was far more consequential than slender membership rolls imply. Consistories maintained rigorous requirements for church membership, signified by the act of taking communion. Members first had to undergo religious education, demonstrate comprehension of teachings through an oral examination, and exhibit a lifestyle consistent with Calvinist morals. Nevertheless, pastors in many areas baptized people (and all recognized Catholic baptism) without holding them to the more strenuous standards for church membership. Thousands of children and adults were educated in church teaching and practiced the Reformed faith in some hybrid fashion, which ministers denounced as vestigial paganism or "Mohammedanism." Thus, Calvinist churches and schools exerted influence beyond those who qualified as church members. Furthermore, clergy collaborated with native linguists to transform oral dialects into written vernaculars, produced a large number of Reformed materials and books of the Bible in local languages, and trained hundreds of indigenous teachers who instructed children and adults in the Reformed faith. In addition, lay deacons managed orphans, poor funds, and other social services in almost every area of Dutch Reformed presence.

Crossing into foreign cultures and trying to produce Christians in societies with little or no exposure to Christianity vexed overseas ministers. Dutch clergy possessed no collective experience to help them navigate the cultural waters of many regions. Calvinists in Formosa, for example, contended with powerful female priests, *inibs*, who called down divine favor by consuming large amounts of alcohol, climbing on raised structures and stripping naked, and vomiting on their followers.[15] In such unfamiliar cultural contexts, what did it mean to be a Protestant Christian? In Europe, an individual had to understand at some level, and assent to, certain doctrinal beliefs, as well as to maintain a particular moral bearing. What must a Javanese, Tupi, or Ceylonese profess, let alone comprehend, to be counted a Christian? What behaviors reflected a genuine conversion in a non-Christian culture? For Calvinists, covenantal theology further complicated matters in that it conditioned the baptism of a child on Christian parentage. Could pastors baptize children of pagans and Muslims only if Reformed members adopted them?

Ongoing correspondence between parties at home and in colonial settlements, along with a burgeoning ethnographic literature, ensured that debates about religion and society in the Netherlands and in the maritime empire informed one another. The thought of Hugo Grotius—humanist, legal theorist, and theologian—bore the mark of engagement with the wider, non-European world. Through his classical training and consumption of ethnographic literature, Grotius learned about a diverse array of societies from the ancient and classical ages down to his present day. He pointed to well-ordered pagan societies in the past and in his own time that illustrated the workings of a balanced political order in which "the name of God is duly honored."[16] Such examples provided models to Christian commonwealths, showing that societies worked best when the civil ruler acted as God's agent. He was also quite cognizant of Dutch Protestant efforts at spreading the gospel in Asia and attempted to engage both a global and domestic audience simultaneously with an irenic, comprehensive vision of Christianity. In 1640 he published *On the Truth of the Christian Religion* (*De veritate religionis Christianae*), one of the first works written by a Protestant as an apologetic guide for Europeans who found themselves in overseas lands surrounded by enemies of Christianity.

Later in the century, Balthasar Bekker, a pastor of the Reformed Church in Amsterdam, drafted a controversial treatise, leading to his expulsion from the church, which argued that practices prosecuted as witchcraft in Europe were really nothing more than pagan superstitions. His *The Enchanted World* (*De betoverde weereld*), published in 1691, called upon Cartesian rationalism to make his case, but he also appealed to the witness of societies around the world. Attention to these societies revealed the global universality of pagan rituals and fables, not only in Asia and Africa, but in Europe as well. Because the Amsterdam church where Bekker served corresponded with all the overseas churches, he had access to firsthand descriptions of indigenous practices as well as the published accounts by missionaries and travelers. Thus, Bekker and Grotius signal that global religious encounters over time necessitated systemic intellectual adjustments within Reformed Protestant Christianity. It is no coincidence that some of the most far-reaching critiques of Christianity's claims to exclusive truth actually came from Dutch and French Protestants residing in Holland in the late seventeenth century.[17]

This study of Calvinism's entanglement in the Dutch empire has two basic aims. First, the analysis brings attention to the sustained Calvinist efforts at spreading a Reformed Protestant influence within the territorial confines of a commercial empire. Calvinist ministers joined the ranks of religious proselytizers and empire builders around the early modern world. Throughout most regions, a very diverse array of messengers, often in the service of imperial states, introduced religious systems into new lands. Catholic missionaries and colonizers converted thousands of Americans and Africans in the Atlantic world and planted congregations across India, China, Japan, and in the societies of maritime Southeast Asia. Emboldened by imperial and commercial expansion, Muslim merchants and Sufi divines pushed the prophet's message deeper into South and Southeast Asia, sub-Saharan Africa, and eastern Europe. Within the Ottoman, Safavid, and Mughal empires that encompassed the traditional heartlands of Islam, widespread efforts at internal consolidation took place that bear a general likeness to religious consolidation in western Europe.[18] These movements were integral to an intense period of global encounter in which a wide current of peoples, goods, texts, ideas, stories, and anxieties ricocheted across land and sea. Thus, Calvinism belongs to early modern world history.

Second, *Global Calvinism* contends that encounters with indigenous societies in the global age of expansion played a vital role in the development of European religious and intellectual history. The enterprise of bringing Christianity and civilization to peoples overseas offered Europeans a lens for viewing their own societies. A byproduct of the far-flung Dutch maritime empire was that Calvinist clergy and laity came into sustained contact with a remarkable variety of religious and cultural practices throughout the early modern world. These observances ranged from all sorts of traditional customs on the Cape of Good Hope, Formosa, Brazil, and New Netherland, to more institutional Islamic, Hindu, and Buddhist conventions across Southeast and South Asia. The sheer scope of these native societies and the wide diversity in their religious traditions confronted Calvinists in colonial societies and in European Reformed circles with an unprecedented array of pastoral, cultural, and intellectual problems.

Thus, the quest to understand the momentous changes in European history, such as the Reformation and Enlightenment, requires the perspectives of world history.

A CONNECTED HISTORY OF MISSIONS AND EMPIRE

Ever since Bartolomé de las Casas (the Dominican who championed the cause of native Americans) wrote *A Short Account of the Destruction of the Indies* in 1542, the topic of European "discovery" and exploration has generated competing narratives. Europeans in the eighteenth and nineteenth centuries idealized the Americas, heralded their own accomplishments in reconnoitering new worlds, and celebrated their mastery over other races. In the twentieth century, Europeans' pride in their cultural dominance gave way to guilt over their ruthlessness. Throughout this long history of writing about the place of America, and to a lesser extent Asia and Africa, within Europeans' imaginations, the prevailing storyline until the last thirty years or so has highlighted Western dominance. Certainly, Spanish, Portuguese, English, French, and Dutch colonization of the Americas and enslavement of millions of Africans provide ample evidence of a rise-of-the-West narrative. In recent scholarship, perhaps the most palpable articulation of this view has come from the modern world systems theory by Immanuel Wallerstein. In this schema, a handful of northern European countries—England, the Netherlands, France—rose as the core powers of a global capitalist structure that dominated commerce and labor beginning in the sixteenth and seventeenth centuries.[19]

While the world systems paradigm still captivates many who seek to explain the long-term effects of colonial hegemony, historians have pushed back against the notion that the West dominated the world in the early modern period. Outside of the Philippines and Cape of Good Hope, Europeans were confined to small fortified outposts in Asia and Africa. As Kenneth Pomeranz, R. Bin Wong, and others have demonstrated, the Qing dynasty in China and the Mughal empire in India remained as the prevailing economic and geopolitical powers in Eurasia into the 1700s. Even in the colonial Americas, the image of European conquest and dominance is much less straightforward than the traditional reading of Spanish and Portuguese bloodletting. The Tlaxcallan ruling council, for example, saw in Hernán Cortés and his small band of Castilian invaders an opportunity to topple the hated Aztec regime in Tenochtitlan and supplied substantial military support that brought down Montezuma's forces. Sexual liaisons between Castilian conquistadors and elite Mexican women helped integrate the foreigners into local social and political structures. Colonists, indigenous peoples,

Africans, criollos, mestizos, and others entangled themselves with one another in multitudinous and multifaceted ways, taking advantage of the fact that the oceans were wide and the king was far away.[20]

The effects of these encounters on Europeans in Europe have attracted sporadic attention, as historians took for granted Western domination in the early modern world. From the 1960s to the 1980s, Donald Lach and others catalogued the massive amount of data that Europeans acquired in their exploration of Asian societies. Despite all the information Lach uncovered about the European discovery of Asia, he did not offer conclusions about how Westerners understood this knowledge, aside from a general sense of wonder. That same expression of wonder and amazement emerges in the work of Stephen Greenblatt as a central theme in Europeans' depiction of their own sense of estrangement in the face of the unfamiliar peoples and lands of the Americas. Beyond an initial fascination at discoveries and explorations, it has been unclear how engagement with the wider world affected Europeans' outlook. In 1992, J. H. Elliott maintained that "the European reading public displayed no overwhelming interest in the newly discovered world of America." Rather, he pointed out that four times more books were published about the Turks and Asia than about peoples in the Americas.[21]

Within the last ten years, historians have begun to revise this assessment, as studies on quite different topics have zeroed in on the effects of globalizing tendencies in the early modern period on Europe. Several have emphasized the Netherlands as a portal through which ideas and goods moved. Lynn Hunt, Margaret Jacob, and Wijnand Mijnhardt, in *The Book That Changed Europe* (2010), for example, traced the influence of Jean Frederic Bernard and Bernard Picart's *Religious Ceremonies of the World* (*Cérémonies et coutumes religieuses de tous les peuples du monde*), contending that it "marked a major turning point in European attitudes toward religious belief and hence the sacred." Both men were Protestants who lived in Amsterdam; Bernard was also the publisher. Appearing between 1723 and 1737, the multivolume *Religious Ceremonies* contained 3,000 pages and 250 plates that depicted all the religious observances Europeans had identified at the time. Hunt, Jacob, and Mijnhardt argue that it "sowed the radical idea that religions could be compared on equal terms, and therefore that all religions were equally worthy of respect—and criticism."[22] Harold Cook's *Matters of Exchange* (2007) moved the time frame back into the seventeenth century and privileged the place of commerce—Dutch overseas commerce, in particular—in the emergence of empirical science in the study of medicine, nature, and financial exchange. Although Cook found little room for religion in his analysis, he makes the important point that the thesis of the German sociologist Max Weber led scholars down errant paths in evaluating the role of religion, specifically Calvinism, in the development of modern science. Weber famously posited that Calvinism's asceticism created the cultural ethos for the Western work ethic and material acquisitiveness. Later, other scholars layered on a few additional steps that ultimately, but erroneously, credited Calvinism with empirically based science.[23]

While Hunt, Jacob, and Mijnhardt rely on a single book to perform a great deal of heavy lifting—the changing of Europe—*Global Calvinism* illuminates the numerous and wide-ranging commentaries about peoples and practices around the world that preceded, encased, and extended beyond Bernard and Picart's *Religious Ceremonies*. Calvinist *predikanten* observed, reflected on, contextualized, and compared their environs, their work, their prospective converts, their backsliding neophytes, and their pagan, Moor, and Catholic enemies in thousands of pages of correspondence to Dutch brethren back home and in a few best-selling tomes. By examining these representations over a long period of time, it is possible to chart the effects of sustained interaction developmentally and reciprocally. Calvinist clergy also joined Cook's naturalists, physicians, administrators, and merchants in the East Indies, Formosa, Ceylon, Brazil, and other company outposts. The attempts by churchmen to make sense of local peoples by placing them in the context of biblical and classical history and by explaining why so frustratingly few of them converted to a deep Protestant faith carried far-reaching ramifications for theologians, philosophers, and naturalists in the Netherlands. Just as Cook showed the effects of overseas commerce on scientific ways of thinking, *Global Calvinism* points to the consequences of prolonged religious encounters on currents of knowing in the Netherlands and, by extension, Europe.

This study reconsiders a celebrated episode of early modern European history—the Reformation—in terms of interconnections with people outside Europe. To that end, *Global Calvinism* builds on recent innovations in world history, including Sanjay Subrahmanyam's notion of "connected history," to probe the unifying features of the early modern period. Subrahmanyam argued for connecting local affairs to global contexts, and he offered an example in the millenarian anxieties that coursed across many parts of Eurasia and America from the fifteenth through the eighteenth centuries. With increased travel by Europeans, Indians, Turks, Chinese, Persians, Afghans, and others, a burgeoning interconnectedness reshaped societies around the world. In Subrahmanyam's words, "The notion of 'early modern' is hence linked, if not directly, then in some important indirect respects, to a changed domain of global interaction that has to do with such diverse matters as the legacy of Chinggis Khan and Timur, the Counter-Reformation and its overseas drive to proselytize, as well as the so-called Voyages of Discovery."[24]

The prospects for a new way of thinking about early modern history have already yielded fruit in several fresh studies on empires and Catholic missions. Laura Hostetler, pulling from the perspective of connected history (*Qing Colonial Enterprise*, 2001), draws parallels between early modern European and Chinese ethnography, both in the service of empire. Similarly, Kaya Şahin's treatment of the Ottoman civil service (*Empire and Power in the Reign of Süleyman*, 2013) makes the case that empire formation across Eurasia shared many elements, including propagation of universal political theologies, centralization of bureaucracies, and adaptation in geopolitical strategies. In the realm of Catholicism, Luke Clossey's examination of Jesuit missionaries (*Salvation and Globalization in the Early Jesuit Missions*, 2008) illustrates that communication between various outposts on the frontier played a far more important role in proselytizing tactics than directives from church authorities in Europe. Karin Vélez's work on the diffusion of early modern Catholicism (*The Miraculous Flying House of Loreto*, 2018) provides an amazing treatment of the shared meanings among multiple communities around the Atlantic world that both connected and distinguished them across space and time. Taking Huron appropriation of the Virgin of Loreto as a case in point, she aptly notes that "Hurons became central to a new 'image' . . . independent of the original Italian shrine."[25] Even more directly to the point of the present study, Simon Ditchfield in many publications has argued that missionary experiences with native peoples in Asia and America were quite suggestive for priests in Europe who were trying to Christianize "the other Indies" of outlying rural communities.[26]

Despite this rich vein of investigation, historians have only lately begun to consider the Protestant Reformation within the framework of global approaches. Historians of the Netherlands have actually taken the initiative in this line of inquiry by examining Protestants' overseas aspirations. Hendrik Niemeijer, Ad Biewenga, and Jur van Goor have produced excellent detailed studies of Dutch Calvinists in Batavia, the Cape of Good Hope, and Ceylon, respectively. More recently, D. L. Noorlander has shown the strong influence of Calvinism in the WIC's imperial agenda, Arthur Weststeijn has illustrated the spiritual hopes that overseas colonies represented for a variety of Protestants, and Andrew Spicer has described the architectural design of Dutch churches in Asia.[27]

The long-standing view in general scholarship has cast Protestant missions before the pietistic revival of the late eighteenth century as inconsequential and irrelevant. Mainline historians, such as Charles Boxer in his classic treatment of the Dutch empire, dismissed Calvinist missionary efforts as unimpressive. Subsequent historians agreed that Calvinists failed to make much of any lasting impression among native societies for a combination of two basic reasons.

First, historians argued that the commercial and imperial priorities of northern European trading companies ran counter to proselytizing. It has become a truism that the VOC's and WIC's drive for profits severely restricted ministers' ability to make Christians. Second, scholars focused on the incongruities between the theological assumptions of Protestant Christianity and the religious cultures in indigenous societies. James Axtell's treatment of Puritan missionary endeavors in North America focused on the futility of acculturating native peoples to Protestant customs. Similarly, other analyses of Protestant missions in New England have drawn attention to the fruitless efforts of pastors to Europeanize natives in preparation for conversion.[28]

This study seeks to show the importance of Calvinism and its missionary aims throughout the Dutch empire. Indeed, the trading companies did give precedence to profits, proselytizing efforts were far smaller in scope than Catholic missions, and Protestants were loath to accommodate much in the way of indigenous religious customs (even though at times compromise was unavoidable). Yet to conclude that trading company officers were somehow secular, in contrast to the zealous religiosity of Catholic empire builders, imposes a modern, anachronistic dichotomy between profane and spiritual that Dutch mariners, merchants, and missionaries did not comprehend. Certainly, company officials favored profits above all else, but only infrequently did they see that priority as being in conflict with the aspiration to spread Protestant Christianity among native peoples. Similarly, to judge Calvinist understandings of religious conversion and culture by Catholic perspectives and strategies necessarily distorts the intentions and outcomes of Dutch efforts. Finally, to evaluate Calvinist missions as unsuccessful in converting large numbers of non-Europeans fails to understand conversion as Dutch overseas ministers and even company personnel conceived it in the seventeenth and eighteenth centuries. *Global Calvinism* presents Dutch Protestant missions on their own early modern terms in the contexts of a confessional public church and a commercial empire.

An examination of Calvinism in the context of early modern global interactions necessitates a varied and extensive combination of primary sources. One important source is the voluminous correspondence between the regional church districts known as classes (singular classis) of Amsterdam and Walcheren, the synods of North and South Holland, and the consistories of congregations overseas. *Predikanten*, with the support of lay elders, composed regular accounts of activities and concerns, yet wrote more frequently in times of heightened confusion, disagreement, or crisis. Accompanying these descriptions were detailed quantitative summaries of baptisms, marriages, congregants, and students enrolled in schools. Dutch representatives responded to these reports and related the major developments taking place in Europe, forming a long-distance and slow-motion conversation about the state of affairs across the Reformed world. These letters give insight into the ways in which Reformed leaders thought about and took action on matters of interest and unease. Church and company records from overseas communities constitute a second key source. Consistory and diaconal records from the East Indies, Ceylon, Formosa, Melaka, Cape Town, and Brazil, as well as edicts and other records issued by colonial authorities, document the sustained Calvinist engagement with indigenous peoples.[29]

Finally, the wide-ranging ethnographic literature, including missionary accounts and treatises, forms a vital means for comprehending how Europeans responded to and represented other peoples. A large body of criticism has injected an ample dose of caution into the use of ethnographic materials. Scholars today cannot take this literature at face value as faithful accounts of native societies. As is the case with all sources, bias runs through ethnographies; European writers in particular projected images of indigenous peoples in keeping with their imperial and missionary programs. Yet even these projections, when interrogated carefully, can reveal a great deal about European perceptions and agendas. Although the scarcity of native sources limits the extent to which we can access native voices, by reading against the grain of these European sources and taking into consideration theoretical work that incorporates the insights of anthropology, we can to some extent mitigate the one-sided nature of the documentation. World history must be a collaborative undertaking. Thus, in addition to these primary materials, the flourishing scholarship on relevant parts of the world and on Catholic, Muslim, and other religious traditions offers a basis for making comparisons and connections in the early modern world.[30]

The global reach of Dutch Calvinism, therefore, offers a unique opportunity to analyze the influence of a Protestant faith and moral outlook in the service of commercial empire and the effects of that engagement on intellectual currents in Europe. This study borrows from the perspective of connected history to present a very different interpretation of Calvinist encounters overseas. Connected history can help us break through the customary bifurcation of the West from the rest of the world, a deeply embedded outlook that has affected historical scholarship for too long. Historians have traditionally treated the Protestant Reformation and European expansion largely as unrelated developments. Thus, the pietistic revivalist movements, the struggles between orthodox and liberalizing parties, and the creeping skepticism that separated faith from rationality all appear to have emerged out of exclusively European historical developments. But as the case of the seventeenth-century Dutch Republic illustrates, people in the early modern period did not think in the bifurcated prejudices of nineteenth- and twentieth-century scholarship. This engagement with the world was especially true in the Netherlands, which invested so much financial and cultural capital in overseas enterprises and constantly absorbed itself with the world beyond Europe.[31] Not only did trading companies remain a vital concern for a wide swath of society, but ethnographers wrote about strange peoples, cartographers mapped global spaces, and vendors retailed goods in open markets. People consumed spices and silks; they read travel accounts, purchased paintings, and pored over maps. Perceptions of the worlds beyond Europe not only made a deep impression on leading figures such as Grotius and Bekker, but they also figured significantly into the major religious and intellectual currents that flowed into the Enlightenment. Is it any wonder that the initial conflicts surrounding skepticism, rationality, and revelation played themselves out so publicly and so extensively in the Netherlands and in the Dutch Reformed Church?

CALVINISM IN GLOBAL CONTEXTS

Following globe-trotting Dutch Calvinists in service of the trade companies plunges us into a jumbled, violent realm of empire, commerce, war, enslavement, and religious conflict. Their journeys and experiences reveal the important roles that Calvinism and its practitioners played in the functions of a commercial empire in the early modern period. Spreading Protestant Christianity into the lands of pagans and Moors and countering the imperial might of Catholic powers infused divine meaning into the Dutch commercial empire. Company officers and church figures regularly praised the opportunity that empire and commerce provided for "propagating the faith of our Lord Jesus Christ in the lands of the heathens and Moors."[32] This expression was not empty rhetoric, but reflected a deeply seated conviction that they lived at a crucial moment in the unfolding of the divine plan for history in which the true Christian gospel was going out to all ends of the earth before the second coming of Christ. Not all company directors or overseas pastors championed this missionary enterprise, yet they all, as Noorlander has pointed out, feared God's wrath.[33]

This book argues that a distinctly Calvinist sense of missionary purpose animated the ethos of the Dutch commercial empire for much of the 1600s, before waning in the early eighteenth century. This perspective permitted Reformed theologians and *predikanten* to revise their stance on enslavement in the 1620s and 1630s. Before, Dutch Calvinists depicted slave trading as a manifestation of Spanish/Portuguese, and not coincidentally Catholic, cruelty foisted on native peoples. But after the conquest of the clove-yielding Banda Islands and sugar-producing plantations in Brazil, Calvinist churchmen justified enslavement as a means to Christianize peoples and save them from the much more oppressive slavery of Muslims and Catholics.[34] Even though the claims belied reality, Calvinism gave missionary cover for the companies' labor strategies.

Calvinism served the Dutch empire in other important institutional ways as well. The regulation of morals through a protocol of religious discipline, for which Reformed churches in Europe were well known, helped to engender a Christian social order in colonial societies. Calvinist consistories labored consistently to regulate sexuality and marriage and crack down on vice and disorder. By calling for the destruction of all other religious sites and the observance of Sabbath rest and worship, ministers sought to reorder space and time according to Reformed Protestant standards.[35] That church officials seldom succeeded in these efforts does not negate the fact that Calvinism served the companies' imperial and commercial interests. Calvinist deacons picked up colonial detritus by providing a modicum of social welfare to orphans, widows, and the most dispossessed in company territories.

Attention to Calvinists at work overseas also gives us insight into the problems and possibilities generated by the attempted indigenization of Protestant Christianity outside the cultural framework it originated. Only a small, in some areas very small, percentage of non-Europeans became full-fledged church members, signified by taking communion at Sunday services between four and six times a year. Consistories in many territories, though notably not Batavia, followed a policy referred to as "dividing the sacraments."[36] This meant the local people and their children could receive baptism, yet were denied communion until they passed an examination of their knowledge of Calvinist teachings and exhibited a European Protestant lifestyle. Although many never took the additional step to become a member, many thousands underwent baptism, attended schools, listened to sermons, and studied catechism lessons in Dutch territories. Thus, they participated at some level in many aspects of church life, but not as a communicant. In overseas territories, *predikanten* also counted baptized noncommunicants in their registers in ways that indicate that church figures regarded them as belonging to the Christian community. These accommodations complicate our assumptions about religious conversion. Calvinists wrestled with the relationship between religion and culture in ways that are reminiscent of the notorious controversies surrounding the Jesuits and Confucian and Hindu rites.

As Dutch *predikanten* sought to indigenize Calvinism around the world, a number of them collaborated with local linguists to translate religious media into regional dialects. The language work overseas among all missionaries paralleled the transformation of "national" vernaculars in Europe. Around the world in the sixteenth and seventeenth centuries, linguists were constructing written, phonetic-based vernaculars from oral dialects. Catholic missionaries produced written translanguages, such as Nahuatl in Mexico, Quechua in Peru, Kikongo in Kongo, Tupian in Brazil; the Dutch fashioned Sinhala and Tamil in Ceylon, Sinkan in Formosa, and Malay in the East Indies.[37]

The challenges of finding an appropriate linguistic medium to communicate Christian teachings sometimes caused intense debates among ministers. The intensity derived in part from competing principles at stake that came to a head in programs of conversion across cultures. Both Catholic and Protestant missionaries desired to make Christianity comprehensible to people in languages and in cultural references they understood without compromising doctrinal purity. Balancing these demands frequently set ministers against one another in disputes that played themselves out around the world from the late sixteenth through the eighteenth centuries.

Calvinist entanglements in empire building and in church planting also left an indelible mark on European thought and culture. The Dutch residing in Asia, Africa, and America had much to explain to themselves and to audiences back home. Over the course of the seventeenth and eighteenth centuries, they composed voluminous descriptions of contemporary societies that historians have mined for ethnographic import. *Predikanten* in the field and religious writers back home also produced comprehensive historical narratives to explain how pagan peoples had multiplied, migrated, and evolved since the Fall. Writers employed a biblical and historical frame of reference to make sense of this wider world they were experiencing at close range. For example, Abraham Rogerius, a minister in India and the East Indies, published *The Open Door to Hidden Heathendom* (*De open-deure tot het verborgen heydendom*, 1651) to expose the dark secrets that Hindu priests used to dupe their people and keep them in subjection to idols.[38] Approximately twenty years later, another *predikant*, Philip Baldaeus, wrote a similar work that linked the fables of ancient pagans with superstitious practices in South Asia. Noting similar elements in pagan stories, he maintained that "the Indians here produced a coarser and clumsier version of idolatry" than the Greeks and Romans.[39]

In the Netherlands, theologians and other thinkers also struggled to make sense of all the religious customs around the world and how they had developed historically. The Arminian theologian Gerardus Vossius published a large compendium of gentile theology that followed in the Neoplatonic teaching of *prisca theologia* that tracked all pagan beliefs back to a single ancient system of thought. From an orthodox Calvinist perspective, Johannes Hoornbeeck, a theologian at the University of Utrecht, attempted a similar project of classifying all the different types of contemporary pagans from those groups described in the Old Testament.[40] These are but a few examples of undertakings in the mission field and in the Netherlands to explain the world that Reformed Protestants were trying to engage.

To account for global Calvinism, chapter 1 provides an integrated overview of the Reformation in the Netherlands and its commercial empire from the revolt against Spain to the fall of the Republic to French forces in 1795. The following three chapters focus on Calvinism's involvement in Christian missions and empire building in the VOC and WIC. Chapter 2 examines the ways in which overseas ministers and church figures in the Netherlands both collaborated with empire building initiatives and conflicted with them. Chapter 3 analyzes Calvinist understandings of conversion and the strategies clergy put in place to bring non-Christian and nominally Catholic peoples to a Reformed Protestant faith. This analysis also focuses on the perspectives of indigenous peoples in their encounters with ministers and company representatives. Chapter 4 explores the VOC's language policy, the translation of religious texts by *predikanten* and native linguists, and the conflicts over culture and communication that ensued. Chapters 5 and 6 return primarily to the Netherlands and turn attention to how Dutch Calvinists and Protestant intellectuals made sense of the wider world. Chapter 5 investigates metahistorical religious narratives composed to understand Calvinism and its place in this newly expanded world. Finally, chapter 6 points to the new ways of thinking that became engrafted into Calvinism and its critics by the eighteenth century.

1

CHRIST, THE FATHERLAND, AND THE COMPANY

Contemporaries inside and outside of the Netherlands puzzled over the remarkable changes in fortune for the Dutch maritime provinces of Holland and Zeeland in the 1600s. Johannes de Laet, a founder of the West India Company, echoed a widely held Dutch Protestant sentiment that their commercial blessing came from the hand of God.[1] "Only the good God must be thanked and praised," he wrote, for the defeat of the Portuguese in Brazil, the success of the company, and the prosperity enjoyed by Netherlanders.[2] While few, if any, people beyond the northern Netherlandish provinces ascribed Dutch success to divine favor, observers from other lands did find their achievements rather extraordinary. The English physician and diplomat William Aglionby noted in 1671 that "the Netherland Provinces have rendred [sic] themselves so conspicuous and considerable amongst the other states of Europe that the sole mentioning of them might suffice to awaken the attention, and invite the regards of all persons."[3] Josiah Child, governor of the English East India Company, found much to admire in Dutch trade and finance.[4] Yet such admiration was usually grudging, since the Dutch made many enemies in the pugilistic early modern world. About the same time, Rijklof van Goens, governor general of the VOC, noted that "[t]here is nobody who wishes us well in the Indies, yea we are deadly hated by all nations."[5]

Historians, too, have found the Dutch Republic and its mercantile empire a fascinating enigma, as they have sought to explain its striking ascent into a "golden age" in the seventeenth century and its gradual demise in the eighteenth. Yet perhaps because of the complexities of the period, studies of the Dutch empire and Reformation have tended to isolate constituent parts of an organic whole. The fragmented narratives have resulted in the neglect of interconnections between Calvinism at home and abroad and entanglements between commerce, empire, and mission. To illustrate these key linkages, this chapter provides an integrated overview of the development of the Dutch Republic, Calvinist mission, and commercial empire. As Dutch merchants and ministers sought to translate their visions in new overseas contexts, they interwove the threads of state building, religious proselytizing, and commercial trading in five distinct phases from the late sixteenth through the eighteenth centuries.

ON THE ROAD TO EMPIRE AND MISSION, 1560s–1620s

This unusual empire that captured the attention of contemporaries and historians grew out of three events that converged at the end of the sixteenth century: the political revolt against Spain, the religious reformation against Catholicism, and the commercial launch of a maritime empire. From the 1560s to the 1620s, religious reformation and war for independence from Spain became embroiled in a global commercial rivalry with all European maritime powers, but chiefly with Portugal. The society that emerged by the early seventeenth century in the northern seven provinces was a decentralized republic led by the commercially driven counties of Holland and Zeeland and ordered by a strident brand of Reformed Protestantism. Thus, the particular articulations of commerce and religion in the Netherlands, forged by war with Spain and Portugal, shaped the global reach of the Dutch Republic and its Calvinist churches.

POLITICAL REVOLT AND RELIGIOUS REFORMATION

In the 1560s, Philip II, the Hapsburg king of Spain, put these forces into motion by seeking to impose strict political, religious, and fiscal controls over his Netherlandish dominions. Elite families in Dutch towns and provinces had long thrived in a highly regionalized political environment; consequently, the centralizing trajectory of the Spanish regime provoked deep hostility among them. These parties came together between 1566 and 1568 to defend local interests and ultimately to rebel against Hapsburg authority altogether.

At the same time, Protestant activists influenced by the teachings of John Calvin and other leaders in the Reformed tradition were spreading their message of reformation across Dutch provinces from Flanders and Brabant in the south to Holland, Zeeland, and Friesland in the north. These Calvinists formed a small but potent movement and created a conspicuous visible presence through open-air "hedge-sermons." Reformers advocated a biblical faith that stressed the sovereignty of God in salvation, demanded moral discipline enforced by church leaders, and roundly rejected the "idolatrous" worship and priesthood of the Roman Catholic Church. To combat this heresy and political sedition, Philip II expanded the number of bishops in the Netherlands from four to fourteen and dramatically increased the number of inquisitors in the provinces.[6] For Dutch nobles and urban magistrates, both of whom showed little enthusiasm for militant Catholicism, these measures violated the assortment of local privileges that they had gained over a long period of time.[7]

Even though most Dutch people were not Protestant, let alone Calvinist, almost all despised the overbearing reprisals of Hapsburg authorities. The combination of religious conviction among a fervent few and a feeling of national insult among a larger populace swelled a powerful tide of anti-Spanish feeling throughout the Netherlands. Active resistance originated from an alliance of Dutch nobles, called Beggars, led by Willem of Orange and supported by zealous Calvinists. After six years of trouble from 1566 to 1572—including widespread iconoclasm, Spanish occupation, harsh military tribunals, and severe taxes—Beggar forces achieved a pivotal victory in the spring and summer of 1572 by invading and subduing most of the chief cities in the province of Holland.[8] Dutch forays and Hapsburg counterattacks in the 1560s and 1570s eventually mired the Low Countries in a struggle for political independence that lasted until the end of the Thirty Years War in 1648. Portugal and its colonies came under the authority of the Spanish crown from 1580 to 1640, which also had the effect of militarizing the enmity between the Dutch and the Lusitanians in the Atlantic and Indian oceans.

In return for their unremitting opposition to Spain, Calvinists gained far-reaching political concessions from rebel leaders. As the northern seven provinces formally pulled away from Spain at the 1579 Union of Utrecht, delegates recognized the Reformed Church as the public church for the provinces of Holland and Zeeland. Gradually the other five provinces followed suit, with Groningen becoming officially Calvinist in 1594.[9] Despite its exclusive status, the Reformed Church was a voluntary body because the Union of Utrecht also guaranteed freedom of conscience in the Netherlands. Freedom of conscience, however, did not entail freedom of religion; civil authorities secularized church property, abolished the Mass, and relegated not only Catholics but also Lutherans, Mennonites, and other Protestants to the margins of society. Catholicism, however, was singled out as particularly harmful to the Republic, leading provincial and national authorities to issue penal codes against priests and Catholic worship. The success of the revolt against Spain enabled Calvinism to gain an abiding influence over Dutch society and culture in the seventeenth century.

Fig. 3.

TRADE AND RELIGION

During the conflict, merchants in Holland and Zeeland sought to take advantage of fluctuations in the market for spices in northern Europe to expand their trading presence in the Mediterranean.[10] Portuguese merchants in Lisbon and Antwerp—the entrepôt of northern Europe—had controlled the market for pepper and fine spices (cinnamon, nutmeg, mace, and cloves) since the early 1500s. The war with Spain did disrupt routes from Antwerp into the northern provinces and Germany in the 1570s and 1580s, and a critical reversal of fortune occurred in August 1585 when Beggars blockaded the Scheldt River estuary, severing Antwerp from international trade.

Antwerp's loss was Amsterdam's gain. Dutch merchants, many of whom had fled war and repression in the Hapsburg-controlled provinces of the Southern Netherlands, expanded beyond the long-standing trade of bulk grain from the Baltic into luxury goods (olive oil, wine, and fine spices) from the Mediterranean. The Dutch saw an opening in the spice market, as demand for pepper remained strong during the 1500s because of Portugal's inability to import a sufficient supply from India and the East Indies.[11] Dutch plans for an integrated and wide-ranging commercial strategy ran into a roadblock in Lisbon, where Portuguese merchants banned their religious, commercial, and political enemies from the spice market.[12] The chance to diversify trade across Europe, combined with the denial to deal in the Lisbon market, prompted Dutch mariners, cartographers, financiers, and merchants in Amsterdam in the 1590s to devise a way to access spices at their points of origin. These efforts, after several misfortunes looking for a northwest passage around Scandinavia, ultimately propelled Cornelis de Houtman around the Cape of Good Hope and into the Indian Ocean.

Dutch Reformed clergy and lay religious partisans ranked among the most enthusiastic supporters not only of war with Spain and Portugal, but also of long-distance trade. Imperial powers (with the exception of China) in the early modern period uniformly institutionalized their religion in territories that came under their control. Yet at the end of the sixteenth century, Dutch geopolitical strategies for advancing trade, including possible territorial conquest, were far from clear. England became the only other country to launch government-backed trading companies at the time, yet none of the syndicates, to the chagrin of Anglican clergy, made the conversion of non-Christians a priority.[13] In the Dutch case, however, influential ministers such as Pieter Plancius, Jacob Arminius, Godefridus Udemans, and Werner Helmichius, along with lay leaders including Reiner Pauw, Johannes de Laet, and Walich Syvaerts, linked Christian missions with overseas commerce.[14] From the beginning, Calvinist overseas missions was tightly interlaced with geopolitical hostility toward Spain and Portugal and with commercial opportunity. The overlapping ambitions for overseas commerce and missions cemented alliances between merchants and Calvinist *predikanten* that led to the formation of monopolistic trading companies staffed with clergy who within a few years expanded their duties into missionary efforts.

TRADE AND EMPIRE

The costs and hazards created by uncoordinated long-distance ventures by small partnerships in hostile waters led to the formation of monopolistic trading companies in the first two decades of the 1600s. Competing *voorcompanieën* (syndicates or protocompanies) from the 1590s merged into larger, better-financed trading companies operating in far-northern, Atlantic, and Asian theaters from 1600 to 1621. During the first two decades of the seventeenth century, the States General approved the charters of the Guinea Company (1600–1621), the Northern Company (1614–1642), and the New Netherland Company (1614–1618), along with the East India (1602–1799) and the West India companies (1621–1674, 1675–1792).[15]

The launch of the East India Company (VOC) into Asian waters signified the most far-reaching commercial undertaking. On March 20, 1602, the States General conferred an exclusive charter for trade in Asia from the Cape of Good Hope to the Straits of Magellan for twenty-one years. According to the charter, the *Heren XVII* (seventeen directors) from four chambers oversaw all operations. In its first two decades, the VOC transitioned from a company seeking spices at their points of production into a commercial imperial power in Asia. The mercantilist outlook of European political and financial elites in this period of global expansion embraced war as a strategy for commercial leverage. Certainly kingdoms across Southeast Asia engaged in conflict to advance trading interests, yet the Portuguese had raised the stakes and level of violence in the early sixteenth century. Afonso de Albuquerque and other admirals introduced the European tradition of armed trading in the Indian Ocean, fortifying control over trade in strategic locations and demanding all vessels carry *cartazes* (permission passes) to sail. Later in the seventeenth century, English and French companies opened fortified trading factors to protect their interests and harass their rivals.[16] The Dutch *voorcompanieën*, which had plied the waters around the East Indies in the late 1500s, tried to avoid armed conflict, yet the VOC's charter rejected this approach as unworkable in light of hostilities with the Portuguese and Southeast Asian rulers.[17]

Granted the right to raise armies, build forts, and negotiate contracts, the VOC gained the capabilities to press its claims and defend itself from rivals in rapidly changing circumstances. Two years earlier, in 1600, Queen Elizabeth I granted a monopoly among English merchants for trading in Asia to the newly formed English East India Company (hereafter EIC). Yet at its founding, the EIC, unlike the VOC, could not sign treaties, take land, or build forts, though over the course of the 1600s the English company acquired these powers.[18] For its part, VOC admirals put their prerogatives to work right away. In 1605, the admiral Steven van der Hagen allied with the raja of Hitu in an improvised attack and capture of Amboina and two years later joined with the sultan of Ternate against the Portuguese. Later in the century, the company gained control of Tidore (1666) from the Spanish, Makassar (1669) from the sultan of Gowa, and Banten

(1682) from the English. During this time, van der Hagen struck trading deals with the rulers of the Ternate, Amboina, and Banda island groups committing them to sell spices only to the "Hollanders" and not merchants of any other "nation."[19] Taking control of Fort Victoria on the island of Amboina, the VOC made it the center of operations until 1619. From these victories, the company sought to impose a monopoly over the "spice islands" that produced almost all of the world's supply of nutmeg, mace, and cloves, though this ambition remained out of reach for several decades.[20]

Enforcing a monopoly on spices in the East Indies committed the Dutch to the bellicose realm of commercial empire. From their base in Melaka since 1511, Portuguese merchants continued to vie for pepper and fine spices, just as English operations continued in Banten, Makassar, and the Banda Islands. Local merchants and rulers also fought for their own leverage in the aggressive commercial environment. In 1607, for example, Bandanese *orangkaya* (trading elites) ambushed and killed forty-seven Dutch personnel, including the admiral Pieter Verhoeven.[21] In light of ongoing hostilities and trade violations, the *Heren XVII* ultimately acquiesced to VOC commanders who advocated a robust military approach to controlling markets. The directors in the Netherlands settled on a mercantilist program to deploy as much force as necessary to achieve company objectives. The *Heren XVII* appointed Pieter Both in 1610 as the first governor general of the VOC. Along with a *Politieke Raad* (Political Council), Both managed all aspects of the company's maneuverings from Asia until succeeded by Gerard Reynst in 1614. The strategy of endowing a mercantile commander on the scene enabled the VOC to adapt quickly to changing situations far from home. During the 1600s, governors of the English East India Company came to acquire a great deal of local authority as well. Initially, the board of directors in London played the leading role in directing operations.[22] Because the exchange of letters from Southeast Asia to Amsterdam or London took anywhere between sixteen and eighteen months, the VOC's reliance on governor generals also handed over, for good and ill, practical control of operations to these political, military, and financial officers.[23]

The governor general Jan Pieterszoon Coen arose as the strongest advocate of force to achieve commercial and geopolitical objectives. Perhaps as much as any VOC officer at the time, Coen recognized and even embraced the mutual relationship between commerce and combat. He wrote to the *Heren XVII* in 1614 "that we cannot carry on trade without war nor war without trade."[24] Coen reasserted monopolistic control over the spice trade in the Moluccan and Banda Islands and wrested control of Banten (temporarily) and Jakarta from the English and the local Muslim prince, Pangeran Wijayakrama. When Coen learned that *orangkaya* in Banda were selling cloves to the English in violation of trade contracts with the Dutch, Coen led an expedition, joined by Japanese mercenaries, and invaded the Banda Islands in 1621, killing or chasing off many natives.[25] He subsequently imported slaves to cultivate spice crops. Two years after the invasion of Banda, Herman van Speult, VOC governor of Amboina, feared that the English (and Japanese) were going to overthrow Dutch rule on the island. He had a number from the English encampment arrested and tortured, which produced confessions to a conspiracy. Van Speult then ordered twenty-one men, including ten who worked for the English East India Company, to be executed—a move that the English referred as the Amboina Massacre. The invasion of the Banda Islands and the Amboina Massacre earned the Dutch a reputation for tenacious military responses.[26]

Coen also initiated an intra-Asian circuit of commerce, with the VOC as a broker among markets. European merchants since the arrival of the Portuguese found that their trade products attracted little interest among Asian buyers, forcing Europeans to purchase Asian goods with silver, which proved quite expensive. Rather than use silver from Europe to pay for Asian goods, Coen fostered a network that traded in Asian goods from one location to another. The creation of an interlocking structure of trade required that the VOC establish a territorial presence in other Asian trading zones. The company had already secured posts on the Coromandel and Malabar coasts at Masulipatnam (1605) and Pulicat (1612). In 1616, the VOC followed with a factory in Gujarat at the port city of Surat, enabling Dutch merchants to pursue goods and markets in inland commercial centers and down the Malabar coast. With holdings in these territories, Coen believed the Dutch could become the major carriers in different trading zones across maritime Asia. As part of this strategy, he also relocated the central operations of the VOC close to the Strait of Sunda. Separating west Java from Sumatra, the strait offered a more strategic nexus for maritime traffic. Consequently, Coen moved the company headquarters to Jakarta, which the *Heren XVII* renamed Batavia. By 1621, the VOC under Coen's aggressive leadership had emerged as a leading commercial player in the East Indies and in South Asia, and as a result committed itself to empire building.[27]

The final component of the unfolding of the Dutch commercial empire by the early 1620s was the introduction of a trading company in the Atlantic along the lines of the VOC. The States General approved the West India Company (WIC) in 1621. Led by the Flemish émigré and ardent Calvinist Willem Usselincx, merchants involved in West Africa, the Caribbean, and South America had put together a plan for an Atlantic trading company in the early 1600s. Yet it did not get off the ground right away because of the Twelve Years' Truce that

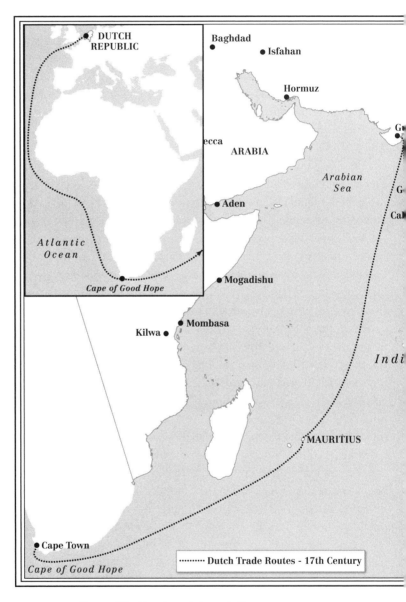

Fig. 4. The Dutch in Asia, 17th Century

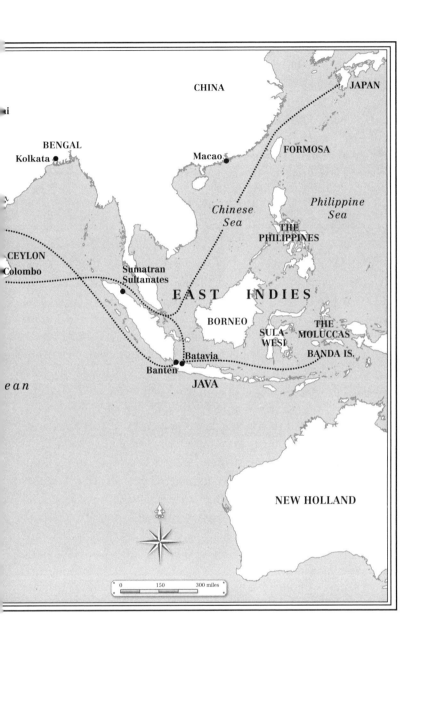

CHINA

JAPAN

BENGAL

Kolkata

Macao

FORMOSA

*Chinese
Sea*

*Philippine
Sea*

CEYLON

Colombo

Sumatran
Sultanates

THE
PHILIPPINES

E A S T   I N D I E S

BORNEO

SULA-
WESI

THE
MOLUCCAS

BANDA IS.

ean

Batavia

Banten

JAVA

NEW HOLLAND

0   150   300 miles

the Dutch negotiated with Hapsburg authorities in 1609. The Spanish king Philip III made it clear in the negotiations that he regarded the creation of such a state-backed trade organization as an act of hostility. Fearing Spanish antagonism, Johannes van Oldenbarnevelt, the Lands' Advocate for the States of Holland, worked to derail Usselincx's efforts and actively discouraged merchants from violating Spanish and Portuguese monopolies and trade restrictions. It was only in the late 1610s, when the truce was set to expire, that planning for a company resumed.[28] Thus by the 1620s, the Dutch had embarked on a maritime empire stretching across the Atlantic and Indian oceans.

CALVINISM AT HOME AND ABROAD

As the VOC and WIC were planting outposts in Asia and the Atlantic, a rigid brand of Calvinism came to occupy a central place in the Dutch Republic by 1620. Because of the revolt, the Reformed faith had risen to a privileged position in the new Republic. Operating within the confessional lineage of Reformed Protestantism, Dutch ecclesiastical organization bore the closest similarities to the churches in Geneva and throughout France. A consistory, composed of *predikanten* and elected lay elders, governed church affairs and upheld the disciplinary standards for remaining a member in good standing, a prerequisite for participating in the Lord's Supper. Within the local bodies, a board of lay deacons collected and distributed alms for the poor, sometimes in collaboration with municipal almoners and sometimes not. Consistories within a region, usually anchored by a sizable city such as Amsterdam, Delft, Middelburg, and Groningen, belonged to a classis, which superintended ecclesiastical affairs in the larger territorial jurisdiction. Classes within a larger area were made up of provincial synods, one for each province except for Holland, which had one in the south and one in the north. Finally, the provincial synods sent delegates to the national synod, though after the Synod of Dort in 1618–1619 the States General did not convoke another nationwide assembly.

It took several decades—from the 1570s until the Synod of Dort—of conflict and compromise to work out the details of the relationship between civil and church authority in this new political environment. The conflict reached its most rancorous levels of hostility in the first two decades of the seventeenth century. At that time, a theological dispute centered on the Calvinist teaching of predestination expanded into disagreements about the relationship between church and state, the treatment of religious dissenters, and the war with Spain and Portugal. The dogmatic quarrel originated between the theologians Jacob Arminius and Francis Gomarius at the University of Leiden. Arminius expressed objections to the Calvinist formulation that God had predestined the saved to eternity in heaven and the damned to eternity in hell before he created the world. For Arminians, these teachings denied humans any agency in their fate and made God out to be the author of sin. Gomarius strongly opposed Arminius's teachings, asserting what became the orthodox Calvinist view, that God conferred salvation or damnation on individuals according to his own counsel before creation. Predestination had always been a staple, albeit contested, tenet of Calvinist theology, though in the highly charged confessional atmosphere of the early 1600s it became more absolute and took on greater centrality in teaching about salvation. The followers of Arminius became known as Remonstrants after 1610, because of a *remonstrance* (protest) that forty or so ministers made to the States of Holland for protection from the majority Calvinist party that wished to subject them to church discipline.[29] Their Calvinist opponents were called Counter-Remonstrants.

Clerics, lay partisans, and political leaders did not allow the controversy to remain strictly theological as Remonstrants sought a more flexible religious outlook that allowed for toleration of other Protestants. Remonstrants advocated government control over ecclesiastical institutions, lest clerics constrain individual consciences. Calvinists aspired to a disciplined social order independent of political authority, which would give clergy outsized influence over public and private life. Thus, church conflicts became enmeshed in power struggles over the war with Spain and administrative authority in the Republic. In 1618, the *stadhouder* (ruling executive) Prince Maurits of Orange-Nassau, a supporter of the Counter-Remonstrants, called for a national synod to address the Arminian articles of faith, which convened at Dordrecht (i.e., Dort) in December. In June of the following year, the synod completely rejected all Arminian teachings. Ministers who refused to accept the resolutions of the synod were expelled from office and banished from the country. Calvinism emerged triumphant in the Dutch Reformed Church and the Dutch Republic, though animosity between Remonstrants and Counter-Remonstrants lingered for decades.[30]

The outcome of these struggles meant that a strict Calvinist form of Reformed Protestantism would shape the approach to mission in the Dutch empire in the seventeenth and eighteenth centuries. Based on his reading of early missionary encounters in Southeast Asia and Brazil, the Utrecht theologian Gisbertus Voetius promoted missions overseas.[31] Other Calvinist theologians and intellectuals, including Johannes Hoornbeeck, Johannes Cocceius, Georgius Hornius, Antonius Walaeus, and Adriaan Reland, devoted their energies to equipping students for service in overseas assignments. Although heterodoxy did seep into the corps, Calvinist *predikanten* and theologians in the Netherlands tried to make sure no Arminian ministers worked in imperial posts.

These ministers took a particularly Calvinist attitude toward planting Christianity in non-European societies. They sought to replicate a disciplined social order and they stressed the importance of adhering to correct doctrine and understanding the Bible from a Protestant perspective. *Predikanten* worked with local linguists to translate catechisms, pedagogical materials, and large portions of scripture, which they used in schools to educate children and adults in the fundamentals of the Christian religion. Though it proved impossible to avoid some accommodation with local customs, Calvinists placed theological principle above pragmatism in converting local peoples. The conflict with Catholicism in Europe reinforced Calvinists' perception that they were combating a worldwide pagan religion, characterized by idol worship and inordinate sensuality.

MISSIONS AND EMPIRE

In the first decades after the inception of the VOC, lay *ziekentroosteren* (comforters of the sick) and ordained ministers made their way to Amboina and Banda in the Moluccan Islands, Banten and Jakarta on Java, and Pulicat on the Coromandel coast. The earliest pastoral personnel were proponents (nonordained apprentice ministers) who served in a variety of capacities. Before the formation of the VOC, Plancius had tried to enlist *predikanten* to accompany fleets, though he had to settle for these less trained recruits.[32] Only months after the initial VOC charter did the *Heren XVII* issue a memorandum, in February 1603, calling for "two suitable and capable persons to present God's Word and to admonish people from Holy Scripture against all the superstitions and temptations of the Moors and Atheists."[33] This resolution did not specify an ordained minister, but still makes clear the goal of spreading the gospel as well as keeping Christians overseas from making missteps into false religion. The missionary and pastoral capacity of *ziekentroosteren*, however, was limited to leading people in prayers, reading from scripture or published sermons, and comforting the ill. Proponents could not preach their own sermons or, more importantly at the time, normally conduct baptisms or perform marriages. After the resolution, ordained ministers did begin to accompany fleets and reside in VOC outposts.[34]

Concerned to instill political loyalty to the company, VOC governors hoped to wean Christians baptized by Jesuits and Franciscans from Catholicism and bring them over to a Protestant faith. Across Asia and the Atlantic, large numbers of Catholic missionaries poured out into the Spanish, Portuguese, and (later) French empires. Jesuits, Franciscans, Dominicans, and other religious orders also went into areas beyond the reach of European empires, most notably China.

These missionaries employed a much more liberal policy of baptizing indigenous peoples than did Dutch Calvinists, who looked for signs of intellectual comprehension and spiritual regeneration before administering the rite. Steven van der Hagen reported in 1605 that the Jesuits boasted that they had baptized some sixteen thousand souls in Amboina and surrounding islands, so Dutch Calvinists certainly had their work cut out for them.[35] Many of these baptized *inlanders* (natives) expected the Dutch to continue to provide religious services as their Portuguese predecessors had. From the point of view of VOC officers in Asian territories, ministers and *ziekentroosteren* were necessary to instill loyalty among local inhabitants. When de Houtman, in April 1608, requested that the *Heren XVII* send a replacement for Johannes Stollenbecker, a minister who wished to repatriate, he wrote that the absence of clergy would cause "offense for the inhabitants who are already Christians, who have earnestly sought that their children be baptized."[36] The *predikanten* Caspar Wiltens and Mathias Paludanus similarly observed that people in Amboina were demanding clerical attention, complaining that the Dutch had betrayed them and denied them spiritual nourishment. The ministers also griped that people baptized by Catholics expected ceremonies abhorrent to Calvinists.[37]

As ministers began gradually to populate settlements in the Moluccas and in Batavia, the Reformed Church took on a distinctly missionary character. One of the earliest statements of a Calvinist sense of mission appeared in the credential letter certifying Wiltens from the Amsterdam classis for service in 1610. The classis resolved that "[t]he opportunity of navigation to the East Indies by the special order and mercy of God in various locations in the East Indies, opens a great door to preach the gospel of our Lord Jesus Christ in the genuine hope that many inhabitants there will be brought to the knowledge of the only true God and to eternal salvation."[38] As the company established alliances in the Moluccas, ministers and *ziekentroosteren* traveled to the outlying islands of Haruku, Saparua, Nusa Laut, Lubeck (Pulau Batjan), and Timor Kupang, to North Sulawesi, as well as to Banten, Jakarta, and Bali.[39] Wiltens, Paludanus, Sebastian Danckaerts, and Adriaan Hulsebos filed reports to the Amsterdam classis and the *Heren XVII* on their travels and corresponded with one another and the governor of Amboina on the state of Christendom across the archipelago. They worked with baptized Christians, preached, and set up schools. Subjects focused on reading and writing in Dutch and learning the basics of Christianity. Almost immediately, Dutch ministers and company officers began translating religious materials into a local Malay vernacular.[40]

The VOC, however, placed limits on the areas where ministers could act as missionaries, as commercial objectives often trumped proselytizing ambitions.

The raja of Hitu in the Moluccan Islands had allied with the VOC to expel the Portuguese, whose aggressive evangelizing stoked resentment. Desiring to mitigate obstacles to trade relations, governors signed commercial treaties in the early 1600s that sometimes included clauses prohibiting conversion. Wolfert Hermanszoon and the ruler of the Banda Islands declared in May 1602, for example, that "each side will serve his God according to the beliefs God has given him without any hatred for the other . . . and both sides will treat one another with friendship and the rest will be entrusted to God who is the judge of beliefs and souls."[41] This rather liberal pact proved in this case to be short-lived, as hostilities over trading violations led to VOC assaults on the islands, culminating in the 1621 conquest. Company governors nevertheless pursued mission-free policies with the sultans of Ternate and Tidore, even inserting promises that each party would return runaways who converted to Christianity or Islam, and upheld the principle of noncoercion throughout the East Indies.[42] The most extreme measure—and the most controversial for Calvinist church personnel—was the treaty between Anthony van Diemen and Tokugawa Iemitsu in November 1640 in which the governor general consented to the shogun's prohibition against all Christian symbols, literature, clergy, or observances in the fort at Deshima.[43]

VOC governors were acting pragmatically in striking these deals, yet they were also abiding by norms broadly accepted by the Dutch at home. One foundational principle at work in VOC diplomacy was the "freedom of conscience" provision enshrined in the 1579 Treaty of Utrecht and widely touted by Netherlanders.[44] It arose during the war for independence out of the need to manage religious pluralities, a challenge that confronted the company in the potentially hostile religious domains of Southeast Asia. A second European-wide standard, inscribed in the Peace of Augsburg (1555) and later in the Peace of Westphalia (1648), was the recognition that the ruler of a territory possessed the right to determine the religion of the realm (*cuius regio eius religio*). The Dutch actually secured alliances with local rulers such as the Muslim sultan of Ternate and the Buddhist king of Kandy because they preferred the VOC to the Portuguese, who gave such free rein to Catholic religious orders. Although Calvinist church leaders complained vociferously about these limits, company governors were appropriating legal principles born out of religious war in Europe that sought to constrain violence. These treaties staked out clear parameters, and *predikanten* did not extend their efforts in areas the VOC declared off limits.

By the 1620s, the general landscape of commerce, empire, and mission in Asia started to come into focus. Under the early governor generals, the VOC planted itself at critical points of production in the Moluccan Islands, negotiated monopolistic contracts with local rulers, and set up headquarters at the strategic point of access at Jakarta. Empire served the needs of commerce, as the Dutch asserted their right to trade wherever they might and to enforce contracts un-failingly. The goal was to make the VOC the principal link in an intra-Asian commercial network. Early governors were Calvinists and saw conversion in stra-tegic areas, namely of Catholics, as conducive to empire building. Company officials and church leaders saw the hand of providence in their enterprises.

A GLOBAL EMPIRE AND WORLDWIDE MISSIONS, 1620s–1660s

In the four decades from roughly the 1620s to roughly the 1660s, the Dutch empire reached its greatest territorial and commercial expanse, comprising stra-tegic geopolitical posts and lucrative financial operations in Asia and the Amer-icas. Christian missions became established as an integral element of colonial societies in the commercial empire and as an important force in Calvinism in the Netherlands. Ministers trumpeted some successes, though the effort to con-vert peoples in the empire presented perplexing challenges both out in the field and at home in the Netherlands.

MISSIONS IN THE NETHERLANDS

Missionary thrusts into Asia and Brazil formed a vital part of Dutch Calvin-ism in the seventeenth century. Ministers and lay elders in church districts cor-responded with overseas consistories, followed their successes and failures, deliberated over their problems, and advised them on doctrinal matters. A num-ber of theologians and *predikanten* composed accounts of paganism, idolatry, Islam, and Judaism from the ancient past to their own day. The theological faculties at the universities of Utrecht and Leiden trained students for mission-ary service and held disputations from the 1630s into the 1660s on mission-related topics. The sharing of information and focus on the prospects of Protestant Christianity around the world and in Europe bred a sense of global Calvinist mission among ministers overseas and at home, theologians, and other intel-lectuals by the mid-seventeenth century.

COMMERCIAL EXPANSION IN ASIA

The VOC, guided by governor generals in Batavia, expanded upon Coen's vision of an intra-Asian network and established the geopolitical basis for its op-erations. To link trading zones across the Indian Ocean, the VOC enlarged its presence at strategic sites in Persia. When a joint English-Persian force ousted the Portuguese from Hormuz in 1622, the VOC moved quickly to open a trading station there and an office in Isfahan. The company merchant, Huybert Visnich, reached a trading agreement with Shah Abbas I, enabling the VOC to become the most important carrier of Persian goods to maritime Asian markets. In South Asia, the company built on its factories at Masulipatnam and Pulicat and developed commercial connections up the Coromandel coast to Bengal between 1620 and 1650. The most important initiative occurred in Ceylon, as the VOC allied with the king of Kandy (in central Ceylon) against the Portuguese, commencing a military campaign that overtook Colombo in 1656 and completely expelled the Iberians in 1658. The company maintained a profitable position in South Asia from its perch in Ceylon until the end of the eighteenth century. With these territorial holdings, the VOC managed to exercise a dominant influence over the flow of pepper, cinnamon, and textiles in South Asia.[45] The VOC governor Rijklof van Goens also carved out fortifications and a small settler colony at the Cape of Good Hope in 1652, which would operate as a provisioning station for Dutch ships in transit between the Netherlands and Asia.

After establishing the VOC in the west, governor generals turned their attention to China and Japan. Unable to gain a foothold on the mainland and repelled from Macau, Coen gained control over Formosa in 1624—which the Dutch held until 1662—then he turned his attention to Japan, which had the richest silver mines in Asia.[46] From 1624 until 1640, the VOC acquired a larger share of trade with Japan, and by 1640 the Dutch had gained the exclusive trading rights in Japan at Deshima Island in Nagasaki Bay. The acquisition of Japanese silver enabled the VOC to trade with the Chinese from Formosa. In South Asia, the company delivered copper to Bengal in exchange for textiles and slaves, which it traded in port cities across the East Indies.[47]

Thus, the VOC adapted itself to the structure of commerce in the Indian Ocean. In a typical cycle, merchants exchanged Chinese wares for Japanese silver, which they then used to purchase additional silks and porcelains from China; they sent these in turn, together with fine spices and Japanese copper, to Gujarat and the Coromandel coast, exchanging them for cotton textiles, which then were traded in Banten, several Sumatran sultanates, and the Banda Islands for pepper and fine spices.[48] Gaining control over the intra-Asian trade enabled the VOC to enjoy enormous success throughout the seventeenth century as the most profitable trade organization in the world, selling spices in Europe for three times the purchase price in Asia. As historians Jan de Vries and Ad van der Woude have observed, "from the perspective of [company authorities in] Batavia, the VOC was a multilateral but highly centralized trading company with a sales office in Europe."[49]

The formation of this comprehensive commercial strategy continued to rely heavily on the armed mercantilism adopted also by the Portuguese, Spanish, and to a lesser extent the English and French. Under Coen, the VOC amassed a considerable military force, with ninety ships, two thousand troops, and twenty forts. He and other governor generals, such as Anthony van Diemen, Rijklof van Goens, and Cornelis Speelman, put these tools to use against the rivals of the company. It was no coincidence that a number of the territories the Dutch secured came at the expense of the Portuguese empire, the *Estada da India*. Between 1605 and 1663, the VOC dealt the Portuguese stinging defeats that sent their Asian empire into irreversible decline. In addition to the acquisitions mentioned above, the Dutch conquered Melaka in 1641, Cochin in 1663, and completely replaced the Spanish in Ternate and Tidore in 1662. The Portuguese did, however, repel Dutch assaults at Mozambique in 1607 and Macau in 1622 and withstood a blockade in Goa from 1637 to 1645. Spain turned the VOC back from Manila several times in the 1640s.[50]

The human production that powered this global commercial nexus came largely from the ranks of free and enslaved Eurasians and Asians, with a relatively small European demographic footprint. After Coen took over the clove plantations in the Banda Islands in 1621, the company began to acquire large numbers of enslaved men and women largely from two circulatory networks. These included the trafficking complexes in eastern Africa (including Madagascar), South Asia (Malabar, Coromandel, Bengal, and Arakan), and Southeast Asia (Malaysia and the East Indies). In the first decades, the VOC purchased the overwhelming share of enslaved peoples, but private free burghers bought and sold them as well. A number of enslaved people did obtain their freedom in Dutch colonies during the period, many of whom remained settled in these societies. A sizable population of Portuguese-speaking manumitted slaves from South Asia, known as *Mardijkers*, formed communities in Batavia and Amboina. Enslaved people constituted half the population in sites along the Dutch commercial archipelago in Asia. In addition to slave labor, large numbers of Chinese migrants from Fujian province on the southeast coast moved into East Indies settlements. Many helped the company broker trade exchanges in the Chinese port cities, where Ming authorities restricted and regulated trade. Other migrants performed "coolie" labor, clearing land, digging canals, and repairing city walls.[51]

Although the governor generals Pieter de Carpentier, Jan Pieterszoon Coen, and Jacques Specx initiated efforts to create settler colonies in Asia, the project never really took off. Between 1622 and 1631, the company brought in almost four hundred girls to Batavia from orphanages in the Netherlands to serve as brides for company employees. The girls did not take well to their new environs, however, and recruiters back home found it difficult to entice female or male Netherlanders to make a home in the faraway tropical lands of Southeast and South Asia. By the early 1630s, the *Heren XVII* and governors in Asia judged that settler colonies composed of sizable European communities were too costly and difficult to manage. While European women, mainly wives or soon-to-be brides of senior officers, did migrate to the colonies in the seventeenth and eighteenth centuries, the VOC did not encourage female migration. European men who married or fathered children locally could not repatriate, nor were they permitted to bring their wives or children to Europe. Although there were many exceptions to company policy, these directives determined the ethnic and social hierarchy in VOC territories. Consequently, VOC colonies in the Dutch Asian empires were composed ethnically of Europeans, Eurasians, Asians, and Africans. The ethnic breakdown in Dutch Asian colonies seems to correlate with Portuguese- and Spanish-held territories in Asia for the same reasons. That is, the Spanish and Portuguese (indeed European generally) demographic presence remained small, few females migrated, and the colonial governments, eventually including the VOC, encouraged marriage to local women. In the Dutch case, European men who did marry non-Europeans ultimately entrenched themselves in local societies and separated themselves from their homelands.[52]

By the 1630s, therefore, the direction of the Asian theater of the Dutch empire had become clear. Under the auspices of the VOC, an archipelago of colonial outposts adapted to the Indian Ocean port city trade by controlling strategic points of production and closely linking the overlapping zones of exchange. The Dutch and European ethnic imprint remained small, as the composition of colonial societies reflected the corporate hierarchy of the VOC and the company opted for a large enslaved labor force.

ORGANIZATION, GROWTH, AND FRUSTRATION IN THE MISSION

Church missions to Asia underwent two important developments from the 1620s to the 1660s. First, governor generals and clergy institutionalized the role of the church in colonial society and organized a program for converting pagans and Moors. In the VOC's second decade, governor generals Coen and de Carpentier sought to impose some structure on church activity. Consequently, in 1624 de Carpentier ratified a church order for Asia, based on the 1619 Synod of Dort. Despite this protocol, the growth of a Calvinist clerical and missionary presence brought the church and the company into a number of conflicts. The 1620s to the 1660s in fact marked one of the most fractious periods in the relations between ministers and company authorities in Asia.[53] From the church's point of view, governor generals neglected to give the *Indisch Sion* the resources to produce an abundant harvest of souls and often failed to respect the traditional prerogatives of consistories. For their part, governors showed little patience with presumptuous ministers who inserted themselves into the affairs of high-ranking officials. And the company sometimes had to contend with ministers who were simply ill equipped emotionally for overseas service. Consequently, in 1643 Anthony van Diemen established a new code that granted more authority to the civil authority—i.e., company rulers—in church affairs than in all other arrangements in the Dutch Reformed world.[54]

Second, these church orders spelled out the missionary character and strategy of the churches in the *Indisch Sion*. Article 8 of the 1624 policy declared the intent of the company and the church to "bring heathens, Mohammedans, and other blind nations" to Christian belief, "especially children." To that end, civil and ecclesiastical authorities agreed that ministers were to preach the gospel in Dutch, Portuguese, and local languages, set up schools to educate children and adults, and produce translations of biblical and pedagogical materials. Governors, as the enforcers of Christian norms, were to uphold Sunday as a day of rest and worship and prohibit non-Christian and Catholic rites in public. The 1643 order reiterated the aim of converting non-Christians and specified the elimination of public displays of Islam and pagan worship, noting that false religions "do not take place in a Christian republic."[55]

In Asian communities, ministers worked with indigenous linguists to learn local languages and translate materials into the vernacular. Many *predikanten* acquired various Malay dialects across the East Indies, Tamil and Sinhalese in South Asia, Sinkan in Formosa, and even a few clergy picked up Tupian in Brazil. Because of the pervasive linguistic presence of Portuguese, company and church personnel became proficient in the language of one of their chief overseas rivals. Within several decades, translated (published and manuscript copies) grammars, catechisms, and books of the Bible appeared in Portuguese, Malay, Sinkan, Tamil, and Sinhalese.

The institutionalization of Calvinism in VOC-held areas contributed to missionary expansion in Batavia, Amboina, Banda, and other locations in the East Indies and across the southwest plains of Formosa.[56] Between 1609 and 1650, the VOC sent 92 ministers and 291 *ziekentroosteren* to the East Indies, South Asia, and Formosa.[57] A number of proponents enlisted in ministerial service in overseas settings. Yet the missionary work of *predikanten, ziekentroosteren,*

and local schoolteachers led to uneven growth of Calvinist congregations overseas. It is difficult to reconstruct quantitative data of converts before the 1670s, but
anecdotal evidence offers an image of a significant number of Asians and Euro-
Asians who were gaining some understanding of Reformed teachings and a
small number who were attaining the difficult status of full-fledged church
members. The most celebrated growth in this period came in Formosa, where
the *predikanten* Robert Junius and George Candidius reported just over 5,000
converts by 1643. Ten years earlier, the minister Helmichius Helmichii counted
1,238 children in the 32 schools scattered across the islands of Amboina. The first
record of church membership in Batavia was not until 1674, when 2,300 members and many more congregants populated the Dutch, Portuguese, and Malay
services. Other locations registered much smaller congregations.[58]

Despite the growth of schools, the translation of materials, and the appearance of converts, Calvinists both overseas and in the Netherlands realized by
midcentury that missions was proving more complicated than they had expected.
The optimism of large-scale conversion of "heathens, Moors, and Jews" gave way
to frustration with the indifference of most native peoples and the equivocation
of many converts. As a result, Calvinists began to take an academic approach to
missionary strategy and gained the theological support of Dutch universities. Beginning in 1634, Gisbertus Voetius and later Johannes Hoornbeeck at the universities of Utrecht and Leiden lectured on Islam and wrote theological works
to open up the study of non-Christian religions to Dutch *predikanten* working
outside the Netherlands.[59] On the mission field, Abraham Rogerius and Philip
Baldaeus, both stationed in South Asia and Batavia, produced extensive and influential accounts of Hindu and Buddhist traditions.[60] They intended to expose
the cryptic rites and myths of "heathenism" to equip theologians and ministers
for missions. Outside of an academic setting, the Reformed classes of Amsterdam and Middelburg, along with the synods of North and South Holland, recruited and vetted ministers and *ziekentroosteren* for overseas service,
corresponded with consistories around the world, dispensed advice, and lobbied
the directors of both the VOC and WIC for resources.

EXPANSION IN THE ATLANTIC

The launching of the West India Company brought together the same strains
of armed commerce, empire, and conversion that drove the VOC in Asian waters.
Willem Usselincx and Johannes de Laet, two leading figures in the company's
early years, imagined a network of settler colonies to plant a Dutch and a Calvinist presence in conjunction with commercial operations not unlike the one

that Coen had envisioned for the Asian empire. Bit by bit, the company pieced together an interlocking commercial enterprise across the Atlantic similar to the intra-Asian trade. Dutch ships attacked Portuguese and Spanish holdings throughout the Atlantic to increase Dutch presence on the west coast of Africa and in the Caribbean, and to conquer Brazil at the expense of their Iberian enemies. A previous Dutch firm, the Guinea Company, had traded for gold along the Gold Coast (Ghana) for a number of years, and the WIC intended to continue this pursuit. The Dutch took Elmina in 1637 and chased the Portuguese out of Luanda and Sao Tomé from 1641 to 1642.[61]

Shortly after the WIC's founding, company fleets launched assaults on Portuguese holdings in Brazil. In 1628, the commander Piet Heijn landed a deep, and lucrative, blow by capturing a Spanish silver fleet off the coast of Cuba. Shortly thereafter, Hendrik Corneliszoon Loncq directed a large fleet that seized Olinda and Recife, and then over the next four years Dutch troops pushed the Portuguese military and colonial authorities out of Brazil. The company took over posts set up by previous expeditions in the Guiana region of Essequibo, Berbice, and Demerara. Shortly after the successful invasion of Brazil, the Dutch conquered Curaçao (in the Antilles) in 1634, but Spanish forces shut them out of Puerto Rico, Cuba, and Chile. Nevertheless, the seizure of the Guinea coast and Brazil, as well as ongoing harassment of Iberian shipping, made the WIC a promising enterprise in the Atlantic.[62]

The West India Company also put down roots in North America, setting up a trading post in 1624 on the southern edge of Manhattan Island, named New Amsterdam. Since Henry Hudson's initial voyage thirteen years earlier, Dutch mariners had explored the region with an interest in the beaver pelt trade. In 1614, the States General issued a four-year charter to thirteen investors for a New Netherland Company. The WIC absorbed all of Dutch mercantile activity shortly after its founding. To substantiate its claim over English objections, the company decided to populate the colony with fifty settlers. There was some disagreement among the *Heren XIX* (not to be confused with the *Heren XVII* of the VOC) over the direction of the settlement. Some, following Usselincx's goal of settler colonies around the Atlantic, pushed for colonization, whereas others advocated for a small trading center similar to VOC settlements in Asia. The WIC came down on the side of colonization, though in New Netherland's first twenty years only a trickle of European migrants moved into New Amsterdam as well as nearby settlements on the North (Hudson) River, Long Island, and Staten Island.[63]

Brazil occupied pride of place within the Dutch Atlantic Empire during the 1630s and 1640s. Johan Maurits of Siegen-Nassau governed the colony from 1637

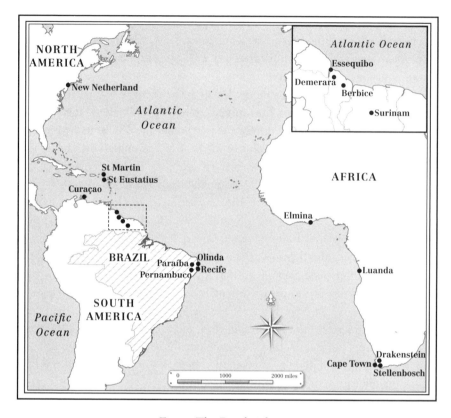

Fig. 5. The Dutch Atlantic

to 1644, and under his rule the company prospered. Maurits attracted a number of artists, naturalists, and financiers to the colony, though enticing only a few of the Protestant settlers who he and others hoped would establish a Calvinist beachhead in South America. Fearful of reprisals from Luso-Brazilian plantation owners, he even allowed the public practice of Catholicism. The Dutch did expel the Jesuits in the newly conquered areas, and Maurits banned other religious orders (Benedictines, Carmelites, and Franciscans) in 1640. In an effort to tempt the large numbers of Sephardic Jews to finance sugar and slaving operations, Maurits also permitted them to worship publicly. These concessions irked Calvinist *predikanten* hoping to transform Brazil into a land of Protestant Christians purged of superstition and false religion.[64]

Conquests along Africa's west coast, in the Caribbean, and in Brazil enabled the WIC to fashion an integrated network of trade in the Atlantic. From Amsterdam, company merchants shipped manufactured items to brokers along the Ivory

Coast and Ghana near Elmina, in exchange for slaves who were then transported to Brazil to labor on sugar plantations. From there, the company exported sugar, molasses, and brazilwood back to the Netherlands. As the company gained control over the Guinea coast, the WIC inserted itself prominently in the slave trade. The traffic in enslaved West Africans aimed at integrating commerce between both sides of the Atlantic, since Brazil's sugar plantation depended heavily on coerced labor from Africa. The growth in human trafficking by the WIC placed the Netherlands among the leading countries in the Atlantic slave trade in the mid-seventeenth century. Between 1636 and 1645, the WIC transported just over 23,000 slaves from West Africa across the Atlantic. Likewise, sugar production rose significantly during Dutch rule, as sugar refineries almost doubled, from 29 to 54, between 1622 and 1660. Company directors expected to insulate this triangular trade from European competitors, according to the mercantilist commercial tendencies of the day. This policy did not work well in practice, however, as Dutch private traders, some of them disaffected former company employees, struck out on their own or went to work for other associations. New Netherland provided fur and timber, but shipped it directly to Amsterdam, and did not participate directly in this commercial nexus.[65]

MISSIONS IN THE ATLANTIC

The WIC's vision of a commercial empire also jibed with a Calvinist commitment to missions in the Atlantic world. De Laet considered the founding of the West India Company to serve "the maintenance of True Religion and the protection of our freedom." Certainly, he had attacking Catholic Spain and Portugal in mind here, yet like so many other leaders in the trading companies, de Laet saw commerce, colonial settlement, and conversion as constituent components of a Dutch empire. His was not a lone voice. D. L. Noorlander's research on the WIC has shown that more than half of the *Heren XIX* members in Amsterdam, and even more in the Zeeland chamber, sat on consistories as lay elders.[66] A global Calvinist mission filtered down to *predikanten* in the Netherlands who preached, taught, and wrote on the joint opportunities for profits and souls. Willem Teellinck, promoter of pietism in the Netherlands, recognized God's business in the Atlantic, declaring that "such works of God have given ever greater operation to opening the eyes of the blind heathens so that they recognize that the Lord Jehovah, indeed the God of Israel, is the true God."[67] Another minister, Godefridus Udemans in Zeeland, praised pious commerce because its "primary fruit is the conversion of the poor heathens"; thus, he admonished company officials, "we cannot pluck this fruit unless this great work is continued."[68]

Translating this vision into a fruitful harvest of souls was closely connected to the fortunes of the WIC, not only in the minds of Calvinist activists but also in the geopolitical realities of the Atlantic theater. Although Dutch ministers served congregations across the Atlantic world during the seventeenth and eighteenth centuries, Brazil during WIC rule formed the only real theater of Calvinist missionary activity. Reformation in Brazil began in earnest only around 1637 with the removal of several problematic clergy and the arrival of the *predikant* Fredericus Kesseler.[69] During this period, perhaps as many as eight thousand Dutch settled in Brazil, out of a total population of around ninety thousand, composed of Portuguese, Luso-Brazilians, indigenous Tupi peoples, and enslaved Africans. Ministers served in the company as early as 1624, and by the 1630s they began to migrate to WIC strongholds in the north, primarily Recife, Olinda, Pernambuco, and Paraíba. By the time of the expulsion of the Dutch, fifty-four clergy had served in the region. Just as elsewhere, these ministers, lay *ziekentroosteren*, and indigenous teachers set up consistories and schools and translated biblical and catechetical materials. Unlike in Asia, the consistories in Brazil formed two classes, one encompassing Pernambuco and environs and the other Paraíba, which together formed the Synod of Brazil. Throughout this period, Dutch Calvinists extended themselves to twenty-two congregations across Brazil.[70]

CONTRACTION IN THE ATLANTIC

The bellicose mercantilism that had served the VOC so well in many areas of the Indian Ocean did not hold up well under the intense competition in the Atlantic. With so many active and armed trading parties in the Atlantic, the WIC could not maintain control over its trading networks and had to give way to Spanish, Portuguese, English, and even private Dutch actors. While the company struggled to sustain profit margins, its grip on Brazil—the linchpin of Dutch intra-Atlantic trade—was always tenuous. After the WIC returned Maurits to the Netherlands in 1644, Dutch rule unraveled in less than a year. Resentful of the rule by Protestant foreigners, the growing encroachments of Calvinists over religious space, the high interest on loans to repair their land holdings, and the immigration of many Sephardic Jews into the WIC's Brazilian domains, planters staged a massive rebellion around Pernambuco in 1645.[71] The insurrection pushed the Dutch to small holdings along the coastline; over the course of ten years, the WIC devoted enormous resources to beat back Luso-Brazilian rebels and the Portuguese forces that came to their rescue. But two major battles at Guararapes in 1648 and 1649 sealed Dutch colonial fortunes in Brazil. By 1653, the Dutch had surrendered Brazil, signaling a critical transition for the com-

pany. It ceased operating as a comprehensive mercantilist corporation inflict-
ing violence as a company strategy and took on the role of specialized trading
to service European colonies in America and the Caribbean.[72]

The loss of Brazil caused immediate problems for the WIC. The loss acceler-
ated a crisis for Dutch commercial fortunes in the Atlantic, since they relied so
heavily on sugar production in Brazil and the slave trade that sustained the plantations there. In addition, Portuguese forces recaptured Angola and São Tomé
in 1648. Prices for WIC shares on the Amsterdam stock exchange fell to 14 guilders per share in March 1650, from 92 guilders in June 1643.[73] Bankruptcy was a
palpable possibility for a corporation burdened by heavy military expenses and
bereft of its primary territorial asset. Although a number of Reformed ministers
continued to work in a missionary capacity to convert small numbers of Portuguese, Luso-Brazilians, Tupi, and Africans, the Dutch Calvinist presence in Brazil eroded quickly after the departure of the company. By midcentury, the
Dutch colonial dream in the Atlantic had come to an end, and the WIC had to
rethink its presence in the Atlantic world. The ambitious missionary dreams of
de Laet and other Calvinist officials sank with the demise of the WIC as a claim-
ant to territorial power.

LOSSES AND GAINS, 1660s–1680s

The three decades after the treaties of Westphalia and Munster (1648) that
ended the Netherlands' struggle for independence formed a critical transitional
period in the Dutch empire and missions. For the first time in its history, the
Republic no longer counted Spain as an existential enemy, and Portugal no
longer represented a serious threat to VOC interests in Asia. The fierce competition that the Dutch Republic and empire faced now came from England
at sea and France on land. During this period of increased competition and
ongoing conflict, the VOC retained its commercial dominance in the Indian
Ocean, while private Dutch merchants exploited commodity markets in the
Atlantic.

As the Dutch lost their footing in Brazil and Formosa, the Calvinist campaign
to convert souls in those regions came to an end. In other VOC territories, a
Calvinist presence grew slowly and steadily in South Asia and the East Indies,
though hardly at all on the Cape of Good Hope. Growing perplexities over identifying genuine conversions in non-Europeans plagued overseas ministers during this period. Discerning the appropriate expectations for converts not raised
in a European Christian context had always troubled ministers, but the issue
began to come to a head again at the end of the century.

ANTIMERCANTILISM IN THE ATLANTIC

The WIC's demise as a colonial power with its mountain of debt forced the company into bankruptcy. The States General revoked its monopoly over Brazilian and Atlantic trade in 1648, though the company had resorted to selling licenses for private trading to shareholders ten years earlier. Ultimately concluded in 1669, the peace treaty with Portugal compensated the WIC with one million guilders' worth of salt from Setúbal, which the company used to recapitalize itself for streamlined carrying operations in the Atlantic. Though a number of schemes were floated or even launched to retake Brazil or to stake a territorial claim elsewhere, most came to naught. Small colonies formed in Guiana and the Caribbean. After the Dutch acquired Surinam from the English in 1667, Netherlanders often referred to it as "New Brazil," a reminder of their once grand colonial aspirations.[74]

Dutch commerce in the Atlantic pivoted quickly in the second half of the seventeenth century in a decidedly antimercantilist direction, servicing colonies and markets within the administrative jurisdiction of the English, Spanish, Portuguese, and French empires. Private companies swiftly took advantage of disruptions to the carrying traffic to the Caribbean plantations. Trading slaves acquired from the WIC on Africa's west coast and spices and linens purchased in Amsterdam, private merchants moved into Spanish territories with little or no fear of assault. With the disruption of sugar production in Brazil because of the war's upheaval, the Caribbean became the hub of sugar production as French planters in Martinique, English in Barbados, and Spanish in Puerto Rico, Cuba, and Hispaniola seized on new prospects for profits in commodities.[75]

The scaled-down version of the WIC under Jacob Ruyghaver also pushed into the Caribbean with slaves from the Guinea coast. In the late 1650s, the Spanish finally removed restrictions on Dutch shipping to its colonies in South America, which proved to be a tremendous boon for the company. The Dutch retained a lucrative trade on the West African Gold Coast with the new WIC well into the eighteenth century. English, French, Danish, and German firms also did business there, making the Gold Coast a busy hub for slaves, gold, and ivory. The WIC delivered the slaves for the *asiento* (exclusive license) the Spanish crown granted to its colonial suppliers of enslaved laborers. Curaçao, occupied by Dutch colonists since 1634, served as the central node of transit in the carrying trade. Traffic moved into Curaçao from West Africa and the Caribbean, and on to Buenos Aires and other sites in South America. Thus, by the 1660s the WIC and private Dutch companies had risen as important players in the carrying trade, especially the slave traffic, across the Atlantic.

By the time the Dutch abolished slave trading between 1814 and 1818, the WIC and other mercantile operations had transported 550,000 enslaved Africans across the Atlantic.[76]

The English now posed the most serious threat to Dutch commerce. In 1651 and 1660, the English Parliament imposed navigation acts designed to prohibit trade between English colonists along the Atlantic seaboard and Dutch merchants. These acts and the seizure of Dutch ships on the sea led to the first of four naval wars between England and the Republic in 1651.

The virtually constant state of war for the next twenty years dealt a serious blow to Dutch shipping and mercantile aspirations in the Atlantic. English fleets, along with a wide cast of privateers, captured, lost, and recaptured Caribbean islands (Saba, Tobago, St. Eustatius, St. Martin, and others), decimated Dutch posts on the African Gold Coast (except for Elmina), and took possession of New Netherland in 1664, renaming it New York. Dutch Calvinist influence there dissipated fairly rapidly, just as it had in the demise of Dutch rule in Brazil. Dutch flotillas did wreak havoc on English (and French) ships and settlements, especially under the admiralty of Michiel de Ruyter, in the Third Anglo-Dutch War of 1672–1674. The Treaty of Breda that settled the Second Anglo-Dutch War in 1667 recognized English possession of New York and Dutch control over Surinam, previously settled by England.[77]

Perhaps the greatest achievement of the Netherlands during this time was that it survived at all. In 1672, Charles II of England and Louis XIV of France joined forces to crush their common foe and its imperial aspirations. Louis XIV's troops invaded the United Provinces from Maastricht in the south, as England blockaded the Channel and went after Dutch ships at sea. Much of the Republic fell to French and other foreign forces, leading to widespread protests against the ineffectiveness of the States General. In 1673, de Ruyter turned back a major English offensive in the North Sea as Spain and the Holy Roman Empire declared war on France, compelling Louis XIV to withdraw his forces from the northern Netherlandish provinces. Nevertheless, the damage was done. With little hope of profitability, the WIC reorganized itself in October 1674 into a vastly scaled down slave-running operation, which it maintained until its ultimate downfall in 1791.[78]

THE END OF ATLANTIC MISSIONS

These hostile circumstances rendered the hope for a Dutch Calvinist bulwark in the Atlantic a lost cause. Ministers and *ziekentroosteren* did serve in Elmina, Curaçao, Berbice, Essequibo, Demerara, St. Eustatius, St. Martin, and other places, but their activity rarely ranged into the area of direct efforts at converting people to Calvinism. Only twelve ministers traveled to New Netherland, the first not arriving until 1650. The settlements in New Netherland were sparsely populated. Ministers in these locations demonstrated little interest in converting native Americans, perhaps because of hostile relations with Algonquin tribes, which had led to warfare between 1638 and 1645. Most ministers betrayed little regard for the capacity of non-European groups to understand or embrace Protestant Christianity. *Predikanten* regularly denigrated Mohicans, Mohawks, and other Native American tribes as treacherous, violent, and uncivilized, perceptions that did not engender missionary zeal.[79] Some clergy in New Netherland attempted to make Calvinists out of African slaves but could only claim sixty converts by the second half of the seventeenth century. Concluding that Africans simply feigned interest in order to improve their lot in life, New Netherland ministers abandoned the effort straightway. There were almost no Catholics in this colony; thus, the main focus of Dutch *predikanten* was trying to stanch defections to the Lutherans, Quakers, Presbyterians, and Congregationalists.[80] Between 1667 and 1680, only one minister and three Dutch Reformed churches had appeared in Surinam.[81]

REENERGIZED MERCANTILISM IN ASIA

The VOC managed to overcome two critical threats to its intra-Asia system from 1650 to 1680, by the tenacious application of armed mercantilism. Two of the forces behind this aggressive policy were governor generals Joan Maetsuijcker (1653–1678) and Rijklof van Goens (1678–1681). Hiring soldiers put out of work by the end of the Thirty Years War, the VOC greatly expanded its military capabilities, fortifying its garrisons with 10,500 troops at midcentury.[82] This bellicose policy enabled the VOC to retain its dominant position in the Indian Ocean until the 1680s against its two greatest challenges: increased competition from the English and French, and conquest of Formosa by Chinese Ming dynasty loyalists.

The expansion of English and French commercial enterprises in India posed a critical threat to the VOC's interconnected commercial networks. Charles II augmented the authority of the English East India Company along the lines of the Dutch, namely to conduct diplomacy, unleash military force, and take control over territory. These powers strengthened the hand of the EIC, which it used to expand English presence in Bombay and Bengal, important sources for textiles, cotton, and silk in the 1660s and 1670s. At the same time, EIC officers managed factories focused on pepper in Banten, cloves in Pulau Run (Banda Islands), and Indian textiles and opium in Makassar. France also sought to enter Asian markets during the reign of Louis XIV. His finance minister, Jean-Baptiste Colbert, created the *Compagnie des Indes* in 1664, which sought outposts in South Asia. Two naval wars between the English and Dutch from 1665 to 1674, however, enabled the VOC to expel the English and consolidate control over the East Indies. In the Second Anglo-Dutch War (1665–1667), the VOC besieged English factories in Makassar and on Sumatra and overtook Makassar with help from the Bugis king of Arung Palakka. The English extended the Third Anglo-Dutch War (1672–1674) into the Indian Ocean, waging unsuccessful campaigns against VOC ships and fortifications on the coasts of Ceylon and Coromandel. Yet by the late 1670s and early 1680s, the governor generals van Goens and Speelman were focused on rooting the English (and Danes) out of the East Indies, which they accomplished by 1682. In the process, van Goens made common cause in 1677 with Amangkurat II, the sultan of Mataram in central Java, who supported company interests in return for military protection. Speelman negotiated arrangements with sultans in Makassar and Java that made them subservient to the company's commercial aims. These successes enabled the Dutch to retain a grip on the intra-Asian trade network, linked from South Asia to the East Indies, despite more intense competition and disturbances in the market for gold and silver specie, into the 1680s. The costs of maintaining dominance through warfare exerted a serious drag on company finances.[83]

Finally, political turmoil in China led Ming loyalists under Zheng Chenggong, also known as the Koxinga emperor, to flee southern China and invade Formosa in 1662, driving the Dutch from their post in the South China Sea. A key element of the VOC's commercial strategy had focused on acquiring silver and gold from Japan, which it traded for Chinese goods, notably silk, through its factory in Formosa. After the Ming invasion, the Chinese took an even harder line against Dutch ships entering their ports. As a result, VOC merchants lost an important item formerly traded with the Japanese at Deshima Island. The company introduced silk from Bengal, but the shogun Tokugawa Ietsuna also began restricting the export of gold and silver. To underwrite trade, the VOC came to depend more heavily on silver coming from Mexico through Amsterdam and Manila, which was costly and subject to disruption. Consequently, critical setbacks in this region posed significant challenges that required company directors in the Netherlands and governors in Asia to reassess their long-term objectives and how to achieve them.[84]

Fig. 6. The VOC in the East Indies

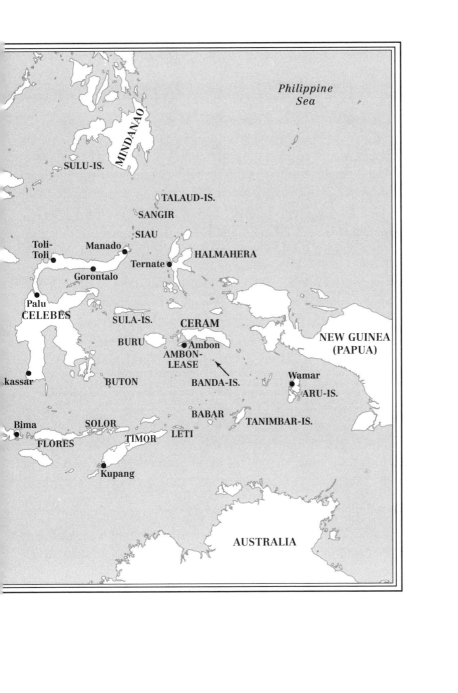

Philippine
Sea

MINDANAO

SULU-IS.

TALAUD-IS.

SANGIR

SIAU

Toli-
Toli   Manado

Gorontalo

Ternate   HALMAHERA

Palu

CELEBES

SULA-IS.   CERAM

BURU   Ambon

AMBON-
LEASE

NEW GUINEA
(PAPUA)

kassar

BUTON   BANDA-IS.   Wamar

ARU-IS.

BABAR

SOLOR   TANIMBAR-IS.

Bima   LETI

TIMOR

FLORES

Kupang

AUSTRALIA

GROWTH IN THE ASIAN MISSIONS

Calvinist missions to Asia continued to grow in the East Indies and began to get underway in Ceylon, but they suffered a major setback with the loss of Formosa. The mission field on the island had looked to be among the most fertile when the energetic George Candidius arrived in 1627, and even more so when the innovative Robert Junius joined him two years later. The company invested a sizable contingent of the Asian pastoral corps in the island in hopes of Christianizing it. By 1659, 28 ministers had served in Formosa, and they claimed 6,078 followers. The ministers worked primarily in the southwest plains adjacent to Fort Zeelandia, the headquarters of the VOC, and set up congregations and schools in Sinkan, Tayuan, Mattauw, Soulang, and Baccloangh. Ministers in the south continued their translation work, and also intermittently taught Dutch in the schools. By the late 1640s, however, the mission in Formosa began to show signs of stress. Junius, one of the most heralded of Dutch overseas ministers, left for the Netherlands in 1643. His departure led to infighting among his successors, Simon van Breen, Joannes Bavius, and Joannes Happart, who charged that he had watered down church standards by baptizing converts before they were properly educated and by incorporating local concepts into Reformed teachings. In 1657, the governor Frederik Coyette approved the establishment of a seminary in Soulang on the southwest coast to train Formosans in Dutch and to teach the Reformed faith in schools throughout the region. By the early 1660s, just before the Chinese invasion, the church had only five ministers on the island, and the schools were the subject of much complaint for the low quality of instruction and indifference of students.[85]

The mission also made slow but steady progress in South Asia and the East Indies. After the VOC commander Gerard Pieterszoon Hulft completely removed the Portuguese from Ceylon in 1658, the Reformed Church started to organize pastoral and missionary work at three nodal points along the coast, Colombo, Galle, and Jaffnapatnam. Philip Baldaeus, one of the most prominent overseas *predikanten* and one who published a description of the region, appeared at Jaffnapatnam 1658. He, along with Antony Hornhovius, and Louis Bogaerd set up consistories in these port towns and soon began to establish schools overseen eventually by both political and church officials. In order not to offend the Buddhist king of Kandy, ministers could not proselytize within the domains under his rule, which were located on the south and east of the island. He did promise to disallow Roman Catholic priests in his realm, though the complaints of Calvinists suggest that the monarch did not consistently enforce the restriction.[86]

The most unusual feature of the missionary terrain in Ceylon, Malabar, and Coromandel was that it centered on a struggle with an overwhelming Catholic presence. Jesuits and Franciscans had baptized tens of thousands of Tamils, Sinhalese, and other South Asian peoples and tried to continue to support them from Goa, the Portuguese metropole in the Indian Ocean, and from a Jesuit mission at Madura on the Coromandel coast. Since Calvinists recognized the validity of Catholic baptism, ministers counted these peoples as "nominal [*genaamd*] Christians." Their numbers were quite large. In annual pastoral reports, the consistory in Colombo reported figures from Ceylon, Malabar, and Coromandel to the Amsterdam classis. In 1711, for example, the consistories in Ceylon listed 160,000 such Christians, and in 1730, 187,133.[87] To bring these Catholics over to Calvinism, the Dutch set up numerous schools and utilized indigenous teachers given some instruction in Reformed teachings.

Locations in the East Indies continued to develop in the second half of the seventeenth century. The two most significant were Batavia and Amboina. The Amboina consistory reported one thousand adult members in 1663, and its ministers made regular visits to a number of schools.[88] Small congregations formed also in Banda, Melaka, Makassar, Ternate, and Tidore.[89] Despite lackluster growth in church membership, schools functioned in many sites across the East Indies at this time, including the Lease Islands of Haruku, Saparua, the villages of Piru, Soahuku, Sepa, Makariki, and Amahai on the island of Seram to the north, the islands of Buru, Manipa, and Boano to the west, (Hitu) Amboina, and the town of Tanunu on Rote Island to the south.[90]

On the Cape of Good Hope, Jan van Riebeeck, the first VOC governor there, expressed optimism at converting the indigenous Khoi Khoi peoples, though that sentiment proved fleeting. Very soon after van Riebeeck's arrival in April 1652, it became clear that misunderstanding and hostility would reign between the Dutch and the Khoi Khoi. The company hoped the pastoral cattle herders would supply fresh meat to the colony—which they refused—and the Khoi Khoi did not expect the European interlopers to stay permanently. Further, the Dutch recoiled at the clothing and customs of the Khoi Khoi and were baffled by their click language. The Khoi Khoi, in turn, thought little of the Dutch. In 1655, the *ziekentrooster* Willem Barentszoon Wijlant described the natives as "a very poor, miserable people in body and soul, deprived of all knowledge of God, they live as cattle. . . . [I]n religion there seems to be no distinction between them and senseless cattle, because they live as beasts that have no work, neither sowing nor planting, nor anything that speaks of God."[91] Throughout this period, Dutch Calvinists cultivated the narrative that the Khoi Khoi lacked a ready capacity for conversion.[92]

Failing a harvest of souls among local peoples, the primary targets for conversion on the Cape of Good Hope were enslaved laborers transported in from other parts of Africa and from South Asia. Soon after arriving in 1652, Wijlant set up a school that provided also for slaves, and in 1685 the company opened a permanent school designated for enslaved adults and children. The three primary congregations at the Cape of Good Hope, Cape Town, Stellenbosch, and Drakenstein, arose during this time, but they exhibited very little missionary character, if any at all. Serving a European population of only several hundred, the churches remained small in the seventeenth century, since they did not take in a large number of converts.[93] The first full-time minister, Johan van Arkel, did not arrive in the colony until 1665, a full thirteen years after the VOC set up shop. Until then, *predikanten* on ships stopping off en route to destinations in Asia performed baptisms and marriages, administered communion, and preached during their stay. Before the second half of the eighteenth century, congregations often had to make do for lengthy periods without a minister.[94]

Across the Dutch commercial empire, three general characteristics of Calvinist church and missionary activity stand out during this period. One is that schools sponsored by the VOC expanded across Ceylon, Malabar, Coromandel, Formosa, the East Indies, and the Cape of Good Hope. Building on educational efforts earlier in the century, ministers and lay officers sought schools as a missionary strategy to Christianize peoples in VOC territories, especially children, sometimes to teach them Dutch and the fundamentals of Reformed Protestantism.

A second and closely related characteristic of Calvinist missionary enterprises at this time was an increased tempo in translation work for use of catechisms, grammars, and portions of the Bible in these schools. Overseas ministers translated instructional materials into Portuguese for all regions (except Formosa), into various Malay dialects for the East Indies, and into Tamil and Sinhalese for Ceylon, Malabar, and Coromandel. In the second half of the seventeenth century, *predikanten* in the East Indies and South Asia extended the linguistic labor of earlier Dutch clergy and company officials to advance translations of the Bible into Malay, Sinhalese, and Tamil. Complete translations appeared in the eighteenth century.

Finally, a third facet of global Calvinism between 1650 and 1680 involved the enlarged operations of diaconates in VOC territories. Jointly chosen by a consistory and town council in most Dutch parishes, lay church deacons of the Reformed Church served those who suffered from poverty or sickness. As the population levels of VOC colonies grew, major reorganizations of diaconates took place at midcentury, transforming their function into comprehensive colonial welfare agencies. A host of social ills, including disease, underemployment, and illegitimacy accompanied rising population numbers, producing widespread poverty.[95] As a result, the VOC enlarged the scope of diaconal operations and (more controversially) began to transform the church office into a colonial social welfare agency.

Van Diemen initiated changes for poor relief in Batavia in 1643, which served as a basis for diaconal operations in other substantive VOC settlements. With company employees who also belonged to the church making up half of the diaconate, the reforms injected VOC influence into the management of poor relief. More importantly, the deacons in Batavia had also taken on the care of orphans, a task that grew significantly in the seventeenth and eighteenth centuries, and management of an *armenhuis* (poorhouse) for those who could not live on their own.[96] Five years later, in 1648, the governor general Cornelis van der Lijn established the diaconate as a separate college from the consistory accountable to the *Politieke Raad* in Batavia.[97] When the VOC established settlements in Melaka, Ceylon, and South Africa in the 1640s and 1650s, the structure of the diaconate in Batavia was replicated in these areas.[98]

The VOC demanded that the Reformed Church customize its mission to outfit the company's imperial and commercial project. The VOC's position relative to the overseas churches does not mean that it was indifferent to the Christian mission or entertained a secular viewpoint, as many historians have claimed. Rather, the Calvinist mission had to be shaped within the framework of a maritime empire. Thus, the Reformed Church's aim to build an *Indisch Sion* as a witness to Protestant Christianity evolved into a religious instrument of empire.

NEW ENVIRONMENTS AND STUBBORN QUESTIONS, 1680s–1730s

It is a long-standing truism among students of Dutch history that the eighteenth century ushered in a new phase in the life of the Republic that contrasted sharply with the "Golden Age" of the seventeenth century. Derided as the "Periweg Period," the eighteenth century in the Netherlands featured economic decline, political retrenchment, and cultural malaise. Many historians have disputed the overdrawn disparity between these eras, yet it is nevertheless true that the Republic faced formidable challenges at home and abroad. The *stadhouder* Willem of Orange invaded England, at the behest of Whigs in Parliament, with a large Dutch armada in November 1688 and triumphed as Willem III (along with his wife, Mary II). This Glorious Revolution brought peace with England, but also committed Dutch financial resources to the ongoing wars with their nemesis, Louis XIV. Two wars that the Netherlands joined against France, the War of the League of Augsburg (1689–1697) and the War of Spanish

Succession (1701–1714), proved tremendously disruptive to trade in the Mediterranean and the Atlantic. Nevertheless, the trading companies adapted to these new environments, as the VOC continued to surpass English, French, and other European corporations in the Indian Ocean and the WIC focused on plantation economies in Surinam, Berbice, and Essequibo.[99]

Calvinists in the Netherlands and the empire engaged in debates about the compatibility of Cartesian philosophy with Reformed theology and Spinozist biblical criticism.[100] In the late 1600s, clerical and lay partisans across the provinces disagreed about the authority and application of scripture, the reality of the devil and angels, and the place of philosophy in Reformed ways of ordering the world. These deliberations correlated with major points of dispute among Calvinists over the administration of the sacraments in non-Christian societies and the translation of the Bible into non-European languages. In this period, Calvinists around the world were grappling with the fundamental question of what it meant to be a Protestant Christian faithful to biblical teachings.

PLANTATION SLAVE COMPLEXES IN THE ATLANTIC

The WIC continued to reinvent itself throughout the vicissitudes of the late seventeenth and eighteenth centuries. Its primary focus centered on the development of plantation economies along the northeastern coastline of South America and the carrying trade in Africa and the Caribbean. Intending to cash in on the lucrative sugar trade, Dutch planters moved into the colonies of Surinam, Berbice, Essequibo, Demerara, and Pomeroon in the 1660s and 1670s. Surinam, the most important of these plantation colonies, came under the authority of a private company, the Society of Surinam, in 1682. The WIC, city of Amsterdam, and Aerssen van Sommelsdijk partnered as the major shareholders in the company. By 1714, Surinam contained 171 sugar plantations, producing 15 million pounds of exports per year, and over 500 plantations by 1740, with dozens in the other locations. The WIC joined with a variety of other syndicates in the carrying trade, concentrating on slaves and gold from West Africa, though in a vastly scaled down capacity. Between 1674 and 1734, the company sent out sixteen ships per year. The company possessed the lucrative *asiento* (until 1701), granting it a monopoly on the shipping of slaves into Spanish American ports. Curaçao in the Caribbean remained the WIC's primary base for reshipping slaves into not only Spanish territories, but others as well, notably the Dutch plantation colonies in South America.[101]

A critical turning point occurred in Dutch fortunes in the Atlantic during and after the War of Spanish Succession (1701–1714). When the outbreak of the war led to a spike in the price of sugar, Dutch planters in Surinam saw opportunities for expanding production and profits. Yet at the war's conclusion, Philip of Anjou, the French Bourbon candidate for the Spanish throne and grandson of Louis XIV, became Philip IV of Spain. The close connection between Spain and France, the archenemy of the Dutch Republic, was disastrous for Dutch merchants in the Atlantic. The new monarch revoked the *asiento* from the WIC conglomerate and awarded it to the French Guinea Company. This loss seriously undercut the WIC's prospects, as it had profited immensely from its privileged position in the carrying trade between Spanish America, the Caribbean, and Spain. As these areas came under French influence, the Dutch were eliminated from all Spanish territories in the Americas, as well as the Mediterranean. The WIC still held on to exclusive contracts for slaves in Surinam and the other colonies on the northeastern coast of South America. This privilege, however, only lasted for twenty more years, as planters complained that the company could not provide an adequate supply of laborers at a competitive price. In 1734, the States General opened slave trading into the area to all merchants, and the WIC could only compete for four more years.[102]

ESCALATING COMPETITION IN ASIA

In the Asian theater of the Dutch commercial empire, important structural shifts in the VOC's role in the Indian Ocean port city network took place in this period. The Japanese shogun's restriction on exports of gold and silver in 1685 and then again in the 1720s, combined with Chinese prohibition of Dutch trading in Canton, deprived the VOC of the currency that made the intra-Asian system work. VOC merchants tried to adapt by using Japanese copper for the regional carrying trade and by procuring Bengali silk for the Japanese exchange. But these measures could do little to satisfy the demand for gold and silver nor prevent the Tokugawa shoguns from curbing the flow of the most valued specie from Japan. Without a substantial Japanese supply, the company had to depend on silver from acquisitions in more expensive markets in Manila and Europe. The constricting East Asian leg of the company's operations raised financing costs, at a time when expenditures were also rising for ships, garrisons, and labor. Between 1680 and 1720, the VOC doubled its labor force, in part to maintain its guard over the monopoly in fine spices in the East Indies and to counteract threats from the English and French.[103]

Yet the VOC continued to be a very profitable company during this period, albeit without the extraordinary (and unsustainable) yields of the midcentury. The Dutch persisted in outpacing English and French shipping into the 1740s.

With the Glorious Revolution, relations between the English East India Company and its Dutch rival eased considerably. Jan de Vries and Ad van der Woude have calculated that the yearly profit from 1680 to 1730 averaged 2 million guilders, compared with 2.1 million guilders during the peak phase from 1630 to 1670. Dutch shipping from the homeland to VOC Asian ports actually increased significantly from the seventeenth to the eighteenth century.[104] Although coffee fell outside of VOC influence in Yemen and Egypt, the company more than compensated by planting coffee plantations in the Priangan region of west Java and dominated the world market for many years.[105] Nevertheless, the VOC competed in a free market in Bengal and Gujarat for products coming into greater demand in Europe, such as cotton, calicoes, and silk. As the volume of trade in textiles grew from European domestic demand, the company's ability to influence pricing in these locations declined. After the 1690s, opium found a stronger market than textiles in the Indonesian archipelago. Tea from China also proved out of the question as VOC ships were barred from Canton. The spice and coffee trade continued to keep the company prosperous, but in the face of increasing competition and changing markets in the Indian Ocean and in Europe.

CONFLICT IN THE ASIAN MISSIONS

The Calvinist missions in Asia carried on in the East Indies, South Asia, and to a much lesser extent at the Cape of Good Hope, primarily through the schools run by local teachers and overseen by *predikanten* and colonial officials. At the universities of Utrecht and Leiden in the 1650s, academic study focused on Islam, and pagan traditions became a higher priority. This academic initiative corresponded to the founding of seminaries at Nallur (near Jaffnapatnam) in 1690 for Tamil-speaking students, at Colombo in 1696 for Sinhalese-speaking students, and later (1735–1745) in Batavia for Malay-speaking students. Directed by *predikanten*, these seminaries trained native men in Reformed teachings and in Dutch so they could teach and enter colonial administration more effectively in schools and potentially undergo ordination as ministers themselves. In concert with language and religious instruction in seminaries, ministers increased attention to translation work, which culminated in complete versions of the Bible in Malay (1733), Tamil (1759), and Sinhalese (1813).[106]

The translation of complicated theological concepts by ministers keenly attentive to nuance led to a number of strong disagreements, the most contested of which was the Malay Bible. Two Batavian *predikanten*, Melchior Leijdekker and Petrus van der Vorm, completed a much-heralded Malay Bible in 1701. Hoping to use it to evangelize among Muslim intellectuals at the court of Johor (on the southern tip of the Malay peninsula), Leijdekker and van der Vorm employed a stylized vernacular, known by the Dutch as High Malay. Long before the translation was finished, Francois Valentijn (a *predikant* in Amboina) criticized the use of this vernacular, arguing that it was useless among the vast number of common folk with whom ministers, *ziekentroosteren*, and teachers interacted on a regular basis. This protracted debate illustrates a great deal about Calvinist attitudes about language, religion, and culture. It is important to note here that the controversy detracted considerably from the mission to convert.[107]

Disputes over the proper linguistic medium for the Bible in the East Indies coincided with an even more hostile disagreement over the administration of the sacraments. Questions and conflicts over whom to baptize, whom to invite to the Lord's Supper, and under what circumstances for each had plagued Dutch Calvinists since the 1610s. A cluster of questions circulated around the world throughout the seventeenth and eighteenth centuries. Since these issues were not only missionary-centered, but were also basic pastoral concerns, queries and discussions also emanated from areas, such as Surinam, St. Eustatius, and Cape Town, that exhibited little to no mission activity. What should an adult understand to receive baptism and to receive communion? How should consistories measure understanding? What behaviors should an adult exhibit in order to obtain sacramental standing? Under what conditions should slaves be baptized and allowed to take communion? Should the standards for partaking in the Lord's Supper be the same as those for baptism? Alternatively, should communicants be held to higher standards? If so, what were they? Fundamentally, consistories struggled to identify who, among non-European peoples, qualified as a faithful Calvinist.

Heated disagreements over translation and sacraments in this period produced enmity among *predikanten* and soured company authorities in Asia on quarrelsome ministers. Not only did these quarrels distract from the mission to convert, but they underscored as well the nettlesome entanglements of religion and culture that bedeviled Calvinists outside of their European heartland.

DECLINING FORTUNES AND DIMINISHING EXPECTATIONS, 1730s–1800

The forces that had long pressed on the Netherlands and its commercial empire conspired in the second half of the eighteenth century to undo the accomplishments of the "Golden Age." The collapse of the East and West India Companies, the loss of empire in Asia, the malaise of Calvinism at home and abroad, and the fall of the Dutch Republic itself occurred almost in tandem by the end of the 1700s. Stagnation, decline, decay, and loss are apt descriptors for most aspects of Dutch society, whether it be political governance, artistic imagination, intellectual innovation, military power, or economic production. No single factor accounts for these coalescing trends, though weakness in each domain affected the other. A minor French incursion in Flanders in 1747 raised popular alarms about the invasions of Louis XIV that humiliated the Dutch and brought to power a *stadhouder*, Willem V, after a hiatus of forty-five years. Perceptions of weakness and decline brought on by the corruption of city and provincial regents set off a long period of struggle between promonarchical partisans of the house of Orange who supported a strong, central authority and prodemocratic activists who wished to wipe the whole corrupt slate of regents clean. Instability in the body politic widened the vulnerability to Dutch forces on land and sea in the Seven Years War (1757–1763) and in the Fourth Anglo-Dutch War (1780–1784), fought in Europe, Asia, and the Atlantic. Disruptions to trade and loss of holdings in the Caribbean and Coromandel, albeit temporary, proved costly for Dutch merchants, companies, and shareholders.[108]

CALVINIST ACCOMMODATIONS

That cultural and religious mainstay of the Dutch Republic, the Reformed Church felt its political and social influence slip somewhat during the latter half of eighteenth century. The Reformed remained the public church and it retained the staunch support of the political establishment. Yet the hardened doctrinaire confessionalism that gave rise to fierce debates over church doctrine, biblical interpretation, and rationalistic philosophy became much less pronounced in the face of an emphasis on heartfelt piety.[109] Calvinist ministers continued to educate their flocks in the scriptures and Reformed teachings to "satisfy the heart and the mind."[110] Among all Christian denominations, religious piety reinforced a commitment to civic virtue and public respectability. The growing acceptance of open Catholic worship and the construction of synagogues outside Amsterdam also signaled the waning of confessional politics dominated by the Reformed Church. Catholic populations continued to grow during this period, and by 1809 the Reformed Church counted for only 55 percent of the Dutch population. Seminary students studying for ordination fell off dramatically from the three to four hundred enrolled in the 1750s to only around forty to fifty by 1790.[111] Far removed from the rancorous struggles over rationalism, the tranquil years of the eighteenth century enshrined respectability, courtesy, and piety as marks of a good citizen and faithful Christian.[112]

FALL OF THE REPUBLIC

The Dutch Republic came to an end in the early months of 1795, as an invading army from France brought to life the Batavian Republic, a democratic government modeled along French Revolutionary principles. Parties in the Netherlands supporting the house of Orange, on the one hand, and a Patriot, democratic regime on the other, had vied for power since 1780. Drawing inspiration from the revolt against Spain and Enlightenment ideals, the Patriot party pushed for a government of the people to complete the task begun by breaking away from Spanish tyranny in the late sixteenth century. Patriots seized on widespread dissatisfaction with political and financial institutions, which even extended to the VOC and WIC for their ineptitude in the Fourth Anglo-Dutch War. A premature Patriot revolution fizzled in the summer of 1787, as Frederick William II, king of Prussia, deployed 26,000 troops to The Hague to reinstall Willem V as *stadhouder*. But in the long term, the house of Orange could not endure; eight years later, Patriot groups cheered on and welcomed French troops into the northern provinces.[113]

LAST GASPS OF A COMMERCIAL EMPIRE

As the Republic was coming to an end in the 1780s and 1790s, the vestiges of what in the seventeenth century had been a thriving commercial empire in the Atlantic were also coming apart. Until the 1770s, however, the plantation economies in South America and the Caribbean churned out between 18 and 20 million pounds of sugar and 6 million pounds of coffee per year to the Netherlands for re-export. From 1764 to 1774, Surinam contained 465 plantations worked by 60,000 enslaved laborers. Yet profits dropped significantly in the 1770s, as a result of a major slave revolt and falling coffee prices. Then later, the Fourth War brought assaults and devastation to St. Eustatius, Surinam, Berbice, Essequibo, and other locations at the hands of the British navy. In the aftermath of the Fourth Anglo-Dutch War, the States General closed the WIC and paid off its remaining shares at a steeply discounted rate. Surinam, Essequibo, Pomeroon, Berbice, Demerara, and Dutch garrisons on Africa's Gold Coast remained technically under the control of the States General, though it exercised little authority over these colonies. In the Americas, only Surinam would survive the Napoleonic Wars under Dutch rule; in Africa, the Netherlands' outposts fell into commercial insignificance in the nineteenth century. Curaçao, St. Maarten, St. Eustatius, Bonaire, Saba, and Aruba continued on as the Dutch Caribbean into modern times. The Dutch Calvinist presence in these territories remained minimal and pastoral by the end of the eighteenth century.[114]

In Asia, the end of the eighteenth century carried the same mortal consequences for the VOC, as the corporation was buffeted by a deteriorating trading
system, betrayed by internal incompetence, and overmatched by British naval and
commercial might. Britain emerged as the dominant European commercial, political, and military power in the second half of the 1700s, with the turning point
in 1757 at the Battle of Plassey. English merchants gained the upper hand in Surat
and Bengal in South Asia and in Canton in the east, elbowing the VOC out of the
growing European market for tea, coffee, cotton, and silk. Obtaining opium from
Bengal, the EIC solved the problem of financing its exchanges for Chinese goods.
The VOC retained control over spices in the East Indies, but demand fell significantly during this period. Governors in the company had adapted to changing
markets and circumstances for almost two hundred years, but at this time it suffered from bad policies, neglected fortifications, and poor decisions. The company
paid its personnel poorly, making it difficult to recruit and retain adequate, let
alone talented, human capital. Earlier in the century, governors allowed the over-
cultivation of sugar plantations around Batavia without sufficient drainage. Standing water created a breeding ground for malaria-carrying mosquitos, leading to a
vicious outbreak of the disease in 1733, followed by a perennially high death rate.[115]
The reputation for unhealthy habitation exacerbated the VOC's problems with
recruitment. Those who did sign on as administrators, merchants, and soldiers
engaged in personal, private trading to augment low wages, which cut into potential profits for the company. Historians of the VOC have pointed to the opaque
bookkeeping practices that provided neither governors nor the *Heren XVII* with
the information they needed to make sound financial decisions. Shady accounting obscured the fact that by the time of the Fourth Anglo-Dutch War in 1780 the
VOC "was not a profitable enterprise—and had not been for some time."[116]

The war with England in effect finished off the VOC. The British besieged
Coromandel, Malabar, and Ceylon, seizing the Dutch fortress at Negapatnam,
destroying ships, and razing fortifications. Across the Indian Ocean, the VOC
lost ships and cargo to destruction and seizure, so that by 1784 the VOC had
sacrificed half of its fleet and forfeited 43 million guilders in financial losses. As
the Dutch Republic faced invasion at home in the 1790s, the king of Kandy
sought to expel the VOC from Ceylon, and the sultan of Golconda pressed on
the Coromandel coast. By the end of the century, the British had taken over all
Dutch outposts in South Asia.[117] Under the newly installed Batavian Republic,
the government attempted to restructure the VOC, but no scheme proved fi-
nancially feasible, and on the last day of the eighteenth century the company
closed its doors permanently. Only the East Indies, Surinam, and the Antilles
survived the Napoleonic Wars as colonies of the Kingdom of the Netherlands.[118]

After the demise of the VOC, Calvinist ministers carried on in their pastoral functions and, by virtue of the educational infrastructure developed over the preceding century, persisted in the evangelical work of spreading the word of God to non-Christians. Consistories in the main hubs of Batavia, Semarang, Makassar, Amboina, Ternate, Banda, Timor-Kupang, and Padang in Indonesia; Melaka in Malaysia; Colombo, Jaffnapatnam, and Galle in Ceylon; and Cape Town continued to report to the classes of Amsterdam and Walcheren on the status of churches and schools in a given year. Overseas ministers went out from these centers to visit the numerous small satellite congregations staffed by *ziek-entroosteren* and schools run by local teachers and to make an accounting of the state of affairs. The annual pastoral reports in these later years of the eighteenth century primarily record the number and location of *predikanten* and *zieken-troosteren* and quantify the Reformed community in all areas, without any substantive narrative about pastoral or missionary work.

The churches in the Moluccas and North Sulawesi, Batavia, and Colombo seemed to hold their own or endure relatively minor reductions, but congregations in Galle, Banda, Ternate, Makassar, Melaka, and others contracted significantly. All churches seemed to settle into a complacent routine in the *Indisch Sion* once the disputes over translation and sacraments ended in the 1730s and the misfortunes for Calvinists multiplied. Consistories lost battles with VOC governors over allowing public worship in Lutheran-constructed churches (in Batavia and Cape Town) and ignoring private Catholic masses. Disease and poor health took their toll on ministers and *ziekentroosteren*; as the company's long-term prospects looked increasingly less promising, recruitment of ordained clergy became more difficult. Calvinists had long complained about the idolatry and immorality of pagans and Moors, but the hopes of converting them, even after all the translation and educational work, seemed distant. Five ministers in Batavia opined in 1737 that the "we must conclude that the desired outcome of the production of booklets . . . that many Jews and Mohammedans would be enlightened did not happen."[119] Later in the century, the Batavia consistory wrote to the Amsterdam classis that ministers came overseas with zeal for converting pagans and Moors, but eventually lost the motivation because of all the hardship and indifference, with the result that wickedness "increased daily."[120] There are many similar complaints, but there is also a striking silence in the sources from the late eighteenth century that betray a loss of enthusiasm for saving souls. The consistory records from Batavia and Colombo, for example, devote almost all attention to recording baptisms and discussing the management of pastoral duties and other administrative matters. As noted earlier, pastoral reports provide quantitative detail about the mission, but very little about church activity. The consistory in Cape Town did give off high heat in May 1744 at the audacity of a Moravian missionary, George Schmidt, who found a receptive audience among the Khoi peoples. The Reformed ministers demanded that the governor expel the "Hottentot converter" from the colony.[121]

Reading and responding to complaints by overseas *predikanten*, ministers across Holland and Zeeland possessed a growing sense that the church needed a different strategy for conversion. Since the arrival of the first personnel, the Reformed Church had always blended parish ministries and their institutional mechanisms with the work of converting non-Christians. Churches, schools, orphanages, translated materials, and catechism classes represented the basic instruments of proselytizing among pagans and Moors. By the late eighteenth century, a new approach began to gain traction among globally minded Protestants in the Netherlands. In 1770, a religious organization in Holland, "the propaganda fidei," sponsored an essay contest on the question of the means to convert the pagan. Initially, no one responded, but the Haarlem Society of the Sciences (*Hollandsche Maatschappij der Wetenschappen*) issued a second call for papers in 1774. Three entries appeared. Each one distinguished between parish ministry to company employees and the exclusively missionary enterprise of evangelizing among non-Europeans. Preachers, teachers, and catechists unfettered by parish responsibilities and trained in pagan religions in a seminary signified a new way of thinking about missions overseas. In the ensuing twenty years, as the VOC and the *Indisch Sion* were winding down, Johannes van der Kemp, a physician from Dordrecht, joined with others to form the Dutch Missionary Society (*Nederlandsch Zendelinggenootschap*) in 1798. To a large extent, this new conversion impulse grew out of a self-perceived need among Protestants to transform Western Christianity and launched the modern approach to missions. Global Calvinism of the early modern period was bounded inseparably by the state, represented by the trading companies, whose goal was to replicate a Christian republic in the territories of the Dutch empire. The attempt to convert pagans and Moors was an interconnected project of empire building, commercial trading, and church planting. The Protestant missionary societies from the nineteenth century marked a new course independent of states and devoted to individualized, transformative conversion. Thus, an era of Calvinism, commerce, and empire had ended and a new one was getting underway.[122]

CONCLUSION

The interwoven threads of political revolt, religious reformation, and commercial empire shaped the history of the Dutch Republic. A society that rejected the religious coercion of the Hapsburgs and that made room for dissenters at the margins adopted Calvinism, a creed not known for accommodation, as the public faith. Though cleaving to theological exclusivism, Calvinists set out to throw open the doors of Protestant Christianity to peoples in Asia, America, and Africa. Empire was the Dutch engine of commerce, just as commerce was the raison d'être of empire. Commerce and empire also operated as the vectors of Calvinism's push into distant lands.

To a large degree but in varying proportions, commerce, state building, and conversion formed the pillars of all early modern empires except the Qing dynasty, which disparaged trade and accommodated most local worship practices. A brief comparison of these components illustrates both equivalent and unique features of Dutch operations. As the public religion of the Dutch Republic, the Reformed Church supported the commercial and imperial aims of the trading companies, just as the VOC and WIC (briefly in Brazil) opened the door for the spread of Protestant Christianity. This mutually supportive relationship thrived in all European Christian and Asian Muslim empires, though the English demonstrated the least inclination to impress their beliefs and practices on others. Aside from the short-lived "Indian Praying Towns" in New England (1646–1675) and the spotty efforts of the Society for the Propagation of the Gospel in Foreign Parts (1701), English Protestants made almost no lasting impression on indigenous peoples. France's trading empire in North America and South Asia with thousands of Jesuits, Capuchins, and Recollects as agents of Catholicization came closest to the Dutch model. The exclusive imprint of the Republic's empire was the integration of missions within the undertakings of private trading companies. As a predominantly commercial enterprise, the Dutch empire, however, stood alone in its commitment to religious proselytization.

In some respects, the interrelations between colonial society and conversion in the Dutch empire bore a closer relation to the Ottoman and Mughal domains than to their Iberian Catholic counterparts. Dutch ministers and lay leaders sought to translate the structural components of the public church in the Netherlands into colonial spaces. These replicated elements were (1) organizational agencies, such as the consistory and the diaconate; (2) indoctrination instruments, including schools, catechetical lessons, and worship services; (3) pedagogical materials, notably catechisms and grammars; and (4) legal sanctions that marginalized all other religious groups. The Ottomans pushed into the Christian lands of Hungary, Serbia, Transylvania, and Romania in the early 1500s, and Mughal emperors incorporated Hindu, Sikh, and Christian communities in their enlarged control over South Asia during the same period. Emperors in both dynasties actively promoted Islam by relocating religious structures in new areas. Ottoman and Mughal rulers patronized scholars, built madrasas, founded waqfs, and erected mosques. These empires also implanted their systems of social organization (known in the nineteenth century as the millet system) that allowed toleration for the "people of the book" (*Ahl al-Kitab*), yet imposed additional taxes and relegated *dhimmi* (protected peoples) to a subordinate status.[123] Like Ottomans and Mughals, the Dutch sought to convert people by importing institutions, cultivating a public presence, and imposing legal prescriptions in the territories they controlled. By contrast, religious diffusion strategies in the Spanish, Portuguese, and Safavid empires incorporated the more assertive tactics of forced conversion, widespread destruction of sacred sites, and aggressive proselytization.

The three chapters that follow detail Calvinism's engagement with commerce, empire, and conversion, and the final two chapters show that the Dutch Republic bore the imprint of that engagement. The enmeshment of commerce, empire, and religion in the seventeenth and eighteenth centuries produced one of the most globalized societies in Europe.

2

CHURCH AND COLONIAL SOCIETY

In March 1654, Nicolaas Verburg, the outgoing governor of Formosa, submitted a report on the state of affairs in his jurisdiction to Joan Maetsuijcker, the governor general in Batavia. Verburg launched into a scathing critique of the missionary labors of the Dutch clergy, who had been engaged in bitter disputes over issues of cultural accommodation in converting natives. He wrote: "It may appear strange to some that I, a political agent, should thus venture to meddle with things belonging to the sphere of the Church; and they may be still more surprised if I enlarge—as it is my intention to do—on the principal methods which have been followed till now for converting the heathen in Formosa. . . ." Verburg believed that governors had a right to weigh in on missionary matters because "all Christian political authorities should be faithful foster-fathers of the Church," just as the clergy should also devote themselves to "promoting the interests" of Christianity.[1] Having justified his standing to comment on church affairs, he criticized the ministers for putting their own interests above those of the missions, for attaching too much importance to theological precision, and for introducing new methods that confused converts.

Verburg's stated conviction that colonial governors ought to act as "foster-fathers of the Church" stands at odds with the prevailing image of VOC and WIC governors.[2] Church sources regularly complained about the companies' penury for missions, and governors routinely clamped down on clergy. Historians have read these complaints and conflicts through modern lenses, leading to a distorted view of religion and commerce in the Dutch empire. Traditional scholarship has imputed to the trading companies a secular, profit-conscious outlook at odds with Christian missions. This ostensible forward-looking ethic contrasts sharply with the regressive spirit of other imperial actors in this period.

Iberian powers bonded crusading with empire building just as Muslim regimes aligned jihad with commercial enterprise. Only British imperialists, also Protestant, stand out with the Dutch as shedding conventional religious sentiments in pursuit of profits and power.[3]

This chapter presents a different vision of Calvinism in the Dutch empire. Calvinism played a central role in the development of the Dutch commercial empire in maritime Asia and the Atlantic (until the loss of Brazil in 1654). The viewpoint expressed in Verburg's report betrays a Christian persona embedded within the leadership of the East and West India companies in the Netherlands and in overseas territories. High-ranking officers held a variety of religious beliefs and attitudes about the Reformed Church. And like Verburg, some governors (such as Jacques Specx) harbored much animosity toward particular ministers. Nevertheless, the companies and their governors promoted a consistent idea of Protestant identity that both overlapped and conflicted with theologically strict notions held by Calvinist *predikanten*.

Colonial governors presided over outposts and territories in the magisterial tradition of councilors and burgomasters in Dutch towns and cities. Regardless of their personal piety, magistrates considered themselves as the *Christelijke overheid* (Christian authority) over their dominions. Rulership had always invoked an ingrained sense of religious stewardship and continued to do so long after the Reformation. Company governors also called forth this understanding in their dealings with *predikanten* and consistories in the empire. Similar to the aims of urban rulers in the Dutch Republic, company officials sought to promote the Reformed Church, manage religious (and ethnic) pluralism, and support a nonideological Protestant social order. In all practical respects, company officials wielded even more power in colonies than city governments did back home. Such Christian management, governors believed, promoted stability in colonial societies.

Both company officials and Calvinist ministers encountered new social problems in VOC- and WIC-held territories. Large-scale enslavement and widespread poverty featuring manumitted slaves, orphans, and abandoned women posed unfamiliar challenges in multiethnic, pluralistic colonial environments. To manage potential disorder, political and ecclesiastical officials worked together, sometimes grudgingly, to translate Dutch traditions across the empire. When these remedies proved unworkable, governors and ministers had to devise new remedies to keep order. As this translation process unfolded, governors and *predikanten* became involved in heated controversies, which often stemmed from divergent views about the place of Calvinism in colonial societies. Sometimes disputes arose simply from personal animosity between two hardheaded men. The struggles over principle and personality were not unique to the trading companies but were commonplace at all times and in all governing bodies in the Dutch Republic after the Reformation.

Despite the quarrels, Calvinist ministers—and the consistories and diaconates they oversaw—contributed crucially to the maintenance of a mercantile empire. A Protestant civilizing process served colonial needs in creating an educated local population and reducing crime, disorder, and unrest. The attention to Christianization also targeted rank-and-file sailors, soldiers, and service personnel for the company. Most did not exhibit an affection for or pursue an affiliation with the Reformed Church. They earned a reputation as a rough and rowdy lot. Among church figures and company governors, distinct points of view over the complex intersections of commerce, colonialism, and Calvinism emerged on a range of issues in the maritime empire. *Predikanten* and governors conflicted over conceptions of a Protestant empire yet converged in many of its practical operations. The central questions that frame this chapter are: How did church and company officials conceive of Protestantism and empire? How did these conceptions translate in concrete efforts to manage the most intractable problems in colonial societies, namely sexuality, poverty, and slavery?

HUGO GROTIUS AND THE PRINCIPLES OF THE DUTCH MARITIME EMPIRE

Imperial apologists in the late medieval and early modern periods blended belief in religious dominion with ideologies drawn from classical world empires to give legitimacy to territorial expansion, commercial entitlement, and colonial rule. European claims in the Americas in the sixteenth and seventeenth centuries were staked to foundational principles of the Roman imperial heritage and to perpetual impulses for Christian mission. This imperial self-image was emphatically cultivated by Spanish, French, and Portuguese monarchs and their theorists, but less so by the English. While writers in this period, such as Richard Hakluyt, Francis Bacon, and William Temple, did utilize the language of empire and monarchy to refer to colonial and commercial activity in North America, the English outlook was more akin to "a protectorate of several interests rather than a universal state."[4] In Spain, on the other hand, the Catholic Monarchs (Ferdinand of Aragon and Isabella of Castile) and then the Hapsburgs (Charles I and Philip II) aggressively promoted Christian proselytizing and conquest as joint ventures reinforced by universalist religious and imperial claims. This conceptual basis for empire grew out of long-standing crusades against Muslim kingdoms in Iberia and the Ottomans in the Mediterranean. Crusading against Muslim powers coalesced with converting pagans, as legitimized by the papal bulls of Alexander VI in 1493. Portugal and France also committed themselves to conversion, sending out and patronizing large numbers of missionary priests from religious orders, most notably from the Society of Jesus.[5]

Positioned against European Catholic rivals, British imperial ideology rested on the pillars of a constructed self-identity that was "Protestant, commercial, maritime, and free."[6] Though some ardent English ministers recognized and acted on opportunities to preach and convert, in general the British demonstrated a reticence for missions until the mid-eighteenth century. The EIC staked out a Protestant religious identity in India and by the 1750s supported missionary work in ways that accommodated the need for trade and peaceful social interaction.[7]

The Dutch overseas enterprise bore the closest resemblance to the English, resting on the pillars of private trading companies rather than centralized, state-directed regimes. The preeminent role of commerce in the Dutch early modern operations has led some prominent historians to conclude that they "were not an imperial power in any meaningful sense, nor ever regarded themselves as such." Connecting empire to universal monarchy and territorial possession, Anthony Pagden asserted: "The claim by English royalists in the 1660s that the Republic of Holland was seeking a Universal Monarchy of the sea was an oxymoron. As every imperialist knew, 'empire' implied rulership, and that, on the British and Dutch understanding of the law of nations, could not be exercised at sea."[8]

It is certainly true that the Dutch did not appropriate the imperial ideology of the Iberian powers.[9] Various theorists pressed the case that the Republic was the quintessential anti-imperialist confederation, freeing Dutch people at home and oppressed populations abroad from Catholic Habsburg tyranny. The *Heren XVII*'s choice of the name Batavia for the VOC headquarters in Jakarta perhaps best exemplifies this anti-imperial ethos.[10] Netherlanders had long identified themselves with the courageous, freedom-loving Batavians who rebelled against the Roman Empire. Throughout the revolt against Spain, Dutch propagandists rallied around the Batavian myth to exhort their people to throw off the yoke of Hapsburg rule.[11] "Batavia" symbolized most poignantly for the Dutch the global extension of these ideals. Yet in advancing the anti-imperial cause, the Dutch were also making the case for taking possession of territory, controlling trade, and making war on those who resisted them, all of which were the basic aspects of empire building.

The principles that underlay the Dutch empire were resistance to Hapsburg imperialism, free trade rooted in natural law, and Protestant witness to Chris-

Fig. 7. Workshop of Michiel Jansz. van Mierevelt (1566–1641),
Portrait of Hugo Grotius, Jurist, 1631; Rijksmuseum Amsterdam

tian truth on a world stage.[12] In the critical first two decades of the seventeenth century, humanists, jurists, theologians, and commercial publicists enunciated these values and wrapped them in a banner of Dutch exceptionalism. The coalescence of revolt against Hapsburg authority, reformation of Christian teaching, and contravention of Portuguese imperial claims pushed Dutch intellectuals not only to justify their rights, but also to consider their historical place in light of biblical and classical ideals. Many theorists, including Caspar Barlaeus, Willem Usselincx, and Johannes de Laet projected republican and Reformed Protestant values on a global seascape. Yet it was Hugo Grotius's defense of commerce and war in the early seventeenth century that staked out the theoretical point of departure for the Dutch empire through the period of company rule.[13]

The circumstance that first prompted Grotius to write occurred in 1603 when Admiral Jacob van Heemskerk seized a Portuguese carrack, the *Santa Caterina*, in the straits of Singapore. Discovering a bountiful cargo worth 3 million guilders, the Dutch were hardly going to return the ship and its cargo to their Portuguese enemies. As the VOC was getting off the ground, the *Heren XVII* enlisted Grotius for their defense. To defend possession of the *Santa Caterina*, he composed *On the Law of Prize and Booty* in 1604–1605. The broader background from which Grotius and others operated was the endeavor by both the East and West India Companies to break into the commercial sea lanes of the Indian and Atlantic oceans against their European rivals.[14] The Iberians asserted monopolistic rights rooted in their claims to the universal authority of the Spanish crown and the sanction of the papacy in bulls at the end of the fifteenth century.[15] From 1605 to the 1620s, Grotius answered these assertions and constructed the ideological framework of the Dutch commercial enterprises in *On the Authority of the Highest Powers in Sacred Matters* (1618), *On the Law of War and Peace* (1625), and *On the Truth of the Christian Religion* (1640). They formed the conceptual basis for the Dutch mercantile empire.

Grotius appealed to three foundations to articulate a theory for international relations and interaction with indigenous societies: natural law, classical history, and the "true" Christian religion. In *On the Law of War and Peace*, he contended that freedom of exchange between societies was an innate law of nature that could not be abrogated by appeals to universal monarchy or papal sanction. Rather, natural law bound all people, regardless of religion, as creatures created by God to a universal set of standards. Free trade represented one of the most basic of these principles. Grotius also marshaled a wide array of Roman, Greek, and Macedonian statesmen, geographers, and historians to provide abundant evidence of long-standing trading networks that predated Vasco da Gama and Afonso de Albuquerque. These regular circuits of exchange, according to Grotius, made a mockery of Portuguese claims to exclusive privileges based on antecedence.[16]

For Grotius, the Spanish and Portuguese violated natural law by conquering societies, ruthlessly exploiting them, and coercing people to trade on terms beneficial solely to Iberian imperial interests. Grotius drew amply from the Black Legend of Spanish Catholic cruelty to dramatize his indictment against Iberian predation.[17] He wrote that the Spanish and Portuguese had brought "despotism . . . to every quarter of the world."[18] This transgression against the natural order of free exchange compelled the Dutch to intervene on behalf of oppressed peoples even though they were infidels. Other Dutch propagandists riffed repetitively on this Grotian chord. To cite just one example, Godefridus Udemans, a Calvinist *dominee* (minister) in Zierikzee (Zeeland) who wrote *The Spiritual Rudder* ('*T geestelyck roer*, 1638), cast the Dutch as allies with indigenous peoples against the Spanish and Portuguese.[19] Grotius pressed this case in the seizure of the *Santa Caterina*, arguing that the King of Johor requested Dutch assistance in his struggle with the Portuguese. The company, as an agent of the duly constituted government of the Republic, was therefore fully justified in retaining the booty as compensation.[20] He continued, "Now we have shown . . . how well it accords with nature's plan and with human brotherhood that one person should give aid to another, and therefore we readily see that the entrance of the Dutch into the war as allies of the King of Johor was permissible. One may go further and say that, since the Hollanders were well able to assist him, they could hardly have remained guiltless while withholding assistance."[21] The Dutch, just like their Batavian forebears, resisted imperial domination, waged war against them at home, and acted on behalf of besieged local rulers across Asia. This Grotian principle became one of the central policies of Dutch empire building in Asia and the Atlantic.[22]

A second Grotian law of nature that shaped VOC and WIC strategy was the tenet that treaties were inviolable (*pacta sunt servanda*). Grotius maintained that once parties engaging in free trade entered into an agreement, the contract was binding and could not be invalidated. The aggrieved party had the right to punish contractual breaches, which in this case meant that a private corporation could legally retaliate and rectify infringements. Even if a party joined a treaty without fully understanding its consequences, suffering as a result in hardship and distress—even slavery—this principle of natural law allowed no occasion for repudiating or redressing its terms. Grotius's defense of the VOC's right to enforce contracts and inflict punishment on transgressing parties justified, in the minds of the Dutch, violence against both native rulers and European interlopers.[23] It was in this legal spirit that Coen punished the rulers of Banda in 1621 by massacring most of the population for violating an exclusive treaty with the VOC. This "colonial empire by treaty" shaped Dutch policy in Asia and the Atlantic, as governors, when possible, pressed native princes and elders into monopolistic contracts and then enforced them with military force.[24]

The obvious paradox, if not outright contradiction, between the enforcement of treaties and the advocacy of free trade as rights derived from natural law enabled the Dutch to present themselves as anti-imperialists, while engaging in war to uphold monopolistic contracts. Grotius's rhetorical and legal mastery was a balancing act that bemused Dutch commercial and imperial rivals. But in terms of imperial ideology, the inviolability of treaties, in combination with the appeal to free trade, gave the VOC and WIC the justification they needed for using force when it suited their commercial and geopolitical aims. The theoretical flexibility enabled companies to pursue monopolistic agreements when possible, as they did in Banda and Jakarta; oust the Portuguese, as they did in

Amboina, Melaka, Elmina, and Luanda; yet also take territorial control where necessary, as in Ceylon, Formosa, Brazil, and the Cape of Good Hope.[25]

Grotius buttressed his application of natural law by delineating the responsibilities required of the Dutch in overseas commerce by what he referred to as true Christian religion. Most historians have glossed over the religious elements in his conceptualization of commercial empire. Those who have recognized his religious references tend to read Grotius as subordinating the interests of Christianity to the priorities of country, company, and even the universal bond of humanity. One scholar of late has observed that in any choice between local non-Christian allies and the Portuguese, Grotius opted for the former. From this perspective, Grotius is said to have essentially advised company directors to "disregard such nebulous notions as Christian fellowship and do their duty as citizens of the world."[26] Unfortunately, this view takes a cynical interpretation of Grotius's own professed statements about Christian responsibility in the service of trade and mission. Grotius exhibited a devout commitment to an irenic Protestant faith and to proselytization of Muslims, Jews, and pagans. Grotius was, after all, a firm supporter of the Remonstrant cause and a participant in the theological disputes of his day. He even paid for his involvement with imprisonment and exile. He wrote commentaries on the Old and New Testaments, a catechism, and treatises on aspects of the Christian life and on the passion of Christ.[27]

Grotius sought to infuse a Protestant Christian ethos into the Dutch commercial empire in two specific ways. First, he contended that pushing the Portuguese and Spanish out of their imperial holdings constituted an act of Christian charity. Grotius grounded that argument in the moral obligations that Christianity imposed on its followers to assist victims of injustice even when other Christians perpetrated the violence. In presenting the case for VOC intervention in Johor, he noted that "Holy Writ . . . bids us deliver the innocent from destruction."[28] And he went on to give numerous examples from the Old and New Testament with their most complete expression in the Golden Rule. The key distinction for Grotius was *true* religion—observance not weighed down by papal pretension and not (false) religion as an excuse for exploitation. He declared, "[T]here is nothing that serves the cause of true religion better than such acts of kindness. . . . The Indian peoples must be shown what it means to be a Christian. . . . Let those peoples look upon their religion stripped of false symbols . . . let them marvel at the faith which forbids that even infidels should be neglected. In achieving these ends, we shall be preparing men for God."[29] The effort to defend societies from predation, according to Grotius, had an evangelical purpose; namely, it gave non-Christians an example of genuine charity that would predispose them to a missionary message.

Second, Grotius promoted the expansion of an ecumenical Christian faith through the Dutch commercial empire. In *On the Truth of the Christian Religion*, he hoped to infuse a missionary dimension into the Dutch trading companies, stating that "my purpose was to benefit all my countrymen, especially sea-faring men, that they might not (as many do) lose and misspend their time. . . . I exhorted them to use the art [of navigation], not only for their own proper gain and commodity, but also for the propagation of the true Christian Religion." In part, he was concerned about the corrosive effects of non-Christian religions and the temptations of the flesh on Protestants going overseas. Grotius thus wrote to give Christians confidence in the truth of their own religion so that they would spurn the superstitions of pagans and "not imitate them in their dissolute and licentious manner of life."[30]

Grotius set forth the fundamental ethical tenets of Christianity, eschewing dogmatic nuances that he believed would present difficulties for peoples beyond Europe.[31] Yet he also sidestepped foundational teachings that most every Christian fully embraced, such as the Trinity, the Incarnation, and the sacraments. Even though he acknowledged that "a great diversity of opinion" existed among Christians, he maintained that "there are some common principles, whereof it is agreed by all."[32] These beliefs included the existence of a transcendent creator, the immortality of the soul, the authority of scripture, the divine power of Jesus Christ, and the moral tenets of Christianity.[33] Grotius presented a universal image of Christendom that he believed would win many pagans, Jews, and Muslims to Christ. The witness to Christianity that Grotius had in mind within the empire focused on ethical principles, avoided theological precision, and manifested itself in a pious manner of life.[34]

Calvinists most assuredly wanted no part of this irenic humanist treatment of Christianity, in Europe or in the empire. In fact, the Calvinists Gisbertus Voetius, Martin Schoock, and André Rivet heaped scorn on Grotius's treatise by accusing him of Socinianism, a rationalist unitarian theology opposed by almost all Protestants and Catholics.[35] The classes of Amsterdam and Zeeland stood adamantly opposed to this sort of appeal; Grotius's version of Christianity was not the brand propagated by overseas ministers. But a broad-based Protestantism did often comport well with VOC and WIC governors, who supported a broad Christian moral order in their colonies and tamped down the clergy-centric zeal of many *predikanten*. As discussed below, individual company directors interacted with clergy in very diverse ways and took different attitudes toward missions. Yet all endorsed a Protestant Christian point of view to order colonial societies and to counter their Catholic rivals.

Grotius advocated for civil control over clergy and ecclesiastical institutions, an outlook adopted unwaveringly by all company governors. Distressed by religious conflict in the Netherlands, Grotius took the position of the Swiss theologian Thomas Erastus that the state should govern the church. Grotius himself argued that clergy should carry out their responsibilities firmly under the control of civil authorities, an arrangement that accorded well with trading companies that promoted Protestant Christianity but could not tolerate an independent clergy. Grotius parted company with Calvinist and Catholic theologians in assigning the management of ecclesiastical institutions to the state. Division over dogma among Christians generated destructive passions that engulfed societies; thus only a civil polity, freed from sectarian partisanship, could preserve "the sacred ministry" so as to propagate "Christ's kingdom." The magistrate "must, in short, countenance the preaching of the Holy Gospel everywhere."[36] Correspondingly, the role of religion was to "make people quiet, obedient, patriotic, and adherents of justice and equity."[37]

The magnitude of his work for the VOC at this critical moment in the imperial launch ensured that Grotius's views gained wide currency among Dutch mercantile interests.[38] Johannes de Laet joined Grotius in presenting the Dutch overseas undertaking as a Protestant check on Iberian Catholic oppression.[39] In 1625, he published the *Description of the West Indies* (*Beschrijvinghe des West-Indien*) in which he chided Philip II of Spain who "would have one believe that all these lands belong to him from the power of a gift from the Pope of the Romans." De Laet went on to decry the wanton desolation that followed in the wake of the Spanish claims to these lands; he charged "the undisputed right (as they call it) of the king of Spain, on which the terrible scattering, destruction, and devastation of the poor inhabitants of the lands is founded, by taking their spaces, robbing them of all their goods, and appropriating everything that is found in their lands."[40] Udemans, in *The Spiritual Rudder,* followed (and cited) Grotius's *On the Law of Peace and War* closely, arguing that, according to natural law, the Dutch had an unfettered right to trade, including the right to defend it by force against the Spanish and Portuguese in Asia and the Atlantic.[41] Likewise, Willem Usselincx, director of the WIC, espoused the Grotian principle that "trade is free for all; and no one in the world has dominion over any particular region."[42] Finally, Caspar Barlaeus, in his detailed panegyric on Dutch Brazil, also echoed Grotius by appealing to natural law as the basis for the Dutch Republic's mercantile empire.[43]

The Grotian assertion of commerce, anti-imperialism, and Protestant identity remained as the standard points of departure throughout the seventeenth and eighteenth centuries. As the enmity with Spain and Portugal receded in the second half of the 1600s, rivalry with Britain and France emerged as the most formidable threats to the Republic's commercial primacy and political independence. Yet competition and even war with these adversaries did not breed the sharp ideology of anti-imperial struggle. Instead, the Republic's identification with commerce became its defining feature, as both the VOC and WIC constantly jockeyed for advantage among indigenous merchants and European powers. The merchant and theorist Pieter de la Court, along with his brother Johan, became a leading spokesman for the synergetic relationship between commercial expansion and republican liberty. The de la Courts "developed a comprehensive theory of commercial reason of state that radicalized the tentative embrace of mercantile colonial enterprise."[44]

Although company governors and directors in the late seventeenth and eighteenth centuries did not expressly convey a pronounced sense of Protestant identity, it nevertheless continued to form an elemental component of the VOC's corporate ethos. The company continued to underwrite the expenses of *predikanten, ziekentroosteren,* teachers, educational materials, and diaconal charity in the East Indies, South Asia, and the Cape of Good Hope. A secretary for the VOC for over fifty years, Pieter van Dam wrote the *Description of the East India Company (Beschrijvinge van de Oostindische Compagnie,* 1701), which revealed the enduring importance of the company's efforts in spreading Protestant Christianity in the Indian Ocean.[45] Van Dam devoted a significant portion of the account, the fourth of four books in the modern published format, to church affairs in Asia. In it he recounted the enormous effort and expense the company shouldered to propagate the word of God among peoples overseas.[46] The section constituted a strident defense of the VOC in its service of the Reformed Church overseas and Christian mission in Asia and South Africa against the complaints of stinginess and control by ministers. Even though he delivered a blistering critique of troublesome *predikanten* with unrealistic expectations, van Dam contended that the VOC for the past ninety years had done its utmost to support the church and spread Christianity in lands under the company's sovereignty. Such an insistent defense of the VOC's support of mission underscores not only the sense of Christian ethos that resonated among company officers, but also its durability in the eighteenth century.

COMPETING VISIONS OF CHRISTIANITY AND COMMERCIAL EMPIRE

COMPANY AND CHURCH ON MISSION

The VOC and WIC (until its ousting from Brazil in 1654) supported the Reformed Church's missionary ambitions within the parameters of the companies' commercial objectives. Patronage and provision from the companies were institutional, not personal. That is, individual governors might throw their own particular backing behind church and mission, while others might display less enthusiasm for the *Indisch Sion*. Regardless of the disposition of a particular governor, company directors in the Netherlands consistently provided for the churches overseas and their evangelical operations. The commitment of the companies to Protestant Christianity manifested itself in two basic ways.

First, VOC and WIC governors upheld as company policy that the Reformed Church was the public faith in lands under their jurisdiction. Promoters of the WIC insisted that the company maintain the Reformed religion and the company even allowed the clergy in Brazil to form classes and a synod. In Asia, the VOC typically opposed the formation of classes; it did allow a classis to form in the Cape of Good Hope in 1746.[47] The *Heren XIX* strongly supported the preservation of the Reformed Church as the public faith in the Americas, delegating "commissioners for ecclesiastical affairs" in Amsterdam for dealing with the churches in Brazil.[48] Because of the political and economic importance of Portuguese planters in Brazil, the governor prince Johan Maurits of Nassau-Siegen allowed Catholics and also Jews to worship openly, which prompted unceasing complaints from Calvinists in the Netherlands and in the Americas.[49] In New Netherland, where there were no Catholics and few Jews, the WIC endorsed the Reformed Church as the only official faith; other Protestant groups had to worship out of the public eye. A church presence came under the most significant restraints in Surinam, where the WIC exerted partial control from 1682 to 1791. In this plantation colony, Lutherans, Moravians, and Jews received permission to worship publicly, and the government even discouraged church workers from trying to convert slaves.[50] The contrast between missionary efforts in VOC territories and the absence of activity in the Dutch Atlantic outside of Brazil is striking. The reasons for this discrepancy are currently not clear and call for further research.

The *Heren XVII* signaled at the outset their intent to maintain the Reformed faith in the VOC's Asian holdings. In 1617 the directors sent instructions to governor general Laurens Reael to set up schools and churches to propagate the gospel.[51] The renewed charter of the VOC in 1622 stipulated that the company must "maintain the public faith."[52] In Batavia, company officials and ministers negotiated agreements about the place of the church in colonial societies by drafting a detailed church order, first in 1624 for all churches in the East Indies, then in an expanded version in 1643 for Batavia that specified the workings of ministries and offices.[53] These church orders represented minor deviations from the Synod of Dort that defined the doctrines and governed the ministries of the Dutch Reformed Church. Consistories and colonial authorities across the Indian Ocean generally followed the principles of these church orders. In Ceylon, the VOC commander in Jaffnapatnam, Anthony Pavilioen, declared his full support for the Reformed Church and its Christianizing mission in 1665: "The most important point in my opinion is that God's Holy Word is now preached in its true spirit. . . . [I]n the meantime it is our duty to promote this object as much as is in our power. . . . [T]he reverend brethren the clergy must be assisted in their high office by the political power."[54] In 1673 the consistory in Amboina adopted its own less detailed regulations, which the church in Ternate affirmed in 1676. In the Cape of Good Hope, churches primarily followed the Synod of Dort, except on the selection of elders and deacons, which derived from the prescriptions at Batavia.[55]

Second, colonial authorities sought to balance church demands for mission with practical diplomatic considerations in a pluralistic religious environment. Some trading outposts, such as the slave running operations in Elmina, Luanda, and Curaçao in the Atlantic or the isolated Deshima Island in Japan, simply did not allow for the development of missionary activity.[56] In the territories where contracts dictated trading relations, such as in Muslim strongholds in the Moluccas, VOC governors agreed to respect the religion of the local ruler. As the Dutch supplanted the Portuguese in the Moluccas, governors sought to avoid instability caused by the forced and/or mass baptisms of their European predecessors. Consequently in Banda, Ternate, Tidore, and other outlying islands, the Dutch included provisos declaring that both parties would recognize each other's religion, promise not to coerce one another's people into conversion, and agree to return defectors.[57] The agreements, however, did not restrict Calvinist ministers from attempting to bring local peoples baptized by Portuguese and Spanish Jesuits into a Reformed Protestant faith. These *inlandse* (native) Christians composed the mission field for Calvinist *predikanten, ziekentroosteren*, and teachers in territories ruled by a Muslim sultan.

In spreading Protestantism only in areas under direct Dutch control, or among Catholics, or with the consent of the local ruler, the VOC was following the standard European principle of *cuius regio, eius religio*—that is, that the ruler determined the official religion of the realm.[58] A resolution ending the religious wars at the Peace of Augsburg in 1555, then reaffirmed at the Peace of Westphalia in 1648, the law recognized the undisputed right of the ruler to establish the state religion. The Dutch employed this European diplomatic principle to navigate religious politics and the parameters of Calvinist mission in the wider world.

Within colonies under the companies' political jurisdiction, governors and councilors followed pragmatic policies that echoed Grotius's call for a general Protestant social order. The Dutch and European, let alone Calvinist, population remained small amid large numbers of non-Christian and Catholic inhabitants within all settlements. Neither the VOC nor WIC intended to alienate indigenous peoples or migrants from outside Europe. In the Netherlands regents had confronted the challenge of managing religious pluralism after the Reformation, as Calvinism endured there as a minority for most of the seventeenth century. In the cities of Holland and Utrecht, provinces that had the largest numbers of Catholics, magistrates sought to control confessional tensions by imposing punitive restrictions (largely fines) on Catholic intrusions into the public sphere. As long as Catholics held services privately and inconspicuously (and paid a fee), and kept their priest out of public view, magistrates tended to overlook their worship practices.

VOC governors adapted this strategy for most of the seventeenth century by issuing restrictive edicts but not enforcing them unless public practice and Calvinist complaints forced their hand. On the other side, consistories regularly pressed governors and councilors in settlements across the empire to ban all non-Reformed worship practices, as fitting in a "Christian republic."[59] The church orders of 1624 and 1643 both completely banned not only the "heathen superstitions" of the Chinese (i.e., Buddhist rituals), but also New Year celebrations and wayang puppet theater, whether public or private. Equating the use of religious imagery with idolatry, Calvinists found these observances particularly objectionable and lumped them all together as *duiveldienst* (devil worship). Until 1642, the VOC did not go so far as to ban Islam explicitly, but the 1624 prescriptions did call on the "political authority" to outlaw circumcision and enforce Sabbath rest "by all kinds of nations."[60] In July 1642, Anthony van Diemen issued a lengthy set of ordinances codified for Batavia that declared "no other religion could be imparted or propagated in secret or public, but the Reformed Christian Religion that is taught in the Netherlands" upon pain of confiscation of property and banishment.[61] Yet from the 1640s into the 1680s, consistories in Batavia periodically protested the presence and use of pagodas, mosques, and madrasas, as well as the popular expressions of Chinese and Javan culture. Governor generals attempted to mollify the consistory with promises, and indeed occasionally they did crack down on Muslim, Buddhist, Catholic, or other devotions.[62] By the 1720s, pluralism in the public sphere became more commonplace and less contested. Over the objections of Calvinist consistories, VOC governor generals allowed Lutherans to establish a public congregation in Batavia, though the Reformed Church was able to resist incursions by other Protestants until the end of the 1700s.[63]

The presence of Catholicism across colonial territories raised serious concerns for the trading companies, yet governors approached the practice of Roman rites

and observances somewhat differently based on the larger geopolitical circumstances. In all areas except Brazil and later Surinam, governors outlawed Roman Catholicism. After the Portuguese and Spanish no longer posed a serious
threat in the East Indies, governor generals customarily took the same stance as
urban regents in Holland: oppose publicly, overlook until conspicuous, take sym-
bolic measures, but in serious cases crack down. In Ceylon, VOC governors
struck hard against Catholicism until the 1750s because of the lingering menace of the Portuguese, whose Asian operations centered on Goa. On the island
and subcontinent, Jesuits had baptized thousands of Tamils and Sinhalese whose
political loyalties gave the VOC cause for concern. The VOC also overlooked
all but the most conspicuous Buddhist practices, though not Islam or Hinduism, in the coastal areas under company rule because the kings of Kandy were
patrons and protectors of Buddhism.[64] WIC governors in Brazil faced the same
quandary with Catholics that plagued VOC officials with Buddhists in Ceylon.
The need to placate large numbers of Portuguese, criollo, and mestizo planters
convinced prince Johan Maurits to allow Catholic worship in Brazil. Since the
company also wished to attract and retain Jewish commercial expertise, governors allowed Jews to construct a synagogue in Recife.[65]

Because governors sought to balance religious pluralism with a distinct Protestant identity, they placed controls over ecclesiastical personnel and institutions. In
doing so, they were following the practice of city governments in the Dutch Republic. In Asia, the governor general in Batavia and regional governors took an
increasingly active role in the 1600s in vetting ministers, arbitrating disputes
among clergy, and assigning them to various locations. The Batavia Church Order
of 1643 stipulated that all ministerial candidates had to be approved by the "high
Christian authority in the city."[66] The issue over the calling and assigning of ministers in Asia came to a head between 1650 and 1653. The Batavia consistory, and
ministers in various territories, objected to political authorities' interference in
church affairs, but the *Heren XVII* backed the standpoint of Joan Maetsuijcker,
giving the governor generals ultimate control over assigning ministers. Nicholas
Verburg, the governor in Formosa who introduced this chapter, stated explicitly
the perspective of the VOC's governors regarding clergy: "The Governor and his
Council should . . . have full power and authority to reprimand and correct any
such ministers or clergymen as should attempt to transgress a regulation which
had jointly been adopted and regarded as definite."[67] In all Dutch territories from
Brazil to the Moluccan Islands, company governors wielded the power to call, re-
locate, discipline, and dismiss ministers—and (as discussed below) they used that
right whenever they deemed necessary. In Formosa and Ceylon, even schools fell
under the jurisdiction of political authorities.[68]

Throughout this period, the institutional maintenance of ecclesiastical affairs reflected the nondogmatic rendering of Protestantism employed by magistrates governing the cities of Holland and advocated by Grotius in *The Christian Religion* and in other writings. Thus, the trading companies, the VOC in particular, appropriated the hard-won civil authority that political entities in the Dutch Republic had gained for themselves and applied it to relations with consistories in overseas environs.

Just as the trading companies supported a Reformed presence that expressed itself in evangelism, Calvinists also threw their support behind commercial empire. As we have seen, Calvinists, such as Usselincx and de Laet, argued that an Atlantic empire would roll back the expansion of the Iberian Catholic powers that warred against Protestants in Europe and terrorized natives in America.[69] For many Dutch Calvinists, trade blended smoothly with mission. Udemans in *The Spiritual Rudder* described an economy of exchange in which "these Indians share liberally with us their materials goods, like silver and gold, diamonds, stones, pearls, spices, sugar, etc. Thus we are responsible for sharing with them our spiritual goods, just as the Jews did at one time with other heathens."[70] Though filled with danger and temptation, overseas commerce was an honorable profession, provided that the merchant conducted business "righteously and in the fear of God," according to Udemans. One of the purposes of his writing was to give guidance to overseas traders so that they might carry out their work as thousands of other pious, patriotic Dutch merchants did at home.[71] Like many other Dutch Calvinists of his day, the *predikant* from Zierikzee, Zeeland, described the commercial and imperial undertakings of the VOC and WIC using the lexicon of piety, Christian charity, and Protestant witness.[72]

Though Calvinists viewed commerce as a godly calling, missionary enthusiasts primarily depicted the trading operations as an instrument in this pivotal moment to throw open the door of the gospel to all people. Many Calvinist writers in the first half of the seventeenth century betrayed a strong sense that they stood at a critical moment in the expansion of Christianity. Udemans concluded that the simultaneity of the "reformation in Europe and the discovery of the Indies" would enable his countrymen to make good use of the door God had opened for the spreading of the gospel.[73] The unprecedented opportunities for propagating the gospel animated Calvinist clerical attitudes about the commercial infiltration into new parts of the world. The convergence of so many political, financial, military, and technological contingencies enabling missionary enterprises appeared to have a divine imprint.

For Calvinists, the perception of providential design was fed by millenarian expectations that coursed through the Netherlands and Europe in the seventeenth century. Initially a prophetic reading of scripture embraced by mystics and nonconformists, millenarianism became increasingly part of orthodox Calvinism by the mid-seventeenth century. The adoption of prophetic theology by Johannes Cocceius, the well-respected though embattled theologian at Leiden in the 1650s, helped millenarianism go mainstream among Calvinists.[74] Many Dutch Calvinists saw themselves as completing the great movement of Christianity from the missionary campaigns of the apostles and early church to the conversion of Europe by Benedictine orders in the seventh and eight centuries.[75] At the same time, the spread of Catholicism by the nefarious Spanish, Portuguese, and French, along with the movement of Islam into eastern Europe, raised the apocalyptic stakes for mission-minded Calvinists.

The "open door" that became a metaphor resonating across Asia, America, and Europe among Calvinists conveyed their sense of providential opportunity for mission offered by empire and trade. The influential University of Leiden theologian Johannes Hoornbeeck described in his *On the Conversion of Indians and Gentiles* (*De conversione Indorum & Gentilium*, 1669) the "remarkable providence of God" that placed Dutch preachers in Africa, Asia, and America. According to Hoornbeeck, the Spanish, owing to providence, excluded Dutch merchants from trade in Europe; "they [Dutch trading companies] went to the most remote dominions of the King of Spain, and as decreed by God, took from the king the position he had denied them."[76] In the spirit of Grotius, Hoornbeeck argued that carving out a place for commerce entailed fighting against the enemies of true religion, defending the homeland, and most importantly, "mak[ing] a way open to propagate the Christian faith among the heathens."[77] Abraham Rogerius's well-worn treatment of Vedic traditions bore the title *The Open Door to Hidden Heathendom.* Ministers in Banda, Ceylon, Cape Town, Brazil, and Formosa celebrated conquest and commercial penetration that threw open the doors wide for converting pagans, Muslims, and Jews.[78] In Formosa, Robert Junius divined God's work in the Dutch conquest of Mattauw in 1636 as a godsend for the mission, exclaiming, "How great has been your acquisition of territory! How wide a door has been opened to us for the conversion of the heathen!"[79]

At direct odds with the companies' assertion of Christian authority, Calvinist clergy held to a forthright clericalism in mission and empire. Originating in Geneva under John Calvin, Calvinist political theory and action in Reformation Europe distinguished itself from other Protestant movements by insisting on the church's independent prerogative in enforcing moral discipline and defining theological orthodoxy. This demand for autonomy meant in practice that the consistory corrected and penalized the sinful behavior of people from all walks of life, even magistrates, nobles, princes, and colonial governors. *Predikanten,*

such as Justus Heurnius, George Candidius, and Philip Baldaeus, drew from
two generations of Calvinist protocol when they called governors to account for
their ethical lapses and for placing restrictions on clergy to carry out moral discipline.[80] Not only did *predikanten* assert their singular ecclesiastical prerogatives, but they also assumed that the spread of the Reformed faith was directly
proportional to and contingent upon the number of ordained ministers in the
mission. Without a doubt the most persistent complaint among ministers both
in the field and in the Netherlands was the acute shortage of clerical labor.[81]
Included in almost every pastoral report from overseas consistories was their unofficial scriptural motto: "The harvest is plentiful, but the laborers are few"
(Luke 10:2 RSV).

POINTS OF NEGOTIATION AND CONFLICT

The two different conceptions about the place of the Reformed Church in
the Dutch empire loomed as points of negotiation that framed interactions between ministers and company officers. Conflicts that arose over principles usually were enmeshed in a thicket of personal animosities, ambitions, and often
bad behavior. High-ranking company officials did not take kindly to clerical intrusion. Jacques Specx, governor general, suspended Justus Heurnius, incarcerated him on the ship *Rotterdam*, and packed him off to Coromandel in 1632
because of a sermon the minister gave that emphasized the church's right to discipline and censure without the interference of political authorities. In the previous three months, Specx had placed political restrictions on ministers and
chastised them for negligence. In April 1630, Specx sanctioned and suspended
the *predikant* Gijsbert Bastionszoon for remaining passive during a murderous
mutiny on a transport voyage from the Netherlands to Batavia.[82] Three days later,
Specx appointed two political commissioners to observe consistory meetings and
report back on their activities to the *Politieke Raad*. Heurnius complained about
the punishment of Bastionszoon and the presence of political officers in church
meetings. Is it not, Heurnius objected, "the *predikanten* and consistory who properly govern the church?"[83] For his complaints and his defiant sermon, Heurnius
was dismissed from service in Batavia.

Specx held a jaundiced view of the clergy, which could only have contributed to his assertion of civil authority over the consistory. Heurnius and his fellow ministers had attempted for several years to reconcile Specx with Anthony
van Heuvel and Jacob Bontius, two members of the *Politieke Raad* in Batavia.
In March 1630, Specx declared he would no longer take communion in the
church in Batavia because he resented the presence of van Heuvel and Bontius.[84]

The falling-out originated from a scandalous episode in Batavia in 1629 involv-ing Specx's twelve-year-old daughter, Saartje. While her father was stationed in Japan, she lived in the home and under the protection of the austere and un-compromising Jan Pieterszoon Coen. In June 1629, Coen returned home to discover Saartje engaged in intimate relations with her sixteen-year-old boy-friend, Pieter Cortenhof. Coen was so outraged that, in consultation with the *Politieke Raad*, on which Bontius and van Heuvel served, the imperious gover-nor general had Cortenhof decapitated and Saartje publicly whipped. Three months later, Jacques Specx came to Batavia to take over as governor general, a position he held for three years.[85]

Heurnius and other *predikanten* looked into the scandal in 1630 because of local unrest over Cortenhof's execution. When Specx withdrew from commu-nion in March 1630, Heurnius obliged van Heuvel and Bontius to abstain as well until all parties reconciled.[86] Dutch consistories were often quite invasive and persistent in matters that laid bare deeply held private wounds. It seems likely that Specx considered the consistory's efforts at making peace between the par-ties to be indiscreet meddling. Thus, after Heurnius's 1632 sermon that defended consistorial discipline, Specx decided to rid himself of a troublesome pastor.

There were numerous other conflicts about the boundaries of civil and church jurisdiction. Between 1659 and 1664, Philip Baldaeus, minister in Galle and Jaff-napatnam, squared off against Rijklof van Goens, governor of Ceylon, over the administration of schools. Like missionaries elsewhere, Baldaeus saw schools as a chief agent of conversion, especially in an environment where many thousands of people had already been baptized by Portuguese Jesuits. The ministers placed their faith in schools to educate these nominal Christians in the Calvinist tradi-tion so they could become full-fledged members. In the 1660s, 18,000 children across Dutch-held Ceylon attended 30 schools.[87] Van Goens had determined that company officials, known as *scholarchen*, would supervise and monitor the schools, though he conceded that *predikanten* could accompany them on visi-tations. This policy resembled arrangements over the administration of schools in Dutch cities. Yet in 1664, Baldaeus complained vigorously to the *Politieke Raad* in Ceylon, to Joan Maetsuijcker, governor general in Batavia, to the *Heren XVII*, and to the classis in Amsterdam. Baldaeus charged that van Goens was tram-pling on the rights of ministers and undermining the mission of the church.[88] After failing to gain support from any quarter, Baldaeus resigned his position in 1665 and returned to the Netherlands.[89]

The company occasionally intervened in confrontations among clergy. In January 1631, Jacques Specx asked the Batavia consistory to send a minister to Amboina to negotiate resentments between Johan du Praet and Wouter

Melchiorszoon. The investigation shed little light on "the secret hatred between them," but revealed both as heavy users of arak, contemptuous of local people, and negligent in various aspects of their duties.[90] Heurnius, who as we have seen was having his own problems with Specx, objected to the governor general's intrusion in consistorial affairs, and using a church officer to do so.[91] As discussed above, Specx cleared Heurnius out within six months.

Other examples of clerical infighting became well known in church and company lore. Twenty years later one of the most quarrelsome *predikanten*, Pieter Appeldoorn, arrived in Batavia, and shortly thereafter Maetsuijcker reassigned him to Amboina. Appeldoorn had already raised strenuous objections to the 1643 church order and protested that Maetsuijcker, as a civil magistrate, should have no role in making pastoral decisions. Once in Amboina, Appeldoorn almost immediately accused his colleague Henricus Hartong of having heretical views on the doctrine of original sin. The dispute escalated into such a distraction that Maetsuijcker sent them both back to the Netherlands in 1654, with Appeldoorn grumbling for years about the "unjust procedures" taken against him.[92] In 1692, Philip de Vriest took umbrage with Johannes Roman, who allegedly rolled his eyes and snickered during a sermon by de Vriest in Colombo. Bitter recriminations ensued that went on for years, pulling the governor Laurens van Pyl and the *Politieke Raad* into the role of arbiter. Eventually a subsequent governor, Gerrit de Heere, suspended Roman from service without pay and shipped him to Batavia in 1699.[93]

In some instances, consistories and governors had to deal with ministers who engaged in erratic behavior quite incompatible with norms for Calvinists, certainly for church leaders. Johannes Anthoniszoon Dubbeltrijck in 1625 in Amboina engaged in such heavy drinking and disorderly behavior that his wife, Hester Jane, left him for another man and sued for divorce.[94] Johan du Praet created scandal in Amboina in 1633 by trading slaves, at roughly the same time that Sebastian Danckaerts and his wife came under fire for engaging in illicit private trade.[95] The proponent Abraham Ruteau got drunk in 1638 and impregnated a woman who was not his wife.[96] In 1664, the church community in Galle wrote to the Synod of North Holland that the *dominee* Johannes Nathaniel Doncker sexually assaulted women, drank heavily, and used profane language.[97] Likewise, George Candidius and Robert Junius in Formosa complained in 1637 about the "godless, offensive, and utterly debauched life" of their ministerial colleague in Formosa, Johannes Lindesheim. The governor Johan van der Burg suspended him for drunkenness.[98] Willem Hendrik Gordon had spoken out against Nicholas Schagen in Amboina in 1692 and for his trouble came under fire for insurrection.[99] Governor Schagen had Gordon incarcerated and even forced him to do hard labor. It is not clear what spurred Gordon or what provoked Scha-gen, but the Walcheren classis stated it was alarmed "that ministers in the East Indies were no longer safe from this type of heavy-handed treatment."[100] The *predikanten* in Middelburg, and undoubtedly their counterparts in Amsterdam, worried about the effects this episode would have on recruiting ministers in the Netherlands. After the governor general Willem van Outhoorn dismissed Gor-don's complaints about mistreatment, he left the East Indies in 1697.[101]

These episodes illustrate the complicated relations between individuals hold-ing clerical and political offices in the trading companies. Even as they negoti-ated the parameters of commercial empire and Christian mission, governors and ministers dealt with the all-too-human frailties of themselves and others. These shortcomings, often covered over by the heroic sheen of missionary service to God and military derring-do for the fatherland, came on full display in tropical environments and unfamiliar cultures far from home. Correspondence from overseas consistories teem with complaints of sickness and longing for hearth and home. Clergy in Formosa, for example, wrote to the Amsterdam classis in October 1652:

> [W]e . . . want to return to our country than live any longer under unbear-able yoke and slander; because of Christ we are exiles from our country, we live in an unhealthy climate having to struggle with many diseases and weak-nesses of the body, we lose our wives and our dearest friends; it is too much for us to endure all these miseries (which are intensified by nuisances and op-pression attacking us from outside); it seems to be a common evil which only threatens the servants of Christ throughout India, but by which they are be-ing assaulted and by which some of them have already been assaulted.[102]

A number of *predikanten* demonstrated exceptional linguistic, evangelistic, and pastoral talent that engaged the challenges of the distant mission field. The large majority went about their tasks competently and quietly. What is worth remembering in this context is that the give-and-take over the rights and respon-sibilities of overseas churches, which flowed from competing conceptions of a Protestant, commercial empire, were intertwined with the personal ambitions and weaknesses of company employees in trying circumstances.

CONVERGENCES BETWEEN MISSION AND EMPIRE

Despite distinct notions of mission and personal shortcomings, Calvinist min-isters and company officers found much common ground. Governors were eager for ministers, elders, and deacons to help construct order out of the messiness of colonial societies. Church leaders, for their part, recognized that company efforts in this domain promoted Christianization among Moors and pagans. *Predikanten* and governors relied on the Dutch customs and institutions that they knew so well to meet the strange new situations in colonial societies. Calvinists cooperated energetically in dealing with the most pressing problems facing colonial territories: regulating marriage and sexuality, alleviating poverty, and adapting to slaveholding.

MARRIAGE AND SEXUALITY

Calvinist consistories joined with company officers to promote Christian marriage as the foundation of the colonial social order throughout all parts of the Dutch empire. Church and political authorities sought to regulate sexuality as a practical means of addressing social problems caused by exploitive partnerships in fluid migration circuits. At the same time, marriage also provided Calvinist *predikanten* with a stratagem to spread the cultural influence of Protestant Christianity. Dutch colonial settlements and outposts overlapped and abutted societies in which people engaged in a variety of sexual practices, from polygamy to child marriage to various forms of nonmarital cohabitation. The disproportionate number of European males to females in colonies added another layer of complication, as men sought sexual partnering through prostitution and other types of extramarital relations with local women, most of whom had not been baptized. Calvinists, of course, condemned these unions as immoral and strove to combat them. Since Reformed churches and colonial governments did not recognize the legitimacy of interfaith relations and non-Christian unions lacked legal standing, it became necessary for a non-Christian partner to convert in order to transact a lawful and Christian marriage.[103] For consistories, Christian marriage represented a catalyst that addressed social ills and promoted the missionary aims of the Reformed Church. Thus, church leaders sought to implant Christian marriage in colonial soil.

Dutch Calvinists characterized the sexual mores of most peoples they encountered in Asia and the Atlantic not just as immoral, but as indicative of cultural degradation. *Predikanten* came from a polemical environment in Reformation Europe in which Catholics and Protestants reflexively accused their religious enemies of sexual immorality. Calvinism's firm theological grounding in the Old Testament prophetic tradition emphasized that concupiscence resulted from religious rebellion.[104] It seemed to many ministers in overseas lands as if the ancient stories of pagan wantonness in the Old Testament had sprung to life. Adriaan Hulsebos from Amboina in 1618 assessed "these Indian quarters" as "almost a new Sodom and Gomorrah" badly in need of "good government" and a "godly magistrate." The Batavian minister Johannes Roman railed in 1648 that the "despicable idolatry" of pagans bore fruit in their "immorality, drunkenness, and lust."[105] Gisbertus Voetius, like most Calvinists, also considered polygamy and divorce among Muslims as evidence of unbridled sensuality. Sebastian Danckaerts claimed that despite Islam's prohibition against adultery, one was ten times more likely to see a Muslim going to a brothel than anyone else.[106] Whether in Formosa, Brazil, Surinam, Cape Town, Ceylon, or the East Indies, Calvinist ministers considered the sexual customs of peoples they encountered as symptomatic of social decadence.[107] As late as the 1720s, the *predikant* Jacob Canter Visscher labeled female temple dancers in Goa as "dancing prostitutes," and their ritual performances as the pinnacle of "wantonness and whoredom."[108]

Calvinist condemnations reduced a wide assortment of sexual and marital customs to a clear-cut violation of the seventh commandment against illegal intercourse. In many territories, marriage and sexuality were framed according to local customs that were antithetical to Christian values. Across the East Indies, villagers tended to take a casual attitude toward premarital sex, yet traditional norms disparaged adultery. Most societies permitted the separation of partners because of unsatisfactory relations.[109] Islam exerted a powerful influence throughout maritime Southeast Asia and thus polygamy was commonly practiced in the Indonesian archipelago and Malaysia. Islamic law also allowed for divorce. Across the Indian subcontinent, child marriage and unions according to caste prevailed among Hindus.

Calvinists also harbored skepticism about conjugal relations outside the bounds of Christianity. In Amboina in 1618, governor Steven van der Hagen and Danckaerts attempted to persuade local couples who had been baptized to marry legally as Christians, even offering them a substantial sum to do so. While Danckaerts did not specify the difference here between an "Amboina marriage" and a Christian one, he did note that they refused because of the "great servitude and the great yoke [that would be] placed around their necks."[110] According to historian Barbara Watson Andaya, "the demand that intercourse should occur only within a lifelong monogamous relationship formally sanctioned by the church introduced local societies to radically new ways of thinking about marriage and family."[111]

The most unfamiliar marriage customs the Dutch encountered were in Formosa. According to church accounts, adolescent boys and girls experimented sexually with few social constraints. Should a female become pregnant, priestesses known as *inibs* induced abortion. After reaching their thirties, men and women began to select long-term mates, though they did so under a shroud of secrecy. Couples lived apart during the day, avoiding social contact, but at night the male partner would visit and sleep with his mate, leaving for his own abode before dawn. Dutch Reformed Protestants cast all of these practices as reprehensible, confirming the moral degradation of non-Christian societies.[112]

Yet the most pernicious sexual threat to the moral order actually came from European (male) employees of the VOC and WIC. Outside of Coen's brief attempt to establish a settler colony in the 1620s, neither the VOC nor the WIC established settler colonies except in the Cape of Good Hope and in New Netherland. In the East Indies, Ceylon, Formosa, and Brazil, only the wives and families of high-ranking officers could join their husbands in overseas posts. Since the settlements of Stellenbosch, Drakenstein, and Cape Town on the Cape of Good Hope functioned as a resupply station for VOC ships on the Asian circuit, the company sought to transplant families and develop a stable population to produce food.[113] New Netherland also developed as a cluster of small settlements as part of Usselincx's vision of establishing Dutch colonies throughout the Atlantic. The colonies did not really take off until after the Dutch loss of Brazil in the 1650s and the transition of the WIC to a slave trading venture. In other VOC and WIC outposts, the companies did not generally encourage European female migration. The dearth of European women was a major driver of the companies' social policies across the empire.[114]

Consistories and company officials waged campaigns against illicit sexuality throughout the seventeenth and eighteenth centuries. VOC and WIC governors outlawed concubinage, polygamy (among non-Muslims), and prostitution, though enforcement proved uneven, much to the dismay of church leaders, who regularly complained about sexual disorder.[115] The VOC and short-lived WIC did not pry too closely into the private marriage customs of other societies or non-Christian groups, such as Muslims, Jews, Buddhists, and Hindus. While people from other traditions regulated marital affairs according to their own conventions, they had to keep a low profile lest a consistory begin a campaign against immorality. Only in the case of Formosa, where seemingly widespread sexual contact and reliance on abortion clearly violated European notions of propriety, did Dutch governors take drastic action.

Consistories across the East Indies kept records not only of marriages, but also of Europeans and Euro-Asian Christians who lived in concubinage, most likely because one of the partners was not baptized. The Batavian consistory drew up a record of concubines, which it turned over to the governor general's office: in October 1644, the register contained 29 people, a number that grew to 110 couples in February 1652.[116] Later in the year, Johannes Roman reported that 75 among the *inlandse natie* cohabitated unlawfully. These couples were both free partners or free and enslaved, some Christian with Christian, but others with partners of mixed religious identities. Apparently, he also conducted oral interviews, recounting that people gave "frivolous reasons" for not marrying, including poverty, debts, and "that the laws of our Christian republic hinder marriage."[117]

It was in these contexts that consistories and companies pressed Protestant Christian ideals for marriage and sexuality in overseas communities. The VOC wanted to make sure that employees and soldiers who took wives locally did so with the understanding that the marriage entailed a long-term financial commitment. In 1645, the *Politieke Raad* in Batavia stipulated that the company would pay employees who married local women on a monthly basis to encourage them to "settle here for life."[118] The VOC on occasions even purchased female slaves from South Asia for resale as brides for company employees in Batavia. Muslims in Banda protested in 1625 that the Dutch were forcing their daughters to go to school so that they would become Christians and then serve as wives for European Christians.[119]

Impediments to marriage, however, sometimes outweighed the benefits of a legal, Christian union. Men could not repatriate once they married a native woman or fathered a child, nor were they permitted to bring their wives or children to Europe.[120] And the church would not marry them unless the women converted to Reformed Christianity. The 1624 church order stipulated that marriages could not contravene the word of God, and permission was at the discretion of the VOC as the civil authority.[121] As a result, many employees and other European burgers pursued partners and prostitutes more enthusiastically than wives among local women. Clergy often complained that the women who did undergo baptism did not properly understand the Reformed faith, which undermined the religious integrity of local congregations. The Batavian consistory, for example, expressed frustration in August 1626 that *inlandse* daughters were far from ready for baptism and that before they married, they must first understand the basics of the Reformed faith.[122]

Consistories hoped to convert nonmarital arrangements into Christian marriages. On a number of occasions, the Batavian consistory discussed the high number of situations in which non-Christians lived together without marrying or a European male lived with a slave he had purchased to serve as a concubine. In 1625, the consistory noted the high percentage of non-Christians from Malabar living together, "with small little creatures overflowing" the settlement. The church leaders discussed launching an initiative to convert them and to persuade them to marry.[123] The consistory determined in 1652 that the *predikanten* should confer with the governor general and *Politieke Raad* to find a means to turn these arrangements into marriages in order to reduce concubinage in the settlement.[124] In a number of cases, couples did eventually wed. Several anonymous natives "living in concubinage" petitioned the Batavian consistory in September and October 1650 to receive baptism so that they could marry. The church officers promised to see to their education so that they could enter the church as married couples.[125]

The requirement of Christian conversion created a host of difficulties, since the task fell to consistories to attest that both partners were Christians in good standing. When a consistory first put down stakes in an area, ministers and elders had to deal with great confusion over marriage requirements and the sexually fluid relations in colonial environments. Batavian clergy described their perplexities in a letter to the *Heren XVII* in February 1621: "[P]eople are coming to us on a daily basis asking to marry, sometimes baptized and sometimes non-baptized . . . sometimes one of the non-baptized partners is willing to be baptized and the other not, sometimes one partner will be capable of becoming a Christian and the other not." Complicating the situation further is that occasionally the female partner is pregnant and does not know the whereabouts of her male companion. To bring some Calvinist order to the situation, the Batavian consistory decided to require those who sought marriage first to receive training in the faith, to be followed by baptism, and then marriage. Inhabitants who refused to become Christian, the consistory concluded, "will be regarded as foreign."[126] Under no circumstances would consistories allow a Christian to marry a pagan or a Muslim.[127]

By the mid-1600s, VOC governor generals had tightened the restrictions for marriages between company employees and local women. Consistories assumed considerable oversight in the administration of marriage, an endeavor that became enveloped in programs of conversion in the empire. Following practice in the Netherlands, the marriage protocol in all overseas territories came under the authority of a *gecommitteerden tot de huwelijkszaken* (civil marriage board). Applicants for marriage came before the committee to certify that they possessed good character, did not fall within the proscribed grades of consanguinity, and had undergone baptism.[128] Even non-Dutch Christian inhabitants seeking marriage had to receive certification of their church membership and good character before applying to the civil board.[129] In all territories, only baptized Christians could marry under the auspices of the colonial government and consistory. Slaves could marry one another only with special approval and with the consent of their owners, though policies with regard to the marriage of an enslaved couple varied by time and location.[130] European men, however, continued to purchase female slaves as concubines; both consistories and colonial authorities pressed men in these situations to marry their concubines. Provided that the couple met these criteria, marriage banns would be read from the pulpit on three subsequent Sundays. If no impediments emerged, then the bride and groom would be married in either a civil or church service shortly thereafter. Consistories had the responsibility for recording marriages.[131]

The combination of the companies' policies and regional patterns of migration produced multiethnic societies overseen by Dutch colonial authorities. In the East Indies and Ceylon, and to a much lesser extent in Brazil, the Cape of Good Hope, and Formosa, European men cohabitated with indigenous women or with mestizas. Consistories pressed these couples to convert and marry. At the top of colonial society stood high-ranking company officers, European males, married generally to European wives, or occasionally to criollas.[132] These men oriented themselves to Europe, sending their sons back home for their education and marrying them to European women. Their daughters they attempted to marry to criollos or high-ranking mestizos. The middling level of society, composed of criollos and mestizos, married among other criollos or Eurasians, and also occasionally among Asians. Within this ethnically amorphous group, intermarriage with partners possessing degrees of European descent determined a family's location on the socioeconomic hierarchy. At the lower end remained Eurasians (and Asians) with greater gradations of Asian heritage. Yet outside of the highest levels of society, the large and unstructured criollo and mestizo groups mixed European and indigenous cultural practices, with heavy doses of local influence. Men and women took European names, dressed in European fashion, and participated in varying degrees in the Dutch Reformed Church. At the same time, however, Eurasian men and women also retained many indigenous worship practices and followed a number of matriarchal traditions.[133]

POVERTY AND CHARITY

While commercial operations in the Dutch empire created remarkable wealth—extraordinarily so in the case of the VOC—many people in colonial societies languished in poverty and suffering. Governors put diaconates from the Calvinist churches on the task of alleviating the economic distress in territories under company control. Arising in the Reformation, the diaconate represented the institutional expression of a steadfast Calvinist commitment to Christian charity. As an integral ministry of the church, diaconates formed in overseas Dutch communities under the authority of consistories. Deacons in colonial societies provided alms to the destitute, managed orphanages, and oversaw almshouses catering to hard-pressed women, children, and men. Company interest and church ministry thus came together in service to the poor. Over

the course of the seventeenth century, however, the religious ministry of the diaconate expanded into a colonial agent of social provision that endured throughout the period of company rule.

The religious character of diaconates that operated in overseas congregations
took shape during the Reformation in the Netherlands.[134] Dutch reformers following the teachings of John Calvin envisioned the diaconate as a return to a
New Testament practice of lay ministry devoted to service of the poor. They believed that charity via a lay diaconate was central to the church's redemptive
mission in society. Calvinist activists inscribed the basic structures of the Dutch
Reformed Church in church orders and synodal statements in the 1570s, giving
the diaconate its distinctive features. Lay deacons served under the authority of
the consistory in each congregation, and they placed priority on relieving the
needs of Reformed church members in good moral standing. City magistrates,
who had traditionally held jurisdiction over charitable institutions within their
domains, often took a dim view of a diaconate beholden only to church authorities and that privileged church members. Negotiations—sometimes rather
turbulent—between city governments and consistories took place throughout
this period, even into the nineteenth century. In general, diaconates remained
under the supervision of consistories, and deacons cooperated with municipal
charitable agencies in all matters of social welfare. In some cases, deacons served
church members, though in other circumstances they reached out to poor people
beyond their congregations.[135]

Diaconates formed alongside consistories in Dutch Calvinist churches overseas. The first deacons appeared in Batavia in 1621, as the ministers and elders
elected one of their own to serve poor church members. The ministers and elders also agreed to talk with the *Politieke Raad* about choosing a free burger to
assist those outside the congregation.[136] The 1624 church order for all churches
of the East Indies provided for deacons to collect and distribute alms according
to the needs of both "inhabitants and foreigners" and to see to it that no one
misused church assets. Deacons were to give an account to the consistory and
the congregation at such times as the consistory deemed appropriate.[137] Despite
the stipulation, charity in early congregations lacked an institutional form and
depended on provision by merchants or other independent actors.[138] No extant
institutional diaconal records remain for any overseas church before the 1650s
at the earliest, and in most cases not until the 1700s. Yet deacons, their alms,
and sometimes their beneficiaries do appear in consistory registers, pastoral reports, correspondence, and VOC documents throughout this period. Consistory
records in Batavia document the petitioners who made their way before the elders and deacons most every week, asking for a few pennies, an increase in their

allotment, or (later) loans.[139] These sources indicate that diaconal funds drew from a variety of sources: the VOC allocated revenues for poor relief, congregants made donations and left legacies, and church officers posted poor boxes into which benefactors could insert coins.[140] The Amsterdam classis sent linen for Brazilians in November 1649, as the uprising against the Dutch created desperate conditions in the colonial settlements.[141]

It took decades for most diaconates to get off the ground, and most struggled, especially in the early years and in outlying areas, as shoestring operations. In 1627, the proponent Pieter Bonnius described the poverty of several women in Malleyen (Ternate) who depended on other settlers, but he made no mention of deacons. A *ziekentrooster* on a visitation circuit in the Moluccas reported in 1628 that there were no deacons in Makian and Batjan, but that merchants and a *ziekentrooster* controlled and distributed funds. Ten years later, Heurnius noted that free burgers were making donations to shore up poor funds in Amboina.[142] The congregation in Makassar represented an outlier, for as late as 1674 the ministers there reported that they had no deacons, perhaps because the ministers claimed that no one there suffered from poverty.[143] Likewise, diaconates were slow to form in New Netherland, Curaçao, and other areas in the Atlantic world.[144]

Even in territories with a significant Calvinist presence, circumstances, especially the lack of adequate resources, did not always allow for the effective operation of a diaconate.[145] The diaconate in Amboina, for example, was sorely underfunded, prompting ministers in Amsterdam to urge the Batavia consistory to support it.[146] Similarly, in Melaka the deacons depended on support from the governor.[147] The mission in Formosa had to cope with the weakest institutional infrastructure among all overseas Calvinist churches. *Predikanten* did not establish consistories in Formosa (Tayouan and Soulang) until 1643, almost twenty years after George Candidius landed on the island.[148] It seems that civil authorities provided whatever social assistance was meted out until consistories were formed. The diaconate in Tayouan emerged in conjunction with the founding of the consistory.[149] It is possible that the subsidies ministers gave children for attending school mitigated the need for a regularized system of assistance in Formosa.[150] While deacons conducted regular relief efforts in Recife, Paraíba, and Olinda, political vulnerability, the renewal of hostilities (after 1643), and the penury of the WIC seemed to overwhelm church resources. Sources from Brazil constantly decried the misery of the local inhabitants and Dutch settlers; the Amsterdam classis took up collections and sent goods on at least two occasions.[151]

With the exception of Formosa and remote villages in the Moluccas, the organization and work of Calvinist deacons hewed fairly closely to the religious lines of charity in the Netherlands. First, just as in the patria, consistories overseas took precedence in selecting deacons and in supervising their work, per the church orders of 1624 and 1643.[152] Second, deacons directed their efforts first and foremost to church members, yet on occasion also assisted those outside their congregations. In Batavia, the deacons pledged before the consistory to serve the church by helping "all good Christians in need, difficulty, and poverty . . . through the appropriate assistance of alms."[153] Since many poor were not church members, the *Politieke Raad* also chose two *huiszittenmeesters* (non-church almoners) to shoulder the responsibility for them.[154] Conversely in Banda, deacons replaced a secular *armenmeester* (poor master) to distribute alms to both "inhabitants and foreigners."[155] Thus, Calvinist poor relief generally exhibited a dual nature, as both a communal service for those of the "household of faith" and a quasi-public provision for local society. Third, deacons met in combination with consistories and made regular reports on their accounts to the consistory. In Batavia, as was probably the case elsewhere in the East Indies, many pleas for assistance came before the joint meeting of the consistory and diaconate.[156] In Melaka, deacons met with the elders and minister and discussed requests from parishioners.[157] Thus in the first forty years or so of a Dutch Calvinist presence in the East Indies, deacons operated along similar principles as in the Netherlands: working under the direction of consistories, making use of church alms, and distinguishing between charity for church members and others in society.

Deacons in Dutch colonial territories had their hands full, particularly as the VOC began to expand their territorial operations in the 1640s and 1650s. Not only did poor relief officers encounter large numbers of widows, orphans, and other dreadfully indigent people, but they also operated in very different circumstances from their counterparts in Europe. Henk Niemeijer for Batavia and the East Indies and Ad Biewenga for the Cape of Good Hope have called attention to the extensive action field of deacons in these colonial territories.[158] In all areas, deacons provided outdoor relief to those in immediate distress and managed institutions, such as poorhouses and orphanages, dedicated to the care of those caught in lingering conditions of deprivation. Deacons also provided loans to settlers, distributed clothes and other goods in extraordinary circumstances, and cooperated with indigenous caretakers in addressing conditions of extreme destitution.

The multiethnic, colonial settings in Asia also presented unique challenges in administering charity and relief services. In the preamble to "Instructions for Deacons and Caretakers of Orphans" ("Instructie voor de diaconen en besorgers der arme ouderloose weesen, weekinderen," 1667), Rijklof van Goens, governor of Ceylon, noted that "because of the many soldiers and other persons who marry native women and then die or experience other misfortunes, the burden of the poor on the government is increasing and expanding daily."[159] Van Goens's casual assessment in Colombo gestures at a universal phenomenon throughout the Dutch colonial world: large numbers of Asian and Eurasian women and children suffering because their European husbands or partners died, repatriated, or relocated in service of the company.[160]

Major reorganizations of social provision took place in VOC settlements in the mid-1600s, transforming the function of overseas diaconates into comprehensive colonial welfare agencies. These renovations corresponded with rising levels of migration and with new VOC conquests in Melaka, Ceylon, and South Africa. Batavia's total population, including Asians, Europeans, and Euro-Asians, grew to 27,000 by 1674, while in South Africa it ballooned from 259 in 1679 to 15,000 in 1795. Three settlements in Ceylon (Colombo, Galle, and Jaffnapatnam) contained almost 4,000 Europeans, but numbered over 420,000 Christians by the 1720s.[161] A host of social ills including disease, underemployment, and illegitimacy accompanied rising levels of population, producing widespread poverty.

As a result, governors in territories under VOC control expanded the scope of diaconates and placed them on a more substantial financial footing. Governor general Anthony van Diemen and the ministers in Batavia laid out more specifically the duties of deacons in the 1643 church order, which served as a guide for diaconal operations in Amboina, Banda, Ternate, Melaka, Ceylon, and the Cape of Good Hope.[162] Chosen annually by the consistory, congregation, and *Politieke Raad*, deacons served two-year terms and remained under the authority of the consistory. They gave regular financial reports and conferred on requests with elders and ministers. The 1643 protocol also specifically mentioned deacons' responsibilities for orphans, a domain of care that had fallen to the church from the outset of the colony. Attention to orphans grew significantly in the seventeenth and eighteenth centuries, as did maintenance of an *armenhuis* (poorhouse) that boarded those who could not live on their own. In addition, deacons offered small loans, oversaw repairs on church property, and worked to ensure that recipients did not misuse church alms.[163]

Five years later in 1648, governor general Cornelis van der Lijn began to pull the diaconate apart from the consistory, having the poor relief officers meet as a distinct college with more direct accountability to the *Politieke Raad* in Batavia.[164] The divergence between consistory and diaconate grew under the tenure of governor general Joan Maetsuijcker in the 1650s and 1660s. As its own separate college, the diaconate thereafter worked more closely with the colonial authorities and less directly with the consistory. Ministers and elders continued to nominate diaconal candidates, and deacons continued to open their account books to the consistory, but only for one day.[165] Deacons conferred with the consistory, but nevertheless acted independently and in concert with colonial authorities. To be sure, ministers regarded this change as a serious breach of ecclesiastical prerogative stipulated by church orders, though deacons strongly approved the transition. Deacons conceived of their office as having equal footing with the consistory and even demanded in the 1650s to play a role in the election of elders.[166] This move occurred during a time of intense conflict between ministers and the colonial government, as governor generals took over the responsibility for assigning ministers to posts across Asia. Consequently, the Batavia consistory appealed to Dutch classes and to the *Heren XVII*, but to no avail.[167]

In terms of poor relief administration, the move by van der Lijn and Maetsuijcker partitioned the diaconate from the consistory, creating a separation that became more pronounced in the late seventeenth and eighteenth centuries. Deacons in Batavia entertained requests for aid independently and took on projects without the approval of the consistory.[168] Managing a substantial budget, deacons allocated relief extensively in Batavia, far beyond the borders of the Reformed congregation.[169] In March 1676, when the deacons complained about a shortage of funds, the minister Theodore Zas suggested snidely that they cease giving assistance to people living in concubinage and preserve funds for church members. Several weeks later another *predikant*, Cornelius Paijs, contended the deacons should cut off monthly stipends to Moors and "heathens."[170] Over the course of the seventeenth and eighteenth centuries, pressing social needs and an insistent government in Batavia effectively transformed the diaconate from an ecclesiastical organ of charity into a colonial welfare agency.

When the VOC established colonies in Melaka, Ceylon, and South Africa in the 1640s and 1650s, the structure of the diaconate in Batavia provided a framework for social provision in these lands. From the outset, deacons in Melaka provided relief to all needy residents, regardless of religious disposition; loaned money; and functioned as the Dutch government's welfare agency.[171] In the early 1660s VOC authorities in Ceylon endowed deacons with comprehensive oversight of welfare provision. In June 1661, Maetsuijcker supplied the governor of Ceylon, Adriaan van der Meijden, with a list of instructions for regulating the diaconate that illustrates its secular footing. Maetsuijcker stipulated that "the deacons should be placed in a position to properly fulfill their functions in compliance with the orders from Batavia and the Fatherland; the clergy shall have no authority over them." Yet the document also indicates that poor relief from the hands of deacons did not extend to the palms of indigenes, Asians, or Eurasians, stating unambiguously that "no alms should be given to any but people of our own race."[172] This provision, if ever enacted, succumbed rather quickly to social reality in Colombo. For only six years later, in 1667, governor Rijklof van Goens released the "Instructions for Deacons and Caretakers of Orphans," discussed above. Further, van Goens's guidelines suggest that people from outside Colombo and foreigners were not excluded from assistance. With regard to the status of the diaconate, the 1667 "Instructions for Deacons and Caretakers of Orphans" reiterated Maetsuijcker's previous directives that the colonial government would choose the deacons, and that they would serve as the only relief agency in the colony.[173]

At the Cape of Good Hope, the company established and administered a relief fund for free burgers in the three communities of Cape Town, Drakenstein, and Stellenbosch before the formation of a consistory or a diaconate. The VOC promoted European migration in order to generate a settler colony of small farmers to produce food to reequip ships for the long voyages. When the first settlers began arriving in 1657, the governor urgently organized a support system for pioneers trying to scratch a precarious living out of a strange land. The first *predikant*, Johan van Arkel, formed a consistory in 1665 after he arrived in Cape Town that selected a member to serve as the church's deacon. Once up and running, the diaconate assumed responsibility for all provision and for policing all recipients under the control of company administrators. Just as in the East Indies and Ceylon, the VOC in Cape Town turned the charitable arm of the Reformed Church into a welfare agency for the entire colony. The diaconate provided outdoor relief to all it deemed worthy and after 1687 supervised the colonial orphanage. The consistory retained the right to nominate a double number of candidates from which the governor selected the deacons. The number of deacons serving at any given time remained small: the Cape Town diaconate consisted of four members for most of the 1600s and 1700s, while Drakenstein and Stellenbosch retained only one or two officers. Revenues came from collections at church services, testaments, gifts, and legal fees.[174] Clearly, the diaconate under the VOC served the secular interests of a commercial, colonial institution.

The structure of church poor relief in the colonies changed little over the course of the eighteenth century. Church and colonial states worked together to support those at the lowest levels of society.[175] The primary function of deacons in VOC settlements was to pick up the pieces of lives broken apart in a grim colonial environment in support of the overseas commercial enterprise. The deacons in Paramaribo (Surinam), for example, paid for the upkeep of "poor young boys" who worked on plantations and lived in almshouses in the eighteenth century.[176] In a fundamental sense, that is the task of any charitable or welfare agency regardless of the setting. And church officers continued to frame their charitable work within a religious purpose. Gerhard â Besten, a *predikant*, lamented the insufficient means to care for the poor in a visitation report from the area around North Sulawesi in 1757. He wanted the church to do more (i.e., post poor boxes) because "this is not only considered a necessary part of the practice of our religion, but it shows God and his people give from the heart."[177]

Yet the VOC's monopoly over political, economic, and social power produced the conditions that impoverished many colonial inhabitants. Dutch colonial outposts ran on extensive slave and coolie labor that suppressed wages severely for free workers.[178] Slaves made up half of the population in Batavia, and enslaved peoples actually outnumbered company employees and free burgers in Cape Town by the end of VOC rule.[179] In a consistory meeting in 1677, the ministers and elders noted the "extraordinary number of black Christians living outside the city whose number extends over eight thousand, which most are poor people who labor for daily rates . . . at coolie wages."[180] At this time, almost eight hundred church members received regular outdoor stipends from the deacons, in addition to those living in the poorhouse and orphanage.[181]

Among the women and men who sought assistance from the deacons, all with their own individual problems and needs, two groups in particular reflected impoverishment wrought by the Dutch colonial enterprise. Native widows and orphans left by European men represented a persistent form of poverty that caught the attention of colonial governors and church officers. As discussed above, the governor of Ceylon cited this problem as justification for reorganizing relief measures in Colombo in 1667.[182] Women often received a regular dole until they married or remarried. Orphans obtained more direct institutional support from deacons that also entailed firmer social and religious controls. In Cape Town, Colombo, and Batavia, deacons coordinated an adoption program that placed children in the homes of Christian parents. Sometimes these children were illegitimate offspring whose parents were neither Christians nor partners. Adopted by Reformed couples, these children would subsequently undergo baptism and receive a Christian education. Adoption became an engine of church growth in Batavia: between 1683 and 1695, church members took in 265 orphans.[183] Fatherless children who did not find a Reformed home and whose mother could not raise them entered orphanages, except in Colombo where orphans continued to live with their mothers but with diaconal support.[184] Deacons managed fairly sizable orphanages in Batavia, Melaka, and Cape Town; the institution in Batavia housed between 80 and 100 orphans in the late seventeenth and early eighteenth centuries. In all orphanages, children received regular instruction in "the fundamentals of the Christian religion," and boys acquired some type of vocational training, whereas girls learned the skills necessary to procure and maintain a good marriage.[185]

Besides vulnerable women and children, manumitted slaves constituted a second peculiar victim of the Dutch colonial enterprise that came within the purview of diaconates. Since Christian slaves received some privileges, such as permission to marry, receipt of a minimal education, and a reprieve from Muslim ownership, those in bondage formed one of the most fruitful mission fields for Reformed preachers. In Cape Town, over two thousand slaves received baptism from 1665 to 1795 and although we do not have the specific figures for other areas, it is likely that many hundreds converted in Batavia and Ceylon during the seventeenth and eighteenth centuries.[186]

Manumitted slaves, with few resources and meager prospects, increased the caseload for church deacons. Some slave owners opted to exercise the Christian virtue of manumission when their slaves had become too old, weak, or sick to retain any labor value. Consequently, the welfare of many of these ex-slaves became the responsibility of diaconates. Deacons in Batavia and Cape Town complained to colonial authorities regularly, beginning in the 1640s, about the burdens created by the growing numbers of ex-slaves.[187] Governors in both colonies responded by imposing financial requirements on owners who manumitted their slaves. In 1708, the colonial government in Cape Town required owners to seek its approval to ensure a freed slave could provide for himself. This policy did not work effectively, and in 1767 the government mandated that owners had to allocate 20 rix dollars to the deacons for each manumitted slave. The fee was raised to 50 rix dollars in 1777, and in 1783 owners had to purchase a twenty-year bond.[188]

The diaconate went through remarkable permutations as it developed out of the Reformation and found a central place in societies in the Dutch empire, especially those managed by the VOC. By the second half of the seventeenth century, deacons primarily served company interests by coping with the human fallout of the VOC's overseas commercial enterprise. Vestiges of confessional charity endured in the activity of deacons, since they continued to assist the church poor and to subsidize the Christian education of impoverished children at all VOC colonies. And caring for the vulnerable, whether they resided in the Netherlands or in Asia, remained a religious duty for Reformed deacons. Yet abandoned or widowed native women, mestizo orphans, and manumitted slaves were particular products of the VOC's colonial project. Company officials shouldered abandoned women and children as a byproduct of male migration and embraced slave labor as a necessity of commercial production. Offering a modicum of provision to the victims helped ensure social order in a colonial regime, a secular undertaking that illustrates the fluctuating functions of the diaconate from Reformation to empire.

Dutch imperial ambitions created a cleavage between the Republic's embrace of liberty and the empire's adoption of slave holding and trafficking. As we have seen, theorists of empire championed the values of freedom from tyranny and bondage that animated Dutch rebels in the war against their Hapsburg overlords. In the lineage of their Batavian forbears, Netherlanders claimed the mantel of freedom as they fought against the "unbearable slavery" of Spanish rule. Dutch nobles and urban regents constantly cited the violation of their "ancient liberties" as just cause for rebellion. It is important to underscore that for Netherlanders in the sixteenth and seventeenth centuries, these liberties were not inherent rights. Rather they derived from an assortment of grants, privileges, and favors given by lords to towns, provinces, and nobles and amassed since the Middle Ages. The radical notion of universal human rights for "life, liberty, and pursuit of happiness" arose out of the Enlightenment in the late eighteenth century. Thus, the Dutch, like all Europeans, recognized degrees of freedom and unfreedom within entrenched premises about the status and privilege imparted by social hierarchy.[189] It is only within this framework that the blithe acceptance of enslavement by the Dutch—or European slaveholders in general—can become comprehensible.

The accumulation of dispensations by Dutch citizens and nobles overlapped with a long-standing view that Dutch soil was free. Just as in England and other northern European countries, it was a deeply held assumption that enslavement could not exist in the Netherlands. Rather, the Dutch regarded bondage as a condition that belonged to the history and culture of other, foreign lands. Dutch communities also expected that because their soil was free, any slaves entering the country would be manumitted. This principle manifested itself in 1596, when the Middelburg city government and the provincial states of Zeeland refused to allow a Portuguese shipper to sell his cargo of 130 African slaves. The magistrates took control of the slaves and granted them their freedom. The fact that the shipper was Portuguese probably had a great deal to do with the outcome in this case, because recent research has shown that enslaved peoples from Africa and the Caribbean did actually reside in the Netherlands in the seventeenth and eighteenth centuries.[190] Dutch statesmen and townsfolk looked past this reality even as they held strongly to their own acquired liberties in political, religious, economic, and social life. Thus, free soil in the Netherlands was more public fiction than fixed principle.

Dutch overseas propagandists, nevertheless, made the most of their liberal heritage in promoting the cause of commerce and empire in Asia and the At-

lantic. Grotius, Usselincx, de Laet, and others promoted mercantile and colonial enterprises as campaigns to defend the natural law of liberty to trade. The
Dutch positioned themselves against the most pernicious threat to freedom on
the seas—Hapsburg tyranny.[191] They insisted that the VOC and WIC operated
in the spirit of Christian compassion to help free and protect innocent native
peoples from the ruthless exploitation of Spanish and Portuguese conquerors.

In Dutch polemical literature, descriptions of merciless enslavement formed
one of the central features of the Spanish and Portuguese empires. Protestants
in the Netherlands and England amplified the Black Legend of the Spanish by
circulating embellished stories and woodcut depictions featuring the enslavement, dispossession, and exploitation of native peoples, revealing the heartless
character of their Catholic enemies. Dutch men and women needed no remind-
ing of Spanish murder, rape, and plunder in their conquests of Mechelen,
Naarden, and Zutphen during the Revolt. Yet drawing from Spanish accounts,
most famously the *Destruction of the Indies* by Bartolomé de las Casas, a host of
statesmen, propagandists, and Protestant activists reprised the Black Legend of
Spanish predation in the Americas. Willem of Orange, Jan van Nassau, Joost
van den Vondel, Godefridus Udemans, Willem Verheiden, Philip Marnix van
St. Aldegonde, and others drew parallels between the Spanish campaign to sub-
jugate the Dutch with the Iberian drive to enslave Americans.[192] Dutch Calvinist theologians, ministers, and lay activists also recounted the horror of slavery
at the hands of the Iberians, contrasting it with true Christian freedom. Usselincx
utilized stories of Spanish and Portuguese slave trading as justification for establishing Protestant colonies in the Americas operating on the principle of love
and equity.[193]

Abhorrence of Spanish and Portuguese slave trading, as presented in the polemics of the Black Legend, masked a much more ambivalent attitude among
Calvinists about slavery even before the capturing of clove fields and sugar plantations in the 1620s and 1630s. Historians have tended to contrast Calvinist attitudes about enslavement before and after the conquests of Banda in 1621 and
Brazil in 1630. The general interpretation posits that Calvinists were largely opposed to slavery previous to these acquisitions, but justified it afterward on the
grounds that they operated a more humane and benevolent form of servitude
than Catholics or Muslims.[194] Yet the evidence upon which this interpretation
rests actually points to an uneasy openness to enslavement in the overseas empire and mission in advance of these conquests.

It is worth remembering that Dutch Calvinists identified closely with the
children of Israel in the Old Testament and read the New Testament and their
contemporary world through the lens of the Mosaic law and prophetic tradition.

Calvinists believed that the presence of sin in the world from the Fall in the Garden of Eden totally corrupted human relations, leading to all sorts of brutalities, such as enslavement. So while slavery might not exist in principle (as it did in reality) in a Christian polity like the Dutch Republic, most Calvinists saw it as a legitimate institution in lands outside Christian Europe. Since one of the guiding modes of operation for the VOC and WIC was to affix themselves to existing networks of exchange, a Calvinist overseas could readily adapt to the province of slavery and slave trading.

Dutch Calvinists themselves wrote little about slavery as a form of physical servitude. When they did, references to it were often ambiguous. Festus Hommius, a Calvinist minister in Leiden, is sometimes put forth as an example of Calvinist opposition to slavery, "condemning any form of slavery as man-stealing," according to one account.[195] Yet Hommius's remark, in a translated edition of an influential catechetical commentary, merely follows a legal maxim laid down in Exodus 21:16, which stipulates that kidnapping a person is punishable by death, regardless of whether the kidnapper sells his victim or is found in possession of him.[196] Perhaps Hommius's use of the term "man-thievery," which was often employed by critics of slave trading, signaled his opposition to the practice. But there was little in the way of an explicit condemnation. Earlier in this work, Hommius commented on slavery, but without giving any insight into attitudes about contemporary practices. In contrasting the spiritual "slaves of Satan" with the "children of God," for example, he commented that "among the Latins slaves were called 'servi' since they were spared; to wit, when they were captured in war by their enemies, they were in danger of being killed but were preserved and spared."[197] In short, Hommius does not appear to offer much in the way of any principled opposition to human enslavement.

Ministers overseas encountered a new world of slaveholding for which they were unprepared when they disembarked from the Netherlands. Silence reigned in the Batavia consistory when the Middelburg classis raised objections around slaveholding outside of the Netherlands. In July 1629, the ministers and elders in Batavia received a letter from their brothers in Zeeland who had written that they considered the "holding of slaves or bondsmen by Christians in the Indies to be unedifying and unlawful."[198] If the Batavian ministers responded, they did not leave a record for posterity, as the consistory register simply moved on to another matter of business. Two years later, Justus Heurnius upbraided Johan du Praet, then serving in Amboina, for trying to purchase as many slaves as possible in Batavia so that he could resell them for maximum profit in his new residence. The stated reason for the censure was actually to put an end to all the "protesting mouths," so that du Praet's ministry would not fall further into disrepute.[199] This objection cited concern for the church's reputation, not for the fact of slave trading itself. Thus, outside of the propaganda against the Spanish and the Portuguese, Calvinist commentary on slavery in the early 1600s was tepid at best, as ministers appeared ready to accommodate themselves to it in the empire.

The Dutch openly embraced slave trading throughout the empire in the 1620s and 1630s with the conquests of the Banda Islands and Brazil. As the East India Company under Jan Pieterszoon Coen overtook the Moluccan Islands in 1605, it did so with the objective of exercising direct control over the production of cloves. Ten years later, the West India Company laid siege to Pernambuco in order to carve out a claim over the lucrative sugar cane industry in Brazil. The success of these companies made it alluring, as it had been for the disreputable Iberians, to acquire extensive and cheap labor to reap the profits offered by cloves, sugar, and later cinnamon in Ceylon, and tobacco and cotton in Surinam. One of the key strategies of Dutch mercantilists in Asia and the Atlantic focused on appropriating existing networks of exchange, a strategy that extended to slavery. In 1638, the Dutch governor of Brazil declared that "it is not possible to effect anything in Brazil without slaves."[200]

Dutch merchants and colonial officials integrated two distinct networks of slavery into their commercial projects. In the Atlantic, the WIC shunned the slave trade in its first decade, but the conquest of Brazil at the end of the 1620s changed the company's course and the direction of the Dutch Atlantic empire. Opportunistic private merchants did conduct slave running operations after the early 1600s, but the company displaced most private trading initially to supply labor for its newly acquired territory. Soon thereafter, the WIC acquired a monopoly from the Dutch States General for slave trading, which it retained until 1734. The capture of Elmina in 1637 completed the circuit from source to market, enabling the company to equip sugar plantations in Brazil as well as to ship human cargo to Spanish, French, English, and Dutch holdings in the Caribbean and South America. Consequently, by 1636 the Dutch slave trade was picking up steam, and between 1630 and 1651 over 31,500 enslaved Africans were transported from West Africa to Brazil. During several stretches in the seventeenth century, from 1636 to 1648, 1662 to 1675, and 1686 to 1689, the Dutch outstripped all of their European rivals in trafficking humans in the Atlantic economy.[201]

From 1662 to 1701, the company also participated actively in the *asiento* system, in which the Spanish crown awarded *asientos* to supply slaves to its American colonies. Johannes Postma, a leading expert on the Dutch Atlantic slave trade, has estimated that Netherlandish merchants shipped 97,000 slaves from Africa to Spanish colonies between 1658 and 1729. Even after the WIC lost its monopoly in 1734, company factors still operated stations along West Africa and in the Caribbean, particularly at Curaçao, the nexus of the enterprise. By the end of the slave trade in 1814, the Dutch had trafficked over 500,000 souls from Africa into the Caribbean and Americas.[202] Whereas the WIC entered the trade specifically to supply its short-lived colony in Brazil, human trafficking became its major commercial staple in the Atlantic.

In the Indian Ocean, the VOC also tapped into the network of enslavement and shipment owing to the need for cheap labor in the Moluccas and Batavia in the 1620s and then later in Ceylon in midcentury. Since commerce in the Indian Ocean depended far less on plantation agriculture, the extent of slaveholding formed a significantly smaller proportion of the overall economy than in the Atlantic. The VOC used slave labor in a variety of company functions, such as ship repair and artisanal industries, as well as for agricultural labor. Dutch settlers and company employees, including *predikanten*, owned slaves too. Not unlike the WIC, the East India Company penetrated preexisting trading networks and came to control them during the course of the seventeenth century. Slave markets existed in three primary circuits: (1) East Africa and Madagascar, (2) the Indian subcontinent along the Bengal and Arakan coasts, and (3) maritime Southeast Asia, especially at Makassar and Bali. The Indian hub accounted for most slaves until the 1660s, when the Mughal empire expanded into the region and eliminated the source. Thereafter the Southeast Asian circuit predominated. Batavia far surpassed all other Dutch settlements in the Indian Ocean in holding the most slaves. The headquarters of the VOC had 16,695 slaves (51.97 percent of the total population) in 1679; Colombo had 1,761 slaves (53.36 percent of the population) in 1694.[203]

The impact of participating in this relatively new world of chattel slavery spawned ongoing discussion among theologians and intellectuals about Dutch Protestant identity in the seventeenth century. To be sure, after the conquest of sites in the Moluccas and Brazil, the empire's future with regard to slavery was never in doubt. At roughly the same time that Coen was invading the Banda Islands, Hugo Grotius was writing *The Law of War and Peace* (1625). In it, Grotius theorized in support of slaveholding, which ultimately came to represent the mainline Dutch view. Grotius maintained that servitude was not the original state of humans in natural law and that "slavery is repugnant to nature." Yet circumstances could alter the natural human condition of liberty. A people had the right to barter their own or their children's freedom, perhaps in response to dire conditions, such as indebtedness or famine. According to Grotius, victors in a just war also possessed the right to enslave the conquered as just recompense. Once someone passed into a state of servitude, the condition was permanent, based on the Grotian principle that treaties were inviolable, unless the owner of his own free will manumitted the slave. Thus, slaves and their offspring, he argued, could be inherited or sold. Many Dutch jurists and theologians adapted Grotius's arguments during the course of the seventeenth and eighteenth centuries.[204]

Dutch Protestants maintained that the colonial Christian republics the VOC and WIC (until 1654) were fashioning offered a compassionate alternative to the brutal servitude at the hands of Muslims, Catholics, or Jews. Christian owners were to treat slaves humanely and to refrain from selling them to Muslims, Catholics, or pagans. More importantly from a Calvinist perspective, enslavement in Dutch territories offered slaves better chances of salvation, for they could hear preaching and receive instruction in the true word of God. The rationale of Christianizing slaves in a benevolent regime of servitude became the standard language of explanation in justifying the use of slave labor in the colonies.[205]

With promoting the gospel in mind, ministers and theologians contended that Christians must present the gospel to their slaves, and should they convert, they should be manumitted, though opinions differed about when that ought to occur. These limits on slaveholding, writers assured, would give slavery a compassionate, Protestant form that stood in opposition to harsh Spanish, Portuguese, or Muslim forms of servitude. Some orthodox Calvinists, most notably Gisbertus Voetius, persisted in opposition to slavery, but their views remained a minority viewpoint. Others in the Voetian camp, such as Cornelis Poudroyen, George de Raad, Jacob Hondius, and Bernard Smytegelt, read the Old and New Testaments as declaring the equality of all peoples under God. Hondius wrote in his *Black Register of a Thousand Sins* (*Swart register van duysent sonden*, 1679), "Church members who buy and sell slaves and trade in such miserable people commit a sin. . . . Reformed members should not taint themselves with such uncompassionate trade. Rather they should act fully in the fear of the Lord, in order that the money they make will be a blessing rather than a curse.[206] In this vein, de Raad warned, "Our country is sinking, and this sin or rather innumerable injustices, which are occurring daily in the slave trade, may be the heaviest ballast which will cause the ship to go down."[207] For these opponents, Protestant morality dictated that as the true people of God, the Dutch must renounce the injustice of bondage and point to a better way.

Despite the objections of a few, no one mounted any serious challenge against or even offered to debate the principle of enslavement during the period of company rule. Even a former slave from Ghana, who converted to Calvinism and was ordained a *predikant*, Jacobus Elisa Joannes, alias Capitein, composed a dissertation in defense of slavery, *Not Contrary to Christian Liberty* (*De servitude*,

libertati christianae non contraria, 1742). Capitein, who served as a pastor in Elmina, maintained that since soul and body are separate, the soul remains free
regardless of the condition of the body. Thus, Christianity and slaveholding are
not incompatible and slave owners need not free slaves who convert.[208] Most
ministers, including those in the mission fields, gave implicit endorsement to
slavery by remaining silent on the issue; others overseas gave explicit approval
by purchasing slaves themselves. Consequently, the discourse on slavery fit
within the framework of Calvinist morality, as the Christian mission of the Reformed Church wedded itself to enslavement in the Dutch empire.

Yet the project to convert slaves was not uniform or consistent across Dutch
settlements, with the most significant and sustained efforts occurring in VOC
territories in Asia and South Africa. Catechetical instruction and baptism
emerged as a matter of attention for the early ministers in the East Indies. Heurnius pushed strongly for converting slaves in the colony and for keeping them
in servitude. Rooted in Aristotelian notions, his rationale focused on the natural servility of Asian peoples. He argued that if manumitted, Asians would seek
out another master, probably even a Muslim and then convert to Islam to please
their new master. The best solution, then, was to maintain slaves in a state of
bondage to a Calvinist owner who would nurture them in the faith. This policy
also corresponded to Calvinists' reading of Genesis 24, in which Abraham had
all of his household, including his slaves, circumcised. Since Calvinists equated
circumcision in the Old Testament with baptism in the New, they considered
slaves as part of a Christian household and thus suitable for baptism after some
basic instruction. Consistories admonished private owners and the VOC to take
their slaves to church on Sundays and allow them to attend catechism lessons.[209]

Teachers and lay *ziekentroosteren* in Batavia, Amboina, Banda, Ternate, and
Melaka in the 1620s, and in Ceylon and the Cape of Good Hope in the 1650s,
offered rudimentary instruction in the faith and then baptism. In the early years,
baptism often was administered fairly quickly. But after ministers became concerned about the authenticity of slave conversions, they became much more cautious. Once baptized, enslaved converts gained a few privileges, including the
right to marry, and they stood a better chance at manumission.[210] In 1648, the
Batavian consistory determined that it would look more favorably on baptized
slaves taking communion once they had met the requirements for baptism.
Other consistories continued to maintain different standards for baptism and
communion, so the total numbers of enslaved converts who were full-fledged
communicants remained lower than in Batavia. From 1688 to 1708, over 4,400
members belonged to the Portuguese-speaking congregation, which was made

up of both enslaved and manumitted Mardijkers.[211] The Reformed Church in fact achieved its greatest success at Christianization in South Africa with slaves. Between 1665 and 1779, ministers baptized just over 2,000 slaves, an average of 15.5 per year, most of whom were owned by the VOC.[212]

Conversely, mission work among slaves in Brazil, New Netherland, Surinam, and the Caribbean received less priority in the beginning and then flagged after a few years. A combination of factors accounted for this scant effort. In Brazil, most plantations remained in the hands of Portuguese or criollo planters during the period of Dutch rule. Those owners had no inclination of giving up their Catholic faith for a Protestant one. Reformed ministers did not, therefore, even have access to most enslaved Africans in Brazil. Protestant plantation owners in Brazil and Surinam resisted Reformed efforts that could impose restrictions on their use of enslaved labor. Giving enslaved workers time off for church and school, in addition to the potential intrusions from *predikanten*, turned hard-bitten planters against churching slaves. The Brazil classis sought to remedy the matter by pressing colonial authorities to compel owners to honor the Sabbath by sending their slaves to church services.[213] But this lobbying came to no avail. Though several ministers did pour energy into converting slaves, the prevailing attitude among Calvinists remained that Africans were not culturally predisposed to accepting the true faith and its disciplinary demands. Although the colony of New Netherland in its first twenty years did make provision for a school for enslaved Africans, of whom at least fifty-six underwent baptism, by the 1660s a similar skepticism had set in. The minister Henricus Selijns explained that they were turning away requests for baptism because of "the worldly and perverse aims" of slaves to better their and their children's lot and to improve their chances of manumission. A similar concern animated ministers in Curaçao, which also experienced a feeble ministerial presence during the seventeenth and eighteenth centuries.[214]

Converting slaves to Protestant Christianity and orienting them to a community of members joined together by sacraments, faith, and moral discipline exposed contradictions that church leadership never resolved. While chapter 3 examines these paradoxes fully, it is worth noting here that Calvinist churches recognized enslaved converts as fellow members and ostensibly as spiritual equals; consistories promoted spiritual and moral growth and worked to provide a basic education. At the same time, enslavement formed such a profound hierarchy that could not be reconciled by notions of spiritual equality or freedom. Even though hampered by these deep inconsistences, the Calvinist missionizing effort threw its full support behind enslavement in the Dutch empire.

CONCLUSION

A Calvinist identity mixed easily with a republican, commercial, and anti-Hapsburg ethos in the seventeenth century to animate the aspirations and ambitions of the VOC and WIC. Ministers sought to spread the cultural and religious influence of Dutch Calvinism within the geopolitical framework of commerce and empire. Despite sometimes divergent visions of mission and empire, church leaders and company officials cooperated extensively in the ordering of colonial societies. *Predikanten* and governors drew from Dutch structures and customs to address their most pressing social problems. Consistories applied Christian norms of marriage and parental responsibility to counter the social effects of rampant sexuality. The requirement of conversion to the Reformed faith for a Christian to be married also abetted the Calvinist missionary agenda. It is unclear how effective the marriage strategy was; consistories continued to complain about extramarital sexuality, yet they approved many candidates for baptism to make a wedding possible. Scholarship has suggested, however, that the offspring from these unions tended to absorb the local, non-Christian religious cultures inherited from maternal kin.

For Calvinists, corralling human sexuality was a long-standing and familiar pastoral concern, but slaveholding and its consequences presented unprecedented quandaries. Most church figures lost little time in the 1630s transitioning from demonizing Spanish and Portuguese slaveholding to adapting to bondage under the VOC and WIC. According to Calvinist writers, Dutch slaveholding would be different, offering manumission to slaves who converted. At best, some Dutch slaveholders manumitted bondsmen and -women at the end of their productive lives, when they could no longer work. At worst, ministers simply stopped proselytizing and baptizing slaves.

It was the church deacons that got stuck with the collateral damage of colonial society—namely, those manumitted slaves, abandoned women, widows, and orphans. Yet in order to make the diaconate somewhat serviceable in these new contexts, VOC governor generals in the mid-1600s had to alter it considerably. They took a confessional organ of the Reformation devoted to church members and made it into a colonial welfare agency tasked with a wider range of social provision. Calvinist ministers and theologians cast their lot with the trading companies to throw open the door of Protestant Christianity to all people. In so doing, they translated Dutch and Protestant institutions and values into new global environments, which often produced remarkable and unintended outcomes.

3

CONVERSION IN THE EMPIRE

The Batavian Church Order of 1643 marked the first European Protestant church document of any kind to put forth a design "to promote the conversion of Heathens." In the first thirty years of the Dutch mission project, clergy in the empire and in the Netherlands had consistently struggled with defining exactly how Protestant Christianity should figure into the lives of people raised outside Christendom. The ninth point in the church's conversion plan sought to provide some clarity, stating: "[I]t should be impressed upon Native Christians that they should conform in their outward behavior after the manner of the Dutch."[1] This prescription, however, could only have perplexed many contemporaries and converts, since the Dutch overseas had earned an international reputation for fighting, drinking, and whoring as much as for anything else. The historian Charles Boxer remarked that it was likely that most Dutch who died overseas did so from drunkenness.[2] Although the Dutch held a different view of themselves, the directive points to the difficulty that church leaders had in discerning how Protestant Christianity should relate to the lived experiences of non-Europeans in colonial settings. It also reveals the reflexive assumption that converts in the empire should act like Reformed Church members in Europe.

The ministers and company officials in Batavia who helped construct the 1643 church order belonged, as did their Calvinist brethren in other lands, to a global movement of proselytization in the early modern period. Riding on the wave of empire building, Christian missionaries from Europe and Muslim divines from Asia worked to convince and compel people to change their religions or purify their practices. Although much smaller in scope than other campaigns, the Dutch Calvinist mission was part of this worldwide religious undertaking. The early modern zeal for gathering converts and for multiplying devoted practitioners led to enormous changes in religious attitudes among peoples throughout the world.

Global Calvinism has largely been left out of this important story, even as a fresh narrative is currently unfolding in exciting new studies of Catholic missions in Latin America and Asia and of Sunni initiatives in eastern Europe and the Balkans. The VOC and WIC committed significant resources to missions, just as Calvinist *predikanten* threw their weight behind long-distance commerce and empire building. But the unsupported judgment in older scholarship about Calvinist indifference to missionary work has clouded the prospects for exploring the global aspirations of the Dutch Reformed Church until quite recently. Jean Gelman Taylor asserted that "Holland's Reformed Church never regarded Indonesia as a mission field."[3] S. D. Franciscus attributed the Reformed Church's "feeble" efforts in Ceylon to a Dutch national trait that disdained proselytizing.[4] Boxer expressed what became a standard view that Calvinist ministers left an unimpressive record of conversion when compared to their Roman Catholic rivals.[5]

Yet Calvinists did go abroad in the service of empire and missions in the early modern period, and their struggles in converting peoples across cultural boundaries corresponded to dilemmas faced by Catholic priests, Sunni ulama, and others. Catholic missionaries sought to find philosophical and cultural affinities with Confucian scholars in China, Hindu Brahmins in India, and devotees of popular cults in central America.[6] The visible religious hybridities that emerged from these approaches—most famously the rites controversies in China and India—generated well-known debates among Catholic authorities about the boundaries of accommodation.[7] Since the thirteenth century, Sufi masters had grafted Islam onto local sacred sites and observances across maritime Asia. Later in the eighteenth century, puritanical Islamist movements in Arabia, the Middle East, and the Sudan sought to purge the local accommodations that Sufi missionaries had allowed in earlier centuries. The porous border between abstruse culture and true religion also plagued Calvinists who attempted to bring Muslims, Hindus, Buddhists, Jews, Catholics, and practitioners of local observances to a Reformed Protestant faith and rule of life.

Missionaries in the field had to carry on, even as they and their colleagues back home grappled with basic questions of faith, affiliation, and religious identity. Native societies and their religious traditions confronted Calvinists in colonial societies and in European Protestant circles with an array of unwieldy pastoral, cultural, and intellectual complications. Calvinists throughout the empire debated what constituted the proper comprehension and practice of Christianity. Under what circumstances could a child or adult undergo baptism? When could baptized men and women take communion? What should happen if con-

verts continued in their old ways? These discussions and disagreements originated in the 1620s and they continued to smolder as late as the 1780s, suggesting
the intractable problems that conversion across cultures presented for Calvinism. Because ministers wrote reports and corresponded with colleagues back
home, and because most returned to the Netherlands, the problems of trans-
planting Calvinism into foreign soil challenged *predikanten* and theologians
within Reformed Protestant networks in northern Europe as well.

Thus, Dutch Calvinists overseas provide a useful opportunity to historicize
Protestant conceptions of conversion as they moved outside of Europe and into
the global orbit in the seventeenth century. This chapter examines the complex
engagements involved in indigenizing Calvinism overseas by focusing on four
questions: What did Calvinists and native peoples understand by conversion?
How did clergy and native teachers execute a missionary strategy? How did
the mission evolve over time? What problems did Calvinists and native converts
encounter?

CONVERTING SOULS AND CHRISTIANIZING SOCIETIES

Calvinists abroad and at home expected to win converts, as ministers threw
open the door of faith to pagans and Moors. The initial supporters of the companies and early pastors expressed this optimism repeatedly. Adriaan Hulsebos,
for example, proclaimed in 1622 that "the Lord by one means or the other and
at some time will be pleased to call many moors and heathens into belief and
eternal salvation."[8] But even after the sanguine prospects for an immediate and
immense impact diminished, Hulsebos's successors appropriated the same language throughout the period of the trading companies. In the 1650s, a Reformed
minister in Gouda predicted that "God has not been pleased until this time to
reveal the saving knowledge of his Son to China and the many lands of the East
and West Indies. So now God will. . . . accomplish the final conversion of the
heathens to Christ, in order to make the Jews jealous" and turn to God.[9] Though
natives frequently showed little affection for Protestant Christianity, *predikanten*
quoted biblical texts that affirmed the inscrutably exultant aims of divine providence. The Amsterdam classis, for example, took solace in Matthew 3:9 (RSV)
that "God is able from these stones to raise up children to Abraham " if he so
chose.[10] Almost fifty years later, the Walcheren classis wrote to the Batavia consistory that "[w]e can do nothing else than be especially joyful when we hear
about the prosperity and health of God's Zion in faraway lands especially those
under the blind heathen."[11] A lexicon of conversion on this score, heralding the
propagation of the faith to blind "heathens," permeated Reformed correspondence,

church registers, ethnographic accounts, and mission treatises throughout the seventeenth and eighteenth centuries.

While the discourse of conversion evoked images of a large-scale crusade akin to Catholic missions, in practice the Reformed approach centered on community formation. This communal outlook was anchored in Calvinism's gestation in the Reformation. As they broke with the Roman Catholic Church, Calvinists in the Netherlands sought to build tightly knit congregations based on preaching the word of God, administering the sacraments of baptism and communion, and implementing moral discipline. Unlike elsewhere in Europe, membership in the Dutch Reformed Church was voluntary. Adults who wished to join the church had to demonstrate knowledge of Reformed doctrine, present proof of baptism, embody evidence of an upright lifestyle, and submit to the discipline of the consistory. A congregation under the authority of a consistory signified in ideal terms a gathered community that Calvinists themselves often referred to as the "household of faith." The Calvinist understanding of community "transcended the limits of parish, city, and province." That is, members of local congregations were united in an international, existential community of like-minded believers.[12]

Baptism marked one's initiation into the religious community. Like most Christian traditions in the Reformation, Reformed Protestantism taught that baptism for both adults and children was a sacrament, meaning a special sign of God's grace to an individual. But unlike Roman Catholicism, Reformed churches did not teach that baptism conferred salvation. Rather, according to the Dutch Confession of Faith, baptism was the rite by which one "is received into God's church and set apart from all other people and alien nations."[13] Calvinists regarded baptism as a sign of the covenantal relationship between God and his people beginning with Abraham. They likened circumcision among the children of Israel in the Old Testament to baptism among followers of Jesus in the New Testament. Since they recognized continuity in the long history of God's people, Calvinists accepted the legitimacy of Catholic baptisms. Catholics who wished to convert to Reformed Protestantism were required, however, to assent to its teachings and consent to its discipline.[14]

The Calvinist approach to conversion as community formation linked baptism to taking communion, or the Lord's Supper, as a sacramental unity. Baptized adults wishing to partake in the Lord's Supper for the first time were required to undertake an examination to demonstrate their knowledge of Reformed teachings. Adults who had not already received baptism had to undergo this examination and the initiatory rite. Once adults had completed these steps, they had to give their assent to Reformed doctrines and to the ecclesiastical discipline of the consistory. Only then could they take communion. All adult church members were expected to take part in the Lord's Supper whenever a congregation offered it, usually between four and six times a year in the Netherlands. Only baptized members given approval by the consistory for proper moral conduct could take communion at the designated worship service, as censured members and nonmembers looked on. For Calvinists, the communion service took center stage in uniting the visible saintly community in corporate worship. It marked the purity and unity of the community in the common meal that commemorated the death and resurrection of Christ. Thus, the sanctity of the Lord's Table had always animated Calvinist church authorities and had given rise to extraordinary pastoral labor in disciplining congregations throughout the Reformed world.[15] Baptism and communion denoted one's entry and honorable standing in the community of believers.

The Sunday service, the sites of both baptism and communion, formed the central act of corporate worship. Calvinists regarded Sunday as the Christian Sabbath, a day of worship in church and rest from labor. Calvinist Sunday worship concentrated on the exposition of the word of God with the proper theological interpretation from Bible passages. Sermons articulated the principles of Holy Scripture necessary for Protestant Christians to understand their moral obligations and cultivate their devotion to God. Preaching also served as a primary means for conversion, inviting all people into a Christian life and a more fervent faith and practice, regardless of their religious commitments. Everyone was encouraged to attend Sunday services to hear the preaching of the word of God.

Most people who affiliated with the Reformed Church in the Netherlands for most of the seventeenth century did not do so as members who took communion. Sometimes called *toehoorderen* (hearers) but more often *liefhebberen* (sympathizers), these individuals attended services and participated in some church functions.[16] Since they had not made a confession of faith and did not submit to the disciplinary authority of the consistory, they were not registered as members and could not take communion. The term *toehoorder* evoked the distinction between "hearers" who passively heard the word of God and "doers" who acted on it (as in James 1:22, RSV).[17] Similarly, *liefhebber* connoted a person who was inclined toward the Reformed faith but did not take the additional steps to join as an official member.

These gradations of affiliation have important implications for Calvinist understandings of conversion that historians have missed. Rather than identifying full-fledged membership as the exclusive index of conversion, contemporary Calvinists recognized all those in different stages toward a Christian life in their congregations and schools as belonging to Christendom. As we shall see below,

Calvinists took a practical pastoral view of conversion as progression in comprehending Christian teaching and performing Christian piety. Molded by these principles, Calvinist ministers went about the task of conversion by creating religious communities based on standards of belief, conduct, and commitment. Thus, Calvinists adapted the institutions and methods of parochial ministry in the Netherlands for overseas missionary ambitions. This understanding of conversion contrasted sharply with the theology of the Roman Catholic Church. Because the Catholic Church operated under a very different conception of the sacraments, its missionaries possessed a much stronger sense of urgency in baptizing non-Christians. According to the Roman view, baptism not only inducted one into the faith, but it also remitted all past and present sins.[18] As a result, Catholic missionaries believed salvation was at stake, so they baptized indigenous peoples liberally, and only later tried to make them better Christians.

For Calvinists, the establishment of a consistory formed a critical first step for the mission in a given area. This action was necessary because consistories oversaw the administration of the sacraments and the disciplinary regime that protected the purity of the community. In March 1622, *predikanten* Hulsebos and Wouter Melchiorszoon, along with Adam Abransen, appealed to Marten Sonck, the governor of Banda, for permission to form a consistory for the orderly administration of the sacraments. By setting forth a "good example of Christendom," they maintained that many "moors and heathens would come to eternal salvation."[19] Hulsebos also organized the first consistory in Batavia in 1620. He and the earliest *predikanten* in the East Indies subsequently set up consistories in Amboina, Ternate, and other locations with satellite congregations and schools in more remote regions.[20] Consistories shouldered the jurisdiction for outlying areas that had no resident minister but were staffed instead with *ziekentroosteren* and sometimes with no church personnel at all. Later as the VOC gained ground in Melaka, Makassar, Ceylon, and the Cape of Good Hope, consistories appeared in due course. Likewise, in the Atlantic world, *predikanten* with the WIC founded perhaps as many as a dozen consistories in the 1630s. Brazil and the Cape of Good Hope were the only colonies in which the Reformed Church instituted a classis. Brazil was divided into two classes, one in Pernambuco and one in Paraíba, which together constituted a synod.[21]

The mission field of Formosa stood out as the exception to the Calvinist approach to conversion that centered on community formation. VOC governors Marten Sonck and Pieter Nuyts lent their political and military support to the ministers George Candidius, who came to Formosa in 1627, and Robert Junius, who arrived two years later. Candidius and Junius preached energetically and taught the Sinkan language to people in the southwestern portion of the island.

Nuyts promised protection to those people who responded favorably to the preachers. With this political backing, Candidius and Junius made significant headway, preaching, catechizing, and waging war on local religious customs. By 1631, Junius reported fifty-one baptisms, and as conquest and conversion proceeded throughout the southwest plains in the 1630s, the number of converts grew substantially, so that by 1643 the ministers counted over five thousand converts.[22] The early mission in Formosa was a storied success that circulated among Protestants in Asia, Europe, and even America, though the mission did run into serious difficulties in the 1650s because of problems in church-run schools and disputes between ministers and colonial governors.

In the earliest VOC settlements, Amboina, Batavia, and Banda, Reformed ministers focused on forming consistories soon after the company established its jurisdiction, setting up schools, and proselytizing. Thus, these areas transitioned fairly quickly from a more Catholic mode of aggressive baptizing to a more cautious focus on community formation.[23] The first consistories did not materialize until 1643 in both Tayuoan and Soulang, the same year in which the first communion service was held. Twelve years had elapsed between the time of the first baptisms and sixteen years since the arrival of the first clergy. Mission strategy in Formosa actually paralleled Catholic approaches to conversion by allowing baptism for prospective converts with few or no preconditions and then by concentrating on education and acculturation. Calvinist missions always hewed closely to the geopolitical parameters of the companies' commercial objectives.

In Formosa, the tactic of baptizing almost anyone willing also fit in well with the VOC's scheme of inserting itself into political divisions among warring tribal societies. For local communities, the promise of military protection by the VOC certainly incentivized conversion. The company beginning under governor Nuyts offered military defense for converts, opening a market for political subjects and religious converts.[24] Governors in Formosa did not have to concern themselves with powerful neighbors who might take such aggressive actions as a threat, as other governors did with the sultans of Ternate and Johor, the Buddhist king of Kandy, or the Luso-Brazilian planters of Brazil. Indigenous peoples in Formosa converted for their own reasons (discussed below), but ministers also sought to bring them along in the Reformed faith through compulsory attendance in church schools. The larger-scale conversion approach in Formosa divided *predikanten* in Southeast Asia and the Netherlands over worries that it compromised orthodoxy. The Formosan case represented a radical departure from the Calvinist approach to conversion in all other parts of the Dutch empire.

Outside of Formosa, Calvinist missions soon settled into a pattern of building communities of Reformed Protestant Christians. These efforts conformed to the political and economic circumstances enveloping the companies in a region. In most areas under VOC and WIC control, such as Batavia, the Moluccan Islands and other East Indies posts, Ceylon, sites on the Coromandel and Malabar coasts, the Cape of Good Hope, and Brazil, *predikanten, ziekentroosteren*, and teachers labored to propagate the gospel. For various reasons only minimal or no mission work beyond pastoral functions in local congregations occurred in New Netherland, Surinam, West Africa locations, and Dutch holdings in the Caribbean. In New Netherland, antagonistic relations with native groups in the 1630s and 1640s and the conspicuous presence of Lutherans and Anglicans retarded missions. Plantation owners in Surinam feared it might hurt production and actively discouraged proselytizing among local and enslaved peoples. In Japan, the shogun Tokugawa Iemitsu prohibited all forms of Christianity on pain of expulsion and possibly even execution, so the Dutch could not worship at all at their post in Hirado (1609–1641) and later on Deshima Island, let alone conduct missionary activity.

One of the largest mission fields for Calvinists comprised native Christians baptized previously by Jesuits and Franciscans, who had accompanied Portuguese operations in the East Indies, Ceylon, southern India, and Brazil. Sebastian Danckaerts remarked that in Amboina, "the natives have learned something about Christianity by the means of the Portuguese . . . but they [the natives] have fallen back even more to worshipping their devils."[25] Cornelis Dedel (a VOC official) concurred, noting that local people claimed to be Christians, but they knew little about the religion and practiced it only in "external ceremonies."[26] Ministers from Recife inherited a huge mission field of Catholics, but a large number of those were Portuguese or Luso-Brazilian. Even more problematic for mission-minded Calvinists, the tolerance of priests in the colony kept most Catholics loyal to the Roman church. In January 1638, the classis in Recife complained that the priests were hampering ministers' ability to attract people to Sunday services. The strength of Catholicism in Brazil made clergy there unwilling to baptize children of Catholic parents until they had undergone education in the Reformed faith.[27] In the early 1660s, after the Dutch had expelled the Portuguese from Ceylon, Philip Baldaeus and Henricus Bongart reported that they had a "church full of European *toehoorderen*" and Christians from the "*inlandse natie*" that needed a thorough Reformed education.[28] Bringing these Catholics over to a Calvinist faith and practice posed immense challenges in no small part because of the stark differences in worship. In Cochin (on the Malabar coast), for example, the minister Jacob Canter Visscher grumbled to the Batavia consistory in the late 1710s that the chances for converting Indians were quite limited because "Roman priests had dangled alluring images before their eyes for so long, which agreed with their heathen idols."[29] In their pastoral accounts to church districts in the Netherlands, consistories in the East Indies, South Asia, and Brazil counted these Catholics in their midst as *gemeene* ("common" or "general') or *genaamd* ("nominal") Christians.[30] Calvinists believed that these Catholics, like *liefhebberen* and *toehoorderen* in the Netherlands, belonged to "Christendom" in their overseas quarters and made it the Reformed Church's mission to make them into good or better Protestants.

Calvinist ministers also devoted much energy to converting peoples who had little to no exposure to any version of Christianity. These peoples included Buddhists, Hindus, and Muslims in the East Indies and South Asia and at the Cape of Good Hope. Calvinists lived among significant numbers of Sephardic Jews whom governor Maurits welcomed to Brazil. The classis in Brazil remarked that the Portuguese thought the Dutch were "half Jews" because of the large migration of Jews into the colony after the WIC conquest.[31] People following these faith practices mixed and mingled a web of local traditions to make sense of the cosmos and give order to their daily lives.

The first step in conversion for all non-Christians and baptized nominal Christians was to display a rudimentary understanding of the faith commensurate with a Protestant standard of life. Though requirements varied by place and time, prospective converts at least had to be able to recite the Ten Commandments, Apostles Creed, and Lord's Prayer from memory and show some understanding of basic concepts. The requirement of comprehension, however, proved a tricky issue that consistories puzzled over throughout this period.[32] Consistories wished to ensure that nominal Christians had a minimal comprehension of fundamental tenets, since native peoples usually had undergone little in the way of education from Catholic missionaries. Calvinist consistories equated a proper manner of life as consistent with following Christian marital and sexual customs, eschewing idolatry and superstition, and avoiding disorderly behavior. Once satisfied that prospective converts had met these requirements, consistories approved non-Christians for baptism. The Reformed Church did not rebaptize nominal Christians. Children of non-Christian parents, however, could not be baptized until they converted and promised to raise their children in the Reformed religion. Slaves had to gain the approval of slave owners before receiving baptism.[33]

Most overseas churches departed from the standards of the Reformed Church in the Netherlands in administering baptism and the Lord's Supper. Consistories harbored anxiety that the newly baptized would scandalize the church community with vestiges of false religion or immorality. Two clergy in Batavia, for example, exclaimed in 1730 that "the minister better not turn his back too quickly [on baptized natives] or they will give themselves over to their idols and to the devil's service."[34] To avoid scandal to the congregation, consistories required additional education and demonstrated maturation in the Reformed faith before granting converts permission to take communion. Derided as "dividing the sacraments," this approach came under harsh criticism by classes in the Netherlands for violating the sacramental unity of baptism and communion. The practice also caused bitter debate between the Batavia consistory—which rejected dividing the sacraments in 1648—and other consistories in the East Indies. As we shall see below, the quarrel and the acrimony it generated stemmed from the difficulty of applying Calvinist principles of community formation to the Christian mission in overseas territories. The steps along the pathway to conversion and sanctification in overseas Calvinist churches were fraught with more complications and ambiguity than the triumphalist expectations of Reformed ministers and theologians in the Netherlands anticipated.

Calvinists conceived of the conversion of souls as interdependent with the Protestant Christianization of societies. In the premodern period, the work of converting individuals generally involved transforming space and time through coercion and compulsion.[35] Within the Dutch empire, the Calvinist missionary project necessitated the Christianization of worship practices, alteration of the sacred landscape, and reconfiguration of the temporal dimensions of social interaction. Ministers overseas and in the Netherlands referred to the Christian societies they were laboring to build variably as a "spiritual Jerusalem," "Christian republic," and in Asia an *Indisch Sion*.[36] The ideal society that Calvinists envisioned in Dutch overseas territories took practical shape as a Christian polity maintained by a judicial structure and cultural ethos. Christianizing public space followed the pattern of Reformed Protestants in Europe who destroyed religious images in churches, dismantled shrines, and repurposed monasteries in territories where they came to power. In the colonies, controlling space meant eliminating the sights and sounds of pagan, Muslim, Jewish, and Catholic observances and upholding Sunday as a day of rest and worship.[37]

Maintaining Sunday as the Sabbath day of rest from labor and of worship in the Reformed community formed a critical component of transforming overseas settlements into Christian republics. Calvinists expected the faithful to rest from their labor, go to church, hear the preaching of the word of God, and participate in religious exercises with family and fellow church members. Calvinists in the Netherlands and the empire lobbied political authorities to legislate a Sabbath so that all people ceased from labor and routine activity and had the opportunity to worship. At the insistence of church leaders, the VOC and WIC enacted laws upholding Sabbath observance for all inhabitants, including Moors and pagans. Yet persistent complaints by clergy indicate that compliance with these ordinances was spotty, even by the company officers themselves.

The resolve to maintain the Sabbath represented a central element in the campaign to Christianize societies contaminated by pagan and Muslim practices. Sabbath observance made headway in this project by Christianizing time, which required the cessation of worldly enterprise for the purpose of worship, prayer, and introspection. More than simply an opportunity to attend church services, the Sabbath created an occasion for people to continue the work of conversion in their lives. Imposing the Sabbath on everyone amounted to a declaration that colonial time was Calvinist. Consistories' insistence on the temporal sacrality of the Sabbath even appeared in the terminology Calvinists used to condemn engaging in worldly activities on Sunday. They denounced working or playing on Sunday as "profaning the Sabbath," connoting contamination, defilement, and desecration.[38]

Christianizing time was closely connected to transforming the religious landscape, so that colonial society appeared visibly as a Reformed Protestant community. In all areas where Calvinists conducted missions, they followed in the wake of company territorial jurisdiction. In the Dutch case, it was inconceivable that missions would go forward outside of the political boundaries of company control. Within those territories, consistories worked to create a Calvinist Christian republic, which entailed eradicating false religion. A wide range of Calvinist clergy, from the theologians Voetius, Hoornbeeck, and Simon Oomius to ministers in the field, assumed that false religion was deeply rooted in the hearts of pagans and Moors and very difficult to remove.[39] Consistories remained wary of the pull of Buddhist pagodas, Muslim mosques, and Hindu temples on native converts who always seemed on the brink of backsliding. The Colombo consistory, for example, argued in January 1689 that pagodas posed a threat to Christian education in Ceylon, because "heathenism" occupied a very long history, whereas true Christianity was a recent arrival on the island.[40] In Brazil, Batavia, Formosa, and the Moluccas, the Dutch feared the deleterious effects of idols, festivals, and mosques on fragile indigenous souls.

In addition to the spiritual menace to new converts, Calvinists argued that the presence of these objects was morally corrosive in a Christian society. They transgressed upon Christian public space, thus mocking religion and civil society, and invited the wrath of God. Consistories in the Netherlands employed the same terminology when condemning Catholic worship to city governments. In these circumstances, Calvinist consistories sought to decontaminate social space by putting regular pressure on governors and political councils to destroy idols, temples, pagodas, and mosques. The trading companies shared these

Calvinist values, yet had to balance them against antagonizing peoples who often wanted little to do with Protestant Christianity. Governors, hoping to avoid alienating local inhabitants and nearby regimes, thus proved reticent about enforcing them with rigor. Major struggles occurred between the companies and consistories in Brazil over Catholicism, in Batavia over Islam and local practices, in Colombo over Buddhism, and in Formosa over traditional practices, all of which illustrate the significance of space in campaigns of conversion for Calvinists.

The overseas settlement that produced the greatest frustration over Catholic worship was Brazil. Priests made their rounds in Ceylon, Batavia, the Cape of Good Hope, and most other Dutch-held locations. But they did so semi-clandestinely. To the umbrage of Calvinist pastors, Catholics (and Jews) practiced openly in Brazil. Governor Maurits allowed priests to continue ministering to Brazilian and Portuguese planters, but what outraged Calvinist ministers was that Catholics still held public processions "in the streets." The classes in Brazil and in the Netherlands protested the "brazen" behavior of priests in Paraíba and the fact that religious orders in Olinda operated two monasteries out in the open. It seems that competition and antagonism were playing themselves out in public religious performance. For in 1640, the Brazil classis complained that the governor had promised an edict to keep the ceremonies inside the walls of their churches "in order not to offend anyone." Governor Maurits did bow to pressure from *predikanten*, expelling the three religious orders still active in the region, Franciscans, Dominicans, and Carmelites, in 1640. After his departure in 1644, Calvinists won other victories leading to greater strictures on Catholic worship and religious space.[41] In all Dutch settlements, the visibility of Catholic observances contested the Calvinist claim on public space, just as the failure of governors to enforce the Sabbath diminished the primacy of Reformed worship.[42]

In Batavia, governor generals beginning in 1643 banned all false religion in principle. Designed to ensure a male child could not become a Muslim, the new policy prohibited circumcision. Nevertheless, governor generals gave Muslims, Buddhists, and others a good deal of practical latitude. From the 1650s to the early 1700s, company generals and consistories in Batavia pushed and pulled back and forth over the public presence of mosques, temples, and displays of local beliefs. Consistories insisted on strict enforcement of the prohibition, but governor generals such as Maetsuijcker retreated from these demands. In 1650 and 1651, Carel Reynierszoon disbanded all public and private services, and demolished a mosque.[43] The consistory declared triumphantly to the Amsterdam classis in 1651 that the progress of the gospel was making great strides, since "the false religion of the Moors is forbidden and the papist religion is banned. Chinese devil worship [Buddhism] has abated and the profanation of the Sabbath is prohibited."[44] Yet private practice of Islam continued, and at least by 1674 a mosque stood in the city, as did several madrasas.[45] By the late seventeenth century, Muslim communities in Batavia functioned largely unimpeded as quasi-autonomous societies under company rule, whereby they regulated themselves according to Islamic law.[46] Consistories fell silent about mosques and madrasas over the course of the eighteenth century, as ministers and elders recognized as a practical matter that they could not eradicate Islam, which had made great gains in the East Indies in the first half of the seventeenth century.

The rites and observances that incorporated images, dancing and festivities, and dramatic symbolism animated consistories the most because of their abhorrence for idolatry. In all Dutch outposts, consistories persisted in their attempts to persuade colonial authorities to take action against Hindu, Buddhist, and shamanistic practices.[47] In Batavia, the consistory targeted wayang street theater, New Year's Eve celebrations, dance festivals, funeral rites, and temple worship among Chinese inhabitants as devilish superstitions that imperiled Christian society.[48] The *Politieke Raad*, growing increasingly concerned with the energy and potential anticolonial energies these celebrations unleashed, began prohibiting the activities in 1668. The council regulated dances and funerary ceremonies by requiring parties to request a license from the colonial government. The consistory also targeted pagodas, constructed as Buddhist shrines in the private domains of Chinese merchants and laborers, but on occasion serving also as public structures in the city. Struggles between the governor general Maetsuijcker and the Batavian consistory came to a head in 1651, as the ministers and elders demanded that a public pagoda be destroyed. Maetsuijcker, not wishing to alienate the Chinese, issued an ordinance to please the consistory, but then neglected to have it carried out.[49] Sometimes, church officials took matters into their own hands. Coming upon a village on the island of Seram in the East Indies, a missionary entourage was so offended by "altars to the devil" that the visitors hacked them into pieces.[50]

The most arduous struggle over pagodas took place in Ceylon, where coastal areas controlled by the VOC abutted lands that remained under the direct authority of the king of Kandy, who was a patron of Buddhist pagodas. While Ceylon consistories opposed the presence of all pagodas, the temple in the city of Kandy caused particular consternation to the Dutch. Known as the Temple of the Tooth because it housed a relic from the Buddha, the pagoda experienced a revival under King Rajasimha II, who reconstructed it after the Portuguese invaded the area in the early seventeenth century. The temple complex reemerged as an important pilgrimage site for Buddhists. As Rajasimha was rebuilding the pagoda, the VOC also constructed a school to instruct new *inlandse* converts in the Reformed faith. Teachers and ministers feared that the presence of the pagoda in close proximity to the school would tug on the souls of these new converts and cause them to backslide into pagan idolatry. Although the Amsterdam and Walcheren classes took the issue up with the *Heren XVII*, the directors merely entrusted their governors to promote cordial relations with local rulers if it best served the company's interest.[51]

Calvinists also opposed any public recognition of other Protestant groups. In the 1700s, Moravian Brethren proselytized aggressively at the Cape of Good Hope and Surinam, while Lutherans working for the VOC at the Cape and in Batavia sought a public presence. Lutheran and other Protestant groups populated New Netherland as well. Calvinists argued that the Reformed Church had undisputed ecclesiastical rights since the early 1600s. Introducing other less pure denominations would "damage" the mission to "*inlandse* Christendom" by tarnishing the "predominance" of the Reformed Church and by confusing unknowing natives.[52] In other words, non-Europeans would not be able to distinguish the right belief and practice maintained in the Reformed Church from the defective tenets of Lutheranism. Thus, religious education and spatial authority formed the two pillars of Calvinist endeavors to Christianize colonial societies in the empire. Even though consistories achieved mixed and uneven success in these undertakings, their strategic importance illustrated the Calvinist missionary project's goal of converting societies in order to save souls.

STRUCTURING MISSIONS

In keeping with its communal identity, the Reformed Church's instruments for conversion arose out of the basic functions of pastoral ministry in Europe. Ministers overseas and in the Netherlands did discuss and devise strategies to convert Moors and "heathens." Yet, like the 1643 Batavian Church Order, these programs—outside of Formosa—always fell back on the regular institutions of parish life in the European Reformation. After deliberating over how best to convert "heathens," the classis in Recife in 1638, for example, endorsed the central ministries of Dutch Reformed churches: preaching the gospel, administering the sacraments, and inculcating discipline among members.[53] Within this parochial framework, the two vehicles for propagating the faith were sermons preached by ministers and, most importantly, schools, run often by native teachers. Consistories set up and oversaw the schools, which taught the fundamentals of the Reformed religion as well as reading and writing, sometimes in Dutch but primarily in local languages. Ministers and lay *ziekentroosteren* also instructed youths and adults in catechetical materials. As we will see below, missionary strategy evolved over the course of the seventeenth and eighteenth centuries, but preaching and teaching remained the basic staples for proselytizing throughout this period.

SERMONS

Predikanten conducted services and preached sermons in Dutch, Portuguese, and often a native vernacular on Sunday and once during the week. Because of the ubiquity of the Portuguese in the Indian Ocean and the colony in Brazil, Portuguese was a translanguage in most regions inhabited by the Dutch. The pervasive influence of Portuguese in Southeast Asia led many peoples in the region to identify the language with Christianity, referring to it as "Kristang."[54] Some ministers also acquired Spanish. It behooved Dutch ministers, in short, to learn the language of their geopolitical and religious enemies. In the East Indies, many clergy developed a facility in Malay; in Ceylon, the indigenous languages were Tamil and Sinhala, though it was not until the very end of the seventeenth century that ministers began regularly acquiring facility in these vernaculars. In Formosa, *predikanten* worked in Sinkan; and in Brazil, a few acquired Tupian, Portuguese, and Spanish.[55] In these regions, ministers and native linguists translated sermons, catechisms, and other materials that could be used by ministers and *ziekentroosteren* who did not speak in local vernaculars. In October 1757 the Colombo consistory, chiding the minister Matthias Wermerskircher for the length of time it was taking him to "make progress in local languages," noted that the church anticipated a learning period of one and one-half years until a *predikant* could preach from the pulpit.[56] Undoubtedly, the acquisition of language varied by minister based on linguistic aptitude and pastoral workload. Consistories pressed governors to compel *inlandse* Christians, including the nominal converts baptized by Catholics, to attend the preaching service on the Sabbath.[57] Although governors did not acquiesce, the church's effort to bring people to preaching from the Bible suggests ministers' strategic thinking about converting souls and Christianizing societies.

Ministers also traveled to small congregations in outlying areas to preach. The most aggressive preaching occurred in Soulang (Formosa) by George Candidius and Robert Junius, where they organized large-scale preaching events in villages under the auspices of the VOC. Not all congregations had ministers, so clergy within a larger colonial site took turns conducting visitations to inspect churches and schools, to baptize converts, to administer communion, to marry Christian couples, to mete out discipline, and to preach. In the absence of an ordained minister, *ziekentroosteren* or laymen read sermons at the Sunday services. These circuits grew to be quite extensive. The Amboina consistory, for example, fairly early in its history extended its reach into eight villages outside Fort Victoria where a *predikant* and elder visited every three months. These sites included Waai, Alang, and Liliboi, about fifteen miles away, but ministers also ventured to the nearby Lease Islands (the Uliassers) of Haruku, Saparua, and Nusa Laut, about thirty-five miles by boat from Amboina.[58] Visitations became more regularized over the course of the 1600s, and by the end of the century ministers and elders were logging even greater distances as the circuits grew. In the autumn of 1693, the Amboina consistory sent out representatives on three occasions to preach, baptize, marry, and administer communion on the island and nearby locations. From August 3 to October 9, for example, Petrus van der Vorm and two elders visited approximately twenty sites on Amboina island, as well as the islands of Nusa Laut, Saparua, Haruku, Seram, Manipa, and Boano. Two months later, Francois Valentijn and an elder traveled to congregations on the south coast of Seram to preach and inspect schools and congregations. Yet a month later, in November, van der Vorm (again) and an elder sojourned for two weeks in the islands of Boano, Seram, Buru, and Manipa to give moral instruction and guidance in various settlements.[59]

Likewise, in Ceylon and Brazil ministers paid regular calls and preached to congregations and communities in the outlying areas around the major colonial sites. In Ceylon, the VOC's chief operations were in Colombo, Jaffnapatnam, and Galle. In November 1737, the consistories listed these locations for Colombo as Negombo, Kalpitiya, Tutucorin, and Kotte; for Jaffnapatnam as Mannar, Trincomalee, and Batticaloa; and for Galle as Matara.[60] In Brazil, the changing landscape because of war made it difficult to set up a stable circuit of traveling preachers. Yet clergy in the principal fortified cities, such as Recife, Frederikstad (today João Pessoa), Olinda, and Fort Maurits, made their way out into the dozen or so smaller congregations. Several ministers, including Vincent Soler and David à Dorselaer, went to preach to native peoples that inhabited the four *aldeias* (mission villages) established by Jesuits in Rio Grande, Paraíba, Itamaraca, and Pernambuco, preaching and teaching in Portuguese, Tupian, and Dutch.[61] In the Cape of Good Hope, clergy from Cape Town made regular visits to Stellenbosch and Drakenstein when resident ministers were installed there in 1686 and 1691, respectively.[62]

Preaching occupied a central place within Calvinist community life—it was indeed one of the three signature marks of a Reformed church—and for that reason only ordained ministers could preach their own sermons.[63] The Batavian consistory declared in 1677 that preaching was the means by which the Word of

God is proclaimed, thus ministers should give as many sermons as they possibly could.[64] Since the early seventeenth century, the Dutch Reformed Church had required extensive theological training for pastors. Yet until the 1640s, *predikanten* assigned to overseas service did not receive any consistent preparation for the unprecedented challenges of proselytizing among non-Christian peoples in non-Christian cultures. Antonius Walaeus, a theologian at the University of Leiden, started a seminary for overseas ministers in 1623 that carried his name, but it folded only ten years later. In the late 1630s, the theology faculty at Utrecht and later in Leiden began to give serious attention to training students for overseas service. Calvinists seemed to believe that a thorough grounding in Christianity, along with the power of the Holy Spirit, was sufficient to preach effectively to pagans and Moors.

By the second half of the seventeenth century, a preaching strategy emerged from an increased academic engagement with paganism and Islam that drew both connections and contrasts with Protestant Christianity. The sermon books of Francis Caron, minister at Amboina, proved quite popular for use by *zieken-troosteren* and other church personnel at the village level.[65] Reformed writers followed St. Paul in recognizing that "all people have a knowledge of God, even though they might appear to be without God or religion."[66] Original sin corrupted human minds. Thus, unregenerate peoples distorted the true worship of God revealed in scripture into the debased worship of created objects and beings through idolatry and empty ceremony. False religions, then, imitated the truth, so that people sought the knowledge of God and the experience of salvation, but did so in perverted observances. Johannes Hoornbeeck, a theologian in the Netherlands, referred to the Hindu practice of cleansing away sin in the Ganges River and revering the Vedas as holy scripture as corrupted attempts to obtain what the Christian gospel generously offered. Preachers were to begin with commonalities between paganism and Christianity, but then lead natives to the basic tenets of Christianity, such as "the nature and condition of man, the origins in creation, the fall from happiness to a state of misery . . . Christ, the savior and how he frees us from damnation, that he is the mediator between God and man."[67] After setting forth Christian truths, the preacher then was to expose the false derivations of pagan ceremonies that misled people into depravity and superstition.

Calvinists took a similar tack in preaching to Muslims. Both Hoornbeeck and Gisbertus Voetius advocated an apologetic approach to Islam focused on championing the Bible to undermine the authority of the Qur'an. To attack the Qur'an, Voetius urged his students to show how it derived from scripture and thus corrupted teachings about the Trinitarian nature of God and the atoning work of

Christ. He also enjoined *predikanten* to study the Qur'an themselves to identify
passages that ran counter to the Bible, natural law, and right reason.[68] Like all
heretics, Muslims, Voetius argued, took portions of scripture and twisted them
into debased forms of beliefs and practices.[69] Adriaan Reland, an orientalist at
Utrecht who wrote an influential treatise on Islam in the early 1700s, also advised ministers that they should appreciate the teachings that Islam and Christianity shared and begin disputations from that standpoint.[70] He put forth a
conversion strategy for Muslims that followed logically from Voetius's emphasis
on recognizing commonalities between Islam and Christianity. Thus, Calvinist preaching in the mission field appealed first to the connections between
Christianity and other religions and then sought to reveal their derivative and
false nature.

SCHOOLS

Preaching announced the Christian message to nonbelievers, but educating
students, especially youthful ones, was the most enduring structural strategy for
indigenizing Calvinism in colonial environments. In 1637, Dutch authorities in
Formosa reported that the industrious labor of Robert Junius to teach the fundamentals of Christianity was "opening their darkened eyes" to the truth.[71] To
that end, the VOC sponsored hundreds of schools for religious and language
instruction in the East Indies, Formosa, South Asia, and the Cape of Good Hope.
On a more limited basis, the WIC also opened schools for missionary purposes
in Brazil, whereas schools in other domains, such as New Netherland, Elmina,
Curaçao, and Surinam, largely served European settlers and company employees.[72] In Asian colonies, the *Heren XVII* even mandated that governors found
schools to spread the Christian religion and promote civilization among "heathen" peoples.[73] The Batavian Church Order of 1643 issued specific guidelines:
"The duty of schoolmasters is primarily to inculcate in the young a fear of the
Lord, to teach them to pray, sing, attend church, and to catechize them; next to
teach them obedience to their parents, the authorities, and their masters; thirdly
to teach them to read, write, and do arithmetic; fourthly, to teach them good
morals and manners; and finally to see to it that no tongue other than Dutch is
used in the schools."[74]

Financed by the trading companies and staffed most often by indigenous
teachers, schools reached tens of thousands of children with Reformed teachings during the seventeenth and eighteenth centuries. In addition to schools,
the church utilized catechists, who often were natives, to teach adults the fundamentals of the Reformed faith. Schools and catechetical practices became pri-

mary instruments for conversion to Reformed Protestantism in the Dutch empire. As a mission strategy, primary education took on increasing importance in the second half of the seventeenth and throughout the eighteenth century as the corps of ordained clergy for overseas churches remained meager. Jointly administered by companies and ministers and often staffed by native teachers, schools functioned as the most efficient means to spread the gospel where a formal pastoral presence was thin.

Schools sprang up most everywhere the Dutch established themselves. The governor Cornelis Matelief established the first Dutch school outside of Europe in Amboina shortly after the VOC put down roots there in 1605. Its first teacher was Johannes Wogma, who gave lessons to Amboinese children in Dutch language, writing, and arithmetic, and taught them several prayers. Although this school closed in 1616, Sebastian Danckaerts opened a new school several years later. By 1633, 32 schools across the East Indies offered instruction to 1,200 students, growing to 46 schools with 3,600 students by 1680, and to 54 schools with 5,190 students by 1700.[75] Batavia boasted 34 teachers in 1706.[76] In Ceylon, approximately 30 schools were in operation in the 1660s with 18,000 students. Intensified missionary efforts in the late seventeenth and early eighteenth centuries spawned more schools. The region of Jaffnapatnam contained 37 schools, while the districts of Colombo and Galle had 29 and 16, respectively.[77] In southeast Formosa, the company and church joined forces to construct 5 schools in in the 1630s in the villages of Sinkan, Bacaluan, Tavocan, Mattauw, and Soulang, with 7 teachers and 395 students. By 1643, 50 native teachers were leading 600 students in these and other sites. As ministers pushed into other parts of Formosa in the 1650s, they opened schools in the north in the settlements of Tamsuy, Kimaurij, and Quelang, and in the south at Pangsoya, Dolatok, Verovorongh, Tapouliangh, and Pangandangh.[78] *Predikanten* and *ziekentroosteren* provided some religious education and catechetical lessons in Cape Town, though largely in an extemporaneous capacity. Regular schools with salaried teachers appeared first in 1676, and by the 1710s the consistory exercised supervision over the religious instruction of slaves, free settlers, and company employees. Schools also sprang up in Stellenbosch and Drakenstein in the early eighteenth century. The consistory at Cape Town expressed an intention to create schools for Khoi children, but linguistic and cultural differences proved too profound to make this goal feasible.[79]

The WIC sponsored schools in the Atlantic churches. The first school in New Netherland appeared in late 1637 or early 1638 in New Amsterdam, under the direction of Adam Roelantsen. During the period of Dutch rule, the company founded eight other schools, in Albany, Breuckelen, Flatbush, New Amstel,

Haarlem, Wiltwyck, New Utrecht, and the Bouwery. Led by *voorlezeren* (salaried readers) and sextons, schools in New Netherland primarily served the
children of Dutch settlers.[80] Closer to the missionary spirit of the Asian consistories, the classis of Brazil declared its aim in 1638 to organize schools to spread
the Christian religion. During the 1630s and 1640s, schools, staffed usually by a
Dutch or sometimes by a Tupi instructor, appeared in all major Dutch settlements.[81] Spanish-speaking teachers also taught reading, writing, and Protestantism to inhabitants of the *aldeias*.[82] Schools in Brazil originally targeted
Portuguese and Dutch settlers, indigenous Tupi inhabitants, and slaves. In 1644,
the classis restricted the scope of the schools by deciding that educating the Tupi
was no longer practical and that *ziekentroosteren* should instruct slaves in segre-
gated meetings.[83] Elsewhere in the Atlantic, the WIC set up schools in Curaçao, Elmina, Luanda, and the Gold Coast.[84]

Setting up schools and managing them were joint ventures between Reformed
ministers, regional governors, and company directors in the Netherlands. In general, clergy exercised supervision over instruction and reported back to consistories and the *Politieke Raden* for a territory. The companies negotiated contracts
and paid wages, though the ministers evaluated the quality of instruction and
made recommendations to company authorities.[85] Mutual jurisdiction varied
somewhat in Ceylon, since masters in the Ceylonese schools performed a number of civic administrative tasks, such as registering births, deaths, and marriages
in a locality. Because of these governmental responsibilities, schools and schoolmasters fell under the authority of *scholarchale raden* (educational councils)
responsible to the governor. A *predikant* did accompany council members on
visitations for religious quality control.[86] The VOC and WIC paid the salaries
of all teachers and underwrote the expenses for all educational materials.[87] The
companies paid teachers (both Dutch and native) primarily in currency, but occasionally supplemented wages with goods in kind. In Ternate in 1628, teachers
received jugs of wine and rice as part of their salaries; the company allotted doles
of rice to native teachers in Formosa.[88] Finally, the VOC and WIC invested
heavily in hundreds of theological books for ministers, grammar books for teachers, translated catechisms, postils, portions of the Bible, and other pedagogical
materials.[89]

While the VOC and WIC exercised jurisdiction over schools, consistories dispatched clergy regularly on circuits to inspect the quality of instruction and the
progress of students. These visitations were supposed to occur at regular inter-
vals. The governor general in Batavia, Johannes Camphuijs, issued general
regulations for schools in the East Indies that stipulated a *predikant* and member of the *Politieke Raad* visit all schools every six months.[90] Rijklof van Goens

decreed in the early 1660s that *scholarchen* and clergy were to inspect schools in their districts every four months.[91] The Colombo consistory stated in 1683 that inspectors visited the schools in the district four times per year.[92] As early as the 1630s, clergy in Formosa visited schools and reported on the progress of Christian education.[93] Although visitation reports abound from the East Indies, Ceylon, and other Dutch territories, it is also clear that contingent circumstances, such as sickness, depletion of the clerical corps, or political instability, inhibited a regular pattern of visitations. During a revival of Buddhism under Vimala Dharma Suriya II, the king of Kandy, in the late 1680s, almost no visitations were carried out around Colombo or Galle.[94] Yet in 1714 the Colombo consistory related that recent visitations gave hope for the "demolition of heathendom and the propagation of true Christianity."[95]

When they did visit schools and outlying congregations, ministers preached, examined the students and schoolmasters, baptized new converts, married couples, and checked the inventory of religious materials. Pastoral inspectors then wrote accounts outlining the "state of native Christendom" within the circuit. The description offered a quantified summary and a qualitative assessment of the progress of the Reformed faith. Petrus van der Vorm, minister in Amboina, drafted one of the most detailed reports from this missionary era. Visiting fifty-two schools in outlying areas and islands, van der Vorm catalogued the number of teachers and students, evaluated their learning, listed the educational materials used, made observations about the natives, described linguistic complexities, and offered recommendations for strengthening the mission.[96] While van der Vorm's account was unusual in its descriptive depth, ministers regularly constructed visitation reports for consistories and colonial authorities, who then distilled them in annual letters for church bodies back in the Netherlands. Ultimately the reports served as the primary source material for a Calvinist missionary narrative of spreading the gospel to pagans and Moors that drew inspiration from the labors of the apostles to the expansion of Christianity in the early middle ages.

Dutch ministers and colonial authorities relied heavily on indigenous teachers to serve as schoolmasters in company schools. Although VOC governors insisted at various times on a Dutch language policy in schools, it never gained traction in local societies. It also took *predikanten, ziekentroosteren,* and other Dutch personnel months and even years to develop facility in local vernaculars and in Portuguese. Consequently, the companies recruited natives with language expertise to teach students to read, write, and comprehend the Reformed faith. Since the VOC inherited the Portuguese school system in Ceylon, it became necessary to replace Catholic priests with local young men who had the ability to teach and do administrative service. Philip Baldaeus worked in the Jaffnapatnam region in the 1650s and 1660s to orient teachers to Reformed teachings and to translate instructional resources into Tamil. The transformation of schools into instruments of Protestant conversion in the southern coastal region around Colombo and Galle did not get underway in earnest until the early 1700s. Yet ministers and company leaders in Ceylon embarked upon the most ambitious training program for indigenous teachers and proponents.[97]

Under the leadership of a veteran company official, Hendrik Adriaan van Reede, the VOC opened a seminary in the small town of Nallur (near Jaffnapatnam) in 1696. Van Reede had observed the revival of Catholicism in the north, which alarmed the governor Laurens van Pyl. To counter this religious and imperial threat and to shore up shoddy schools, the company established a seminary to train indigenous youths in Dutch and in the Reformed faith. The minister Adriaan de Meij, proficient in Tamil, assumed rectorship of the school, which took in twenty-four students. The seminary functioned well for the first fifteen years, graduating teachers and commissioning five native proponents in 1704.[98] However, the shrinking corps of Dutch overseas ministers, none of whom were skilled in Tamil, led to a decline in the quality of instruction, and the seminary closed in 1722. Students from Nallur had already been transferring to a seminary in Colombo, created in 1696 and directed by the minister Johannes Ruël, who had gained capability in Sinhalese in the early 1690s. The seminary soon surpassed its counterpart in Nallur and remained an important training ground for teachers and proponents throughout Dutch rule in Ceylon.[99]

In the East Indies, the VOC made extensive use of native teachers, training them on a more informal basis than in Ceylon. Dutch schoolmasters in Amboina eventually gave way to indigenous leaders in the 1620s and 1630s. In Batavia and the Moluccan Islands, the early ministers Sebastian Danckaerts and Justus Heurnius worked directly with native teachers and leaders to teach them basic Christian tenets, reading, and writing. It is likely that Dutch *ziekentroosteren* and lay readers also provided training to local schoolmasters. Efforts at inculcating Dutch language proficiency in students and teachers were no more successful in the archipelago than anywhere else, thus Portuguese and Malay endured as the linguistic media in the schools of the East Indies. More institutionalized forms of teacher education appeared later in the seventeenth century. The consistory and *Politieke Raad* in Batavia founded a short-lived Latin School (1642–1656, 1666–1670, 1745–1755) that produced a few ministers and teachers. Local catechism teachers who gave lessons in homes and neighborhoods proliferated in Batavia, growing to thirty-four by 1706. The Amboina Church Order of 1673 required native teachers in remote areas to come into the city to attend classes and take examinations every two to four weeks.[100]

In the mission fields of Formosa and Brazil, clergy and governors utilized native schoolmasters less effectively, and at the Cape of Good Hope not at all. With the surge of conversions in Tayouan in the 1630s, Candidius and Junius scrambled to field a teaching corps to indoctrinate the novices.[101] In 1636, Junius enlisted a number of company soldiers to learn local vernaculars so that they could teach and at the same time prepare promising indigenous students for teaching roles. In the 1630s, the classis in Brazil was also searching for indigenous, Portuguese-speaking teachers for their schools, though the results seem meager at best.[102] In Formosa, the lack of sufficient clerical oversight coupled with the abundance of linguistic uncertainty inhibited the development of an operative network of native schoolmasters. A seminary launched in Soulang in 1657 was taking shape to deal with these obstacles when rebel Ming Chinese forces led by Zheng Chenggong (Koxinga) expelled the Dutch from the island.[103]

Overseas clergy recognized that schoolmasters, largely consisting of native teachers, represented the best hope for the success of global Calvinism. This recognition is what prompted consistories to devote so much time and energy to inspection rounds. Rightly or wrongly, inspectors often drew a direct connection between the industry and piety of a schoolmaster and the progress of students in the Reformed faith. The Colombo consistory credited schoolmasters in 1683 with providing education that was leading to the conversion of people from paganism to true religion and from concubinage to Christian marriage.[104] The Amboina minister Francis Caron remarked in November 1672 that the teachers in Hatala and Kielang were industrious and their students performed well, giving parents confidence to send their children to school.[105] Similarly in Sepa (Seram) in 1675, the minister Pieter Durant praised the schoolmaster for producing excellent students.[106] The consistory in Amboina even credited native *predikanten* in 1720 for setting a great foundation for the Christian community in Hitu, which had since gone into decline.[107] Jacob Montanus in Ternate advised against allowing Marcus de Rosario to leave his post on the island of Sangir in November 1675 because children needed an experienced master like him to "bridle the wonderful humors of these people and lead their limited and narrow souls."[108] Likewise, the visitor Gellius Cammiga praised Domingos Mangus in Batjan as a most capable master whose labor bore fruit.[109] Inspectors consistently equated the ability of students and their desire to learn with the work of industrious, reliable, and devout native schoolmasters.[110]

While capable schoolmasters were praised by *predikanten* for furthering student achievement, they got the blame in cases where inspectors perceived religious education as failing. Pieter Noot, a minister in Ternate, explained in 1703 that only when a schoolmaster learns the religion himself will a student comprehend it; thus, the ignorance of teachers in north Sulawesi meant that in many areas "no Christianity can be found."[111] The Dutch resorted to clichéd caricatures of native behaviors and customs to account for shortcomings in teachers that manifested in student apathy, which in turn amounted to a failure in mission. One standard complaint was that indigenous people lacked discipline in composure and behavior. Inspectors referred to this character flaw often to explain why parents did not send their children to be educated. In 1674, inspectors lamented the anger and vindictiveness of a teacher whose deportment kept children in the village of Akoon (Nusa Laut) away from the classroom.[112] At about the same time, the insolence and drunkenness of a teacher in the village of Baguala (Ambon) was said to have discouraged parents from sending children to school.[113] In September 1757, Gerhard â Besten described schoolmasters on the coast of Celebes and northern islands as "ferocious as rolling sea waves," screaming at students like a pagan priest rather than behaving like a Christian educator.[114]

A second character flaw was the supposed incuriosity and smug ignorance of non-Europeans.[115] Inspectors typecast many teachers as apathetic and conniving, such as the schoolmaster Bastiaen Loho in Attingola in 1720, who reportedly "lived like a heathen," spending most of his days in the forest and in gardens.[116] Nicolas Verburg, governor of Formosa in 1654, decried the teaching corps there as "unprofitable servants, who lack all Christian virtues" and "are of no possible use in converting the heathen."[117] *Predikanten* made similar complaints about teachers and pupils in Ceylon.[118] In 1669, the minister Simon de Buck lamented that on the island of Saparua (near Amboina) students only attended when the visiting minister did. Local villagers laid culpability with the schoolmaster, who enjoined the students to do work for him rather than to study their lessons.[119] The lack of curiosity and laziness of teachers as expressed in reports endured throughout this period. In Ternate, the superstition of schoolmasters confounded students (1769), indifference kept students hunting and fishing (1774), and dullness mired students in ignorance (1781). It is hardly surprising that Calvinist ministers from the Netherlands characterized native peoples and teachers in these condescending tones.[120]

Many of the ministers' criticisms reflected more the disconnectedness of the visiting *predikanten* from local culture than an accurate description of the work of indigenous catechists and teachers. In most villages, the schools functioned reasonably well. Local teachers went fishing and worked in other capacities to supplement the low salary and late pay by the company.[121] Yet it is also important to realize that the bitterness and recrimination arose from the ministers' realization that the progress of global Calvinism rested on the backs of native teachers.

Schools utilized a range of religious materials, outside of the scriptures, that ranged from catechisms, sermons, and other miscellaneous and devotional texts. These sources presented the basic teachings of orthodox Calvinism as it emerged in the Dutch Republic at the Synod of Dort in 1619. Although Reformed ministers translated portions of scripture, the translation of the full Bible did not get underway in earnest until the second half of the 1600s.

Company authorities attempted to employ a mixture of compulsion and compensation to entice parents to send their children to company schools. On Mondays, Tuesdays, Thursdays, and Fridays, the school day for children in the East Indies customarily lasted two hours in both the morning and afternoon broken by a two-hour interval; on Wednesdays and Saturdays, students attended only the morning session. Since parents depended on the labor of children, the loss of productivity, in addition to any hostility to Dutch rule, acted as a strong disincentive for school attendance. To combat this impediment, governors attempted to subsidize school attendance by providing a staple to families whose children attended school. Families in Banda received twenty pounds of rice per month as compensation.[122] In the 1630s, the classis in Brazil pressed the WIC to subsidize students for Christian education in Dutch schools.[123] In Ceylon and Formosa, school attendance was compulsory for Christians, though difficult to enforce. In the former, boys were to attend school until age twelve and girls until age ten, or their families faced a fine.[124] When governor Gerard Joan Vreeland dropped the requirement in 1751, attendance dropped significantly.[125] Children in Formosan villages attended mornings and afternoons five days per week, whereas adults attended two hours per day for one week a month. Those who attended somewhat faithfully were awarded a dole of rice, but those who failed to appear on a regular basis were fined a deerskin.[126] Ministers in the Cape considered making education a requirement for the Khoi people, but their migratory patterns and their hostility to the Dutch rendered compulsory schooling impractical.[127]

TRACKING MISSIONS

The Calvinist mission to convert peoples within the orbit of the Dutch empire developed through three general phases during this period. The initial phase, from the 1610s until the late 1640s, was set in motion by the first face-to-face encounters between ministers and Muslims, Hindus, Buddhists, non-European

Catholics, and practitioners of local religions. Reformed *predikanten* going abroad most likely would have possessed some familiarity with Islam through medieval commentators, such as George Elmacinus and Aben Ezra, and contemporary history writers, including Paul Jovius and Hugo Grotius. Although Dutch merchants traded and allied with Muslims from various polities, Calvinist clergy held Islam in contempt, and in the early seventeenth century deemed it worthless for study. Dutch intellectuals exhibited even less understanding about and far more disdain for Vedic or magico-religious traditions. Calvinists lumped them all together as paganism (also gentilism and heathenism). For *predikanten*, "heathen" religions simply confirmed the depravity of human societies outside a state of grace by idol worship and sexual disorder. Ministers in the East Indies, Ceylon, Formosa, and Brazil, often employing Old Testament analogues of idolatrous pagans, conveyed a profound sense of estrangement from Asian, American, and African peoples and societies.[128] Danckaerts grumbled that the Amboinese were "poor blind people and idolatrous Indians, being slaves of the devil," and they "serve the devil and many devils" in worshipping idols.[129]

Ministers involved in this early period of Dutch discovery gave little if any consideration to learning about non-Christian religions. In fact, the soon-to-be overseas proselytizer Justus Heurnius wrote in a 1618 missionary manifesto that effective evangelism required no knowledge in letters or philosophy, but only faith in God's power to save. Heurnius even dismissed the linguistic difficulty of mission, citing the presence of the Holy Spirit who gave the apostles the power to speak in many languages at Pentecost.[130] The Reformed theologian Johannes Cocceius composed an *Oration on the Religion of the Turks* in 1625 that attempted little more than to put on display the well-worn tropes of lust and sensuality among Muslims. He believed that once the word of God would go forth into the world, converts would stream into Christendom one hundredfold.[131] Calvinists in the mission field also did not seem to think it necessary to contest Muslims intellectually. In a conversation with a group of Muslim elders at Rosengain (Banda Islands) in 1622, the Calvinist minister Melchior Meinertszoon Vitriarius avoided discussing Muslim teachings and their relationship to Christian beliefs. At one point in the dialogue, an elder asked him what he knew about Islam. Vitriarius answered that Muslims believed in Muhammad rather than Christ and the Qur'an rather than the Bible. He added that Muslims practiced circumcision and polygamy and abstained from pork and alcohol. Finally, Vitriarius noted that he "found it advisable to speak no longer" about their religion, but rather simply to "disclose the foul deeds of Muhammed."[132]

By the mid-seventeenth century, the mission entered into a second phase characterized by an academic scrutiny of Islam and paganism in the Netherlands and in Asia. Chapters 5 and 6 examine thoroughly this new engagement with world religions, but a brief account is worthwhile in this context to illustrate the evolution of Calvinist mission in response to global interactions.

It was around the mid-1600s that Reformed scholars in the Netherlands and clergy in the empire began to undertake serious study of other religions, after several decades of complexity and confusion on the mission field. Gerardus Vossius and Johannes Hoornbeeck wrote large tomes on worldwide paganism from the ancient period to their own day. In *On the Conversion of Indians and Gentiles* (1669), Hoornbeeck placed emphasis on "the methods developed from within the academy and from within the church" to convert gentiles. In two earlier works on false religions published in 1653 and 1655, he incorporated a treatment of Islam to arm overseas ministers to defend their faith more effectively. Hoornbeeck worked in conjunction with Gisbertus Voetius at Utrecht from 1644 to 1654 to prepare ministers to confront Islam. In 1655 Voetius produced *On Muhammedanism* (*De Muhammedismo*) for students going to Hungary, Transylvania, and the East Indies. Voetius, Hoornbeeck, and Cocceius (at the University of Leiden) lectured on Islam and sought to give specific theological training to their students. The maturation of Calvinist perspectives on Islam was reflected in the work of Adriaan Reland at the University of Utrecht from 1701 to 1718. He authored *On the Muhammedan Religion* (*De religione Mohammedica*) in 1705, a highly influential work that signified a decisive pivot to a more balanced view of Islam among European intellectuals.

This academic emphasis produced two effects in the overseas mission: renewed attention to educating native teachers and increased translation of scriptural texts. The seminaries in Nallur and Colombo in the 1690s formed the most exemplary and durable institutional effort to train native teachers and proponents in Reformed theology. A seminary in Soulang (Formosa) in 1657 and a Latin school in Batavia in 1745 proved unworkable, but the impetus for them nevertheless grew out of the increasing attentiveness that Dutch Calvinists gave to scriptural texts on the mission field.[133] Simon Cat, a pioneering leader of the seminary in Colombo, cited Hoornbeeck's *On the Conversion of Indians and Gentiles* in making the case for seminaries in Ceylon and elsewhere in Asia. He also pointed to Voetius's work in arguing for ecclesiastical autonomy to carry out a worldwide mission.[134] The Colombo seminary, along with its counterpart in Nallur, proved to be the most durable Reformed institutions for training ministers and teachers in VOC territories. Supporting the seminaries, governor Gustaaf Willem van Imhoff established a printing press in Colombo that turned out an abundance of religious literature.[135] Although ministers and governors in other areas were not able to establish seminaries, consistories did preoccupy themselves in their visitation circuits with the quality of instruction, even though they lacked a formal, centralized means to provide for it.

Ministers also contributed to a more systematic and nuanced perception of Hinduism, Buddhism, and the religious environment of maritime Southeast Asia. Not only did *predikanten* reflect on their interactions and labors, but three of them wrote highly influential treatises.[136] Stationed in Ceylon and Batavia, Abraham Rogerius published *The Open Door to Hidden Heathendom* in 1651, and Philip Baldaeus brought forth *A True Account and Refutation of East Indian Idolatry* (*Nauwkeurige en waarachtige ontdekking en wederlegginge van de afgoderij der Oost-Indische heydenen . . .*) in 1672. These writers joined with other Protestant and Catholic theologians and ethnographers to make sense of the cosmologies, myths, and rites of old Abrahamic rivals and newly encountered peoples. Fifty years later in Amboina, Francois Valentijn published a multivolume description of the East Indies, *Old and New East Indies* (1724–1726). In it, Valentijn provided an adept treatment of local customs and practices under the general rubric of "heathenism" and a more concise description of Islam in the region.[137]

A second effect of academic study in the mission field was an increased attention to translating large portions of scripture into the dominant languages of Ceylon and the East Indies. As discussed above, Dutch *predikanten* had utilized translated religious materials such as catechisms, books of prayers and creeds, and sermons since infiltrating various regions of Asia. Ministers had rendered portions of scripture into Portuguese and Malay, but almost nothing into Tamil or Sinhalese. The theological approach by scholars at Utrecht and Leiden, however, led in the second half of the 1600s to a greater emphasis on translating larger sections of the Bible. The purpose, as stated by the Batavia consistory in the early eighteenth century, was to prove to Muslims "that the Bible is the Word of God."[138] The ministers, citing Reland yet relying on their own experiences, asserted that Muslims' devotion to the Qur'an as the word of God made it very difficult to convert them to Christianity.[139] Even as early as the 1630s, Heurnius worked on portions of the New Testament, but he redoubled his efforts in the 1640s and 1650s, producing Malay versions of the book of Acts and the Gospels. A decade later in 1662, Daniel Brouwerius completed the book of Genesis and the New Testament, also in Malay. A number of other *predikanten* and *ziekentroosteren,* such as Valentijn, Nikolaas Hodenpijl, and Simon de Lange, produced unpublished versions of the New Testament from the 1650s to the 1690s.[140] At the end of the seventeenth century, Melchior Leijdekker and Petrus van der Vorm, ministers in Batavia, translated the entire Bible into a Malay vernacular; completed in 1701, the translation was not published until 1733. The dialect they chose, referred to as "High Malay" by the Dutch, derived from Muslim intellectual circles at the court of Johor on the southern tip of the Malay peninsula. Translation work in Ceylon proceeded more slowly, though by 1739 clergy had produced a Sinhalese version of the Gospels, and in 1759 Philip de Melho, a Tamil minister, put forth a New Testament in his native tongue.[141]

In the 1720s or 1730s the overseas missionary project morphed into a third distinct phase, distinguished by a more cosmopolitan Calvinism. Dutch consistories exhibited a staid perseverance as they continued to inspect schools and congregations in outlying areas and report on the state of Protestant Christianity in the East Indies, South Asia, the Cape of Good Hope, and to a very limited degree in the Atlantic. A sense of decline, however, loomed over the work of overseas ministers, even though the church continued to grow in Batavia and Amboina.[142] The consistory in Batavia in 1739 lamented the loss of the church's influence across Southeast Asia, placing the blame on the lack of ministers and teachers.[143] Throughout the eighteenth century, the shortage of *predikanten* grew more acute, as Batavia and other consistories attributed flat growth among "heathens and Moors" to the lack of church personnel.[144] While the harvest of souls remained small, ministers counted baptisms, marriages, and new communicants. Consistories in Colombo, Jaffnapatnam, Banda, Amboina, Ternate, Batavia, and other areas reported regularly that Moors and "heathens" sought baptism, and annual pastoral reports quantified new converts, members, and schoolchildren.[145] The accounts give ample quantitative evidence of ongoing engagement through mission, but at the same time the records appear rote and formulaic. Consistory meeting minutes by the late 1730s from Colombo and Batavia are largely devoted to lists of baptisms and adoptions and to routine administrative matters, such as the preaching and inspection rotation, visitation districts, and appointment of *ziekentroosteren* and schoolmasters.[146] Annual reports from overseas consistories to church districts in the Netherlands similarly consist primarily of such enumerations and of notations of ministerial assignments. In November 1777, the *Politieke Raad* in Batavia issued a list of reforms to promote the "propagation of religion in foreign lands." The councilors recommended enforcing the Sabbath, upholding the bans against non-Reformed religions, recruiting more *ziekentroosteren* and better schoolmasters, and raising the monthly salaries of overseas ministers to 130–150 guilders (up from 90–100) if they signed on to a second five-year contract.[147] Consistories had pushed for all these measures since the early 1600s. A proposal coming 150 years later offered nothing further in tangible action points beyond the church orders of 1624 and 1643 and lacked the ebullient optimism of the early 1600s.

At the same time, ministers also betrayed a more nuanced understanding of Islam, Hinduism, and Buddhism. Valentijn in *Old and New East Indies* unmistakably regarded Islam as a false religion, but his sharpest reproaches grew out of missionary frustration at the resistance of local Muslims to the Christian message. Yet he also noted the piety and industry of some Muslims.[148] Valentijn told a personal story about being allowed to observe prayers at a "temple" in Hila (Amboina) in 1687. He conversed extensively with a Muslim "priest" he knew well, Hassan Soeleyman, about his religion and the service.[149] Valentijn described an episode in 1706 when as chaplain in the army he befriended a "Makassar Captain," Daeng Matàra, "one of the most sensible Mohammedans."[150] In his description of Ceylon, Valentijn went into detail about the characteristics of Buddhism and Hinduism in South Asia and commented on a large corpus of religious writings in the Vedic tradition. He even thought it worthwhile to append certain "moral lessons" by Hindus and Buddhists "so that one may not have too low [an] opinion of Cinghalese and Malabar writers."[151]

Although few writings by orthodox Calvinists about Hindus and Buddhists exist for the eighteenth century, in those that do, a few episodes intimate a culturally flexible view among ministers. The *predikant* Jacob Canter Visscher, for example, came to regard Hindu images as artifacts of exoticism rather than instruments of the devil. In 1758, the consistory in Colombo began to rethink their stance against toleration of an adherence to Buddhism and Catholicism among natives. The ministers and elders reasoned:

> The native inhabitants, notwithstanding their many weaknesses and insouciance in matters of religion . . . generally have these tendencies or rather superstitions that they, although they know better, will not change their religion without regard or reason, and would rather bring up their children in the same way. As a result of this, it happens that through our unwisdom in treating and dealing with them less tolerantly, they become obstinately more and more hardened in heart and so seek to promote (the interests of) their blind religion.[152]

These attitudes signified marked shifts from the standard Calvinist view of idolatry as devil worship to be eradicated to stay the wrath of God. In the same period in Batavia, the consistory agreed to send a minister to give a prayer at the public execution of some captured pirates. In their deliberations, the church authorities conveyed an attitude of benevolent condescension more evocative of philosophical radicals in Amsterdam and Paris than of the likes of Voetius and Hoornbeeck. The scribe wrote: "[T]he unbelievers or heathens or Mohammedans, people who not only have few and vague notions of their own religion, but whom one, considering their humanity and humanly speaking, and unless one would resort to miracles, should consider to be unable to grasp those truths put before them in their last hours." With little hope that the prayer might induce the malefactors to convert at the end of their ropes, the consistory nevertheless resolved to carry out the public prayer.[153]

During all phases of the mission, but especially in the last interval, Calvinists kept count of its progress, charting ebbs and flows through quantitative reports. These accounts became much more comprehensive at the end of the 1600s and arose as fairly systematic in layout in the mid-1700s. Before the late 1600s, figures of converts, baptisms, schoolchildren, and nominal Christians frequently turn up in correspondence, but the detailed quantitative description of the mission was really a feature of the last phase of global Calvinism. The most extensive that have survived come from the East Indies and South Asia. Most Christian churches and missions, regardless of confessional disposition, relied on numerical computation to evaluate their degrees of growth. For Dutch Calvinists, and perhaps other groups as well, the use of quantitative reports reflected their attention to the community and its organic development over time. That said, there were very few accounts of individual conversion in Dutch Calvinist sources in overseas environments. Perhaps one reason was that one never knew how a story might end. One of the most celebrated episodes in global Calvinist lore ended in tragedy. A young Khoi woman in Cape Town named Krotoa converted, received baptism in 1662, and took the name Eva. She embraced Christianity, learned Dutch, adopted European customs, and even married Peter van Meerhoff, a surgeon for the VOC. Unfortunately, when van Meerhoff died several years later, Eva found it impossible to navigate the liminal waters between indigenous and colonial cultures. She turned to prostitution, fell prey to alcoholism, and abandoned her children. She died unhappily in a Dutch prison on Robben Island in 1674.[154]

Individuals disappoint, yet it was also the paramount importance of community to Calvinists that rendered personal conversion stories less meaningful than corporate spiritual growth. If taken in conjunction with the other records that consistories produced, especially the *notulen* (minutes) of its disciplinary proceedings against wayward members, these reports do tell a story about conversion with a uniquely Calvinist flavor. They chronicle a community establishing its ministries, preaching the gospel, helping the poor, and leading a faithful remnant from all the nations through the baptismal waters to the communion table, signifying the purity and unity of the body of Christ. Recording the disciplinary interventions of ministers and elders, consistory registers bore witness to the condemnation of sin, correction of moral error, and reconciliation of a transgressor to the community. While these are individual stories, the focus is not on the individual, but on a religious community attempting to work out its sanctification before God and the world. Therefore, the quantitative reports fit in with a Calvinist vision of conversion by calling attention to the community and by taking the spotlight off the individual convert.

The numerical accounts charting the development of the mission point to two essential dynamics in the quest for converts by global Calvinists. First, overseas ministers conceived of Christian identity as a layered affinity that ranged from full (communicant) membership to nominal baptism. Church officials distinguished between members (*ledematen*), nominal, common, or general (*genaamd* or *gemeene*) Christians, and the recently baptized (*gedoopt*), but often included students in all of these categories. In Jaffnapatnam in December 1663, for example, Philip Baldaeus and Johannes a Breijl counted 93,787 "Christian souls," which consisted of 62,558 native nominal Christians, 15,012 schoolchildren, 15,614 baptized children (Dutch, mestizo/a, enslaved, and native), 443 school graduates, and 160 couples married by a Dutch minister.[155] In every mission territory, a vast chasm yawned between the number of communicant members and nominal Christians. The Colombo district in 1693 offers an example of the discrepancy between the numbers of members and nominal Christians, as the consistory counted over 17,000 Christians but only several hundred were members. And in 1758, 1,000 members in Colombo were enveloped within a sea of 64,149 common Christians.[156] A similar taxonomy and discrepancy existed in the Moluccas, where the most extensive reports have survived. The Amboina consistory in 1716 enumerated the Christian community there as 1,431 members, 17,145 nominal Christians, 4,881 schoolchildren, 8,377 school graduates, and 1,389 new baptisms, for a total of 33,223 souls.[157] Ternate's Christian population ranged from 20,000 to 32,500 between 1710 and 1757, whereas communicants fluctuated from between only 66 and 210 members. Similarly, Banda claimed between 2,300 and 3,600 nominal Christians from 1740 to 1780 but only from 201 to 143 members during the same period. The Cape of Good Hope mustered only 160 members by the 1690s.[158] As we will see below, a very wide distance separated the commitments to Calvinism among full members at the top of the Christian pyramid from the hybridities of nominal Christians at the base.

Second, numerical descriptions in the various regions illustrate the slow, uneven, and anemic growth of church membership throughout many regions from the late seventeenth through the late eighteenth century. Unfortunately, the fragmented nature of quantified accounts does not allow for an aggregate evaluation of church development, though comparing figures across place and time does reveal important trends. The congregation in Batavia, serviced by the most clergy, grew steadily over the course of this period, from 2,300 members in the 1670s to 5,000 by 1700, and to 10,000 by 1800. Amboina hovered between 1,300 and 1,600 in the mid-eighteenth century, amid a population of around 30,000 nominal Christians. Amboina experienced considerable growth in the second half of the 1700s, with church membership reaching 3,395 in 1790, while the number of nominal Christians dropped to 23,558.[159] Outside of Batavia and Amboina, the numbers of members in the East Indies and South Asia remained low, especially in relation to nominal Christians.[160]

Only a fraction of baptized Christians within the Calvinist overseas mission qualified as full-status members, submitting to the discipline of the consistory and participating in the Lord's Supper. Ministers did add converts to church rolls, baptizing children and adults regularly. The Batavia consistory exclaimed in 1701 that "119 people have been led out of heathendom this past year" through baptism; three years later a consistorial scribe documented that 497 people had joined the ranks of Christendom within the year.[161] In almost every area under VOC and WIC control consistories added a significant number of converts to their community. Most of these were children either of baptized local parents or of adopted European Christian guardians. Adults also requested baptism, which they received after some instruction or made a confession of faith (if previously baptized by a Catholic priest). Non-European Christians were expected to attend church and school; in the East Indies, Formosa, and South Asia, they were subject to a fine for absenteeism. Nevertheless, most did not attain sufficient knowledge and/or exhibit suitable piety to be admitted to communion. Only in Batavia after 1648 did the consistory insist on the same standards for baptism and communion. The divergence between Calvinist expectations for full membership and the varying levels of observance by converted peoples in the Dutch empire produced enormous frustrations for consistories that ultimately carried long-term consequences for Protestantism in Europe.

DECODING CONVERSION

Calvinists in service of commerce, empire, and conversion entered diverse and unfamiliar religious topography in Asia, America, and Africa. *Predikanten* encountered Muslims in sea lanes, ports, and markets across the trading zones of the Indian Ocean and Mediterranean Sea. In VOC lands, the most concentrated communities of Muslims emerged in the East Indies and to a lesser extent in Ceylon and the Cape of Good Hope. Sunni Muslim traders and Sufi divines from the early Shafi'i legal tradition had set down firm religious roots in the East Indies and South Asia long before the arrival of the Portuguese. The arrival of Islam into these regions occurred intermittently between the thirteenth and sixteenth centuries via Arab trading networks that crisscrossed the Indian Ocean.

Arab merchants set up posts along the southern coast of Ceylon, while Muslims from India, China, and Arab lands traded at sites along the coasts of Sumatra, Malaya, East Java, and the straits of Melaka. Many of them settled locally, married, and spread their influence and religion among the inhabitants. By the time of Tomé Pires, the Portuguese apothecary who wrote *Suma Oriental* based on his experiences in Melaka between 1512 and 1515, most of the rulers in the coastal settlements of Sumatra and Aceh were Muslim. Significant Muslim enclaves also developed in primarily Tamil-speaking regions in northern Ceylon, which maintained tenuous connections to kindred settlements in southern India. The Portuguese waged intense campaigns against Moors in Ceylon, forcing many to flee to the highlands of Kandy and the east coast around Batticaloa.[162] By the time of the VOC's appearance on the island, Islam was on the wane, yet West Java (including Jakarta), the Moluccan Islands, Banda, Ternate, and Tidore all had either Muslim rulers and/or sizable Muslim populations.[163]

At the Cape of Good Hope, Islam arose during the period of VOC rule. The strategic location of the settlement brought a wide variety of travelers to the southern tip of Africa, some of whom were Muslim. A community first appeared in the 1600s and grew over the course of the 1700s to such an extent that at the end of the century a local imam appealed to the *Politieke Raad* to allow the construction of a mosque. Proselytizers made strong inroads among enslaved laborers at the Cape.[164]

Islam became thoroughly indigenized in Ceylon and the East Indies. The intermarriage among Tamils and Sinhalese resulted in the absorption of local customs into Islam. Tamil became the native language for Muslims in Ceylon; women interacted more freely with men than in Arab lands; marriage ceremonies featured pomp and ceremony. In the East Indies, the influence of Sufi divines from the thirteenth to the fifteenth century engendered a blending of local shrines, holy figures, and observances into Islam. Sufis and practitioners of Sufism embraced many local aspects of folklore and observance, which alleviated the demands and perplexities of adopting an exclusive religious creed. Michael Pearson has observed that "Muslim proselytizers succeeded in part because they did not press too hard, but rather were prepared to tolerate 'deviations' and a rather syncretic form of Islam."[165] Scholars of Indonesian Islam have highlighted a "mystic synthesis" between Islam and traditional practices, particularly in the premodern period.[166]

The same trade routes and migration patterns that brought Islam to South and Southeast Asia had also earlier transported Hindu and Buddhist traditions to Ceylon and the East Indies. Vedic observances, myths, and social structures had developed in Ceylon in concert with their counterparts in southern India since 1500 BCE. The ancient Hindu epic the *Ramayana* refers to the island as

Lanka, intimating a long shared, albeit obscure, cultural history. If the origins of Hindu practices were shrouded in the opacity of an undocumented distant past, the origins of Buddhist teachings and rites are discernible. At the instigation of emperor Ashoka in the third century BCE, monks made their way into Ceylon, spread the tenets of the Buddha, and cultivated the notion that the island held a special destiny for a pure understanding of enlightenment. More practically, Sinhalese kings adapted the pageantry of Buddhist ceremonial ritual to sacralize and thus validate their authority. In time, kings of Kandy became the primary patrons of monasteries and temples, wrapping their legitimacy in the mantel of Theravada Buddhism. Sacred objects, temples, and rituals expressed the close association between Kandyan rulership, Buddhist mythology, and the ideological unity of the Sinhalese people. This religious and political cohesion was represented most profoundly in the Tooth Relic (of the Buddha) that was brought into Ceylon in the early 300s CE. At the political and societal level, Buddhism served as a centralizing force, yet at the popular level its disciplines blended with local folklore, astrology, and magico-religious practices. Ceylonese Buddhism made way for Hindu deities such as Indra, Vishnu, and Skanda within Sinhalese temples, as well as Hindu rites and stories. Thus, Hindu, Buddhist, Muslim, and traditional conventions had coexisted and overlapped in Ceylon long before the arrival of the Portuguese and Dutch.[167]

Penetrating maritime Southeast Asia in the 500s and 600s, Hindu and Buddhist traditions alike predated Islam at least by several centuries in Java, Sumatra, and the Moluccan Islands. Buddhist monks and pilgrims traveling on board commercial craft between China and India came onshore at ports in the southern peninsula and archipelago, introducing the Vedic teachings to elites and common folk. Kings in Java and Sumatra found that the social organization, epic mythology, and political theology in Hindu beliefs enhanced their claims to territorial sovereignty and social authority. The epic poems the *Mahabharata* and the *Ramayana* became incorporated into Javanese mythical tropes. Wayang theater, depicting episodes from the *Mahabharata* in popular public venues, formed a widespread media for the diffusion of Southeast Asian and Indian mythological narratives. The Shailendra dynasty in eighth- and ninth-century Java patronized Buddhist monks and endowed temples in the central region of the island. Buddhist and Hindu traditions developed alongside one another, but in the preceding centuries before the appearance of Europeans, the religions actually integrated central elements into an overarching cosmology that recognized two distinct, but correspondent, paths to salvation. Temples were devoted to both the Buddha and Shiva, and shrines within large sacred compounds were dedicated to both figures.[168]

In South and Southeast Asia, the formal religious structures of Islam, Buddhism, and Hinduism mixed with a wide variety of local folklore and magical appeals to the supernatural. Aboriginal peoples in Formosa, Khoi Khoi in South Africa, Tupi in Brazil, Algonquins in New Netherlands, and Caribs in the West Indies also employed shamans, prophets, and priestesses to protect themselves from calamity and provide for their progeny. Without a creed or priestly hierarchy, people recognized divinity in the sun, moon, and stars and felt the spiritual presence in animated and vegetative life. Stories, passed down orally, told of their origins, their place in the cosmos, and their hopes for a better future. In most Dutch-controlled areas outside of Formosa, New Netherland, and the Cape of Good Hope, Calvinists encountered these traditions, along with the more codified religious structures of Islam, Buddhism, and Hinduism, in the wake of mostly superficial Catholic missionary campaigns. Thus, Dutch Calvinists not only faced a bewildering host of practices and mythologies on the mission field, but they also set for themselves the profound task of persuading people to reject religious fluidity, assimilation, and hybridity in favor of an exclusive confessional creed with strict disciplinary boundaries.

People responded to the global Calvinist mission in a wide variety of ways, despite the fact that the ministers themselves were really only interested in the one-dimensional narrative that heralded the spread of the gospel. Dutch accounts of proselytizing thus necessarily masked the many complexities that impinged upon local religious experience. What Calvinists considered backsliding, obstinacy, moral weakness, worldly motivation, or ingrained superstition is better understood from indigenous perspectives as the adaptation of Christian conversion within autochthonous cultural and political frameworks. To gain a fuller understanding of conversion, it is important to resist the reductionist archetypes of spiritually blind and immoral pagans and Moors conjured in the sources and read between the lines to reconstruct themes in indigenous perspectives on Calvinism and conversion.

The sources do demonstrate that overlapping local matrices of political authority, culture, and kinship were foremost considerations affecting indigenous attitudes to altering their religious affiliations. Ministers often presented religious choice in their writings as a moral, personal decision largely untethered from the social forces that encased individuals. A typical case appeared in the village of Lirong (Talaud Island) in 1706, as clergy noted that a chieftain desired to become a Christian not for any "worldly reasons," but through "the internal counsel of his heart and soul."[169] Along those lines, another political leader "laid aside all the foulness of Muhammad's teaching," thankful that his "eyes have been opened to Jesus Christ."[170] Reports from visitations highlighted the activity of ministers admonishing, persuading, preaching to, and debating with village notables to forsake superstition and embrace the gospel. The minister Jan de Graaf represented a standard image, writing about his travels in the Banda Islands and archipelagoes to the southeast (Kei, Aru, Tanimbar) and southwest (Babar, Damar, Kisar, Wetar) in June 1692, when he "seriously admonished" the elder of Toterquera to take action against persistent pagan practices, "sharply questioned" him about unbaptized schoolchildren, and "demanded" to know his motives for adopting Christianity.[171] The visitation accounts by ministers and elders discussed above featured the *predikant* presenting "heathens" and Moors with the spiritual and moral consequences of true faith and false religion.[172]

Yet the sources also reveal how profoundly religious belonging was embedded in the social and political fabric of local life. Religious choice and identity rarely, if ever in the premodern world, existed outside the various structures of everyday existence. Just as Calvinists viewed conversion as joining a community, peoples around the early modern world also associated religious affiliation as inherent to community maintenance. The embeddedness of religious performance within a communal context posed a formidable obstacle to Calvinists who tried to persuade people to change their beliefs and practices. The encroaching expectations of neighbors and long-standing customs of the community highlighted the implacable and foreign qualities of Calvinism for many local peoples. Representatives from Wodgier (Aru), for example, declined the invitation to become Christians in 1646 because they found the dominance of clergy to run counter to their custom of not "having one person over another." Similarly, the elder in nearby Wokam rejected Calvinist overtures, saying that "he preferred to walk in his own traditions."[173] Minister Cornelius de Leeuw lamented in April 1673 that children of Christian parents in Manipa (government of Amboina) kept "going over to the Moors" because the parents did not properly understand the demarcations of Christianity and they mingled too freely with Muslim neighbors. "Familiarity with Moors endangers Christians," he concluded.[174] The consistory in Colombo remonstrated bitterly in the 1680s about the rebuilding of the renowned Kelaniya Buddhist temple because they believed that the presence of the shrine and the pilgrims flowing into it would erode the faith of Sinhalese Christians.[175] In Formosa, Sinkans responded to Candidius's preaching by declaring their preference for their priestesses and "our customs [which] have been handed down from generation to generation and cannot be done away with."[176] The classes in Brazil opposed tolerance for Jews because the clergy complained that they were leading Christians to abandon their religion.[177]

The fear of temptation from the old pagan or Moorish life was of long standing among Calvinists. From an indigenous perspective, observance, ritual, and tradition were closely connected to community cohesion. Ministers in Amboina as early as 1619 had recommended isolating Muslims so that they would not create an obstacle to converting others.[178] Another minister recognized the religious attachments that marriage and family obligations carried, commenting that "nuptial contracts and dowries among Muslims" caused the greatest hindrance slowing the advance of Christendom.[179] One unnamed woman in Pey Noessa (Amboina) did defy her father in 1682 by becoming a Christian, though she expressed to the consistory her fear of her father's wrath.[180] By the same token, Calvinists whenever possible used the leverage of marriage (to Christians) to compel conversion, a demand that people everywhere seemed to accept as normative. The historian Ad Biewenga concluded that membership in the Reformed Church at the Cape of Good Hope conformed to marriage and family networks.[181] Muslim elders in villages across Ternate and Makassar believed it important to carry on the religious traditions of their forefathers, just as inhabitants continued to uphold conventional festivities, fetishes, and fashions. Johannes Ruiterus, a minister on the Coromandel coast, cited the extensive presence of fortunetellers, teachers, and magi in a temple in Tranquebaar that anchored the local community and gave Buddhism renewed legitimacy in the eyes of native Christians.[182]

As Calvinists tried to disrupt these observances and establish new moral systems and codes, peoples felt drawn to their time-honored deities in times of sickness, in maintaining social harmony, and for validating sexual customs.[183] As discussed above, the Kelaniya pagoda in Kandy, outside Colombo and near to a Dutch school, exerted a strong pull on Christians to go back to their familiar ways.[184] In Formosa, the female priests known as *inibs* wielded such an influence over new native Christians that the VOC banished 250 of them into the mountains. The governor of Formosa, Francis Caron, grumbled in 1646 that those "witches work more mischief among the converts than [Christian] teachers, with all their labour, can do them good."[185] The seductions of idols, images, and superstitions became all the more intractable for Calvinists in areas patrolled by Catholic missionaries, such as South Asia and Brazil. In Cochin, for example, the minister Jacob Canter Visscher (as noted above) lamented the connection between Catholic religious imagery and ceremonial forms in Hinduism and Buddhism.[186] Priests in Brazil regularly warned Portuguese and creole planters that they needed to be faithful to the Roman church even when ruled by Dutch heretics who tolerated Jews.[187] Local shamans, imams, and spiritual mediators emphatically reminded men and women of their obligations to community standards. Muslim religious leaders regularly repudiated Calvinist ministers and dissuaded parents from sending their children to Dutch schools.[188] A shaman ("priest of Baal") in Tanimbar confronted the *predikant* Jacob Vertrecht before villagers in 1646 arguing that he had no experience in their language, he would not be willing to accept their religion, and he would reproach them for not following beliefs that they could not comprehend. Their priest concluded that if they converted, they would simply be pretending to be Christians.[189] A Calvinist minister in Amboina complained bitterly in 1635 that they had preached there for thirty years to no avail, so the only recourse was for the VOC to compel obedience to Protestant Christianity.[190]

In many situations native peoples who converted or expressed interest in Reformed Christianity visualized it as a new instrument to secure the prosperity and protection they sought in traditional observances. The first ministers in the East Indies and Formosa occasionally recorded their surprise that people often would ask to be baptized without hearing so much as a word of the Protestant gospel. Some in the Indies had already undergone baptism by Jesuits. A number of scholars have noted the connections between healing and funerary rituals across Southeast Asia associated with water and the attractions of Christian baptism.[191] Similar associations abound in Dutch sources. In the 1650s, Formosans complained that they were made to go to school with little hope of getting baptized.[192] A chieftain just outside Makassar in 1695 asked ministers for prayers for healing in the Sunday worship service even though he did not believe in the Trinity and worshipped "devils."[193] Ministers in Formosa were struck by the obsession converts in Sinkan, Bakloan, Solang, and Mattau gave to prayer and kneeling before hunting and before laboring in the fields. Indeed, after local peoples credited their traditional deities with providing abundant rice harvests, Robert Junius and George Candidius lost little time emphasizing God's power to bless and curse harvests. *Predikanten* in the 1630s argued that rice crops were much more plentiful since Formosans had converted to the true faith and turned from their idols.[194]

The lever of local political authority formed perhaps the first and foremost local consideration in decisions about conversion. Throughout the Dutch empire, Calvinist missions only operated within territorial conquest or treaties that company officials struck with local rulers. The VOC and WIC permitted schools, churches, and the other instruments of conversion directed at non-Christians only within company jurisdictions or if allowed by indigenous authorities. Both trading companies hoped that global Calvinism would instill loyalty among local inhabitants, and ministers were only too happy for the support of the colonial arm. In many Asian societies, individuals did not make a religious choice based on their personal commitments, rather people followed the religious preferences of their rulers. Rulers made geopolitical calculations that carried religious implications. These decisions also proved paradoxical for *predikanten*. Colonial political initiatives opened the door to missions, but ironically, they also impeded what Calvinists regarded as a genuine conversion—that is, one based solely on spiritual convictions. Yet as evidence will show below, native peoples saw little to no distinction between political and spiritual motives for altering their religious identity. Caspar Wiltens, the first Dutch Calvinist overseas minister, put it this way: "[T]hese people do not understand what religion is as a thing, what does it do, what is it good for, and what lies in it."[195] For native societies, religious affiliation usually commanded political cooperation. Wiltens went on to observe:

> It is unheard of in this region that a Moor would become a Christian unless he considers himself in great need. Also the grandfather of this king [raja of Batjan] who in former times was a Christian and with all his people through the pressure of the Portuguese sought protection against the king of Ternate. Later in order to win the friendship of the king of Ternate, he became a Moor again with all his people. . . . [I]t is not heard here that one would accept a religion through debates, instruction, or consideration of the truth. They always have other motives and then come saying make me a Christian without having any question what it means to be a Christian or what one should believe or must do.[196]

Throughout the period of company rule, inhabitants within the Dutch empire from Brazil to Amboina aligned their religious affiliations in keeping with political, social, or economic needs. Leaders in Sinkan in the late 1630s recognized conversion to Calvinism as a means to express loyalty to the VOC and secure protection from their hostile neighbors in the Siriyan plains.[197] In the Sinhalese-speaking regions of Dutch Ceylon, Buddhists counted on and received protection from the kings of Kandy. Consequently, VOC governors and Calvinist ministers had to tread gingerly around Buddhists and temple observances.[198] In Brazil, the plantation owners at the heart of the sugar industry never really accepted WIC rule, and they rejected Calvinism outright. To placate this population, Johan Maurits of Nassau-Siegen and other governors went against the Dutch policy operative in other imperial holdings and forged a pluralistic religious environment.[199] Yet pluralism failed to win over this important constituency who identified so closely with Portugal and Rome.[200] For those planters who might show interest in the Reformed faith, the priests whom Nassau-Siegen and other governors allowed to remain threatened Catholics with excommunication.[201] At the same time, the WIC allied with the indigenous Tupi people against the Portuguese. Because the Dutch freed Tupis from Portuguese enslavement and domination, they proved more receptive to Calvinist teachers.[202] The fragmented nature of political authority across the East Indies, Formosa, and the Tamil-speaking region of northern Ceylon meant that choices about religious affiliation were usually made at the village level. And usually, to the chagrin of Calvinists, they did not, at least initially, involve a belief or interest in a set of teachings.[203] A very diverse range of contingent circumstances influenced these decisions.

Following the European principle of *cuius regio eius religio*, the VOC recognized the right of rulers to determine the religion of their realms. The company allowed Calvinist missions in territories ruled by either a Christian or a sympathetic ally.[204] In these cases, regional dynamics exerted considerable influence over whether a particular ruler might convert to Christianity and/or permit proselytization in his domain. A delegation from the Amboina consistory, for example, learned in May 1645 that the people in the village of Kaibobo (West Seram) seemed inclined to follow the Christian religion, so that they could throw off the "yoke" of the Muslim ruler of Ternate.[205] When the VOC eventually persuaded the sultans of Ternate to give up their claims to Amboinese territories in 1676, *predikanten* hoped that they could now take advantage of the opportunity to preach and teach among Muslims in previously disputed regions.[206] Sometimes the key rivalries were quite parochial. The elder of Haturewan (West Seram) refused missionary overtures in 1674 because he feared the wrath of the Muslim raja of Sisiulu.[207] In 1678, ministers awaited the outcome of skirmishes among villages on Seram's southern coast to determine their prospects for conversion in the area.[208] When local authorities agreed to baptism, it generally followed that their subjects would convert or at least that ministers were free to open schools and churches. The ruler of Tagulanda (Ternate) accepted baptism in October 1673 and consented to have his subjects educated in the Christian faith.[209] David Bintang and Paulo Carbou, elders in Manipa, promised to have their villagers take baptism as they arranged for the baptism of their own sons.[210] In Formosa, the company and the church regarded the lack of a central power as an advantage for bending villagers to colonial and Christian rule.[211]

Within a community, baptism also afforded privileges that attracted villagers, so that their lives functioned more easily as affiliates of the Reformed Church. Consistories more often than not went along with these enticements yet became preoccupied with the authenticity of conversion. The Batavian minister Johannes Roman complained in 1648 that local people who came to the consistory to be baptized did not have spiritual interests in mind but wanted to marry or be freed from enslavement.[212] Membership in the Reformed Church bestowed social privileges in a colonial, slaveholding environment. Reformed deacons managed an extensive network of poor relief that attracted the attention of local people. Although deacons did offer assistance to those outside the church, the prospect of increased access to alms for baptized Christians could have only attracted people in desperate circumstances.[213] The VOC stipulated that their personnel could only marry Christians, thus compelling many Asian women who had marriage prospects with European men to seek baptism. Free Asian and Eurasian converts also received protection from enslavement for debts and authorization to marry a Christian. Enslaved converts, too, received privileges that were not inconsequential: the right to marry, to avoid sale to Muslims, and to stand a better chance at manumission than non-Christians.[214]

Occasionally sources allow vivid glimpses into the quotidian concerns that circulated around questions of conversion and religious identity. A prospective convert in Amboina, a man named Sahahelou, approached Johannes Bartholomeus, an English pastor, one night in October 1676 seeking baptism for himself and his family. Bartholomeus suspected that the request had more to do with an accusation that Sahahelou had pilfered pepper from VOC inventories and feared the consequences coming his way. Nevertheless, since he promised that he and his family would undergo a Christian education, Bartholomeus permitted it.[215] Cornelius van der Sluys and Jan Claaszoon from the Amboina consistory could barely contain their amusement at the interest elders at Kaibobo on Seram Island showed for the "gifts" and "benefits" as a condition for baptism.[216] The consistory in Ternate baptized the king of Kaudipan, who turned from Islam, even though the ministers and elders noted that he "mingled the request for religion with several aspects of worldly advantages," including protection from a nearby enemy.[217] When Jan de Graaf asked the elder of Touterquera (Pulau Leti) why he had become a Christian, he answered straightforwardly that it gave him greater dominion over his people and that the VOC offered him secure protections. Disheartened, de Graaf admonished him to undertake a more complete Christian education to instill a fear of God in his conscience.[218]

These indigenous perspectives on religious belonging and affiliation stood out quite sharply from Calvinist expectations about conversion, and they remained consistent over the course of the seventeenth and eighteenth centuries. Natives frequently rejected an affiliation with the Reformed Church because it was associated with Dutch trading companies and its requirements were at variance with local needs. Those people who did espouse Calvinism through baptism, education, or even church membership adapted a Reformed faith and sense of belonging to their local, social, political, and economic circumstances—as well as their religious aspirations. They did not tend to turn away from traditional customs and observances. Dutch ministers and consistories countered these "superstitions" through education, stressing the exclusiveness of the Reformed faith and the discipline required of its members. As the low number of full members, signified by taking communion, attests, most native converts did not altogether embrace the absolute disciplinary boundaries of the Reformed Church.

The practice of Calvinism by native peoples, thus, exhibited significant religious hybridity. Not only did non-Europeans take a more flexible view toward religious belonging than the Dutch, but colonial patronage, or what Calvinists called "worldly motives," encouraged plural affiliations. The Batavian consistory lamented to the governor in 1653 that the Chinese and "heathens" who claimed they were Christians did so with little love or knowledge of the truth.[219] Consistories held out suspicion that some local people sought conversion in order to procure church alms from deacons.[220] An implacable foe of dividing the sacraments, the Batavia minister Hendrick Heideggers complained in 1730 that many "inlanders" sought baptism to procure "worldly" privileges from the church. Likewise, the Colombo consistory compared Tamil and Sinhalese converts to opportunists in the late Roman Empire who requested baptism to gain political advantages.[221] Nonreligious motivations attracted many to seek baptism, but afterward such converts appeared less than enthusiastic about the religious commitments of church membership. As one minister put it, they "show no inclination to approach the table of the lord [and] have no love for God."[222]

Quantitative reports featured "nominal Christians" as those who were baptized and bore some affinity with the Reformed Church. Calvinists considered them Christians, even though they continued to follow pagan, Moorish, and papist traditions. In the early eighteenth century, ministers and elders in Batavia and Colombo made the distinction between "mouth professors" (*mondbeleijders*) and "true and worthy members of Christ" who understood God's truth. The Amsterdam classis expressed hope that these converts would show forth their calling not only in teaching, but in maintaining a "holy walk," and thus serve as witnesses to the power of faith in the midst of "idolatrous heathendom."[223] Similar distinctions echoed across other territories. Baldaeus wrote that those who identified as Christians in South Asia and Ceylon "know how to discourse rationally of the Ten Commandments, and the other points of the Christian doctrine, [yet] they still retain many of their pagan superstitions." He complained that they continued to avoid eating meat, despite Christian liberty in eating and drinking.[224] Indeed, many Christians in Ceylon attended Reformed church services and sent their children to company schools, yet also participated in ceremonies and festivities held at Buddhist and Hindu temples.[225] Muslim converts to Christianity in the East Indies continued to avoid pork, circumcise their sons, and observe sholat (five daily prayers). In Brazil, classis delegates reported to

Amsterdam that African Christians there refused to attend church, worked on the Sabbath, and engaged in illicit sexual practices.[226] In all regions controlled by the VOC and WIC, clergy lamented that indigenous people persisted in worshipping idols, praying to devils, and engaging in traditional superstitions. Indeed, many converts found a hybrid affiliation with the Reformed Church to satisfy a variety of needs.

For Calvinists in the empire and in the Netherlands, the discrepancy between their expectations and the realities surrounding conversion of pagans and Moors posed serious intellectual problems. Theologians and ministers conceived of conversion as an altered religious identity that led the novice into greater comprehension of Christian teaching and more complete embodiment of Protestant morality ("after the manner of the Dutch" according to the 1643 Batavian Church Order). The paltry membership registers across mission fields in the empire throughout this period made it perfectly clear that few embraced the faith in those terms. While church leaders blamed the meager resources, the pluralistic religious identities of native Christians confounded Calvinists, who lashed out at the insolence of the Moors, the idolatry of pagans, and the decadence of societies around the world. These frustrations raised profound questions about the possibility of non-European people living as Reformed Protestant Christians. The perplexities over what constituted a Christian among societies beyond the Atlantic played themselves out in debates among Calvinists in a pernicious dispute over the administration of the sacraments of baptism and communion.

The quandary of religious hybridity and identity surfaced with the first ministers in the East Indies and persisted until the trading companies closed their doors on global Calvinism. At issue were the requirements and expectations for people who desired baptism and communion but had little or no introduction to Protestant Christianity. In 1617, for instance, Meijnert Meijnertszoon, a *predikant* working at Banda Niera, wrote, "It worries me that so many people are baptized here, it seems better to wait until they are taught first. I have also spoken out against this to Caspar [Wiltens], who responded that this was the way it was done before his time. It is an old, harmful practice that for definite reasons [we] here can no longer neglect to report."[227] The previous practice certainly referred to the liberal policy of Catholic missionaries within the fold of the Portuguese empire. Reformed ministers expressed concerns about baptizing people with no education in the faith across the East Indies, Formosa, Ceylon, the Cape of Good Hope, Brazil, the Caribbean, and Surinam. Baptizing children and adults with little discrimination, as well as recognizing Catholic baptisms, produced an influx of initiates in Dutch missionary territories who understood very little about Christianity in general and Calvinism in particular. As we have seen, clergy complained in reports, letters, and consistory meetings that these natives usually reverted to their former practices.[228]

The consternation about baptism touched on fundamental practices of the faith and exposed the tensions between Reformed theology and the cultural landscapes within the orbit of the VOC and WIC. Reformed theology linked baptism to communion in a sacramental union; thus, all adult Christians in good standing were expected to take part in the Lord's Supper whenever a congregation offered it. As the "gathering of God's people," the Lord's Supper represented the pure eucharistic assembly of saints. The sanctity of the Lord's Table had always animated Calvinist church authorities and had given rise to extraordinary pastoral labor in disciplining congregations throughout the Reformed world.[229] Therefore, initiating someone into a congregation before he or she was prepared intellectually and morally or baptizing the child of non-Christian parents could cast tremendous dishonor on the Reformed community. When an Asian convert and communicant continued to engage in traditional religious observances, it made a mockery of what Calvinists considered sacred and invited the wrath of God. Because the Catholic Church taught that baptism remitted original sin, its missionaries possessed a much stronger sense of urgency in baptizing non-Christians. According to the Roman view, baptism not only inducted one into the faith, but it also remitted all past and present sins. In the wake of all the Jesuit activity in the region, Calvinist ministers faced a difficult dilemma: defer baptism and risk losing them or baptize them and risk disgracing the religious community. For those already baptized by Catholics, Dutch ministers did not allow them to take communion, but tried to educate them in the Reformed faith so that they could participate as full-fledged, communing members.

Overseas clergy attempted to accommodate the hybridity of non-European Christians by maintaining different levels of association with the religious community. Ministers permitted baptism for those who professed faith and exhibited a minimal comprehension of Reformed teachings, but they withheld communion until converts demonstrated a clear knowledge of the faith and a moral lifestyle. Those who had received a Catholic baptism also needed to make a profession and show comprehension to become a bona fide member and take communion. Consequently, a wide chasm yawned between baptism and communion.[230] Under this policy, large numbers of Asian converts, almost entire congregations, could claim a Reformed Protestant identity but never took communion.[231]

Dutch church authorities beginning in the 1620s and throughout this period expressed strong opposition to administering sacraments in any protocol that deviated from the standard Reformed practice.[232] According to the Synod of Dort, the sacraments, the word of God, and discipline formed an inviolable unity.[233] Delegates from the Dutch classes interpreted this provision to mean that all baptized members were to partake of the Lord's Supper. Denying the Lord's Table until they became better Christians, therefore, violated the sacramental unity of the Reformed community and the universality of the Reformed communion. Orthodox critics labeled this accommodating missionary approach as "dividing the sacraments," which became the stock epithet for the dispute.[234] While no Reformed *predikant, ziekentrooster,* or elder contested the unity of the sacraments in any theological sense, the problems that arose in overseas churches were practical ones that necessitated adjustments for the hybrid religious identities of native peoples. Orthodox opponents in the Netherlands and in Asia, however, likened this incremental strategy to accommodation, for which the Jesuits were infamously known.[235]

Since the sacraments marked entrance into and unity within the community of believers, they formed essential signifiers of Reformed Protestant Christianity. Consequently, disputes over who and under what circumstances someone could be baptized or take communion grappled with the question of just what constituted a Reformed Protestant Christian in the varied global and colonial contexts that existed outside the Netherlands. Such disputes plagued all overseas churches off and on for over a hundred years, including in Ceylon, Formosa, Cape Town, Brazil, the Caribbean, and Surinam. Ministers in Banda debated among themselves in November 1623 about the propriety of baptizing children of Muslims.[236] In 1636, questions came from Brazil about whether to baptize children of non-Christians, and from Angola and Curaçao about the baptism policy for orphans of "heathens."[237] The Curaçao church asked in 1661 about the propriety of dividing the sacraments.[238] The Reformed Church inherited thousands of baptized Catholics when the Dutch wrested Ceylon from the Portuguese, which generated many questions about administering the sacraments.[239] In 1650 both the Palicatta community (on the Malabar coast) and the Batavia consistory complained to the Amsterdam classis that requiring local people to undergo an extensive education before baptism caused many to seek baptism from Catholic missionaries instead.[240] In 1667 and 1670, Amboina advised the Amsterdam classis that it was considering making exceptions to the Dort canons in baptizing adults and children.[241] In 1679, the consistory at the Cape of Good Hope made the same petition.[242]

The challenges brought on by religious hybridity provoked the struggles that Dutch Protestants faced in relating the sacraments to cultural assumptions in overseas societies. Contrary to traditional interpretations of Protestant missions, Dutch ministers did make allowances for indigenous cultures and sought to figure out how Reformed tenets applied in a colonial and decidedly non-Christian milieu. Determining how to translate a Reformed theology of the sacraments within Asian societies essentially entailed deciding how to recognize a Protestant Christian among non-European peoples. Creating Reformed Christians out of Moors and pagans who had been enculturated in strange and exotic customs presented challenges for Calvinist *predikanten.*

What did conversion mean to Dutch Calvinists and to indigenous peoples? Informed by a keen awareness of cultural hybridities across early modern societies, recent scholarship on Catholic missions has made it obvious that religious interactions among European missionaries and indigenous peoples were far more complex and inconclusive than traditional notions of conversion have suggested. Pierre Dumonceaux observed almost forty years ago that Europeans did not hold to any fixed notion of conversion; rather, it could convey a range of connotations. Despite any such flexibility, Karl Morrison has surmised that the possibility of an abrupt change from one religion to another or from unbelief to belief is a concept rooted primarily in Western culture.[243] Missionary sources often invoked the Augustinian ideal of a transformative psychological and epistemological event, yet Allan Greer has argued convincingly from his work on the Iroquois that this totalizing conception of "a sudden rebirth that wipes out preexisting identities was impossible."[244] Other scholars analyzing Catholic attempts at conversion in various parts of Asia, America, and Africa have shown that missionaries in the field tempered such idealistic expectations, appealing to commonalities in local belief and practice and accepting negotiated compromises.[245] Many thousands of indigenes did undergo baptism, partake of sacraments from Catholic priests, and adopt Christian teachings, yet native peoples situated these new observances within customary ways of believing, praying, and performing.

Reformed Protestants in the empire and the Netherlands frequently waved the bright banner of Christian missions, though making converts on the ground proved complicated and ambiguous. The quarrels about dividing the sacraments illustrates that identifying genuine converts perplexed Calvinist ministers, and the persistence of the conflict suggests that no option satisfied ministers fully. Insisting on higher standards for communion, as the dividers advocated, effectively meant that most baptized natives counted as Christians in name but somehow not in substance. Many converts thus occupied a liminal religious site between the sacramental poles of baptism and communion.

CONCLUSION

The missionary goals of propagating the Reformed faith and building religious communities of converted pagans and Moors animated Dutch Calvinists in the age of merchant empire. Nearly a thousand *predikanten* and many more lay *ziekentroosteren* went into VOC and WIC settlements expecting to establish a worldwide community of Calvinist believers. Utilizing and collaborating with native linguists and teachers, ministers organized and oversaw hundreds of schools across Dutch outposts in the Indian and Atlantic Ocean basins. Despite a small overseas pastoral corps, clergy did plant congregations of baptized native peoples around the world, regularly counting, classifying, and reporting on the souls inside and outside their churches and schools. The gradient nature of church affiliation in the Netherlands, with members, sympathizers, and hearers, gave pastors a flexibility to count as part of the Christian community both baptized natives with little knowledge and commitment and those who met the more rigorous disciplinary requirements for church membership.

The complications and compromises inherent in forming Calvinist Christians among peoples with different assumptions about conversion, however, obscured this achievement. Not only have historians largely looked askance at the global Calvinist mission, but Reformed ministers preoccupied themselves with the perceived shortcomings of converts. The Dutch Protestant conception of conversion as a transformative process that would gradually put to flight long-established habits of mind and soul and purify worldly motives ran aground on the cultural hybridities of Asian, African, and American peoples. Natives who affiliated to some degree with the Reformed Church appended that Protestant identity to Hindu, Buddhist, Muslim, and/or shamanist affinities. What Calvinists regarded as vestigial idolatry and innate superstition, overseas converts considered time-honored strategies for prosperity and security that could coexist with Christian observances. This inclusive approach to worship and belief also played into the patronage offered to converts by the trading companies. Though Calvinists roundly condemned "worldly motivations," they were the very same pressures and incentives that ministers wrung from colonial authorities. These paradoxes illustrate the uneasy but indispensable relationship between the projects of conversion and commercial colonialism in the Dutch empire.

4

LANGUAGE AND SALVATION IN THE EMPIRE

A nine-year stretch among Tamils and Sinhalese in South Asia confirmed to Philip Baldaeus that Dutch simply would not work as the language of Calvinist missions. As he wrote in the 1660s,

> It is beyond dispute that the low-Dutch tongue is not so proper to propagate our religion here as the Malabar and Portuguese; and consequently, that the ministers of the Gospel sent into those parts should rather apply themselves to these languages, than to impose their own upon the new converts, which always meets with great difficulty, and can't be introduced without vast trouble and charges: besides, that it is much more reasonable one man should accommodate himself to many, than these to one man.[1]

Baldaeus's practical skepticism aligned with the observations of most other ministers that Asians, Africans, and Americans showed little interest in learning the Dutch language.[2] Calvinists chalked this indifference up to the complexity of their language and the provincialism of their potential converts. Sebastian Danckaerts wrote in the early 1620s that teaching Dutch to Amboinese children was futile because of the difficulty of the Dutch language. Caspar Wiltens complained they never learned more than seven words.[3] Across the way in Formosa thirty years later, the consistory in Tayouan expressed serious reservations about a Dutch language initiative, noting that Formosans "are most anxious to . . . be freed from the burden of daily attending the schools."[4] At the end of the century, clergy in Colombo feared that it was simply too much to expect Sinhalese students to learn Christianity in the foreign language of Dutch.[5] Native peoples left no stated record of their perspective on acquiring Dutch, but it seems likely that they could find little incentive for learning it, since a facility with a regional vernacular or Portuguese enabled them to communicate with most anyone outside their city or village. Whatever attractions conversion to Calvinism held, they generally were not sufficient to compel people to learn very much Dutch.

Faced with a strong motive for translation, Calvinist overseas ministers collaborated with indigenous linguists to learn new languages for preaching, teaching, and translating religious materials—catechisms, prayers, sermons, formularies, and large portions of scripture (even the entire Bible when it came to Portuguese, Malay, Tamil, and Sinhalese)—in order to present the soul-saving message of Protestant Christianity to pagans and Moors. Dutch and native translators incorporated European syntax and grammatical rules into local vernaculars, producing what scholars of colonial Spanish America have called translanguages.[6] The Dutch indeed joined a throng of merchants, imperialists, and evangelists in the unprecedented level of translation work being undertaken around the early modern world. Missionaries played a formative role in the creation of widely accessible linguistic media in the Americas, portions of Africa, and Asia, and in the destruction of countless oral dialects in these areas. Jesuits and native linguists fashioned Quechua in the Peruvian Andes, while Franciscans produced Nahuatl from oral dialects in central Mexico. A marked uptick in the translation of texts was not simply a western European phenomenon, but converting knowledge into different linguistic systems appeared as a central feature of Turkish, Persian, and Indian scholarship as well. Madrasas in Anatolia featured treatises on medicine, astronomy, astrology, and pharmacology that Ottoman scholars translated from Persian and Arabic into Turkish. Intellectuals such as Kâtib Celebi in the first half of the seventeenth century borrowed from translated Western geographic, medical, and astronomical texts extensively from the sixteenth century onward.[7] Unfortunately, the roles of Protestant empire and missionary endeavor have largely fallen outside the scholarship on this broad range of global translation activity. Studies of Protestantism in Europe have long identified translation as a critical component of the application of scripture to society and culture, which indicates the importance of translation to the conversion of peoples overseas.

The missionary effort to penetrate these language systems in highly diverse linguistic landscapes ran up against VOC officials who tried to implement a Dutch language policy in Asia (the WIC accepted the prevalence of Portuguese in Brazil). In the East Indies, Formosa, Ceylon, and the Cape of Good Hope, churches and colonial agencies went back and forth between indigenous, Portuguese, and Dutch language programs. Ultimately, Dutch ministers and native translators produced written vernacular texts in Malay, Sinkan, Sinhalese, and Tamil, disseminating them across Ceylon, Formosa, and the East Indies.

This chapter tracks the language work among both Dutch and native church personnel and conflicts between evangelistic aims and imperial objectives over language that lingered in the empire until the early eighteenth century. From there, the analysis focuses on the cultures of translation that enmeshed Dutch pastors and local peoples. This study highlights the European translation cultures broken apart by new global environments and the constraints of language dictated by divergent cultural expectations.

LINGUISTIC BACKGROUNDS

CULTURES OF TRANSLATION IN EARLY MODERN EUROPE

The Renaissance and Reformation produced a diverse translation movement that transformed European society by making biblical, classical, scientific, and other sources of knowledge far more accessible than ever before. Utilizing insights from cultural anthropology, Peter Burke has adopted the phrase "cultures of translation" as shorthand for the attempt to place the systems of rendering texts within the full range of their social contexts.[8]

The translation cultures instrumental to these powerful intellectual and religious currents shaped Dutch missionary linguistics in the seventeenth and eighteenth centuries. Close criticism of classical and sacred texts by humanists across Europe inculcated heightened awareness of the historical evolution of grammar and rhetoric. At least in northern Europe, textual criticism of the Bible and the early church fathers was closely related to a movement of religious reform. As the "prince of the humanists," Erasmus illustrated vividly the integration of spiritual piety with philological analysis of scripture, publishing a Greek New Testament in 1516, correcting mistakes in the Latin Vulgate, and reexamining key passages with attention to spiritual devotion rather than external ritual and ecclesiology.[9] The biblicism in northern European humanism, combined with the advent of Protestantism in the sixteenth century, gave new impetus to making the word of God accessible to people through translating scripture into vernacular languages. Lefevre d'Etaples brought forth an early French Bible in 1530, Martin Luther a German Bible in 1534, Miles Coverdale an English version in 1535, as translations proliferated across Reformation Europe.[10] Dutch versions of the Bible circulated throughout the sixteenth century, although a definitive edition, the States Bible (*Statenvertaling*), did not appear until 1637.[11]

Since Bibles were beyond the financial reach of many families, Protestant educators—as well as Catholic theologians—condensed the essential elements of their faith into catechisms and confessional statements. Composed by Guido de Brès in 1561, the Belgic Confession of Faith captured the fundamental tenets of the Dutch Reformed Church; it and the Heidelberg Catechism (1563) formed the central educational texts for congregations. Catholic authorities, however, recognizing an evangelical hermeneutic in these and other works that sought to appeal directly to the laity and rendered key passages in line with a Protestant outlook, upheld the authority of the Latin Vulgate at the Council of Trent and condemned "twisting the text to . . . [an] individual meaning in opposition to that which has been and is held by holy mother church."[12] To counteract defective versions in English, Catholic translators at the English College in Douai produced a complete English edition of the Vulgate by 1609.

These momentous shifts in language use shaped Dutch and all European missionary enterprises in four important respects. First, making texts accessible obliged *predikanten* to place emphases on literary education that, in the Dutch context, were exemplified by the extensive networks of schools maintained by the VOC and to a lesser extent by the WIC. At times, these schools taught Dutch, and in most times, native languages or Portuguese. Regardless of language, Calvinists believed that reading and writing were critical for students to understand the precepts of Protestant Christianity. The instruction of children and adults remained a consistent priority for the Dutch, thus schools always appeared in a newly penetrated region, even before consistories and sometimes before congregations. *Predikanten* also sought to direct seminaries in Formosa (Soulang), Nallur (Jaffnapatnam), Colombo, Batavia, and the Netherlands dedicated to training indigenous men to teach in the company schools.[13]

Second, rendering religious texts from Greek and Latin into "national" vernaculars in Europe oriented translators toward native dialects and transformed them into translanguages across regions that comprised different linguistic groups. Unlike the Portuguese and Spanish, the Dutch (as we shall see below) were unable to inculcate the use of their language extensively among free or enslaved inhabitants. This failure was not for lack of motive or effort. Dutch theologians and ministers believed that Dutch provided a fuller range of linguistic expression to relate the subtle truths of Protestant Christianity than local languages. Simon Cat, *predikant* in Colombo, argued in 1690 that the Dutch language was more expansive in meaning and richer in understanding than other tongues.[14] Undoubtedly, this perspective stemmed from a native affection by the Dutch for their own mother tongue over an acquired Asian or American language. Despite strenuous (albeit uneven and intermittent) efforts on the part of *predikanten* to impart Dutch, local people found it too difficult and impractical, according to Baldaeus and other ministers.

The analogies between classical Greek and Roman informed the basic strategies of missionary and native linguists in developing and endorsing translanguages. Calvinists worked with indigenous translators to identify a mother tongue in a region, codify it, impose European grammatical rules on it, translate materials into it, and then promote it. Singling out a particular vernacular, sometimes an oral one, from among very diverse linguistic environments, they projected it as the standard mode of written communication. For Dutch translators, these local means of expression took on the form of a vernacular that they could classify according to European linguistic categories. For example, the minister Petrus van der Vorm characterized the Amboinese Malay language as the "mother tongue" for the inhabitants of the neighboring locations of Leitimor, Hitu, Nusa Laut, Lease, Buangbesi, Seram, Manipa, and Buru. Yet each group spoke their own dialect, a linguistic relationship that van der Vorm compared to Old Greek and Attic, Aeolic, Doric, and Ionic.[15] In Batavia and Amboina, consistories compared the relationship between certain oral idioms of Malay and the written "High" form at the court of Johor to the correlation between Latin and national languages in Europe. Calvinist *predikanten* in Ceylon, Formosa, and the East Indies strove to identify a mother language and establish it as a basic language of education in company schools.[16]

The movement toward more national vernaculars in sixteenth-century Europe was replicated in the homogenization of native dialects in overseas environments by missionary translators. Jesuit translators, for example, identified a "single republic" among Andean peoples and fashioned a Quechua "national" language for them.[17] The Dutch also tended to regard the peoples of Formosa, Ceylon, South Africa, and Brazil as confederations of people with an overarching national identity, and Dutch language workers thus sought to match these "national" groupings of people with a specific translanguage. Calvinists, hoping to homogenize vernaculars, however, were stymied by the sheer diversity of dialects in the East Indies and Formosa. Clergy on visitation circuits, suspecting that converts did not understand teachings because of linguistic differences, issued additional calls for homogenization of and education in instructional languages.[18]

The third way in which changes in language use in Europe influenced overseas missions lay in the close critical attention to texts. This analytical focus, combined with a renewed realization that language conveyed the special revelation of God, instilled a precision about linguistic meaning in translation projects. Calvinists in Europe had devoted considerable intellectual energy to distinguishing their beliefs and practices from those of Catholics and other Protestants. The sharpened sense of confessional identity produced a preoccupation with theological precision among the major denominations by the early seventeenth century. Within the Dutch Reformed tradition, the concern for biblical orthodoxy produced intense theological quarrels over, among other issues, predestination, human agency, original sin, and Sabbatarianism.

The enduring struggle to define belief and practice precisely through language accompanied the Dutch into the global mission field, as *predikanten* sought theological exactness in translated texts. During a heightened concern with orthodoxy in Formosa in 1648, ministers Johannes Happart and Simon van Breen refused to use materials produced by Robert Junius, including a book of prayers, a catechism, and sermons, allegedly because of doctrinal and linguistic sloppiness.[19] In Colombo, it took seven years (1751–1758) for the consistory to approve Philip de Melho's Tamil translation of the New Testament over concerns that errors jeopardized the work's orthodoxy.[20] The only translated product by a Calvinist in Tupian, a 1641 translation of the Heidelberg Catechism, was rejected in the Netherlands because it did not replicate the Dutch version exactly. Although the WIC printed it, the catechism remained in a company warehouse and seemingly was never used.[21]

Finally, linguistic expertise bestowed cultural capital in the formation of new social hierarchies overseas. Facility in language and translation instilled a sharpened sense of intellectual self-possession that compensated in part for a diminished social status in colonial societies. Consequently, criticism from a colleague over linguistic capability often sparked a protracted debate that not infrequently devolved into bitter animosity. When the consistory in Colombo allowed for the reexamination of de Melho's translation in 1752, the examiners were cautioned to "avoid immoderate and irrelevant comments unlike the previous commentators."[22] Disputes over the most appropriate Malay version of the Bible engulfed consistories in Batavia and Amboina and in church districts in the Netherlands for over thirty years, from the late 1690s to 1733, generating volumes of incendiary correspondence. In November 1697, the Batavia consistory responded that they found it insulting and offensive that ministers in North Holland would presume to take a position on the matter, since they knew nothing about the language.[23] In April 1689, Joan Fereria d'Almeida, who had converted to Calvinism from Roman Catholicism, endured much criticism for his Portuguese translations of the Old and New Testaments. Feeling remorse over prolonged and animated arguments regarding his translation work, Fereria asked that references to disputes be withdrawn from the consistory's records. "To my great regret," he stated, "several questions and misunderstandings have arisen between me and this assembly from 1683 to 1686 over the revision and correction to my Portuguese translation of both the Old and New Testaments . . . which troubled me;

so it is my humble, reverent, and earnest request that the resolutions proposed about the book be expunged or scratched out because I am an old and weak person and desire that this happen before I die so I might go to the grave with greater peace of mind."[24]

LINGUISTIC LANDSCAPES OVERSEAS

The spindly contours of the Dutch empire placed Reformed ministers in quite variegated linguistic environments. Yet the one common language to almost all of the areas of active Reformed proselytizing was Portuguese. The extraordinary success of the Portuguese empire in the sixteenth century and the extensive mission activity of Catholic priests made it a translanguage throughout the littoral of the Indian Ocean and in Brazil, the crown jewel of Portugal's Atlantic dominions. Simultaneous to the implanting of the formal, written language, the ubiquity of Portuguese merchants in the trading emporia of the port cities along the Indian Ocean facilitated the cultivation of an oral, pidgin version of Portuguese across maritime Asia. Consequently, Portuguese in some form was utilized throughout the Indian subcontinent, the Malaysian peninsula, Burma, Siam, Tonquin, Cochinchina, Macau, Kamaran (Persia), Basra, and even Mecca.[25] Most people without expertise in a local language relied on Portuguese to communicate. The Dutch, therefore, preached, taught, and translated religious material in Portuguese throughout all VOC lands except Formosa.

The majority of the local languages in the East Indies, Formosa, and Ceylon belonged to the vast Austronesian language family that stretched from Madagascar across maritime Southeast Asia and the Pacific. Scores of dialects had developed across the East Indies from Malaysia and Sumatra to Java, Sulawesi, and the Moluccas. By the time Europeans arrived in the early sixteenth century, several forms of Malay had spread across the archipelago, functioning as media for interaction among people from different islands and the Malaysian peninsula who each also spoke their own native vernacular. The long-standing commercial activity in the region had both created a need for a common means of communication and contributed to the expanding utility of Malay across space and time. Thus, traders from areas such as Java, Melaka, Makassar, and Timor mixed Malay into their own native dialects. Referred to as "Low" or "Bazaar" Malay, this oral tongue was an assorted and extemporized mix that derived from a written, formal language used at the courts of Johor, Aceh, Ternate, and Makassar. Seeking to convert souls, Muslim mystics and proselytizers contributed to the spread of what became known as "High Malay," employing it to explain the tenets and prayers of Islam. The Muslim missionary campaign imparted an

Arabic influence to the language. High Malay also functioned as a language of contact for diplomatic interactions among political rulers. Europeans compared High Malay, the translanguage of literate elites, to Latin in western Christendom, and Low Malay to the "national" vernaculars expanding there in the sixteenth and seventeenth centuries.[26] As Dutch merchants made their way into this world, they utilized both forms of Malay, as well as native dialects, to negotiate with princes, transact business, and spread Christianity. VOC officials and Dutch ministers also acquainted themselves with local dialects and relied heavily on native translators to navigate this linguistic thicket.

Lying at the northernmost end of the Austronesian language family, Formosa is considered the point of origin for the diffusion of these related languages. When the Dutch made contact with the island in the 1620s, it was home to twenty different ethnic groups, speaking at least twenty-eight distinct languages within three primary ethno-linguistic groupings.[27] The VOC carved its initial toehold at Tayouan on the southeastern coast of Formosa in 1624 and from there consolidated military and political control over adjacent areas in stages: first into the southern coastal regions in the 1630s and then toward the northern and central districts in the 1630s and 1640s. From the Favorlangh River to the Tamsay River, the southwestern Formosan plain came under the most direct management by the VOC, and accordingly it experienced the heaviest missionary operations, though preaching, baptizing, and church planting; they accompanied VOC conquests in the north and central regions as well. Moving into these areas meant that Dutch ministers came into increasing contact with a bewildering array of languages. In the vicinity of Tayouan, Siriyan (Sinkan) was widely used, but Favorlangh, Tackays, and Quataongh were also significant. To the south, Tapouliangh, Parruam, and Tonghtoval possessed wider resonance than other more insular dialects.[28]

Meanwhile, the languages that confronted Dutch merchants and ministers in Ceylon and the Malabar and Coromandel coasts belonged to an Indo-Aryan ancestry, having displaced native Austronesian structures more than two thousand years earlier. Aryan communities introduced Sinhalese vernaculars, which became subjected to a number of extraneous morphological and syntactical conventions, as Malay, Arabic, and Dravidian speakers traded with Ceylon merchants. Pali and Sanskrit also exerted influence as Buddhist and Hindu religious figures spread new rites and myths across the island. Dravidian vernaculars from southern India, particularly Tamil, predominated in northern Ceylon, whereas Malayam, Kannada, and Telugu held sway in Malabar and Coromandel. One of the most able Dutch translators of Sinhalese, Johannes Ruël, was greatly helped in his task by grammars in Tamil and Sinhalese produced by Jesuits in

Ceylon.[29] Thus by the time of the Dutch arrival, previous translation work had facilitated the prevalence of Sinhalese dialects in central and southern portions of the island, while Tamil languages flourished in the north.

In the Atlantic basin, where Dutch trading outposts and settlers dotted the coastlines by the 1630s, Netherlandish people encountered a vast array of very different linguistic systems and language groups, ranging from Algonquin in northeastern America, to Tupi-Guarani in Brazil, to Akan in Ghana, to Bantu in Luanda, to Khoisan on the Cape of Good Hope, to Carib and Arawak in Surinam. Missionary engagement with American and African languages, however, was largely limited to Tupian in Brazil, as attempts to convert natives and slaves elsewhere were ephemeral. The first Reformed Protestant to describe and work in the language was the French Huguenot minister Jean de Léry, who had voyaged to an island off the coast of Rio de Janeiro and then onto the mainland in 1556–1557, where he lived among the Tupi people.[30] Eighty years later, Dutch ministers in Paraíba, Recife, and Bahia actually benefited immensely from the linguistic work of Jesuits in the acquisition of Tupian. Beginning in the late 1500s, missionaries from the Society had rendered the Tupian vernacular in written form with grammatical and syntactical structure. Dutch clergy utilized these resources in their missionary campaigns.[31] During the Dutch sojourn in Brazil, *predikanten* also had to navigate creole varieties of Portuguese and Spanish. Thus, although the Dutch faced quite unfamiliar linguistic environments, the diversity itself had facilitated the creation of pidgin and trade dialects, along with pedagogical materials that they could use to navigate these terrains and equip themselves to render materials in appropriate translanguages.

LANGUAGES FOR EMPIRE AND MISSIONS

LANGUAGE POLICY IN THE EMPIRE

The renowned Spanish humanist and grammarian Antonio de Nebrija famously observed in 1492 that "language has always been the companion of empire," as Spain prepared to follow up its conquest of Granada with an imperious Castilian language agenda.[32] Among the early modern European imperial powers, Spain and Portugal ranked far and away as the most successful in injecting their languages into new territories, including the Americas, the Philippines, and trading hubs of the Indian Ocean. Regardless of linguistic allegiances, all imperial powers had to fashion a structure of communication that would best promote political loyalty and social order. Since religious proselytizers often made common cause with empire builders, an appropriate idiom for conversion could either support or controvert imperial language policy. As Dutch overseas operations unfolded in the seventeenth century, company governors and church leaders grappled with how best to achieve the aims of both empire and mission in many foreign linguistic environments.

Company and church authorities held up Dutch as the ideal idiom for as many inhabitants as possible in their overseas realms. Yet the combined realities of the dominance of Portuguese, the unpopularity of Dutch, the scarcity of language instructors, and the urgency of Christian missions ultimately proved too much for that linguistic aspiration. For most of the seventeenth century, the VOC and overseas churches tussled back and forth over a language policy until finally coming to accept a two-tiered status quo. In this state of affairs, Dutch church workers and other company employees worked mainly through Portuguese or native vernaculars when interacting with most residents. A few local people did, however, learn Dutch and worked in collaboration with *predikanten* and *ziekentroosteren* to reach people in their communities.[33]

This circuitous development is important for understanding the diverse social, cultural, and political contexts that encased verbal and written language use among *predikanten*, native linguists, and company authorities. The geopolitical strategies in combating the Portuguese and the divergent needs of clergy and colonial authorities led the Dutch overseas to veer in different directions at different times to devise a linguistic medium of exchange.

A DUTCH LANGUAGE POLICY

In the East Indies, Ceylon, Formosa, and the Cape of Good Hope, the VOC and Reformed Church initially sought to teach Dutch in schools and impart the language in the colonial settlements. Some schools in these regions offered Dutch, but its availability was limited and it was not compulsory. In the Atlantic, schools in New Netherland and Brazil gave language instruction only sporadically to people who were not Dutch. The WIC's brief and tenuous grip on Brazil meant that Dutch functioned almost exclusively as intercompany and interchurch means of communication. Although governors occasionally voiced a desire to implant Dutch in order to displace Portuguese, they, as well as ecclesiastical officers, acquiesced to the linguistic dominance of Portuguese out of the political necessity of placating the local population.[34]

Meanwhile, in June 1641 half a world away, the increasing alarm over the prevalence of Portuguese in the East Indies and other VOC operations prompted governor general Anthony van Diemen to make a bold proclamation. Batavia and other areas had experienced an influx of Portuguese-speaking migrants from

South India and from Melaka after the VOC conquest in 1641. Van Diemen, witnessing company personnel marry Portuguese- and Malay-speaking women, became concerned about the light cultural presence of the Dutch throughout the region. He therefore declared war on the Portuguese language, which threatened "to eventually gain the upper hand and suppress the language of our mother country, which would not be proper in view of our main important political considerations." He issued a number of restrictive measures and then ordered that schoolmasters "make sure that in the schools no language other than Dutch is used."[35] Van Diemen also instructed governor Maximiliaan le Maire in Formosa to promote knowledge of the Dutch language in schools there.[36] In Ceylon, Rijklof van Goens declared his intention in 1659 and again in 1668 "to eliminate the Portuguese language and import our own language to expand the gospel better." In March 1668, he convened a meeting with the consistory in Colombo to develop a plan; two years later he proposed a school in Jaffnapatnam attended by both Tamil- and Dutch-speaking students so that they might learn from one another.[37]

Governors in New Netherland and of small outposts in the Atlantic did not express a need for any language policy. Portuguese posed no geopolitical threat, and Calvinist missions did not receive priority in these areas. The VOC (at the Cape) and WIC did set up schools that utilized Dutch as the language of instruction. But there was no sustained effort to promote the language or to translate materials into other vernaculars. When he was governor at the Cape, van Goens issued a Dutch language policy for the colony in 1658, which was directed at slaves.[38] Yet governors or ministers did not attempt in any consistent fashion to assimilate the indigenous Khoi Khoi people into the settlements, and *predikanten* almost completely ignored them. The migratory people spoke a Khoisan vernacular, characterized by click consonants. Colonial and church officers considered it utterly incomprehensible and *predikanten* did not expend any effort to learn the language. Only a very few Khoi Khoi gained any knowledge of Dutch. Some European settlers did speak Dutch, which evolved into the modern language of Afrikaans in the second half of the eighteenth century.

Ministers generally supported initiatives to promote facility with Dutch, even though most reflected Philip Baldaeus's skepticism about its practicality, cited at the beginning of this chapter. Alarmed that baptized converts did not truly grasp Reformed religion, the Banda consistory in April 1622 refused to allow a baptized member to take communion unless he or she could understand Dutch.[39] Consistories set up schools in the Banda Islands, Amboina, and Batavia for instruction in the Christian faith in Dutch as well as in local Malay dialects.[40] In 1643, the Batavian Church Order sought to impose the exclusive use of Dutch in schools, but it quickly faltered.[41] In 1648, the Tayouan consistory, with the support of the governor, Pieter Anthoniszoon Overtwater, launched an educational initiative to teach Dutch in the schools in the vicinity. In the villages of Soulang, Sinkan, Bakloan, Tavakan, Mattau, Tevorang, Dorko, and Tirosen, parents were required on pain of a fine of a deerskin to send their children to these schools in the mornings and afternoons, "in accordance with the Dutch custom."[42] In discussions surrounding the establishment of a seminary in Colombo in the 1690s, Simon Cat strongly advocated the spread of Dutch to advance the kingdom of God on the island. Cat maintained that Sinhalese children could learn "our language" if they could be separated from their parents in a school setting where they had to speak and write Dutch.[43]

The seminary projects in Nallur and Colombo at the end of the 1600s occasioned a great deal of rethinking about conversion and language strategies. Cat, a promoter of the seminary in Colombo and author of a Sinhalese grammar, argued forcefully for a vigorous Dutch language program to Laurens Pyl, the governor in Ceylon. To make his case, Cat appealed to the unusual theory of Johannes Goropius Becanus, a sixteenth-century linguist, physician, and Dutchophile from Antwerp. Goropius contended that Dutch (Flemish) was the world's oldest language, spoken in the Garden of Eden by Adam and Eve, and the etymological ancestor of all linguistic systems. This schema drew derision from most linguists and other European humanists, though it had an ardent following among a small number of Dutch-speaking intellectuals. It is not clear how seriously Cat held to Goropian theory, yet the missionary linguist did appropriate it to make a central point about the exemplary quality of the Dutch language. Arguing against the prevalent view among *predikanten* that Dutch was too obscure and incomprehensible to Asians, Cat expostulated that "our language has always been an unalloyed Heavenly Language and a most intelligent tongue from antiquity transmitted through other languages such as those of the Celts, Chaldeans, and Hebrews, manifesting itself in not only many other languages, but especially in the first inhabited parts of the world, and having shared qualities with Greek and Latin." He went on to extol the expansive capacity of Dutch in illuminating the meaning of concepts. Cat concluded that seminaries should spread knowledge of Dutch so that books can be read and understood in order to bring the word of God to the Ceylonese people.[44] Though all overseas personnel would not have gone as far as Cat, governors, ministers, and lay leaders regarded Dutch as a fitting instrument for political assimilation and the fullest medium for carrying forth the gospel.

Cat was responding in part to the truism that had emerged over the course of the seventeenth century that native peoples found the Dutch language exceedingly arduous to learn. Baldaeus, as we saw at the outset of this chapter, admitted that teaching Dutch to Asians and Euro-Asians was a frustrating endeavor. The earliest ministers in the Moluccas, including Casper Wiltens, Adriaan Hulsebos, and Sebastian Danckaerts, commented to their colleagues in Batavia, Amsterdam, and Walcheren on the failure of the Amboinese and Bandanese to develop any sort of facility with Dutch. Wiltens wrote to the Amsterdam classis in 1616 that Dutch was more difficult to learn for adults than Latin.[45] At the beginning of the Dutch language push in Formosa in 1648, the scribe of the Tayouan consistory even expressed astonishment at the notion that "other nations or peoples should be taught to speak our language."[46] Initially, the ministers in Formosa judged that indigenous children were picking up the language quickly, though by the mid-1650s their optimism had cooled. By 1656, the *Politieke Raad* in Formosa reported to the governor general Joan Maetsuijcker that the clergy were divided on preaching and teaching in Dutch; some opted for it, while others chose local vernaculars.[47]

VERNACULAR STRATEGIES IN THE EAST INDIES, FORMOSA, AND CEYLON

An overriding missionary impulse worked against any VOC governor's pro-Dutch language project. Since schoolmasters and *predikanten* found students less than enthusiastic about learning Dutch, most schools in the East Indies and Ceylon resorted to Portuguese, Malay, Tamil, or Sinhalese within a short time.[48] The Reformation principle of *sola scriptura* provided a compelling impetus to put the word of God into the hearts and minds of the people as quickly as possible, so that they could absorb it into their lives. Thus, the first criterion for a missionary language was that it be intelligible to the converted. This ideology had motivated Protestant translation movements in developing national vernaculars in Europe, a trajectory that also supported political autonomy among rising states. In the imperial setting, however, it worked against a normative Dutch-only policy.

Along with the practical evangelical purpose, analyzing languages stimulated a more abstract intellectual preoccupation for Calvinists in the Netherlands and in Asia. An abiding fascination with the families of language and their linkages to a global, biblical narrative had transfixed humanists across Europe since the fifteenth century. The antiquarian study by humanists—both Protestant and Catholic—engaged the problem of language after the Fall. A universal language, they believed, fragmented at the tower of Babel and continued to disintegrate down through history. Since humanists took language as historical and contingent, the wide diversity of vernaculars contained the linguistic residue of the diffusion of peoples and cultures, undocumented and thus unknown, but nevertheless signified in the languages of the world. Some intellectuals sought to reconstruct or rediscover this lost universal language, while others posited connections among vernacular diversity as a necessary consequence of the Fall but one that linked societies to a common historical and linguistic development.[49] The mission field served as a linguistic laboratory for Dutch Protestants fascinated by the presence of paganism in a global historical narrative.

At the same time, Dutch linguists recognized that translation was not a transparent, straightforward process of restating concepts from one language into another. Because of the vast number of dialects and vernaculars present in South and Southeast Asia, Dutch *predikanten* had to pick and choose dialects that seemed most appropriate for cultivating a translanguage. This linguistic transformation had been well underway in Europe since the sixteenth century, spurred on by Protestants who were attempting to translate the Latin Vulgate into national vernaculars. Consequently, homogenizing linguistic differences for the sake of conversion was a missionary program that Dutch Calvinists were quite familiar with before the rise of an overseas empire. It proved to be a model that ministers in all areas drew from when constructing written vernacular languages from the diverse oral modes of communication prevalent in the East Indies, Formosa, and Ceylon. The linguistic endeavors of Dutch imperial agents and clergy in the Indian Ocean world contrasted with their strategies in Brazil, where the Dutch simply borrowed from and built on the work of Portuguese priests who had already done extensive work in Tupian. In both settings, however, missionary labor and the imperial ambition of the trading companies shaped European "representation of linguistic structure."[50]

Although overseas ministers clearly recognized that translating Calvinism into the written and spoken word was vital to missions, a significant number clung to Dutch. *Predikanten* generally signed five-year contracts (though some served for much longer), which hindered the acquisition of a new language. The report on minister Jacob Canter Visscher in Cochin observed that he did not neglect Dutch services, but had preached only once in six years in the local language and even then was not understandable.[51] Others cited age, fragile health, or intellectual incapacity to tackle the challenge of learning a new and unfamiliar language.[52] To a large extent, the workload of a pastor overseas, unless given release time for language study, greatly limited the opportunity for acquiring local linguistic facility. Wilhelm de Bitter, a minister in Banda, spoke for a large number of his brethren in September 1672 when in a letter to the governor general Joan Maetsuijcker he catalogued a list of circumstances that precluded them from learning Malay. De Bitter complained that no materials, such as dictionaries or grammars, were available, and no opportunities, given the small staff, were open to them. He also pointed out the discrepancy between the local vernacular and the Malay as presented in Batavia and Amboina.[53] As noted by an Amboina schoolmaster, Zacharias Caheying, in 1670, linguistic fragmentation characterized all theaters of missionary activity.[54] Petrus van der Vorm in June 1692 reported to Batavia that the languages in the Amboina region were quite distinct from those in Java. Harmanus Kolde de Horn, visiting the island of Haruku from Amboina in May 1694, remarked that he decided not to administer the Lord's Supper because he had not mastered Malay and could not read a sermon in the language.[55]

The persistence of Portuguese and a pro-Dutch language policy also retarded a commitment to learning native languages. In Ceylon, the study of Sinhalese and Tamil did not get off the ground comprehensively until the early 1700s. Aside from Baldaeus, Cat, and Ruël, very few Dutch ministers in South Asia possessed any facility in these languages. It was not until the impetus for the Nallur and Colombo seminaries that ministers began to be appointed with the specific charge of learning either Sinhalese or Tamil.[56] In 1730, a minister in Cochin could reassure Batavia that the ministers in South Asia had taken to heart the need to learn the language of the *landaard* (national character).[57] Similarly in Formosa, after the departure of Candidius and Junius and the advent of governor Overtwater's pro-Dutch initiative in 1648, a complacency about Sinkan and Favorlang set in among *predikanten*. The emphasis on Portuguese after the influx of Portuguese-speaking peoples in Batavia undermined the study of Malay there during the middle of the 1600s.[58]

In times and places of linguistic deficiency (among Dutch clergy), native interpreters and teachers came to the fore even more than usual. Chapter 3 examined their critical role in education, yet they also taught *predikanten* languages and translated for them. Most often these local language workers only rarely emerge in the sources. Caheying wrote of his visit to Manipa: "I do as much as possible to make myself understood and have someone here who can translate my words."[59] In May 1693, Cat acknowledged that "native linguists have taught me that Malabar [Tamil] and Sinhalese have an extensive commonality, so that they share many words and also a [grammatical] construction."[60] More specifically, he mentioned working with Pieter Jaas, a Sinhalese teacher in Colombo; Wieh Kramazinga, also in Sinhalese; and Modeljar don Antonio, an expert in Portuguese.[61] Tamil proponents and ministers, including Adriaan de Meij and Jan Phillipszoon (Jaffnapatnam), Philip de Melho (Colombo), and Philip Emmanuelszoon (Negombo), played vital roles in translating materials in South Asia.[62] The Amboina consistory promoted Rogier Hendrickszoon from lay reader to proponent in 1625 because his native fluency in Malay would enhance the quality of sermons there.[63] Daniel Gravius credited native linguists for assisting him in translating catechisms and prayers into Sinkan.[64]

With the support of native linguists, Dutch Calvinists translated religious materials into local languages for almost two hundred years. Frederick de Houtman, the brother of Cornelis, who led the first Dutch expedition to the East Indies, produced the first Dutch-Malay dictionary in 1603, which he composed while imprisoned by the sultan of Aceh (Alauddin Riayat Shah ibn Firman Shah) from 1599 to 1601. Eight years later, Albert Ruyl, a merchant for the VOC, constructed the first work in Malay for local consumption, translating the Ten Commandments, Lord's Prayer, Apostles Creed, along with a primer for teaching children titled *ABC Letters* (*Sovrat ABC*). In the following year, Ruyl published a longer work, *Mirror of the Malay Language* (*Spieghel van de Maleysche taal*), which combined a translation of Philip Marnix van St. Aldegonde's catechism along with the materials in the *ABC Letters*, several additional prayers, and edifying dialogues.[65] Sebastian Danckaerts contributed a Malay translation of the Heidelberg Catechism in 1629.

Ministers and lay linguists continued to revise and expand these materials during the 1600s. Johannes Roman, a minister in Batavia, brought forth a new Malay grammar in 1647 and enlarged upon Danckaerts's translated catechism; Josias Spijlardus translated the catechism *The Way to Heaven* (*De Weg naar de Hemel*) in 1657, which Francis Caron reproduced in 1683; Frederick Gueynier compiled a dictionary in 1677; Isaac Thije released another catechism in 1680; Melchior Leijdekker also issued a catechism, with prayers and other materials, in 1688. In addition, sermons by Casper Wiltens, Francis Caron, and Justus Heurnius were rendered in Malay and circulated among congregations.[66] Containing documents central to a Reformed Protestant education, these texts constituted a practical compendium of doctrine, moral directive, and language instruction.

Translation of portions of scripture into Malay got underway as well, though this project proceeded much more slowly owing to the grander scale of intellectual labor involved and because of disputes over language. Ruyl published a Malay version of the Gospel of St. Matthew, along with some of the Psalms, in 1629—one of the first translations of one of the gospels into a non-European language—and nine years later he produced the Gospel of St. Mark in Malay. In Melaka, the head merchant, Johan van Hazel, rounded out the synoptic gospels by translating St. Luke and St. John in 1646, followed by fifty of the Psalms in 1648. Revising the work of Ruyl and van Hazel, Justus Heurnius produced a Malay version of the Gospels, the Acts of the Apostles, and the full Psalms in 1652. Ten years later, the minister Daniel Brouwerius in Batavia completed a Malay translation of Genesis and a much-maligned edition of the New Testament. A number of other nonpublished translations abounded, including ones by Nikolaas Hodenpijl (a *predikant* in the Moluccas and Batavia), Simon de Larges (a *ziekentrooster*), and Francois Valentijn (a minister in Amboina). All of this language work culminated in the complete translation of the Bible undertaken by Melchior Leijdekker, minister of the Malay congregation in Batavia, and brought to completion by Petrus van der Vorm after Leijdekker's death in 1701. Leijdekker and van der Vorm utilized High Malay, which provoked a protracted dispute over which vernacular best suited the mission (discussed below) and delayed the actual publication of the Leijdekker translation until 1733.[67]

In Formosa, Dutch ministers also focused on translating materials into local languages. Since the Portuguese had no presence on the island, governors did not have to fret about the Lusitanians' linguistic influence, but ministers also could not rely on it as a medium of expression. Spain held a small colony on the northern coast from 1626 to 1642, but the Spanish presence was quite limited. More problematic for Dutch *predikanten* was the fact that Formosans possessed no written language. In this fragmented and nebulous linguistic environment, George Candidius and Robert Junius settled on Sinkan, a Siriyan dialect prominent in the southwestern coastal plain where the VOC concentrated its activities, as the language of salvation. Junius created a phonetic alphabet with Latin script and constructed a syntax in the 1630s and early 1640s. He translated three catechisms, a formulary, and a grammar.[68] After the Dutch expulsion of the Spanish from the north in 1642, the minister Simon van Breen moved into the area around Favorlang. Like Junius, he produced a grammar and catechism, yet he did so by combining elements of two vernaculars, Tarrokaysian and Favorlang. By the mid-1640s, van Breen had set up six schools offering lessons in Favorlang and Protestant Christianity. Later, in 1650, the minister Jacob Vertrecht completed an authorized catechism for schools in the north, *Teachings for Use in the Schools of the Favorlang District* (*Leerstukken ten gebruikke der schoolen van't Favorlang district*). Because of concerns that Junius had reduced Reformed teachings to simplified and local applications, in 1649 a team of pastoral and native translators revised his catechism and formulary according to the Heidelberg Catechism and other solidly orthodox pedagogical materials. Johannes Happart, Daniel Gravius, and Antony Hambroek collaborated on a Sinkan translation of the Gospels of St. Matthew and St. John in the 1640s and 1650s. Utilizing both Dutch and Siriyan, these works became important not only for the Dutch missionary effort but also for later British Protestant missions in the nineteenth and twentieth centuries.[69]

In Ceylon, translation projects in Tamil and Sinhalese circulated primarily in manuscript form for the first several decades, and most materials did not get published until the early eighteenth century. Until that time and even thereafter, Dutch clergy often conceded the pervasiveness of Portuguese and simply used the language of their Catholic forebears.[70] Philip Baldaeus, self-taught in Sinhalese and Tamil, compiled grammars in both languages, in 1658 and 1671 respectively. He also managed to publish a work in Tamil that included the Lord's Prayer, Apostles Creed, catechism, and several prayers, and completed, along with Adriaan de Meij, a translation of St. Matthew in manuscript form.[71] De Meij eventually turned out a New Testament in Tamil, which became important for later translators seeking to construct an authorized version. Simon Cat and Johannes Ruël, both heavily involved in the seminary at Colombo, translated materials into Sinhalese for the native students. Cat collaborated with local linguists to translate portions of the Bible and other materials in Tamil, which were published later in the eighteenth century.[72] He also produced a catechism in Sinhalese. Ruël composed sermons in Sinhalese and published the first grammar of the language in 1700, *Grammar or Singhalese Linguistics* (*Grammatica of Singaleesche taal-kunst*), which became the standard language reference until the nineteenth century. Published and manuscript versions of catechisms, grammars, dictionaries, and sermon collections circulated across Ceylon and the southern coasts of India.[73]

A conflict emerged between Cat and Ruël in the late 1690s that illustrates the complex personal and linguistic engagements that often roiled the mission. Cat and Ruël spearheaded the effort in the Sinhalese language in the seminary at Colombo, and both played integral roles in the seminary and in the production of translations. Cat had served in Ceylon for thirty years and was dean of the very small pastoral corps on the island. His linguistic work led him to theorize extensively about language. As discussed previously, he expounded on the theories of Johannes Goropius, who argued for the antiquity of the Dutch language. Prolix with quill and ink, Cat conjectured widely on the relationship between languages and pondered the cultural embeddedness of morphology and semantics. Ruël's star rose shortly after his arrival in Colombo, and he achieved recognition as the most able European linguist in Sinhalese. He served as rector of the seminary from 1697 until his death in 1701.[74]

The men's dispute erupted shortly after Ruël stepped up as rector, when each criticized the other's translation work. Neither took the critique very well. Given both ministers' involvement in the seminary and in language work, it seems likely that personal rivalry also came into play, at least on the part of Cat, who documented his complaints thoroughly in church records. The episode blew up when

Ruël found a number of errors in Cat's catechism and prayers, even claiming that his work was beyond saving simply by revision. So the new rector set out to substantially revise and retranslate the catechism and prayers. Shortly thereafter, in October and November 1697, Cat drafted a repudiation of Ruël's work and went before the consistory in Colombo to have it removed from use. Whereas Ruël had simply pointed out Cat's errors, Cat argued that Ruël's entire approach to translation was off base and that his work did not communicate a sense of true meaning in Sinhalese.[75] The dispute encapsulated the differing modes of European language work that shaped Dutch translation experiences overseas.

Four years earlier, when he was working in both Tamil and Sinhalese, Cat had written a lengthy exposé on the proper approach to translation from a European to a Ceylonese language. The primary task for translation, he maintained, was to convey meaning in the "sense of the language." With this phrase, which he used repeatedly, he referred to the humanist translation principle *ad sensum*, which gained favor in Europe at the end of the sixteenth century. Humanists, champions of rhetoric, fiercely attacked the literalistic (*ad verbum*) translation dogma, which had prevailed in the Middle Ages.[76] Cat called on the humanist ideal of rendering texts according to their general meaning to support his approach. The problem, as he defined it, was that translators employed synonymous vocabulary from one language into another, but often the translated words were removed from the circuit of meaning and style in one language and placed into another communicative system with very different linkages of meaning and style. He reiterated this approach to the consistory, maintaining that Ruël's catechism and prayers conveyed a "mistaken and bad sense" of Reformed doctrine owing to improper translation.[77]

Ruël's pitfall, according to Cat, was that he did not rely on a "good reliable" Dutch translation of the catechism from the Latin. This charge, again, seems to follow from his previous claim that translators needed to absorb inherent meaning of a text in order to render its essence into another vernacular. In the 1693 exposé, he made an analogy to the translation of the Bible into European vernaculars during the Reformation. "Our old Dutch translation," he reminded readers, came from the high German Bible of Martin Luther, who believed in the truth of scripture and understood the path to salvation. Though littered with "many mistakes," the Dutch translation was used in Reformed churches across the Netherlands until a team of translators produced an authoritative and accurate version in the 1637 States Bible. Yet because the translators grasped the true spirit of the language and the word of God, they brought the word of salvation and light of the gospel—the true meaning of scripture—to the Dutch people. Conversely, the revisions to the Vulgate were undertaken by "unbelievers"—

Catholic translators who lacked the illumination of Protestant linguists to comprehend the authentic purpose of scripture. Thus, they manufactured versions that kept people in "the darkness of popedom." For Cat, translators had to be embedded in the culture and the semantic aspirations of the text to convey "an essential sense in the [local] manner of speaking."[78]

Ruël did not respond to Cat's theories, at least in the extant church correspondence, but simply requested that the consistory submit his catechism to a committee of native linguists who could judge the quality of his work. The consistory held a number of meetings, conferred with the governor Gerrit de Heere and his office, and recommended that an examining committee be formed. On November 2, the governor appointed the ministers Isaack van der Banck, Rudolph Meerland, and Johannes Berghuijsen, the VOC officers Abraham Venie and Gregorius de Costa, and unnamed native linguists, and charged them with this task.[79] The committee examined Ruël's catechism and Cat's detailed critique, then invited both *predikanten* (separately) to defend their views. After reading the materials, interviewing Cat and Ruël, and deliberating among themselves, the committee upheld Ruël's translation on every point. Cat complained vehemently about the decision and charged that the native linguists were cowed by Ruël, a lament that the consistory rejected.[80] Shortly thereafter, the consistory and governor de Heere demanded that Cat show remorse for his unsubstantiated allegations, promise not to speak or write about the issue again, and bundle up all his "papers" and submit them to the Amsterdam classis and Batavia consistory.[81] Both missionary linguists died soon afterward, Ruël in 1701 and Cat in 1704.

Although Cat lost his case in whole, the episode nevertheless suggests how assumptions about language and translation could become wrapped up in personal animosity, perhaps heightened by the intense experience of living abroad. Humanistic assumptions about the historical and social contingencies of semantics and aesthetics overlapped with the Protestant preoccupation with inflecting languages as closely to an orthodox understanding of religious truth as possible.

The translation work of Cat and Ruël stimulated the publication of scripture and catechetical materials in Ceylon in the early 1700s. The establishment of the first printing press in Ceylon in 1737 by the governor G. W. Baron van Imhoff was a major technological development.[82] Not only allowing for the printing of religious materials, it also inspired translation activity on sections of the Bible. Shortly after the press became operational, the Colombo consistory, with the approval of van Imhoff, appointed a team to create published Sinhalese translations of the Gospels, as well as catechisms and prayers from manuscript copies.[83] Two years later, the consistory approved the translation of St. John and the other three Gospels for use in Sinhalese vernacular schools. Other *predikanten*, such as J. P. Wetzelius and Willem Konijn, constructed catechisms focusing on biblical history and theology intended for children, adult catechumens, and more advanced students in the seminaries. In 1739, Wetzelius and Konijn finalized a revised version of the Gospels in Sinhalese, and thirteen years later the consistory authorized a new edition of Cat's dictionary, with some emendations.[84]

The church sought to increase accessibility to scripture and Reformed teachings in Tamil as well. Bartholomeus Ziegenbalq, a Lutheran pastor at the Danish colony of Tranquebar on the Coromandel coast translated the first Bible into Tamil by 1714. At the instigation of governor van Imhoff in 1740, the minister Adolf Kramer and later J. P. Wetzelius, along with native linguists, set out to prepare an authorized Reformed edition of a Tamil New Testament utilizing the Ziegenbalq work, the older version by Adriaan de Meij, and Baldaeus's translation of St. Matthew.[85] Calvinists found fault with the Ziegenbalq work because of a perceived Lutheran outlook informing the translation, nor did they consider it linguistically sophisticated.[86] The project progressed fitfully for almost a dozen years before the consistory assigned Philip de Melho, a native Tamil speaker, to collaborate with native proponents and bring an entire New Testament to fruition.[87] De Melho devoted a substantial amount of time and energy to the translation, and he also worked on the Heidelberg Catechism, which was eventually finished by S. A. Bronsveld in May 1753 and published in the following year.[88] Throughout the 1750s, the Colombo consistory worked at producing new translations or revising previous ones for sermons, portions of the Bible, catechisms, and other educational materials.[89]

Led by de Melho and native proponents, the translation of a Tamil New Testament proceeded in earnest. On September 30, 1755, the *Politieke Raad* for Ceylon authorized translation work that would lead to a completed New Testament.[90] Henceforth de Melho, as he moved through the remaining books of the New Testament, periodically submitted his additional work piecemeal for revision by a committee that including the ministers Bronsveld, F. Janszoon, P. de Silva, and J. J. Fybrands. Once changes were made and the text approved, the consistory and the *Politieke Raad* rendered their judgment and ultimate endorsement. After all the approvals, the printers published the additional material as offprints to supplement the previously translated sections.[91] De Melho completed the Tamil translation of the New Testament in 1756, and it was published three years later.[92]

During Dutch rule in the seventeenth century, Brazil served as a counterpoint to the efforts in Asia to envelop the Calvinist message in local vernacular languages. Portuguese remained the translanguage in Brazil that connected all the disparate ethno-linguistic groups, from Portuguese and creoles, to Luso-Brazilians and Luso-Africans, Tupi and Africans. Dutch ministers largely relied on Portuguese and Spanish to reach the diverse, multiethnic groups across the colony. Some *predikanten* had facility in these languages, as well as French, but not all did. The WIC purchased Spanish and Portuguese editions of the Bible, the Psalms, the Heidelberg Catechism, and a range of educational and polemical texts. A handful of *predikanten* attempted to learn Tupian, but most relied on Portuguese, Spanish, and native translators. In 1637 and 1638, ministers in Recife tried to create separate boarding schools for Tupi children and adults, with instruction in Tupian and Dutch, but the natives demonstrated little enthusiasm for the arrangement and the plan was quickly abandoned.[93] David à Dorselaer produced a Heidelberg Catechism in Portuguese, Tupian, and Dutch in the early 1640s, though it was not published. Johannes Apricius, a teacher, *ziekentrooster*, and minister in Brazil from 1644 to 1654, completed a dictionary and worked on a new edition of the Heidelberg Catechism.[94] Purchasing published translations from Europe, the WIC shipped Portuguese and Spanish Bibles beginning in the 1630s. Unlike other areas of Dutch missionary activity, these translated portions of scripture did not come from local ministers on the ground.[95]

A TWO-TIERED APPROACH

Across the empire, company initiatives to promote Dutch widely among local populations, governors, *predikanten*, and teachers faltered. In Brazil, a structured program of training Brazilians, Africans, or Portuguese criollos never got underway. In 1625 the WIC trained six young men from the Potiguara tribe in Dutch in the Netherlands and made use of them as translators in the 1630s.[96] But this effort remained an isolated episode in Brazil. Despite more sustained initiatives in Asia, governors, ministers, and schoolmasters were ultimately unable to instill Dutch in religious and educational instruction, much less in routine discourse. Though the circumstances varied according to VOC settlement, a two-tiered general pattern prevailed throughout the East Indies, Formosa, and Ceylon. Consistories appropriated a local vernacular, along with Portuguese for a wide indigenous and creole audience, extending training in Dutch only for a small number of local young men who wished to undertake administrative and church work as schoolmasters, linguists, *ziekentroosteren*, or proponents.

In the East Indies, governor generals periodically followed van Diemen's Dutch-only policy by issuing proclamations to support the colonizer's language and to suppress that of their European rivals. Joan Maetsuijcker claimed in

1674 to have supported the spread of Dutch, though he admitted it had been in vain. He attributed the failure to Dutch inhabitants themselves, who "consider it such a mark of prestige to be able to speak a foreign language."[97] While there is likely a grain of truth to his lament, the most substantial force behind linguistic dominance was the migration of the Portuguese-speaking Mardijkers from South Asia and Melaka.[98] Despite Maetsuijcker's commitment to Dutch, an overwhelming percentage of the population in Batavia used either Portuguese or Malay as their primary language.[99] Although teachers continued to employ Malay in schools throughout the East Indies, it underwent a decline in use in church services in Batavia. Between 1662 and 1669, Batavia did not have even one Malay-speaking minister among its pastoral corps.[100] As the leading entrepôt for slave labor shifted to Makassar in the 1660s, Malay did reemerge as a primary language for worship. Nevertheless, not all Dutch ministers acquired the language after the mid-seventeenth century. From the 1670s until almost the end of VOC rule in the East Indies, governor generals, notably Rijklof van Goens (1678–1681), Johannes Camphuis (1684–1691), and Reinier de Klerk (1777–1780), reiterated a Dutch-only policy in schools, though largely with little effect.[101]

One important reason these linguistic aspirations failed in the East Indies and throughout the empire was that Reformed consistories readily accepted the ubiquity of Portuguese and gradually constructed regional languages out of local vernaculars. Ministers reasoned that the best means to reach local people was by using a language that they already spoke, or one close to it. In Batavia, the consistory made use of Mardijkers as catechists throughout Portuguese-speaking neighborhoods in the city. Malay- and Dutch-speaking instructors gave catechism lessons, but Portuguese dominated, at least until the eighteenth century when a Malay vernacular began to close the gap with Portuguese. In a 1706 list of 4,873 catechumens, 4,440 took instruction in Portuguese, 323 in Malay, and 110 in Dutch. In the more than two hundred churches across Java, Sumatra, Sulawesi, and the Moluccas, Malay and Portuguese remained the primary languages in churches and schools. In Batavia at the end of the seventeenth century, church services in Portuguese and Malay were held twice a week, but only once in Dutch.[102] Schools continued to teach Dutch until they fell into decline in the eighteenth century.

Portuguese and Malay served as the vernaculars of the masses, while Dutch remained the language of the elite in the East Indies. For the mission, consistories identified young men who appeared promising as teachers, *ziekentroosteren*, and perhaps even *predikanten*. Supported by the VOC, consistories established seminaries for these young men. One, the *Seminarium Theologicum*, opened in

Batavia in 1745 and lasted until 1755, when governor general Jacob Mossel closed its doors for financial reasons. Although Portuguese and Malay were allowed, the primary courses of study were in Dutch and Latin, the most fundamental linguistic means to impart the mysteries of the Reformed faith.[103]

The most expansive dual language strategy in the Dutch empire was embarked on, by the VOC and the church in partnership, in Formosa. In the 1640s, the consistory and colonial government, with the encouragement of van Diemen in Batavia, initiated a Dutch language policy to overcome the linguistic diversity that hampered missionary work and administrative centralization. This project reversed the trend of proselytizing and preaching in vernaculars, with an emphasis on Sinkan in the region around Tayouan carried out by the first generation of *predikanten* in the 1620s and 1630s. The consistory in Tayouan expressed optimism about the success of Dutch, especially among children, since *predikanten* perceived that Formosans had better memories and linguistic facilities than natives in the Moluccas and Java. In February 1648 governor Pieter Overtwater, determining that Dutch would be the language of instruction in schools, provided for grammars, catechisms, and prayer books. Yet the Dutch program did not push out the missionary drive to develop portions of the Bible, catechisms, and grammars in Sinkan and Favorlang, but actually complemented instruction in schools. The Sinkan gospels translated by Happart, Gravius, and Hambroek, the Favorlang catechism of Vertrecht, and a Dutch/Sinkan Heidelberg Catechism in 1650 allowed ministers, native linguists, and students to go back and forth between languages.[104]

The language policy became embroiled in personal conflicts between the governor Nicholas Verburg and the clergy who complained about one another to the governor general in Batavia. The ministers in Batavia also did not appreciate the independent streak of the Tayouan consistory, which appointed its own minister in 1651. Verburg was highly critical of the missionary tactics of the clergy and poor teaching in the schools. He did not explicitly single out Dutch language instruction as a culprit, but he did extol the methods of Junius in the 1630s, who worked in Sinkan and localized Christian teachings. By contrast, the contemporary crop of ministers gave emphasis to doctrinal precision at the expense of student accessibility.[105] The *predikanten* themselves, according to the Formosan *Politieke Raad* in November 1656, remained uncertain about language preference, "some being desirous of employing the Dutch, others the Formosan language."[106] Several months later, the ministers remained divided, but proposed the following February a bilingual policy. Adults would be taught in their native language, and children would learn Dutch but continue to recite prayers in their own tongue. Further, in the villages of Sinkan, Soulang, and Mattauw the government would set up colleges to teach young, native men Dutch and theology. In that way, the Formosans would be fulfilling the prophecy of Isaiah 66: 21: "out of the converted heathen, I will take some for priests and Levites, that is preachers and teachers of the holy gospel."[107] This principle formed the basis of a dual language policy. It took several years, but a seminary did open in Soulang in 1659. Schoolchildren received a religious and language education in Sinkan in the morning and Dutch in the afternoon.[108] The arrangement lasted only three years until the Chinese invasion in 1662. As Dutch clergy were departing the island ahead of the invading forces, an entry in the day register at Fort Zeelandia noted bitterly that local people "are delighted that they are now freed from attending the schools. Everywhere they have destroyed the books and utensils. . . ."[109]

In Ceylon, the Dutch language ambitions for the native people that governor Rijklof van Goens embraced and that Philip Baldaeus dismissed in the 1660s never materialized. The pervasiveness of Portuguese and the dearth of Dutch-language instructors rendered the project unrealistic. Nevertheless, the seminary in Colombo—established in 1696, temporarily closed from 1698 to 1704—developed into a center for theological and linguistic training until the end of Dutch rule in Ceylon in 1797.[110] From 1704 until 1760, at least 130 Sinhalese, Tamil, and mestizo students "from the most honorable castes" trained in Dutch, Portuguese, and Reformed theology at Colombo. Beginning in the late 1730s, the VOC sent the two best students each year to the Netherlands to complete their studies, and over the course of this period a handful of students passed proponent exams. Others who completed their studies worked as schoolmasters or took positions with the company.[111] The overriding purpose was to have local young men present the gospel to local people in local languages, offering an indigenous image of Calvinism to native peoples. As the Colombo consistory explained to the Walcheren classis in December 1712, teachers would be able to teach "the fundamentals of the Christian religion through Christianizing and catechizing."[112] A scribe went on to note in the following year that the seminary had just dispatched graduates to the Malabar and Coromandel coasts because of their training and their ability to speak Tamil.[113] In the last decades of the seminary, it functioned exclusively to train native schoolmasters.[114]

The intermittent commitment to vernacular communication and to a Dutch lingua franca resulted in a layered linguistic structure in VOC territories in the eighteenth century. For native teachers, proponents, and other church workers close to the heart of the Calvinist mission, Dutch held the place of prominence, whereas Portuguese, Malay, Sinkan, Tamil, and Sinhalese variously functioned as popular linguistic media.[115] The seminaries in Nallur and Colombo educated top-tier native young men, skilled in Tamil or Sinhalese, in Dutch, and in Reformed theology, to serve as teachers in the school system, as ministers, and as lay workers in congregations. The Nallur seminary persisted until 1723, and the Sinhalese until 1797. Seminary graduates served as teachers in either Dutch- or indigenous-language schools.

TRANSLATION PRINCIPLES IN CONFLICT: TWO CASES

Thus far this chapter has shown that the trading companies and ministers wavered between promoting Dutch language acquisition, acceding to the prevalence of Portuguese, and constructing a standard vernacular translanguage from the various local dialects. These approaches were often in conflict with one another, as the need to convey the gospel in languages people could understand ran against company ambitions of inculcating political loyalty against their Portuguese rivals. When *predikanten* settled on a vernacular strategy by the end of the seventeenth century, they struggled with the difficulty of producing a standardized linguistic medium that accommodated the evangelical goal of conversion with a need for theological uniformity and depth. While a countless number of disagreements arose, two quite acrimonious debates caught the attention of imperial and ecclesiastical parties across the Dutch empire. For the present study, they cast a revealing light on Dutch and local language cultures during a period of heightened linguistic encounter.

LOCAL ASSIMILATION VS. UNIVERSAL TRUTH IN THE SINKAN CATECHISM

The unease between assimilating Christian teaching as it came out of Reformation Europe into decidedly different cultures and retaining orthodox doctrinal standards plagued all missionary initiatives in the early modern period. In Dutch operations, deep uncertainties about the conditions for baptism and admitting non-Europeans to communion accompanied missionary and pastoral activity throughout this time. Since religious truth was embedded in language, this tension also surfaced in the translation of educational materials that summarized doctrinal tenets. Theological precision reigned. The Amsterdam classis, for example, rejected a summary of doctrine in Spanish in 1637 by Vincent Soler because it contained unspecified errors.[116] One hundred years later, J. P. Wetzelius in Colombo recommended inserting "Jehovah" in the Lord's Prayer, but his consistorial colleagues would only approve it if an explanatory note were added that "the word 'Jehovah' is God's remembrance name of old and it cannot be suitably translated by a corresponding word in other languages."[117] One of the most controversial disputes, and one that highlights the intersection of language and truth, occurred in Formosa between 1646 and 1652, pitting the celebrated overseas minister Robert Junius against his more prosaic successors in the Tayouan consistory.

Beginning in the late 1620s, as we have seen, Junius and George Candidius preached, instructed, and set up schools in the villages to the north and west of Tayouan. As part of their Protestant instincts to vernacularize the Christian message, they developed lexicons and written aids in the 1630s, and Junius created a Shorter Catechism, then a longer version, as well as a Formulary that contained prayers, the Ten Commandments, and Articles of Faith. He also produced three published sermons all in the Sinkan vernacular. Junius utilized these texts in educating new and potential converts, focusing on memorization, the standard European pedagogy. As students successfully repeated the correct answers to questions from the Shorter Catechism, along with the Ten Commandments and Articles of Faith, Junius judged them sufficiently informed in the faith to warrant baptism. He reported remarkable progress in spreading the gospel in the villages around Tayouan, and by 1643, when he departed for the Netherlands, the missions there seemed to hold great promise.[118] He returned home to much acclaim in Reformed ecclesiastical circles, took a pastoral position in Delft, and cast himself as an expert on missions and the Sinkan language.

The approach Junius took in translating the Reformed faith into Sinkan sought to root teachings within people's local experiences and observances that reflected universal principles. In trying to explain the transgression of Adam and Eve in the Garden of Eden, Junius drastically changed the setting in his Formulary. "Question 47: In what way did Adam and Eve transgress God's word? Answer: They ate from the apples in the midst of the field. Question 48: Was it a great sin that they ate of the apples and fruit in the midst of the field? Answer: Yes, for God said, 'Those fruits are mine, [but you may] eat freely of the fruits growing on the borders of the field.'" He rendered the prohibition against murder in the Ten Commandments as "Thou shalt not murder another man and abort children," taking aim at headhunting and compulsory abortion. The Shorter Catechism presented hell as a "pit beneath the earth" populated by biting centipedes and snakes.[119] These represent some of the most explicit examples of assimilation, but throughout his published work Junius relied on vivid, local images that were immediately familiar to Formosans.

Ongoing efforts to standardize a vernacular in Formosa led the Tayouan consistory in 1646, three years after Junius's departure, to decide on revising his texts. Johannes Happart and Johannes Bavius took on the task that summer. Digging into Junius's works, they determined that his catechism "was so ill chosen and the order followed was so unsuitable, that it was impossible to improve it. . . . [I]n its present form, the catechism was not fit to be used as a Christian formulary in the schools of Formosa."[120] The consistory assigned Simon van Breen to devise a new catechism.

The criticism of Junius's catechism became thickly ensnared in a personal dispute between him and Happart, Bavius, and van Breen. Happart had written to a colleague in Batavia in October 1645 regretting Junius's departure and fearing the missions would "fall into decay."[121] Yet over the next several years the Tayouan ministers experienced a falling out with Junius as word began to trickle out in correspondence from the Netherlands that Junius had criticized the state of mission work in Formosa to the *Heren XVII*, complaining about the lack of energy among the other ministers.[122] Incensed, Happart and Bavius responded at length on November 3, 1648, with substantial countercharges against Junius's ostensible missionary successes and his moral character.[123] Junius appeared before the Amsterdam classis in September 1649 to answer these charges and explain to the ministers "how he tried to convert the blind heathen." His colleagues in the Netherlands assured him that they held him in high regard and advised him to put the matter behind him.[124]

The classis regarded the Tayouan ministers as overly sensitive and personally vengeful, jealous of an exceptionally able and pious brother. The delegates in the Netherlands expressed repugnance at Happart, van Breen, and Bavius for slandering the honor and industry of such a committed pastor to the Formosans, and accused van Breen of scheming for authority over the villages of Sinkan, Bakloan, and Tavakan, even though he had admitted earlier that "he could not write a word of the language himself without assistance."[125] In turn, van Breen and Happart cast the classis representatives as badly informed dupes of a grandstanding cleric who criticized his brothers to brandish his own inflated accomplishments. Over the course of four years, the ministers in Tayouan and the delegates for overseas affairs from the Amsterdam classis exchanged several letters disputing Junius's missionary work and the condition of Formosan Christianity. Eventually by 1652, Junius and the Formosan ministers agreed to allow the rancor to "pass into oblivion."[126]

Even though high-octane animosity fueled the exchanges, the linguistic dispute nevertheless involved defining the boundaries between assimilation and orthodoxy. The first charge lodged against Junius was that his linguistic skill in Sinkan was "slovenly" to such an extent that "no meaning can be attached to his words." They cited a consistent mistranslation that conflated prayer with confession, and noted that he rendered "Hallowed be thy name" in the Lord's Prayer to "We praise thy name."[127] They concluded that "we are quite sure that

Mr. Junius is not sufficiently acquainted with the elements of the Sinkan language."[128]

The second criticism by the Formosan ministers singled out Junius's adaptation of Christian teaching to engage local customs and practices. In the November 3, 1648, letter to Amsterdam, they objected that Junius in his sermons denounced "the customs and manners of the heathens without expounding the principles of Christianity."[129] From their point of view, Junius sacrificed comprehension of Christian truth on the altar of moral propriety. Certainly, all Dutch clergy found practices such as headhunting, animal sacrifices, uninhibited sexuality, and abortion as reprehensible evils that had to be extinguished. But here the Tayouan *predikanten* protested that he had subverted the gospel message by neglecting universal doctrines, thereby reducing Christianity to a set of social values. This emphasis on cultural assimilation left converts and students ignorant about the faith. Previously, in March 1646, when the ministers were initially deliberating how to emend Junius's Shorter Catechism, they identified a basic problem, namely that "knowledge [ought to be] joined to virtue," so that "godliness [may] be inculcated in the hearts of the inhabitants."[130] The proper course, according to van Breen and Happart, was first to implant knowledge of Christianity, and then "virtue" (i.e., moral decorum) would ensue. And that Christian knowledge was the orthodox Calvinist one contained in the Dutch Confession of Faith and Heidelberg Catechism. Consequently, the Tayouan ministers believed that Junius erred egregiously as both a translator and a preacher when he represented the sixth commandment in an applied Formosan context—as thou shalt not "murder another man" (headhunt) and "abort children." To remedy these acculturated translations, van Breen and Happart scrapped Junius's work and started over using the Heidelberg Catechism as the textual model for a new Sinkan catechism and formulary.[131] Whereas Junius worked directly with Sinkan himself, the other ministers started with the Dutch documents and collaborated with Formosan linguists to translate the materials into Sinkan.[132]

The Amsterdam classis to which Junius had defended himself in 1648 sided with him. The classis delegates argued in a November 1648 letter to Tayouan that it was necessary for pioneering ministers, such as Junius and Candidius, "to regulate their acts according to the age, time, and capacities of these simple and benighted people. It is by degrees that we attain the greater perfection; and the work itself that has been done by Mr. Junius testifies to its not having been done in vain."[133] The Amsterdam delegates viewed the Tayouan consistory's current attention to universal doctrine as necessarily built on the initial successes of assimilation established by Junius. It is likely that this generous view of accommodation aimed at conciliation between all the ministers and mollification of a highly regarded *predikant.*

Emphasizing the need to privilege local settings, governor Verburg also articulated the case for local assimilation. For Verburg, an emphasis on theological purity in a missionary setting like Formosa would always be misguided. He defended Junius's assimilationist approach and condemned his orthodox critics. In 1654, he reported to Maetsuijcker in Batavia that "zealous and pious clergymen began the good work of converting the heathen here, but considering the capacity of their scholars [indigenous schoolmasters], they embodied the fundamental principles of Christianity in a catechism, which was very easy to understand. Their successors, however, flying above the lowly things beneath them, and unwilling to continue building on a foundation laid by others, have done away with this catechism and have introduced new and higher things; so that many a scholar has become bewildered, and many have gone backward."[134] Despite Verburg's grievance, the orthodox approach won out and supplanted an assimilationist strategy in Formosa, which proved to be the general pattern among Calvinist missions in the early modern Dutch empire.

SEARCHING HIGH AND LOW FOR A MALAY TRANSLATION OF THE BIBLE

The most protracted and bitter dispute involving a translation took place in the early eighteenth century over the production of a Malay Bible. The debates over a High or Low Malay translation of the Bible were the imperial refractions of long-standing Renaissance and Reformation translation debates, which had real political and theological consequences in both Europe and Asia. Since the early 1600s, missionary and lay translators had labored to put catechisms, prayers, sermons, and New Testament texts into a standardized Malay vernacular. This translation work attempted to homogenize the diffuse forms of spoken and written Malay that circulated across the East Indies and interacted with local indigenous languages. Dutch schools, which utilized Malay as a primary language of instruction especially in the eighteenth century, helped to facilitate its strength as a common regional vernacular.[135] Other distinct forms of Malay cohabited and overlapped in the linguistic landscape. Referred to as Johor-Malay or Riau-Malay, a stylized literary form of Malay was cultivated at the court of Johor and prevalent in erudite Muslim circles in Melaka. A language of intellectuals, "High Malay," as the Dutch called it, did not filter down to the everyday discourse of common people. Contemporaries distinguished it from "Low" or "Bazaar" Malay, which emerged as a heterogeneous and improvised oral patois used for trade and practical purposes. It was a pidgin variety that derived from the High and more standardized expressions of Malay.[136]

Dutch ministers had translated biblical texts into Indian Ocean languages since the early seventeenth century, and the appearance of a New Testament by the Batavian minister Daniel Brouwerius in 1668 marked an important juncture in the project to translate the entire Bible into Malay. Unfortunately, Brouwerius's translation was not well received either by the Batavian consistory, by other clergy in the region, or by the colonial government. According to a number of reports, Brouwerius either poorly translated or even embarrassingly mistranslated a number of passages, which rendered the text unusable. Apparently, he did not work from a consistent vernacular, but combined a number of dialects, some in Low Malay, which did not make sense to people from one region to another. Nor did he understand Malay syntax very well. A Portuguese convert to the Reformed faith, Brouwerius also used a number of Portuguese spellings. The results could be amusing. For example, he translated "saint" as "sakti" because it sounded like "sanctus," but the term actually means "sorcerer" in Malay. And the passage from Genesis 13:2 (RSV), "Abraham was very rich in livestock, in silver, and in gold," somehow came out as "Abraham was a very rich man because he was a beast."[137] Clearly, this translation would not work, especially for Dutch *predikanten* who were finely attuned to semantic nuances. Brouwerius's disappointing attempt at a Malay New Testament nevertheless spurred work on an authoritative translation of the Bible, an endeavor accomplished by Melchior Leijdekker, with assistance from Petrus van der Vorm. Leijdekker began his translation work shortly after his arrival in Batavia in 1678 and worked on it until his death in 1701.[138]

Leijdekker, a theologian and physician from Zeeland, arrived in the East Indies in 1675. Serving first as a chaplain to the fleet commanded by the VOC admiral Cornelis Speelman, he received a call to service in Batavia three years later. There, he immersed himself in the written literary expression of Malay.[139] Because he had earned wide respect as a linguist and because of his ongoing labor on a Malay Bible, the Batavian consistory endorsed his efforts by granting him its authorization in 1691, and a year later gave him a reprieve from his pastoral duties to expedite this work. Setting himself on the task, Leijdekker chose High Malay in part because he believed it possessed the linguistic depth to convey divine truth with proper elegance and in part because Dutch Calvinists hoped to use scripture to convert Islamic elites. By November 1700, Leijdekker had worked all the way through the Old Testament and the Gospels, and was well into the Pauline epistles when he became seriously ill. He died the following March, having reached Ephesians chapter 6. After his death, his Batavian colleagues called on Petrus van der Vorm, also a highly respected scholar of oriental languages, to complete Leijdekker's work. Van der Vorm, who had served as a minister in the East Indies since 1689, picked up where his predecessor had left off in Ephesians. He finished the translation in 1701.[140]

In the late 1680s a minister in Amboina, Francois Valentijn, challenging the value of a High Malay translation, began working on his own version of the Bible in Low Malay. In the autumn of 1694, Valentijn appeared before the Amboina consistory and received its official authorization to undertake a translation. In September, the Amboina consistory notified the Batavia ministers that this work was in progress.[141] Shortly thereafter, Valentijn returned to the Netherlands, arriving in August 1695. Fifteen months later, Valentijn solicited support from the synods of North Holland and South Holland, along with classes of Amsterdam and Walcheren, for his Low Malay translation with the *Heren XVII*. He was, he said, preparing a Bible in the common language used and understood by the people of the East Indies. The Dutch delegates in these districts felt compelled to back a project to make scripture accessible to as many people as possible and the ministers gave their approval.[142] The Walcheren classis expressed support for Valentijn's cause, yet thought wider deliberation was in order.[143] These ministers actually reiterated the need to train people in the Dutch language because of the linguistic prerogatives of imperialists, observing that "when Greeks, Romans, and Franks conquered, they implemented their language."[144]

Yet vernacularization was a fundamental Protestant linguistic principle in Europe and around the world. *Predikanten* in the field, from Baldaeus to Junius to Ruël, had promoted the cultivation of vernacular language and willingly resorted to Portuguese (and Spanish in Brazil) to reach native Christians and prospective converts. Rendering the gospel in the vernacular of the people perfectly animated the missionary language commitments of Dutch Calvinists. Throughout Protestant Europe, translators of the Bible sought to find and construct a vernacular as universal and accessible as possible. Peter Burke has pointed out that Martin Luther avoided translating the German Bible into his own Saxon tongue, but rather tried to find a "kind of koine that drew on different dialects."[145] Dutch Calvinists also strove to fashion a common language in the fullest measure, mixing idioms and vocabularies from Brabant and Holland. The States Bible of 1637 was the product of a translation commission whose delegates hailed from different linguistic regions of the country.[146] The implicit analogies to the struggle against Catholic scholasticism that kept scripture imprisoned in a language unknown to most Europeans clearly resonated with the ministers and theologians in these ecclesiastical bodies. According to Valentijn's application of the Protestant-oriented language culture, High Malay signified Latin and linguistic obscurity, whereas Low Malay connoted the word of God in the vernacular of the people.

When the Batavia consistory heard the news of the Dutch delegates' decision to support the Valentijn project, the brothers were outraged that fellow *predikanten* half a world away with no expertise in Malay would presume to intervene. The ministers Augustin Thornton and Melchior Leijdekker himself wrote on behalf of the consistory in November 1697 to the synod of North Holland, "[W]e wish you had been pleased to consult with us in this weighty matter because we here understand the Malay language better than those in Holland." The ministers and elders in Batavia both criticized Valentijn's reliability as a translator and rejected Low Malay as an appropriate linguistic medium for the Bible. They noted that translation work should be done carefully, collaboratively, and slowly, with significant time allowed to complete, correct, and revise. Flawed translations, such as Heurnius's version of the Gospels and Brouwerius's rendition of the New Testament, stemmed from hasty and sloppy work. It seemed highly unusual, and thus suspect, for a minister to work on a translation in complete isolation, as Valentijn did.[147] The Batavian consistory was incredulous that Valentijn alleged to have picked up the language well enough to preach in three months and to translate the entire Bible in two years.[148] The consistory also raised doubts about the quality of Valentijn's Malay because of errors he made in his sermons. Ultimately, however, the Batavian brothers could not render a judgment because he refused to share the manuscript with them.[149] Regarding Valentijn as a charlatan, they accused him of misleading the ministers in Europe by playing on their Protestant evangelical aspirations.

Leijdekker and Thornton argued that Low Malay did not constitute a genuine language, but was akin to doggerel "monk Latin" and "street Portuguese" in Goa, Macau, and Ceylon. Low Malay, in their view, lacked a stable syntax, orthography, and standard grammar. As an informal oral medium, Low Malay was a mixture of common Malay, indigenous vernacular, and Portuguese expressions, and varied considerably from one area to the next. Valentijn's assertion, they contended, that Low Malay represented a national translanguage of the East Indies was just not true. Since the medium drew from so many diverse and often unidentifiable sources, it was not possible to translate words consistently. The Batavian ministers invoked Brouwerius, saying that his failure to locate the origin and etymology of words and his reliance on flimsy syntax rendered sections in his New Testament nonsensical. Valentijn, they suggested, was proceeding down the same path, much to the derision of Calvinism in the Indies.[150]

Valentijn responded to the criticisms of the Batavian consistory in a pamphlet, "Door of Truth" ("Deure der waarhijd"), published in Holland in 1698, in which he defended a Low Malay translation. Writing from Dordrecht, Valentijn attempted to answer the charges of Leijdekker, Thornton, and the Batavian consistory point by point. On Batavia's claim of prerogative to judge the quality of language, Valentijn assailed the ministers for both their presumption and their ignorance. Only one person on the consistory there, he alleged, actually understood common Malay, and no one had the theological learning to assess a Bible translation. Moreover, Leijdekker was one of but a handful of Christians throughout the region who could read High Malay.[151] On the other hand, he (Valentijn) often received compliments on his linguistic ability; people who heard him preach said that "no one has a clearer understanding of the Malay language" than he did.[152] The criticisms and quibbling about syntax and grammar, thus, had no basis, since only Leijdekker possessed the expertise to make linguistic judgments.

Leijdekker, according to Valentijn, was pursuing a humanistic philological preoccupation and not Christian mission. The Batavian *predikant* only wanted a High Malay version because "he cared more about learning the language than he did for Christendom learning the Christian religion."[153] Just as humanists in Europe adored classical Greek and Latin, the enthusiasts for High Malay studied it "only for their pleasure as an object of study, like a master who wishes to teach it to a prize student. But we are talking here about schoolchildren and the priority ought to be for them to understand the Word of God."[154] The Batavian ministers believed the High Malay vernacular to be closer to Semitic languages because it utilized a number of loan words from Arabic. Valentijn, however, did not yield an inch. If High Malay were such a fertile idiom, he asked, why had no one translated materials into it before Leijdekker? As for the consistory's criticism of Brouwerius, Valentijn admitted he had made mistakes, but at least his New Testament was in a vernacular people could understand. Leijdekker's insistence on purity of language would only put the word of God out of reach of most people.[155] Valentijn maintained that "throughout this land, [Batavia] wanted to compel people to learn a new language, High Malay, on the grounds that they would better understand our religion, to come hear sermons in church; a proposition which all people who do not have this type of motivation and who are more practical will certainly reject. They [the Batavian ministers] must recognize that this is the best means to get people who are not already staying away, to go away because what desire can someone have to hear preaching or the catechism in a language that he does not understand?"[156]

In reiterating the argument for Low Malay, Valentijn appropriated the Protestant principle of making scripture available to the common person. Valentijn echoed the case for vernacular languages that other ministers had made through the years, namely that preachers and teachers of the gospel ought to meet native Christians and prospective converts on their own vernacular turf rather than trying to compel entire populations to learn an unfamiliar language. Valentijn identified Low Malay as the way forward to preach "in the power of the spirit." Invoking St. Paul, he wrote that "the gospel should not be preached with human wisdom, but in the power of the Spirit. We believe not in human wisdom, but in God's power. Christ and the gospel are offensive to Jews and foolishness to Greeks."[157]

Valentijn was a controversial figure in his own day, and he is much more generally known to subsequent generations of historians, ethnographers, and orientalists than Leijdekker, largely because of his widely read *Old and New East Indies* (*Oud en Nieuw Oost-Indien*, 1724–1726). Valentijn came to the East Indies initially in 1686, serving in Amboina, other sites in the Moluccas, and briefly in Batavia before returning to the Netherlands in 1695. For ten years, he and his family lived in Dordrecht, where he was a minister. In 1705, he returned to the mission field in Batavia and Amboina until he repatriated a second and final time in 1713.[158] Yet Valentijn left himself vulnerable to the charge of acting in bad faith. He refused to share his translation with anyone and never mentioned any problems over syntax or semantics which translators inevitably encounter. Even the Amboina consistory refused to recommend Valentijn's translation because he would not let them inspect it.[159] Subsequently, historians have argued that his translated manuscript could have come from the work of Simon de Larges, a *ziekentrooster* in Amboina who died in 1677. According to the historian J. L. Swellengrebel, Valentijn came into possession of the translation through the death of a third party, Jacobus de Bois, in 1687. When Valentijn died himself in 1727, the manuscript disappeared.[160]

All the controversy over the two versions led the VOC to lock the High Malay translation of Leijdekker and van der Vorm away in a chest in the Batavian consistory chamber until a definitive decision could be reached. It remained there for twenty-two years.[161] The disagreement over language acquired the added venom of antagonistic church bodies, since the Batavian ministers were outraged at the Amsterdam classis and the Synod of North Holland for inserting themselves into a language dispute about which the ministers knew next to nothing. The consistories of Amboina and Batavia were also squaring off over the acrimonious "dividing the sacraments" controversy. The persistence of Valentijn, along with the ill feeling among church bodies, the painstaking pace of Reformed church deliberations, and the vast distances between the Netherlands and the East Indies, combined to stretch the process out for years. In 1723, the *Politieke Raad* in Batavia appointed a committee of four linguists to revise the

High Malay version, chaired by the Makassar *predikant* George Werndly. Consulting biblical texts in many different languages, the committee worked for five years to square the Leijdekker translation with a more standardized Malay. After much consideration and argument, the company published and distributed the revised version of Leijdekker and van der Vorm: the New Testament in 1731 and the entire Bible in 1733. The Werndly-Leijdekker Bible remained the standard Malay version until the twentieth century.[162]

For the purposes of this chapter, this dispute elucidates principles of translation that came into conflict in the linguistic crucible of the foreign mission field. The position on the utility and function of language that Valentijn and his colleagues in Amboina held vis-à-vis their brethren in Batavia derived from two distinct European perspectives. Those who promoted the High Malay version operated from a humanistic language culture that privileged written classical language cultivated by learned elites and promoted linguistic transfer through a formal educational structure. The Batavian consistory thus put forth a case for High Malay rooted in humanistic assumptions about language that had prevailed since the Renaissance. These ministers likened High Malay (sometimes referred to as classical Malay) to Greek or classical Latin, and Low Malay to a barbarian tongue. These ministers contended that Christianity had to be translated into a linguistic medium with semantic substance, which could function as a legitimate lingua franca, and that that would gain the respect of nonbelievers, especially Muslims.[163]

Conversely, the Low Malay stance of Valentijn relied on a language culture championed by Protestants to make religious truth accessible in the everyday discourse of a people or nation.[164] In Europe these ideologies overlapped extensively as mainline Protestants promoted study of classical languages while also seeking to bring the Bible into a vernacular common to most people. Both Batavia and Amboina cast their claims to a particular vernacular within those familiar and accepted European programs. But in the mission field, the competition between Valentijn in Amboina and Leijdekker in Batavia brought linguistic elegance and Protestant accessibility into competition with one another.

Leijdekker, van der Vorm, and their defenders also hoped their High Malay edition would appeal especially to Muslims. Leijdekker's translation reflected the distinctive Arab influence that pervaded literary circles in Johor and Melaka. Valentijn had criticized the High Malay version as being "half written in Arabic."[165] Van der Vorm corresponded with and made contributions to Adriaan Reland's *On the Religion of Mohammed*, known for its nonpartisan and detailed account of Islam. A chief worry with biblical translation by the Batavian consistory involved the reputation of Christian missions among Muslim literati in

Johor and Melaka. Additionally, after the Leijdekker translation was finally approved by the VOC, a very serious deliberation took place over what script the Bible should be written in. Many in Batavia argued for Arabic script so that Muslims might have a stronger inclination to read it.[166] The company, however, determined that the Bible would be published with Latin script. Thus, it stands to reason that Leijdekker and van der Vorm wanted to present scripture in as eloquent and persuasive linguistic medium as possible for Muslims.

Just as the Batavian consistory effectively identified the shortcomings of the Low Malay strategy, the Amboina brethren's criticisms of the Leijdekker translation also hit home. For most Malay-speaking people, the Leijdekker Bible was written in an abstruse, perplexing vernacular that they did not understand and ultimately did not care to learn. As Swellengrebel assessed the work, the Leijdekker translation was very difficult for Christians to understand. Part of the ambition of a High Malay version infused with Arabic words was to attract Muslims, but it also failed in that regard.[167] The quest for a standard vernacular proved elusive to Dutch Reformed clergy in the early modern period. Yet in terms of language use in the East Indies, the struggles of the Dutch ultimately produced a split between the formal, written language used by ministers and colonial authorities, on the one hand, and the fluctuating "low" varieties of oral discourse that took place on the ground, on the other.[168] Despite all the efforts the Dutch invested in schools, the educational structure that ministers and colonial authorities put in place could not overcome this divide.

As this episode demonstrates, European cultural assumptions about language did not work well in areas that did not share the same deep-seated inclinations. The attempt to translate the Bible became constructed in European disputes over European problems, problems that simply did not exist in Southeast Asia. The debate also reveals the considerable impact of indigenous societies on Europeans and their linguistic ambitions, compelling Dutch theologians and faculty in Europe to devoted study of oriental languages and cultures.

CONCLUSION

Ironically, the marks the Dutch left in the linguistic fields of the early modern world were vernacular footprints put down by ministers and native linguists. As a language of empire and missions, Dutch never really got off the ground in any VOC or WIC holdings, except at the Cape of Good Hope in the late eighteenth century. In the towns of Cape Town, Drakenstein, and Stellenbosch, Afrikaans began to emerge as a distinct language from the pidgin Dutch spoken among a growing population of European settlers. Generally, however, the territories of the

Dutch empire in the period of company rule were kept deliberately small, spatially diffuse, and sparsely populated with Dutch settlers, factors that counteracted a Dutch language policy. The VOC and WIC, in any case, supported such a policy only with ambivalence and inconsistency. The most potentially potent means for inculcating the Dutch language were the instruments of the Calvinist mission: schools, churches, and religious media. Yet the Protestant translation culture of vernacularizing the journey to salvation and sanctification stood at odds with the imperial project of promoting loyalty to the company through language and culture.

Dutch *predikanten* schooled in Protestant universities and formed in Calvinist intellectual circles absorbed the translation cultures of the Renaissance and Reformation. Steeped in a humanistic ethos, ministers set up schools that focused on transmitting Protestant principles in young minds through a literary education. Translators placed a premium on theological precision, which often sparked fierce, persistent, and acrimonious personal quarrels. In these schools and in their translation work, *predikanten* worked with native linguists to identify the relationship between a mother tongue and local idioms. This effort stemmed from their understanding of the relationship between Latin and national vernaculars. On every occasion except the conflict over High or Low Malay in Bible translation, missionary linguists opted for what they regarded as the vernacular of the people or "nation"—Sinkan in Formosa, Tamil and Sinhalese in Ceylon and South Asia. Often Portuguese stood in for a national vernacular. In pursuing this linguistic strategy, Dutch Calvinists operated in continuity with the Protestant translation culture of the Reformation that prized vernacular translation. In the Leijdekker-Valentijn debate, the humanist commitment to an elite classical form triumphed so that Calvinists could present scripture to Muslim elites in as compelling language as possible. The disputes over how to convert pagans and Moors, how to distinguish between religious demand and cultural adiaphora, and how to transmit the word of God across languages exerted far-reaching influences on Protestantism in Europe.

5

IDENTITY AND OTHERNESS IN THE REPUBLIC AND THE MISSIONS

Jacob Haafner, an enlightened ethnographer and a critic of Dutch missions, catalogued in an 1806 essay the failures of pastors and preachers to reap the abundant harvest of souls that church leaders had once predicted. The reasons he gave sounded much like the accusations Protestants had hurled against Spanish and Catholic missions: imperial cruelty, clerical arrogance, and theological chicanery. Yet a fundamental reason Haafner dwelled upon, and one that was common among Calvinists, was that pagans could relate to Catholic missions because of the external nature of their worship practices, with the array of rites, images, and objects; Calvinists, on the other hand, overburdened locals with disciplinary "rigor . . . no small impediment for the spreading of the Gospel; they [missionaries] want to make these sons of Nature and Liberty into complete duds fit for nothing but singing and dancing; they deny them the use of all their customs and habits, even those that have no bearing on their so-called Christian religion at all; they want to make them live perfectly like the most scrupulous Christians."[1] Haafner's dichotomy between fussy Calvinist moralists and "the sons of nature and liberty" revealed a perceived sense of cultural incompatibility between Reformed Protestantism and indigenous societies beyond the Atlantic and Mediterranean.

By the late eighteenth century, Reformed church leaders overseas and in the Netherlands, too, possessed a more realistic, even pessimistic, appraisal about the prospects for instilling Calvinism in the colonies and outposts of the VOC than they did in the 1600s. Ministers had long conveyed an ample measure of distrust about the religious sincerity of many indigenous converts. But beginning in the 1720s and 1730s, a more constricted outlook about mission emerged in correspondence and in consistory records overseas. The *Indisch Sion* came to bear a more pastoral than missionary character, as consistories increasingly looked inward, shepherding their flocks, attending to administrative matters about baptism and marriage, and discussing the need for proselytizing initiatives without in fact doing much about them. Outside ecclesiastical circles, intellectuals were even pondering the very point of Christian missions. Haafner had drafted his treatise as an entry in an essay contest sponsored by the free-thinking Teylers Theological Society. The question posed by the directors was "What has been the use of missionary societies in the past two centuries and what can be expected of the activities of missionary societies in the future?"[2] Learned societies such as this one and the questions they posed helped create the impetus for launching new Protestant missionary enterprises in the late 1700s. These differed from the global Calvinism of the early modern period, as they came under the auspices of ecclesiastical structures, sought out independent financing, and emphasized emotion in religious life. The Dutch Missionary Society, modeled on the London Missionary Society, emerged in these circumstances in 1797.[3]

Throughout the two-hundred-year experience of missions within a commercial empire, Dutch Calvinists regularly reflected on their enterprise among unfamiliar societies and eccentric customs. The aspiration for a global Calvinism, the sustained interaction with native peoples, and the mystifying task of converting them manifested themselves in narratives that mission-minded writers constructed to make sense of the wider world. By the time Cornelis Houtman set sail for the Spice Islands in 1595, a broad Dutch audience had already scrutinized distant lands and populations from the well-known accounts by Bartolomé de las Casas, Francis Xavier, Jean de Léry, José de Acosta, and others. The outset of the Calvinist mission with its fluctuating fortunes prompted the Dutch to begin writing themselves about religious beliefs and practices in Asia, America, and Africa. A range of Dutch writers produced a voluminous literature on the lands and peoples of the world, just as artists and cartographers created visual depictions of newly globalized spatial dimensions.

An imperative for Protestant writers was to calibrate a biblical and humanist outlook with ongoing fluidities in the mission. From the 1620s to the 1720s, a number of Dutch Reformed theologians and ministers composed narratives in keeping with the prevailing sentiments in the mission. In the early days, Hugo Grotius, Godefridus Udemans, and Gerardus Vossius published influential volumes within quite different genres that attempted to provide globally minded Protestants with a hermeneutic for reading world religions and expressed confidence in the human capacity for religious conversion. As momentum in the mission seemed to stall in the 1650s, the overseas ministers Abraham Rogerius and

Philip Baldaeus and the academic theologians Gisbertus Voetius, Johannes Hoornbeeck, and Simon Oomius wrote detailed critiques of "heathenism," "Mohammedanism," and Judaism, not only to better equip overseas ministers but also to account for the difficulty of converting non-Christian peoples. They sought to expose the dark deceptions of priestly classes that twisted religious truth and misled benighted souls in much the same way that Catholic ecclesiastics betrayed Christians in Europe. Godefridus Carolinus, a minister in Barneveld and Harderwijk (both in the province of Gelderland), composed his own survey of contemporary "heathendom" following similar methodological lines, yet with a somewhat more optimistic assessment of pagan religions. Finally, in the early eighteenth century, Adriaan Reland, the orientalist at Utrecht, and Francois Valentijn, a *predikant* in Amboina, took an even more measured approach, especially toward Islam. They even seemed ready to concede the nearly impermeable power of culture in shaping religious belief and moral practice that had impressed Jacob Haafner eighty years later.[4]

This chapter maps the evolution of Calvinist narratives of religious identity and otherness as part of the ongoing need to reconcile a Protestant biblical paradigm with the hard realities of the world. The chapter draws from a body of Dutch Reformed writers across different genres to analyze shifting perspectives among intellectuals whose primary intent was to narrate the place of non-Christian religions in light of a Protestant vision of the world. Most of the Dutch travel accounts and ethnographic descriptions already studied by scholars were put to different purposes, and thus they fall outside this study. Careful investigation of Reformed Protestant writings about the non-Christian world illustrates the intellectual responses to and constructions of paganism and Islam across time.

THE COMMENSURABILITY OF PROTESTANT CHRISTIANITY, 1620s–1650s

Calvinists in the Netherlands threw their support behind the launch of the trading companies, portraying commerce as a providential means to propagate the gospel around the world. Pieter Plancius insistently organized among fellow Amsterdam clergy to recruit ministers for overseas service and schmoozed among financiers to bankroll them. Johannes de Laet and Willem Usselincx pressed for a West India Company to land a blow for Calvinism in the Atlantic. *Predikanten* in the Amsterdam and Walcheren classes commissioned overseas ministers "so that many inhabitants . . . will be brought to the knowledge of the only true God and to eternal salvation."[5] Ministers and theologians throughout the Dutch Reformed world announced triumphantly that they were throwing open the door widely for all peoples, which would inaugurate the second coming of Christ. Encouraging reports of early contacts in the Moluccas, Formosa, and Brazil rippled through the networks of affinity and vocation that connected Calvinist clergy, intellectuals, and partisan activists in the Netherlands. Hugo Grotius, Gerardus Vossius, and Godefridus Udemans belonged to this moment; their engagements with world religions bore its imprint.

The narratives composed by not only these writers but also other theologians and ministers later in the 1600s were part of a broader and ongoing production of knowledge about the interface between Protestant Christianity and other religions. Joke Spaans has established that the comparative studies of religion that began to appear in the sixteenth and seventeenth centuries initially were constructed on the foundation of ancient authorities and from there were "fed by a mounting stream of information about the overseas world, also as an empirical science."[6] Grotius, Vossius, Rogerius, Hoornbeeck, Oomius, Valentijn, et al. certainly framed their accounts based on classical and contemporary sources, yet they also reframed them based on travel and letter writing by Calvinist consistories overseas and church districts in the Netherlands. This "geography of knowledge" ran from the far-flung mountains of the Moluccan Islands, to the island of Manhattan, to the southwest plain of Tayouan, to the forests of Pernambuco, to the theology faculties in Utrecht and Leiden, to consistory chambers and pulpits across the Dutch provinces.[7] Letter writing from a diverse array of geographical spaces connected the circuits through which communication about missionary encounter traveled. Out of that communication network, writers in the Netherlands produced narratives to realign a Reformed Protestant vision of the world and history with the messy experiences on the mission field.

Overseas consistories wrote habitually to the classes of Amsterdam and Walcheren and the synods of North and South Holland to report on affairs and to seek advice on thorny pastoral questions.[8] These letters from overseas consistories were read at classis and synod meetings. Clergy and elders from all churches within a regional classis attended its meetings, and representatives from classes participated in the larger regional synod meetings. The issues of the mission field even came to the attention of the delegates at the famous national synod of Dort meeting between November 1618 and May 1619. A minister to the East Indies, Adriaan Hulsebos, had requested from the synod clarification on the propriety of baptizing children of Moors and "heathens."[9] The canons provided that baptism and communion were an inviolable unity that could not be divided, which Dutch ministers interpreted to mean that all adult baptized members had to meet the same requirements for participating in the Lord's Supper.[10]

The regional organizational structure of the Dutch Reformed Church ensured that ecclesiastical and political leaders across Holland and Zeeland, as well as other provinces, heard about the workings of overseas ministers in various locales. This correspondence reaffirmed the tightly connected boundaries of the worldwide Calvinist community of believers. In most every piece of correspondence, scribes affirmed these global confessional bonds by giving thanks for their brothers in either a distant non-European land or in Europe. The Amsterdam classis in its 1679 letter gave thanks, for example, for the health and growth in "God's church in Ceylon" and expressed encouragement at the strong condition of the kingdom of God in Batavia.[11] In reiterating their hopes for the spread of the gospel in Ceylon, the Galle consistory wrote to the Amsterdam classis in January 1668 that the ministers and elders there trusted that the king of Kandy's heart lay in God's hands, giving them hope for "the prosperity of the church and the company."[12] In assessing the state of the church worldwide, the Amsterdam classis concurred that "God has the kings of the world in his hand."[13]

Congregants could also hear personally from *predikanten* who had repatriated. A number of them, including several who were quite well respected such as Sebastian Danckaerts, George Candidius, Justus Heurnius, and Robert Junius, had returned from Asia and America and taken up pastoral posts in the Netherlands. One of the most ardent early proponents of missions, Heurnius had composed an enthusiastic exhortation in 1618, six years before he himself embarked on overseas service. Danckaerts published a historical account of his experiences in Amboina in 1621.[14] Gisbertus Voetius wrote that he conferred with overseas ministers, including his "friend" Heurnius, on the best strategies for spreading the Reformed gospel.[15] Finally, over the course of the seventeenth century, a number of company governors and merchants added to this body of knowledge by publishing descriptions of various locales and accounts of voyages in the line of duty. Although these works did not aim at narrating the progress of Calvinist missions, they did keep tantalizing images of world religions before the large book-reading market in the Netherlands.[16]

It is also worthwhile to bear in mind that Calvinists in the Netherlands and across Europe had always maintained a keen international perspective. The Amsterdam consistory contributed to the ransoms for Protestants captured by Muslim pirates off the coast of north Africa. At the end of the sixteenth century, consistories across the Netherlands periodically sent funds to Calvinist communities in the southern Low Countries under duress from forces loyal to Spain. In the early eighteenth century, the Amsterdam classis sent funds to a fledgling Dutch Reformed congregation in Pennsylvania.[17] This international outlook found expression in correspondence between Dutch church districts and consistories overseas. Correspondents regularly assessed the state of Calvinist Christianity, mentioning developments from across the world in their letters.

For example, in letters from the Netherlands and overseas outposts in the late seventeenth century, ministers discussed their concerns about threats from Catholic France. In May 1682, the Amsterdam classis described a darkness enveloping the worldwide community of Reformed Christians. The ministers in Amsterdam were particularly anxious about the persecution of French Calvinists by Louis XIV. French Catholic aggressiveness also made for misery among Reformed Protestants in England and Scotland. The classis compared the situation to that of the children of Israel threatened by Jezebel, who desired to make them offer themselves to idols.[18] In October 1685, just after the Act of Revocation that outlawed Protestantism in France, the Amsterdam ministers wrote to Colombo that the Reformed Church in France was severely pressed, as true Christians often had been throughout history. Many Dutch feared for their own safety at the hands of "bloodthirsty Jesuits" and the French king.[19] The Colombo consistory responded by encouraging the faithful to stand fast "like holy prophets and apostles in times past," and then took up a collection for Huguenot refugees.[20] Several years later, the Amsterdam classis wrote to Batavia about the continuing distress coming out of France and that "faithful brothers" in the Palatinate were being sentenced to galley ships.[21] When possible, Dutch churches also relayed positive news about the fortunes for Reformed Protestantism in Europe, as for example in December 1720, when the Amsterdam classis rejoiced that their brothers in the Palatinate had gained a measure of liberty from Catholic authorities.[22]

Grotius, Udemans, and Vossius certainly give evidence of a knowledge flow streaming from the mission field into the cities and towns of the Netherlands. Calling the missionary project "a second Reformation," Udemans described in *The Spiritual Rudder* (1638) the schools that had opened in Amboina since the 1620s. He referred to twenty-nine schools, with thirty to sixty children in each, operating in the mountains and villages and undergoing regular inspections by consistories. Schoolmasters, he noted approvingly, read sermons on Sundays in Malay.[23] Grotius wrote that he wanted to arm his countrymen with truth as they made "incursions with pagans, such as live up in Arabia and Guinea; or upon the Mahumetans, as those under the dominion of the Turks, the Persians, and Carthegenians; and lastly upon the Jews, at this day professed enemies of Christianity."[24] He went on to add that his treatise would arm Christians to refute the errors of the enemies of the faith.[25] Vossius also followed Dutch enterprises and delved deeply into Jesuit and other ethnographic writing. He utilized, for example, José de Acosta for his description of Andean and Mexican customs,

Jean de Léry for examples of hornets in Brazil, and Jan Huygen van Linschoten for material on China and Japan. He also cited Dutch efforts to alleviate poverty among the Tupi, indicating that he had access to the stories of missionary encounter and pastoral work overseas.[26] Vossius remarked on Dutch navigational observations about the movement of sea currents and winds from the Moluccas to the Cape of Good Hope, praising that same navigation as that which "allows us to announce the salvation of the Gospel, just as our Savior commanded us."[27] These writers, in other words, were knowledgeable about and engaged with missions; let us see how their works sought to make sense of them.

Grotius, Udemans, and Vossius wrote for distinct purposes, and their narratives fell into very different literary genres. Grotius's intent in his relatively brief exposition *The Christian Religion* (1640) was to defend the superiority of a non-dogmatic Christian faith against other religions.[28] The treatise originated as an expansive prose summation of a poem in Dutch which Grotius published in 1622.[29] In *The Christian Religion*, he hoped to make the case for an ethics-based, nondogmatic, and unifying Christianity at home and abroad. Grotius's approach and spirit were grounded in the Christian humanism of Erasmus and Juan Luis Vives, which aspired for religious unity and biblical piety. Grotius drafted the work to set forth the fundamental ethical tenets of Christianity, eschewing dogmatic nuances that would present difficulties for peoples beyond Europe.[30] A 2004 study by J. P. Heering maintains that Grotius "was consciously addressing non-Christians, and allowed himself to be guided by the rhetorical rule that if one wishes to convince, one must base an argument not on one's assumptions but on those of one's audience." Though Calvinists criticized *The Christian Religion* as Socinian, the work became quite popular among Protestants and Catholics across Europe, going through four Latin editions and translated into English, German, French, Swedish, Greek, and Persian. Ultimately, *The Christian Religion*, written for a global audience of Christians and non-Christians, belonged to a Christian humanistic tradition.[31]

Udemans, a staunch orthodox minister and theologian—he served as a leader of the Counter-Remonstrant party at the Synod of Dort—wrote *The Spiritual Rudder* out of concern for the moral hygiene of Dutch merchants and company personnel in the East and West India Companies. Udemans represented the moral reservations of many clergy vis-à-vis the seductions of commerce and the degeneracy of riches,[32] and produced a 600-page volume to this end.[33] In Grotian fashion, Udemans advocated for commerce, arguing that merchants' work was a proper, Christian calling. At the same time, he fully recognized that human greed and lust for profits could contaminate and destroy the soul of a well-intentioned commercial enterprise. Above all, he feared that Christian missions would get drowned out by service to Mammon. Udemans took it upon himself to advise the directors of the trading companies, overseas partisans, fellow *predikanten*, and anyone else who might read his work to keep their focus on spreading biblical Christianity and pay heed to the sins of the flesh.[34] Just as Grotius saw conversion of non-Christians as an antidote to Christian divisions, Udemans believed missions would keep merchants on the straight and narrow godly path.

Vossius's work belonged to a very different genre altogether: it was a massive and exceptionally erudite history of pagan religions from the ancient and classical past down to his own day. Based on classical, Christian, and Jewish materials, as well as contemporary travel and ethnographic accounts, Vossius attempted to "show that the characters of the different polytheistic religions are really Biblical characters in disguise." A close friend of Grotius, Gerardus Vossius shared a fascination with the worship practices of people around the world and also sought to interpret them within a universal historical framework. Both Grotius and Vossius wrote as Christian humanists and Protestants striving for religious unity. A minister and a theologian at the University of Leiden, Vossius became chair of the theological faculty in 1614, but had to resign five years later for his Arminian sympathies in the face of Counter-Remonstrant pressure after the Synod of Dort. He later became a professor of rhetoric and Greek at Leiden, then received a prebendaryship at Canterbury Cathedral in 1629; he returned to the Netherlands to teach at the Amsterdam Athenaeum in 1632, where he worked until his death in 1649. Vossius was highly esteemed for his immense erudition in Greek and Hebrew and in the study of history. In 1641, he published *The Theology of the Gentiles*, which went through several editions until 1700. The historian Richard Popkin has argued convincingly that Vossius offered an apologetics to "provide intellectual Christians of his time with a way of understanding how most of the world had strayed, and had subsequently confused or debased, the original revelation."[35]

The disparities in genre and audience among these works by Grotius, Udemans, and Vossius point to the importance of the wider religious world in the intellectual, clerical, and academic networks across the Dutch Republic. Despite the different contexts for these works, all three authors readily accepted the straightforward transferability of Protestant Christianity across world societies. From this premise, they sought to appropriate universal religious taxonomies that linked contemporary beliefs and observances to worship practices going back in time. That is, to understand pagans, Moors, and Jews of their own day, it was necessary to expose their roots in the distant past and trace their continuities to the present. In so doing, they collapsed the almost endless record of non-Abrahamic belief and practice into the universal religion of paganism.

Grotius, after laying out the case for the superiority of Christianity in the first three books of *The Christian Religion*, offered a refutation of the three other world religions: paganism, "Mohammedanism," and Judaism. He claimed that "paganism . . . cannot be said to be one religion . . . since some practitioners adore the stars, others the elements, and others various animals."[36] Yet throughout his polemic, he actually employed paganism as a singular universal category for all religions outside the Abrahamic traditions. Grotius contended that all pagans believe in many gods, adore evil spirits, embrace licentiousness as a religious exercise, and venerate the created order. Medieval writers typically referred to all non-Christians and non-Jews as pagans, yet Grotius and other Dutch Protestant writers imputed a theological cohesion to paganism.[37] The pagans that Grotius referred to in *The Christian Religion* were Greeks, Romans, and Egyptians from antiquity; and from his own day he included Persians, Arabians, Ethiopians, Guineans, and collectively the "people of America and Africa . . . who sit in the darkness of paganism."[38] These contemporary adherents to paganism, according to Grotius, were a far cry from the religion practiced in its golden age in Greece and Rome. Paganism went into decay—though it is unclear when—because it depended on human rather than divine agency. Now, he asserted (erroneously), "if we behold all the kingdoms and states that are among Christians and Mahumetans, we see none in paganism except as a memory in books."[39]

Throughout his other writings, Grotius took a historicist and anthropological approach to pagan societies, identifying common functions of pagan religious habits across great distances of time and space and contextualizing them within their own contemporary settings. As in *The Christian Religion*, his other works typecast pagan observances as a range of eclectic external religious expressions practiced by peoples around the world since the fall of Adam and Eve. Yet he also recognized a commonality in all of the myths and rituals. For example, in his commentary on the Old Testament, he noted the lineage of pagan gods and rituals from the ancient Phoenicians and Egyptians to the Greeks and Romans of classical antiquity to the observances of contemporary pagan societies.[40] From its high point in classical Greece and Rome, he observed, paganism had fragmented and devolved into an array of idle superstitions and licentious activities.[41]

Grotius's treatment of paganism past and present stands out for its relatively gentle treatment of its observances. *The Christian Religion* unquestionably cast pagans as impious, sexually immodest, sometimes cruel, and always misguided; yet Grotius did not accuse paganism of diabolism (though he did note that some pagans worshipped evil spirits), and nowhere in the work did he rail against idolatry. Grotius's outlook ran counter to the views of most Reformed Protestant theologians for whom idolatry—that is, the use of religious imagery and ceremonies that distorted the image of the true and infinite nature of God—was the defining feature of pagan observance.[42] It thus seems rather odd that Grotius did not even mention idolatry in *The Christian Religion.* In his commentaries on the Old Testament, too, Grotius took up a historicist interpretation of the children of Israel and the Decalogue, which led him to depart radically from most theologians within the Reformed faith. Without a doubt, Grotius considered idolatry to be superstitious, but for him it was not a violation of divine law. In his treatment of the second commandment (prohibiting the worship of graven images), he argued that the ban was simply a historical and temporary injunction to the Hebrews. Relying heavily on the twelfth-century Jewish philosopher Maimonides (Moses ben Maimon), Grotius contended that the decree was intended to keep the Israelites from imitating their pagan neighbors, which potentially could lead them down a wayward path to polytheism. Commenting on the Decalogue, Grotius classified the prohibition of graven images not as the condemnation of an essentially evil practice, but rather as a constructive admonition against customs that could cloud a true understanding of God. He observed that the commandment came historically just after the Hebrews had fled Egypt, and thus the proscription served to prepare them for settlement in a new land. Grotius also drew out a contemporary application of his radically historicist reading of the second commandment: the prohibition against religious imagery did not extend to Christians.[43]

Vossius's *Theology of the Gentiles* traced the practices and beliefs of pagans within a metahistorical schema from the ancient Egyptians forward; it had an extensive influence on European thinkers in the seventeenth and eighteenth centuries, especially in England.[44] Like Grotius and Hebraists of the day, Vossius was heavily indebted to Maimonides. Vossius's son Dionysius even produced a Latin translation of Maimonides's *Laws of Idolatry* (*Mishneh Torah*), which the elder Vossius annotated and had published in 1642, shortly after his son's death.[45] The eminent and wide-ranging Jewish intellectual provided a captivating analytical point of departure for Protestant thinkers concerned with idolatry in Europe and in diverse global environments. He portrayed the recourse to idol worship by the Jews in the Old Testament as originating from their acceptance of Egyptian cults during their enslavement, as presented in the book of Exodus.[46] The immateriality and utter transcendence of God, which was coarsely distorted by any visual or physical depiction, resonated powerfully with Reformed Protestants. For Vossius, Maimonides also offered a means to track the development of false worship from ancient times.

Vossius took up the intellectual challenge of providing an overarching explanation for the multiplicity and diversity of pagan practices across the world. His knowledge of the classical corpus was immense and, like Grotius, he drew heavily upon it to link contemporary pagan practices with what he regarded as their origins. Here are just a few of numerous examples: In searching for the antecedents to "demon worship" among Brahmins in Calcutta, Indians in Mexico, and Tupis in Brazil, Vossius said that "if we look back in time, we find that the demons were worshipped by ancient Saxons," and even further back by the ancient Egyptians.[47] Attention to the presence of snakes in the religious imagination occupied Vossius in books three and four as he tracked down reports of serpentine veneration in recently explored lands in the Americas and related these to folklore in the ancient world. On belief in the transmigration of souls, he drew connections between Egyptians, Druids, and ancient Persians and contemporary pagans in India, America, and Africa. Similarly, he correlated the worship of many creatures, from elephants, monkeys, cows, crocodiles, and all sorts of insects in ancient Egypt, Mesopotamia, and Phoenicia with cults in Mexico, the Caribbean, and Peru.[48]

The endeavor among Reformed thinkers (such as Vossius) to explicate the history and culture of non-Christian peoples blended with the antiquarian interests of not only Jesuits and humanists, but also Neoplatonists and rationalists of different stripes. With the revival of classical literature in the Renaissance, Neoplatonists in the fifteenth century such as Marsilio Ficino, Pico della Mirandola, and Nicholas of Cusa had revived the search for an ancient revelation given to sages, such as Moses, Hermes Trismegistus, Plato, Pythagoras, Zoroaster, and others, which found its most perfect expression in Christianity. This *prisca theologia* remained a highly influential concept in the sixteenth and seventeenth centuries, linking antiquarian study to ethnography, as a broad spectrum of writers with their own distinct interests sought to contextualize the practices and beliefs of recently discovered peoples.[49] Dutch Reformed writers appropriated *prisca theologia* as well, since it seemed to agree with St. Paul's declaration that God made evident to all peoples "his invisible attributes, his eternal power, and divine nature."[50]

Prisca theologia was the interpretive lens through which Vossius presented his extraordinarily vast historical survey of pagan rites and practices. He attempted to show by amassing a seemingly infinite number of examples that all societies bore God's stamp revealed in nature. The worship practices of pagans indicated that the creation always led back to the creator; in the same way, a reflective examination of the natural world always directed one back to God. This inseparable bond of creation to creator was manifested in the worship practices of pagans as they identified the divine principle in the celestial spheres, the forces of nature, and the creatures in the earth. Throughout the four volumes, Vossius catalogued the objects of devotion in nature by societies down through history, from the golden calf in Egypt to the worship of spirits among Moabites, Babylonians, Zoroastrians, Manichees, to worship of the stars, sun, and moon, to the veneration of creatures of land, water, and air by Finns, Laplanders, and "northern peoples."[51] The universal human impulse to worship objects of nature demonstrated for Vossius that nature revealed God, compelling all people to search out the divine within the created order.

Alongside nature, God had imparted a special, direct revelation to Adam, Noah, Abraham, then Moses, but also to other ancient figures outside the Old Testament and the Hebrew tradition. The Hebrews recorded aspects of this *prisca theologia*, though Vossius conceded that some tenets were probably lost or corrupted over time. The Old Testament preserved the most complete and faithful rendering of this divine revelation, since the texts constructed around other ancient holy figures had been lost, if they ever existed at all, and thus transmission of these traditions was accomplished orally. Over time, *prisca theologia* became obscured because of human sensuality and priestly deception, but also as a result of linguistic confusion. In one well-known example, Vossius argued that priests wrongly translated as *numina* (names or concepts) what should have been rendered as *numen* (divine presence). Consequently, religious figures transferred the allegiance owed to God to physical aspects of the creation. Though these degradations bred all sorts of superstition and idolatry, they also functioned as signs of a universal theology embraced by the ancient sages and contemporaneously represented by Christianity.[52] Vossius's purpose ultimately was not simply explication to a European Christian world seeking understanding. Rather, his massive work attempted a comprehensive taxonomy of pagan rites and observances. If theologians could understand all the false worship practices and how they pointed to a universal system of belief, it would provide a strategy for discourse and proselytizing among pagans.

Godefridus Udemans in *The Spiritual Rudder* also labored under the supposition that all non-Abrahamic traditions were part of a comprehensive world religion. He reminded readers that the "heathens who made God out of flesh and blood" were just "like our forefathers" who converted at the preaching of monastic Christian missionaries a thousand years earlier. Udemans believed that Hollanders in the Middle Ages served idols of the Roman god Mercury and the Egyptian deity Isis. The only distinction Udemans made between his Dutch ancestors and "Indians, Egyptians, and Moors" was racio-ethnic: the latter descended from Noah's cursed lineage through Cham (Ham), whereas Europeans came from the line of Japheth.[53] To illustrate the spiritual blindness and ignorance of pagans, Udemans moved cavalierly and seamlessly between the customs of the

Chinese, Indians, Mexicans, and Peruvians. Perhaps following Jean de Léry, Udemans, like other Dutch writers, considered Brazilians (Tupi peoples) the most degraded, castigating them as devil worshippers and cannibals. Even Vossius depicted them as filthy cannibals, and Caspar Barlaeus claimed that they listened to the counsel of devils.[54] However, Udemans alleged that superstition and idolatry in Asia possessed less offensive features because of the long presence of Christian communities, beginning with the evangelical mission of St. Thomas the apostle.[55] False religion did not prevent some societies from achieving high levels of civic morality, as sometimes pagans put Christians to shame. Greeks, Romans, Indians of South Asia ("Brahmins"), and Japanese gained Udemans's admiration for social discipline and political virtue. He concluded that divine grace extended to pagans, enabling them to develop governments to rein in excesses, and that [European] "Libertines and other low Christians . . . are no better than blind Heathens, who have as much political understanding and life as they [Libertines] do."[56] So Udemans did recognize variations, but the different customs and level of civilization did not obscure the fact that all pagan peoples shared a religious genealogy from the ancient past to the present characterized primarily by the worship of the creation rather than the creator.

Grotius, Vossius, and Udemans had much less to say about Muslims than about pagans. Humanists in the Renaissance had attempted to uncover the origins of the Turks and the rise of other Muslim peoples and empires, but often relied on age-old religious caricatures.[57] These Dutch writers followed the same story lines. Of the three, Grotius devoted the most attention, allocating one chapter in *The Christian Religion*, yet he simply repeated the polemical tropes of medieval and contemporary writers. Grotius attacked Muhammad as a thoroughly evil and insatiably lustful figure, and assailed Islam as a coercive and bellicose religion. The precepts that Grotius identified as key to Islam were revenge, divorce, polygamy, circumcision, and the prohibition of alcohol. For Grotius and other Calvinists, the only theological aspect of Islam worth stating was that it was "contrary to the law of Moses and the disciples of Jesus."[58] Udemans did not discuss Islam at all in *The Spiritual Rudder* and only brought Muslims into view when discussing conditions under which a Christian might marry, trade with, or serve under a non-Christian party. Undoubtedly Udemans held nothing but contempt for Islam, at one point calling the religion "the abomination of Muhammad," yet it did not merit any more of his attention.[59] Vossius, for his part, made mention of Moors and Turks, but merely in passing, which is not surprising given his analytic focus on paganism.[60]

The relative inattention to Islam reflected the casual attitude Calvinists took toward the belief systems of other religions in this period. The study of Islam and Arabic sources was attracting serious attention among a wide array of Protestant and Catholic scholars in the early seventeenth century, but this interest had not yet filtered into a Calvinist missionary outlook. Just as one broadly brushed category of paganism fit all non-Abrahamic faiths, Islam attracted no serious consideration among missionary-minded Calvinists. The only Dutch Calvinist treatise dedicated to Islam in the early seventeenth century appeared in 1625 by Johannes Cocceius, who simply recapitulated medieval and contemporary Christian commentators.[61]

Cocceius's emphases in the *Oration on the Religion of the Turks* reflected the predominant Christian sentiments inherited from the Middle Ages, as he essentially treated Islam as a heresy that arose with Muhammad. Like all heresies and deceptive teachings, it emerged because of divine punishment for the moral laxity of Christians and the diabolical aspirations of false prophets.[62] Cocceius, however, cited a fairly specific period for the divine wrath, and a cause: the "depraved" Byzantine ruler and "blasphemer" emperor Heraclius (610–647).[63] Cocceius noted that during and after his reign blasphemies circulated throughout the eastern empire, the most heinous being Muhammad's teachings. Giving no analysis of these teachings, the Calvinist theologian devoted most of his attention to the evil character of the prophet, his profound misreading of the Christian scriptures and history in the Qur'an, and the religion's appeal to fleshly decadence. In fact, he noted, one characteristic that Muslims and pagans shared was a predilection for carnal pursuits and external rites, though Cocceius acknowledged that Muslims rejected religious images. Like pagans, Muslims possessed no valid conception of the spiritual, but relegated all aspects of religion and law to the body. Nevertheless, Cocceius expressed confidence in his later eschatological writings that large numbers would be converted to Christianity in due course. Cocceius did not alter or add to the basic views about Muslims that he put forth in the *Oration*, but over the course of his life he did develop an expansive eschatological theology that envisioned the mass conversion of Muslims in the immediate future.[64]

A second theme running through these works by Grotius, Vossius, and Udemans upheld the moral and rational capacity of non-Christian peoples to convert. For Grotius, those who had departed from the true worship of God were ripe for conversion to an ecumenical, nondogmatic Christianity. For that purpose, he appealed to the reason and moral conscience of pagans, Jews, and Muslims to consider Christianity's "superiority in the great holiness of laws and precepts, as well in matters pertaining to the worship of God, as likewise in things concerning other matters," such as the responsibility to one's neighbors.[65] Grotius's allegiance to the free moral agency of all people led him to put forth his ecumenical form of Christianity, which he judged would find a ready audience among pagans, Jews, and Muslims. In order to appeal to a rational moral conscience, he avoided the puzzling (if fundamental) Christian doctrines, such as the Trinity, the Incarnation, the Resurrection, and the Sacraments. Instead, he called attention to the "common principles" agreed to by all Christians, including a transcendent creator, the immortality of the soul, the authority of the Bible, the divine power of Christ, and basic Christian morality. For Grotius, a universal image of Christendom would, he said, win many "heathens, Jews, and Turks" to Christ.[66] Not only did he repeatedly express the strong hope for the conversion of non-Christians, but his conception of the possibilities for a universal faith stemmed from his confidence in the free moral will of peoples around the world.[67] One of his proofs for the existence of God was the "light of reason . . . manifested in all nations," except those overcome by "savagery."[68]

One of the foremost theorists of natural law in the seventeenth century, Grotius maintained that universal moral principles, discernible through observation and reason, governed all societies throughout the world since its creation. His adherence to a transcendent law that formed the basis for any legitimate adjudication between all polities diverged from common European taxonomic premises that privileged allegiance to Christian theology and morality. Thus, the understanding of world societies that Grotius presented cast all peoples as moral and rational citizens compelled by universal standards.[69] Grotius, consequently, rooted his narrative of the wider world in the premise of the commensurability of societies. His humanistic training, his work on behalf of the VOC, and his interest in the conversion of pagans, Jews, and Muslims immersed him in the history and development of peoples around the world throughout his life.

In Vossius's application of *prisca theologia*, pagans exerted moral and rational capacities similar to Grotius's understanding. In their telling, pagans possessed knowledge of God through nature and an ancient theological tradition, albeit corrupted over time.[70] Pagans had turned the image of God into false representations and idols. Evil spirits also played a pernicious role in human affairs by deceiving people into the worship of false gods. Yet both Vossius and Grotius believed that all people, except the most debased, wished to worship the true God and turned to the divine for protection and blessing. In this regard, Vossius related false worship and idolatry to medicinal therapies. In the latter section of book four, for instance, he gives examples of the medicinal properties that peoples ascribed to insects. Various past and present cultures used snails for eye and stomach maladies, beeswax for neck and throat ailments, spiders for wounds, and millipedes for tumors of the ear.[71] Then Vossius went on to show how certain societies venerated insects: Egyptians revered beetles, Thessalonians adulated ants, and in Canaan flies won place of honor. Over time, the names for these insects became corrupted and mistranslated so that later writers believed them to signify devils, such as Beelzebub in Canaan. Thus, Vossius argued that what contemporary writers contended was diabolism was nothing more than pagans venerating animals, fish, birds, and even insects that they believed had healing properties. He concluded, "it is though there is a kind of sentient being that leads humans, as if by the hand, to the worship and love of God the creator."[72]

The optimistic views of Vossius and Grotius on the ability of pagan peoples to undergo Christian conversion stemmed from at least two impulses. One was their own theological stance regarding the ability of humans to make independent moral choices. As classical humanists and Arminians, they believed that humans possessed free will and were not predestined to an eternal fate. It makes sense that they would consider all people reachable, except those who seemed given over to extreme practices, such as cannibalism and unrestrained sexuality. But another reason was that they wrote in a period in which a general sanguine outlook about the possibilities for success on the mission field gripped a large number of Dutch Protestants in the early years of empire.

As a good Calvinist, Udemans did not believe that humans exercised free will, of course, but rather understood that they were by nature in bondage to sin. Udemans considered some pagans reprehensible, calling American Indians "savage" and "dumb" and judging that Brazilians were "bewitched by the devil,"[73] Udemans nevertheless displayed confidence in the power of the gospel and supposed that pagans in the East and West Indies would turn to Protestant Christianity. As noted previously, he did not condemn pagan societies carte blanche, and on occasion even praised their virtues. Other Calvinists did too. In 1654, Arnold Montanus, a Calvinist teacher and theologian, wrote of Brahmins that "the conscience of the blind heathens burn a sun of virtue that numbs the dim light of Christians."[74] Theologically, Udemans, like most Calvinists, accepted that God held even sinners accountable as moral and rational beings, and mandated that preachers bring the word of God to them. Influenced by currents of millenarianism circulating in Reformed orbits, Udemans also had faith that the end times—a period of worldwide conversion—were at hand.[75] In the *Spiritual Compass* he had stated that "in these times we expect the conversion of the Jews and the fullness of the heathens as the apostle prophesied."[76] Consequently, he resolved that the Reformed Church and the trading companies must seize the opportunity to "bring these blind heathen to knowledge of the Lord Jesus Christ."[77] Positioning Dutch commerce and Protestantism against the backdrop of the Spanish and Portuguese empires, Udemans argued that only a Reformed civilizing effort could lead pagans to the knowledge of God and establish justice in those lands. Otherwise the "Indians" would denounce the Dutch as harshly as they did the Spanish and Portuguese.[78] For Udemans, pagans possessed the moral and rational capacity to convert, as God so pleased, and he anticipated an abundant harvest of souls.

Hugo Grotius, Gerardus Vossius, and Godefridus Udemans not only reflected general Dutch Protestant attitudes about overseas missions in these writings; they also calibrated their construction of world religions in correspondence with optimistic hopes for widespread conversion. To manage the immense and incomprehensible knowledge about peoples and customs from the flood of ethnography and information flowing into Europe, they resorted to universal religious taxonomies as organizing principles. The bewildering breadth of non-Abrahamic religious observance was shoehorned into the capacious category of paganism. From Canaanites to Chaldeans, Brahmins to Brazilians, and Greeks to Guineans, pagans shared a common religious lineage characterized by confusing the creation with the creator. This reading of world religions enabled intellectuals, theologians, and ministers to apply their knowledge of classical authors to interpret contemporary customs. Such an uncomplicated hermeneutic also imputed a moral and rational facility to peoples around the world, which facilitated Christianity's straightforward commensurability with these cultures. Grotius and Udemans called for the direct preaching of the gospel, with no attention to how that message might be received.[79] Vossius's commitment to *prisca theologia* implied that pagan religions were already quite close to Christianity in their ultimate aims and functions.

PREOCCUPATIONS WITH INTRACTABILITY, 1650s–1670s

In the mid-seventeenth century, the cause of global Calvinism both encountered new opportunities for growth and suffered some significant setbacks. Since their inception, the VOC and WIC had employed dozens of clergy and even more *ziekentroosteren*, had subsidized the production of religious materials, and had hired many native and Dutch schoolmasters. Breaking new ground, the VOC established itself in Ceylon, the Coromandel and Malabar coasts, Melaka, and the Cape of Good Hope. Though new territories in the Indian Ocean loomed in the Calvinist imagination, the WIC lost all hope for a permanent conquest of Brazil, and with it the prospects for an Atlantic mission dimmed.

In Asian missions, the expectation for a wholesale conversion of pagans, Moors, and Jews was languishing at the indifference and backsliding of prospective converts, giving rise to a perception of regression among overseas ministers.

In the East Indies at the time, the churches remained small, school attendance was spotty, and neophytes often seemed equivocal about the new faith. Over five thousand Formosans had undergone baptism in the 1630s and 1640s, though by the 1650s ministers and governors were pointing fingers over whom to blame for relapsing converts. The Reformed faith was also proving slower to get off the ground in Ceylon and the Cape of Good Hope than ministers had originally hoped.[80]

Also by the mid-seventeenth century, *predikanten* and *ziekentroosteren* had preached and interacted with a wide variety of people and had developed a much greater appreciation not only for the difficulty of converting pagans and Moors, but also for the complexity in even determining what behaviors and beliefs to expect of a non-European Protestant Christian. This uncertainty had led to the "dividing sacraments" controversy of the 1620s to 1648, pitting the Batavia consistory against the classes of Amsterdam and Walcheren over whom to baptize and permit to communion. One can feel the exasperation of Johannes Roman, a minister in Batavia, who lamented in 1648 that new converts often "imagine themselves already to be good Christians . . . being wise and satisfied in their own eyes, yet continue as in previous times after the desires of heathens, walking in immorality, lust, drunkenness, and despicable idolatry."[81]

These inclinations convinced many Dutch that indigenous Christians, having been raised in idolatrous environments, suffered from an enculturated moral weakness. The consistory in Banda, for example, had declared in January 1624 that "heathens and Moors" who professed belief in Christ "were still very weak" and vulnerable to the pull of the flesh toward prostitution and adultery.[82] Likewise, the consistory in Colombo objected to the close proximity of a Buddhist pagoda in Kandy to a Dutch school because the ministers feared that the temple's very appearance and the Buddhist pilgrims it attracted would lure new Christians back into old ways.[83] In Formosa, ministers fretted about the influence of *inib*s (female priests) on new native Christians.[84] In competing for souls with Jesuits and other Catholic missionaries, Calvinist ministers considered themselves at a decided disadvantage because, as we saw Jacob Haafner assert at the outset of this chapter, papist idolatry always played well with pagan idolatry.[85] By this time, the standard terminology that Dutch Calvinists employed for all Vedic and local practices in all of these regions was *duiveldienst* (devil worship). Even worse for the mission, Muslims had gained the reputation of being aloof toward Christianity. In August 1625, Anthony Dircksen in Banda wrote to Batavia that "Moors had little in interest in Christendom."[86] Voetius wrote in the 1650s that forty years of missionary experience in the East Indies had taught Calvinists that Muslims were very difficult to convert.[87] Consistories across the

East Indies noted on many occasions that Moors exhibited an antipathy toward Christianity and only expressed interest in baptism in order to marry a Christian or to gain the favor of the company.[88]

The observations and assessments of the sad state of the *Indisch Sion* prompted Abraham Rogerius to compose a detailed description of "heathendom" from his experiences. *The Open Door to Hidden Heathendom*, published in 1651, exerted an enormous influence in Europe by virtue of translations into German (1663) and French (1670). Scholars working on Western imperialism in South Asia regard *The Open Door* to be the foundational European treatment of Hindu religion and culture until the nineteenth century.[89] It sparked the imagination of Johannes Hoornbeeck and Philip Baldaeus to follow with similar works in 1669 and 1672, respectively. Gisbertus Voetius produced a number of works on paganism derived from theological disputations he held for his students at Utrecht. The work of Rogerius and Jesuit missionaries likewise inspired Godefridus Carolinus, a *predikant* in Gelderland, to assess pagans in Asia, Africa, and the far reaches of northern Europe in a treatise on contemporary paganism in 1661. In the same period, Hoornbeeck, Voetius, and their former student Simon Oomius also brought forth detailed critiques of Islam.[90]

Taken together, these works signal a turning point in the Calvinist narrative of world religions. Whereas in the first half of the 1600s overseas ministers showed little interest in learning about other religions, in the latter half theologians in Dutch universities began providing academic training that incorporated a focus on paganism, Islam, and Judaism, an initiative that in the East Indies, Ceylon, and Formosa spurred an additional emphasis on scriptural translation and teacher training. An inherent part of this project involved revising the Protestant and humanist narrative from the apparently outdated optimistic vision of the early 1600s. The works by Rogerius, Baldaeus, Hoornbeeck, Voetius, and Oomius conjured darker images of the sinister grip of a generalized priestly class over duped followers and the destructive power of false religion over decadent cultures.

It was his own experiences with Hindus and Buddhists on the Coromandel coast and his concern over the lack of progress in the mission that moved Abraham Rogerius to write his treatise on Vedic traditions and practices. Rogerius attended the Walaeus Seminary at the University of Leiden, established to train students for overseas service, and set sail for Batavia in 1630. From 1632 to 1642 he worked as a pastor at Pulicat on the Coromandel coast, where he interacted with Hindus and established a cordial relationship with at least one Brahmin. At the end of this period he transferred to Batavia, where he was stationed until 1647 when he returned to the Netherlands.[91] Soon after arriving in Batavia, he proposed to the consistory there that he write a treatise he had tentatively titled "A Priest of Baal: A True Life Description of the Life of the Brahmins," based on his encounters in South Asia.[92]

Rogerius undertook this account to sound the alarm to the Dutch Calvinist world that the conversion of pagans in Asia was proving far more complicated than expected. In one of his last consistory meetings in Batavia, on September 23, 1647, he expressed concern to colleagues about the state of Christendom in Asia, pointing out that the Dutch classes, especially the Walcheren district, were not taking the arduous difficulties of overseas ministers seriously. The VOC, he charged, was allowing pagan blasphemies to go unchecked in public, even on the Sabbath.[93] Given that the Christianization of space and time were key elements in Calvinism's conversion strategy, this routine profanation of the Sabbath and the public presence of Buddhist temples undermined the missionary work of the ministers. Even more problematic, leaders in the Netherlands were simply not paying attention. A year after his protest to the Batavia consistory, he appeared before the Amsterdam consistory to press these concerns.[94] It seems that he thought the Reformed church leaders in the Netherlands were too busy congratulating themselves on the success in Formosa—being trumpeted by Robert Junius since his repatriation in 1643—yet overlooked the complaints and frustrations of most ministers.

To this end, Rogerius sought to expose the deceptions in paganism, based on his labor at Pulicat, and drafted a Latin work, *Gentilism Exposed* (*Gentilismus reseratus*).[95] From this treatise, the publisher Francis Hackius brought forth a book in Dutch, *De Open-Deure tot het Verborgen Heydendom* (*The Open Door to Hidden Heathendom*), two years after Rogerius's death in 1649. Jacobus Sceperus, a Calvinist minister in Gouda (where Rogerius lived), edited the work and wrote an introduction; Andreas Wissowatius, an antiquarian and Socinian, added a preface and made extensive annotations throughout.[96] Thus, the full body of *The Open Door* was a collaborative effort in which Sceperus and Wissowatius utilized Rogerius's point of view to reflect on the seemingly impenetrable nature of pagan idolatry to a European audience. *The Open Door* followed Grotius, Vossius, and Udemans in situating observances in a universal, metahistorical narrative, but it departed from them in alleging the deceptive seductions of a priestly class.

Sceperus framed Rogerius's analysis by presenting the Vedic (Hindu) traditions of Asia as layers of mysterious rites and obfuscatory fables deployed by a caste of priests to conceal the kernel of true religion from ordinary people. As denoted in the title, the work therefore intended to open the doors to expose the deceptions of Brahmin priests. Rogerius claimed to have based his account on extensive conversations with a Brahmin named Padmanaba with whom he became acquainted at Pulicat. The genuine voice of a Brahmin priest lent the work an element of authenticity often present in Jesuit accounts but absent in previous Protestant treatments.[97] The scholar Joan-Pau Rubiés, however, has cautioned against reading native voices in missionary ethnographic works as genuine; rather, the appropriation of intermediaries such as Padmanaba enabled Rogerius and his counterparts to construct a case for authenticity.[98] Rogerius put forth the standard Calvinist view that the light of nature provided all people clear evidence of a transcendent, moral creator, leaving all people with a yearning for knowledge of that God.[99] Brahmins, like all other pagan priestly figures— including Catholic ones in Europe and around the world—had distorted the truth of godly religion with superstitions and legends that concealed God's revelation and enslaved practitioners to idolatry and immorality. Interestingly, Caspar Barlaeus in his account of Brazil maintained that the priests of the Tupi kept them in darkness through fear, which suggests the extensive reach of this trope.[100] For his part, Wissowatius in an annotation speculated that Brahmins had come into contact with divine teachings through communities of "St. Thomas Christians," descendants of Syriac converts along the Malabar coast who traced their origins to the apostle.[101] *The Open Door* charged that "the laws of the Vedas and the secrets of their religion are not made public to the Sudras, that is, the common people of their nation."[102]

Rogerius laid out the fundamental principles of Vedic religion and where they deviated from the gospel, illustrating that Christian teachers might appeal to prospective converts' "taste for God."[103] Because pagans were given by their fallen nature to sensuality, they exchanged divine truth for worship of things in the created order. So when Brahmins encountered the truth of the gospel, they naturally twisted it into superstitious fables. Brahmins, for example, took the religious truth of a divine mediator for human sin and transformed it into a fable of Vishnu who manifested himself in beastly incarnations as a fish, turtle, boar, and elephant.[104] *The Open Door* noted, too, that Brahma created the world and also took human form, representing another pagan myth that accorded with scriptural truth.[105]

Reminiscent of the work of Grotius, Vossius, and Udemans, *The Open Door* pointed to Hindu beliefs that correlated with a long tradition of pagan folklore that stretched back to a distant past in Mesopotamia and Egypt. Rogerius and Wissowatius (in his annotations) asserted that contemporary observances in South Asia shared a basic similarity to ancient paganism because they developed out of a common intellectual and religious heritage. Just as Christianity emerged out of Judaism, so also did contemporary Vedic practices derive from an older pagan lineage. Just as Jews passed down their teachings in oral and written forms, pagan forefathers bequeathed their traditions through subsequent generations.[106] In emphasizing continuity over time, *The Open Door* maintained that Brahmins appropriated the pagan past of the Chaldeans and Persians to carry out divination rituals, just as Indian astrological tenets grew out of ancient pagan superstitions.[107] Even when it did not draw a historical connection between contemporary and past practices, *The Open Door* called attention to common patterns among various pagan societies. For example, the work compared illicit marriage customs in India with German, Roman, and Greek practices; omens with ancient pagan signification; oath-swearing rituals with Chaldean and Persian practices; and views about the devil with Japanese beliefs.[108] Comparisons such as these invited the reader to draw connections among pagan practices around the world since ancient times.

Like writers in the earlier period, Rogerius and his editors were trying to fit these unfamiliar practices into the biblical and classical framework that shaped a seventeenth-century European outlook on the world. Having emerged from a century of schematizing doctrine and worship formed by the confessional struggles of the Reformation, Calvinists in the seventeenth century conceived of religion as a system of belief and practice. *The Open Door*, in seeking to explain Hindu practices, projected a known religious system onto a miscellany of cults, deities, stories, and rituals. In short, it imparted theological significance to idolatry.[109] The reference to "Heathendom" in the title revealed the aim of imposing theological structure on missionary frustration. By framing Hindu tenets within a global and biblical narrative, the work gave the exotic other a sense of familiarity. These teachings and observances, inherently strange and foreign to Europeans, were rendered as a recognizable tradition, reflecting pagan practices described in the Old and New Testaments.[110] Hindu observances might still remain bizarre to Reformed Protestants, but they nevertheless now fit within an overarching narrative that made sense of a tradition even while condemning it as false worship.

This attempt to unravel the mysteries of paganism made its mark on standard works that appeared in the 1660s and 1670s. The theologians Voetius and Hoornbeeck completed treatises on converting pagans around the world, the overseas minister Baldaeus dissected idolatrous false worship in South Asia, and the minister Carolinus surveyed contemporary pagandom. Voetius's *Gentilism and the Calling of Gentiles*, published in 1655 and 1676, expanded on theological debates held at Utrecht in 1638 on the topic of presenting the gospel to pagans.[111] Hoornbeeck, one of the most important advocates of orthodox Calvinism and Dutch overseas missions in the seventeenth century, had studied under Voetius, with whom he developed a keen commitment to proselytizing among pagans, Muslims, and Jews, as well as exposing the errors of non-Reformed Christians. His *Summa on Controversies with Infidels*, published in 1653, became a standard work for Dutch ministers. In August 1690, Simon Cat marshaled an argument of Hoornbeeck's in a treatise as support for the establishment of the seminary in Colombo.[112]

At roughly the same time, Carolinus reconstructed the pagan religion as he believed it was practiced in his day, relying on missionary writings, travel accounts, and public VOC records. He also corresponded with Georgius Hornius, another theologian at Leiden who twenty years later wrote a church history from the creation of the world to 1666. Carolinus referred to Voetius's discourse *On Atheism* (1645), but did not indicate an awareness of his or Hoornbeeck's volumes on paganism. While recovering from an illness, Carolinus began reading travel literature and "descriptions of Heathenish lands," in which he "found very strange and wonderful things concerning the Religion of the Heathens." Surprised that no one had yet attempted a serious, comprehensive survey of contemporary paganism in Asia, Africa, and Europe, he took the initiative to write "a general and also short description of the Heathen Religion, as it has now and for some years past been found across the world and is still practiced [there]."[113] Carolinus's comparative survey circulated broadly among Dutch readers; Hoornbeeck cited it in his discussion of Peruvian worship of Pachacama as the divine creator of the world.[114]

A few years later, in 1672, Baldaeus, a minister in various stations in Asia from 1655 to 1666, published *True Account and Refutation of East Indian Idolatry*, a detailed ethnographic description of the lands and peoples of South Asia, including a critique of paganism in South Asia. Like Voetius, Carolinus, and Hoornbeeck, Baldaeus relied heavily on Rogerius's *The Open Door* but went further than his predecessor in highlighting the degenerate effects of idolatry on societies.[115] Although Baldaeus utilized Rogerius, as well as a number of other Reformed treatises, honestly, he also plagiarized copious sections from a text by a Portuguese Jesuit, Jacob Fenicio.[116] The fact that Baldaeus claimed these sections as his own points to the overlapping perspectives of world societies by writers from divergent confessional camps. For European Protestants, both Rogerius's and Baldaeus's works collectively gave sharp clarity in the 1670s to the universal character of paganism and the moral corrosion of idolatry.

All of these writers sought to expose the true nature of paganism, although they took different approaches in doing so. Carolinus came down closer to Grotius and Vossius, who considered paganism a natural religion. Surveying pagan sects in Japan, China, the East Indies, Siam, India, Guinea, the Cape of Good

Fig. 8. Abraham Bloteling (1634–1690), after J. v.d. Sijdervelt,
Portrait of Philip Baldaeus, 1671; Rijksmuseum Amsterdam

Hope, Muscovy, and Lithuania, Carolinus attempted to demonstrate the shared general characteristics of these religions and their recognition of a single God.[117] Yet he also believed that diabolism was behind their superstition, idolatry, and spiritual blindness.[118] Voetius and Hoornbeeck placed all the diverse rites and stories within the framework of a common pagan religion that came into being with the fall of Adam and Eve.[119] These pagan tendencies, they argued, derived from the natural religion implanted in the heart of Adam and Eve at creation. Further, their turn to a sinful state did not erase natural religion, for they and all humans possessed an innate awareness of God and desire to worship him.

The loss of innocence, however, perverted their understanding of God, such that humans worshipped creatures and objects of nature in place of the divine. Hoornbeeck's approach followed the schema put forth by Vossius and Grotius, who took inspiration from Maimonides's account of idolatry. Yet he and Voetius both cast paganism in very dark terms as the enemy of true religion, impious, profane, the domain of idolaters and idol worshippers. Voetius distinguished between pagans who worshipped devils and less extreme Epicureans, but for him they all denied the transcendent nature of God and thus were atheists.[120]

Baldaeus's purpose was more immediate, namely to illustrate the horrors of idolatry and to refute Hindu errors, but he also framed his account along the lines of Rogerius. Like his predecessor, Baldaeus claimed he gained much of his knowledge from a Brahmin priest (in his case unnamed) and promised readers he would lay bare "[t]hese and similar absurdities that are the secrets of the Brahmins, which they do not wish to reveal to the people."[121] Baldaeus maintained that heathens encountered the basic truths of the gospel, but in their blindness and sensuality had distorted them into idolatrous falsehoods. He described Buddha as a religious figure who had supernatural origins and powers, a white man living in a land of black people. Noting that whiteness denoted virtue, Baldaeus asserted that these features were Christlike and therefore indicated that Asians had heard about the true messiah, but twisted the truth into a lie that they could fashion into an idol.[122] Like other Reformed intellectuals, Voetius and Hoornbeeck endorsed the notion of a global gentilism and related it more directly to the mission fields in which Calvinists were laboring.[123]

Similar to other Calvinists, all of these writers equated paganism with idolatry. Idolatrous worship, Voetius and Hoornbeeck contended, arose in tandem with paganism, as people defected from true devotion to God and became enslaved to their fanciful, sensual imaginations, leading to impiety and injustice.[124] The earliest pagans worshipped aspects of nature, especially the sun, moon, and stars, but then ascribed human features to deities, and finally came to associate the divine with many other creatures.[125] According to Voetius, pagans worshipped aspects of nature even as they rejected obedience to God.[126] Preying on pagans all over the world, demons kept people in a state of spiritual and moral blindness by manipulating imitations of true worship with idols, divinations, and incantations.[127] Voetius and Hoornbeeck traced the historical evolution of idolatry from the Chaldeans and Egyptians encountered by the Israelites to the Greeks, Romans, and Germans and down to the pagans of contemporary times in Asia, Africa, and America.[128] Hoornbeeck explained that pagans acquired the name after Christianity became the official religion in Rome in the fourth century and they fled the cities to the *pagani* (countryside), where they established themselves and practiced their superstitious rites. While pagans over the ages and across vast spaces performed different rites, constructed distinct legends, and appealed to different gods, their universal characteristic, according to Hoornbeeck, was idolatry.[129] He maintained that although pagans did exhibit a diversity in their practices and some were more barbarous than others, they all had abjured the worship of the true God, and "many among them are highly addicted" to idolatry and superstitions.[130] Western Christendom, Hoornbeeck contended, did not escape the scourge of gentilism; rather, its coexistence with Christianity in the late Roman Empire and early Carolingian period led to a blending that resulted in the idolatrous errors of Catholicism.[131]

These Calvinist writers at midcentury followed Vossius, Grotius, and Rogerius in imposing an overarching unity on all pagans by drawing connections between the fables of ancient pagans and superstitious practices in the contemporary world. Carolinus's survey sought to show that despite their very diverse practices, contemporary pagans shared similar commitments to a priesthood, imagery, nature, pilgrimages, feast days, and an afterlife.[132] Also noting parallel elements in pagan stories, Baldaeus maintained that "these Indians are coarser and more lumpen idol worshippers than the Greeks and Romans of old."[133] Likewise, Arnold Montanus observed characteristics among pagans across time and attributed the combination of similarities and differences to great migrations of people across the world after the Flood.[134] For Baldaeus, though, the false teachings and delusions of contemporary Hindus were a far greater danger than the mythological legends of the ancients, because they led people into idolatry. He asked rhetorically, for example, "[D]o we see here something other than the old errors of the learned Greeks and Romans cooked in another pot, and like a reheated cabbage stewed differently and drenched in a strange sauce?" Brahmins constituted a much more insidious threat because they tried to cloak their idolatry in fanciful fables.[135] In other passages, Baldaeus related Hindu beliefs to those of ancient Egyptians, Persians, Greeks, and Romans. In making these links, Baldaeus not only appealed to Rogerius and his own missionary experiences, but he also utilized Vossius's *Theology of Gentiles* and his son Dionysius's *On Idolatry*.[136] Like, Rogerius, Voetius, and Hoornbeeck, Baldaeus lumped Catholic superstitions and heresies in Europe in with the idolatrous worship by pagans.[137]

Another important motif in *The Open Door* that Hoornbeeck, Baldaeus, and to a certain degree Carolinus enunciated more fully was the moral pollution that accompanied false worship. Embracing the Old Testament prophetic tradition and the moral judgments of the church fathers, Reformed Protestants since the early sixteenth century had associated idolatry with sexual impurity. Calvinists in the Netherlands and elsewhere considered idolatry as spiritual adultery and supposed that all sorts of sexual impropriety flowed from the worship of false gods.[138] Antonius Walaeus, the Leiden theologian who trained a number of the early overseas ministers, also argued that idolatry introduces libertinism in a society, so pagan idols must always be removed.[139] Hoornbeeck and Baldaeus adopted the explanatory power of this principle in assessing the moral condition of pagan peoples. Hoornbeeck asserted that as pagans inclined themselves to the devil, "they were given over . . . to concupiscence."[140] He went on to assert that pagans were far more wicked than Muslims or Jews because of their idolatry, observing that idol-worshipping pagans in Asia, Africa, and America went about in shameful nudity and engaged in fornication, polygamy, incest, pederasty, sodomy, and prostitution.[141] Baldaeus concurred that a pervasive idolatry, inextricably intertwined with sensuality, formed the guiding principle for how pagans responded to religious truth, whether revealed generally through nature or specifically through biblical revelation. Baldaeus compared the Christian doctrine of creation, namely that God brought the world into being through his Word, with the Hindu teaching that Ishvara, Vishnu, and Brahma acted creatively only through gods with bodily forms. He remarked sneeringly that in Hinduism, "all things have their origins from the virile member of their God."[142] Carolinus devoted long sections to pagan sexual practices and commented that "prostitution and adultery are both quite customary among the heathens . . . prostitution is most common under them and hardly counted a sin."[143]

The works of Voetius, Hoornbeeck, Carolinus, and Baldaeus perpetuated the universality of gentilism set forth by Grotius, Vossius, and Udemans, yet moved away from the optimistic view of the moral and rational potential of pagan peoples. The interactions of *predikanten* with peoples apathetic to the Calvinist mission and with converts who incorporated old practices and beliefs into their new identity echoed in the narratives of Rogerius, Voetius, Carolinus, Hoornbeeck, and Baldaeus. Carolinus wrote, "[S]o now at long last there is the preaching of the gospel to them, though not so much with any fruit . . . and many [preachers] cannot by any means break through their ungodly religion."[144] Idolatry and superstition, manipulated by fraudulent priests, had corrupted the souls of individuals and corroded the bases of societies in the pagan worlds outside Europe. From a sense of frustration in the mission fields, Calvinist theologians and ministers relied on metahistorical narratives to chart the grim grip of false religion that made genuine conversion so elusive. Within these narratives, the wide diversity of myths and rites of myriad peoples took on a common religious identity signified by the use of religious imagery in worship and healing. Idolatry became the hermeneutic for reading not only these constructed religious systems, but also the societies in which Calvinists sought converts.

Ministers in the East Indies also discovered themselves foundering when it came to making headway against Islamdom. The truism that Muslims were obstinate and hostile to Christianity circulated from the Moluccan Islands to Amsterdam and Zeeland in correspondence and reports.[145] In the Moluccan Islands and in Batavia, Islam reinforced family networks and community solidarity, which meant that changing religious identities (i.e., conversion) introduced the possibility of social instability. The small number of Muslims who did convert almost always did so for the sake of marriage to a Christian.

The impetus for a revised narrative and for a more studied approach to Islam came from faculty and students at the universities of Utrecht and Leiden. Abraham Rogerius and Philip Baldaeus spent most of their careers as clergy in South Asia at Ceylon and the Coromandel coast, where only small enclaves of Muslim communities resided. Perhaps for that reason, Rogerius did not write about Islam at all, and Baldaeus allotted a minuscule three and one half out of 901 pages in his *True and Exact Description*.[146] Voetius, at the University of Utrecht, took up his quill against the religion at the request of his students who expected that they "would come into contact" with Muslims as ministers in Hungary, Transylvania, and the East Indies.[147] Voetius had studied Arabic and the Qur'an even before coming to Utrecht, and once there he lectured regularly on Islam, recognizing that Calvinists going out into Asia needed advanced preparation to confront the Islamic challenge and to convert Muslims. His *On Muhammedanism* was based on a disputation he held for students on March 25, 1648, which he edited in 1653 and eventually published in 1655 as part of a theological compendium, *Select Disputations*. Hoornbeeck's contribution to the subject was a very long chapter (roughly 121 pages) devoted to Islam in his 1653 work *Summa on Controversies with Infidels, Heretics, and Schismatics*.[148] Simon Oomius followed in 1663 with a much more detailed critique, *The Opened and Revived Muhammedisdom or Turckdom*, that ran to over nine hundred pages. Although Voetius and Hoornbeeck did not cite each other, their arguments against Islam bore strong similarities and shaped a generation of students, including Oomius, who referenced them both throughout his work.

These writings, considered in light of the work on paganism in this period, constituted part of a new approach to world religions. Yet unlike the darker constructions of paganism, Dutch Calvinism's response to Islam assumed that it was possible to convince Muslims of the truth of Christianity. Following the lead of Voetius and Hoornbeeck, students and later ministers began to engage Muslim theology and the Qur'an seriously in order to refute them. Voetius drew from an extensive array of traditional and contemporary writings about Islam and quoted from fifty of them. These included the widely circulated volume by Thomas á Jesu *Attending to the Salvation of All Peoples* (*De procuranda salute omnium gentium*, 1613) that figured heavily in many studies of paganism and Islam, as well as William Rainolds's *Calvinism-Turkism* (*Calvino-Turcismo*, 1597), which compared Calvinist teachings to Muslim ones, and Mattheus Sutlivius's *Turko-Papism* (*Turco-Papismo*, 1599), which returned the polemical fire to Catholics.[149] Oomius also utilized these writers, but relied heavily as well on the orientalists Edward Pococke and Thomas Erpenius (English and Dutch, respectively) and the Swiss theologian Johan Heinrich Hottinger. The latter, whose second edition of *The History of the Orient* (*Historia orientalis*) appeared in 1660, proved especially important for Oomius's goal of tarring Socinians with an Islamic brush.[150]

Voetius argued that in order to defeat Islam, Protestant Christendom needed the equivalent of a Collegium Romanum devoted to the study of the Qur'an in Arabic and able to train Calvinist *predikanten*. Lamenting the lack of study of Middle Eastern and Asian languages in Europe, he called for building a library of Muslim writings in their original languages. Voetius recommended that students study Arabic, philosophy, and theology to ready themselves for battle with Muslims.[151] Citing Voetius, Oomius also contended that it was important for overseas ministers to understand the Qur'an so that they could dispute with Muslims more effectively.[152] As Protestants gained the requisite expertise, they should then set out to refute Islamic teachings by focusing on what Voetius regarded as weaknesses in the Qur'an's status as a source of divine revelation. He believed that undermining the authority of the Qur'an ought to serve as the key apologetic strategy for Christian missionaries, since it formed the basis of religious authority in Islam. Using arguments from the natural world, philosophy, and reason, Christians could contradict the teachings of Islam in the Qur'an, thus eroding its authority. Voetius followed with a summary of examples of the chief teachings of Islam, drawing contrasts with Christians ones.[153] Similarly, Oomius devoted over three hundred pages to scrutinizing Islamic theology and religious practices.[154] In so doing, Voetius, Hoornbeeck, and Oomius placed the Calvinist engagement with Islam on an academic footing, having faith that theological debate would win the day.

For Voetius, the adherence to the Qur'an explained why Muslims clung to a "steadfast faith" and would not consider the claims of Christianity. He went on to observe that the Qur'an ascribed an important role for Christ in Islam, effectively camouflaging the truth of Christianity.[155] In essence, Voetius thought that Christians had trouble converting Muslims because Islam had an answer for Christianity. Hoornbeeck, too, gave priority to the corrosive influence of the Qur'an, maintaining that it adulterated the Old and New Testament in many places; by miscasting scripture, it inoculated Muslims against the truth of Christianity.[156] Thus, both theologians advocated an apologetic methodology focused on championing the Bible to undercut the scriptural legitimacy of the Qur'an. To mount an attack, Voetius urged his students to show how Islam's holy book, though derived from the Bible, corrupted teachings about the Trinitarian nature of God and the atoning work of Christ. He also enjoined *predikanten* to study the Qur'an themselves to identify passages that ran counter to the Bible, natural law, and right reason.[157]

In narrating early Islam historically and unpacking its theology, Voetius cast the religion as an apostasy that combined elements of many heresies, from Arianism to Nestorianism, and paralleled Socinianism and spiritualist Anabaptist sects in Europe. Oomius not only gave extensive treatment to the parallels between Islamic and Socinian theology, but he even sketched out Muslim influences on unitarians from Miguel Servetus and Faustus Sozzini to Remonstrants such as Hugo Grotius and Johannes Uytenbogaert.[158] Voetius and Hoornbeeck claimed that, like all heretics, Muslims took portions of scripture and twisted them into corrupted forms of beliefs and practices.[159] It was a standard view among Calvinists that Islam was an amalgam of Christian heresy (Nestorianism), paganism, and Judaism.[160]

Yet Voetius and Oomius also read Islam through the lens of Calvinist polemics against Catholic theology.[161] As Voetius saw it, Muslims practiced works righteousness—a common accusation against Catholics as well—so they could merit their way into an "eternal life of carnal pleasures like a foul animal."[162] Charging Islam with idolatry, Voetius claimed that Muslims followed pagan practices of worshipping the moon and turning toward a fixed point (Mecca) to pray. Voetius also followed a host of previous writers in attributing Friday as the Muslim day of public prayer to the Arab veneration of the goddess Venus, whose day for cultic devotion fell on the same day.[163] And similar to the Catholic Church, Muslims followed a "religious order through popes, which are called muftis, and other leaders of a religious life, namely bishops, priests, learned doctors, and lawyers."[164] Oomius learned well from Voetius because he not only parroted these points, but also asserted that both "papists" and "Mohammedans" spread their religion through violence, prohibited their members from converting, embraced a cycle of fasting and luxuriant feasting, gave themselves over to external ceremonies, worshipped saints, and promoted pilgrimages.[165] Voetius, Hoornbeeck, and Oomius agreed that Catholicism made it much more complicated to convert Mus-

Fig. 9. Anna Maria van Schurman (1607–1678), *Portrait of Gisbertus Voetius*, 1647; Rijksmuseum Amsterdam

lims, who equated the Roman church's use of religious images with idolatry among all Christians.[166] All three hoped that a deeper theological understanding of Islam would equip *predikanten* in Asia to defend their faith and find more converts among Moors and Turks. In this way, the theology faculties in Utrecht and Leiden became participants in the global struggle with Islam.

The decadent carnality that Reformed writers ascribed to paganism applied also to Islam, functioning as a moral debility that fettered Muslims to falsehood and blinded them to religious truth. For Calvinists, the practice of polygamy was nothing more than legalized adultery, a concession to the unbridled libido of Muslims. Christian polemicists of all stripes cast Muhammad as a concupiscent unable to restrain his sexual desires. In an age in which sexual othering was a standard means by which European Christians identified their confessional enemies, polygamous marriage justified for Calvinist and Catholic writers the categorical denunciation of Islam as a religion imbued with sensuality. The Dutch merchant and commander of the ship *Batavia* Francisco Pelsaert wrote that the palaces of Muslim rulers in India (mahals) were "adorned with lascivious sensuality, wanton and reckless festivity."[167] Viewing Islam through this prism, Reformed Protestants read carnality into various Muslim teachings. Oomius went on to argue that the virtues that writers ascribed to some Muslims, such as their piety, zeal, and almsgiving, were actually only "apparent virtues" (*schijn-deugden*), because they were not reconciled to Christ. Consequently, their works were not pleasing to God and of no substance.[168]

An element of Muslim teaching that drew much attention from Calvinists was the Islamic conception of heaven as a sensual paradise in which the denizens consumed wine, hunted ducks, and engaged in seemingly unending sex with multiple partners. Baldaeus characterized it this way: "In paradise . . . they [men] pass their time in pleasures with certain most beautiful women created for that purpose by God, whilst their wives shall look through a grate and be spectators of the enjoyments of their husbands with these most beautiful women, who shall not be subject to the monthly times or child bearing, and the men as vigorous as Mahomet himself, who gloried in his having outdone by double the number of Ovid himself." Muslims, thus, "are extremely addicted not only to lust, but also to sodomy itself and combination with brutes."[169] So even though Muslims rejected idolatry, Calvinists believed that their core social observances enthusiastically embraced carnality.

The complexity of navigating culture in the quest to convert people to Protestant Christianity thwarted the buoyant expectations of Calvinists. Writers at midcentury labored to better equip theologians and ministers in the confrontation with entrenched false religion. In these works, Rogerius, Baldaeus, Hoornbeeck, Voetius, Oomius, and to a lesser extent Carolinus created a bleak narrative that cast doubt on the faculty of pagans and Muslims to receive, understand, and accept the gospel. By distorting tenets and concocting credulous tales, priests shrouded the features of Vedic religions that might lead a person to religious truth. Idolatry and superstition worked their wicked woe, leading communities and individuals down the diabolical path to perversion and inordinate sensuality. Voetius and others were so obsessed with the relationship between idolatry and sexual disorder that they assigned paganism a contaminating role in Islam. Nevertheless, there was still hope. The effort to train and educate Calvinists assumed that debate and refutation could still convince nonbelievers, especially Muslims, of the superiority of Christianity. So Calvinism geared itself up for struggle with powerful adversaries that held sway in the lands of the Dutch empire.

DETACHMENT AND OTHERNESS, 1700s–1720s

Calvinist missions grinded on at the end of the seventeenth and beginning of the eighteenth centuries. Ministers and native linguists devoted much time and attention to translating the Bible into Tamil, Sinhalese, and Malay. *Predikanten* could still get quite animated about matters central to their faith, as bitter debates over dividing the sacraments (for the second time) and the Malay Bible stirred up consistories in Batavia and Amboina. And on occasion, ministers sounded the familiar triumphalist refrain, such as when, in 1698, Francois Valentijn proclaimed that the time was now ripe for God to "touch their hearts through the working of his spirit."[170] A gritty perseverance among Dutch consistories informed his yearning; ministers and elders continued to visit outlying areas, oversee schools, make inroads among village leaders, and report on the state of Protestant Christianity in the far reaches of the Indian Ocean. Yet the pace of conversions had not picked up, and ministers concerned themselves primarily with pastoral, rather than missionary, issues. Calvinists began to take a more cavalier and cosmopolitan attitude toward other practices and beliefs intimating that religion largely became a marker for cultural difference.

Only two works appeared during this time that carried out an analytical portrayal of other religions in the vein of narratives from earlier in the century. The most widely read and only historical and descriptive account written by an overseas Dutch Calvinist *predikant* in the eighteenth century was *The Old and New East Indies* by Francois Valentijn, an encyclopedic work spanning five large volumes that also included Siam, Vietnam, Cambodia, Laos, China, Japan, Ceylon, the southern coasts of India, and other areas. Although Valentijn borrowed copiously from many writers, his elegant prose and detailed descriptions of peoples, places, and historical events made it the most important work by a Dutch writer on South and Southeast Asia until modern times.[171] The second significant book, on Islam, was by Adriaan Reland, a professor of oriental languages at the University of Utrecht; published in 1705, this highly influential work reflected a decisive pivot to a more balanced view of Islam among European intellectuals. Despite their vastly different intentions, Valentijn and Reland both conveyed a measured approach toward Islam and a detachment toward other religions.

For all his geographical and topical coverage, Valentijn displayed a rather tepid interest in describing religious traditions, save for narrating the work of Reformed ministers. In several thousand double-columned pages, he devoted less than a hundred to Asian religions, and even then most of what he wrote was derivative and superficial. For example, he sidestepped discussing "the heathen religion" in Java, instead referring "curious readers" to the works of Rogerius and Baldaeus, which focused on South Asia.[172] And although he included sections on the "religious affairs" of people in most of the regions he covered, the accounts were terse and unoriginal. The pagans of Amboina, he complained, worshipped the sun, moon, and too many other bodies to enumerate. Holding to the universality of paganism, he maintained that pagan beliefs were indistinguishable from the old Eastern beliefs filtered through the Greeks and Romans.[173] His most extensive look at Islam required only a little over two pages, which he inserted in the section on Java. This treatment enabled him to avoid considering Islam altogether in his account of Celebes; he simply directed those who might want more detail to his brief discussion regarding Java.[174] Perhaps Valentijn's rather meager treatment of the religious practices of Asians reflected his own personal indifference. He earned a reputation among contemporaries and also historians as a half-hearted minister more interested in intellectual pursuits and making an income on the side than in pastoral duties, especially conducting visitations.[175] It also seems likely that Valentine was simply responding to his reading market, which by now had acquired a tired sense of familiarity with Muslim, Hindu, Buddhist, and local observances and a growing perception of intractable cultural difference between East and West.

When Valentijn did discuss religious traditions, he relied heavily on seventeenth-century writers, such as Grotius, Voetius, Hoornbeeck, Rogerius, and Baldaeus, rather than on personal experience.[176] Like those writers, Valentijn conceived of faith and worship in his own day as deriving historically from four world religions: pagandom, Judaism, Islam, and Christianity. In some instances, he made distinctions between Roman Catholicism and Reformed Christianity, and in one case he categorized Buddhist observances on Java as the "Chinese [heathen] religion," and the observances of the Siamese as "heathens in the manner of Indians and Ceylonese," by which he meant Hindus.[177] Nevertheless, by the eighteenth century the notion that a universal religion known as "heathendom" comprised all the non-Abrahamic beliefs and traditions around the world had long become a truism for Reformed Protestants. For this reason, Valentijn noted that it was not necessary to describe the "heathen religion" on Celebes, because "it is nothing different from the heathen religion of the Amboinese, Ternatens, Javanese, and all other eastern peoples."[178] Pagan religion certainly had nuances, he conceded here and there, but all practitioners from ancient times to his present day shared several fundamental characteristics: they all worshipped entities within the created order; they constructed idols; they succumbed to diabolical seduction (though this dimension receives much less attention in Valentijn than in earlier writers' works); and they labored under the burdens imposed by a self-serving clergy. These elements united pagans in India, China, the East Indies, Africa, and the Americas, and of course manifested themselves in Europe through the Catholic Church.

The focus on scriptural texts and the continued attention to missions in both Southeast Asia and the Netherlands yielded a more informed engagement with Islam by the early 1700s. Although the harvest of souls remained small, ministers noted baptisms and marriages of converted Muslims throughout the eighteenth century. Consistories in Banda, Amboina, Ternate, and Batavia reported regularly that Moors and pagans sought baptism, and annual pastoral reports quantified new converts, members, and schoolchildren.[179] The accounts give ample quantitative evidence of ongoing engagement through missionary work, but they do not provide a qualitative basis with which to evaluate Calvinists' attitudes toward Islam.

Valentijn possessed an adept understanding of the history of Islam in the region, an extensive knowledge of its teachings, and a perceptive awareness of local practice. He recounted the arrival and spread of the religion, which he dated to the 1400s, by Sunni Arab traders into the Moluccas, Java, and Ternate. Across regions, he noted the varying levels of commitment to Islam among ruling dynasties and their outlook toward other religions, especially Christianity. Occasionally citing Voetius and Hoornbeeck, Valentijn described the central tenets of Islam in generally neutral terms, while making no effort to disguise his contempt for the religion, calling it "a cancer and a pest." He belittled the Qur'an as a "work of deceit" and Muhammad as a "foul adulterer."[180] His most trenchant criticisms, however, grew out of missionary frustration at the resistance of local Muslims to the Christian message. He disparaged Muslims for their rote and thoughtless conformity to religious observance and for their obstinate refusal to reconsider their traditions. Explaining why few Muslims converted to Christianity, Valentijn contended that adherence to Islam required little effort. He did credit Islam for introducing greater literacy in Malay, though not Arabic, and for doing away with idols and superstitions followed by pagans. Noting their industry, he spoke respectfully of Muslims' practice of praying five times during the day and of ritual washing.[181] Valentijn told a personal story about being allowed to observe prayers at a "temple" in Hila (Amboina) in 1687 and conversing extensively with a Muslim "priest" he knew well, Hassan Soeleyman, about his religion and the service.[182] Valentijn also described an episode in 1706 when, as a chaplain in the army, he befriended the "Makassar Captain" Daeng Matàra, "one of the most sensible Mohammedans." In one conversation, Matàra located the origins of Islam in Makassar with a certain merchant, Datuk Bendang, who introduced the religion in 1605.[183]

The abiding effort to understand Islam in order to convert Muslims reached its apex in the Netherlands in the early eighteenth century with the work of Adriaan Reland. A brilliant linguist with a wide reach, Reland possessed outstanding facility in a range of Asian languages, including Arabic, Persian, Hebrew, and Malay; he also excelled in the cartography of Palestine, Persia, and Southeast Asia. The son of a minister, Reland grew up in a solidly Calvinist milieu, and he remained loyal to the orthodox version of Reformed Protestantism throughout his life. He received his education and held a faculty appointment from 1701 to 1718 at Utrecht, the intellectual bastion of orthodox Calvinism in the Netherlands. Utrecht had also developed a robust global outlook under Voetius and Hoornbeeck that Reland inherited. His *On the Mohammedan Religion* was translated into Dutch, English, French, German, and Spanish. Perhaps because it exposed Catholic misreadings and took a relatively neutral stance toward Islam, the work made the Index of Prohibited Books in 1722.[184]

The premise underlying *On the Mohammedan Religion* was that Christians had to understand and even appreciate Islam before they could engage Muslims successfully. Reland thus summarized Islamic teachings in Latin and Arabic and corrected thirty-nine views wrongly ascribed to Muslims.[185] Like Voetius, furthermore, he argued that it was essential for Christian theologians to study the Qur'an in Arabic.[186] He also criticized and refuted many incorrect portrayals of Islam by Christian apologists who relied uncritically on Latin texts and medieval commentators, pointing out to readers that they should not judge any religion based on the writings of its detractors. After all, he reminded Calvinists, Roman Catholics wrongly accused Protestants of despising good works, of making God the author of sin, and of disparaging Mary, the mother of Christ, and the saints.[187] Likewise, Christians should not take criticisms of Islam at face value, especially by those works not based on Arabic. He even included Hoornbeeck's *Summa controversarium* in a list of books not rooted in Arabic sources and that thus "fantasized" about Islam.[188] Working from Arabic sources, Reland refuted erroneous charges that Muslims taught, for example, that God existed in bodily form, that hell and providence did not exist, and that God was the author of sin.[189]

Reland argued that the problem with many Christian polemicists was that they did not take seriously the similarities between Christianity and Islam that they themselves recognized. Rather, he advised that Christians should appreciate what Islam and Christianity shared in common and begin disputations from that standpoint.[190] The conversion strategy followed logically from Reland's emphasis on recognizing commonalities. Ministers could highlight the points where the Qur'an departed from the teachings of the Old and New Testament. Moreover, he declared that Muslims were not as crazy as Christians had characterized them. Islam could not, Reland continued, have spread so widely across Asia, Africa, and Europe had it not enticed many as an appealing and genuine religion.[191] He quoted Ludovico Marracci, a contemporary Catholic orientalist, who observed that Islam seems at first glance to accord with the laws of nature, whereas the Christian mysteries of the Trinity, Incarnation, and Resurrection seem far-fetched.[192]

On the Mohammedan Religion sought to convey a comprehensive and accurate understanding of Islam, shorn of long-held misconceptions and caricatures that had plagued Christian missionaries, but not at the expense of his own faith. Reland remained fully within the Calvinist orbit in the University of Utrecht, and his work seems to have escaped controversy among Reformed church authorities. He continued to work uninterrupted on orientalist scholarship at the university until his death in 1718. Even though Reland's work belonged to global Calvinism, he was participating in a broad reappraisal of Islam that took hold among orientalists in Europe in the late 1600s and early 1700s.[193] Steeped in Arabic, Persian, and other European languages, these scholars, including many whom Reland esteemed, such as Edward Pococke, Eusebius Renaudot, and Ludovico Marracci, translated texts and engaged in comparative study of languages, literatures, and cultures.[194]

CONCLUSION

As *predikanten* and *ziekentroosteren* embarked on ships headed to distant outposts in the Indian and Atlantic oceans, Dutch Reformed Protestants (Calvinists and Arminians) sought to make sense of the world the evangelists were encountering and their place in it. Ever since the *Magdeburg Centuries* was first published between 1559 and 1572, Protestants had been writing histories to demonstrate that they were the true descendants of apostolic Christianity and to point out where the Roman church had diverged from it. Humanists, too,

resorted to historical study to recapture the classical past and to trace the evolution of law, language, and custom. Writings by Dutch authors describing many
new lands and peoples proliferated through the Golden Age. Yet Grotius, Vossius, and Udemans operated with a different objective, namely to provide a narrative of Dutch Protestantism in light of this auspicious opportunity to take the
gospel around the world. They worked from St. Paul's principle in Romans 1:20
that God had implanted in all people a nascent awareness of his divine nature.
Utilizing biblical and classical examples, they forged all observances and beliefs
into four universal religions: paganism, Judaism, Christianity, and Islam. Calvinists expected a global gathering of souls leading to the second coming of
Christ.

In the mid-seventeenth century, Calvinists in the empire and Republic continued to have hope for an abundant harvest of souls, yet with a greater awareness of the cultural obstacles involved. Local peoples who did convert often did
not demonstrate the lifestyle transformation expected of them, and they cared
little for Protestant teachings. Rogerius, Baldaeus, Hoornbeeck, Voetius, Carolinus, and Oomius wrote between the 1650s and 1670s to help their co-religionists
understand paganism and Islam and also to recalibrate the narrative to account
for slow and uneven growth. Adopting the taxonomies of the earlier writers, the
midcentury Calvinists stressed the dark clouds of priestly deception that kept
people from the true divine nature and the pernicious effects of idolatry that
enmeshed societies in sexual licentiousness. Hoornbeeck, Voetius, and Oomius also read Islam through the lens of paganism and sensuality. While the mission slogged on, by the 1720s Calvinists had developed diminished expectations
for the mission field. Valentijn wrote from a more aloof perspective, and Reland
granted Islam a fair amount of respect. Culture, it seemed, formed an almost
impermeable barrier to conversion to Calvinism.

After Reland and Valentijn, no more ambitious narratives of world religions
or dissections of Islam appeared from Dutch Calvinists in the eighteenth century.
Perhaps Calvinists and their missions, with no new crises on the horizon, did
not need a new grand arc. A contrary vision, however, was emerging, reflected
in the publication of Jean Bernard and Bernard Picart's *Religious Ceremonies
and Customs of All Peoples of the World* (*Cérémonies et coutumes religieuses de
tous les peuples du monde*) between 1723 and 1737.[195] A vast multivolume work,
Religious Ceremonies was preoccupied in the same type of project as Dutch
Calvinists—that is, to comprehend the diversity of world religions in light of new
knowledge or perspective. In this case, Bernard and Picart hoped to use rationality and relativism to present all religions as authentically as possible. Though
at the opposite end from Calvinist articulations of history, *Religious Ceremonies*

carried the imprint of Calvinist accounts. Picart and Bernard employed Rogerius for South Asia and leaned almost exclusively on Reland for Islam. Furthermore, the universal categories first put down by Grotius and then utilized in all other Dutch accounts formed the major divisions that shaped Bernard and Picart's analysis. The connections between Calvinist world narratives and the comprehensive analyses in *Religious Ceremonies* suggest that the inspirations and methods for the rationalism of the eighteenth century could come from unlikely sources.

6

GLOBAL CALVINISM AND THE
PAGAN PRINCIPLE

The Dutch Calvinist missionary Jacob Canter Visscher, stationed in Cochin from 1717 to 1724 and then in Batavia until 1735, had always been a connoisseur of travel literature. Perhaps for that reason, he composed memoirs about the people and places he encountered during his service in South Asia, based on letters he had written to family and friends at home. Like most travel accounts, Visscher's contained the usual descriptions of ornate pagan temples, alien sexual practices, and dark-hued bodies. Buried in one letter to his mother in Harlingen (Friesland), an account of a perplexing episode from 1717 stands out from the usual ethnographic fare, at least from a Dutch Calvinist minister. Toward the end of that year, according to Visscher, forces under the direction of the VOC had laid siege to an area around Calicut. Following the assault, soldiers plundered a Hindu temple and made off with some of the religious images. Soon after, Visscher crossed paths with the soldiers and their loot. Rather than admonishing them for preserving pagan idols or insisting that they be destroyed, Visscher actually pressed the soldiers to share a portion of their bounty with him. He wrote, I "collected [from the soldiers] many heathen idols that were taken out of the temple, which I keep as a memento."[1]

This Jacob Canter Visscher is the same *predikant* who complained to the Amsterdam classis at roughly the same time that Catholic missionaries had seduced pagans by "dangling alluring images before their eyes."[2] Perhaps because of his grounding in Reformed theology, he felt immune from the pull of pagan idols that prevailed over superstitious and decadent societies. Perhaps Visscher saw the images as keepsakes to show others back home and tell them about his days on the mission field converting strange peoples. Perhaps he simply found them interesting for reasons he could not describe. Regardless, it is remarkable that what once were diabolical idols for Calvinist missionaries had become, at least for one minister, souvenirs of a distant culture.

Calvinists like Visscher went out into the world to convert non-Christians, yet infidels also made their way into the cities and towns of the Dutch Republic. Pagan and Muslim men and women who had converted to—and then backslid from—Calvinism filled the pastoral reports that were read at synod and classis meetings across the Netherlands. Hindu and Buddhist images, much like those collected by *dominee* Visscher, crept into the curiosity cabinets of cosmopolitan elites; the Amsterdam burgomaster Nicolaes Witsen owned twenty-three idols. Brahmins in India, *inibs* (female priests) in Formosa, Tupi cannibals in Brazil, and fetish worshippers in Africa showed up in books, pictures, and maps for sale in Dutch shops.[3] Japanese samurai, Americans in headdress, and African villagers snuck into paintings of biblical scenes by famous Dutch masters, including Rembrandt and Ferdinand Bol. Willem Konijn, a minister in Ceylon who overlapped with Visscher in South Asia, sent local sketches of the Buddha (and Buddhist holy sites) to collectors in Amsterdam, who misidentified the figure as Adam. As these cases attest, Calvinists and other Dutch Protestants had complicated relationships with pagans and their idols.[4]

This chapter explores the ways in which global Calvinism played out among broad circles within Protestantism and wider swaths of intellectuals in the Dutch Republic. Historians have brought attention to the global knowledge flowing through Holland. Amsterdam functioned as the "metropolis of print" about Asiatica for western Europe. In one of the world's most active book and art markets, accounts of faraway places, maps and geographies charting distant spaces, and paintings, woodcuts, and engravings of mysterious peoples found their way into Dutch homes. Benjamin Schmidt has argued that a growing enchantment with overseas societies contributed to exceptionalist constructions of "Europe" by Western writers. Joan-Pau Rubiés has corroborated the substantial role that ethnology played in the formation of comparative and universal approaches to religion that were characteristic of the Enlightenment.[5]

For the Dutch, Calvinism, owing to its missionary project and participation in commercial empire, lay at the center of this engagement with world societies. Calvinist missionaries grappled intensely with the complexities of translating Protestantism within unfamiliar cultures, and they brought those struggles home. The geographical dimensions of the knowledge that they generated connected the mysterious places where they toiled to the interlinked church and social networks across the Netherlands. Overseas societies thus gained a powerful presence within Dutch towns and cities, contributing over time to an ambient global perspective that framed religious and intellectual discourses. Yet it has been easy to overlook global influences on central debates over the place of religion and morality in society. For example, historians routinely pass over René Descartes's confession of his debt to "the great book of the world" and his observation that often even "savage and barbarous . . . nations make an equally good if not better use of their reason than we do."[6]

The following analysis shows how Calvinists appropriated paganism, and to a lesser extent Islam, to provide new perspectives on religious and intellectual struggles in Europe. Paganism in particular manifested itself in at least two ways among Dutch Protestants. First, Calvinists who operated within the institutional framework of the Reformed Church came to identify central tenets of rationalism as pagan. For these Calvinists, the pagan principle—which they had long combated in overseas churches—confused the worship of God with (some aspect of) the created order. Their Socinian, Libertine, and Spinozist opponents resembled pagan idolaters and atheists because rationalists elevated human reason on a par with direct (scriptural) revelation. Second, Reformed Protestants of varying intellectual commitments used either the praise or criticism of pagans and Muslims as thinly veiled attacks on their enemies in Europe. For these Protestant intellectuals, paganism gave insight into European superstitions. The first half of this chapter analyzes the readings of paganism, and to a lesser extent Islam, among orthodox Calvinists in their networks of correspondence and theological writings. The second half examines several examples of (mostly) heterodox Protestant thinkers and their engagement with paganism.

CONSEQUENTIAL CONJUNCTURES

The Calvinist missions overseas gave rise to a comparative outlook that informed the approaches that Protestants in the Netherlands took toward new rationalist trends in Protestantism and customary antagonisms with Catholicism. A global outlook on missions came at a crucial moment in the mid- to late 1600s as it converged with the emergence of Cartesian and Spinozist influences within Protestantism in the Netherlands and Europe.

THE CENTRALITY OF MISSIONS WITHIN DUTCH CALVINISM

The world formed the backdrop against which everyday life played out in the "Golden Age" of the Dutch Republic. A long line of writers, including such figures as Olfert Dapper, Arnold Montanus, and Willem Bosman, drafted texts about exotic Asian, African, and American lands. Though they displayed little interest in analyzing cultures or religions in any pan-historic context, these and other writers detailed the customs and practices of people in various parts of the world. Dutch intellectuals, including Calvinists, debated the merits of Confucianism as Sinophilia found a warm reception in the Republic in the 1600s.[7] Writers were joined by an equally long list of artists, perhaps most notably Romeyn de Hooghe, Theodore de Bry, Jacob van Meurs, and Cornelis de Bruijn, who sketched eye-popping images of those strange bodies described in textual accounts. And this period was just as golden for cartography with the likes of Abraham Ortelius, Jodocus Hondius, and Willem Janszoon Blaeu, who mapped the spaces of this endlessly fascinating world. Benjamin Schmidt has labeled the Netherlands in this period "an entrepôt of exoticism," as a flood of media depicting flora, fauna, people, architecture, religions, customs, and landscapes streamed through the Republic at the height of the VOC's power.[8] Those visual and textual images reminded the Dutch of their place in an increasingly interconnected world and beckoned them to imagine strange lands. This global tableau also called out to serious-minded Calvinists, who were puzzling out how to make foreign peoples good, God-fearing, idol-hating Protestants.

By the 1630s, global missions took on increasing significance and became central to Dutch Calvinism as ministers overseas labored at converting pagans and Moors. These struggles pulsed through the intellectual core of the missionary project, centered at the universities of Utrecht and Leiden. As we have seen, Antonius Walaeus, a theologian at Leiden, had opened a seminary to train *predikanten* for overseas service in 1623, though it closed after ten years. Shortly thereafter, in 1634, Gisbertus Voetius joined the faculty at Utrecht and took on a leading academic role in supporting the global spread of Calvinism. A delegate at the Synod of Dort in 1618–1619, Voetius had called on his fellow members there to declare formally their commitment to "the propagation of the gospel in the East Indies and other places."[9] With the Ottoman empire on Europe's eastern frontier, an absorbing concern with Islam animated Voetius. He learned Arabic, lectured on Islam and paganism, and wrote about missions.

Voetius regularly held disputations with students on a variety of theological matters. On many topics, he subsequently drafted an expanded treatment of the issues under discussion, and published them in theological compendia, which appeared in five volumes from 1648 to 1669. A number of the disputations were devoted to critiquing non-Christian religions and converting infidels. Thus, the conversion of non-Christian peoples around the world, including Europe, occupied the center of Dutch Calvinist intellectual life in the seventeenth century.

Voetius did not sketch out a new theological structure for missions, but rather he described the Calvinist community-building approach to conversion already on the ground in Southeast Asia and Brazil.[10] Since the earliest treatises came thirty years after the start of missionary activity in the Moluccan Islands, Batavia, Formosa, and Brazil, the global mission actually gave impulse and direction to his writings on this and related topics. In several places, he referred specifically to his experience following missions or counsel he received from former overseas ministers. For example, he wrote that "experience has taught me" that consistories and classes should call missionaries. He gave "serious consideration" to the advice of a "learned *predikant* who spent eighteen years declaring Christ in the East Indies" on the need to learn local languages. A letter sent by "a faithful minister of the word" in the East Indies confirmed for Voetius the need to take a slow approach to conversion. And his "good friend Justus Heurnius" advised him on the need for rigorous education and repetitive messaging in sermons to inculcate godliness among pagans.[11]

Following missionary practice in the East Indies since the 1610s and 1620s, Voetius placed emphasis on building church communities under the auspices of a Christian political order as the basis for converting infidels.[12] Ministers had established consistories to administer the sacraments, preach the gospel, and impose moral discipline, while they set up diaconates to distribute alms to the poor. Time and again they declared triumphantly that establishing these parochial offices would "throw open the door" to pagans, Muslims, and Jews. Decades later, Voetius endorsed this strategy.

Although Voetius applauded the missionary work underway in Asia and the Americas, he expressed frustration with the limitations imposed by the Dutch trading companies. In a treatise titled *Planting Churches* he complained, "Our ministers, working among pagans there, are often impeded by rulers, military commanders, and merchant leaders; they sometimes have dealings with such men, who are more worthy of the workhouse [than of such high positions]. The fact that ministers sometimes enter into commercial contracts with pagans is no small impediment to conversion."[13] The principle at stake for Voetius was that it was the responsibility of church bodies (consistories, classes, and synods) to authorize missionaries, though he fully accepted that they could accompany trading companies.[14] And yet in practice, governor generals of the VOC assigned ministers to posts across the Indian Ocean, over the strong objections of Calvinist clergy in the empire and Republic. Voetius followed Catholic authorities, notably Philip Rovenius, Apostolic Vicar of the Holland Mission, in calling for ecclesiastical autonomy over missions. Referencing Rovenius's *Treatise on Missions* (*Tractatus de missionibus*, 1621), Voetius wholeheartedly endorsed his denunciation of Jesuit missionaries, though naturally he departed from Rovenius in rejecting the authority of the pope to call and send missionaries.[15]

Voetius prescribed a process for planting churches that tracked the playbook of overseas Calvinist ministers in Southeast Asia and Brazil. Among pagans, Muslims, and Jews, *predikanten* should first seek out people who seemed amenable to the Christian message and educate them in the faith through catechism lessons. Out of those prospects, ministers were to evaluate and then recruit the most competent to profess their faith, receive baptism, and participate in the life of the congregation. This church-planting protocol, he believed, followed the examples of St. Paul and the apostles. The New Testament model provided the best opportunity to establish new communities of faith that in turn would herald the gospel among non-Christians, leading to the salvation of many.[16] Focusing on New Testament examples, Voetius stressed that overseas ministers should cultivate church communities, live among pagan families, and make disciples of them.

Voetius also held that an understanding of philosophy—by which he meant Aristotelian scholasticism—was vital for effective proselytizing among sophisticated non-Christians. Philosophy, he contended, gave missionaries intellectual weapons to counter pagan and Muslim thought and to defend scripture as the word of God whose dictates and promises extended to all peoples. Voetius also argued that demonstrating a knowledge of philosophy would impress non-Christians with the intellectual acumen of Calvinist *predikanten* and help them appeal to natural law in debating with Muslims.[17] Yet he did not believe it necessary to send learned men into all areas of the mission field. In pagan regions that possessed little political order and barbarous customs, Calvinists could make do with "unlettered" and "unlearned" men equipped with godliness and knowledge of the scriptures. In societies that demonstrated a high level of order and knowledge of philosophy and science, only distinguished *predikanten* should be sent. Voetius proposed that the most knowledgeable ministers be reserved for Japan and China because of the intellectual achievements of those civilizations.[18]

Voetius also displayed a familiarity with the most divisive question for clergy both overseas and in the Netherlands related to the conversion of non-Christians: whether to establish different criteria for allowing prospective converts to receive baptism and to partake of the Lord's Supper. The proposed policy by overseas ministers to "divide the sacraments" sought to lower the barriers to church membership through a more graduated set of requirements for knowledge and behavior in societies with only a passing acquaintance with Christian teachings. Voetius emphatically affirmed the resolution of the Synod of Dort that the sacraments were bound together in an inviolable unity.[19] This view meant that potential converts had to meet the requirements for both baptism and communion before they could be admitted as members, a practice most overseas consistories apart from Batavia did not follow.

Simon Oomius devoted several pages in his *Opened and Revived Muhammedisdom or Turckdom* (1663) to the best means for converting Muslims. He stressed it was incumbent upon Christians to obey Christ's mandate to preach the gospel to all peoples and for trading companies to support learned ministers overseas. Following Voetius and many others, he also advocated the study of languages, especially Arabic for those *predikanten* working among Muslims. Finally, he urged Christian magistrates and states to set up academies and colleges to train capable young men who could accompany ambassadors and merchants to propagate the gospel in Muslim lands.[20] As this shows, the missions already underway in Asia and America and the problems ministers faced were shaping theological reflections at Utrecht on the conversion of far-off peoples.

The global Calvinist missionary project also exerted an enormous influence on faculty at the University of Leiden. Since the late sixteenth century, Leiden was already a leading center for the study of Asian languages and cultures. The university claimed such humanistic luminaries as Joseph Scaliger, Thomas Erpenius, and Jacob Golius; it also owned an extensive collection of Arabic manuscripts.[21] Johannes Hoornbeeck joined the theological faculty at Leiden in 1654, carrying his devotion to missions with him. There he was joined by associates Johannes Cocceius and Georgius Hornius, who were also committed to spreading Calvinism overseas. The latter, for example, engaged in a long dispute with Isaac Vossius, son of Gerardus Vossius, over the value of Confucian thought for Christians in Europe.[22] Hoornbeeck composed comprehensive works on setting heretics right in Europe and converting pagans, Moors, and Jews around the world.[23] Hoornbeeck's efforts shared both the pedagogical aims of Voetius's treatises and the interpretive ambitions of Calvinist narratives that sought to recontextualize the missionary project in light of its adversities in the mid-1600s.

Cocceius lectured and wrote about missions throughout the course of his career, doing so within the framework of his view of the church, the unfolding drama of salvation throughout history, and the looming imminence of the end times. His inaugural oration at the University of Leiden in 1648 was devoted to Judaism and the conversion of the Jews. In this speech, he called out to the audience that "we are seeking people" to carry God's message to "faraway lands."[24] Although Cocceius's enunciation of mission appears throughout his voluminous body of writing, the most well-developed exposition appeared in his *Summa on Theology* (1662).[25] In this treatise, Cocceius rolled out the missionary calling of the church from the prophets in the Old Testament through the work of the apostles in the New Testament. W. J. van Asselt, a theologian specializing in Cocceius's work, described his devotion to mission as part of his "prophetic theology." That is, for Cocceius the direction of history was leading to the worldwide conversion of pagans, Muslims, and Jews.[26]

The development of the Calvinist missions and Cocceius's expectations for their success substantiated his millenarian outlook. By the 1660s, Cocceius had worked out an eschatological scheme that recognized the events of his own day as signs of the impending return of Christ. One of the essential prophetic marks was the church's return to biblical Christianity (in the Reformation) and its going forth into all the world.[27] Protestant missions to Muslims functioned as a key component in the process of salvation for Cocceius. He coupled an exegesis of Romans 6:12 that mentions kings in the east with an interpretation of Isaiah 19:23 that prophesies Egypt's and Assur's return to the Lord.[28] These passages, according to Cocceius, indicated that the gospel would reach Muslims (the people of Assur) and that they would convert on a large scale. Cocceius made a distinction between previous missionary movements and those of his own time that would lead to a worldwide conversion of Jews, Muslims, and pagans, writing: "[T]hey preach Christ, but the seed does not take, as the good earth does, to produce fruit, yet it is clear that when pagans come and live in peace with the faithful and reject hatred, then it can be said rightly that the pagans will enter that heavenly city."[29] In his schema, Cocceius linked the conversion of Muslims to the salvation of the Jews, which would trigger the second coming of Christ. On other occasions, he represented the full conversion of pagans as a precursor to the (Christian) salvation of the Jews.[30] Although the order of the ingathering of Jews, Muslims, and pagans varied in his writings, his theological understanding of his own day was predicated on the global missions carried out in Asia and the anticipation of their success. Cocceius believed that this prophetic theology—which assigned a central place to missions—could demonstrate the truth of scripture to skeptics and rationalists alike.[31]

THE IMPORTANCE OF COMPARATIVE OBSERVATION

Outside the intellectual atmosphere of Dutch universities, Calvinist ministers, theologians, and intellectuals also read about and responded to the highs and lows of the mission fields, just as their overseas brethren tracked the state of Reformed Christianity in Europe. The dissemination of information about the state of Dutch Calvinist conversion efforts spread far beyond the Netherlands. In 1699, for instance, Increase Mather, the Puritan divine in the Massachusetts Bay Colony, composed an account titled *On the Progression of the Gospel to India*.[32] Using letters from Dutch overseas clergy, Mather related conversions taking place in Ceylon, the opening of the seminary in Jaffnapatnam, and "Mohammedans" coming to the Christian faith in Amboina.[33]

The correspondence and circulation of letters consolidated Dutch and overseas consistories into a worldwide Calvinist body pursuing Reformation wherever possible. In other words, the mission field was not just overseas; it was a global one that also included Europe and the Netherlands. Theaters of activity from diverse and distant spatial vantage points gave Calvinists the opportunity to make comparisons among religions between one region and another. They used the lens of the struggle against Catholics and rationalists (Libertines, Socinians, Cartesians, and Spinozists) in Europe to inform their understanding of the missions overseas. And the battle against paganism overseas reoriented Calvinists in their contests over rationalism in Europe. Their biblicist and classical training enabled Calvinists to elongate the field of comparison through time. The universalizing religious taxonomies of Grotius, Vossius, Hoornbeeck, et al. opened the way to a rich cache of analogies for the sake of understanding the fortunes of true religion past and present, from the children of Israel to the early church to international Reformed Protestantism.

The relevance of comparative analysis across space and time to comprehend Calvinism's place and progress in the world manifested itself in a variety of writings by Dutch partisans. The classes of Amsterdam and Walcheren, as well as the synods of North and South Holland, received letters regularly from consistories around the world describing the state of missions in their regions. Reading, discussing, deliberating, and responding to reports from Batavia, Formosa, Amboina, Banda, Ternate, Colombo, the Cape of Good Hope, Brazil, New Netherland, Curaçao, Surinam, and other locations necessarily invited Dutch ministers to observe and compare the circumstances affecting Calvinism worldwide. As firm believers in direct divine involvement in the world, they relied on comparative readings of remarkable events to discern the signs of the times in the contemporary struggle between good and evil.

Dutch Calvinists construed the causal hand of providence in the contingencies affecting the mission, the empire, and the Republic. No events were random; they happened for a purpose. Godefridus Udemans and Hugo Grotius discerned a divine plan at work in the conjuncture of the Reformation with the discovery of the Indies. As Udemans wrote in 1638, "[T]he lord wishes to show that now the time has come that the gospel of the kingdom should be preached throughout the entire world."[34] Beyond the missions, the Dutch scrutinized and interpreted providence in the newsworthy events of the day. In June 1693, for example, Samuel Trezel, secretary to the deputy for Indian affairs, wrote to the Batavia consistory that God had once again demonstrated his goodness and care for their country, as a "very evil, horrible design" by the king of France against the life of *stadhouder* Willem III was uncovered and foiled. Since Calvinists, like most Christians of the time, believed that God intervened directly in the world, they regarded spectacular environmental events as evidence of divine judgment. In the same letter, Trezel described an earthquake felt in the Netherlands, an ordinary phenomenon in the "hot" lands of the Indies but uncommon in the Netherlands. He went on to note reports of earthquakes in Jamaica and Sicily and called on people to consider the meaning of "such noticeable judgments of God."[35]

Calvinists infused meaning in their reading of world societies through analogies from the Bible and church history. These stories became the language of explanation for the course of the gospel through history and in contemporary times. Because *predikanten* overseas considered themselves to be carrying on the work of the great commission back to the time of the apostles, church districts in the Netherlands often attempted to buoy ministers' spirits with stories from the early followers of Christ.[36] Attempting to encourage a Dutch community in Albany, New York, in April 1699, for example, the Amsterdam classis reminded leaders there of the example of St. Paul's patience: although he longed for heaven, the apostle contented himself with his earthly ministry in order to nurture young congregations.[37] A minister in South Asia sought to explain the false practices of Christians in the region by invoking the story of St. Thomas as the first missionary to India in 52 CE. He converted many people to the true religion, but over time Roman Catholic missionaries contaminated those congregations.[38] In Colombo, the consistory compared local conversions based on "worldly motives" to the windfall of new Christians in the Roman Empire after the emperors attached themselves to the religion.[39] The fall of Formosa to the Chinese greatly saddened Calvinists, for it represented the loss of a promising mission field. A melancholy scribe from Holland utilized the story of Naomi's despondency over her social dislocation and bereavement in the book of Ruth to capture the disappointment that Calvinists felt. In the story (Ruth 1:20), Naomi wept, "[N]o longer call me Naomi, but call me Mara for the Lord has dealt bitterly with me." The scribe echoed this lament: "unfortunate Formosans, with tears in their eyes" could likewise "say no longer call me Formosa [which means beautiful], because all my beauty and adornment have gone away and God has left me wounded."[40]

A common theme in these biblical analogies was the Calvinist identification with the children of Israel, for they gave witness to the struggles of the people of God against powerful enemies.[41] Here are a few examples. Citing the story of quarrels between Abraham and his nephews in Genesis 13, the Batavia consistory emphasized in October 1784 the need for the Dutch churches to stay united during a difficult political and economic moment. The moral of unity and loyalty would not have been lost on any Calvinist, for in this account Abraham's nephew Lot went out from his kinsfolk and settled in the city of Sodom, leading his family to moral disaster.[42] Likewise, bullied by Catholic France in the south, the Amsterdam classis in 1682 took solace in the long suffering of Israel, which God continually delivered out of its troubles against large and fierce enemies.[43] Over a hundred years later, the *predikanten* in Batavia sought to comfort the brothers in Amsterdam by cloaking them in the image of the ancient Jews. In 1786, under assault from France, Batavia offered prayers for the rebuilding of Solomon's temple in Jerusalem that was destroyed in the sixth century BCE, declaring their hope "that the fallen walls of the Dutch Jerusalem may be rebuilt."[44]

Thus, ministers in the Netherlands and overseas conceived of one broad mission field extending from the apostles down to their own day in which *predikanten* were working to preach the word of God, administer the sacraments, and establish morally disciplined communities. Voetius regarded the Reformation as a missionary movement in which the Reformers meant to bring the church back to true religion. Following in the footsteps of the Hussites and Waldensians in the late Middle Ages, Protestant Reformers planted churches and propagated the faith in Germany, the Netherlands, France, Scotland, and England.[45] And now the Dutch were extending that influence along trading circuits in Asia and the Atlantic. The Amsterdam classis made connections between the mission abroad and at home, giving thanks in September 1675 that the ministers in Ceylon were bringing out many souls from "blind heathendom" and that God was also pouring out his "gracious love onto our darkness in the Fatherland."[46] Similarly, in November 1720 the Colombo consistory responded to a letter from the Walcheren classis that the brothers rejoiced to hear about the preaching of the word of God in all the kingdoms of the world.[47] Hoornbeeck included French Huguenots and English Puritans in North America as part of the global spread of the Reformed faith.[48] An anonymous local ruler in Patani (North Molucca) who converted in 1610 even had learned to consider himself as part of universal body of Christians. A Dutch scribe and native linguist produced a statement in which the elder realized that "God had been pleased" to allow the Dutch to come into his land so that he "could receive knowledge of Christ" and the "right fundamentals of Christian belief."[49]

RELIGIOUS THREATS AT HOME

As Calvinists sought to propagate their faith in new lands, they also had to contend with serious threats to Protestantism in their own backyard. Beginning in the second half of the seventeenth century, Dutch Calvinists saw themselves engaged in an existential struggle for the future of Christianity against two enemies: a revived Catholicism on the one hand, and an emergent rationalism on the other. Both endangered, from a Calvinist viewpoint, the biblical foundations of revealed religion and made Christians susceptible to the paths of idolatry and atheism. By virtue of the large presence of Catholics in the Netherlands, Dutch political authorities, primarily city magistrates in the provinces of Holland and Utrecht, tolerated Catholic worship under certain circumstances. As long as Catholics worshipped privately in hidden locations, kept symbols of Roman religion out of the public sphere, and paid "recognition money" to the sheriff, local authorities usually looked the other way. Catholicism actually underwent a resurgence in the early 1600s, and by midcentury one-third of the adult population in the Netherlands were Catholic.[50] On the international scene, the rise of the Jesuits as a force in Baroque Catholicism and the aggression of Catholic France put Dutch Protestants on their guard. In 1672 and 1684, Louis XIV's armies invaded the Netherlands and many feared the Republic was on the verge of collapse. Calvinist ministers and theologians consistently sought greater strictures against Catholic worship, called the wayward to repentance, and engaged in theological polemics against the Roman faith.

At the same time, an even greater menace appeared from several Protestant sources. Because of its relatively benign religious climate, the Republic, especially the cities of Holland, had attracted sizable groups of non-Calvinist Protestants. Mennonites and other Baptist sects had nurtured healthy communities even before the revolt against Spain. An eclectic and amorphous collection of spiritualists, known as Libertines (because they opposed Calvinist strictures on discipline and orthodoxy), overlapped and interacted with Mennonites and Remonstrants.[51] Finally, Socinians had migrated from Poland into Holland beginning in the sixteenth century, though more so in the seventeenth century because of persecution in the 1630s and 1660s. Followers of Fausto Sozzini, Socinians rejected the Trinity, emphasized the ethical teachings of Jesus, and supported complete freedom of religious thought. Historians of theology have regarded Socinianism as the "first form under which rationalism . . . emerged in the Protestant church."[52] Socinians found a friendly reception among Remonstrants, Libertines, and Mennonites and became instrumental in all of these networks. Calvinists considered the primacy that Socinians accorded to human reason as undermining the Protestant commitment to scripture alone (*sola scriptura*) as the revealed word of God.

The rationalism of the Socinians and other Protestants blended well with the rise of Cartesian thought in the 1640s. Living in Franeker (Friesland), Amsterdam, and The Hague from 1628 to 1649, René Descartes published his *Discourse on Method* in 1637. Shortly thereafter he attracted the ire of orthodox Calvinists (most famously Voetius), who began attacking the *Discourse* in print in 1641. Descartes sought to overturn the Aristotelian and scholastic explanation of natural knowledge, an explanation that Calvinist theology (and missions) accepted. For Voetius, the idea that human reason should serve as the basis for interpreting the Bible, religion, or nature posited a rational autonomy he equated with atheism. True religious knowledge came only from God, via the Holy Spirit, illuminating the mind of an individual and giving him or her the ability to have faith.[53] The long-standing Aristotelian scholastic system that had established proof of God's existence was under attack, and its demise, in the view of orthodox Calvinists like Voetius, would result in a conception of God bound by nature and reason. That Cartesian philosophy was seeping into heterodox Protestant denominations seemed, for Calvinists, to betray the biblicist legacy of the Reformation.

In the 1650s, the dispute over the rationalist trends in Dutch Protestantism spilled over into orthodox Calvinism and threatened to fracture it. Cartesian thought appealed not only to Remonstrant, Socinian, and Mennonite intellectuals already predisposed to deploy rationalism, but also to Calvinists who sought weapons against skepticism. Abraham Heidanus, a prominent theologian at Leiden from 1648 to 1676, and Christopher Wittichus at Nijmegen and Leiden from 1658 to 1687 believed that philosophical reasoning gave surer footing in defending orthodoxy against those who rejected their absolutist position on scripture. The ongoing tension between orthodox Calvinism and Cartesianism now became folded into a contentious theological dispute between Voetius and Cocceius over observance of the Sabbath. This conflict kept the problem of the Bible, rationalism, and skepticism alive as a contested issue among orthodox Calvinists from the 1650s well into the eighteenth century.

Cocceius rejected a literal reading of all portions of the Bible, particularly the Old Testament. With regard to the Sabbath, he argued that the injunction to keep the fourth commandment no longer applied after the advent of Christ and the New Testament. The Dutch Reformed Church had always held to a strict Sabbatarian observance; ministers often complained to city and company officials about profane activities taking place on Sundays. Beyond the particular impasse on Sabbath observance, Cocceius's method of interpreting the Bible highlighted the obscurity of many passages, the difficulty of understanding them in their own historical contexts and of applying them in a meaningful contemporary way. Cocceius maintained that certain episodes, such as Moses parting the Red Sea and Joshua commanding the sun to be still in the sky, should be understood figuratively, not as literal, historical events.[54]

For Calvinists such as Voetius, Cocceian hermeneutics seemed to embrace a natural and rational means of apprehending God and divine truth that corresponded to Cartesian methods. Voetius regarded Cocceius as a Cartesian because of his rejection of a literal interpretation of scripture. From the opposite angle, Heidanus, Wittichus, and other Cocceians also recognized the affinity between Cartesian philosophy and this more critical, historical approach to scriptural interpretation.[55] For his part, Cocceius did not admit to being a follower of Descartes and claimed not to have considered his writings very carefully. Cocceius did, however, acknowledge that God made himself known by processes and means that were natural to humans and that God accommodated himself to human capacities. For most Reformed Protestants on either side of the divide, Cocceianism and Cartesianism went hand in hand.[56]

PAGANISM AS A LENS

The comparative approaches that the global mission stimulated gave Calvinists nuanced ways of seeing these religious struggles and intellectual debates in Europe, ones that historians have not yet recognized. Religious cultures around the world formed a lens through which orthodox Calvinist *predikanten* and polemicists, particularly those who fell into the Voetian camp, looked in an effort to understand, explain, and discredit old and new enemies. They began by imposing the universal classifications of paganism, Mohammedanism, and Judaism on all worship practices and beliefs. Whereas Judaism and Islam were composed of self-identifying religious constituents, paganism represented an all-inclusive, amorphous category. Participants in the mission to propagate the gospel thus began to attribute similar characteristics of pagans overseas to their rivals in Europe. The malleability of paganism made it conducive for broad polemical applications, and the cultural geography constructed in the world narratives of Grotius, Vossius, Rogerius, Hoornbeeck, and others reinforced these comparisons. Having observed the beliefs and behaviors of apostates, idolaters, devil worshippers, and pagans across the world for over two generations, orthodox Calvinists by the 1640s were primed to identify these characteristics in their enemies: Catholics and rationalists. A key figure in the process of applying paganism to European religious conflicts was the great theologian of Calvinist missions, Gisbertus Voetius.

In four disputations on atheism held in 1639 (published in 1648), Voetius sought to expound on atheism as a phenomenon that not only was afflicting Christian Europe, but was inherent in other religious traditions as well. For Voetius, anyone who even implicitly denied the transcendence of the triune, creator God or who reduced the divine to the level of nature engaged (in principle) in atheism. Consequently, Voetius's understanding of atheism was rather elastic and enabled him to fold in Libertines, Socinians, Cartesians, deists, Epicureans, Machiavellianists, and spiritualist sectarian groups alike.[57] Because pagans in their worship practices attributed divine characteristics to nature, they, too, were atheists.[58] "[W]hen [one] transfers divine attributes of the true God, as the Gentiles, Mohammedans, and Jews do, they deny God," he wrote; "or those who have worshipped religion or reason, they also deny God either completely, or in principle, or in great part."[59] Thus, pagans, Muslims, and Jews not only qualified as atheists, but they served as the paragon of atheism by which groups in Europe were judged. Voetius did differentiate between Libertines, who he conceded functioned as a "secondary category of atheists," and those degenerate pagans "who live as beasts." Nevertheless, "Libertines, infidels, and enthusiasts" opposed scripture, subverted it to the light of nature, and consequently betrayed themselves as atheists.[60] In this regard, he ridiculed Descartes's famous dictum, *Cogito ergo sum*, by rendering it as "I think therefore I am, the idea of which is in me—by this notion, together with [his] prior skepticism, all natural and acquired knowledge is erased."[61] Voetius maintained that rationalists fell prey to atheistic principles that were first revealed in paganism.

In five disputations related to gentilism between 1638 and 1652, Voetius drew even sharper connections between pagans and rationalists. He described pagans as impious, profane, and idolatrous people who worship things of nature rather than God. Following the standard view among orthodox Calvinist writers, he contended that they all derived from one religious association: "one community begat a multitude."[62] Consequently, he went on to assert that "gentiles are all profane men of the world, Epicureans, Libertines, and similar people who have abandoned the pure worship of God."[63] Again Voetius made distinctions among levels of pagan decadence, claiming that in the East and West Indies, Brazil, and South Asia they worship devils, whereas in many ancient (Romans, Greeks) and contemporary (Chinese, Japanese) societies they have attained high levels of sophistication.[64] Despite the distinctions, equating God with nature was a pagan principle. The affinities of pagans from ancient peoples to contemporary "Socinians, Enthusiasts, and Papists" constituted the same error of containing God in or reducing God to nature.[65] For Voetius and like-minded thinkers, these peoples were instrumental in helping them dissect their new enemies in Europe.[66]

Other Calvinist partisans made connections between Socinians and Muslims. Georgius Hornius, a theologian at Leiden, declared that if Socinians were pagans, they were "much smarter" than "Heathendom." Rather, he saw European rationalists as treading down the path to "Turkdom and Atheism."[67] Simon Oomius, in a comparison of teachings about Christ, credited Muslims for clarity of expression, in contrast to Socinians who used "ambiguous words to deceive the simple and untrained" lay person.[68] Oomius, however, did not content himself with highlighting parallels, but went further to draw linkages between Islam, the Spanish theologian and humanist Miguel Servetus, Socinians, and Remonstrants. He claimed that Servetus acquired his anti-Trinitarian theology from Muslim teachers in Africa. Prominent Socinians were the most ardent defenders of Servetus because many of their beliefs aligned with Islam. Socinians, Oomius observed, did not attempt to convert Muslims in Transylvania because they agreed about the nondivine nature of Christ. Oomius took another step in Islamizing his enemies, calling attention to the resemblances between Muslim and Socinian doctrines. In that context, Oomius presented evidence that the well-known Remonstrants Hugo Grotius and Johannes Uytenbogaert had wavered somewhat on Socinianism, a fact that implicated them as secretly sympathetic to Islam.[69]

Yet paganism triumphed as the most dominant trope for discrediting Calvinists' religious enemies. Since the early sixteenth century—long before the Dutch became world traders—Reformed Protestants had accused Catholics of practicing pagan idolatry. Ulrich Zwingli in the 1520s invoked analogies of "heathen idolatry" in his call for reforming Catholic worship, and Heinrich Bullinger in the 1530s identified pagan elements in the Mass and cult of saints. Throughout the Reformation, the charge of pagan idolatry resounded as a routine polemical screed by Protestants of all stripes against religious imagery in Catholic worship.[70] And on the mission field, as we have seen, Calvinist clergy drew close correlations between "papist" and pagan idolatry. The Colombo consistory wrote in February 1691 that because of the Portuguese priests in the area, he and his pastoral colleagues were having to "rescue [natives] from both their old heathenism and their new papist superstition."[71]

The contribution that global Calvinism made to this construction in the seventeenth century was the folding of Catholicism into a metahistorical narrative of paganism. According to Johannes Hoornbeeck, the development of images and ceremonies in Christianity arose in the late Roman Empire and early Middle Ages, as bishops absorbed and appropriated traditional gods and rites into their churches. Just as the kingdom of Israel under Jeroboam incorporated idols—and incurred God's wrath at the hands of the Assyrians—so too had Christian leaders deviated from the true biblical path. Thus, they opened the door to local variations of the pagan practices that entrapped people worldwide.[72] For Calvinist apologists in the late seventeenth century, then, Catholicism belonged to the world narrative of paganism from which Calvinists and other Protestants were extricating themselves.

Calvinists' long engagement with paganism abroad gave them new perspectives on rationalist theological groups in the Netherlands. In the 1690s, a number of Socinians migrated into the Netherlands, fleeing another wave of persecution in Poland. They made headway into latitudinarian Baptist and Remonstrant groups, provoking alarm from Dutch Calvinists.[73] The Walcheren classis wrote to the Batavia consistory in May 4, 1694, that Socinian and Libertine writers were putting out "pernicious books which attempt to proclaim Christendom in order to bring people to heathen sentiments."[74] It is not clear to which "pernicious books" the classis scribe referred, but the charge of cloaking paganism under the guise of Christian teachings equated Socinianism with the religion of pagans from around the world. As we shall see, the accusation of paganism was not simply a random insult; it belonged to Calvinist polemical discourse of the seventeenth century.

The classis's remark reflected a Calvinist tendency to use constructions of paganism to unmask rationalist theological tenets in Europe. The Amsterdam classis fifteen years later wrote to ministers and elders in both Colombo and Batavia warning them about the works of Willem Deurhoff, a quirky philosopher accused of spreading Socinian and Spinozist views. Amsterdam Calvinists feared that a follower of Deurhoff was corresponding with "Indian *predikanten*" to spread his ideas and books among the Indians. On several occasions earlier in the 1600s, the Batavia consistory had investigated rumors of Socinianism among their ranks.[75] Charging Deurhoff with slandering the Reformed Church, the classis argued that he made no distinction between creatures and the creator, making God out to be a part of nature, ascribing fleshly characteristics to angels, and describing Jesus as just another human. Calvinists believed that the same critical error that led pagans to worship idols, also a confusion between creation and creator, was leading Deurhoff into "atheism." The affinities between "Indian" idolatry and Libertine atheism provoked concern among the Amsterdam pastors that his writings would be particularly appealing to natives and "lead to a harvest for Deurhoff among the Indians."[76]

Often when ministers or theologians appraised rationalist theological programs, such as Socinianism or Libertinism, they utilized similar language to identify the root problem, just as Calvinists had done with paganism since the early 1600s. In expressing its disdain for Spinozism, for example, the Batavian consistory described it in 1719 as presuming a "worldly deity" (*wereldse godheid*) that "gives idolatry an evangelical luster." The intrinsic idolatry of Spinozists, according to the Batavian brothers, was that they ascribed divinity to "all people and things."[77] From Grotius to Valentijn, Dutch Protestant writers had distinguished pagan practices and beliefs as mistaking the profane objects in creation for the divine. Consistories in both Batavia and Colombo promised to remain on the lookout for these heresies in their domains, lest they corrupt weak, native Christians struggling to free themselves from idolatry. Three years later, in 1722, a scribe from the Walcheren classis decried the "lustful men" who wished to act as prophets to Israel, namely Libertines and Spinozists who rejected Trinitarian Christianity and espoused the eternal natural birth of God the Son.[78] The organic nature of God that Calvinists attributed to theological rationalists paralleled their critique of divine incarnations in Vedic traditions. Fifty years earlier, Philip Baldaeus had ridiculed Hindu notions in South Asia as enmeshed in the generation of their own gods.[79] These examples indicate not only that Calvinists drew analogies between pagans around the world and rationalists in Europe, but that ministers and theologians also put into service their long experience interacting with and writing about pagans to critique Libertines, Socinians, and Spinozists. Since, according to Calvinist thinkers, all peoples worshipped and believed within the framework of the four basic religions (Judaism, Christianity, Islam, and paganism), it made sense to categorize rationalists as holding on at least partially to pagan errors.

Dutch Calvinists looked for lessons from the global missions of the seventeenth century. Writing in the late 1630s, Udemans exhorted readers to discern the lessons of missionary work among the Indians. Societies overseas had much to teach the Dutch, he believed. For those who paid attention, it taught over a dozen lessons, ranging from a renewed appreciation of God's greatness to a recognition of the humanity of all peoples, to the judgment of God on sin and unbelief. He also believed that examples from pagans were instructive for Europeans, asserting that "we can observe in the Indians, as in a mirror, what people are by the light of nature without knowledge of Christ and the light of rebirth, to wit [they are] as dumb and unwise as the offspring of a wild ass."[80] Udemans's blatant condescension should not distract us from his larger point, namely that the world was a great looking-glass that brought into sharper relief the effects of sin, error, grace, and faith. Pagans illustrated a Calvinist state of nature in which the devil preyed on the "children of disobedience" through idolatry, which also undoubtedly for Udemans served as a moral warning to European Catholics. Yet Udemans contended that pagans could teach Europeans certain virtues woefully absent in many Christians, qualities such as simplicity, peaceful social relations, and industriousness.[81]

By the late seventeenth century, entanglements with native societies had made their mark on the Dutch Reformed Church in ways that would have taken even *dominee* Udemans by surprise. As he had hoped, planting Calvinist communities overseas and converting non-Christians occupied an important place in the theological faculties at Utrecht and Leiden, in the intellectual labor of Dutch writers, and in the deliberations of classes and synods in the Netherlands. Yet he could only have speculated about the geography of knowledge that spanned the parameters of the Dutch empire from the Moluccas to Brazil. The commitment to missions forged a global, comparative outlook among the orthodox leadership in the Dutch Reformed Church. This comparative approach converged with the increasing attractions of rationalist assumptions in heterodox Protestant circles and in theological debates among mainline Calvinists. Reformed church officials regularly expressed anxiety about encroaching Libertinism, Socinianism, and Spinozism in the Republic and about conniving Jesuits gaining the upper hand in other parts of Europe.[82]

Global comparisons gave orthodox Calvinists a new way of seeing their enemies and their intellectual threats. Constructed by writers over the course of the 1600s, paganism became a hermeneutic for condemning rationalist tenets held by heterodox groups, and it always came in handy for ostracizing Catholicism. But paganism represented more than a polemical label. For Calvinists in a global struggle to spread biblical Christianity, underpinned by special revelation, the pagan principle elevated things of nature, including human reason, and confused them with the divine. This idolatry, according to Calvinists, was consistent in the universal religion of paganism across the world and now had resurfaced in Europe.

GLOBAL IMPRINTS

Many intellectuals in the seventeenth and eighteenth centuries were utilizing societies outside Europe as a mirror to reflect on institutions, customs, belief systems, and ways of thinking within Europe. René Descartes, as previously noted, claimed to have begun his search for a new method of reasoning after reading from "the great book of the world." Although it is unclear what exactly constituted this world, he gave some indication, advocating the study of world societies "so that we may judge our own more beneficially and not think that all that differs from our customs is ridiculous and against reason, as those do who have seen nothing of the world."[83] Jean Bernard and Bernard Picart's *Religious Ceremonies of the World* (1723–1737) floated "the radical idea that religions could be compared on equal terms and all religions were worthy of respect . . . [and that] individual ceremonies and customs . . . reflected truths relative to each people and culture."[84] The appropriation of knowledge about world societies in the service of Europe was possible because of the fundamental intellectual and cultural transformations that had taken place over the course of the seventeenth century.[85] These thinkers, like many Dutch Protestants, found that the wider world helped put Europe into a different focus.

The analytical and rhetorical strategies that writers used to bring a global perspective to bear on domestic issues were comparative in nature. As we have seen, Calvinists corresponding within institutional ecclesiastical networks employed comparative observation to dissect enemies at home and abroad. Along with observation, a common tactic used by a variety of intellectuals consisted of what one scholar has recently called "shame praising," a rhetorical device that involved lauding virtues of foreign peoples to cast shame on groups, especially rivals, at home.[86] Montesquieu, for example, in the *Persian Letters* (1721), used the fictitious Iranian travelers Usbek and Rica to deliver biting social commentary on French society and religion.[87] Voltaire famously touted Confucian philosophy as a guiding system of thought for reforming Western civilization in a more humane fashion and as an antidote to the superstition and oppression wrought by Christianity.[88] Within the Dutch Reformed Protestant fold, Georgius Hornius and Isaac Vossius debated the value of Confucian thought for the construction of a more tolerant, rational society in Europe.[89] Similarly, other French intellectuals, such as Denis Diderot and René-Francois Chateaubriand, inspired by reports of the expeditions by Captain James Cook in the Pacific, saw the innocence and simplicity of Pacific Islanders as an antidote to the decadence and corruption of Europe.[90]

A broad swath of Protestant groups on the fringes of Calvinism or outside it altogether felt the influence of the ongoing engagement with the wider world. In the two hundred years since Christopher Columbus's first transatlantic voyage, the inundation of material goods, textual and visual images, and information flows about peoples and places worldwide had woven a global orientation into the discursive fabric of Dutch cultural and intellectual life. Consequently, writers took knowledge constructed from interactions half a world away for granted, and it in turn became insinuated in a variety of sources (often in obscure formulations, at least for readers today). A consistent encompassing awareness of the exotic world inscribed itself into debates on theological and philosophical questions, discussions of moral reform, and questions of legal sovereignty. The remainder of this chapter looks at examples of how entanglements of the type that energized Dutch Calvinists played out across European Protestant thinking, and how a global perspective refracted across a spectrum of thinkers.

UNIVERSAL RELIGIOUS PRACTICES AND BELIEFS

Pierre Bayle, the renowned French Huguenot who fled persecution to the Dutch Republic in 1681 and lived in Rotterdam until his death in 1706, betrayed a deep preoccupation with non-European societies and figures from ancient to contemporary times. Shortly after landing in Rotterdam, Bayle published *Miscellaneous Observations on the Comet of 1680* (1682) to argue against supernatural causes for astronomical events. Fifteen years later, he produced one of the most controversial and influential works of the early Enlightenment, *An Historical and Critical Dictionary* (1697). An elusive and enigmatic thinker, Bayle claimed to be a faithful follower of John Calvin, yet his critics, most notably his Reformed colleague in Rotterdam Pierre Jurieu, criticized him as an atheist. Scholars who have studied his thought have come to very different conclusions about the intent of his writings, though two of the leading scholars of his work, Richard Popkin and Elisabeth Labrousse, consider Bayle to have combined skepticism with a positive moralism.[91] While not disputing skepticism as a tool for philosophical exploration, Jonathan Israel offers a judicious view of Bayle as "a towering, rigorous rationalist at once exceptionally cautious and timid, but also in a furtive fashion, highly adventurous and innovative."[92] Regardless of his precise intellectual bearing, Bayle's relevance to this study arises from his enduring affiliation with Calvinism during his residence in Rotterdam.

Though unwilling to learn Dutch, Pierre Bayle engaged consistently with the intellectual and cultural debates in the Republic. Historians have traditionally considered Bayle somewhat removed from Dutch controversies because of his linguistic limitations and his antipathy for theological divisions among Voetians and Cocceians.[93] Yet more recently, scholars have recognized Bayle's continual involvement and significant influence in Dutch Protestant circles. He followed the refutation of Cartesian thought by Voetius and other orthodox opponents, for example, in Adrien Baillet's 1691 French-language biography of Descartes. Bayle maintained regular contacts with many Dutch Calvinist colleagues and esteemed the work of Abraham Heidanus and Christopher Wittichus. Likewise, Bayle's works remained popular among the sizable Dutch public who read French.[94]

Bayle and his *Dictionary* illustrated the centrality of comparative analysis (and of shame praising here and there) to combat religious dogmatism and intolerance. In so doing, he used the examples of personages, religions, and customs in Asia, Africa, and America to comment on moral deficiencies in Europe and to establish universal characteristics among all people. In the vein of his Dutch confreres, Bayle also sought to establish linkages between various forms of thought across continents, including parallels between Spinozism and paganism in South Asia, the East Indies, and the Far East. Bayle's work thus reflected both Dutch Calvinists' obsessions with non-Christian societies and their use of the wider world for analyzing religious and intellectual currents in Europe. Like

Fig. 10. Gille Edme Petit (1696–1760), *Portrait of Pierre Bayle*,
before 1760; Rijksmuseum Amsterdam

Dutch authors, he appropriated a vast ethnographic and antiquarian literature, exploiting travel writings, missionary accounts, and classical authors extensively as the basis for knowledge of world societies.[95] In both the *Dictionary* and *Miscellaneous Observations,* Bayle relied on ancient and contemporary writers to critique commonly accepted European attitudes and practices that ran counter to his views about the true teachings of Christianity. He drew extensively from Jesuit ethnographers, including José de Acosta for Peru and Guy Tachard, Louis le Comte, Charles le Gobien, and Jean Crasset for East Asia. But he also utilized the French Calvinist Jean de Léry for Brazil, the Dutch writers Olfert

Dapper and Willem Bosman (in French translation) for Africa, and an account by the Calvinist *predikant* George Candidius for Formosa.[96] In *Miscellaneous Observations*, he availed himself of VOC embassy reports from China.[97]

Although Bayle digested a large amount of missionary literature, he directed sharp criticism at Christian proselytizers overseas, especially those from Catholic religious orders. He compared the suppression of the Huguenots in France, leading to the revocation of the Edict of Nantes in 1685, with Jesuit and Franciscan heavy-handedness in the Spanish and Portuguese empires. Bayle viewed the Jesuits in particular as a destabilizing force and predicted major social disruptions in China as missionaries and their converts came to undermine the legitimacy of the emperor. He even turned the tables on readers by asking them to consider the social upheaval should the Ottoman sultan send missionaries into western Europe to convert Christians to Islam.[98] In various entries Bayle called into question the ethics of proselytizing in other cultures, yet his primary emphasis pressed the irrationality of religious intolerance. In this regard, his treatment of Muslim lands, especially the Ottoman empire, made Christian bigotry highly conspicuous. For example, in the *Dictionary* entries on "Job" and "Mahomet," Bayle, leaning heavily on Paul Ricaut's account and Oqier Ghislain de Busbecq's published correspondence, made the case that the Turks displayed far more humaneness than Christians did toward practitioners of other faiths.[99] Having suffered persecution in France, his reading of these sources taught him that Christians failed to act compassionately despite the mandates from scripture, whereas Muslims practiced tolerance even though, according to Bayle, the Qur'an sanctioned religious violence.[100] (For example, he made the point, as many Christian writers did, that Islam advanced by the sword. In fact, he regarded it as a "Mahometan practice" that the king of France adopted in Europe.)[101] In the end, Bayle considered Europeans just as cruel and barbarous as other societies around the world. He used Jean de Léry's and Cieza de Leon's works on Brazil and Peru respectively to draw analogies between the practice of cannibalism in the Americas and the bloodletting that occurred between Catholics and Protestants in the French wars of religion.[102] Drawing on the black legend of Spanish conquest and inquisitorial harshness, he went so far as to aver that "popery exceeded the cruelty of cannibals."[103]

A comparison of people and practices around the globe demonstrated to Bayle universal characteristics of societies regarded by Europeans as essentially different from their own. Just as Dutch Reformed ministers and theologians were drawing parallels among various "false beliefs" and worship practices across the world, Bayle also employed a comparative method to bring a new perspective on European religious culture. One of the central arguments in *Miscellaneous*

Observations was that Europeans exhibited the same penchant for superstition and idolatry that plagued pagan peoples. Bayle believed that, the world over, the devil pursued similar strategies to divert people from the true worship of God. Those who touted omens in floods, earthquakes, and comets duped simple people into revering external and empty rituals, folklore, and false deities that, if left unchecked by reason or religion, fostered increasingly crude and cruel superstitions. As Bayle pointed out, astrology was practiced to assist emperors at the Mughal and Safavid courts.[104] But, he mused, "we do not need to go out looking into a land of infidels filled with countless superstitions and errors . . . there is no necessity to go far to find what we are looking for: has not our own western world, with all the lights of Christianity, been completely infatuated by horoscopes for centuries?"[105] The tales that missionaries told about barbarous idolatry in the Indies overlooked the fact that such criticism applied to European Christians as well.[106] From Bayle's reading of world history past and present, Europeans exhibited as much superstition as the people missionaries were trying to convert overseas.

Bayle's comparative methodology led him down some of the same paths as orthodox Dutch Calvinists who fought against the influence of rationalist currents in Protestant communities. Namely, he equated paganism found in the ancients—and in his own day in India, China, Japan, and the East Indies—with Spinozism in the Netherlands. His study of religions from the past and their contemporary manifestations also led him to conclude that Spinozism actually revived in Europe a common tenet in paganism. According to Bayle, Spinoza's conception of the divine as self-subsistent, encompassing both matter and spirit, reflected the teachings of Anaximander and Thales. Both taught, like Spinoza, that the divine was the principal originator of all things, emanating from and exuding through them. Referencing the travel account of Francois Bernier, he attributed these views to Hindus, Sufi Muslims, and Zoroastrians in Asia, but argued as well that Spinozism "very much prevails in the East Indies. . . . This is a universal doctrine of the Gurus, pagans in the East Indies; and that very same doctrine constitutes to this day the cabala of the Sufis, and of the greatest part of the men of letters in Persia." These Asian forms of thought, Bayle did admit, went beyond Spinoza's formulation, in that the Supreme Being was understood as producing not only souls "out of its own substance" but also all corporal entities in the universe.[107] Bayle's formulation followed the long-standing conceit of universalizing paganism from the ancient period to the present and applying it to rationalist tendencies in Europe. Calvinists had been engaged with paganism since the early 1600s, and Bayle's analysis certainly corresponded to their method of observation and conclusion about their enemies.

Throughout the *Dictionary* Bayle pointed to parallel observances among peoples of different faith traditions. For example, he noted that many Muslims offered prayers to Fatimah, just as many Christians venerated Mary.[108] Often arguing against the unique character of a particular religion, Bayle identified analogous characteristics of worship and belief.[109] He argued that Hindu Brahmins held to views about the impersonal nature of the divine and embraced a passivity that "has great affinity" with Quietists in Europe. In fact, he asserted that the "doctrine of Brahmins is less dreadful than our mystics."[110] The diversity exhibited by societies around the world in regard to religious worship actually masked the basic sameness of all peoples. "[W]ith so much diversity among men, on the manner of serving God," he claimed, "certain notions and passions act equally in all countries and in all ages. That the Jew, the Mahometan, the Turk, the Moor, the Christian, the Infidel, the Indian, the Tartar, the Islander, and the inhabitant of Terra Firma . . . are so alike in regard to their operation of the passions, they are in that respect copies of each other throughout the world."[111]

In other cases, the examples from world societies served as cautionary tales for people in Europe. The superstition that Europeans encountered in America, Africa, and Asia provided instruction for Christians about the wiles of the devil. Relying on a variety of sources, Bayle contended that reports of observances in Peru, Mexico, and Japan underscored how the devil used superstition and idolatry as the most reliable instruments to divert people from worship owed to God alone.[112] Christians risked falling under the same misconceptions by ascribing paranormal characteristics to the natural processes of the universe. Christians should remember that, lest they fall in line with the "posterity of these pagans and . . . give in to idolatry as readily as do pagans."[113] The profound errors that Europeans witnessed in world societies only confirmed for Bayle that idolatry was a greater evil than atheism, as idolaters were much harder to convert.[114]

European interactions with peoples around the world and Dutch overseas engagements were inviting a broad range of intellectuals in the Netherlands to reflect on universal patterns of belief and practice. These global perspectives come to the fore in a variety of writers. The Calvinist orientalist Adriaan Reland, for one, composed in 1705 the most balanced treatment of Islam by a European, *De religione Mohammedica*, one remarkably free from polemical condemnations. It is important to note that although historians often cast Reland as an early Enlightenment figure, the primary influence on his resolve to undertake a treatment of Islam was the global Calvinist mission. In the preface, he explained: "[M]y labors shall make way for others for the triumph of the truth and the evangelical faith and the ultimate aim of our actions, the glory of the only and one god, father, son, and holy spirit."[115] The unfulfilled opportunity that Dutch overseas enterprises offered for spreading the gospel and converting Muslims frustrated Reland, just as it had tantalized Grotius, Voetius, Hoornbeeck, and others before him. Like many Calvinist church leaders in the Netherlands, he charged that the trading companies were not doing enough to convert Muslims. Many Netherlanders, he contended, went overseas to make money, not to save souls.[116] "Do we not have much contact with Mohammedans in Constantinople, along the borders of Hungary and Turkish lands, on the coasts of Africa, in Syria, Persia, and the East Indies, where, in our colonies and in places where we seek to make money, many Mohammedans live?" For Reland, the fact that Islam is in "the mouths of so many, demanded a call to arms for the study of the entire body of literature."[117] Thus, it was his awareness of Dutch entanglements in these lands and his sense of urgency about the Calvinist mission that prompted his study of Arabic and Persian literature focusing on the Qur'an. Alexander Bevilacqua has shown that Reland also utilized Malay manuscripts brought to Holland by merchants and ministers from the East Indies to parse uncertain linguistic expressions in the Qur'an.[118]

Reland's work became instrumental among European intellectuals engaged in resituating the place of religion in society in the early Enlightenment. To cite just one example, Bernard Picart and Jean Bernard leaned heavily on Reland for their depiction of Islam in the widely influential *Religious Ceremonies of the World*.[119] They marshaled his appeal to persuasion and rejection of coercion in religious matters with a long quote from the French edition of *On the Religion of the Mohammedans*: "[We must allow] full and complete liberty for each to follow his own lights and to believe true that which appears to him to be such. For there is nothing more absurd than to want to oblige people to receive as truth that which they do not regard as true."[120]

Along similar lines as Pierre Bayle, Abraham Heidanus, inclined to Cartesian thought, argued that the witness of world societies in which Dutch overseas *predikanten* had operated actually showed that idolatry was far worse in Europe than in Asia, Africa, or the Americas. Resorting to some shame praising, he asserted, "[N]owhere is the existence or practice of idolatry found more prevalently than in Christianity, either in various corners of Europe or spread throughout the world. For across the world it is primarily practiced among the pagans in Asia, Africa, and America—since Turks nor Jews nor any of the sects that have separated from the Roman Church can be accused of idolatry."[121]

From even more different points of view, Andreas Wissowatius and Antonius van Dale argued that just as pagan priests kept the secrets of their religion from

Fig. 11. Pieter van Gunst (1659–1732), after Johan
George Callasius, *Portrait of Adriaan Reland*, 1712–1731;
Rijksmuseum Amsterdam

their people, so also did the Catholic ecclesiastical establishment in Europe. Wis-sowatius was a Socinian who supplied the annotations to Abraham Rogerius's *The Open Door*, while van Dale was a Mennonite minister steeped in classical learning. The Socinian Wissowatius shared the agenda of the Calvinist Rogerius of revealing the deceptions of pagan priests to Indian peoples. Arguing in a 1703 work that Catholic teaching relied heavily on pagan logic and metaphysics, rather than on the plain teaching of scripture, he asked rhetorically, "[I]f we wish to persuade deists, heathens, Jews, and Muslims to accept the Christian religion, then I (have to) ask whether we don't have to accomplish this through proofs from the author of the Christian religion, along with his and the religion's own properties and effects through reasoned argument?" For Wissowatius, the plain teaching of scripture provided clear answers to questions, unlike pagan and metaphysical obfuscations.[122]

Van Dale wrote influential historical treatments of idolatry, superstition, and divination at the end of the seventeenth and beginning of the eighteenth centuries. One of the central themes throughout his treatises focused on the nefarious duplicity of pagan (in which he included Roman Catholic) priests in foisting myths about miracles, devils, oracles, and other supernatural phenomena onto hoodwinked peoples. Although van Dale's concerns centered on paganism in the biblical and classical periods, he occasionally gestured toward its universal characteristics that also manifested themselves in his own day. For example, he remarked in *Dissertation on the Oracles of Ancient Pagans* (1683) that belief in the devil, as exhibited among pagans, was "a human inclination or art." Certain pagan prophecies had, moreover, spread from the ancient Greek *Sibylline Books* out to various peoples throughout Asia, including Arabs. Van Dale, like other Protestant writers, linked atheism with paganism; in paganism, he commented, "no greater seed of atheism has been sown—before the light of the gospel and the knowledge of the true God and religion had dawned like a radiant sun with its rays—than the relentless assault of pretended miracles and oracles of heathen gods and goddesses."[123]

THE DEVIL ABROAD AND AT HOME

The most controversial episode in which a theorist appealed to the testimony of societies outside Europe occurred in the early 1690s with the publication of Balthasar Bekker's anti-witchcraft treatise, *The Enchanted World* (1691). At roughly the same time that Pierre Bayle was working on his *Historical Dictionary*, Bekker, a Reformed minister in the Amsterdam consistory, was taking aim at common understandings of witchcraft in Europe. *The Enchanted World* made Bekker a pariah among orthodox Calvinists and led to his expulsion from the Reformed Church. In the book, Bekker argued that practices prosecuted as witchcraft in Europe were really nothing more than pagan superstitions and that "the Empire of the Devil is but a chimera and that he has neither such a power, nor an administration as is ordinarily ascribed to him."[124] Despite efforts to censor it, *The Enchanted World* quickly sold out of two editions; it was subsequently translated into German (1693), French (1694), and English (1695). Outside of the Reformed Church, a number of Protestant figures supported him, including van Dale, Johannes Duijkerius, Ericus Walten, and Pieter Rabus.[125]

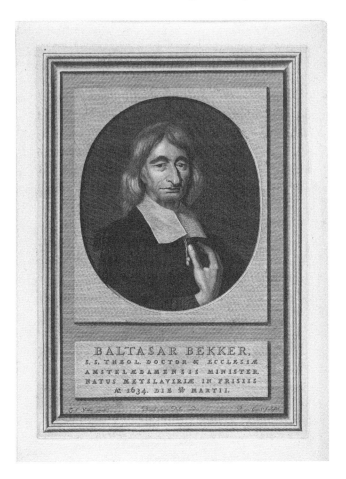

Fig. 12. Pieter van Gunst (1659–1732), after Zacharias
Webber II, *Portrait of Balthasar Bekker*, after 1694;
Rijksmuseum Amsterdam

Over the course of the sixteenth and seventeenth centuries, secular and ecclesiastical authorities across Europe had pursued an extensive campaign against
witchcraft. The best estimates from recent scholarship, based on archival sources,
put the total number of prosecutions around 110,000, with approximately 50,000
executions in the early modern period. For reasons that still are not clear, prosecutions and executions in the Netherlands were quite rare. By the late 1600s,
the scale of prosecutions had fallen off so sharply as to be nonexistent in the
Netherlands, yet Calvinists, as missionary encounters clearly illustrate, continued to believe in the reality of Satan and demons and their active involvement
in the idol-worshipping world.

Within this context, controversies over biblical hermeneutics, not only in Dutch universities but in the court of popular opinion as well, spilled over into questions about the existence of the devil. Certainly, as many historians have pointed out, the implications of Cartesian and Spinozist thought played a central role in these discussions and disputes. Bekker was himself a moderate Cartesian.[126] He took the view, as did others with these leanings, that the terms and language God used in the Old Testament were intended to accommodate the Hebrews, immersed as they were in pagan cultures of the time.[127] But these forms of instruction no longer applied after the coming of Christ. Undertaking a thorough examination of the devil in both Old and New Testaments, Bekker contended that all references depicted Satan in allegorical and metaphorical language connoting evil or sinfulness. Although Bekker did not deny the existence of the devil, he argued that no one in scripture—or anywhere else for that matter—ever had dealings with him.[128]

Most Calvinists, like other Protestants and Catholics, drew the conclusion from missionary enterprises that the devil and witchcraft were alive and well in the wider world. Heidanus maintained, for example, that world societies demonstrated that "in many parts of Africa, Asia, and America . . . the devil or some subspecies of devil is worshipped in horrendous and terrible forms and as idols."[129] True Christians throughout the world and at all times had suffered under persecution of the devil, who was responsible for introducing Islam in the east and pagan popery in the west.[130]

Bekker, like Bayle, certainly called upon rationalism to make his case, but what scholars have overlooked was the influence of his mindfulness about Dutch entanglements with pagans in Asia and the Atlantic. Bekker actually called for the witness of societies around the world in making his case against the devil. He even declared in his preface that the examples he would give from around the world and from the past "[are] enough to satisfy those [readers] who totally reject the principles of Descartes."[131] That is, a global perspective provided a new vantage point from which to view common assumptions and accepted practices in Europe. Attention to world societies revealed the global universality of pagan rituals and fables, not only in Asia and Africa but in Europe as well. Since the Amsterdam consistory to which Bekker belonged corresponded with all the overseas churches, he was deeply ensconced in the information flows about pagans and Moors in the Dutch empire. In *The Enchanted World,* he laid out the religious geography of Hinduism in South and Southeast Asia. In this section, Bekker, when describing the beliefs of Javans, referred to the Dutch East India Company operations in the East Indies.[132] He also cited and quoted extensively from the works of Abraham Rogerius and Philip Baldaeus. He quoted Baldaeus on "contemporary heathen" tenets concerning the relationship between body and soul and employed Rogerius as a source for explicating indigenous practices on the Coromandel coast.[133] Furthermore, Bekker made the point that although Baldaeus treated idolatry and superstition extensively, the only place he ever brought up a diabolic practice (divination) was in reference to the "conjuration of serpents" on the Malabar and Coromandel coasts and among the Sinhalese in Ceylon.[134]

Bekker also read widely among other missionaries and ethnographers. He lamented that Godefridus Carolinus, a Reformed minister in Gelderland who mined fifty ethnographic sources for his *Contemporary Heathendom* (1661), "did not live long enough to write" about the pagans in the Americas; had he done so, it would have spared Bekker from "extracting from a great many writers."[135] Bekker did lean heavily on Carolinus and "a great many writers" extensively throughout the work, especially in chapters 5 and 11 that discussed contemporary pagan practices and in 7, 9, and 10, devoted respectively to Asia, Africa, and the Americas. In total, ten chapters, out of twenty-four in book one, focused on pagans past and present, with two dedicated to Jewish customs and one to Muslim ones.[136] Some of the writers Bekker utilized included (Jesuits) Nicolas Trigault, Martinio Martini, and Athanasius Kircher on the Chinese, and Arnold Montanus, Jean de Léry, Richard Blome, and Thomas Gage on the Americas.[137] Thus did the wide diversity of practices and beliefs about the spirit world find their way to Balthasar Bekker in Amsterdam.

At the beginning of *The Enchanted World*, Bekker held up a comparative approach, so familiar to Dutch Calvinists, to make his case. He wrote, "In the first book I go to work introducing the reader to the entire work, to which in the first chapter I investigate throughout all the world where this view [incarnation of the devil] has its origin. . . . I seek first in the ancients, and afterwards in contemporary books of all sorts of peoples, religions, and opinions which are now current in the world, distinguishing between pagans, Jews, Muslims, and Christians."[138] Bekker's view of the global religious map was remarkably similar to the seventeenth-century vision laid out by Hugo Grotius, Gerardus Vossius, and Johannes Hoornbeeck. Bekker posited that "[t]he inhabited world is divided into three great islands. . . . [I]n the northern part of Europe . . . most of the inhabitants still live in heathendom. In Asia, Christians hardly make up a tenth of the people, and about a third remain under the law of Muhammad, so the greatest portion are still heathen. North Africa is Muslim; in the eastern half of the continent half-Christians and Muslims constitute a third, but still two-thirds are heathenish. The new world . . . lies completely in heathendom except for the small number of Christians who have come out from Europe."[139]

From there, Bekker surveyed understandings of the devil in these traditions. Muslims and Jews, for example, hold that the devil ranks among the created angels.[140] It was among pagan religions, which maintained a "uniformity in belief," that Bekker contended the devil acquired a reputation for terrible power that could disrupt and destroy the lives of men, women, and children. And Christians, over time, took on many of the beliefs and practices of pagans in the classical world, one of which was their construction of diabolism.[141] He noted that Christians acquired their pagan belief in the devil initially from Greek and Roman societies. Thus, Muslims and Jews hold to a closer biblical standard in their teachings about the devil than do Christians because of the latter's adoption of pagan beliefs and observances.

Bekker was able to chart this appropriation because he had observed that "similar doctrines and practices are also seen among present day heathens," and he concluded that "people must not be cast as sorcerers and witches and this false attribution applies to the same prejudice as so-called devil worship."[142] Like many other Reformed thinkers across the seventeenth century, Bekker viewed those many diverse groups who emphasized ceremony, ritual, and imagery in worship as belonging to a universal religion that Calvinists consistently referred to as paganism, heathenism, or gentilism.[143] Consequently, he moved back and forth through pagan as well as Muslim and Jewish history to provide evidence that what Europeans were prosecuting as witchcraft derived from ancient pagan practices absorbed by Christianity over the years. Since Bekker and other seventeenth-century intellectuals believed that paganism formed a unity stretching from the distant past to his present day, modern-day pagans offered a laboratory of sorts for all pagan beliefs and practices. His survey, relying on ethnographic sources and his knowledge of Dutch exploration, trade, and missions, was meant to show that witchcraft was a mere illusion. Using Carolinus and Rogerius, he noted that on the Coromandel coast local peoples believe in good and bad gods and malevolent spirits, and that the Siamese revere some "wicked gods." On Java, Sumatra, and the Coromandel coast, many held to a belief in the transmigration of souls, but Bekker emphasized that although these peoples used objects to worship a supreme deity— i.e., practiced idolatry—this did not equate with witchcraft. Moreover, just because missionaries and Christian writers categorized many of these rites as devil worship or sorcery did not make them so. Rather, Christians tended to conflate diabolism with age-old superstitions about good and bad spirits.[144] Similar views about the movement of the soul outside of the body at death or even before existed in Ethiopia, Guinea, the Caribbean, and Guatemala. Bekker explained that "[w]e find that on the one hand peoples differ extremely in their views of Gods and Spirits, yet on the other hand, they are wonderfully united about them."[145] For Bekker, this meant that universally people, whether ancient or modern, whether European, Asian, African, or American, shared five basic beliefs: (1) in a supreme divinity, (2) in spirits that are distinct from human souls, (3) in spirits as either good or evil, (4) in an afterlife for humans, and (5) in moral accountability.[146]

The fatal error in paganism, according to Bekker and other Calvinists, was a confusion between the creator and the created. That confusion provided the intellectual rationale not only for idolatry but also for notions of magic. The Voetian tradition identified this pagan principle as the source of atheism. Yet Bekker followed other Calvinists, such as Rogerius and Baldaeus, as well as non-Calvinists, including Wissowatius and van Dale, who laid the blame on pagan priestly castes that devised the concept of magic and brandished it in rituals in order to empower themselves and to dupe the laity into subservience.[147] In many pagan regions, Bekker noted, a priesthood characterized by divination mediated the ascent to political and social power. These practices, as many overseas ministers testified, were simply false religions and superstitions, possessing no ontological basis. In essence, sorcery and witchcraft, the common currency of pagan religious power, was nothing more than a ruse.

Bekker also devoted attention to diabolical elements within Judaism and Islam, though much less so than with paganism. With Judaism, Bekker made no appeal to contemporary practices, but to practices in the Old Testament and the apostolic period. In tracing the origins and development of a personal evil force in Jewish thought, he relied heavily on Maimonides, but he turned to other writers as well, including Johannes Hoornbeeck and his refutation of Judaism in *Summa on Controversies*.[148] Bekker discussed the Jewish view of angels and devils, the fall of Adam and Eve, and the development of cabbalism, divination, and astrology. Just as Christians adopted practices from their pagan neighbors, so also did Jews incorporate rites and folklore from the Egyptians and peoples they encountered in Canaan.[149] And in his own day, Bekker claimed that Jews believed themselves to be harassed by devils, tried to harness the mystical sources of nature through cabalistic practices, and conjured spirits, all of which, he said, sprang from the bosom of paganism. In one cursory chapter, Bekker dealt with Islam on the matter of devils and magic. Although he did describe teachings about angels, the spirit world, hell, and Satan, he considered Muhammad's teachings on the subject, as depicted in the Qur'an, to parallel Jewish and Christian teachings based on the Old Testament. In contrast to the lengthy descriptions and interpretive connections on paganism and Christianity, Bekker treated Islam as a set of beliefs and practices largely unrelated to contemporary attitudes and observances about witchcraft.[150]

The Enchanted World outraged the Dutch Reformed establishment. In the summer of 1692, the Synod of North Holland censured Bekker and pressed the Amsterdam city council—which controlled the appointment of Reformed ministers—to remove him from his post. Ultimately, the magistrates did suspend him, but without depriving him of his salary and his position. Three years after the book's publication, around 170 works had appeared, mostly attacking it.[151]

Jacob Koelman, a severely Voetian clergyman, rose up as one of the fiercest antagonists of Bekker, publishing several highly critical works and condemning him as a Socinian and Cartesian. In a 1692 treatise, Koelman tried to reverse the argument based on Bekker's appeal to pagan practices, asserting that Bekker made God's explicit declarations about the spiritual world and morality, which all Christians accepted, out to be "a pagan sentiment." Furthermore, Koelman charged that Bekker considered those faithful Christians who understood God's Word "as the simple and naked truth" to be "bewitched" themselves.[152] That is, to Bekker, Calvinists were the real devil worshippers. The archorthodox minister went on to lump Bekker in with atheists, Libertines, Sadducees, Cartesians, Spinozists, and pagans whom Calvinists had warred against for decades. Accusing Bekker of harboring pagan sympathies and neglecting in his blindness the diabolical nature of pagan idolatry and false worship, Koelman charged that these new pagans in Europe conceived of God in natural and "fleshly" terms.[153]

Other anti-Bekker publications worked from the same premises. Johannes van der Waeyen, a theologian at Franeker and another Calvinist critic, ridiculed him in a 1696 pamphlet for allegedly assuming that Christians can discover truth in the "fables of pagans." Van der Waeyen continued that although pagans themselves actually believe they are praying to demons, Bekker cannot recognize this because he has rejected the reality of the devil. This rejection, according to van der Waeyen, amounted to a Socinian view not just of the devil, but also of God, creation, and paganism.[154] This orthodox Calvinist reading saw the neopagan Bekker refusing to recognize diabolism or evil in the practices of pagans down through history and to his present day.

The controversy over the devil that erupted in the Reformed Church was not simply a product of the creeping influence of rationalism in Protestant thinking. Rather, the crisis around the devil grew out of a long gestation of comparative observation among Calvinists and other Protestants about people around the world and a preoccupation with paganism, which converged with the development of rationalist tendencies in the seventeenth century.

RELIGION AND CULTURE: REDRAWN LINES

These examples from Europe illustrate the ways of seeing that influenced debates over rationality and religion, as well as the natural and the supernatural, at the end of the seventeenth century. There is also evidence from the mission field that pastors were coming to different conclusions about religion and culture in non-Christian societies. Jacob Canter Visscher in Cochin opened this chapter by treating Hindu images—once regarded as diabolical instruments—simply as cultural artifacts of an exotic religion. This chapter will now close with another episode from South Asia, this time in Negapatnam just across the peninsula from Cochin on the Coromandel coast in the 1680s. The incident suggests how ministers and company officers were redrawing the lines between religion and culture.

Sometime in 1683, Jacob Joriszoon Pits, chief merchant of the VOC, attended a function hosted by a local official, along with several other company personnel including Willem van Dielen, an elder in the Reformed Church. At this business meeting, the host offered as entertainment for his guests a troupe of local women who danced and sang in the traditional Bharatanatyam style of South Asia. These dances were performed at weddings and other festive occasions, but also in religious ceremonies in Hindu pagodas and before images of deities there. Calvinists in Europe fiercely denounced dancing of most any type, and consistory records throughout the Reformed world teem with disciplinary cases involving members who participated in or sponsored dances, which were often customary as part of wedding festivities. In Asian territories, Calvinists unfailingly and vehemently opposed almost all public expressions of popular culture because they often contained religious elements at odds with Christian teaching and the frivolity they exuded provided occasion for sin. Such demonstrations included wayang theater, new year celebrations, processions, and other public spectacles. With regard to the Hindu dances, the Dutch customarily referred to the women performers as *dansenhoeren* (dancing prostitutes). It is possible that this 1683 case involved devadasi, women who belonged to temples where they conducted rituals and performed songs and dances as acts of worship. And indeed, the devadasi sometimes were associated with prostitution, especially later from the nineteenth century to the present. Yet it is also likely that the language used by Calvinists simply connoted the sensuality of the performances that the Dutch considered immoral.

When the only Reformed minister in Nagapatnam, Johannes Ruiterus—newly arrived from the Netherlands—discovered the participation of Pits, van Dielen, and other church members in the affair, he immediately took disciplinary action by censuring them, suspending them from the communion service that was only two weeks away, and prohibiting them from serving as witnesses in an upcoming baptism. Although his stance was quite consistent with Reformed attitudes and disciplinary procedures, his actions upset high-ranking company officials, who apparently considered it necessary to accommodate manifestations of local culture for commercial purposes. Part of the conflict grew out of personal animosity between Ruiterus and the VOC government. For his part, Ruiterus had a reputation for prickliness, and he was less than impressed with the state of the church building on his arrival.[155] Pits considered the newly arrived minister unfamiliar with local customs; he also believed that walking out of the event would have insulted his host, disadvantaging the VOC's prospects. When the governor of Ceylon refused to allow Ruiterus's censure to stand, he quickly resigned, producing complaints among company officials and some congregants that they no longer had pastoral services.[156]

The conflict prompted Ruiterus to write to the ministers and elders in Batavia and to the clergy in the Synod of South Holland for their assessment of the situation. In his letter to Batavia, Ruiterus framed the affair around four central questions. First, could a church member in good conscience watch the dances of Moors and pagans? Second, should a church member who participated be permitted to take communion? Third, could a censured church member serve as a witness to a baptism? And fourth, might a minister resign his service and deprive the community of religious services?[157] In his missive to the synod in October 1684, Ruiterus, however, cast the first and fourth questions in very different language. In the first, he asked whether Reformed members might "mix with prostitutes of heathen services with much frivolous, hellish licentiousness" during a period when the members should have been preparing for a communion occurring two weeks after the encounter. And in the fourth, he queried if the company could compel a minister in a moral question of this nature.[158]

The Batavian consistory's response, which the ministers and elders discussed in an October 30, 1685, meeting, was remarkable. They concluded that the dances did not constitute an offense, but represented traditional "civic recreation" according to local cultural tastes. The Batavian leaders acknowledged that "under the heathens, this dancing supports these women and they dance and sing in pagodas and before idols." Nevertheless, they pointed out, the performances were not "songs to devils" but were traditional folk songs. Furthermore, the consistory noted, the VOC needed to conduct business in pagan lands, and it was that same company that provided the church with the opportunity to spread the gospel to pagans and Moors. Because Pits, van Dielen, and the others "had done nothing sinful," the consistory concluded, any form of spiritual punishment would be unjust. Finally, the Batavian church officers expressed surprise that Ruiterus had "laid aside his service and did so quite suddenly."[159]

The synod's understanding of the conflict balanced the need of the company to do its business in a pagan society with the demand to protect the moral authority of the overseas clergy and congregation. In a letter to the States of Holland, the synodal delegates stated that they recognized the company's need to make profits, but the charges of consorting with prostitutes threatened the integrity of the entire congregation; for that reason, the consistory might need to be dissolved.[160] Ruiterus appealed to the synod to assist him with his appeal to the directors of the VOC for compensation for lost wages, but the church's support failed to convince the company officers. Ruiterus returned to the Netherlands in July 1686.[161] For its part, the Synod of South Holland cast its full support behind the *predikant* at Nagapatnam. They recommended compensation to Ruiterus of 1,400 guilders for damages, complained about the corruption of the East Indies churches, and called on company directors to uphold discipline in the colonies. The synodal delegates also condemned in typically harsh Calvinist terms the dancing as "devilish," the women as prostitutes, and the whole affair as a debacle.[162]

Nevertheless, the outlook of the consistory in Batavia about this encounter reveals a significant shift in attitudes about Hindu religious culture and perhaps about other observances outside of Europe. Since the earliest days of the mission in the East Indies—seventy years previous—consistories had regarded practices involving dancing, women, and imagery as religious in nature, and as forming some of the most offensive manifestations of diabolism. For Calvinists coming out of Reformation Europe, with all of its violent conflicts surrounding worship, images were idols and idolaters were blasphemers in the grip of demons. The immoral nature of dancing, in this case by women referred to as prostitutes, offered no possibility for accommodation. This stance had been the policy and practice of the Dutch Reformed Church throughout the early modern period, and Ruiterus represented that viewpoint. For the most part, Dutch overseas ministers had stood uniformly in opposition to such practices, unlike Catholic missionaries who diverged fiercely over tolerable "civil practices" and idolatry. The Jesuits Robert Nobili and Matteo Ricci, for example, argued that some Brahmanical and Confucian practices were civil acts and did not constitute superstition.[163] For Calvinists, apparently, seventy years of interacting with Muslims, Hindus, Buddhists, and others had altered the worldview of clergy overseas. The Batavian consistory considered Ruiterus to be a reactionary. For many Reformed clergy overseas, the diabolical religious practices that had so alarmed their predecessors for many decades had receded to the status of innocuous exotic customs by the late seventeenth century.

CONCLUSION

Calvinist entanglements in missions and empire building left indelible marks on the Reformed Church and on Protestant intellectuals in the Dutch Republic. The desire to implant Protestant Christianity in new territories pulled university faculties as well as synods, classes, consistories, and congregations into a sustained engagement with many different peoples. A geography of knowledge that spanned from Asia to the Atlantic invited Calvinists to contextualize European religious and intellectual currents in light of customs, beliefs, and practices around the world. Riding on the wake of the encounter with world societies via trade and travel, Calvinist missions became an important part of a broad globalization of Dutch society in the seventeenth and eighteenth centuries.

The influence of these international interconnections refracted quite distinctly among various thinkers and networks of like-minded partisans. Calvinist ministers and theologians embedded in the ecclesiastical establishment manipulated the prism of the wider world to decipher rationalist views, thus revealing a particular form of paganism that flattened the categorical differences between creator and creature. Denying the transcendence of God, these Libertines, Spinozists, and radical Cartesians fell into the same trap of atheism as pagans. The growing familiarity with pagan superstitions through sustained interactions invited a range of Calvinists and Protestants, from Jacob Canter Visscher to Pierre Bayle and Balthasar Bekker, to attribute universal characteristics to religious observance and belief. This domestication of paganism undermined a belief in the intervention of the devil in human affairs and the natural world. A more granulated understanding of Islam led Adriaan Reland to emphasize its reasonableness, which freethinkers such as Jean Bernard and Bernard Picart used to illustrate the anthropological functions of religion across the world. The missionary enterprise to convert pagans, Muslims, and Jews produced transformations within Reformed Protestantism in surprising ways.

CONCLUSION: THE EARLY MODERN LEGACY OF GLOBAL CALVINISM

The last gasps of the VOC and WIC became quickly overwhelmed by convulsions from the Batavian Revolution and Napoleonic Wars, which brought an end to the Dutch Republic and forever changed its commercial empire. Sandwiched between France and England, the Netherlands fell to French forces in 1795, and in the ensuing eighteen years Britain eventually came into possession of all Dutch overseas territories except several posts on the West African coast, which were subsequently sold to the British in 1872. After the defeat of Napoleon and the restoration of European monarchies in 1815, the new Kingdom of the Netherlands regained control over Surinam, Curaçao, and the East Indies. In the Southeast Asian archipelago, the Dutch waged a series of bloody wars in Borneo, Sumatra, and Java to oust local rulers and put down rebellions. All Dutch colonies came under direct administration by the Dutch government. The Netherlands lost Ceylon, posts on the Malabar and Coromandel coasts, the Cape of Good Hope, Essequibo, Berbice, and Demerara.[1] Although Calvinist missionary projects did not come to an end with the demise of the trading companies—ministers, elders, and deacons continued to serve congregations and oversee schools—the missionary drive in the East Indies, South Asia, and the Cape of Good Hope diminished significantly in the last half of the eighteenth century.

A new missionary vision was afoot in the Dutch Reformed Church in the last decades of the 1700s. Linked to a broader evangelical impulse among several Protestant denominations, Calvinists strove to identify potential missionaries in their communities and find ways to fund them. The pietistic fervor of the Second Great Awakening instilled a commitment to missions directed toward pagans and Muslims among Protestants in the Netherlands, England, Germany, and the United States. In contrast to the confessional public church approach of early modern Dutch Calvinism, these evangelical societies sought to fund missions independently and to free missionaries from colonial constraints. Missionary-minded folk reached across denominational boundaries to promote collaboration among Lutheran, Reformed, Anglican, and other evangelical associations. The groups emphasized special training for missionaries, preaching the simple word of God free from theological controversies, and translating the Bible into as many languages as possible. In the Netherlands, these pietistic activities culminated in the formation of the Dutch Missionary Society in 1797, modeled on the London Missionary Society, founded two years earlier. Global Calvinism thus transitioned into a new era.[2]

A keen awareness of the enduring efforts of Dutch ministers to spread Reformed Christianity and promote commercial empire in the seventeenth and eighteenth centuries shifts the ground on which assumptions about Protestantism have stood since the nineteenth century. The new pietistic initiatives of the missionary societies marked a signal departure from the church-planting approach of overseas ministers working for the trading companies. Studies of Protestant missions have denigrated conversion work in the earlier period either as "trade churches" under the thumb of the companies or as a precursor to the great age of missions in the nineteenth and twentieth centuries.[3] As a result, a long-standing conceit of scholarship has identified the Protestant Reformation, especially in its Calvinist manifestation, with an insular cultural ethos, a prejudice that has permeated, popular opinion and even international policy making. Few historical developments in fact have served this traditional narrative of Western exceptionalism and rise of modernity as the Protestant Reformation.

This study, in contrast, has shown that Calvinism, just like Catholicism, Islam, Judaism, Buddhism, and Hinduism, belonged to the global interactions that reshaped all regions of the world. The iconic image of the severe Dutch Reformed *dominee* clad in the black gown with white preaching tabs overlaid, thus obscured, the invisible reality of worldwide Calvinism. Mostly buried in the thicket of ecclesiastical reports and ethnographic descriptions, indigenous people—teachers, linguists, elders, deacons—perpetuated Calvinism among Tamil, Sinhalese, Sinkan, Malay, and Tupi men and women, boys and girls. Thousands of others appropriated Calvinism in countless ways into their cultures, belief systems, and social interactions. Reformed churches stood against the local skyline in Colombo, Jaffnapatnam, Batavia, Amboina, Cape Town, and other centers of VOC authority. By the end of the eighteenth century, thousands of non-European people had engaged with Reformed Protestant Christianity.

The missionary character of early modern Calvinism, as it had emerged in seventeenth-century Netherlands, was encased in a commercial empire. Once

Calvinism cast its lot with this empire, ministers and lay activists became participants in the development and maintenance of colonial societies. Just as Catholic missionaries (notably Jesuits), Muslim ulama, and Sufis acted as agents of empire, so did Calvinist *predikanten*, proponents, and *ziekentroosteren* involve themselves in the nitty-gritty aspects of colonial life. They bought and sold slaves, and married women and men into the Reformed Church; deacons oversaw the raising of orphans and ameliorated the suffering of the sick, feeble, and disabled. It is difficult to imagine how the VOC or WIC could have managed colonial societies without the support of the Dutch Reformed Church.

Dutch Calvinist strategies for converting non-Christians grew out of the confessional church structure in the Netherlands. Ministers abroad and church leaders at home envisioned the *Indisch Sion* and its Atlantic equivalents as the public church that consistories cultivated and political authorities promoted. Thus, *predikanten* attempted to translate a state-supported ecclesiastical structure in the East Indies, Formosa, Ceylon, Cape of Good Hope, Brazil, and other company-held territories. Just as in the Netherlands, ministers preached the gospel, consistories governed morals, schoolmasters indoctrinated youths, and deacons helped the poor. Magistrates (or company officials) were to promote conversion by banning all other religions, policing public space, enforcing the Sabbath, and subsidizing church ministries. Calvinists believed that as this organizational scheme was transplanted in overseas sites, a wide door of conversion would be opened to many peoples. *Predikanten* conceived of conversion as the entrance into a community of believers and practitioners, from full-fledged communicant members to affiliates (*liefhebberen* and *toehoorderen*), with varying allegiances to the church. As Peter van Rooden has argued, it was inconceivable that conversion could operate outside this confessional state structure.[4] Early modern Calvinist missions, therefore, were embedded in a conceptual framework very different from that of the modern Protestant missionary initiatives that got underway at the end of the eighteenth century.

These facets of empire building gave pastors opportunities to compel individuals to meet basic requirements for affiliating with the Reformed Church. While missionary pastors and company officials found common cause in many ventures, they also frequently clashed over the priority of missions and the extent of church influence in colonial society. Calvinists in overseas territories, just as in Dutch cities, operated from a theocratic social vision that chased false religion to the margins of society and ordered space and time according to a biblicist Protestant framework. Company officials for the VOC and WIC pursued the more balanced latitudinarian approach favored by most city governments in the Netherlands. In so doing, they protected freedom of conscience and man-

aged pluralism by blending periodic doses of coercion with long spells of con-
nivance. Though Calvinists had originally imagined a great harvest of souls via
the circuits of the trading companies, by the mid-1600s figures such as Gisbertus Voetius and Johannes Hoornbeeck came to chafe under the constraints of
governors like Joan Maetsuijcker, Rijklof van Goens, and Prince Johan Maurits
of Nassau-Siegen.

The key elements of Calvinist missions in this era were commitments to community formation as the destination of conversion, to vernacular language as
the linguistic means of evangelism, and to education as the strategy of religious
indoctrination. Working from the European parochial model, Calvinist missionaries attempted to form cohesive religious communities rooted in biblical
teachings and moral discipline. It is only possible to understand Dutch strategies in light of these allegiances. The extensive networks of schools functioned
to try to inculcate the necessary understanding and comportment to enable individuals to function in such a religious community. Working with native linguists, missionaries translated catechisms, prayers, sermons, and the scriptures
into Malay, Tamil, Sinhalese, Sinkan, Tupian, Portuguese, Spanish, and French.
Protestant and humanist principles of translation converged and sometimes
collided as missionaries sought both elegance and accessibility in vernacular
editions. The missionary impulse to vernacularization undermined the companies' campaign to instill Dutch as a viable colonial language.

Missionaries in many respects achieved their stated goals of preaching the gospel to "heathens, Moors, and Jews" and spreading the influence of Protestant
Christianity. Nonetheless, Calvinist expectations about the prospects for large-
scale conversion diminished significantly by the mid-eighteenth century. Certainly, the standard pastoral complaint of a meager ministerial corps carried
considerable weight in any reflection on the progress of missions. Yet the crucial factor that rendered the number of full-fledged members smaller than Calvinists had hoped was their steadfast association of conversion with community
formation. Historians have noted that Protestant emphasis on theological precision and moral inflexibility hindered their ability to convert Native Americans.[5]
Yet that unwillingness to accommodate local beliefs and customs derived from
a stalwart obligation to religious community, embodied through moral discipline
and symbolized by the sacraments of baptism and communion. A fear of divine
wrath for the moral contamination of the community animated Calvinists in
Europe from the early sixteenth century on, and they fixated similarly on defilement and scandal in the territories within the empire. A keen sensitivity to
orthodoxy plunged missionaries, pastors, and theologians in the Republic and
empire into bitter conflicts over the division of the sacraments periodically from

the 1620s to the 1720s. Divisions over translation of the Sinkan catechism in the 1640s and the Malay Bible in the first three decades of the 1700s distracted pastors from missions and embittered company governors toward ecclesiastics. Precision was a straightforward strategy for navigating the border between religion and culture in unfamiliar lands by (largely) obliterating that border. But stiff standards bred skepticism about the authenticity of conversion and thus one's standing in the community, which could only persuade nominal Christians and the newly baptized to seek a sense of belonging, protection, and support elsewhere.

Ultimately, Calvinist community formation could not compete effectively with the structures of belonging and protection already in place in many locations in the East Indies, South Asia, Cape of Good Hope, and Brazil. Formosa, Amboina, and Batavia represented the exception here, as VOC territorial control in the southwestern plain of Tayouan, the Amboinese islands, and northwestern Java did induce many indigenous people to accept Reformed Protestantism. In other areas, however, missionaries and their surrogates in effect were asking native peoples to abandon beliefs and customs and adopt radically new ones in order to belong to a new community. While Calvinists hoped to help save souls, spiritual well-being was inextricable to the embeddedness in a local association of families, friends, and supporters. As the missionary Caspar Wiltens exclaimed in 1615, Moluccans did not conceive of religion "as a thing," that is, as beliefs separate from the pragmatic necessities of everyday existence.[6] Calvinists also recognized the pragmatism of true religion as they tried to avoid divine wrath, as they pointed out to peoples that prosperous harvests followed from their conversions, and as they thanked God for victories over their enemies. Yet missionaries failed to recognize or remedy the fact that they were appealing to people to adopt foreign beliefs that would uproot them from their families, social networks, and political allegiances. Joining a Calvinist community through conversion did confer benefits: the opportunity to receive poor relief, the license to marry a Christian, the prospect of company employment, and, for slaves, the possibility of eventual manumission. Yet for many Africans, Asians, and Americans these advantages paled in comparison to the risks. Apostasy by Muslims, Jews, Hindus, Buddhists, and local practitioners carried serious consequences.

Conversion as community formation took time and involved assimilating old and new beliefs and practices. Studies of Christianization in Central and South America and Islamization in South and Southeast Asia demonstrate that the adoption of new deities, supernatural figures, and myths occurred in very gradual processes of integration that offered religious techniques for immediate needs. Without an offer of political protection or community formation that met pragmatic needs, Calvinism could only establish a cultural presence in many theaters of missionary activity, one that faded fairly quickly with the loss of territorial holdings by the trading companies.

As the Netherlands became globalized in the seventeenth and eighteenth centuries, entanglements with the wider world affected Dutch Calvinism in fundamental ways. Planting churches and converting non-Christians persisted as an aspiration in the theological faculties of Utrecht and Leiden and in church districts across Holland and Zeeland. The networks of correspondence between overseas churches and the classes of Amsterdam and Walcheren as well as the synods of North and South Holland kept alive a discourse about pagans, Muslims, and Jews. Reformed writers sought to situate world religions in historical and comparative contexts as missions evolved. The knotted religious and cultural perplexities involved in translating Calvinism in foreign lands and combating a resurgent Catholicism and burgeoning rationalism in Europe fostered a global perspective that reoriented Calvinism in at least three dimensions.

First, the long and tangled encounter with non-Christian beliefs and practices, especially "paganism" as constructed by Calvinists, bred a universal and genealogical outlook on contemporary religious alignments. The wider world—its people and their customs—became a lens through which Calvinists scrutinized European religious and intellectual culture. Reformed Protestants came to see false religion in their own day as part of a long and diffuse lineage of idolatry and superstition that originated with the Fall and manifested in diverse expressions across the world. Paganism, characterized by idolatry, sensual ceremonies, diabolism, and unrestrained sexuality, had over time metastasized and taken root in all spaces of human habitation. Dutch overseas ministers bore witness to the living legacy of this idolatrous genealogy. The fundamental error of paganism in all its expressions was confusion of the divine with the natural world, so that creatures, celestial bodies, human forms, and material substances emerged as objects of worship or voices of revelation. At the end of the seventeenth century and beginning of the eighteenth, this pagan principle also gave Calvinists a way to understand the assault of not only Catholics but also rationalists (particularly Socinians and Spinozists) on scripture. These rationalist groups, Calvinists believed, elevated human reason as a source of knowledge that contested special revelation, which constituted idolatry. Thus, Calvinists were not reactionaries who simply resisted new forms of rational thought in the age of Enlightenment; rather, a global perspective led them to equate rationalism with a neopagan movement in Europe.

Second, by the early eighteenth century the study of non-Christian religions spawned by engagement in the mission fields had given Calvinists a much better understanding of Islam and the Vedic traditions in South Asia. The study of Arabic and eastern languages had received serious attention in Dutch universities since the late sixteenth century. With missions underway, theologians in the mid-1600s also began to acquire facility in Arabic. At the same time, Gisbertus Voetius, Johannes Hoornbeeck, Georgius Hornius, and (a little later) Simon Oomius were making Islam a focus of academic inquiry. This attention converged with lengthy treatises by Abraham Rogerius (*The Open Door to Hidden Heathendom*) and Philip Baldaeus (*True Account and Refutation of East Indian Idolatry*) on Hinduism and Buddhism in South Asia. Other works appeared as well. The scholarly pursuits concentrating on Islam culminated in the early eighteenth century with Adriaan Reland's *On the Muhammedan Religion*, which provided a detailed and fairly benign view of Islam. To be sure, the production of knowledge about Islam and other religions aimed above all to demonstrate the superiority of Christianity and to deconstruct the errors of competing faiths. And Calvinists did not countenance Hindu, Buddhist, or other religions they classified as pagan. The relics collected by Jacob Canter Visscher, Nicholas Witsen, and others that found their way into curiosity cabinets in the Netherlands suggest that even Dutch Calvinists had domesticated pagan objects. The Batavian consistory's 1685 rebuke of *predikant* Johannes Ruiterus in Nagapatnam for censuring church members who attended a meeting with exotic dancing suggests that ministers were grappling with the differences between culture and religion. Batavia's view that such dancing was nothing more than local "civic recreation" signified a transformation had already taken place among a number of Calvinists. The profusion of knowledge generated by missionaries, travel writers, and other ethnographers across Europe, to which these Calvinist works belonged, led eighteenth-century writers to take a more comparative and relativistic view of world religions.

Third, the comparative reflection on world religions provided intellectuals within the broad Reformed Protestant camp experiential knowledge with which to adjudicate the case against and for diabolism. Mining the writings of Calvinist missionaries, Balthasar Bekker took the readers of his *Enchanted World* on a global survey of pagans, Muslims, and Jews to argue that "the empire of the devil is but a chimera." His work influenced those inclined already to embrace his premises, including a range of Protestants from Antonius van Dale to Johannes Duijkerius to Pieter Rabus. The orthodox Calvinists who inveighed against Bekker charged him, as they did Socinians, Spinozists, and Libertines, with imbibing paganism. Jacob Koelman and Johannes van der Waeyen made the claim that Bekker could not see the devil because he was a pagan himself. They also charged that Bekker slandered faithful Calvinists as devil worshippers because they recognized him at work among idols and sorcerers. Thus, paganism became fodder for both heterodox Protestants and orthodox Calvinists. Despite the fury directed against Bekker, the devil loomed less large in the Reformed Protestant reading of malevolence in other societies and their own than it had for most of the sixteenth and seventeenth centuries.

Ironically, outside of certain Calvinist enclaves such as the Cape of Good Hope, Amboina, and Batavia, the most far-reaching effects of overseas missions was on Reformed Protestant domains in the Netherlands. The struggle of converting peoples in the empire, along with the rising challenges of rationalist currents in European Protestantism, converged on Dutch Calvinists in the seventeenth century. Worldwide networks of correspondence, the study of paganism past and present, and missionary accounts of many varieties of false religion facilitated the rise of comparative observation as a mode of analysis among Dutch Calvinists.

In the second half of the seventeenth century, this comparative approach and the global perspective that underlay it refracted in distinct manifestations among a wide range of Protestant intellectuals in the Netherlands. Orthodox Calvinists in the vein of Gisbertus Voetius and Jacob Koelman, who rejected rationalist tendencies, appropriated critiques of paganism into polemical campaigns against a host of "Libertines" that embraced Cartesian, Socinian, and Spinozist perspectives. The pagan principle that Voetius, Hoornbeeck, and others identified was the elevation of creation, including human reason, to the level of the divine. The confusion between creation and creator constituted both idolatry and atheism that led away from a biblical understanding of God. For other orthodox Calvinists, such as Jacob Visscher, Adriaan Reland, and Francois Valentijn, the sustained proximity to exotic practices and images bred a familiarity that ultimately rendered diabolical idols as cultural artifacts, erotic religious dance as civic custom, and the scourge of Islam as a rational, albeit erroneous, religion. Finally, for other heterodox Calvinists such as Balthasar Bekker and Pierre Bayle, *malificia* and miracles faded into obsolescence. These instances suggest that developments long considered as exclusively and insularly Western, such as Calvinism and perhaps even Enlightenment, were entangled in indissoluble ways not yet fully understood with global patterns in the early modern period.

Appendix

AUTHORS AND WORKS DISCUSSED
IN CHAPTERS 5 AND 6

Philippus Baldaeus, *Nauwkeurige en waarachtige ontdekking en wederlegginge van de afgoderij der Oost-Indische heydenen* (*True Account and Refutation of East Indian Idolatry*), 1672.

Pierre Bayle, *Dictionnaire historique et critique* (*Historical and Critical Dictionary*), 1697.

Pierre Bayle, *Pensées diverses écrites à un docteur de Sorbonne, à l'occasion de la comète qui parus au mois de Décembre 1680* (*Miscellaneous Observations on the Comet that Appeared in December 1680*), 1683

Balthasar Bekker, *De betoverde weereld: zynde een grondig ondersoek van 't gemeen gevoelen aangaande de geesten, derselver aart en vermogen, bewind en bedryf: also ook 't gene de menschen door derslever kraght en gemeenschap doen* (*The Enchanted World*), 1691.

Godefridus Carolinus, *Het hedendaagsche heidendom: of beschrijving vanden godtsdienst der heidenen* (*The Present-Day Heathendom*), 1661.

Johannes Cocceius, *Rede over de godsdienst der Turken/Oratio de religione Turcarum* (*Oration on the Religion of the Turks*), 1625.

Johannes Cocceius, *Summa theologicae ex scripturis repetita* (*Summa on Theology*), 1662.

Antonius van Dale, *Verhandeling van de oude orakelen der heydenen* (*Discussion of the Ancient Oracles of the Heathens*), 1718.

Sebastian Danckaerts, *Historisch ende grondich verhael vanden standt des Christendoms int quartier van Amboina* (*Historical and Fundamental Account of the Condition of Christianity in Amboina*), 1621.

Hugo Grotius, *De veritate religionis Christianae* (*On the Truth of the Christian Religion*), 1640.

Justus Heurnius, *De legatione evangelica ad Indos capessenda admonitio* (*Admonition for Undertaking the Evangelical Mission to the Indies*), 1618.

Johannes Hoornbeeck, *De conversione Indorum & Gentilium libri duo* (*On the Conversion of Indians and Gentiles*), 1669.

Johannes Hoornbeeck, *Summa controversarium religionis cum infidelibus, haereticis, schismaticis* (*Summa on Controversies with Infidels, Heretics, and Schismatics*), 1653.

Jacob Koelman, *Het vergift van de cartesiaansch philosophie grondig ontdekt* (*The Poison of Cartesian Philosophy Thoroughly Exposed*), 1692.

Arnold Montanus, *De wonderen van 't Oosten* (*The Wonders of the East*), 1651.

Simon Oomius, *Het geopende en wederleyde Muhammedisdom of Turckdom* (*The Opened and Revived Muhammedisdom or Turkdom*), 1663.

Adriaan Reland, *De religione Mohammedica libri duo* (*On the Mohammedan Religion*), 1717.

Abraham Rogerius, *Het open-deure tot het verborgen heydendom* (*The Open Door to Hidden Heathendom*), 1651.

Godefridus Udemans, *'T geestelyck roer van't coopmans schip* (*The Spiritual Rudder of the Merchant's Ship*), 1640.

Francois Valentijn, *Oud en nieuw Oost-Indien* (*Old and New East Indies*), 1724–1726.

Gisbertus Voetius, *De atheismo* in *Selectarum disputationum theologicarum, pars prima,* 114–225 (*On Atheism*), 1648.

Gisbertus Voetius, *De gentilismo et vocatione gentium* in *Selectarum disputationum theologicarum, pars secunda,* 579–648 (*On Gentilism and the Calling of the Gentiles*), 1655.

Gisbertus Voetius, *De Judaismo* in *Selectarum disputationum theologicarum, pars secunda,* 77–124 (*On Judaism*), 1655.

Gisbertus Voetius, *De Muhammedismo* in *Selectarum disputationum theologicarum, pars secunda,* 659–83 (*On Muhammedanism*), 1655.

Gisbertus Voetius, *De plantatoribus ecclesiarum* in *Selectarum disputationum theologicarum, pars secunda,* 552–78 (*On the Planting of Churches*), 1655.

Gisbertus Voetius, *De praejudiciis verae religionis* in *Selectarum disputationum theologicarum, pars secunda,* 539–51 (*On the Foundations of True Religion*), 1655.

Dionysius Vossius, *De idolatria* (*On Idolatry*), 1642.

Gerardus Vossius, *De theologia gentili et physiologia Christiana liber I & II* (*Theology of the Gentiles*), 1641.

Gerardus Vossius, *De theologia gentili et physiologia Christiana liber III & IV* (*Theology of the Gentiles*), 1668.

[Johannes van der Waeyen], *Balthazar Bekker, en insonderheyd sijner voedsterlingen onkunde, onbescheidenheyd en dwalengen* (*Balthasar Bekker, and in Particular His Nurturers: Ignorance, Immodesty, and Error*), 1696.

Andrzej Wiszowaty, *Die vernünfftige religion* (*The Rational Religion*), 1703.

ABBREVIATIONS

ANRI	Arsip Nasional Republik Indonesia (Jakarta). Archief van de Kerkeraad van de Nederduits Gereformeerde Gemeente te Batavia.
ATB	H. E. Niemeijer and Th. van den End, eds. *Bronnen betreffende Kerken School in de gouvernementen Ambon, Ternate en Banda ten tijde van de Verenigde Oost-Indische Compagnie 1605–1791.* 4 vols., 6 parts. The Hague: Huygens ING KNAW, 2015.
KITLV	Koninklijk Instituut voor Taal-, Land- en Volkenkunde (Leiden) (Royal Netherlands Institute of Southeast Asian and Caribbean Studies).
NA VOC	Nationaal Archief (The Hague). Archief van de Verenigde Oostindische Compagnie.
OHZ	J. A. Grothe, ed. *Archief voor de Geschiedenis der Oude Hollandsche Zending*, vols. II, V, VI. Utrecht: C. van Bentum, 1885–1891.
1401 OSA	Het Utrechts Archief 1401. Oud Synodaal Archief van de Nederlandse Hervormde Kerk.
RSV	Revised Standard Version (of the Bible).
SA 379	Stadsarchief Amsterdam 379. Classis Amsterdam van de Nederlandse Hervormde Kerk.
UA 52-1	Het Utrechts Archief 52-1, nr. 212. Acta van de classicale vergaderingen van Pernambuco, Brazilia, 1636–1644.
ZA	Zeeuws Archief (Middelburg). Archief van de Classis Middelburg 28.1. Nederlandse Hervormde Kerk, Classis Walcheren/Classis Middelburg.

NOTES

INTRODUCTION

1. De Vries and van der Woude, *First Modern Economy*, 383–84.
2. Mak, *Kleine geschiedenis*, 107–9, 123, 124, 126.
3. Prak, *Dutch Republic*, 226.
4. Barend-van Haeften and Paasman, *Kaap: Goede Hoop*, 23–28.
5. Prak, *Dutch Republic*, 226; Subrahmanyam, "Forcing the Doors of Heathendom," 137–38; Safier, "Beyond Brazilian Nature," 171.
6. Van Groesen, *Representations of the Overseas World*, 139–42, 354.
7. Boxer, *Dutch Seaborne Empire*, 149. F. A. van Lieburg shows that only 650 can be documented from the sources. This number does not include *predikanten* who went into the Atlantic outposts. For a quantitative discussion of church personnel in the VOC, see van Lieburg, "Personeel van de Indische kerk," 76–78. See also Meuwese, "Disciplinary Institutions," 254, 259.
8. Nagtegaal, *Riding the Dutch Tiger*, 16–18; Blussé and van Veen, *Rivalry and Conflict*, 78–82, 95–102; Israel, *Dutch Republic*, 327, 934–38.
9. Chiu, *Dutch Formosa*, 194; Arasaratnam, "Protestants," 24–26; Niemeijer, *Calvinisme en koloniale stadscultuur*, 179–92.
10. For several examples, see NA VOC, nr. 11160, "Walcheren Classis to Batavia Kerkeraad," April 1, 1692; December 20, 1706; November 31, 1718. Also SA 379, nr. 188 (East Indies), "Batavia Kerkeraad to North Holland Synod," October 15, 1744 (362).
11. Niemeijer, *Calvinisme en koloniale stadscultuur*, 212–13. Also see Niemeijer, *Batavia*.
12. Arasaratnam, "Reverend Philippus Baldaeus," 32; Chiu, *Dutch Formosa*, 198; Niemeijer, *Calvinisme en koloniale stadscultuur*, 187.
13. Boneschansker, *Nederlandsch Zendeling Genootschap*, 15; Biewenga, *Kaap de Goede Hoop*, 174–78.
14. Haefeli, *Dutch Origins*, 123–25, 153–66, 277; Jacobs, *New Netherland*, 174–79; Meuwese, "Disciplinary Institutions," 253–65.
15. Chiu, *Dutch Formosa*, 186.

16. Grotius, *De imperio summarum potestatum*, 1:169; Keene, *Beyond the Anarchical Society*, 50, 56–57.

17. Bekker, *De betoverde weereld*, unpaginated preface; Hunt, Jacob, and Mijnhardt, *Book That Changed Europe*, 45–47, 79–80; Israel, *Dutch Republic*, 674–76.

18. Hsia, *World of Catholic Renewal*, 165–93; Levtzion, "Toward a Comparative Study of Islamization"; Antov, *Ottoman "Wild West*," 272–81; Şahin, *Empire and Power*, 208–10; Krstic, *Contested Conversions to Islam*, 165–74.

19. Elliott, *Old World and New*, 3–5; Wallerstein, *Modern World-System I*.

20. Pomeranz, *Great Divergence*, 31–68; Wong, "Search for European Differences," 453–54, 460, 468–69; Richards, *Mughal Empire*, 185–204; Hassig, *Mexico and the Spanish Conquest*, 89–94; Restall, *Spanish Conquest*, 44–76; Elliott, *Empires of the Atlantic World*, 3–87.

21. Lach, *Asia in the Making of Europe*; Greenblatt, *Marvelous Possessions*; Elliott, *Old World and New*, 12. See also van Groesen, *Representations of the Overseas World*, 12–16.

22. Hunt, Jacob, and Mijnhardt, *Book That Changed Europe*, 1.

23. Cook, *Matters of Exchange*, 83–84.

24. Subrahmanyam, "Connected Histories," 749.

25. Vélez, "Transatlantic Gifts of the Hurons," 39.

26. Ditchfield, "Decentering the Catholic Reformation," 196–97.

27. Niemeijer, *Calvinisme en koloniale stadscultuur* and *Batavia*; Biewenga, *Kaap de Goede Hoop*; van Goor, *Jan Kompenie as Schoolmaster*; Noorlander, *Heaven's Wrath*; A. Weststeijn, "Colonies of Concord"; Spicer, "Dutch Churches in Asia." See also Joke Spaans's excellent introduction to *Johannes Hoornbeeck*, 1–34.

28. Boxer, *Dutch Seaborne Empire*, 149–50; Furber, *Rival Empires of Trade*, 325–27; Taylor, *Social World of Batavia*, 21–23; Ricklefs, *War, Culture, and Economy*, 3–15; Joosse, "Scoone dingen sijn swaere dingen," 58–59; Bertrand, *L'Histoire à partes égales*, 232–33, 254–55; Axtell, *Invasion Within*, 131–78, 271–74. For an astute discussion of the failure by Protestants on the mission field and its ramifications, see Fisher, "Native Americans, Conversion, and Colonial Practice," 103–7. For a recent effort to reassess Protestantism in global contexts, see Rublack, *Protestant Empires*.

29. In addition to an array of published records and ethnographic materials across the Dutch empire, this study is based on the following archival collections: SA 379, nrs. 158, 163–170, 184–189, 191–192, 201–207, 212; NA 1.04.02 VOC, nrs. 11160–11162, 4712, 4778; NA 1.11.01.01, nr. 1373, Resoluties van de Gereformeerde kerk te Malakka, 1655–1695; 1401 OSA nrs. 1325–1362; UA 52-1, nr. 212, Acta van de classicale vergadering van Pernambuco, Brazilië, 1636–1644; KITLV, nrs. H80, H216; ZA, nrs. 65–70, 73; ANRI, nrs. 5–18, 156, 158, 160, 162, 163, 164.

30. Relevant works not cited elsewhere in the introduction include Baer, *Honored by the Glory of Islam*; Bethencourt, *The Inquisition*; Burke, *Cultural Hybridity*; Cañizares-Esguerra, *Puritan Conquistadors*; Clossey, "Merchants, Migrants, Missionaries"; Ditchfield, "What Did Natural History Have to Do with Salvation?"; Greer and Mills, "Catholic Atlantic"; Gregerson and Juster, *Empires of God*; Johnson, *Cultural Hierarchy in Sixteenth-Century Europe*; Kidd, *Forging of Races*; MacCormack, "Gods,

Demons, and Idols"; Prosperi, "'Otras Indias'"; Rafael, *Contracting Colonialism*; van Ruymbeke and Sparks, *Memory and Identity*; Schwartz, *All Can Be Saved*; Selwyn, *A Paradise Inhabited by Devils*; Sheehan, "Altars of the Idols"; and Strasser and Tinsman, "It's a Man's World?"

31. Schmidt, *Innocence Abroad*, 10–11.
32. For a few examples, see SA 379, nr. 164 (East Indies), "Walcheren Classis to Batavia Kerkeraad," September 14, 1649 (53); van Boetzelaer van Asperen en Dubbeldam, "Correspondentie Adriaan Hulsebos," 21 (February 7, 1618); van Boetzelaer van Asperen en Dubbeldam, *Protestantsche Kerk*, 12.
33. Noorlander, *Heaven's Wrath*, 9–10.
34. Frijhoff and Spies, *Dutch Culture*, 1:110–12; Postma, *Dutch in the Atlantic Slave Trade*, 10–14.
35. For one example, see van der Chijs, *Plakaatboek*, 2:169–70 (March 7, 1650).
36. C. Parker, "Converting Souls," 50–71.
37. Burke, *Languages and Communities*; Durston, *Pastoral Quechua*, 33; Lockhart, *Nahuas after the Conquest*, 306, 469; Swellengrebel, *Leijdeckers voetspoor*, 9; Koschorke and Mottau, *Colombo Consistory Minutes*, 13 (October 9, 1737), 24 (March 28, 1740), 55 (November 2, 1750); Heylen, "Dutch Language Policy, 216–20.
38. Rogerius, *Open-deure*, 4–6, 86, 114.
39. Baldaeus, *Oost-Indische heydenen*, 63.
40. Vossius, *De theologia gentili*; Hoornbeeck, *Summa controversarium*.

1. CHRIST, THE FATHERLAND, AND THE COMPANY

1. Noorlander, "'Calvinism and Directors," 74.
2. "Daer voor de goede Godt alleen ghedanckt ende ghepresen moet wesen." De Laet, *Kort Verhael*, 31.
3. Aglionby, *Present State*, unpaginated preface.
4. Child, *New Discourse of Trade*, 24–25, 31, 66. The treatise first appeared in 1668.
5. Quoted in Boxer, *Dutch Seaborne Empire*, 94.
6. Rogier, *Geschiedenis van het Katholicisme*, 1:201–416; Kaplan, *Calvinists and Libertines*, 8–11.
7. Tracy, *Founding of the Dutch Republic*, 64–67; van Gelderen, *Political Thought*, 24–36.
8. Arnade, *Beggars, Iconoclasts, and Patriots*, 212–20.
9. Delegates from all provinces confirmed the public status of the Reformed Church in a special convocation known as the First Great Assembly in The Hague in 1651. Israel, *Dutch Republic*, 707–9.
10. Oddly enough, Dutch commerce actually prospered amid war, as merchants even traded heavily with their Spanish antagonists. De Vries and van der Woude, *First Modern Economy*, 370.
11. De Vries and van der Woude, *First Modern Economy*, 383.
12. Israel, *Dutch Primacy*, 30, 46–52, 68.
13. Carson, *East India Company and Religion*, 3–11.

14. Evenhuis, *Ook dat was Amsterdam*, 2:316–17, 322–23; van Boetzelaer van Asperen en Dubbeldam, *Protestantsche Kerk*, 10; Keuning, *Petrus Plancius*, 52.

15. Israel, *Dutch Republic*, 321–22, 326–27; de Vries and van der Woude, *First Modern Economy*, 397–98; van Tielhof, "*Mother of all Trades*," 117.

16. Tracy, "Dutch and English Trade," 242–46; Tracy, "Introduction," 6–20.

17. Van der Chijs, *Plakaatboek*, 1:1–2 (March 20, 1602); Borschberg, *Hugo Grotius*, 68–72.

18. Erikson, *Between Monopoly and Free Trade*, 70–71.

19. *Corpus Diplomaticum*, 1:35–36 (Ambon, March 3, 1605), 36–41 (Banda, July 13, 1605), and 50–53 (Ternate, May 26, 1607).

20. Steensgaard, *Asian Trade Revolution*, 131–33; de Vries and van der Woude, *First Modern Economy*, 385.

21. Burnet, *East Indies*, 102.

22. Erikson, *Between Monopoly and Free Trade*, ix.

23. Gaastra, *Geschiedenis van de VOC*, 36–39, 43–44.

24. Quoted in Boxer, *Dutch Seaborne Empire*, 107.

25. Niemeijer, "Als een Lelye onder de doornen," 3–4.

26. Clulow, *Amboyna, 1623*, 27–49; see also Games, *Inventing the English Massacre*.

27. De Vries and van der Woude, *First Modern Economy*, 386–87; Gommans, "Continuity and Change," 197–202; Chaudhuri, *Trade and Civilisation*, 82–83.

28. Israel, *Dutch Republic*, 325–26.

29. Kaplan, *Calvinists and Libertines*, 229.

30. C. Parker, "Reformed Protestantism," 198–200.

31. Van Andel, *Zendingsleer*, 15–37.

32. Evenhuis, *Ook dat was Amsterdam*, 2:317–18; Keuning, *Petrus Plancius*, 52–53.

33. "Twee geschikte ende bequame persoonen, omme Gods Woort voor te dragen, ende 't volck jegens alle superstitie ende verleydinge der Mooren ande atheïsten uyt de H. Schrifture te vermanen." "Resolutien der Vergadering van de Zeventien aangaande het kerkelijke," *OHZ* V:1 (February 27, 1603).

34. Van Boetzelaer van Asperen en Dubbeldam, *Protestantsche Kerk*, 12.

35. *ATB* I:1, "Tekstfragment over religie uit een eerste Nederlandse beschrijving van Ambon," 7 (1605).

36. "Overmits tot ergernisse van de inwoonders die alreede christenen sijn soude strecken, dewelcke ernstelick versoucken dat haer kinderen mochten ghedoopt werden." *ATB* I:1, "Resolutie van Gouverneur Frederick de Houtman en Admiraal Paulus van Caerden en de Scheepsraad betreffende de aanstelling van ds. Johannes Stollenbeckeer," 9 (April 9, 1608).

37. "De predikanten Wiltens en Paludanus aan Bewind. Der O.-I. Compagnie," *OHZ* V:23 (July 29, 1612).

38. "Also by gelegenheid van de Oost-Indische scheepsvaert door bysondere schickinge en genade Gods, in verscheyde plaetsen van Oost-Indien een grote deure geopend is om het Evangelie onses Heren Jesu Christi, te predicken, met merckelicke hope, dat daer door vele inwoonders tot de kennisse des enigen waren Gods end also tot eeuwige salicheyt sullen worden gebracht, gelijck daer van alrede eenige goode be-

genselen werden gespeurd." "Credentiebrief door den Amsterdamsche Kerkenraad gegeven aan Caspar Wiltens," *OHZ* V:10 (December 23, 1610).

39. Hägerdal, *Lords of the Land,* 33–40.
40. The first materials actually came from Frederick de Houtman, who constructed a grammar in 1603 and then later translations of the Ten Commandments, Lord's Prayer, and a catechism by Philips van Marnix, St. Aldegonde. Van Boetzelaer van Asperen en Dubbeldam, *Protestantsche Kerk,* 16; Collins, *Malay, World Language,* 27–42.
41. "Sal yeder sijn Godt dienen, na tgelove hem Godt gegeven heeft, sonder den eenen den anderen te haten ofte eenighe oorsaecke te gheven daer questie uijt soude mogen rijsen, dan sullen malcanderen in all vruntschap aen wedersijden bejegenen ende de rest Godt bevelen die vant gelove ende gemoet is ende sijn sal." *Corpus Diplomaticum,* 1:23 (May 23, 1602).
42. *Corpus Diplomaticum,* 1:64 (July 1609); Steenbrink and Aritonang, "Arrival of Protestantism," 115–16.
43. *Corpus Diplomaticum,* 1:338–39 (November 8, 1640).
44. Niemeijer, "Dividing the Islands," 278–79; Steenbrink and Aritonang, "Arrival of Protestantism," 116.
45. Chaudhuri, *Trade and Civilisation,* 85, 92–94; de Vries and van der Woude, *First Modern Economy,* 386–87; Israel, *Dutch Primacy,* 184–87; de Bruijn, "Iranian Studies," 161–62.
46. Blussé, *Visible Cities,* 20–24.
47. Shimada, *Intra-Asian Trade,* 64, 118–24; Israel, *Dutch Primacy,* 171–74. See also Andrade, *How Taiwan Became Chinese.*
48. Prakash, *Dutch East India Company,* 27–29, 133–36, 144; Gaastra, *Geschiedenis van de VOC,* 124–40.
49. De Vries and van der Woude, *First Modern Economy,* 392.
50. Israel, *Dutch Primacy,* 175, 181–87.
51. Vink, "'The World's Oldest Trade,'" 74, 78–81; Bosma and Raben, *Being "Dutch" in the Indies,* 47–48.
52. Niemeijer, *Batavia,* chap. 1; Bosma and Raben, *Being "Dutch" in the Indies,* 34–35; Taylor, *Social World of Batavia,* 17, 28–29; Subrahmanyam, *Portuguese Empire in Asia,* 228–36; Rafael, *Contracting Colonialism,* 18. Only on the Cape of Good Hope, where the VOC put down stakes in 1652, did the company cultivate a colony of settlers, in order to provide fresh food to crews stopping for a respite on their way to and from their Asian destinations.
53. See *ATB* IV, "Kerkordre voor de kerken in Oost-Indië (1624)," 98–110. On this fractious period, see Niemeijer, *Calvinisme en koloniale stadscultuur,* 97–103.
54. See KITLV, nr. H80, "Kercken ordeninge gestelt voor de gemeente van Batavia," Anthonio van Diemen.
55. KITLV, nr. H80, "Kercken ordeninge gestelt voor de gemeente van Batavia," Anthonio van Diemen; *ATB* IV, "Kerkordre voor de kerken in Oost-Indië (1624)," 98–110.
56. Japanese authorities strictly prohibited VOC employees from any public practice of Christianity on Deshima Island. Proselytization was out of the question.

57. Van Lieburg, "Personeel van de Indische kerk," 73.

58. Junius's and Candidius's numbers are reported in Kuepers, *Dutch Reformed Church in Formosa*, 21; *ATB* I:1, "Helmichius Helmichii to Anthonio van den Heuvel," 145 (June 8, 1633); Niemeijer, *Calvinisme en koloniale stadscultuur*, 212; *ATB* III, "Banda Kerkeraad to Batavia Kerkeraad," 95 (August 28, 1643); *ATB* II:1, "Petrus Schotte to Batavia Kerkeraad," 89–92 (August 9, 1632).

59. Van Andel, *Zendingsleer*, 16–18, 57–59; for Voetius's theological work in the service of missions, see van Asselt, *Voetius*; Jongeneel, "Voetius' zendingstheologie."

60. See Rogerius, *Open-deure*; Baldaeus, *Oost-Indische heydenen*.

61. Emmer, *Dutch in the Atlantic Economy*, 21, 38, 42–45, 67, 79, 81.

62. Israel, *Dutch Primacy*, 160–65; Noorlander, *Heaven's Wrath*, 88–92.

63. Jacobs, *New Netherland*, 32–43.

64. Van Groesen, "Introduction," 8–10; Israel, "Religious Toleration," 17–27.

65. Meuwese, *Brothers in Arms*, 304–5 (Dutch slave trade between 1636 and 1645); Israel, *Dutch Primacy*, 163 (sugar production in Brazil); de Vries and van der Woude, *First Modern Economy*, 398–400; Antunes, Odegard, and van den Tol, "Networks of Dutch Brazil," 79–82.

66. Noorlander, "Calvinism and Directors," 79–80; see also Noorlander, *Heaven's Wrath*, 36–58.

67. "Dusdanige wercken Gods hebben oyt ende oyt groote operatie ghegeven tot openinghe der oogen selve blinde Heydenen, om te bekennen dat de Heere Iehova, even de God Israels, de ware God is daer het al aen hanght." Teellinck, *Davids wapentuygh*, 50.

68. "De voornaemst vrucht, is de bekeeringhe van die arme Heydenen: dese vrucht en konnen wy niet ter dege plucke ten zy dat dit groote werck ghecontinueert worde." Udemans, *Geestelyck roer*, 353.

69. ZA, nr. 73, "Brazil Classis to Walcheren Classis," August 19, 1637; UA 52-1, 18v, March 3, 1637; Noorlander, *Heaven's Wrath*, 115–18.

70. Noorlander, *Heaven's Wrath*, 113; Schalkwijk, *Dutch Brazil*, 48, 68, 70, 88. 97.

71. Israel, *Dutch Primacy*, 168–69; Israel, *Dutch Republic*, 935. For growing Calvinist intrusions, see Noorlander, *Heaven's Wrath*, 114, 127–34.

72. Klooster, *Dutch Moment*, 134–35.

73. Israel, *Dutch Primacy*, 168.

74. Klooster, *Dutch Moment*, 90–96.

75. De Vries and van de Woude, *First Modern Economy*, 465.

76. Postma, *Dutch in the Atlantic Slave Trade*, 27–41, 289–91, 302.

77. Klooster, *Dutch Moment*, 102–3, 106; Koot, *Empire at the Periphery*, 47–48, 106–7, 137–38.

78. Klooster, *Dutch Moment*, 106; Israel, *Dutch Republic*, 796–815.

79. Jacobs, "Jonas Michaelius," 73–75.

80. Haefeli, *Dutch Origins*, 96, 188, 211, 216, 221, 228–29.

81. Meuwese, "Disciplinary Institutions," 262.

82. Israel, *Dutch Primacy*, 245.

83. Sutherland, "On the Edge of Asia," 64; Ricklefs, *History of Modern Indonesia*, 93–95; de Vries and van der Woude, *First Modern Economy*, 430, 433; Israel, *Dutch Primacy*, 253; Chaudhuri, *Trading World of Asia*, 315–28.

84. Clulow, *Company and Shogun*, 207, 259; de Vries and van der Woude, *First Modern Economy*, 434.

85. Chiu, *Dutch Formosa*, 181, 202; Kuepers, *Dutch Reformed Church in Formosa*, 40.

86. Franciscus, *Faith of Our Fathers*, 8; van Goor, *Jan Kompenie as Schoolmaster*, 7, 30–33; Arasaratnam, "Reverend Philippus Baldaeus," 27, 29.

87. NA VOC, nr. 11160, "Colombo Kerkeraad to Walcheren Classis," December 9, 1711; NA VOC, nr. 11162, "Batavia Kerkeraad to Diederik Dueren," August 18, 1730.

88. *ATB* I:1, "Ambon Kerkeraad to Amsterdam Classis," 306 (September 8, 1663).

89. Steenbrink and Aritonang, "Arrival of Protestantism," 110–17.

90. See, for example, the reports in *ATB* I:1, 313–28, 336, 339, 350, 355, 357, 413.

91. ". . . dese inwoonders, is een seer arm elendich volck na siel ende na lichaem; berooft van alle kennisse Godts; leven als het vee, so dat gij niet en kont bemercken datse eenyge maniere van godtsdienst hebben ofte datter iets is, die sy eenige eer oft dienst bewisen, maer schint in dat stuck tusschen haer ende het onvernuftige vee van religie ofte godtdienste geen onderscheyt; want sie leven als beesten, die ock nergens geen werck van hebben, noch van saeyen ofte van planten, ofte dat men haer iets toepraet van godt, sie hebben der geen werck van; sodat het haest schint onmogelijck te sijn om haer tot die kennisse der waerheyt te brengen, want haer spraecke nyet wel is te leeren." "De Ziekentrooster Willem Barentsz. Wylant to Classis van Amsterdam" [20 April, 1655], in Spoelstra, *Bouwstoffen*, 1:4.

92. Biewenga, *Kaap de Goede Hoop*, 158; Elphick and Shell, "Intergroup Relations," 186–87.

93. "Capetown Kerkeraad to Amsterdam Classis" (July 4, 1697), "Joh. Godefr. D'Ailly to Amsterdam Classis" (April 19, 1708), in Spoelstra, *Bouwstoffen*, 1:120–22; Biewenga, *Kaap de Goede Hoop*, 204, 206.

94. On the lack of ministers to marry and baptize, see "Zesde Brief van Pieter van der Stael to Classis Amsterdam" (March 31, 1662), in Spoelstra, *Bouwstoffen*, 1:18–21.

95. Bosma and Raben, *Being "Dutch" in the Indies*, 27–31; Niemeijer, *Calvinisme en koloniale stadscultuur*, 305–8; Schutte, "Company and Colonists," 289; Wagenaar, *Galle*, 95–97.

96. The deacons had assumed management of the poorhouse and orphanage sometime before the 1643 church order, though the precise date is not clear. KITLV, nr. H80, "Kercken ordeninge gestelt voor de gemeente van Batavia," Anthonio van Diemen. See also Mooij, *Bouwstoffen protestantsche kerk*, 1:496 (March 6, 1637), 1:515 (February 8, 1638); Niemeijer, *Calvinisme en koloniale stadscultuur*, 308–10.

97. Mooij, *Bouwstoffen protestantsche kerk*, 2:68 (February 10, 1648).

98. NA VOC 1.11.01.01, nr. 1373, Kerkelijk Archief van Malakka, November 20 and December 17, 1648 (49–51); SA 379, nr. 201 (Ceylon), "Instructie voor de diaconen en besorgers der arme," August 6, 1667 (58–61); Chiu, *Dutch Formosa*, 123; Biewenga,

Kaap de Goede Hoop, 136–37; *ATB* I:1, "Kerken-Ordeninge van Amboina," 393–98 (April 4, 1673).

99. For an overview of this period, see Israel, *Dutch Republic*, 807–1130.

100. On the development of biblical philology and its importance in the seventeenth century, see van Miert, *Emancipation of Biblical Philology*; Touber, *Spinoza and Biblical Philology*.

101. De Vries and van der Woude, *First Modern Economy*, 467–68; Israel, *Dutch Republic*, 950, 969.

102. De Vries and van der Woude, *First Modern Economy*, 468.

103. Nierstrasz, *In the Shadow of the Company*, 77–78; de Vries and van der Woude, *First Modern Economy*, 436–37.

104. De Vries and van der Woude, *First Modern Economy*, 447; see Bruin, Gaastra, and Schöffer, *Dutch Asiatic Shipping*.

105. Breman, *Mobilizing Labour*, 11, 61, 65–72.

106. Van Goor, *Jan Kompenie as Schoolmaster*, 45–46, 57; Groeneboer, *Gateway to the West*, 44–45; Swellengrebel, *In Leijdeckers voetspoor*, 19; Koschorke and Mottau, *Colombo Consistory Minutes*, 277–78 (October 24, 1759); Somaratne and Somaratna, "History of the Sinhala Bible."

107. Swellengrebel, *In Leijdeckers voetspoor*, 13–20.

108. Schama, *Patriots and Liberators*, 26–33, 54–63.

109. This transition from confessionalism to pietism has not been studied closely for the Netherlands and only recently has come into focus for Dutch scholars. (Joke Spaans, for example, is completing a book on this subject.) Nevertheless, the move away from the confessional politics of the seventeenth century to a heartfelt Christian piety remains quite clear.

110. Spaans and Touber, "Introduction," 8–9; van Rooden, *Religieuze regimes*, 23, 115.

111. De Kok, *Nederland op de breuklijn*, 292–93; Israel, *Dutch Republic*, 1019, 1024, 1029–32, 1111.

112. Spaans and Touber, "Introduction," 9.

113. Israel, *Dutch Republic*, 1109–21.

114. Israel, *Dutch Republic*, 1115.

115. Harmen van den Brug, *Malaria en malaise*. See, for example, SA 379, nr. 189 (East Indies), "Banda Kerkeraad to Johannes Temming," May 26, 1754 (1–4); SA 379, nr. 189 (East Indies), "Banda Kerkeraad to Heren XVII," September 2, 1754 (17–20).

116. De Vries and van der Woude, *First Modern Economy*, 448–53 (quote on 454).

117. Van Eyck van Heslinga, *Van compagnie naar koopvaardij*; Schrikker, *Dutch and British Colonial Intervention*, 131–40.

118. De Vries and van der Woude, *First Modern Economy*, 455–56.

119. ". . . de uijtwerkinge vandie boekjes van den Professor Kallenberg, dat daar door so veele Joden en Muhamedanen zijn verligt geworden waar op wij antwoorden dat de zaak in den daadt soo niet en is . . ." SA 379, nr. 188 (East Indies), "Redenen en Motiva waarom de onderschreven predikanten genoodsaakt zijn geweest de voormelde

geschriften te verwerpen en tegens de Maleidse Bijbels druk met eene Arabise Letter to protesteren," December 30, 1737 (216).

120. SA 379, nr. 188 (East Indies), "Batavia Kerkeraad to Amsterdam Classis," November 27, 1747 (475–76).

121. "Ds. F. Le Suer to Amsterdam Classis" (May 13, 1744), in Spoelstra, *Bouwstoffen*, 1:204–5. See also Gerstner, *Thousand Generation Covenant*, 87.

122. Van Rooden, *Religieuze regimes*, 66, 122, 132–34; Lamping, "Nederlandsch Zendeling Genootschap," 235–40.

123. Dale, *Muslim Empires*, 56–57, 61–62.

2. CHURCH AND COLONIAL SOCIETY

1. "Ex-Governor Verburg's Report on Mission Work in Formosa," Campbell, *Formosa*, 292–97 (quote on 293) (March 10, 1654).

2. This view is undergoing revision. D. L. Noorlander (*Heaven's Wrath*, 3–8) has recently called attention to the religious motives of WIC governors.

3. There is a vast literature discounting religion as a factor in the development of the VOC and WIC. For a few examples, see Reid, "Early Southeast Categorizations of Europeans," 287–92; Riemersma, *Religious Factors*, 28–30; Taylor, *Social World of Batavia*, 21–22. For a discussion and criticism of this literature, see Noorlander, *Heaven's Wrath*, 4–7.

4. Pagden, *Lords of All the World*, 127. David Armitage in fact has shown that the notion of a British empire did not really emerge until the "late seventeenth century at the earliest" (*Ideological Origins*, 7).

5. Pagden, *Lords of All the World*, 11, 15–16, 31–34; Marcocci, *A consciência de um império*, 107–44.

6. Armitage, *Ideological Origins*, 8.

7. Carson, *East India Company and Religion*, 2, 13–16.

8. Pagden, *Lords of All the World*, 4.

9. Gijs Kruijtzer points out the exaggerated nature of Pagden's view in "European Migration," 141–42.

10. Koekkoek, Richard, and Weststeijn, "Visions of Dutch Empire," 85–86.

11. C. Parker, "To the Attentive, Nonpartisan Reader," 60–61.

12. The anti-Hapsburg motivation greatly diminished after the Treaty of Münster in 1648, in which Spain recognized Dutch independence.

13. A. Weststeijn, "Republican Empire"; Borschberg, "Hugo Grotius's Theory," 45–47.

14. Van Ittersum, *Profit and Principle*, 1.

15. Van Ittersum, *Profit and Principle*, 490; Kruijtzer, *Xenophobia*, 34; Terjanian, *Commerce and Its Discontents*, 118–24.

16. Grotius, *De ivre Belli*, 147; Grotius, *De jure praedae*, 1:241–42, 255, 345–47 (English), 2:107, 113–14, 154–55 (Latin).

17. Van Ittersum, *Profit and Principle*, 81.

18. Grotius, *De jure praedae*, 1:345 (English), 2:155 (Latin).

19. Schmidt, *Innocence Abroad*, xvii–xxi.

20. Clulow, *Company and Shogun*, 148–50.

21. Grotius, *De jure praedae*, 1:314 (English), 2:142 (Latin).

22. A. Weststeijn, "'Love Alone Is Not Enough,'" 30–37; Kruijtzer, *Xenophobia*, 34.

23. Van Ittersum, *Profit and Principle*, xxii.

24. A. Weststeijn, "'Love Alone Is Not Enough,'" 37–39; van Goor, *Jan Pieterszoon Coen*.

25. Clulow, *Company and Shogun*, 214.

26. Van Ittersum, *Profit and Principle*, 58.

27. See, for example, Grotius, *Annotationes in Vetus Testamentum*; Grotius, *Annotationes in Novum Testamentum*; Grotius, *Baptizatorum puerorum institutio*; Grotius, *Christus patiens*.

28. Grotius, *De jure praedae*, 1:314 (English), 2:142 (Latin).

29. Grotius, *De jure praedae*, 1:316 (English), 2:142 (Latin).

30. "Propositum enim mihi erat, omnibus quidem civibus meis, sed praecipue navigantibus, operam navare utilem, ut in longo illo marino otio impenderent potius tempus, quam quod nimium multi faciunt, fallerent. Itaque sumto exordio à laude nostrae gentis, quae navigandi solertia ceteras facile vincat, excitavi eos, ut hac arte, tanquam divino beneficio, non ad suum tantum quaestum, sed & ad verae, hoc est Christianae religionis propagationem, uterentur." Grotius, *De veritate religionis Christianae*, 2–3. "Secundò in vivendi modo licentioso, nec aliam habente legem, quam à cupiditate dictatam." Grotius, *De veritate religionis Christianae*, 368.

31. Heering, "Grotius," 49.

32. "Sic & discrepantia illa opinionum inter Christianos impedire nequiit, quominus de praecipuis, id est de praeceptis illis, ex quibus Christianam religionem maxime commendavimus, satis constet." Grotius, *De veritate religionis Christianae*, 50. See also Heering, "Grotius," 49.

33. Grotius, *De veritate religionis Christianae*, 44–218.

34. Grotius, *De ivre belli*, 439.

35. Heering, "Grotius," 50. See also Oomius, *Muhammedisdom of Turckdom*, 318.

36. Grotius, *Imperio summarum potestatum*, 1:169.

37. Grotius, *Imperio summarum potestatum*, 1:175.

38. In the prelude to the negotiations with Spain that led to the Twelve Years Truce (1609–1621), Grotius lobbied the *Heren XVII* and Dutch diplomats to stand firm against Spanish insistence that they withdraw from their overseas outposts. He also participated actively in discussions in the 1610s for the formation of the West India Company that ultimately came to fruition in 1621. Although Grotius fled the Netherlands after the crackdown on Remonstrants in 1619, he nevertheless continued to support and advise the VOC directors in an unofficial capacity, and his brother and son obtained positions as attorneys for the company. Terjanian, *Commerce and Its Discontents*, 118–24; Wilson, "VOC, Corporate Sovereignty," 330–34; Hayton, *South China Sea*, 38; van Ittersum, "Long Goodbye," 386–411.

39. A. Weststeijn, "Republican Empire," 496.

40. "Den koningh van Spaegnien ofte om eyghentlijcker te spreecken van Castilien ende, Leon, wil hebben datmen geloove alle dese Landen hem te behooren uyt kracht van een gifte des Paus van Roomen." "Uyt welcke insinuatie ende protestatie men kan sien het onghetwijfelt (soo sy het noemen) recht van den koningh van Spaegnien op de Landen van West-Indien ende waer op ghegrondt zijn gheweest de schrickelijcke verstroyinghen vernielinghen ende verscheuringhen van de arme inghesetenen van die landen in neminghe van hare plaetsen beroovinghe van alle hare goederen ende toe-eygheninghe van alles 'tgene daer in die landen wordt ghevonden" (De Laet, *Beschrijvinghe des West-Indien*, unpaginated preface).

41. Udemans, *Geestelyck roer*, 648, 650, 671.

42. *Schuyt-praetgens, op de vaert naer Amsterdam, tusschen een lantman, een hovelinck, een borger ende schipper* (1608), quoted in Schmidt, *Innocence Abroad*, 181. Schmidt (*Innocence Abroad*, 368n110) points out that this work was likely not written by Usselincx, but by someone within his close circle of associates.

43. A. Weststeijn, "Republican Empire," 503; Borschberg, *Hugo Grotius*, 61–62; Borschberg, *Singapore and Melaka Straits*, 70.

44. A. Weststeijn, "Republican Empire," 507; see also A. Weststeijn, *Commercial Republicanism.*

45. Van Dam composed the account over the course of an eight-year period at the behest of the *Heren XVII* to provide an accurate recounting of the company's governance and trade from its origins to the present time. Not published until 1927, *The Description* was a voluminous work meant only for the eyes of the directors. See A. Weststeijn, "VOC as a Company State," 17–20.

46. Van Dam, *Oostindische Compagnie, vierde boek*, 4–278.

47. Biewenga, *Kaap de Goede Hoop*, 119. Thank you to Joke Spaans for pointing this fact out to me.

48. Schalkwijk, *Dutch Brazil*, 85.

49. UA 52-1, nr. 212, 124r (January 5, 1638).

50. Meuwese, "Disciplinary Institutions," 260, 262–63.

51. Van der Chijs, *Plakaatboek*, 1:38–39 (August 22/November 3, 1617).

52. Van der Chijs, *Plakaatboek*, 1:108 (December 4, 1622).

53. See 1401 OSA 1353, "Kercken Ordeninge Gestelte over de Kercken in Oostindien," October 16, 1624; *ATB IV*, "Kerk ordre voor de gemeente te Batavia (1643)," 111–26.

54. *Instructions from the Governor-General*, trans. Pieters, 107.

55. *ATB I:1*, "Kerken-Ordeninge van Amboina," 392–98; Biewenga, *Kaap de Goede Hoop*, 118, 134. Rijklof van Goens, governor in Ceylon, made minor modifications to the 1643 church order for use in South Asia. Van Goor, *Kooplieden, predikanten*, 110.

56. The VOC's willingness to eschew all religious activity on Deshima was a sore spot among church leaders. See, for example, ZA, nr. 65, 112r (April 12, 1657).

57. *Corpus diplomaticum Neerlando Indicum*, 1:23 (Banda, May 23, 1602), 1:36–41 (Banda, July 13, 1605), and 1:50–53 (Ternate, May 26, 1607); Steenbrink and Aritonang, "Arrival of Protestantism," 115–17.

58. My thanks to Hendrik Niemeijer for directing me to this line of interpretation.

59. Examples of prescriptive activity include SA 379, nr. 184 (East Indies), "Adriaan Hulsebos to Martin Sonck," May 1, 1622 (23–24); SA 379, nr. 184 (East Indies), "Banda Kerkeraad to Willem Janssen," February 7 and 8, 1625 (126–27), SA 379, nr. 184 (East Indies), "Willem Janssen to Banda Kerkeraad," April 1, 1625 (131–32); SA 379, nr. 163 (Amsterdam), "Amsterdam Classis to East Indies," December 12, 1641 (94–95); SA 379, nr. 164 (Amsterdam), "Amsterdam Classis to Batavia Kerkeraad," September 11, 1651 (112); SA 379, nr. 165 (Amsterdam), "Amsterdam Classis to Heren XVII," September 22, 1656 (28–29); SA 379, nr. 185 (East Indies), "Batavia Kerkeraad to Amsterdam Classis," January 19, 1651 (121); SA 379, nr. 185 (East Indies), "Batavia Kerkeraad to Amsterdam Classis," January 19, 1654 (376); SA 379, nr. 186 (East Indies), "Amboina Kerkeraad to Amsterdam Classis," September 3, 1676 (366).

60. *ATB* IV, "Kerkordre voor de kerken in Oost-Indië (1624)," 109; *ATB* IV, "Kerkordre voor de gemeente te Batavia, 7 December 1643," 125.

61. Van der Chijs, *Plakaatboek*, 1:474–75 (July 5–7, 1642).

62. For consistorial complaints in Batavia about Buddhist, Muslim, and indigenous practices, see Mooij, *Bouwstoffen protestantsche kerk*, 1:699 (March 22, 1644), 2:22–23 (October 1, 1646), 2:52 (September 23, 1647), 2:128 (June 7, 1649), 2:188 (March 6, 1651), 2:198 (July 3, 1651), 2:210 (October 9, 1651), 2:215 (December 4, 1651), 2:354 (March 2, 1654), 2:389 (July 27, 1654), 2:587 (November 20, 1659), 3:208 (April 16, 1674), 3:453 (May 27, 1680), 3:458 (August 12, 1680), 3:491 (December 28, 1681).

63. SA 379, nr. 188 (East Indies), "Batavia Kerkeraad to Amsterdam Classis," November 27, 1747 (477–78); "Cape of Good Hope Kerkeraad to Amsterdam Classis" (July 17, 1741), in Spoelstra, *Bouwstoffen*, 1:190–91 (June 7, 1742), 1:192–95 (July 12, 1748), 1:218–21; van Goor, *Jan Kompenie as Schoolmaster*, 87–88.

64. Van Goor, *Jan Kompenie as Schoolmaster*, 8, 30–35, 125; SA 379, nr. 201 (Ceylon), "Colombo Kerkeraad to Heren XVII," January 19, 1689 (187–91); Niemeijer, *Calvinisme en koloniale stadscultuur*, 124–35.

65. For Calvinist complaints, see UA 52-1, nr. 212, 130r–131v (April 20, 1640), 132v–135v (November 21, 1640), 138v, 141v, 142v (July 18, 1644).

66. *ATB* IV, "Kerkordre voor de gemeente te Batavia, December 7, 1643," 112.

67. "Ex-Governor Verburg's Report on Mission Work in Formosa," Campbell, *Formosa*, 294 (March 10, 1654).

68. In Ceylon, beginning in 1664, company administrators, known as *scholarchs*, oversaw and inspected schools accompanied by a *predikant*. Government officials appointed and dismissed teachers. See Arasaratnam, "Reverend Philippus Baldaeus"; SA 379, nr. 168 (Amsterdam), "Amsterdam Classis to Colombo Kerkeraad," November 8, 1672 (68). Likewise, schools came under the jurisdiction of judicial officers in Formosa. See "Ex-Governor Verburg's Report on Mission Work in Formosa," Campbell, *Formosa*, 296 (March 10, 1654).

69. Schmidt, *Innocence Abroad*, 175, 219.

70. "Overmidts dese Indianen soo liberael zijn ons mede te deelen van hare vleeschelijcke goederen, als silver ende gout, diamenten, gesteenen, peerlen, specerien, suycker etc. So zijn wy den schuldich haer van onse gheestelijcke goederen deelachtich te

maken ghelyck de Joden eertijts den andere Heydenen gedaen hebben." Udemans, *Geestelyck roer*, 119.

71. Udemans, *Geestelyck roer*, unpaginated preface, 4–5.

72. Benjamin Schmidt (*Innocence Abroad*, 244–46) points out the tension that Udemans and other Calvinists felt between the godly calling of commerce and all the worldly temptations it posed.

73. "De reformatie in Europa, ende de ontdeckinge vande Indien, zijn den vast ontrent eenen tijdt geschiedt daermede de heer heft willen toonen dat nu den tijdt ghekomen was dat het Evangelium des Coninckrijcx door de gheheele wereldt soude gepredickt worden." Udemans, *Geestelyck roer*, 120.

74. Van der Wall, "Mystical Millenarianism," 37–39.

75. Udemans, *Geestelyck roer*, 290–91; Hoornbeeck, *De conversione*, 196–205; Rogerius, *Open-deure*, unpaginated preface; van Asselt, "Motieven en perspectiven," 232.

76. Hoornbeeck, *De conversione*, 9.

77. Writing in the 1660s, Hoornbeeck perhaps betrayed disappointment that the companies were not doing more as he lamented, "If only it had always been sought with equal effort." Nevertheless, he expressed gratitude that "we cannot deny that at least God in his great providence has given opportunity for sowing seed abundantly in spiritual things, thus we should not only promote our own affairs, but also the things of God and his kingdom." Hoornbeeck, *De conversione*, 10.

78. SA 379, nr. 184 (East Indies), "Banda Kerkeraad to Batavia Kerkeraad," August 20, 1624 (279); van Boetzelaer van Asperen en Dubbledam, *Protestantsche Kerk*, 12; Mooij, *Bouwstoffen protestantsche kerk*, 1:477 (April 24, 1636), 1:774 (October 2, 1645), 2:569 (September 12, 1658).

79. Chiu, *Dutch Formosa*, 192.

80. ANRI, nr. 162, "Corte relatie van Georgio Candidio op Ternaten," [n.d.] (18); Arasaratnam, "Reverend Philippus Baldaeus," 34; Mooij, *Bouwstoffen protestantsche kerk*, 1:340, 342 (April 15, 18, 1632).

81. Almost every letter from consistories in Asia to Dutch church districts registered this complaint. For several examples, see KITLV, nr. H216, October 24, 1731 (81); SA 379, nr. 201 (Ceylon), "Philippus Baldaeus to Amsterdam Classis," August 10, 1668 (74–75).

82. This episode was the well-known tragic tale of the shipwreck of *Batavia* in June 1629. After the ship ran aground off the coast of western Australia, mutineers took control of the situation, murdering more than a hundred passengers. Bastianszoon's own wife and daughter were victimized. Specx charged that he stood by passively as these events took place. Callenbach, *Justus Heurnius*, 163–66.

83. Mooij, *Bouwstoffen protestantsche kerk*, 1:340–42 (April 15, 18, 1630) (quote on 342); van Troostenburg de Bruijn, *Oost-Indische predikanten*, 25–26.

84. Mooij, *Bouwstoffen protestantsche kerk*, 1:335–38 (March 18, 22, 1630).

85. Van Boetzelaer van Asperen en Dubbledam, *Protestantsche Kerk*, 51–54.

86. Mooij, *Bouwstoffen protestantsche kerk*, 1:335 (March 14, 1630); 1:337–38 (March 18, 1630).

87. Arasaratnam, "Reverend Philippus Baldaeus," 32.

88. ANRI, nr. 162: "Instructie voor den dessave over d'provintien van Jaffnapatnam, R. van Goens," July 26, 1661 (515); "Instructie 1665, Instructie voor de Scholarchen des eijlants Ceylon," 1665 (517); "Philip Baldaeus, Joh. A Rueijll, Bart. Heijnen to R. van Goens," June 22, 1665 (519).

89. Franciscus, *Faith of Our Fathers*, 11; Arasaratnam, "Reverend Philippus Baldaeus," 33–35.

90. *ATB* I:1, "Ambon Kerkeraad to Batavia Kerkeraad," 115–16 (May 22, 1631), "Verslag door Ds. Sebastiaan Danckaerts," 116–19 (quote on 118) (June 16, 1631); Mooij, *Bouwstoffen protestantsche kerk*, 1:364 (January 2, 1631), 1:374–78 (July 3, 1631).

91. Van Boetzelaer van Asperen en Dubbledam, *Protestantsche Kerk*, 53.

92. ZA, nr. 65, April 16, September 24, 1654 (109r–109v).

93. For detailed accounts of the dispute, see NA VOC, nr. 11160, "Colombo Kerkeraad to Walcheren Classis," December 6, 1699; NA VOC, nr. 11160, "Joh. Roman to Walcheren Classis," December 21, 1701; ANRI, nr. 5, January 18, 25, 1700.

94. Mooij, *Bouwstoffen protestantsche kerk*, 1:221 (September 25, 1625), 1:223 (October 14, 1625), 1:224 (October 18, 1625); van Boetzelaer van Asperen en Dubbledam, *Protestantsche Kerk*, 29.

95. "Sebastianus Danckaerts aan Bewindhebbers der O. I. Compagnie," *OHZ* VI:154 (April 9, 1631); Callenbach, *Justus Heurnius*, 147.

96. Mooij, *Bouwstoffen protestantsche kerk*, 1:526 (October, 4, 1638).

97. SA 379, nr. 201 (Ceylon), "Colombo Kerkeraad to North Holland Synod," January 4, 1664 (44–46).

98. Blussé, van Opstall, Yung-ho, et al., *Dagregisters*, 1:310 (February 24, 1637).

99. NA VOC, nr. 11160, "Walcheren Classis to Batavia Kerkeraad," May 4, 1694.

100. "Dat de heeren broederen predikanten in oost-indien niet langer secuijr soude sijn tegens sodanige extravagantie handelingen. . . ." NA VOC, nr. 11160, "Walcheren Classis to Batavia Kerkeraad," December 1, 1695.

101. See also NA VOC, nr. 11160, "Walcheren Classis to Batavia Kerkeraad," October 18, 1696. For other complaints about the Dutch clergy, see SA 379, nr. 167 (Amsterdam), "Batavia Kerkeraad to Amsterdam Classis," October 25, 1780 (5–15); SA 379, nr. 168 (Amsterdam), "Amsterdam Classis to Suriname Kerkeraad," December 11, 1696 (232); SA 379, nr. 169 (Amsterdam), "Raaden van Suriname to Heeren Directouren," May 2, 1701 (2–4).

102. "Formosa consistory to Amsterdam Classis, October 26, 1652," quoted in Kuepers, *Dutch Reformed Church in Formosa*, 38.

103. Malherbe, "Illegitimacy and Family Formation," 1153; van der Chijs, *Plakaatboek*, 1:539 (1642).

104. See C. Parker, "Diseased Bodies."

105. Mooij, *Bouwstoffen protestantsche kerk*, 2:86–87 (August 10, 1648); "Adriaan Hulsebos to Steven van der Hagen, February 7, 1618," quoted in van Boetzelaer van Asperen en Dubbeldam, "Correspondentie Adriaan Hulsebos," 22.

106. Voetius, "De Muhammedismo," 153; Danckaerts, *Historisch ende grondich verhael*, 12.

107. For other examples, see SA 379, nr. 201 (Ceylon), "Heere Hendrick Adriaen van Rhee to Draeckesteijn Heere van Meidrecht," September 11, 1690 (197–218); SA 379, nr. 185

(East Indies), "Actum Palliacatta Kerkeraad," October 7, 1650 (99–103); SA 379, nr. 212 (Brazil), "Recife Classis to Amsterdam Classis," November 23, 1649 (188).

108. Van der Pol, *Mallabaarse brieven*, 110.

109. Andaya, *Flaming Womb*, 88.

110. "Want dit trouwen achten sy vry voor eene groote servituyt ende meenen hier door al een groot jock op den hals te hebben." Danckaerts, *Historisch ende grondich verhael*, 26.

111. Andaya, *Flaming Womb*, 100.

112. "George Candidius to Jan Pieterszoon Coen, August 20, 1628," Campbell, *Formosa*, 93–97.

113. Biewenga, *Kaap de Goede Hoop*, 211–12.

114. Taylor, *Social World*, xxvi. In Batavia, governor general Maetsuijcker increased the quota of European women in 1669 for a brief period. Taylor, *Social World*, 15.

115. See, for example, Mooij, *Bouwstoffen protestantsche kerk*, 1:97 (January 15, 1621), 1:102 (January 28, 1621), 1:103–5 (February 4, 1621); "Antwoort op de voorstaende remonstrantie," *OHZ* VI:25–27 (April 1, 1625); SA 379, nr. 184 (East Indies), "Banda Kerkeraad," June 10, 1623 (75); SA 379, nr. 184 (East Indies), "Banda Kerkeraad to President ende sijne Raad," August 17, 1623 (79–82).

116. Mooij, *Bouwstoffen protestantsche kerk*, 1:724 (October 10, 1644), 2:78 (May 18, 1648), 2:226 (February 26, 1652).

117. Mooij, *Bouwstoffen protestantsche kerk*, 2:264–65 (December 2, 1652) (quote). For accounts in other areas, see Mooij, *Bouwstoffen protestantsche kerk*, 1:356 (September 26, 1630), 1:449 (September 7, 1634).

118. Van der Chijs, *Plakaatboek*, 2:90 (1645).

119. Mooij, *Bouwstoffen protestantsche kerk*, 1:221 (September 25, 1625). To promote marriage among native and Eurasian children raised as Christians and baptized in orphanages, the Batavian consistory established in January 1638 that when the orphans left to get married, the deacons would award them 20 Realen. They provided 30 Realen to orphans born in the Netherlands. Mooij, *Bouwstoffen protestantsche kerk*, 1:515 (January 25, 1638).

120. Van der Chijs, *Plakaatboek*, 2:226–27 (June 3, 1655), 4:89 (October 16, 1716), 4:213 (August 17, 1728). There were many exceptions to company policy, though these directives determined the ethnic and social hierarchy in VOC territories. See Taylor, *Social World*, 17.

121. *ATB* IV, "Kerkordre voor de kerken in Oost-Indië (1624)," 104; *ATB* IV, "Kerkordre voor de gemeente te Batavia, 7 December 1643," 120.

122. Mooij, *Bouwstoffen protestantsche kerk*, 1:256 (August 6, 1626).

123. Mooij, *Bouwstoffen protestantsche kerk*, 1:214 (August 7, 1625).

124. Mooij, *Bouwstoffen protestantsche kerk*, 2:234 (April 8, 1652).

125. Mooij, *Bouwstoffen protestantsche kerk*, 2:166–67 (September 19, 1650), 2:171 (October 31, 1650).

126. "Wyders also ons voor desen als noch dagelyck voorvalt dat verscheyden persoonen hun soecken in den houlicken staet te begeven ende dat somtyts met gechristende

ende somtyts met ongechristende perturen . . . ende de ongeschristende partuuren somtyts worden bevonden d'eene gewillich d'ander gewillich, d'eene bequaem d'ander niet om sich tot het Christendom ende den H. doop te begeven." Mooij, *Bouwstoffen protestantsche kerk*, 1:149–50 (February 3, 1621).

127. Mooij, *Bouwstoffen protestantsche kerk*, 1:152 (June 28, 1621); van der Chijs, *Plakaat-boek*, 1:539 (July 1642).

128. Bosma and Raben, *Being "Dutch" in the Indies*, 28–29; van der Chijs, *Plakaatboek*, 1:536–43 (July 1642), 2:226–27 (June 3, 1656).

129. Mooij, *Bouwstoffen protestantsche kerk*, 1:227 (November 6, 1625), 1:644 (March 26, 1643).

130. Van der Chijs, *Plakaatboek*, 2:346–47 (March 22, 1661), 2:397 (May 29, 1665).

131. Mooij, *Bouwstoffen protestantsche kerk*, 1:163–64 (November 13, 1621).

132. Blussé, *Strange Company*, 158–59; Bosma and Raben, *Being "Dutch" in the Indies*, 27–28.

133. Taylor, *Social World*, 8, 15–19, 28–29.

134. For treatments of the relationship between Reformed Protestantism and humanistic reform programs, as well as the debates surrounding them, see Safley, *Reformation of Charity*; Grell and Cunningham, *Health Care and Poor Relief*.

135. C. Parker, *Reformation of Community*, 98–122.

136. Mooij, *Bouwstoffen protestantsche kerk*, 1:153 (February 21, 1621).

137. *ATB* IV, "Kerkordre voor de kerken in Oost-Indië (1624)," 102.

138. SA 379, nr. 184 (East Indies), "Batavia Kerkeraad to Banda Kerkeraad," August 10, 1622 (39); "Corte aenwisinge van den stant des godsdienst ende schoole op Amboyna," *OHZ* VI:154 (April 9, 1631); *ATB* II:1, "Rapport van Krankbezoeker Cornelis Jacobsz Wodway," 76–77 (August 26, 1628); *ATB* I:1, "Rapport door Justus Heurnius," 225 (1639).

139. For a few examples in Batavia, see Mooij, *Bouwstoffen protestantsche kerk*, 1:205 (February 27, 1625), 1:228 (November 13, 1625), 1:299 (January 1, 1629), 1:382 (August 14, 1631), 1:499 (May 25, 1637).

140. For the various sources of funding, see *ATB* I:1, "Ambon Kerkeraad to Batavia Kerkeraad," 234–35 (September 6, 1643), *ATB* I:1, "Amboina Kerkeraad to Batavia Kerkeraad," 266 (May 1, 1649).

141. SA 379, nr. 212 (Brazil), "Recife Classis to Amsterdam Classis," November 23, 1649 (188–90); SA 379, nr. 163 (Amsterdam), "Acta Amsterdam Classis," December 1646 (148).

142. *ATB* II:1, "Ternate Kerkeraad," 65 (September 15, 1627); *ATB* II:1, "Rapport van Krank-bezoeker Cornelis Jacobsz Wodway," 76–77 (August 26, 1628); *ATB* I:1, "Rapport door Ds. Justus Heurnius," 225 (1639).

143. ANRI, nr. 156, May 14, 1674. The absence of poverty could have been a result of the very small size of the congregation. The ministers reported in 1739 that there were only 83 church members and 243 nominal Christians. ANRI, nr. 158, October 15, 1739.

144. Noorlander, *Heaven's Wrath*, 99, 147, 171.

145. The Walcheren classis remarked on the paltry funding for diaconates in Asia in SA 379, nr. 164 (Amsterdam), "Walcheren Classis to Amsterdam Classis," September 14, 1649 (53–54).

146. SA 379, nr. 163 (Amsterdam), "Amsterdam Classis to Batavia Kerkeraad," January 2, 1640 (66).

147. NA VOC 1.11.01.01, nr. 1373, Kerkelijk Archief van Malakka, September 3 and 20, 1648 (47–49).

148. "Formosa Consistory to Amsterdam Classis," Campbell, *Formosa*, 194 (October 7, 1643).

149. "Minute-Book of the Castle of Zeelandia," Campbell, *Formosa*, 200–201 (March 29–November 14, 1644); Chiu, *Dutch Formosa*, 123.

150. "From the Tayouan Account-Book," Campbell, *Formosa*, 167–73 (November 1638–October 1639).

151. SA 379, nr. 163 (Amsterdam), "Amsterdam Classis to Brasilia," October 1, 1646 (148); SA 379, nr. 212 (Brazil), "Recife Kerkeraad to Amsterdam Classis," November 23, 1649 (188).

152. *ATB* IV, "Kerkordre voor de kerken in Oost-Indië (1624)," 101–2; *ATB* IV, "Kerkorde voor de gemeente Batavia, 7 December 1643," 113–15.

153. Mooij, *Bouwstoffen protestantsche kerk*, 1:132–33 (January 6, 1622).

154. Mooij, *Bouwstoffen protestantsche kerk*, 1:152–53 (not dated, but presumed after February 1621).

155. SA 379, nr. 184 (East Indies), "Banda Kerkeraad to Willem Janss Gouverneur van Banda," April 2 and 3, 1625 (137–38).

156. For a few examples in Batavia, see Mooij, *Bouwstoffen protestantsche kerk*, 1:205 (February 27, 1625), 1:207 (April 17, 1625), 1:208 (May 15, 1625), 1:212 (July 24, 1625), 1:216 (August 28, 1625), 1:218 (September 12, 1625).

157. For several examples, see NA VOC 1.11.01.01, nr. 1373, Kerkelijk Archief van Malakka, September 20 and November 20, 1648 (49, 50–51).

158. Niemeijer, *Calvinisme en koloniale stadscultuur*, 279–338; Biewenga, *Kaap de Goede Hoop*, 136–56.

159. "Aengesien d'opsicht en sorge der armen ende nood-druftige weesen deser stede mitsgaders de goederen en inkomen daer toe behoorende tot noch den diaconen aenbevelen ende van den aenbeginne aen vertrout geweest is, ende door erveringh ondervonden wort, dat door de menigste der soldaaten ende andere persoonen met inlandsche vrouwen getrouwt wesende, der selver afsterven overtheydt en anderen ongevallen den last der armen daghelix toeneemt en vermeerdert." SA 379, nr. 201 (Ceylon), "Instructie voor de diaconen en besorgers der arme ouderloose weesen, weeskinderen, waernaer in t'beidenen, onderhoude, en besorgen derselver soo veel als d'ordinaire armen op Col. saken te [illegible] te reguleeren," August 6, 1667 (58–61; quote on 58).

160. Extensive slave-holding drove down wages for free burgers, whose livelihoods were circumscribed by the VOC's commercial monopoly. For the circumstances that fostered colonial poverty in Cape Town and Batavia, see Biewenga, *Kaap de Goede Hoop*, 136; Niemeijer, *Calvinisme en koloniale stadscultuur*, 329.

161. Bosme and Raben, *Being "Dutch" in the Indies*, 16; Niemeijer, *Calvinisme en koloniale stadscultuur*, 212–13; Arasaratnam, "Protestants," 19; Schutte, "Company and

Colonists," 298; Guelke, "Freehold Farmers and Frontier Settlers," 66; Wagenaar, *Galle*, 45–46.

162. See *ATB* I:1, "Kerkenordening voor Ambon, 4 April 1673," 396 (April 4, 1673). For Banda, see SA 379, nr. 184 (East Indies), "Banda Kerkeraad to Willem Janss. Gouverneur van Banda," April 2 and 3, 1625 (137–38); for Ternate, see *ATB* II:1, "Consideratiën van Ds. Cornelis de Leeuw op Manado," 184 (February 13, 1681); *ATB* II:1, "Rapport betreffende een visitatie Ds. Gellius Cammiga," 349 (November 23, 1693).

163. The deacons had assumed management of the poorhouse and orphanage sometime before the 1643 church order, though the precise date is not clear. KITLV, nr. H80, "Kercken ordeninge gestelt voor de gemeente van Batavia," Anthonio van Diemen; Mooij, *Bouwstoffen protestantsche kerk*, 1:496 (March 2, 1637), 1:515 (January 25, 1638).

164. Mooij, *Bouwstoffen protestantsche kerk*, 2:67 (January 27, 1648). In an edict from the *Politieke Raad* in 1656, it was noted that the deacons and the consistory had not been a single college since 1648. Van der Chijs, *Plakaatboek*, 2:213–14 (January 18, 1656).

165. See, for example, Mooij, *Bouwstoffen protestantsche kerk*, 2:636 (March 5, 1663), 2:637 (March 8, 1663), 3:35–36 (January 19, 1668), 3:236 (March 4, 1675); van der Chijs, *Plakaatboek*, 2:213 (January 18, 1656), 2:332 (March 8, 1660), 2:334 (March 23, 1660).

166. The *Politieke Raad* rejected this proposal. Van der Chijs, *Plakaatboek*, 2:213–14 (January 18, 1656). For episodes in the long-running battle between deacons and consistories in Batavia, see Mooij, *Bouwstoffen protestantsche kerk*, 2:239–40 (May 17, 1652), 2:256–59 (October 17, 1652), 2:277–78 (February 3, 1658), 2:279 (February 17, 1653), 2:288–89 (April 3, 1653), 2:362–63 (March 26, 1654), 2:470 (January 17, 1656), 2:482–83 (May 1, 1656), 2:526–27 (February 12, 1657), 2:587 (February 20, 1659), 2:624–25 (April 17, 1662); SA 379, nr. 186 (East Indies), "Batavia Kerkeraad to Amsterdam Classis," January 22, 1657 (39–44); SA 379, nr. 186 (East Indies), "Batavia Kerkeraad to Amsterdam Classis," January 14, 1659 (141).

167. "Batavian Kerkeraad to H. H. XVII, January 29, 1657," in van Dam, *Oostindische Compagnie, vierde boek*, 162–63. See also Niemeijer, *Calvinisme en koloniale stadscultuur*, 279–83.

168. In the 1650s, for example, the deacons collaborated with the *Politieke Raad* to purchase and renovate a building for the orphanage. The consistory objected that the deacons had done this work without its knowledge and should have asked the ministers and elders to advise them. Mooij, *Bouwstoffen protestantsche kerk*, 2:502–3 (October 16, 1656), 2:586 (November 17, 1659). After the partition in 1648, no petitions from individuals for poor relief are listed in the consistory records.

169. In 1644, the deacons expended almost 6,600 Realen during the calendar year, most of which went to "inlanders." Mooij, *Bouwstoffen protestantsche kerk*, 1:741–43 (January 30, 1645).

170. Mooij, *Bouwstoffen protestantsche kerk*, 3:281–82 (March 16, 1676).

171. NA VOC 1.11.01.01, nr. 1373, Kerkelijk Archief van Malakka, November 20 and December 17, 1648 (51); Hussin, *Trade and Society*, 206–7, 277.

172. "Instructions to the governor," June 1661, in *Instructions from the Governor-General*, trans. Pieters, 8. The instructions also specified that if circumstances warranted, the consistory could "communicate with the consistory."

173. SA 379, nr. 201 (Ceylon), "Instructie voor de diaconen en besorgers der arme ouder-loose weesen, weeskinderen, waernaer in t'beidenen, onderhoude, en besorgen der-selver soo veel als d'ordinaire armen op Col. saken te [illegible] te reguleeren," August 6, 1667 (58–61). In Ceylon, it was a requirement that a recipient had to be at least a nominal Christian. Wagenaar, *Galle*, 95–97. The Amsterdam classis expressed reservations about the policy as it would give more control over poor relief to civil officers. SA 379, nr. 168 (Amsterdam), "Amsterdam Classis to Predikanten van Cey-lon," October 29, 1668 (37).

174. Biewenga, *Kaap de Goede Hoop*, 134–38. Pieter van Dam noted that the deacons at the Cape operated according to the model in Batavia. Van Dam, *Oostindische Com-pagnie, vierde boek*, 27.

175. For the Moluccan Islands, see *ATB* I:2, "Rapport betreffende een visitatie," 410 (November 1757); *ATB* II:2, "Rapport betreffende een visitatie," 77 (1706); *ATB* II:2, "Rapport betreffende een visitatie," 103 (February 1709); *ATB* II:2, "Rapport betref-fende een visitatie," 152 (November 1, 1724); *ATB* II:2, "Rapport betreffende een visitatie," 179 (June 1727); *ATB* II:2, "Rapport van een visitatie," 219 (April 6, 1729); *ATB* III:1, "Jaarrekening van de Bandase Diaconie over 1789–1790," 510–11 (February 28, 1790); van der Chijs, *Plakaatboek*, 4:10 (February 3, 21, 24, 1711), 4:92–93 (February 13, 1717).

176. SA 379, nr. 166 (Amsterdam), "Extracten der brieven van buiten ontvangen begin-nende met 't jaar 1759," April 7, 1759 (1).

177. "Niet alleen als een noodzakelijk gedeelte in de oefening van onzen godsdienst moet aangemerkt, alzoo men daardoor toont Gode en zijn evenmensch op het hart te draa-gen." *ATB* II:2, "Ternate Kerkeraad to Batavia Kerkeraad," 291 (September 1, 1757).

178. Niemeijer, *Calvinisme en koloniale stadscultuur*, 329.

179. Freund, "Cape under Transitional Governments," 330.

180. "Omdat in de gemelte buijten stede, een wtsteckende groot aental van swarte Chris-tenen woonen, welk getal streeckt tot acht ende meer duijsende menschen, welck alle meest arme lijden sijn, die haer cost so int bos, met dachhuijr te wercken, tuijnen te cultiveeren, als oock in de stadt met op de passer te sitten, met coolij-loon, ende soo voorts moeten soecken." Mooij, *Bouwstoffen protestantsche kerk*, 3:353 (September 16, 1677).

181. Niemeijer, *Calvinisme en koloniale stadscultuur*, 329.

182. SA 379, nr. 201 (Ceylon), "Instructie voor de diaconen en besorgers der arme ouder-loose weesen, weeskinderen, waernaer in t'beidenen, onderhoude, en besorgen der-selver soo veel als d'ordinaire armen op Col. saken te [illegible] te reguleeren," August 6, 1667 (58).

183. Niemeijer, *Calvinisme en koloniale stadscultuur*, 307.

184. SA 379, nr. 201 (Ceylon), "Instructie voor de diaconen en besorgers der arme ouder-loose weesen, weeskinderen, waernaer in t'beidenen, onderhoude, en besorgen

derselver soo veel als d'ordinaire armen op Col. saken te [illegible] te reguleeren," August 6, 1667 (58–61).

185. Biewenga, *Kaap de Goede Hoop*, 153–54; Niemeijer, *Calvinisme en koloniale stads-cultuur*, 314–19.

186. Elphick and Shell, "Intergroup Relations," 189; no specific number of slave baptisms are available for Batavia. In the second half of the seventeenth century, the consistory there adopted more stringent standards for baptism than the churches in South Africa. Nevertheless, it is clear that hundreds of slaves did experience some level of catechism instruction. Niemeijer, *Calvinisme en koloniale stadscultuur*, 187–89.

187. Mooij, *Bouwstoffen protestantsche kerk*, 2:4–5 (February 5, 1646), 2:22 (September 24, 1646).

188. Elphick and Shell, "Intergroup Relations," 204–6; Bosma and Raben, *Being "Dutch" in the Indies*, 47.

189. Ward, *Networks of Empire*, 21.

190. Vink, "Freedom and Slavery," 29. Recent research has shown slaves did reside in the Netherlands in a state of servitude in the seventeenth and eighteenth centuries, although officials and townsfolk overlooked their presence. Hondius, "Access to the Netherlands," 372–95.

191. Schmidt, *Innocence Abroad*, 189.

192. Schmidt, *Innocence Abroad*, 73–104.

193. Van Asselt and Abels, "Seventeenth Century," 355.

194. Marcus Vink ("Freedom and Slavery," 28) has concluded that the prevailing attitude among the Dutch Reformed in the late sixteenth and early seventeenth centuries was opposition to slavery. Referencing Justus Heurnius's opposition to slavery, Willem Frijhoff and Marijke Spies (*Dutch Culture*, 1:110–11) have argued that "there was initially opposition to slavery in every form."

195. Van Asselt and Abels, "Seventeenth Century," 355.

196. Ursinius, *Schat-boek*, 2:403, 429, 435.

197. "Wy waren van naturen kinderen des toorns, vyanden Godts, en Slaven des Satans: maer ons van zyne tyranny verlossende, en ons die waardig waren dat hy ons had laten verloren gaan, heeft hy ons, dat zalig is, tot kinderen Godts en tot zyne Slaven of dienst knegten gemaakt. Want by de Latynen worden Slaven servi genaamt, on datze behouden waren, te weten, wanneer ze in den oorlog gekregen van hunne vyanden, in gevaar waren om gedoodt te worden, behouden en gespaart wierden. Deze Heerschappij van Christus is een byzonderen Heerschappij die zig alleen over de Gemeente uytstrekt." Ursinius, *Schat-boek*, 1:317. Grotius, *De ivre belli*, 635–36.

198. Mooij, *Bouwstoffen protestantsche kerk*, 1:316 (July 12, 1629).

199. Callenbach, *Justus Heurnius*, 147.

200. Quoted in Boxer, *Dutch in Brazil*, 83.

201. Postma, *Dutch in the Atlantic Slave Trade*, 14, 21, 303.

202. Postma, *Dutch in the Atlantic Slave Trade*, 33–35, 54–55, 299; van Welie, "Patterns of Slave Trading," 167.

203. Vink, "'The World's Oldest Trade,'" 139–46.

204. Grotius, *De ivre belli*, 635–36. For one adaptation of Grotius's argument, see, for example, Udemans, *Geestelyck roer*, 648, 650, 671.
205. Frijhoff and Spies, *Dutch Culture*, 1:112.
206. Vink, "Freedom and Slavery," 19–21 (quote on 19).
207. George de Raad, *Bedenckingen over den Guineschen slaef-handel* (1665), quoted in Vink, "Work of Compassion," 472.
208. G. Parker, *Agony of Asar*, 40–43.
209. Niemeijer, *Calvinisme en koloniale stadscultuur*, 176.
210. Niemeijer, *Calvinisme en koloniale stadscultuur*, 177–78.
211. Bosma and Raben, *Being "Dutch" in the Indies*, 47–48.
212. Elphick and Shell, "Intergroup Relations," 188–89.
213. UA 52-1, nr. 212, 121v–122r (January 5, 1638).
214. Haefeli, *Dutch Origins*, 125–29 (quote on 129); Noorlander, *Heaven's Wrath*, 176–77, 187–88.

3. CONVERSION IN THE EMPIRE

1. Van der Chijs, *Plakaatboek*, 2:56 (January 31, 1643).
2. Boxer (*Dutch Seaborne Empire*, 235) thought the English were similarly prone.
3. Taylor, *Social World of Batavia*, 22.
4. Franciscus, *Faith of Our Fathers*, 4.
5. Boxer, *Dutch Seaborne Empire*, 149–50. A large number of other historians have come to a similar conclusion: see Furber, *Rival Empires of Trade*, 325–27; Ricklefs, *War, Culture, and Economy*, 18–19; Bertrand, *L'Histoire à partes égales*, 232–33, 254–55. Other explanations have emphasized either the alleged antagonism of Calvinist theology, i.e., predestination, to proselytizing or the unwillingness of Reformed Protestants to accommodate local observances at any meaningful level. See Elphick and Shell, "Intergroup Relations," 186; Axtell, *Invasion Within*, 31–78.
6. Burke, *Cultural Hybridity*, 9–11, 42–44; Ditchfield, "Decentering the Catholic Reformation."
7. Zürcher, "Jesuit Accommodation"; Hsia, *World of Catholic Renewal*, 166–77; Thornton, "African Catholic Church," 151–60. Yet less visible, and thus less contentious, appropriations of Catholic Christianity by native peoples also produced enduring synthetic blending of religious cultures. Filipinos, Kongolese, Mexicans, and many other peoples incorporated Catholic images and rituals within the cultural matrices of their traditional beliefs and practices.
8. "Selfs veeler mooren ende heijdenen die de heere door deen oft d'andere middel, d'eene of dandere tijt, mede ten gelove ende eeuwighe salicheijt . . . mochte gelieven te reopen." SA 379, nr. 184 (East Indies), "Banda predicanten to Marten Sonck," March 17, 1622 (3). Opening the door became the choice metaphor for the opportunities global Calvinism afforded for conversion. For other examples, see "Credentiebrief door den Amsterdamschen kerkeraad gegeven aan Caspar Wiltens," *OHZ* V:10 (December 23, 1610); SA 379, nr. 184 (East Indies), "Banda Kerkeraad to Batavia

Kerkeraad," August 20, 1624 (279); SA 379, nr. 185 (East Indies), "Paliacatta Kerkeraad to Amsterdam Classis," October 7, 1650 (102).

9. "Doch al hoewel het Gode niet ghelieft en heft tot op desen tijt, de Saligh-makende kennisse sijns Soons te laten komen, tot in Chinâ, en vele ghewesten van de Oost ende West-Indien. . . . Nu schijnt God met ernst te willen bevorden. . . . Door de laetste bekeeringhe der Heydenen, tot Christum, sal Godt der Ioden jaloers maken." Rogerius, *Open-deure*, unpaginated preface by Jacob Sceperus, a *predikant* in Gouda.

10. SA 379, nr. 164 (Amsterdam), "Amsterdam Classis to Batavia Kerkeraad," September 11, 1651 (112).

11. "Het kan ons niet anders dan tot zonderlinge verheuging zijn, wanneer wij dan bloei en het goede van Gods Zion ook met verre landen, en met naamen onder de blinde Heidenen mogen hooren." NA VOC, nr. 11160, "Walcheren Classis to Batavia Kerkeraad," December 20, 1706.

12. Kaplan, "Dutch Particularism," 249–51.

13. Bakhuizen van den Brink, *Belijdenisgeschriften, vergelijkende teksten*, 127.

14. Berkhof, *Systematic Theology*, 641–42. For Calvinists' view of baptism, see Spierling, *Infant Baptism*, 31–60.

15. Bakhuizen van den Brink, *Belijdenisgeschriften, vergelijkende teksten*, 133–35; C. Parker, "Moral Agency and Moral Autonomy," 44.

16. For an example, see Mooij, *Bouwstoffen protestantsche kerk*, 3:275 (January 20, 1676).

17. "Be doers of the word, and not hearers only."

18. Schroeder, *Canons and Decrees*, 53–54; Hsia, *World of Catholic Renewal*, 165–77.

19. SA 379, nr. 184 (East Indies), "Banda predicanten to Marten Sonck," March 17, 1622 (3).

20. Niemeijer, *Calvinisme en koloniale stadscultuur*, 91; ATB II:1, "Verklaring van de Compagniesdienaren Pouwelis Adriaensz, Frans Bruys, Nicolaes van Dortmont, Hendrick Harouse, Joos de Lampreel, en Daniël Otten ten laste van ds. Georgius Candidius," 9–10 (March 21, 1626); Steenbrink and Aritonang, "Arrival of Protestantism," 112; Niemeijer, "Als een Lelye onder de doornen," 6–8.

21. Schalkwijk, *Dutch Brazil*, 67–68, 70–73, 82; Biewenga, *Kaap de Goede Hoop*, 119.

22. SA 379, nr. 191 (Formosa), "Tayouan Kerkeraad to Amsterdam Classis," October 7, 1643 (77–80); Kuepers, *Dutch Reformed Church in Formosa*, 10–21; Chiu, *Dutch Formosa*, 198.

23. Niemeijer, "Als een Lelye onder de doornen," 7–9.

24. Chiu, *Dutch Formosa*, 190; "George Candidius to Gov. General Coen," Campbell, *Formosa*, 97–100 (February 1, 1629).

25. "Nu dese Nativers soo wat Christelijckheyts door desen middel vande Portugijsen gheleert hebbende . . . ende sijn wederomme meer tot haere Duyvellarije vervallen." Danckaerts, *Historisch ende grondich verhael*, 15.

26. "Cornelis Dedel to Bewindhebbers der I. O. Comp.," OHZ V:74–75 (August 6, 1616).

27. UA 52-1, 118v (March 3, 1637), 121v (January 5, 1638).

28. SA 379, nr. 201 (Ceylon), "Colombo Kerkeraad to North Holland Synod," [n.d., before October 3, 1662] (5–6).

29. "Voor eerst geen kans om het geloof uit de gemoederen te verjagen om dat de Christenen van de gereformeerde kerk geduiring om gingen met die van de Roomse in welcke de beelden dienst aanlachelijck voor het oog door haar groote pragt en overeenkomende met de heidense afgoden." NA VOC, nr. 11160, "Batavia Kerkeraad to Walcheren Classis," November 20, 1719. From a different perspective, Simon Ditchfield ("Translating Christianity," 195) has argued that the materiality of Catholic worship actually enabled Catholicism to become the first world religion.

30. This nomenclature was universal. For examples, see *ATB* I:2, "Rapport betreffende een visitatie van kerken en scholen in Hitu en Leitmor," 430–40 (April 1759); *ATB* II:2, "Resolutie van de Politieke Raad van Ternate met bijliggend rapport betreffende een visitatie van kerken en scholen in Noord-Sulawesi en op de Sangihe-eilanden," 327–34 (late 1769); *ATB* III:1, "Banda Kerkeraad to Batavia Kerkeraad," 418–20 (August 15, 1750); NA VOC, nr. 11160, "Batavia Kerkeraad to North Holland Synod," November 16, 1699; NA VOC, nr. 11160, "Batavia Kerkeraad to Walcheren Classis," November 1, 1717; NA VOC, nr. 11160, "Batavia Kerkeraad to Walcheren Classis," November 7, 1718; NA VOC, nr. 11160, "Batavia Kerkeraad to Walcheren Classis," November 9, 1722; NA VOC, nr. 11162, "Batavia Kerkeraad to Diderik Durven," August 18, 1730; SA 379, nr. 188 (East Indies), "Amboina Kerkeraad to Amsterdam Classis," September 20, 1731 (113); SA 379, nr. 188 (East Indies), "Amboina Kerkeraad to Amsterdam Classis," September 23, 1737 (129); SA 379, nr. 188 (East Indies), "Batavia Kerkeraad to Amsterdam Classis, November 27, 1737 (132–44); ANRI, nr. 158, "Makassar Kerkeraad to Batavia Kerkeraad," October 15, 1739; ANRI, nr. 158, "Makassar Kerkeraad to Batavia Kerkeraad," October 4, 1753; ANRI, nr. 158, "Makassar Kerkeraad to Batavia Kerkeraad," October 20, 1758; ANRI, nr. 158, "Makassar Kerkeraad to Batavia Kerkeraad," October 14, 1772; ANRI, nr. 158, "Makassar Kerkeraad to Batavia Kerkeraad," October 9, 1784.

31. UA 52-1, 121v (January 5, 1638).

32. Consistories deliberated over the extent to which prospective converts were sincere and comprehending of Christian teachings. See Koschorke and Mottau, *Colombo Consistory Minutes*, 55 (November 2, 1750); Mooij, *Bouwstoffen protestantsche kerk*, 2:518 (December 21, 1656), 3:42 (March 26, 1668), 3:43 (April 16, 1668), 3:107 (October 19, 1670); "Tayouan Consistory to Amsterdam Classis," Campbell, *Formosa*, 241 (November 3, 1648); NA VOC, nr. 11160, "Walcheren Classis to Colombo Kerkeraad," October 15, 1698; NA VOC, nr. 11160, "Colombo Kerkeraad to Walcheren Classis," December 1705; NA VOC, nr. 11160, "Colombo Kerkeraad to Walcheren Classis," November 13, 1722; NA VOC, nr. 11162, "Batavia Kerkeraad to Diderik Durven," August 18, 1730; "Amboina Gov. to Gov. Gen. Coen," *OHZ* VI:74–75 (September 10, 1628); SA 379, nr. 185 (East Indies), "Walcheren Classis to Amsterdam Classis," August 22, 1645 (54); SA 379, nr. 185 (East Indies), "Batavia Kerkeraad to Amsterdam Classis," January 19, 1651 (125); SA 379, nr. 186 (East Indies), "Batavia Kerkeraad to Amsterdam Classis," December 17, 1663 (214–15); ZA, nr. 68, "Colombo Kerkeraad to Walcheren Classis," January 3, 1681.

33. SA 379, nr. 206 (Cape of Good Hope), "Cape of Good Hope Kerkeraad to Amsterdam Classis," 1679 (54).

34. NA VOC, nr. 11162, "Batavia Kerkeraad to Diderik Durven," August 18, 1730.

35. Baer, *Honored by the Glory of Islam*, 6.

36. NA VOC, nr. 11160, "Walcheren Classis to Batavia Kerkeraad," April 1, 1692; SA 379, nr. 164 (Amsterdam), "Amsterdam Classis to Batavia Kerkeraad," September 11, 1651 (112); SA 379, nr. 168 (Amsterdam), "Amsterdam Classis to Batavia Kerkeraad," October 3, 1670 (56); SA 379, nr. 185 (East Indies), "Batavia Kerkeraad to Gov. Gen.," January 21, 1655 (457); van Boetzelaer van Asperen en Dubbeldam, "Correspondentie Adriaan Hulsebos," 2, 3, 4 (1943), 22 (February 7, 1618); 1401 OSA, nr. 1328, "Batavia Kerkeraad to South Holland Synod," November 6, 1724.

37. On attempts to enforce stronger moral order and eliminate other religions, see SA 379, nr. 185 (East Indies), "Batavia Kerkeraad to Gov. Gen.," January 21, 1655 (455–59); "Remonstrantie van den kerkeraad op Banda," *OHZ* V:139–41 (May 1, 1622); "Classicale Vergaderinge [Brazil]," *OHZ* II:221, 227 (March 3, 1637); Mooij, *Bouwstoffen protestantsche kerk*, 3:686 (July 29, 1686), 3:697 (January 6, 1687); ZA, nr. 68, "Batavia Kerkeraad to Walcheren Classis," November 22, 1681.

38. See Mooij, *Bouwstoffen protestantsche kerk*, 2:53 (September 23, 1647), 2:187 (March 6, 1651), 2:633 (November 13, 1662), 3:235 (February 4, 1675), 3:292 (July 13, 1676); "Remonstrantie van den Kerkeraad op Banda," *OHZ* V:139–41 (May 1, 1622); "Classicale Vergaderinge [Brazil]," *OHZ* II:240–41 (January 5, 1638), 282, 288 (November 21, 1640).

39. Hoornbeeck, *De conversione*, 230–33; Voetius, *De gentilismo*, 604–5; Oomius, *Muhammedisdom of Turckdom*, 24, 34–49 (chap. 5; N.B.: the pagination starts anew in this chapter).

40. See, for example, SA 379, nr. 201 (Ceylon), "Colombo Kerkeraad to Heeren XVII," January 19, 1689 (183–92); ZA, nr. 66, "Colombo Kerkeraad to Walcheren Classis," January 19, 1689.

41. Noorlander, *Heaven's Wrath*, 128–34.

42. UA 52-1, 124v–125v (January 5, 1638), 130r–130v (April 20, 1640); "Acta Classis Brasiliana," *OHZ* II:282 (November 21, 1640); SA 379, nr. 163 (Amsterdam), "Amsterdam Classis to Brazil Classis," November 21, 1640 (98); SA 379, nr. 163 (Amsterdam), "Remonstrantie to Heeren XIX," July 9, 1646 (142–43).

43. Van der Chijs, *Plakaatboek*, 2:152 (March 7, 1650).

44. SA 379, nr. 164 (Amsterdam), "Batavia Kerkeraad to Amsterdam Classis," December 18, 1651 (133).

45. SA 379, nr. 186 (East Indies), "Batavia Kerkeraad to Amsterdam Classis," January 25, 1657 (70–71).

46. Niemeijer, *Calvinisme en koloniale stadscultuur*, 138–43.

47. SA 379, nr. 185 (East Indies), "Batavia Kerkeraad to Amsterdam Classis," January 19, 1651 (121).

48. SA 379, nr. 185 (East Indies), "Batavia Kerkeraad to Gov. Gen.," January 21, 1655 (455–56).

49. Niemeijer, *Calvinisme en koloniale stadscultuur*, 147–62.

50. SA 379, nr. 186 (East Indies), "Amboina Kerkeraad to Amsterdam Classis," September 3, 1676 (366).

51. SA 379, nr. 168 (Amsterdam), "Amsterdam Classis to Walcheren Classis," September 30, 1689 (205–6); NA VOC, nr. 11160, "Walcheren Classis to Colombo Kerkeraad," February 17, 1690; NA VOC, nr. 11160, "Walcheren Classis to Batavia Kerkeraad," April 19, 1691; 1401 OSA, nr. 1327, "Colombo Kerkeraad to South Holland Synod," November 20, 1730.

52. SA 379, nr. 164 (Amsterdam), "Resolutie van de XVII op versoeck van de kerk op niew Nederlandt in Niew Amsterdam nopende de Luthersche aldaer," February 26, 1654 (159); SA 379, nr. 188 (East Indies), "Batavia Kerkeraad to North Holland Synod," October 23, 1744 (379–82); SA 379, nr. 207 (Cape of Good Hope), "Cape of Good Hope Kerkeraad to Amsterdam Classis," March 27, 1767 (200–202).

53. "Classicale vergaderinge gehouden in Brasil," *OHZ* II:235–36 (January 5, 1638).

54. Ostler, *Empires of the Word*, 390.

55. Niemeijer, *Calvinisme en koloniale stadscultuur*, 112–14; van Goor, *Jan Kompenie as Schoolmaster*, 39, 49, 57, 59; Schalkwijk, *Dutch Brazil*, 176–85; Chiu, *Dutch Formosa*, 197.

56. Koschorke and Mottau, *Colombo Consistory Minutes*, 56–57 (December 16, 1750), 168 (October 25, 1757); SA 379, nr. 201 (Ceylon), "Colombo Kerkeraad to North Holland Synod," [no date, before October 3, 1662] (4–7); Franciscus, *Faith of Our Fathers*, 10. By the 1730s, it seems clear that most ministers could preach in either Portuguese, Tamil, or Sinhala.

57. For Ceylon, see "Instructions to Anthony Pavilionen," [after November 1663], in *Instructions from the Governor-General*, trans. Sophia Peters, 93.

58. *ATB* I:1, "Verslag van de Kerkenraad van Ambon," 182–88 (September 14, 1635).

59. *ATB* I:2, "Rapport betreffende een visitatie van kerken en scholen in Hitu," 48–55 [1693]; "Rapport betreffende een visitatie van kerken en scholen op Haruku en de zuidkust van Ceram," 55–58 [Oktober 1693]; *ATB* I:2, "Rapport betreffende een visitatie van kerken en scholen op Buru, Manipa, Buano, Piru, en Tanunu," 58–61 [November 1693].

60. Two additional churches were listed: at Cochin on the Malabar coast and at Nagapatnam on the Coromandel coast. SA 379, nr. 188 (East Indies), "Batavia Kerkeraad to Amsterdam Classis," November 25, 1737 (139–44).

61. Schalkwijk, *Dutch Brazil*, 70–71, 75–76, 152–53, 171–77.

62. Biewenga, *Kaap de Goede Hoop*, 118.

63. On the importance of preaching, see SA 379, nr. 188 (East Indies), "Redenen en motiva . . . tegens de Maleijdse Bijbels druk met une Arabise letter te protesten," December 30, 1737 (214–15).

64. Mooij, *Bouwstoffen protestantsche kerk*, 3:352 (September 16, 1677).

65. For a comprehensive list of materials used by Reformed church workers, see *ATB* IV, 127–61.

66. Baldaeus, *Oost-Indische heydenen*, 1.

67. Hoornbeeck, *De conversione*, 176.

68. Voetius, *De Muhammedismo*, 142, 151–52.

69. Voetius, *De Muhammedismo*, 141–42, 148.

70. Relandus, *De religione Mohammedica libri duo*, unpaginated preface.

71. Blussé, van Opstall, Yung-ho, et al., *Dagregisters*, 1:327 (April 10, 1637).

72. Niemeijer, *Calvinisme en koloniale stadscultuur*, 96; Noorlander, *Heaven's Wrath*, 118, 174–79, 188; SA 379, nr. 206 (Cape of Good Hope), "Cape of Good Hope Kerkeraad to Amsterdam Classis," July 4, 1697 (57).

73. Van Dam, *Oostindische Compagnie, vierde boek*; van Boetzelaer van Asperen en Dubbeldam, *Protestantsche Kerk*, 4–5.

74. "Het ampt van de schoolmeesters is vooreerst de jonge jeucht de vreese des Heeren in te scherpen, haer t'onderwijsen in de fundamenten van de christelijcke religie, haer te leeren bidden, singen, met haer te kerck te gaen, te catechiseren. Ten anderen haer to leeren hare ouders, overheden ende meesters te gehoorsamen. Ten derden haer te leeren lessen, schrijven ende cijfferen. Ten vierden haer te leeren alderley goede zeden ende manieren, ende eyntlijck te betrachten dat in de schoolen geen andere als de Nederlantse tale gebruyckt werde." *ATB* IV, "Kerkorde voor de gemeente te Batavia, 7 december 1643," 123.

75. "Joh. Wogma to H. H. Bewindhebbers der O.I.C.," *OHZ* V:6–8 (August 14, 1608); Steenbrink and Aritonang, "Arrival of Protestantism," 104–5; Niemeijer, "Orang Nasrani," 129–30.

76. Niemeijer, *Calvinisme en koloniale stadscultuur*, 187.

77. Arasaratnam, "Reverend Philippus Baldaeus," 32; van Goor, *Jan Kompenie as Schoolmaster*, 110, 114, 116; NA VOC, nr. 1160, "Batavia Kerkeraad to Walcheren Classis," November 5, 1714.

78. SA 379, nr. 191 (Formosa), "Tayouan Kerkeraad to Amsterdam Classis," October 7, 1643 (77–78); Chiu, *Dutch Formosa*, 193–202, 208.

79. NA VOC, nr. 11160, "Walcheren Classis to Cape of Good Hope Predicanten," [no date, immediately after February 17, 1691]; SA 379, nr. 206 (Cape of Good Hope), "Cape of Good Hope Kerkeraad to Amsterdam Classis," September 26, 1742 (391); Biewenga, *Kaap de Goede Hoop*, 157–64, 179; "De Kerkenraad van Drakensteyn aan de Classis Amsterdam," (April 4, 1703), in Spoelstra, *Bouwstoffen*, 1:31–34; "De Kaapsche Kerkenraad aan de Classis Amsterdam," (April 2, 1706), in Spoelstra, *Bouwstoffen*, 1:36–38; "De Kerkenraad te Kaapstad aan de Classis Amsterdam," (June 15, 1730), in Spoelstra, *Bouwstoffen*, 1:162–63.

80. Kilpatrick, *Dutch Schools*, 139–40.

81. Schalkwijk, *Dutch Brazil*, 142–44, 190.

82. "Classicale vergaderinge gehouden in Brasil," *OHZ* II:235–236 (January 5, 1638).

83. "Classicale vergaderinge gehouden in Brasil," *OHZ* II:235–236 (January 5, 1638), 317–18 (July 26, 1644).

84. Noorlander, *Heaven's Wrath*, 76, 179, 188.

85. See *ATB* I:1, "Fragment uit een verslag van Gilles Seys betreffende Ambon," 92 (May 7, 1627); *ATB* I:1, "Brief van Justus Heurnius aan Gouverneur-Generaal Hendrik Brouwer," 132 (May 25, 1632); *ATB* I:1, "Notities van Ds. Daniël Sonnevelt betreffende kerk van Ambon," 238 (May 30, 1644); *ATB* I:1, "Reglement aangaande de schoolmeesters en scholen in Leitmor," 319–20 (March 3, 1666); *ATB* II:1, "Brief van schoolmeester Hendrick van Hengel," 173 (July 24, 1628); *ATB* II:1, "Brief van school-

meester Andries Fortados aan Gouverneur Cornelis Francx," 143 (March 23, 1673); *ATB* II:2, "Ternate Kerkeraad aan Batavia Kerkeraad," 279 (September 1, 1757); Noorlander, *Heaven's Wrath*, 91, 195.

86. 1401 OSA, nr. 1327, "Colombo Kerkeraad to South Holland Synod," November 13, 1722.

87. See *ATB* II:1, "Rapport betreffende een visitatie van kerken en scholen in Noord-Sulwesi en op de Sangihe-Eilanden," 367 (August 18, 1694); SA 379, nr. 201 (Ceylon), "Jaffnapatnam Kerkeraad to Walcheren Classis," November 25, 1670 (101–3).

88. *ATB* II:1, "Brief van schoolmeester Hendrick van Hengel aan de Batavia Kerkeraad," 73 (July 24, 1628); Blussé, van Opstall, Yung-ho, et al., *Dagregisters*, 1:122 (February 26, 1648).

89. See for example, *ATB* I:2, "Kort ontwerp van de staat der Ambonese kerken en scholen," 8–9 (June 12, 1692).

90. Van der Chijs, *Plakaatboek*, 3:129 (April 4, 1684). At the end of the 1600s, the Amboina consistory attempted to conduct visitations every six months. *ATB* I:2, "Kort ontwerp van de staat der Ambonese kerken en scholen," 10 (June 12, 1692).

91. Van Goor, *Jan Kompenie as Schoolmaster*, 110–11.

92. SA 379, nr. 201 (Ceylon), "Colombo Kerkeraad to Amsterdam Classis," January 17, 1683 (138).

93. Blussé, van Opstall, Yung-ho, et al., *Dagregisters*, 1:402–4 (February 7, 1638); "Tayouan Day Journal, 11 November 1647 till 9 January 1648," Campbell, *Formosa*, 225–26 (December 5, 1647); "Council of Formosa to Governor General and Councillors of India," Campbell, *Formosa*, 291 (February 26, 1654).

94. Van Goor, *Jan Kompenie as Schoolmaster*, 34, 114.

95. NA VOC, nr. 11160, "Batavia Kerkeraad to Walcheren Classis," November 16, 1716; NA VOC, nr. 11160, "Colombo Kerkeraad to Walcheren Classis," December 8, 1717.

96. *ATB* I:2, "Kort ontwerp van de staat der Ambonse kerken en scholen," 7–29 (June 12, 1692).

97. Van Goor, *Jan Kompenie as Schoolmaster*, 112–13; NA VOC, nr. 11160, "Walcheren Classis to Colombo Kerkeraad," [no date, immediately after January 25, 1693]; NA VOC, nr. 11160, "Batavia Kerkeraad to Walcheren Classis," January 15, 1699; NA VOC, nr. 11160, "Colombo Kerkeraad to Walcheren Classis," December 1705.

98. NA VOC, nr. 11160, "Colombo Kerkeraad to Walcheren Classis," December 7, 1718; November 14, 1721; November 13, 1722.

99. Van Goor, *Jan Kompenie as Schoolmaster*, 38–40, 45–49, 57–60.

100. Steenbrink and Aritonang, "Arrival of Protestantism," 105–8, 114, 123–24; Niemeijer, *Calvinisme en koloniale stadscultuur*, 187; van Boetzelaer van Asperen en Dubbeldam, *Protestantsche Kerk*, 245–46.

101. Blussé, van Opstall, Yung-ho, et al., *Dagregisters*, 1:331 (April 30, 1637), 332 (May 7, 1637), 404 (February 7, 1638).

102. "Classicale vergaderinge gehouden in Brasil," *OHZ* II:223 (March 3, 1637); "Acta van de gemeente t'samenkomste, bestaende beyde Classes, Reciffo, Pernambuco," *OHZ* II:317–18 (July 18–26, 1644); Schalkwijk, *Dutch Brazil*, 143–44.

103. Chiu, *Dutch Formosa*, 198–202.

104. SA 379, nr. 201 (Ceylon), "Colombo Kerkeraad to Amsterdam Classis," January 17, 1683 (139). For other positive assessments of Ceylonese schoolmasters and students, see NA VOC, nr. 11160, "Batavia Kerkeraad to Walcheren Classis," November 5, 1719.
105. *ATB* I:1, "Rapport betreffende een visitatie van kerken en scholen op Leitmor, Buano, Manipa, Hitu, and Piru," 380 (November 30, 1672).
106. *ATB* I:1, "Ambon Kerkeraad to Batavia Kerkeraad," 471 (October 1675).
107. *ATB* I:2, "Ambon Kerkeraad to Batavia Kerkeraad," 314 (September 19, 1720).
108. *ATB* II:1, "Rapport betreffende een visitatie van kerken en scholen op Ternate, Obi, Batjan, Makian, Tidore, Manado, Tahulandang, Siau, en Sangihe," 156 (November 17, 1675).
109. *ATB* II:1, "Rapport betreffende een visitatie van kerken en scholen op Batjan en Makian," 372 (June 8, 1695).
110. For other examples, see *ATB* I:1, "Rapport betreffende een visitatie van kerken en scholen op Saparua en Nusa Laut," 500 [January 1677]; *ATB* I:1, "Rapport betreffende een visitatie van kerken en scholen op Haruku en de zuidkust van Ceram," 503 (February 23, 1677); *ATB* I:2, "Rapport betreffende een visitatie van kerken en scholen op Haruku en de zuidkust van Cerram," 56 [October 1693]; *ATB* I:2, "Rapport betreffende een visitatie van kerken en scholen op Haruku en de zuidkust van Ceram," 78 (May 31, 1694); *ATB* II:1, "Ternate Kerkeraad to Batavia Kerkeraad," 201 (September 1, 1683); *ATB* II:1, "Ternate Kerkeraad to Batavia Kerkeraad," 301 (October 17, 1691); *ATB* II:2, "Rapport betreffende een visitatie van kerken en scholen in Noord-Sulawesi en op de Sangihe-Eilanden," 93 (November 2, 1707); *ATB* II:2, "Rapport betreffende een visitatie van kerken en scholen op Makian, en Batjan en op de Sangihe-Eilanden," 217 (April 6, 1729); *ATB* II:2, "Rapport betreffende een visitatie van kerken en scholen op Batjan en op de Sanigie-Eilanden," 299 (August 30, 1762); *ATB* II:2, "Ternate Kerkeraad to Batavia Kerkeraad," 347 (September 23, 1774); *ATB* III:1, "Banda Kerkeraad to Batavia Kerkeraad," 278 (June 14, 1688). There were occasions when an inspector complained about the quality of the students, but nevertheless praised the schoolmaster; see, for example, *ATB* I:2, "Rapport betreffende een visitatie van kerken en scholen op Saparua, Nusa Laut, en de zuidkust van Ceram," 114 (July 1695); *ATB* I:2, "Ambon Kerkeraad to Batavia Kerkeraad," 297 (May 22, 1715).
111. *ATB* II:2, "Ternate Kerkeraad to Batavia Kerkeraad," 43 (January 3, 1703).
112. *ATB* I:1, "Gerrit van de Voorde to Gouverneur Anthonio Hurdt," 460 (July 21, 1674).
113. *ATB* I:1, "Rapport betreffende een visitatie van kerken en scholen op Leitmor, Buano, Manipa, Hitu, en Piru," 375 (November 30, 1672).
114. *ATB* II:2, "Ternate Kerkeraad to Batavia Kerkeraad," 283 (September 1, 1757).
115. See, for example, Blussé, van Opstall, Yung-ho, et al., *Dagregisters*, 1:364 [July 1, 1654].
116. *ATB* II:2, "Rapport betreffende een visitatie van kerken en scholen in Noord-Sulawesi en op de Sangihe-Eilanden," 123 [October 1720].
117. "Ex-Governor Verburg's Report on Mission Work in Formosa," Campbell, *Formosa*, 296 (March 10, 1654).

118. NA VOC, nr. 11160, "Batavia Kerkeraad to Walcheren Classis," November 5, 1719.

119. *ATB* I:1, "Rapport betreffende een visitatie van kerken en scholen op Haruku, Saparua, Nusa Laut," 340 (July 19, 1669).

120. *ATB* II:2, "Ternate Kerkeraad to Batavia Kerkeraad," 283 (September 1, 1757); *ATB* II:2, "Ternate Kerkeraad to Batavia Kerkeraad," 330 [1769]; *ATB* II:2, "Rapport betreffende een visitatie van kerken en scholen in het gouvernement Ternate," 351–53 (September 23, 1774); *ATB* II:2, "G. J. Huther aan de Politieke Raad," 369–70 (July 18, 1781). For other complaints about the lack of learning among native teachers, see *ATB* I:1, "Rapport betreffende een visitatie van kerken en scholen op Haruku, Saparua, en Nusa Laut," 340–41 (July 19, 1669); *ATB* I:1, "Rapport betreffende een visitatie van kerken en scholen op Ambon, Manipa, Buano, Ceram, Saparua, en Nusa Laut," 449 [May 1674]; *ATB* I:1, "Rapport betreffende een visitatie te Kamarian," 478–79 (March 9, 1676); *ATB* II:2, "Ternate Kerkeraad to Batavia Kerkeraad," 325 (September 10, 1767); *ATB* II:2, "Rapport betreffende een visitatie van kerken en scholen op de Sandihe-Eilanden en in Noord-Sulawesi," 368 (April 27, 1781).

121. Henk Niemeijer, personal correspondence, April 17, 2020.

122. Steenbrink and Aritonang, "Arrival of Protestantism," 114.

123. "Classicale vergaderinge gehouden in Brasil," *OHZ* II:235 (January 5, 1638).

124. NA VOC, nr. 11160, "Colombo Kerkeraad to Walcheren Classis," December 1705.

125. Van Goor, *Jan Kompenie as Schoolmaster*, 32, 110–11.

126. "Hans Putman to the Governor General and Councillors of India," Campbell, *Formosa*, 149 (October 7, 1636); "Ex-Governor Verburg's Report on Mission Work in Formosa," Campbell, *Formosa*, 296 (March 10, 1654); Blussé, van Opstall, Yung-ho, et al., *Dagregisters*, 1:314 [January 1654]; Chiu, *Dutch Formosa*, 196.

127. "De Kaapsche Kerkeraad aan de Classis Amsterdam," (July 4, 1697), in Spoelstra, *Bouwstoffen*, 1:31–32.

128. See, for example, KITLV, nr. H216, "Batavia Kerkeraad to Amsterdam Classis," November 20, 1719; "R. Junius to the Council at Batavia," Campbell, *Formosa*, 144 (n.d., before October 5, 1636); "The Council of Formosa to the Governor General and Councillors of India," Campbell, *Formosa*, 316 (March 2, 1658); SA 379, nr. 185 (East Indies), "Batavia Kerkeraad to Gouverneur General," January 21, 1655 (455–59); SA 379, nr. 186 (East Indies), "Batavia Kerkeraad to Amsterdam Classis," November 15, 1655 (17–18); Valentijn, *Oost-Indien*, 1:40.

129. ". . . Die arme blinde menschen ende Afgodische Indianen sijnde Slaven van de Duivels. . . . gedient den Duyvel ofte veel met den Duyvel." Danckarts, *Historisch ende Grondich Verhael*, unpaginated preface.

130. Heurnius, *De legatione evangelica*, 39–46.

131. Cocceius, *Godsdienst der Turken*, 37, 39, 46–47, 52.

132. "So dat wij raetsaem vanden hier van niet langer te spreeken ende hebben de reden omgewendt, ende de grouwelijcke daden van Mahumet ontdeckt." SA 379, nr. 184 (East Indies), "Wouter Melchiorsz, Martinus Sonck," August 31, 1622 (55).

133. Chiu, *Dutch Formosa*, 202; van Boetzelaer van Asperen en Dubbeldam, *Protestantsche Kerk*, 245.

134. SA 379, nr. 201 (Ceylon), "Consideratie wegens een Cingalees seminarium," August 6, 1690 (258–60).
135. Van Goor, *Jan Kompenie as Schoolmaster*, 83.
136. Voetius utilized Rogerius as well. See Voetius, *Appendicula de precatione ad orientem*, 270.
137. Vossius, *Theologia gentili*; Voetius, *Selectarum disputationum theologicarum*; Rogerius, *Open-deure*; Hoornbeeck, *De conversione*; Baldaeus, *Oost-Indische heydenen*; Valentijn, *Oost-Indien*.
138. ANRI, nr. 8, December 20, 1737.
139. 1401 OSA, nr. 1348, "Batavia Kerkeraad to South Holland Synod," March 30, 1738.
140. Van Boetzelaer van Asperen en Dubbeldam, *Protestantsche Kerk*, 121–22.
141. Van Goor, *Jan Kompenie as Schoolmaster*, 84–85; Hudson, *Protestant Origins in India*, 143.
142. See, for example, ZA, nr. 67, "Walcheren Classis to Heren XVII," October 12, 1773.
143. ANRI, nr. 8, May 5, 1739.
144. ZA, nr. 67, "Walcheren Classis to Heren XVII," February 9, 1764 (1–13).
145. See the pastoral and visitation reports in *ATB*, I:2; II:2, II:1 passim. See also ZA, nr. 67, "Amsterdam Classis to Walcheren Classis," November 12, 1772; ZA, nr. 69, "Batavia Kerkeraad to Walcheren Classis," October 24, 1782.
146. See, for example, ANRI, nr. 9, April 21, May 8, 1741. ANRI, nr. 12, September 26, 1757; March 19, April 2, 1759. ANRI, nr. 13, August 29, 1761; February 5, July 23, August 6, August 25, 29, September 11, 25, 1765; August 6, 26, 1766. ANRI, nr. 14, November 26, December 3, 22, 1766; November 23, 1767; August 11, September 19, 1768; September 21, 1769; September 10, 1778. ANRI, nr. 15, September 25, 1777. ANRI, nr. 17, March 6, June 26, July 10, 1783; January 8, 22, March 20, September 18, 1784; April 6, 1786. Koschorke and Mottau, *Colombo Consistory Minutes*, 25 (June 24, 1740), 40 (June 10, 1743), 44 (April 13, 1744), 45 (June 15, 1744), 46 (July 8, 1744), 56 (December 5, 1750), 59 (January 28, December 2, 1751), 75 (March 7, 24, 1752), 82–83 (June 23, 1752), 85 (July 24, 1752), 91 (December 7, 1752), 94 (March 21, 1753), 136 (February 23, 1756), 137 (April 9, 1756), 139 (May 19, 1752), 166 (October 10, 1757), 168 (October 25, 1757).
147. ANRI, nr. 16, September 25, 1777.
148. Valentijn, *Oost-Indien*, vol. 3, pt. 1, 1, 3, 25.
149. Valentijn, *Oost-Indien*, vol. 3, pt. 1, 23–24. See also Steenbrink, *Dutch Colonialism*, 39–40.
150. Valentijn, *Oost-Indien*, vol. 3, pt. 2, 233. This episode is recounted in Steenbrink, *Dutch Colonialism*, 38–39.
151. Arasaratnam, *Ceylon*, 51.
152. Koschorke and Mottau, *Colombo Consistory Minutes*, 216 (September 7, 1758).
153. "Ongelovige of heidenen of Mahomedaan, menschen die niet alleen van haar eijge religie seer weijnige en duystere begrippen hebben, maar die men ook naar den mensch en menschelijke mogelijkheit gesproken ten ware men sijne toevlugt tot buyten gewoone wonderwereken wilde neemen moet reckenen niet vatbaar te zijn voor die waarheeden welke hen in dit hun laaste uur worden voorgehouden." ANRI, nr. 13, January 11, 1761.

154. Biewenga, *Kaap de Goede Hoop*, 158; Elphick and Shell, "Intergroup Relations," 186–87.

155. SA 379, nr. 201 (Ceylon), "Den gehelen toestant der kercken en schoolen int ryck Jaffnapatnam," December 1, 1663 (39).

156. Van Goor, *Jan Kompenie as Schoolmaster*, 113–14; SA 379, nr. 166 (Amsterdam), "Batavia Kerkeraad to Amsterdam Classis," October 28, 1758 (6).

157. SA 379, nr. 187 (East Indies), "Amboina Kerkeraad to Amsterdam Classis," September 17, 1716 (205).

158. *ATB* IV, "Verzamelstaten van de kerken en scholen in het gouvernement Ternate," 187–93; *ATB* IV, "Verzamelstaten van de kerken en scholen in het gouvernement Banda," 194–96. ZA, nr. 66, "Batavia Kerkeraad to Walcheren Classis," September 6, 1694.

159. Steenbrink and Aritonang, "Arrival of Protestantism," 122–23; *ATB* IV, "Verzamelstaten van de kerken en scholen in het gouvernement Ambon," 176–77.

160. Ternate reported 262 members and 10,362 nominal Christians in 1700; Banda, 200 members and 1,750 nominal Christians in the 1780s; the Cape of Good Hope, around 300 members in 1700; and Ceylon, around 2,000 members and over 64,000 nominal Christians in the 1780s. *ATB* II:1, "Rapport betreffende een visitatie van kerken en scholen in Noord-Celebes en op die Sanghe-Eilanded," 389 (September 18, 1696); SA 379, nr. 188 (East Indies), "Batavia Kerkeraad to Amsterdam Classis," November 25, 1737 (139–44); SA 379, nr. 188 (East Indies), "Batavia Kerkeraad to Amsterdam Classis," January 26, 1739 (298–303); SA 379, nr. 189 (East Indies), "Batavia Kerkeraad to Amsterdam Classis," [1760] (264–91); *ATB* III, "Banda Kerkeraad to Batavia Kerkeraad," 477–78 (August 26, 1768); *ATB* IV, "Verzamelstaten van de kerken en scholen in de gouvernementen Ambon, Ternate, en Banda," 175–96; Niemeijer, *Calvinisme en koloniale stadscultuur*, 174, 212–13; SA 379, nr. 201 (Ceylon), "Colombo Kerkeraad to Amsterdam Classis," January 20, 1690 (178); SA 379, nr. 206 (Cape of Good Hope), "Cape of Good Hope Kerkeraad to Amsterdam Classis," July 4, 1697 (57–58); "De Kaapsche Kerkeraad aan de Classis Amsterdam," (July 4, 1697), in Spoelstra, *Bouwstoffen*, 1:31–32; "Joh. Godefre. aan de Class Amsterdam," (April 19, 1708), in Spoelstra, *Bouwstoffen*, 1:120–22; Biewenga, *Kaap de Goede Hope*, 204, 206.

161. SA 379, nr. 158 (Amsterdam Acta), "Batavia Kerkeraad to Amsterdam Classis," November 14, 1701 (445); SA 379, nr. 158 (Amsterdam Acta), "Batavia Kerkeraad to Amsterdam Classis," December 1, 1704 (476).

162. The revered Sufi sheikh Yusuf Makassari was sent into exile to Colombo (from Makassar) by the VOC in 1684. Although the extent of his work in Ceylon is not known, it is likely he acquired a significant following among Muslims there. He was sent into exile a second time in 1694 to the Cape of Good Hope. Ricci, *Banishment and Belonging*, 3, 12, 35, 133, 230n19.

163. Ricklefs, *History of Modern Indonesia*, 6–11; Ricklefs, *Mystic Synthesis*, 17–22; Reid, "Islamization of Southeast Asia," 14–17, 23; Arasaratnam, *Ceylon*, 117–22; McGilvray, *Crucible of Conflict*, 21.

164. Elphick and Shell, "Intergroup Relations," 191–93.

165. Pearson, "Conversions in South-East Asia," 54.

166. Ricklefs, *Mystic Synthesis*, 21–22. For hybridization among Muslims in Ceylon, see Arasaratnam, *Ceylon*, 120–21.

167. Malalgoda, *Buddhism in Sinhalese Society*, 12–17, 22–25; Raghavan, *India*, 25–26, 56.

168. Klokke, "Hinduism and Buddhism," 17–19, 23–25; Steenbrink and Aritonang, *History of Christianity*, 25, 73; Geertz, *Religion of Java*, 5.

169. *ATB* II:2, "Rapport betreffende een visitatie van kerken en scholen in Noord-Sulawesi en de Sangihe-Talaud Archipel," 75 (1706).

170. *ATB* II:1, "Rapport betreffende een visitatie van kerken en scholen op Ternate, Obi, Batjan, Makian, Manado, Tahulandang, en Siau," 135 [October 1673].

171. *ATB* III, "Rapport betreffende een visitatie van kerken en scholen op de zuidwester-eilanden," 290 (June 6, 1692).

172. For another example of this pattern, see SA 379, nr. 186 (East Indies), "Amboina Kerkeraad to Amsterdam Classis," September 8, 1663 (206).

173. *ATB* III, "Verslag van Ds. J. Vertrecht betreffende een reis naar Tanimbar, Kei, en Aru," 132–33, 139 (April 9, 1646). For similar responses, see *ATB* I:1, "Rapport betreffende een visitatie van kerken en scholen op Ambon, Manipa, Buano, Ceram, Saparua, en Nusa Laut," 450 (May 1674); ANRI, nr. 164, December 13, 1742.

174. *ATB* I:1, "Rapport betreffende een visitatie van kerken en scholen op Manipa, Buano, en Ceram," 519 (April 3, 1678). The opposite situation occurred in the Aru Islands (Banda) in 1704, when four Muslims asked to be baptized. The pastor determined that baptism appealed to them because they associated with Christians in their community. *ATB* III, "Rapport betreffende een visitatie van kerken en scholen op de Aru-Eilanden," 331 (April 28, 1704).

175. SA 379, nr. 201 (Ceylon), "Colombo Kerkeraad to Heeren Seventiende," January 19, 1689 (183–92).

176. "G. Candidius to Gov-general J. P. Coen," Campbell, *Formosa*, 95 (August 20, 1628).

177. UA 52-1, 135v (November 21, 1640); ZA, nr. 73, "Brazil Classis to Walcheren Classis," November 4, 1641. For examples of Calvinist fears about intermingling among native Christians and non-Christians, see *ATB* I:1, "Rapport betreffende een visitatie van kerken en scholen op Ceram," 372 [November 1672]; *ATB* I:1, "Rapport betreffende een visitatie van kerken en scholen op Ceram," 399–400 (April 28, 1673).

178. Van Boetzelaer van Asperen en Dubbeldam, "Correspondentie Adriaan Hulsebos," 44 (July 1, 1619).

179. *ATB* I:1, "Rapport betreffende een visitatie van kerken en scholen op Manipa, Buano, Hitu, Ceram, en Haruku," 484 (May 9, 1676).

180. *ATB* I:1, "Rapport betreffende een visitatie van kerken en scholen op Buru, Manipa, Buano, Ceram, en Haruku," 545 [November 1682].

181. Biewenga, *Kaap de Goede Hoop*, 182.

182. OSA Kolonien, nr. 67, "Johannes Rutherus to Heeren Bewinthebberen Oost indische Compag" [n.d, immediately after September 1686].

183. *ATB* II:1, "Rapport betreffende een visitatie van kerken en scholen op Ternate, Obi, Batjan, Makian, Manado, Tahulandang, en Siau," 134–36 [October 1673]. For other

examples of the tenacity of local religious culture on converts, see KITLV, nr. H216, "Batavia Kerkeraad to Amsterdam Classis," June 8, 1753; Mooij, *Bouwstoffen protestantsche kerk*, 1:221 (September 25, 1625), 2:50 (August 27, 1647); *ATB* I:1, "Ambon Kerkenraad to Batavia Kerkenraad," 93 (May 7, 1627); *ATB* I:1, "Rapport betreffende een visitatie van kerken en scholen op Ambon, Manipa, Buano, Ceram, Saparua, en Nusa Laut," 441 [May 1674]; SA 379, nr. 166 (Amsterdam), "Colombo Kerkeraad to Amsterdam Classis," January 22, 1766 (119).

184. Van Goor, *Jan Kompenie as Schoolmaster*, 131–32; SA 379, nr. 201 (Ceylon), "Colombo Kerkeraad to Heeren XVII," January 19, 1689 (183–92).

185. "Gov. Caron to President Overtwater and the Formosa Council," Campbell, *Formosa*, 219 (November 5, 1646); "Formosa Council to the Gov. Gen. and Councillors of India," Campbell, *Formosa*, 288–89 (October 30, 1652).

186. NA VOC, nr. 11160, "Batavia Kerkeraad to Walcheren Classis," November 20, 1719.

187. Schalkwijk, *Dutch Brazil*, 164–65.

188. SA 379, nr. 184 (East Indies), "Adriaen Hulsebos to Marten Sonck," May 1, 1622 (24); SA 379, nr. 184 (East Indies), "Banda Kerkeraad," June 18, 1625 (217–19). See also *ATB* I:1, "Rapport betreffende een visitatie van kerken en scholen op Ambon, Manipa, Buano, Ceram, en Nusa Laut," 442 [May 1674]; *ATB* II:1, "Rapport betreffende een visitatie van kerken en scholen op Ternate, Obi, Batjan, Makian, Manado, Tahulandang, en Siau," 136 [October 1673].

189. *ATB* III, "Verslag van ds. J. Vertrecht betreffende een reis naar Tanimbar, Kei, en Aru," 141 (April 9, 1646).

190. *ATB* I:1, "Ambon Kerkeraad to Batavia Kerkeraad," 186 (September 14, 1635).

191. Chiu, *Dutch Formosa*, 213–15.

192. "Formosa Council to the Gov. Gen. and the Councillors of India," Campbell, *Formosa*, 291 (February 26, 1654).

193. ANRI, nr. 156, October 14, 1695.

194. "Robert Junius to Amsterdam Chamber of the East India Company," Campbell, *Formosa*, 140 (September 5, 1636); "Governor van der Burg to the Gov. Gen. and the Councillors of India," Campbell, *Formosa*, 179 (November 4, 1639); "Commissioner Nicolaas Couckebacker on his mission to Tonking and his visit to Formosa," Campbell, *Formosa*, 182 (December 8, 1639); Chiu, *Dutch Formosa*, 213–14.

195. ". . . Dat dese lieden niet wel en weten wat de religie voor een dinck is, wat mer mede doet, waert goet voor is, ende watter aen is gelegen." "Caspar Wiltens to Amsterdam Classis," *OHZ* V:51 (May 31, 1615).

196. "Dat is een sake die ongehoort is, ten sy dat hy daerdoor weet te geraken uyt eenen grooten noot. Also is den grootvaeder van desen Coninck eertijts Christen geworden met alle sijn volck, omme van de Portugysen beschermt te werden tegen de Coninck van Ternate, ende naemaels, om te vriendschap van den selfden Coninck te gewinnen, wierd hy weder Moors met alle sijn volck, uytgenomen dese, . . . want hier en is geen saecke soo ongehoorde, als dat yemandt een religie soude aengenomen door dispoteren, door onderrichtinge, ofte uyt consideratie van de waerheyt. Sy hebben altijdt eenige andere motyven, ende dan comen se, seegende maeckt my Christen, sonder

eens gevraecht te hebben wattet in heeft Christian te sijn, ofte wat men gelooven ende doen moet." "Caspar Wiltens to Amsterdam Classis," *OHZ* V:58–59 (May 31, 1615).

197. Chiu, *Dutch Formosa*, 193.

198. Van Goor, *Jan Kompenie as Schoolmaster*, 30–31.

199. UA 52-1, 130r (January 5, 1638).

200. The Portuguese, creoles, and mestizos in Brazil found Dutch policies and attitudes alien. Calvinists ministers complained that the Portuguese regarded them as half Jewish because of the WIC's open acceptance of Jews in the colony. UA52-1, 20v (January 5, 1638).

201. The classis of Brazil complained about this obstruction. UA52-1, 139r (January 18, 1641).

202. Schalkwijk, *Dutch Brazil*, 172–75.

203. Mooij, *Bouwstoffen protestantsche kerk*, 3:107 (October 19, 1670).

204. See Niemeijer, "First Protestant Churches," 57–59.

205. *ATB* I:1, "Ambon Kerkeraad to Batavia Kerkeraad," 247 (May 28, 1645). For examples of Muslim influence on local villages to the dismay of the Dutch, see Mooij, *Bouwstoffen protestantsche kerk*, 2:23 (October 1, 1646); "Ex-Governor Putmans to Directors of the Amsterdam Chamber," Campbell, *Formosa*, 158 (August 2, 1637).

206. *ATB* I:1, "Andreas Eldercampius to Amsterdam Classis," 497 (November 24, 1676).

207. *ATB* I:1, "Rapport betreffende een visitatie van kerken en scholen op Ambon, Manipa, Buano, Ceram, Saparua, en Nusa Laut," 445 [May 1674].

208. *ATB* I:1, "Ambon Kerkeraad to Batavia Kerkeraad," 525 (May 28, 1678).

209. *ATB* II:1, "Rapport betreffende een visitatie van kerken en scholen op Ternate, Obi, Batjan, Makian, Manado, Tahulandang, and Siau," 134–35 [October 1673].

210. *ATB* I:1, "Rapport betreffende een visitatie van kerken en scholen op Manipa, Buano, Hitu, Ceram, and Haruku," 484 (May 9, 1676).

211. "G. Candidius to Gov. Nuyts," Campbell, *Formosa*, 89–90 [1627].

212. Mooij, *Bouwstoffen protestantsche kerk*, 2:86 (August 10, 1648). For other examples, see Mooij, *Bouwstoffen protestantsche kerk*, 1:149 (February 3, 1621); 1401 OSA, nr. 1328, "Batavia Kerkeraad to South Holland Synod," November 1723; NA VOC, nr. 11162, "Batavia Kerkeraad to Gov. Gen. Diderik Durven," August 18, 1730; *ATB* I:1, "Rapport betreffende een visitatie van kerken en scholen op Leitmor, Buano, Manipa, Hitu, en Piru," 376 (November 30, 1672).

213. Mooij, *Bouwstoffen protestantsche kerk*, 3:281–82 (March 16, 1676).

214. Blussé, *Strange Company*, 166–67.

215. *ATB* I:1, "Rapport betreffende een visitatie van kerken en scholen op Ceram," 493–94 [October 1676].

216. *ATB* I:1, "Rapport betreffende een visitatie te Kamarian," 475 (January 13, 1676).

217. *ATB* II:1, "Rapport betreffende een visitatie van kerken en scholen op Ternate, Obi, Batjan, Makian, Manado, Tahulandang, en Siau," 138 [October 1673].

218. *ATB* III, "Rapport betreffende een visitatie van kerken en scholen op de zuidwester-eilanden," 290 (June 6, 1692).

219. SA 379, nr. 185 (East Indies), "Batavia Kerkeraad to Gouverneur Generale ende Raden van India," January 4, 1653 (298).

220. NA VOC, nr. 11162, "Batavia Kerkeraad to Gov. Gen. Diderik Durven," August 18, 1730.

221. NA VOC, nr. 11162, "Batavia Kerkeraad to Gov. Gen. Diderik Durven," August 18, 1730; SA 379, nr. 201 (Ceylon), "Colombo Kerkeraad to Amsterdam Classis," December 29, 1684 (148–49). The Walcheren classis remained steadfastly opposed to dividing the sacraments throughout this period; see ZA, nr. 66, "Acta," May 21, 1732.

222. Mooij, *Bouwstoffen protestantsche kerk*, 2:86 (August 10, 1648).

223. SA 379, nr. 169 (Amsterdam), "Amsterdam Classis to Batavia Kerkeraad," November 29, 1725 (242–45).

224. Baldaeus, *True and Exact Description*, 814.

225. SA 379, nr. 169 (Amsterdam), "Amsterdam Classis to Batavia Kerkeraad," November 29, 1725 (242-45).

226. "Classicale vergaderinge gehouden in Brasil," *OHZ* II:240 (January 5, 1638).

227. "Want men doopt hier veele persoonen (t'welck mijns bedunckens) beter waer gelaten tot dat se eerst geleert waren, gelijck ick oock selve tegens Casparum geseyt hebben, die mij daerinne gelijck gaff, maer t'zelve al meede dede, om dattet hier andere voor zijn tijt gedaen hadden, en also ist een oude quade gewoonte; can oock om seeckere reedenen niet nagelaten worden, hier te lange te verhalen." Van Boetzelaer van Asperen en Dubbeldam, "Correspondentie Adriaan Hulsebos," 16 (April 21, 1617).

228. Van Boetzelaer van Asperen en Dubbeldam, "Correspondentie Adriaan Hulsebos," 40 (n.d., after December 19, 1618 and before July 1, 1619); SA 379, nr. 184 (East Indies), "Banda Kerkeraad to Willem Janss. Gouverneur van Banda," January 23, 24, 1625 (120).

229. Bakhuizen van den Brink, *Belijdenisgeschriften, vergelijkende teksten*, 117.

230. The consistories in Banda and Batavia even resolved in April 1622 not to allow a baptized member to take communion unless they grasped the Dutch language to ensure that they understood the word of God. SA 379, nr. 184 (East Indies), "Resoluties, Banda Kerkeraad," April 26, 1622 (15). For questions arising in the Cape of Good Hope, see SA 379, nr. 206 (Cape of Good Hope), "Resolutie genomen in Politicquen Rade," March 22, 1666 (41–48).

231. Ministers attempted to accommodate children of non-Christians, stipulating that they could receive baptism as long as members in good standing sponsored them and promised to see that they were raised in the Reformed faith. SA 379, nr. 184 (East Indies), "Resolutie vande doop der volwassen ende jonghe kinderen van moorse ofte heijdense," August 9, 1622 (34).

232. SA 379, nr. 184 (East Indies), "Banda Kerkeraad to Batavia Kerkeraad," August 20, 1624 (277–80); SA 379, nr. 184 (East Indies), "Banda Kerkeraad to Batavia Kerkeraad," May 12, 1625 (298–300); SA 379, nr. 185 (East Indies), "Walcheren Classis to Batavia Kerkeraad," August 22, 1645 (83); SA 379, nr. 185 (East Indies), "Palliacatta Kerkeraad to Broederen ende Medewerkeren inde huijse van den Heeren," October 7, 1650 (102).

233. Bakhuizen van den Brink, *Belijdenisgeschriften, vergelijkende teksten*, 223, 252.

234. The documentation relevant to this dispute is massive. For several collections of documents, see NA VOC, nr. 11162, "Stukken bestemd voor de classis Walcheren betreffende het geschil tussen ds. Le Boucq en den van de Kerkeraad in Batavia over het

toedienen van de doop met of zonder belijdenis aan pas bekeerde inheemsen en de bijwoning van het avondmaal van deze bekeerden," 1730–1736; 1401 OSA, nr. 1341, "E. F. Le Boucq to South Holland Synod," December 15, 1724; 1401 OSA, nrs. 1339–1340, "Stucken, rakende het Geschil der Sacrament-scheiding."

235. Van Boetzelaer van Asperen en Dubbeldam, "Correspondentie Adriaan Hulsebos," 79 (September 1, 1620); NA VOC, nr. 11162, "Batavia Kerkeraad to Gov. Gen. Diderik Durven," August 18, 1730; SA 379, nr. 187 (East Indies), "Extract den Synodaale Resolutien, Synodus Suijd Holland," 1726 (268–70).

236. SA 379, nr. 184 (East Indies), "Doop der kinderen op Angola," "Resolutie nopende de doop der school kinderen op Poulouaij," December 14, 1643 (129).

237. SA 379, nr. 163 (Amsterdam), "Brazil Classis to Amsterdam Classis," June 8, 1636 (28–29).

238. SA 379, nr. 165 (Amsterdam), "Acta Amsterdam Classis," May 30, 1661 (75).

239. SA 379, nr. 201 (Ceylon), "Antwoort op seker Extract . . ." October 2, 1696 (87–99); SA 379, nr. 201 (Ceylon), "Colombo Kerkeraad to Amsterdam Classis," December 29, 1684 (144–50). Ceylon consistories practiced a policy of dividing the sacraments; see Schutte, "Gereformeerd Ceylon," 183.

240. SA 379, nr. 164 (Amsterdam), "Acta Amsterdam Classis," August 7, 1651 (109–10); SA 379, nr. 185 (East Indies), "Batavia Kerkeraad to Amsterdam Classis," January 19, 1651 (125). See also SA 379, nr. 185 (East Indies), "Palliacatta Kerkeraad to Broederen ende Medewerkeren inde huijse van den Heeren," October 7, 1650 (102).

241. SA 379, nr. 186 (East Indies), "Amboina Kerkeraad to Amsterdam Classis," September 26, 1667 (296–98); SA 379, nr. 186 (East Indies), "Amboina Kerkeraad to Amsterdam Classis," September 1670 (329–30).

242. SA 379, nr. 165 (Amsterdam), "Acta Amsterdam Classis," September 4, 1679 (194).

243. Dumonceaux, "Conversion, convertir"; Morrison, *Understanding Conversion*, 185–86. See also Luria, "Rituals of Conversion," 73, 77.

244. Greer, "Conversion and Identity," 177.

245. Hsia, "Translating Christianity, 88; Županov, "Twisting a Pagan Tongue," 110; Gose, "Converting the Ancestors," 140–43.

4. LANGUAGE AND SALVATION IN THE EMPIRE

1. Baldaeus, *True and Exact Description*, 793.

2. "Caspar Wiltens to Amsterdam Classis," OHZ V:73 (1616). Simon Cat in Ceylon lobbied for a seminary in Colombo to train native teachers in Dutch so they could educate children in native languages. SA 379, nr. 201 (Ceylon), "Consideratie wegens a Cinghalees seminarium," August 6, 1690 (228).

3. Danckaerts, *Historisch ende grondich verhael*, 9, 25.

4. "From the Minute Book of the Church at Tayouan," Campbell, *Formosa*, 310.

5. NA VOC, nr. 11160, "Walcheren Classis to Colombo Kerkeraad," October 15, 1698.

6. See Hanks, *Converting Words*, 10–11, 17, 19.

7. Günergun, "Ottoman Encounters"; Alam and Subrahmanyam, *Writing the Mughal World*, 28–29. For some of the most important works on missionary translation not cited elsewhere in this study, see Hsia, *Jesuit in the Forbidden City*; Lockhart, *Nahuas after the Conquest*; Hovdhaugen, "Missionary Grammars"; Rafael, *Contracting Colonialism*; Cohen, "Mediating Linguistic Difference"; and Ditchfield, "Translating Christianity," 189–90.

8. Burke and Hsia, *Cultural Translation*, 11.

9. Wandel, *Reformation*, 72–78.

10. Wandel, *Reformation*, 78–80.

11. Burke, *Towards a Social History*, 18.

12. Wandel, *Reformation*, 110.

13. There were occasional discussions about a seminary in Batavia, and the governor general Gustaaf Willem Baron von Imhoff did open one in 1745, but it lasted only ten years. The VOC had also sponsored the Walaeus Seminary at the University of Leiden in 1622 to train ministers for Asia, but it, too, closed after only ten years. At the end of the eighteenth century, the VOC and church leaders considered opening a seminary in the Netherlands for Dutch and foreign students for the East Indies, South Asia, and the Cape of Good Hope. See van Boetzelaer van Asperen en Dubbeldam, *Protestantsche Kerk*, 244–47; NA VOC, nr. 4712, "Gecommitt. Bewendh. en verdere Gevolmachtigen tot zaaken van 't Vaderlandsche Seminarium to Gouverneur Generale ende Raden van India," October 19, 1792; ZA, nr. 65, "Acta Walcheren Classis," July 1, 1621 (5r–5v); SA 379, nr. 168 (Amsterdam), "Amsterdam Classis to Colombo Kerkeraad," April 12, 1689 (200); 1401 OSA, nr. 1328, "Batavia Kerkeraad to South Holland Synod," November 27, 1747.

14. SA 379, nr. 201 (Ceylon), "Consideratie wegens a Cinghalees seminarium," August 6, 1690 (242–43). Simon Ditchfield ("Translating Christianity," 190) has observed that Jesuits often complained that local languages in the Americas lacked the linguistic depth to convey Christian concepts.

15. *ATB* I:2, "Kort ontwerp van de staat der Ambonse kerken en scholen," 11 (June 12, 1692).

16. NA VOC, nr. 11160, "Walcheren Classis to Batavia Kerkeraad," January 6, 1700; NA VOC, nr. 11160, "Batavia Kerkeraad to North Holland Synod," November 16, 1699.

17. Durston, *Pastoral Quechua*, 32–33.

18. *ATB* I:1, "Gouverneur Artus Gusels to Batavia Kerkeraad," 158 (September 25, 1633); "Kort ontwerp van de staat der Ambonse kerken en scholen," 18–25 (June 12, 1692).

19. "Tayouan Consistory to Amsterdam Classis," Campbell, *Formosa*, 237–39 (November 3, 1648); SA 379, nr. 191 (Formosa), "Tayouan Kerkeraad to Amsterdam Classis," November 10, 1650 (88–91).

20. Koschorke and Mottau, *Colombo Consistory Minutes*, 75 (March 7, 1752), 76 (March 24, 1752), 80–81 (May 25, 1752), 101 (June 15, 1753), 134 (January 2, 1756), 170 (November 15, 1757), 172 (December 7, 1757), 176 (March 17, 1758), 182 (June 9, 1758).

21. The Amsterdam classis also refused to approve a short summary (*Cort begryp*) of Reformed teaching in Spanish by the minister in Brazil, Vincent Solerus. See

Noorlander, *Heaven's Wrath*, 177–78; Schalkwijk, *Dutch Brazil*, 157; UA 52-1, 120v (January 5, 1638).

22. Koschorke and Mottau, *Colombo Consistory Minutes*, 75 (March 7, 1752).

23. NA VOC, nr. 11160, "Batavia Kerkeraad to Walcheren Classis," November 25, 1697; NA VOC, nr. 11160, "Batavia Kerkeraad to North Holland Synod," November 16, 1698.

24. "Alzoo in dese Eerw. vergadering van het jaar 1683 tot het jaar 1686 eenige questien en misverstant tusschen mij en dezelve tot mijn groot leetwezen over de revisie en correctie van mijne Portuguesche translatie beide des O. en N. Testaments, en daarover verscheide resolutien to boek gestelt, waarover ik mij beswaart en ongerust bevinde: zoo is mijn ootmoedig, nederig, en ernstig verzoek, dat dezelve geroijeert of doorgehaalt mogen warden, alzoo is alreede een oud en zwak mensch ben en wensche weld at zulkx voor mijn dood geschieden, opdat ik dezen aangaande des te geruster ten graven mog te deelen." Mooij, *Bouwstoffen protestantsche kerk*, 3:802 (April 3, 1689). A multiyear conflict between Philip de Vriest and several ministers in Colombo had some roots in criticism of his facility in Tamil. ANRI nr. 5, March 1700.

25. Groeneboer, *Gateway to the West*, 23–26.

26. Sneddon, *Indonesian Language*, 84–85; Ewing, "Colloquial Indonesian," 227.

27. Chiu, *Dutch Formosa*, 5–6.

28. Chiu, *Dutch Formosa*, 197–99.

29. NA VOC, nr. 11160, "Rapport van de Colombo Kerkeraad to Gouverneur Gerrit de Heere," December 2, 1699; Seboek, *Current Trends in Linguistics*, 736–37.

30. See de Lery, *History of a Voyage*, 178–95.

31. Lee, "Language and Conquest," 143.

32. Gilbert, *In Good Faith*, 1–18.

33. For another example of tensions between promoting a European language or an indigenous translanguage and accepting local linguistic diversity, see Betancourt, "Colonialism in the Periphery."

34. Because congregations made no sustained efforts to offer instruction in Dutch, clergy preached in Portuguese, Spanish, French, and Tupian. Schalkwijk, *Dutch Brazil*, 152–53, 166.

35. Van der Chijs, *Plakaatboek*, 1:459–60 (June 1641); see also 1:542, 547, 575 (July 1642).

36. Heylen, "Dutch Language Policy," 223; Ginsel, *Gereformeerde Kerk op Formosa*, 103.

37. Simon Cat related these events in a history of efforts to inculcate Dutch in an extended appeal in 1690 to establish a seminary. SA 379, nr. 201 (Ceylon), "Consideratie wegens a Cinghalees seminarium," August 6, 1690 (234); Hovy, *Ceylonees plakkaatboek*, vol. 1, 49–50 (November 14–21, 1659).

38. Groeneboer, *Gateway to the West*, 39.

39. SA 379, nr. 184 (East Indies), "Resoluties, Banda Kerkeraad," April 26, 1622 (15).

40. SA 379, nr. 184 (East Indies), "Banda Kerkeraad to President ende sijne Rade," June 6, 1623 (70–72); SA 379, nr. 184 (East Indies), "Banda Kerkeraad to Gouverneur Willem Janss.," February 7 and 8, 1625 (127–30); Mooij, *Bouwstoffen protestantsche kerk*, 1:144–45 (July 31, 1622); *ATB* I:1, "Caspar Wiltens to Amsterdam Classis," 51 (May 31, 1615).

41. Van der Chijs, *Plakaatboek*, 2:52 (December 7, 1643).

42. "Tayouan Consistory to Amsterdam Classis," Campbell, *Formosa*, 242 (November 3, 1648); "Ex-Governor Verburg's Report on Mission Work in Formosa," Campbell, *Formosa*, 296 (March 10, 1654).

43. SA 379, nr. 201 (Ceylon), "Consideratie wegens a Cinghalees seminarium," August 6, 1690 (242–43). For the same proposal for the Moluccas, see "Adr. Blocq to Steven van der Haghen," *OHZ* V:91–92 (November 6, 1617).

44. "Onse taele is immers . . . een onvermenghde cierlijcke rijcke en verstandige spraacke d'outheijd der selver haalen sommige af vande kelten en van die met de Chaldeen en Hebreen die niet alleen in veele andere maar bijsonderlijk in d'eerste benaem-inghe vande deelen des weerelts, een de selve zijn, daar mede nog de griecke not de latijnse eenige gemijnschap hebben." SA 379, nr. 201 (Ceylon), "Consideratie wegens a Cinghalees seminarium," August 6, 1690 (239).

45. "Casparus Wiltgiens to Amsterdam Classis," *OHZ* V:73 (1616).

46. "Tayouan Consistory to Amsterdam Classis," Campbell, *Formosa*, 242 (November 3, 1648).

47. "Governor and Council of Formosa to Governor-General Maetsuycker and the Councillors of India," Campbell, *Formosa*, 301 (November 30, 1656).

48. Groeneboer, *Gateway to the West*, 29–39, 55.

49. Bono, *Word of God*, 60, 67, 74.

50. Errington, "Colonial Linguistics," 19–21 (quote on 20).

51. ANRI, nr. 163, May 2 and 4, 1725.

52. SA 379, nr. 201 (Ceylon), "Hendrick Adriaen van Rhee to Draackesteijn heere van Meidreght," September 11, 1690 (213–14).

53. *ATB* III, "Noodzakelijk vertoog door ds. W. de Bitter aan de Hoge Regering te Batavia," 242–44 (September 1672). For similar complaints, see *ATB* II:2, "Rapport betreffende een visitatie van kerken en scholen op Batjan en Makian," 131 (June 3, 1722); *ATB* II:2, "Ternate Kerkeraad to Batavia Kerkeraad," 133–34 (September 2, 1722); *ATB* II:2, "Ternate Kerkeraad to Batavia Kerkeraad," 137 (June 26, 1713).

54. *ATB* I:1, "Brief van schoolmeester Zacharias Caheying aan Gouverneur Jacob Cops," 342 (September 20, 1670).

55. *ATB* I:2, "Kort ontwerp van de staat der Ambonse kerken en scholen door ds. Petrus van der Vorm," 19–22 (June 12, 1692); *ATB* I:2, "Rapport betreffende een visitatie van kerken en scholen op Haruku en de zuidkust van Ceram," 74 (May 31, 1694). For similar remarks, see *ATB* III:1, "Noodzakelijk vertoog door ds. W. de Bitter aan de Hoge Regering te Batavia," 234–41 (September 1672).

56. Van Goor, *Jan Kompenie as Schoolmaster*, 39.

57. ANRI, nr. 163, May 2, 1725, July 24, 1730.

58. Niemeijer, *Calvinisme en koloniale stadscultuur*, 113–17; Heylen, "Dutch Language Policy," 231.

59. *ATB* I:1, "Brief van schoolmeester Zacharias Caheying aan Gouverneur Jacob Cops," 342 (September 20, 1670).

60. "Mijn wierd van taalkundige inlanders onderrigt dat de mallabaarse en singaleese tale een groote gemeinschap hadden met malkanderen soo ten opsight van veele

gemeine woorden als ten opsight vande constructie." SA 379, nr. 201 (Ceylon), "Simon Cat to Thomas van Rhee Gouverneur van Ceylon," May 28, 1693 (298).

61. SA 379, nr. 201 (Ceylon), "Simon Cat to Thomas van Rhee Gouverneur van Ceylon," May 28, 1693 (298–300).

62. Koschorke and Mottau, *Colombo Consistory Minutes*, 35 (March 16, 1742), 76 (March 24, 1752).

63. *ATB* I:1, "Johannes du Praet to Batavia Kerkeraad," 75 (July 17, 1625).

64. "Tayouan Consistory to Amsterdam Classis," Campbell, *Formosa*, 239 (November 3, 1648).

65. Sneddon, *Indonesian Language*, 83.

66. Van Boetzelaer van Asperen en Dubbeldam, *Protestantsche Kerk*, 121–23; Thianto, *Way to Heaven*, 18–60.

67. Swellengrebel, *Leijdeckers voetspoor*, 11, 14; van Boetzelaer van Asperen en Dubbeldam, *Protestantsche Kerk*, 121–22.

68. See SA 379, nr. 192 (Junius Catechism), "Ordinair Formulier des Christendoms D. Junio of syn vertrec gelaten inder dorpen Solang, Sinckan, Mattau, etc.," 1647.

69. Heylen, "Dutch Language Policy," 211–22; Davidson, *Island of Formosa*, 48; Groeneboer, *Gateway to the West*, 50; "Tayouan Council and Consistory Minutes," Campbell, *Formosa*, 218–19 (August 16, 1646), "Tayouan Consistory to Governor-general and Councillors of India," Campbell, *Formosa*, 235, 239–40 (November 3, 1648); SA 379, nr. 191 (Formosa), "Tayouan Kerkeraad to Amsterdam Classis," November 10, 1650 (88–91); Chiu, *Dutch Formosa*, 197–200.

70. Van Goor, *Jan Kompenie as Schoolmaster*, 41–42.

71. Koschorke and Mottau, *Colombo Consistory Minutes*, 24 (March 28, 1740); Arasaratnam, "Reverend Philippus Baldaeus," 31; van Boetzelaer van Asperen en Dubbeldam, *Protestantsche Kerk*, 125; SA 379, nr. 201 (Ceylon), "Simon Cat to Thomas van Rhee Gouverneur van Ceylon," May 28, 1693 (298).

72. Koschorke and Mottau, *Colombo Consistory Minutes*, 55 (November 2, 1750).

73. Wickramasuriya, "Printing Press," 287–88; van Goor, *Jan Kompenie as Schoolmaster*, 58–59.

74. Van Troostenburg de Bruijn, *Oost-Indische predikanten*, 370–71; Wickramasuriya, "Printing Press," 287.

75. SA 379, nr. 202 (Ceylon), "Extraordinaire kerkelijke vergadering," November 13, 1697 (144–48).

76. Durston, *Pastoral Quechua*, 228–30.

77. SA 379, nr. 201 (Ceylon), "Simon Cat to Thomas van Rhee Gouverneur van Ceylon," May 28, 1693 (270–74).

78. SA 379, nr. 201 (Ceylon), "Simon Cat to Thomas van Rhee Gouverneur van Ceylon," May 28, 1693 (275–78).

79. SA 379, nr. 202 (Ceylon), "Extraordinaire kerkelijke vergaderingh," November 19, 1697 (179).

80. SA 379, nr. 202 (Ceylon), "Extraordinaire kerkelijke vergaderingh," November 21, 1697 (149–53); November 25, 1697 (155–63); November 27, 1697 (164–67).

81. SA 379, nr. 202 (Ceylon), "Raport gedaen . . . tot het examineren den verschillen tusschen . . . Simon Cat en Johannes Ruell," [November 1697] (188–99). The Colombo consistory summarized the dispute to the Walcheren Classis in correspondence received in Middelburg in October 1698; see NA VOC, nr. 11160, "Walcheren Classis to Colombo Kerkeraad," October 15, 1698.
82. Wickramasuriya, "Printing Press," 288.
83. Koschorke and Mottau, *Colombo Consistory Minutes*, 13 (October 9, 1737); ANRI, nr. 8, July 14, 1738.
84. Koschorke and Mottau, *Colombo Consistory Minutes*, 13 (October 9, 1737), 20 (May 14, 1739), 89 (October 6, 1752); van Goor, *Jan Kompenie as Schoolmaster*, 84–85.
85. 1401 OSA, nr. 1328, "Batavia Kerkeraad to South Holland Synod," January 26, 1739; Koschorke and Mottau, *Colombo Consistory Minutes*, 24 (March 28, 1740), 28 (October 18, 1740); ANRI, nr. 9, November 14, 1740. The *Politieke Raad* supported the translation projects in both Sinhalese and Tamil, occasionally making inquiries into the status of the work. Koschorke and Mottau, *Colombo Consistory Minutes*, 35 (March 16, 1742). Twenty-five years later, Nicholas Dal, a Lutheran pastor at Tranquebar who worked extensively on a Portuguese Bible, wrote to the Batavian consistory for financial support, but the Dutch ministers and elders were reticent to assist him. ANRI, nr. 8, January 29, 1739.
86. SA 379, nr. 204 (Ceylon), "Colombo Kerkeraad to North Holland Synod," December 1, 1739 (19).
87. Koschorke and Mottau, *Colombo Consistory Minutes*, 154–56 (June 24, 1757).
88. Koschorke and Mottau, *Colombo Consistory Minutes*, 55 (November 2, 1750), 98 (April 30, 1753), 100 (May 21, 1753). De Melho also wrote an anti-Catholic polemical treatise, and undertook scripture translation. Koschorke and Mottau, *Colombo Consistory Minutes*, 59 (January 14, 1751).
89. Koschorke and Mottau, *Colombo Consistory Minutes*, 96 (April 13, 1753), 98 (April 30, 1753), 99 (May 3, 1753), 100 (May 21, 1753), 101 (June 15, 1753).
90. This date was specified in a later consistory meeting. Koschorke and Mottau, *Colombo Consistory Minutes*, 134 (January 2, 1756).
91. Koschorke and Mottau, *Colombo Consistory Minutes*, 154 (June 24, 1757), 172 (December 7, 1757), 173 (December 19, 1757), 176 (March 17, 1758), 182 (June 9, 1758).
92. Koschorke and Mottau, *Colombo Consistory Minutes*, 134 (January 2, 1756); van Troostenburg de Bruijn, *Oost-Indische predikanten*, 291–92.
93. Schalkwijk, *Dutch Brazil*, 187–88.
94. Schalkwijk, *Dutch Brazil*, 176, 181.
95. Schalkwijk, *Dutch Brazil*, 154–55.
96. Schalkwijk, *Dutch Brazil*, 168–69.
97. Groeneboer, *Gateway to the West*, 38.
98. *Mardijkeren* denoted free descendants of migrants from South Asia who were brought to the East Indies as slaves by the Portuguese.
99. Groeneboer, *Gateway to the West*, 63.
100. Niemeijer, *Calvinisme en koloniale stadscultuur*, 113–16.

101. Groeneboer, *Gateway to the West*, 41–42.

102. Niemeijer, *Calvinisme en koloniale stadscultuur*, 187–89.

103. Groeneboer, *Gateway to the West*, 44–45.

104. This paragraph and the succeeding one were closely informed by Heylen, "Dutch Language Policy," 200–237.

105. "Ex-Governor Verburg's Report on Mission Work in Formosa," Campbell, *Formosa*, 293–94 (March 10, 1654).

106. "From the Governor and Council of Formosa to Governor-general Maetsuycker and the Councillors of India," Campbell, *Formosa*, 301 (November 30, 1656).

107. "Ende oock sal ick uijt d'selvige dat is, uijt de bekeerde heijdenen, eenige tot priesters ende tot Leviten, dat is tot praedicanten ende leeraers de H. Evangelij." ANRI, nr. 162, February 23, 1657.

108. Groeneboer, *Gateway to the West*, 48–51.

109. "Extracts from the Zeelandia Day-Journal," Campbell, *Formosa*, 318 (May 17, 1661).

110. Van Goor, *Jan Kompenie as Schoolmaster*, 60.

111. Van Goor, *Jan Kompenie as Schoolmaster*, 69–71, 77–83.

112. NA VOC, nr. 11160, "Colombo Kerkeraad to Walcheren Classis," December 9, 1712.

113. NA VOC, nr. 11160, "Colombo Kerkeraad to Walcheren Classis," December 1713.

114. Van Goor, *Jan Kompenie as Schoolmaster*, 62.

115. 1401 OSA, nr. 1327, "Colombo Kerkeraad to South Holland Synod," December 9, 1712; Groeneboer, *Gateway to the West*, 51–55.

116. Schalkwijk, *Dutch Brazil*, 157.

117. Koschorke and Mottau, *Colombo Consistory Minutes*, 13 (October 9, 1737).

118. "Formosa Consistory to Amsterdam Classis," Campbell, *Formosa*, 193 (October 7, 1643); Heylen, "Dutch Language Policy," 209–13.

119. "First Shorter Catechism by the Rev. R. Junius," Campbell, *Formosa*, 341, 338; "A Larger Catechism by the Rev. R. Junius," Campbell, *Formosa*, 360; Heylen, "Dutch Language Policy," 220, 338.

120. "Minutes from the Tayouan Council and Consistory," Campbell, *Formosa*, 218 (August 16, 1646).

121. This letter was summarized in "From the Amsterdam Classis to the Consistory of Tayouan," Campbell, *Formosa*, 246 (November 3, 1648).

122. "From President Overtwater to the Governor-general and councillors of India," Campbell, *Formosa*, 232 (November 2, 1648); "From the Tayouan Consistory to the India Committee of the Amsterdam Classis," Campbell, *Formosa*, 242–43 (November 3, 1648).

123. "Tayouan Consistory to India Committee of the Amsterdam Classis," Campbell, *Formosa*, 237–38 (November 3, 1648); SA 379, nr. 164 (Amsterdam), "Amsterdam Classis to Tayouan Kerkeraad," October 4, 1649 (48–50). Please note that in the latter document, the Amsterdam Classis reprised the ministers' complaints about Junius.

124. SA 379, nr. 164 (Amsterdam), "D. Robertus Junius," September 6, 1649 (43–45).

125. SA 379, nr. 164 (Amsterdam), "Amsterdam Classis to Tayouan Kerkeraad," October 4, 1649 (48–50).

126. SA 379, nr. 164 (Amsterdam), "Amsterdam Classis to Tayouan Kerkeraad," October 4, 1649 (48–50); SA 379, nr. 164 (Amsterdam), "Amsterdam Classis to Formosa Kerkeraad," October 3, 1650 (75–78); SA 379, nr. 164 (Amsterdam), "Amsterdam Classis to Tayouan Kerkeraad," September 11, 1651 (114–15). This affair is recounted in the letters in Campbell, *Dutch Formosa*, 236–49.

127. "Tayouan Consistory to Amsterdam Classis," Campbell, *Formosa*, 238–39 (November 3, 1648).

128. "Tayouan Consistory to Amsterdam Classis," Campbell, *Formosa*, 244 (November 3, 1648).

129. "Tayouan Consistory to Amsterdam Classis," Campbell, *Formosa*, 240 (November 3, 1648).

130. "Minutes of the Taiwan Council and Consistory," Campbell, *Formosa*, 218 (August 16, 1646).

131. "Tayouan Consistory to Amsterdam Classis," Campbell, *Formosa*, 238 (November 3, 1648).

132. Heylen, "Dutch Language Policy," 221.

133. "Amsterdam Classis to Tayouan Consistory," Campbell, *Dutch Formosa*, 247 (November 3, 1648).

134. "Ex-Governor Verburg's Report on Mission Work in Formosa," Campbell, *Formosa*, 293–94 (March 10, 1654).

135. Errington, "Colonial Linguistics," 29.

136. Groeneboer, *Gateway to the West*, 24–25; Swellengrebel, *Leijdeckers voetspoor*, 8–9; Sneddon, *Indonesian Language*, 84–85.

137. NA VOC, nr. 11160, "Walcheren Classis to North Holland Synod," July 18, 1699; Swellengrebel, *Leijdeckers voetspoor*, 11–13.

138. Swellengrebel, *Leijdeckers voetspoor*, 13–14.

139. Sneddon, *Indonesian Language*, 84–85; van Troostenburg de Bruijn, *Oost-Indische predikanten*, 258.

140. Van Troostenburg de Bruijn, *Oost-Indische predikanten*, 258–59; Swellengrebel, *Leijdeckers Voetspoor* 14.

141. *ATB* I:2, "Ambon Kerkeraad to Batavia Kerkeraad," 80–81 (September 29, 1694). For the consistory's support of Valentijn's Low Malay translation, see *ATB* I:2, "Ambon Kerkeraad to Batavia Kerkeraad," 187–93 (September 27, 1698).

142. NA VOC, nr. 11160, "Batavia Kerkeraad to Walcheren Classis," November 25, 1697; 1401 OSA, nr. 1338, "Batavia Kerkeraad to North Holland Synod," November 19, 1699.

143. NA VOC, nr. 11160, "Walcheren Classis to Batavia Kerkeraad," January 15, 1699.

144. NA VOC, nr. 11160, "Walcheren Classis to Batavia Kerkeraad," January 6, 1700.

145. Burke, *Early Modern Dutch*, 18.

146. Burke, *Early Modern Dutch*, 18–20.

147. NA VOC, nr. 11160, "Batavia Kerkeraad to Walcheren Classis," November 16, 1698, copied in "Walcheren Classis to Batavia Kerkeraad," January 6, 1700. See also NA VOC, nr. 11160, "Batavia Kerkeraad to Walcheren Classis," November 25, 1697. Note

that that the Walcheren Classis received the letter in October 1698. The Batavia consistory complained later that Valentijn would not even show it to his fellow ministers in Amboina. NA VOC, nr. 11160, "Beswarissen vande broederen van Amboina tegen de Maleysche oversettinge van Godt Woord door D. Valentijn uit het extract van haren brief aan de kerkeraad van Batavia," September 27, 1698.

148. NA VOC, nr. 11160, "Batavia Kerkeraad to Walcheren Classis," November 16, 1698, copied in "Walcheren Classis to Batavia Kerkeraad," January 6, 1700.

149. *ATB* I:2, "Batavia Kerkeraad to Noord-Holland Synod," 135–47 (November 15, 1697).

150. *ATB* I:2, "Batavia Kerkeraad to Noord-Holland Synod," 135–47 (November 15, 1697); NA VOC, nr. 11160, "Batavia Kerkeraad to Walcheren Classis," November 16, 1698, copied in "Walcheren Classis to Batavia Kerkeraad," January 6, 1700. See also 1401 OSA, nr. 1338, "Amboina Kerkeraad to South Holland Synod," September 25, 1700.

151. *ATB* I:2, "Deure der Waarhijd," 151–53 (1698).

152. *ATB* I:2, "Deure der Waarhijd," 165 (1698).

153. *ATB* I:2, "Deure der Waarhijd," 153 (1698).

154. *ATB* I:2, "Deure der Waarhijd," 164 (1698).

155. *ATB* I:2, "Deure der Waarhijd," 161–63 (1698).

156. "By al het welke niet die groote verbystering komt, dat men een geheel land en volk dwingen wil om een nieuwe Taal, of hoog Maleitsch te leeren om de gronden van onzen Godsdienst te beter te verstaan, in de kerk te komen hooren prediken; een zaak, die alle menschen, die buiten drift zyn, en reden gebruiken willen, zekerlyk zullen afkeuren, en van welke zy moeten bekennen, dat dit regte middle was, om de Inlanders, zoo zy niet reeds weg bleven, weg te jagen: want was lust kon iemande hebben in een Taal, die hy niet verstaat, te hooren prediken, of te Catechizeeren." Valentijn, *Omstandig verhaal Amboina, Oost-Indien*, 3, 89.

157. Valentijn, *Omstandig verhaal Amboina, Oost-Indien*, 3, 89.

158. Van Troostenburg de Bruijn, *Oost-Indische predikanten*, 441–42.

159. NA VOC, nr. 11160, "Beswarenissen vande broederen van Amboina tegen de Maleysche oversettinge van Godt Woord door D. Valentijn uit het extract van haren brief aan de kerkeraad van Batavia," September 27, 1698; *ATB* I:2, "Ambon Kerkeraad to Batavia Kerkeraad," 187–94 (September 27, 1698).

160. Van Troostenburg de Bruijn, *Oost-Indische predikanten*, 442; Swellengrebel, *Leijdeckers voetspoor*, 15. For several published fragments of the Valentijn edition, see *ATB* IV, 165–69.

161. SA 379, nr. 169 (Amsterdam), "Amsterdam Classis to Colombo Kerkeraad," November 8, 1701 (24); Swellengrebel, *Leijdeckers voetspoor*, 14; van Boetzelaer van Asperen en Dubbeldam, *Protestantsche Kerk*, 154.

162. Swellengrebel, *Leijdeckers voetspoor*, 16–19.

163. NA VOC, nr. 11160, "Walcheren Classis to Batavia Kerkeraad," January 6, 1700.

164. *ATB* I:2, "Ambon Kerkeraad to Batavia Kerkeraad," 190–91 (September 27, 1698).

165. Valentijn, *Omstandig verhaal Amboina, Oost-Indien*, 3, 79.

166. See, for example, SA 379, nr. 188 (East Indies), "Advijs vande ondergetekende onder-ling Augustinus Thornton in kerkenrade," December 19, 1737 (149–56); ANRI, nr. 8, December 20, 1737.
167. Swellengrebel, *Leijdeckers voetspoor*, 174–75, 178.
168. Errington, "Indonesian's Development," 272.

5. IDENTITY AND OTHERNESS IN THE REPUBLIC AND THE MISSIONS

1. "Voorts is de gestrengheid der Protestantsche Zendelingen ook hier geen gering be-letsel tot de verbreiding van het Evangelie; zy willen van deze zonen der Natuur en Vryheid volkomene suffers maken, tot niets geschikt dan tot zingen en bidden; niet en eeniger hunner gewoonten en gebruiken, ook dezulken niet, die geene de minste betrekking tot hunnen zo den Christeyke Godsdienst hebben, wil men hun veroor-loven; men wil hen volmaakt als de naauwstgezette Christenen doen leven." Haaf-ner, *Onderzoek*, 107.
2. Boneschansker, *Nederlandsch Zendeling Genootschap*, 23–25, 163–64.
3. Lamping, "Nederlandsch Zendeling Genootschap," 235–40.
4. See the appendix for a list and brief description of the authors and works treated in this chapter.
5. "Also by gelegenheid van de Oost-Indische scheepsvaert door bysondere schickinge en genade Gods, in verscheyde plaetsen van Oost-Indien een grote deure geopend is om het Evangelie onses Heren Jesu Christi, te predicken, met merckelicke hope, dat daer door vele inwoonders tot de kennisse des enigen waren Gods end also tot eeuw-ige salicheyt sullen worden gebracht, gelijck daer van alrede eenige goode be-genselen werden gespeurt." "Credentiebrief door den Amsterdamschen kerkeraad gegeven aan Caspar Wiltens," *OHZ* V:10 (December 23, 1610).
6. Spaans, "Introduction," 3.
7. Harris, "Mapping Jesuit Science."
8. The overseas churches corresponded regularly with the classes of Amsterdam and Walcheren (Middelburg). To gain some sense of this voluminous correspondence, see *Inventory Classis van Amsterdam van de Nederlandse Hervormde Kerk 1885–1951 (–1971)* (Stadsarchief Amsterdam), 35–42.
9. Schutte, "Between Amsterdam and Batavia," 35.
10. Bakhuizen van den Brink, *Belijdenisgeschriften, vergelijkende teksten*, 252. This judg-ment continued to be cited during the seventeenth century as the issue kept popping up. See SA 379, nr. 168 (Amsterdam), "Amsterdam Classis to Amboina Kerkeraad," November 19, 1668 (42).
11. SA 379, nr. 168 (Amsterdam), "Amsterdam Classis to Ceylon Kerk," [immediately be-fore May 1, 1679] (130); SA 379, nr. 168 (Amsterdam), "Amsterdam Classis to Batavia Kerkeraad," May 1, 1679 (131–32).
12. SA 379, nr. 201 (Ceylon), "Colombo Kerkeraad to Amsterdam Classis," January 6, 1668 (72–73).

13. SA 379, nr. 168 (Amsterdam), "Amsterdam Classis to Batavia Kerkeraad," October 3, 1670 (57). For other descriptions of the state of affairs in Europe, especially in political and religious matters, see SA 379, nr. 168 (Amsterdam), "Amsterdam Classis to Kerken op Ceilon," September 24, 1669 (47); SA 379, nr. 168 (Amsterdam), "Amsterdam Classis to Batavia Kerkeraad," November 5, 1669 (49).

14. Heurnius, *De legatione evangelica*; Danckaerts, *Historisch ende grondich verhael.*

15. Voetius, *Politicae ecclesiasticae*, 325–26, 341, 342.

16. See, for example, Caron, *Beschrijvinghe*; van Goens, *Javaensche reyse*; van Twist, *Generale beschrijvinghe van Indien.*

17. SA 369, nr. 170 (Amsterdam), "Amsterdam Classis to Predikanten van Nieuw York," December 1730 (59).

18. SA 379, nr. 168 (Amsterdam), "Amsterdam Classis to Batavia Kerkeraad," May 13, 1682 (152–54). See also SA 379, nr. 168 (Amsterdam), "Amsterdam Classis to Batavia Kerkeraad," December 8, 1682 (160–63); SA 379, nr. 168 (Amsterdam), "Amsterdam Classis to Batavia Kerkeraad," December 6, 1695 (227–28).

19. SA 379, nr. 168 (Amsterdam), "Amsterdam Classis to Colombo Kerkeraad," October 18, 1685 (187–88).

20. SA 379, nr. 201 (Ceylon), "Colombo Kerkeraad to Amsterdam Classis," January 13, 1687 (165–67).

21. SA 379, nr. 168 (Amsterdam), "Amsterdam Classis to Batavia Kerkeraad," November 29, 1700 (267–68).

22. SA 379, nr. 169 (Amsterdam), "Amsterdam Classis to Batavia Kerkeraad," December 1720 (168–71).

23. Udemans, *Geestelyck roer*, 330–32.

24. "Neque enim deesse materiam, cum per longinqua itinera passim incurrerunt, aut in Paganos, aut in Sina & Guinea; aut in Mahumetistas, ut sub imperio Turcae, Persiae, & Poenorum; tum vero Iudaeos, & ipsos jam Christianismi professsos hostes." Grotius, *De veritate religionis Christianae*, 2–3.

25. Grotius, *De veritate religionis Christianae*, 3.

26. G. Vossius, *De theologia gentili I & II*, 27, 57–58, 70.

27. G. Vossius, *De theologia gentili III & IV*, 750–51.

28. Grotius, *De veritate religionis Christianae*, 1–2.

29. See Grotius, *Bewijs van den waren godsdienst.*

30. Heering, "Grotius," 49; Heering, *Grotius as Apologist*, xix, 40, 64, 72.

31. Heering, *Grotius as Apologist*, 73 (quote), 199–230.

32. See Schama, *Embarrassment of Riches*, 323–39.

33. He produced a similar work earlier, *Spiritual Compass* (*Geestelick compas*), which set forth the Christian values for all overseas traders and travelers. In the dedication to *Geestelyck roer* (3), Udemans stated that it was an expansion of the *Spiritual Compass*. The *Geestelick compas* did not address non-Christian religions.

34. Udemans, *Geestelyck roer*, 286–302; Schmidt, *Innocence Abroad*, 244–46.

35. Popkin, "Polytheism, Deism, and Newton," 28–29 (quotes); Rademaker, *Vossius*, 249–50, 283.

36. "Nam si paganismum dixeris, nomen unum dixeris, non religionem unam. Nam nec idem adorabant: alij enim astra, alij elementa, alij pecudes, res non subsistentes." Grotius, *De veritate religionis Christianae*, 54.

37. Abulafia, *Christians and Jews*, 45, 79, 85–86, 128.

38. "Americae & Africae populous paganism tenebris obsitos." Grotius, *De veritate religionis Christianae*, 81.

39. "Nam if oculos circumferas per quotquot sunt imperia Christianorum aut Mahumetistarum, videbis paganismi nullam nisi in libris memoriam." Grotius, *De veritate religionis Christianae*, 89.

40. Laplanche, "Grotius et les religions," 56; Grotius, *Annotationes in Vetus & Novum Testamentum*, 10, 12, 13, 24, 36.

41. Grotius, *De veritate religionis Christianae*, 3–5, 9–10, 88–92.

42. Hoornbeeck, *De conversione*, 11–16; Baldaeus, *Oost-Indische heydenen*, 1–4, 5, 32, 40; Rogerius, *Open-deure*, 158, 163–65, 179, 184.

43. Laplanche, "Grotius et les religions," 55, 59–62; Grotius, *Annotationes in Vetus & Novum Testamentum*, 32–37.

44. Discussed in Popkin, "Polytheism, Deism, and Newton," 29–32.

45. Stroumsa, *New Science*, 91.

46. Stroumsa, *New Science*, 91.

47. "Quod si seculis aliquot retro tempora legamus, competiemus itidem, daemonas ab antiquis esse Saxonibus cultos, quibus ante tempora Karoli M." G. Vossius, *De theologia gentili I & II*, 56–60 (quote on 60).

48. G. Vossius, *De theologia gentili III & IV*, 790, 1134–39, 1507, 1520–1644.

49. Johnson, *Cultural Hierarchy in Sixteenth-Century Europe*, 27–28; Nongbri, *Before Religion*, 86–95.

50. Romans 1:20 (Revised Standard Version).

51. G. Vossius, *De theologia gentili I & II*, 19, 29–42, 71–85, 99.

52. Mulsow, "Antiquarianism and Idolatry," 200–203; Popkin, "Crisis of Polytheism," 11.

53. Udemans, *Geestelyck roer*, 119–22.

54. G. Vossius, *De theologia gentili I & II*, 57–58; Barlaeus, *Nederlandsch Brazilië*, 325–26.

55. Udemans, *Geestelyck roer*, 123–27.

56. "Dat de Libertijnen, ende andere lauwe Christenen, die altijdt roemen op haer natuerlicke verstandt ende politijck leven, indien sy niet voorder en komen datse niet een hayr beter en zijn dan de blinde Heydenen, die naer advenant soo wel politijck verstandt, ende een politjck leven hebben als sy doen." Udemans, *Geestelyck roer*, 131.

57. Meserve, *Empires of Islam*, 4–5, 16–17.

58. Grotius, *De veritate religionis Christianae*, 64–70 (quote on 70).

59. "Grouwel van Mahometh." Udemans, *Geestelyck roer*, 454.

60. See for example, G. Vossius, *De theologia gentili III & V*, 1011–12.

61. *Oratio de religione Turcarum* was originally written in Greek as a linguistic exercise. It was later translated into Latin by John Creighton and published as part of Cocceius's *Opera Anecdota* in 1707. Thus, it was unknown to the public until almost forty

years after Cocceius's death in 1669. When he wrote this work, Cocceius's library contained at least twenty works on Islam or Arabic, including ones by Jacob Golius, Thomas Erpenius, Georg Elmacini, Georg Nisseli, Joseph Scaliger, Luis Vives, and others. Cocceius owned a French translation of the Qur'an. Van Amersfoort and van Asselt, *Liever Turks dan Paaps?*, 12–14.

62. Cocceius, *Godsdienst der Turken*, 47–48.

63. Cocceius, *Godsdienst der Turken*, 40.

64. Van Asselt, "Structural Elements," 92–93; van Asselt, "Motieven en perspectiven," 227–28.

65. "Quo Christiana religio omnes alias, quae aut sunt, aut fuerunt, aut fingi possunt, exsuperat, est summa sanctitas praeceptorum, tum in iis quae ad Dei cultum, tum, quae ad res caetereas pertinent." Grotius, *De veritate religionis Christianae*, 42–43 (quote on 43).

66. Grotius, *De veritate religionis Christianae*, unpaginated preface.

67. Keene, *Beyond the Anarchical Society*, 50–57.

68. "Alterum argumentum, quo probamus, numen esse aliquod, sumitur à manifestissimo consensu omnium gentium, apud quas ratio & boni mores non plane extincta sunt inducta feritate." Grotius, *De veritate religionis Christianae*, 3–4.

69. Keene, *Beyond the Anarchical Society*, 50.

70. G. Vossius, *De theologia gentili I & II*, 18, 23, 48.

71. G. Vossius, *De theologia gentili III & IV*, 1582–84, 1588, 1603, 1606–7.

72. "Providentiam numinis divini clarrisime elucere: eoque nullum plane esse animantium genus, quod non hominem quasi manu ducat ad Dei creatoris notitiam amorem ac cultam." G. Vossiusi, *De theologia gentili III & IV*, 1644–47 (quote on 1647).

73. Udemans, *Geestelyck roer*, 122.

74. "In de gemoederen van het blinde Heydendom brant so een heldere Son van deugden die het flauwe licht der Christenen verdooft." Montanus, *Wonderen*, 26.

75. Udemans, *Geestelyck roer*, 120; see also Heurnius, *De legatione evangelica*, 22–23.

76. "In den welcken wy verwachten de bekeeringhe der Joden ende de volheyt der heydenen daer van den Apostel geprophetheert heeft." Udemans, *Geestelick Compas*, 168.

77. Udemans, *Geestelyck roer*, 118.

78. Udemans, *Geestelyck roer*, 337.

79. Heurnius also called for the preaching of the gospel to be "plain and simple" without any intellectual adornment. Heurnius, *De legatione evangelica*, 1–8; Callenbach, *Justus Heurnius*, 84.

80. "Tayouan Consistory to Amsterdam Classis," Campbell, *Formosa*, 236–44 (November 3, 1648); Niemeijer, *Calvinisme en koloniale stadscultuur*, 174; SA 379, nr. 212 (Brazil), "Recife Kerkeraad to Amsterdam Classis," November 23, 1649 (188–89); Franciscus, *Faith of Our Fathers*, 4–7.

81. "Wanen sich selve al goede Christenen te zijn . . . maer zijn alrede in haren oogen wijs en versadigd geworden, volbrengen als in den voorgaenden tijd haeres levens den wille der Heidenen, wandelende in ontuchticheden, begeerlijkheden, drinkerijen,

ende grouwelijke afgoderijen." Mooij, *Bouwstoffen protestantsch kerk*, 2:86 (August 10, 1648).

82. SA 379, nr. 184 (East Indies), "Banda Kerkeraad to Willem Janss., Gouverneur van Banda," January 2, 1624 (94).

83. Van Goor, *Kooplieden, predikanten*, 125; SA 379, nr. 201 (Ceylon), "Colombo Kerkeraad to Heeren Bewindthebberen Zeventiende," January 19, 1689 (184–89).

84. "Council of Formosa to the Governor-General and Councillors of India," Campbell, *Formosa*, 288–89 (October 30, 1652).

85. See similar comments by a minister on the Coromandel coast in the early 1700s: NA VOC, nr. 11160, "Batavia Kerkeraad to Walcheren Classis," November 20, 1719.

86. Mooij, *Bouwstoffen protestantsche kerk*, 1:221 (September 25, 1625).

87. Voetius, *De Muhammedismo*, 72, 145; see also Oomius, *Muhammedisdom of Turckdom*, 24, 34–49 (chap. 5; N.B.: the pagination starts anew in this chapter).

88. See, for example, Mooij, *Bouwstoffen protestantsche kerk*, 1:149 (February 3, 1621), 222 (October 9, 1625).

89. Rubiés, *Travel and Ethnology*, 309–10; Neill, *Christianity in India*, 419; Mitter, *Much Maligned Monsters*, 51.

90. Hoornbeeck, *De conversione*; Baldaeus, *Oost-Indische heydenen*; Carolinus, *Heidendom*; Voetius, *De gentilismo & vocatione gentium* in *Selectarum disputationum pars secunda*, 579–648; Hoornbeeck, *Summa controversarium*; Voetius, *De Muhammedismo*, 59–101 (Dutch text) and 140–55 (Latin text); Oomius, *Muhammedisdom of Turckdom*. See also Loots and Spaans, *Johannes Hoornbeeck*; and Schuringa, "Embracing *Leer* and *Leven*," 29–31. Please note that I have not included Georgius Hornius's *Kerkelycke historie van scheppinge des werelts to 't jaer des heeren 1666* (1685) because it is primarily a history of Judaism and Christianity with only ancillary discussion of paganism or Islam. In his coverage of world history, Hornius covers only up to 1623 and thus gives no consideration to Calvinists' missionary aspirations.

91. Van Troostenburg de Bruijn, *Oost-Indische predikanten*, 358–59.

92. Mooij, *Bouwstoffen protestantsche kerk*, 1:687 (December 7, 1643).

93. Mooij, *Bouwstoffen protestantsche kerk*, 2:52–53 (September 23, 1647).

94. Van Troostenburg de Bruijn, *Oost-Indische predikanten*, 358.

95. Van Troostenburg de Bruijn, *Oost-Indische predikanten*, 359.

96. Interestingly, Wissowatius was a Unitarian and his interest in Rogerius lay in demonstrating the universality of all religions. Noak, "Glossaries and Knowledge-Transfer," 257–59; Rubiés, *Travel and Ethnology*, 310.

97. Rogerius, *Open-deure*, unpaginated preface.

98. Rubiés, "Ethnography and Cultural Translation," 303–8.

99. Rogerius, *Open-deure*, unpaginated preface, 103.

100. Barlaeus, *Brasilia*, 252–53.

101. Rogerius, *Open-deure*, 55.

102. "Ja, selfs de Wetten van haren Vedam, ende de ghcheymenissen hares Gods-dienst niet en openbaren aen de Soudraes, aen den gemeynen Man, onder hare eygen Natie." Rogerius, *Open-deure*, unpaginated preface.

103. Rogerius, *Open-deure*, unpaginated preface.
104. Rogerius, *Open-deure*, unpaginated preface, 39, 55.
105. Rogerius, *Open-deure*, 114.
106. Rogerius, *Open-deure*, unpaginated preface.
107. Rogerius, *Open-deure*, unpaginated preface, 37–38, 86.
108. Rogerius, *Open-deure*, 42–49, 56–57, 86, 91.
109. Rubiés, *Travel and Ethnology*, 311.
110. Rogerius, *Open-deure*, 114.
111. Voetius has been miscast as the first Protestant to develop a theology of missions (see van Andel, *Zendingsleer*; and Jongeneel, "Voetius' zendingstheologie"). This claim is misleading because it imposes a post-1800 understanding of missions onto the seventeenth century, which takes Voetius out of context. Voetius was indeed a supporter of missions, but he did not write about them cohesively or comprehensively. In fact, the vision he put forth of missions was derived largely from what he understood that overseas ministers and *ziekentroosteren* were already doing. The global Calvinist vision that Voetius and others advocated for was the planting of Reformed churches overseas to convert pagans, Muslims, and Jews in the lands occupied by the VOC and WIC. This view is quite different from modern missions managed by missionary organizations and devoted to converting individuals outside the boundaries of a political state. For a critique of these interpretations, see van Rooden, *Religieuze regimes*, 134–35.
112. Oomius, *Muhammedisdom of Turckdom*, 103, 109, 160, 189, 374, 491, 497; SA 379, nr. 201 (Ceylon), "Consideratie wegens a Cinghalees seminarium," August 6, 1690 (258).
113. ". . . heeft het my gelust by een te vergaderen een algemeine en evenwel korte beschrijving van de Heidensche Godsdienst, so als die nu en enige Jaren herwaarts over de Wereld bevonden is en noch geoffent word . . . vond ik daer in seer vremde en wonderlijke dingen den Godsdienst der Heidenen rakende." Carolinus, *Heidendom*, unpaginated dedication.
114. Hoornbeeck, *De donversione*, 231–32.
115. Voetius, *De idolatria indirecta et participata* in *Selectarum disputationum pars tertia*, 270.
116. Baldaeus probably acquired the text at a Jesuit seminary in Jaffnapatnam (Ceylon) after the Dutch took control of the region. See Joel Charpentier, ed., *The Livro seita dos Indios Orientais (Brit. mus. ms. Sloane 1820) of Father Jacobo Fenicio, SJ* (Uppsala: Almqvist & Wiksell, 1933). See also Neill, *Christianity in India*, 382–83; Lach and van Kley, *Century of Advance*, 494.
117. Carolinus, *Heidendom*, unpaginated dedication, 2–6, 21–31, 41–54, 151–79.
118. Carolinus, *Heidendom*, unpaginated dedication, 41, 54, 75, 87, 100, 151, 193–99, 227.
119. Voetius, *De gentilismo & vocatione gentium* in *Selectarum disputationum pars secunda*, 580–82; Hoornbeeck, *De conversione*, 11–16.
120. Voetius, *De gentilismo & vocatione gentium* in *Selectarum disputationum pars secunda*, 579, 582, 585. Carolinus cited Voetius (*On Atheism*) to disagree with him and dispute the notion that pagans were atheistic. Carolinus, *Heidendom*, 1–6.

121. "Deze en diergelijke ungerijmtheden zijn de geheymen der Brahmines, die zy aan het volk niet willen openbaren." Baldaeus, *Oost-Indische heydenen*, 12; see also unpaginated preface, 1, 5, 40.

122. Baldaeus, *Oost-Indische heydenen*, 126–29.

123. Voetius, *De gentilismo & vocatione gentium* in *Selectarum disputationum pars secunda*, 585–86, 590, 633–34.

124. Hoornbeeck, *De conversione*, 11–14; Voetius, *De gentilismo & vocatione gentium* in *Selectarum disputationum pars secunda*, 580–82, 592–94. Carolinus did not push these conclusions, but he did identify pagan practices with idolatry. Carolinus, *Heidendom*, 75, 151.

125. Hoornbeeck, *De conversione*, 27–28.

126. Voetius, *De idolatria indirecta et participata* in *Selectarum disputationum pars tertia*, 235–36.

127. Voetius, *De gentilismo & vocatione gentium* in *Selectarum disputationum pars secunda*, 585.

128. Hoornbeeck, *De conversione*, 19–74; Voetius, *De gentilismo & vocatione gentium* in *Selectarum disputationum pars secunda*, 580, 581, 590.

129. Hoornbeeck, *De conversione*, 10–11, 158.

130. "Ergo & colendum Deum esse, & non per idolatriam aut multiplicem superstitionem, sed abjurata quoque omni (cui plurimi inter illos sunt addictissimi) magia hic docendum." Hoornbeeck, *Summa controversiarum*, 62.

131. Hoornbeeck, *De conversione*, 13.

132. Carolinus, *Heidendom*, 100, 140, 151, 160, 165, 238.

133. "Deze Indianen hier in wel grover ende plomper Afgoden-dienaars, als weer eer de oude Grieken ende Romeynen." Baldaeus, *Oost-Indische heydenen*, 63.

134. Montanus, *Wonderen*, 112–13. Two influential studies on the connections between comparative religion and antiquarianism and biblical exegesis are Rossi, *Dark Abyss of Time*; and Levitin, "From Sacred History."

135. "Maar zien wij hier ijets anders dan de oude dwalingen der geleerste Grieken en Latijnen in een andere pot gekookt, en artici verwarmde kool anders gesmoort, en met een vreemde sausse overgoten?" Baldaeus, *Oost-Indische heydenen*, 40.

136. Baldaeus, *Oost-Indische heydenen*, 5, 6, 40, 52.

137. Baldaeus, *Oost-Indische heydenen*, 52, 122, 134. Voetius, *De gentilismo & vocatione gentium* in *Selectarum disputationum pars secunda*, 600; Voetius, *De idolatria indirecta et participata* in *Selectarum disputationum pars tertia*, 234–35, 268. Carolinus also gestured in this direction, as many of the pagan customs he describes (confession to a priest, a mediatorial clergy, use of images and temples, pilgrimages, feast days, veneration of a female deity) correspond to Catholic ones. Carolinus, *Heidendom*, 78, 100, 140, 151, 160, 165. For other examples by Calvinist writers, see Polyander à Kerckhoven, Rivet, Walaeus, and Thysius, *Synopsis purioris theologiae*, 199–214.

138. See C. Parker, "Diseased Bodies," 1265–97.

139. Walaeus, *Loci communes s. theologiae* in *Opera omnia*, 1:256.

140. "... Sed Diabolo mancipati, & suis, quibus ille in ipsis dominator, concupiscentis." Hoornbeeck, *De conversione*, 11; see also 14–15, 27.
141. Hoornbeeck, *De conversione*, 164, 168, 169. See also Barlaei, *Brasilia*, 257.
142. "Alle dingen haer beginzel hebben uyt het membrum virile van haren Godt." Baldaeus, *Oost-Indische heydenen*, 137.
143. "Van hoerery en overspel beide seer gebruikelijk onder der heidenen sullen te gelijk spreken. De hoererey is meest gemein onder haar en minst voor sonde gerekent." Carolinus, *Heidendom*, 179–203 (quote on 193).
144. "So is ook tot haar ten langen lesten de prediking des Evangeliums overgekomen, doch niet met so veel vruchts, of het Heidendom blijft noch aan allen kanten in sijn wesen, en velen konnen door geen middelen van haar ongoddelijcken Godtsdienst afgetrokken worden." Carolinus, *Heidendom*, unpaginated dedication.
145. Mooij, *Bouwstoffen protestantsche kerk*, 1:221 (September 25, 1625).
146. Baldaeus, *True and Exact Description*, 581–84. In the first Dutch edition, *Naauwkeurige beschryvinge*, seven out of 198 pages were devoted to Islam (28–35).
147. Voetius, *De Muhammedismo*, 140; see also Jongeneel, "Voetius' zendingstheologie," 119–22.
148. Hoornbeeck, *Summa controversarium*, 70–191.
149. Voetius, *De Muhammedismo*, 140–43, 150–51.
150. Mulsow, "Socianianism, Islam," 559–60.
151. Voetius, *De Muhammedismo*, 148–51.
152. Oomius, *Muhammedisdom of Turckdom*, 24–26, 135–42 (chap. 5).
153. Voetius, *De Muhammedismo*, 152–53; Steenbrink, *Dutch Colonialism*, 49–54.
154. Oomius, *Muhammedisdom of Turckdom*, 230–566.
155. Voetius, *De Muhammedismo*, 145.
156. Hoornbeeck, *Summa controversarium*, 167.
157. Voetius, *De Muhammedismo*, 142–43, 151–52.
158. Oomius, *Muhammedisdom of Turckdom*, 308–29.
159. Voetius, *De Muhammedismo*, 141–42, 148; Hoornbeeck, *Summa Controversarium*, 135–44.
160. Voetius, *De Muhammedismo*, 144; see Hornius, *Kerkelycke historie*, 151.
161. Cornelis Uythage, a Reformed philosopher at the University of Leiden, argued in 1666 that Muhammad was a greater antichrist than the papacy. Uythagius, *Anti-Christus Mahometes*, unpaginated preface, 10, 53–58, 113–18, 240, 269–70. Uythage came under censure by the Leiden consistory for his claim, since it contradicted the Reformed teaching that the pope was the antichrist. Vermij, "Ruzie over de antichrist," 209–10. Many thanks to Joke Spaans for pointing this work out to me.
162. "In carnalibus voluptatibus, immo & plusquam brutalibus spurcitiis consistente: cujus consequenter ipsa bestiae participes sint futurae." Voetius, *De Muhammedismo*, 143.
163. Voetius, *De Muhammedismo*, 143.
164. "Ecclesiae institutae formam & regimen, per Papam, quem Muphti appellant, aliosque sacrorum praefectos Episcopos scilicet, Sacerdotes, Legisperitos seu Doctores, Judices." Voetius, *De Muhammedismo*, 144.

165. Oomius, *Muhammedisdom of Turckdom*, 425–27, 429–30, 444, 452–66, 521–22, 543, 547, 566, 36–41 (chap. 5).

166. Voetius, *De Muhammedismo*, 145; Hoornbeeck, *Summa controversarium*, 176; Oomius, *Muhammedisdom of Turckdom*, 42–49 (chap. 5).

167. Moreland and Geyl, *Remonstrantie of Francisco Pelsaert*, 64.

168. Oomius, *Muhammedisdom of Turckdom*, 149–50 (chap. 5).

169. Baldaeus, *True and Exact Description*, 582.

170. *ATB* I:2, "Deure der Waarhijd," 156.

171. Steenbrink, *Dutch Colonialism*, 38.

172. Valentijn, *Oost-Indien*, 4:1.

173. Valentijn, *Oost-Indien*, 3:2–3.

174. Valentijn, *Oost-Indien*, 3:233.

175. Niemeijer, "Orang Nasrani," 140–45.

176. Steenbrink, *Dutch Colonialism*, 41.

177. Valentijn, *Oost-Indien*, 3:91, 4:2.

178. Valentijn, *Oost-Indien*, 3:232.

179. See, for example, the extensive pastoral and visitation reports in *ATB* I:2, II:2, II:1 passim.

180. Valentijn, *Oost-Indien*, 4:3.

181. Valentijn, *Oost-Indien*, 3:25.

182. Valentijn, *Oost-Indien*, 3:23–24; Steenbrink, *Dutch Colonialism*, 39–40.

183. Valentijn doubted this account, noting that Portuguese sources attributed the arrival of Islam into Makassar at the hands of the king of Ternate in 1580. Valentijn, *Oost-Indien*, 3:233. This episode is recounted in Steenbrink, *Dutch Colonialism*, 38–39.

184. Hamilton, "Adriaan Reland and Islam," 243–44.

185. Relandus, *De religione Mohammedica libri duo*, 124–25.

186. Relandus, *De religione Mohammedica libri duo*, unpaginated preface.

187. Relandus, *De religione Mohammedica libri duo*, unpaginated preface.

188. Relandus, *De religione Mohammedica libri duo*, unpaginated preface.

189. Relandus, *De religione Mohammedica libri duo*, 142–54, 166–77.

190. Relandus, *De religione Mohammedica libri duo*, unpaginated preface.

191. Relandus, *De religione Mohammedica libri duo*, unpaginated preface.

192. Relandus, *De religione Mohammedica libri duo*, unpaginated preface.

193. See Irwin, *For Lust of Knowing*; and Malcolm, *Useful Enemies*.

194. Van Amersfoort and van Asselt, *Liever Turks dan Paaps?*, 115, 116, 122.

195. See Hunt, Jacob, and Mijnhardt, *Book That Changed Europe*.

6. GLOBAL CALVINISM AND THE PAGAN PRINCIPLE

1. "Als gevolg van deze plunderingen heb ik vele heidense afgodsbeelden gekregen, die uit de temple meegenomen waren, en nog door mij als herinneringe bewaard worden." Van der Pol, *Mallabaarse brieven*, 107. Although the time between the collection of the images and the writing of the letter is unclear, it seems certain that he

had no intention of parting with the images; perhaps he kept them for a considerable time.

2. "Voor eerst geen kans om het gelooff uit de gemoederen te verjagen om dat de Christenen van de gereformeerde kerk geduiring om gingen met die van de Roomse in welcke de beelden dienst aanlachelijck voor het oog door haar groote pragt en overeenkomende met de heidense afgoden." NA VOC, nr. 11160, "Batavia Kerkeraad to Walcheren Classis," November 20, 1719.

3. Schmidt, *Inventing Exoticism*, 6, 173, 195, 251–56, 272; Hunt, Jacob, and Mijnhardt, *Book That Changed Europe*, 38–39; Vink, *Encounters on the Opposite Coast*, 142.

4. T. Weststeijn, "Een wereldse kunst," 17–21, 29, 31–32.

5. Schmidt, *Inventing Exoticism*, 6; Rubiés, *Travel and Ethnology*, 308–20. See also Vink, *Encounters on the Opposite Coast*, 142; and Hunt, Jacob, and Mijnhardt, *Book That Changed Europe*, 38–39.

6. "Le grand livre du monde"; ". . . et depuis, en voyageant, ayant reconnu que tous ceux qui ont des sentiments, fort contraires aux nôtres ne sont pas pour cela barbares ni sauvages, mais que plusieurs usent autant ou plus que nous de raison." Descartes, *Méthode*, 8, 14.

7. See T. Weststeijn, "Spinoza Sinicus."

8. Schmidt, *Inventing Exoticism*, 1–23 (quote on 6).

9. The synod ratified the resolution, though it never appeared in the official version of the acta. Van Andel, *Zendingsleer*, 16.

10. For the argument that Voetius crafted a missionary theology, see Jongeneel, "Voetius' zendingstheologie."

11. Voetius, *Politicae ecclesiasticae*, 326, 341, 342.

12. Voetius, *De plantatoribus ecclesiarum* in *Selectarum disputationum pars secunda*, 552–62.

13. "Quod Ecclesiae sole hoc non possint agere: absque dependentia à mercatoribus, eorumque praefectis: quorum corda, bursas, naves, castella, praesidia non habent in manu suâ. . . . Quod Ministri nostrates inter Gentiles istic laborantes, saepe impediantur a Politicis, Militaribus, Mercurialibus Praefectis: inter quos intercurrunt nonnunquam, ergasterio quam munere illo digniores. Quod subinde mercuriales contractus cum infidelibus istic gentium ineantur, qui conversioni non parum obsunt." Voetius, *De plantatoribus ecclesiarum* in *Selectarum disputationum pars secunda*, 553–65 (quote on 562). See also van Andel, *Zendingsleer*, 27.

14. Voetius, *Politicae ecclesiasticae*, 324–26.

15. Voetius, *Politicae ecclesiasticae*, 322–23, 324–25; Jongeneel, "Voetius' zendingstheologie," 121–22, 124.

16. Voetius, *De plantatoribus ecclesiarum* in *Selectarum disputationum pars secunda*, 552–55.

17. Van Andel, *Zendingsleer*, 172; Goudriaan, *Reformed Orthodoxy*, 31.

18. Voetius, *Politicae ecclesiasticae*, 334–35.

19. Van Andel, *Zendingsleer*, 28.

20. Oomius, *Muhammedisdom of Turckdom*, 130–31, 139–42, 145–46 (chap. 5; N.B.: pagination begins anew in chapter 5).

21. Hamilton, "Study of Islam," 174–76.
22. T. Weststeijn, "Spinoza Sinicus," 537–41.
23. Baldaeus, *Oost-Indische heydenen*; Hoornbeeck, *De Conversione*.
24. Van Asselt, "Motieven en perspectiven," 230–31.
25. Coccejus, *Summa theologicae*, 751–58. Please note that I have used his second edition (1665).
26. Van Asselt, "Motieven en perspectiven," 228; van Asselt, "Amicitia Dei," 40.
27. Van Asselt, *Coccejus*, 74, 76.
28. Van Asselt, "Structural Elements," 91–92.
29. "Praedicant Christum & non excipere semen, vt terram bonam, ut fructificent: clarum est, quando gentes accedunt, & cohabitant fidelibus, & blanda loquuntur, & odium abnegant, tum recte dici gentes intrare in civitatem sanctam." Coccejus, *Summa theologicae*, 848.
30. Van Asselt, *Coccejus*, 76.
31. Van Asselt, "Amicitia Dei," 40.
32. Mather, *De successu*. Europeans often referred to all of Asia as India. Given the content of the work, it seems clear that was what Mather did here.
33. Mather, *De successu*, 7, 12–15.
34. "De reformatie in Europa ende de ontdeckinge van de Indien, zijn den vast ontrent eenen tijdt gheschiedt daermede de here heft willen toonen dat nu den tijdt ghekomen was dat het Evangelium des Coninckrijcx door de gheheele wereldt soude gepredickt worden." Udemans, *Geestelyck roer*, fol. 60v. Note that this work is inconsistently paginated.
35. NA VOC, nr. 11160, "Walcheren Classis to Batavia Kerkeraad," June 25, 1693.
36. SA 379, nr. 168 (Amsterdam), "Amsterdam Classis to Batavia Kerkeraad," October 3, 1670 (53–57).
37. SA 379, nr. 168 (Amsterdam), "Amsterdam Classis to Henricus Selijns, predicant Nieuw York," April 23, 1699 (245–46).
38. KITLV, nr. H216, "Batavia Kerkeraad to Amsterdam Classis," November 20, 1719.
39. SA 379, nr. 201 (Ceylon), "Colombo Kerkeraad to Amsterdam Classis," December 29, 1684 (149).
40. "Dat ongeluckige Formosa mach met tranen inde ogen, gelijck eertijts Naomi seggen noemt mij niet meer Naomi maer noemt mij Mara, soo oock noemt mij niet Formosa, want sij heeft meer reden als eertijts Godts klagende kercke om te suchten en te seggen, noemt mij niet Formosa, want al mijn schoonheit, al mijn cieraedt is van uijt wechgegaen, en wat smerte." SA 379, nr. 168 (Amsterdam), "Amsterdam Classis to Batavia Kerkeraad," October 3, 1670 (56).
41. SA 379, nr. 201 (Ceylon), "Consideratie wegens a Cinghalees seminarium," August 6, 1690 (265).
42. SA 379, nr. 167 (Amsterdam), "Batavia Kerkeraad to Amsterdam Classis," October 30, 1784 (121–22).
43. SA 379, nr. 168 (Amsterdam), "Amsterdam Classis to Batavia Kerkeraad," May 13, 1682 (154).

44. ". . . vervallen muuren van Nederlands Jerusalem mogen opgebouwd worden." SA 379, nr. 167 (Amsterdam), "Batavia Kerkeraad to Amsterdam Classis," October 30, 1786 (227).

45. Voetius, *De plantatoribus ecclesiarum* in *Selectarum disputationum pars secunda*, 541–45.

46. SA 379, nr. 168 (Amsterdam), "Amsterdam Classis to Colombo Kerkeraad," September 5, 1675 (104); see also SA 379, nr. 168 (Amsterdam), "Amsterdam Classis to Batavia Kerkeraad," October 13, 1675 (106).

47. NA VOC, nr. 11160, "Colombo Kerkeraad to Walcheren Classis," November 7, 1720.

48. Hoornbeeck, *De conversione*, 205, 260–65.

49. NA VOC, nr. 4778, "Majores der geotroijeerde Generale Oostindische Compagnie," November 1, 1610.

50. C. Parker, *Faith on the Margins*, 17.

51. For an excellent treatment of the Libertines, see Wielema, *March of the Libertines*.

52. Schneckenburger, *Vorlesungen über die Lehrbegriffe*, 30, quoted in Goudriaan, *Reformed Orthodoxy*, 37.

53. Goudriaan, *Reformed Orthodoxy*, 37–38.

54. Israel, *Dutch Republic*, 662, 666.

55. Israel, *Dutch Republic*, 666.

56. Van Asselt, *Federal Theology*, 78–83.

57. Voetius, *De atheismo* in *Selectarum disputationum pars prima*, 117–18.

58. Voetius, *De atheismo* in *Selectarum disputationum pars prima*, 137–39.

59. "Quando attributa divina & qualis sit verus Deus: aut verus Deus, seu quis sit ille verus Deus ex exemplo Gentilium, Mahumedisterum, Judaeorum negatur; aut religio seu ratio colendi: Deum indirecte negatur, sive in totum, sive quod ad principalem, sive quod ad magnam partem." Voetius, *De atheismo* in *Selectarum disputationum pars prima*, 122.

60. Voetius, *De atheismo* in *Selectarum disputationum pars prima*, 133.

61. "quales Cogito ergo sum, et, cujus idea est in me, illud ipsum & c. inducto prius scepitismo, omnique notitia naturali insita & acquisita erasa." Voetius, *De atheismo* in *Selectarum disputationum pars prima*, 214.

62. "Multitudienem ex una familiâ progentam." Voetius, *De plantatoribus ecclesiarum* in *Selectarum disputationum pars secunda*, 582.

63. Voetius, *De plantatoribus ecclesiarum* in *Selectarum disputationum pars secunda*, 580.

64. Voetius, *De plantatoribus ecclesiarum* in *Selectarum disputationum pars secunda*, 586, 590, 592.

65. Voetius, *De plantatoribus ecclesiarum* in *Selectarum disputationum pars secunda*, 600.

66. See Goudriaan, *Reformed Orthodoxy*, 71, 90, 97, 108, and 135 for similar views among later Reformed intellectuals.

67. ". . . veel slimmer als 't Heydendom is." Hornius, *Kerkelycke historie*, 229.

68. Oomius, *Muhammedisdom of Turckdom*, 307.

69. Oomius, *Muhammedisdom of Turckdom*, 300–324, esp. 315–18.

70. See, for example, Rainoldus, *De Romanae Ecclesiae idololatria*, 411; Viret, *De la vraye et fausse religion*, 219–21. See also Sheehan, "Introduction," 567–68; Johnson, "Idolatrous Cultures," 607–13.

71. SA 379, nr. 201 (Ceylon), "Colombo Kerkeraad to Amsterdam Classis," February 5, 1691 (269).

72. Sheehan, "Introduction," 45–48.

73. Visser, "Mennonites and Doopsgezinden," 332–33.

74. NA VOC, nr. 11160, "Walcheren Classis to Batavia Kerkeraad," May 4, 1694. Overseas churches followed debates with rationalists closely and stood in solidarity with their Calvinist brethren in the Netherlands. In 1709, for example, the Colombo consistory wholeheartedly endorsed the condemnation of Frederik van Leenhof, a minister in Zwolle accused of Spinozism. See SA 379, nr. 203 (Ceylon), "Colombo Kerkeraad to Batavia Kerkeraad," December 23, 1709 (81–84); SA 379, nr. 203 (Ceylon), "Colombo Kerkeraad to Amsterdam Classis," December 10, 1710 (85–86).

75. The Walcheren classis noted rumors of Socinianism among overseas communities. ZA, nr. 65, "Vergaderinge gehouden op Maert 24, 1642," March 24, 1642 (75–77). See also Mooij, *Bouwstoffen protestantsche kerk*, 3:130 (August 10, 1671).

76. SA 379, nr. 169 (Amsterdam), "Amsterdam Classis to Batavia Kerkeraad," December 1708, 70–72 (quote on 71); SA 379, nr. 169 (Amsterdam, "Amsterdam Classis to Colombo Kerkeraad," [December 1708] (65–68). See also 1401 OSA, nr. 1328, "Batavia Kerkeraad to South Holland Synod," November 6, 1724.

77. NA VOC, nr. 11160, "Batavia Kerkeraad to Walcheren Classis," November 20, 1719.

78. NA VOC, nr. 11160, "Walcheren Classis to Batavia Kerkeraad," [November 1720]; December 2, 1712; October 1, 1722. Antonius Walaeus made this same point in *Loci communes s. theologiae* in *Opera omnia*, 1:257.

79. Baldaeus, *Oost-Indische heydenen*, 137.

80. "So konnen wy in de Indianen, als in eenen Spieghel aenmercken, wat dat de menschen zijn van natueren, sonder de kennisse Christi; ende het lich der weder-geboorte, te weten so dom ende onverstandigh, als een veulen van eenen Woudt-ezel." Udemans, *Geestelyck roer*, 122.

81. Udemans, *Geestelyck roer*, 112–39.

82. See, for example, NA VOC, nr. 11160, "Amsterdam Classis to Batavia Kerkeraad," [December 1718].

83. "Il est bon de savoir quelque chose des moeurs de divers peoples, afin de juger des nôtres plus sainement, et que nous ne pensions pas que tout ce qui est contre nos modes sont ridicule et contre raison, ainsi qu'ont coutume de faire ceux qui n'ont rien vu." Descartes, *Méthode*, 5.

84. Hunt, Jacob, and Mijnhardt, *Book That Changed Europe*, 1–2.

85. Pagden, *Fall of Natural Man*, 199–201.

86. Malcolm, *Useful Enemies*, 37; also 38, 412. I am grateful to Joke Spaans for pointing out this book and approach to me.

87. Mauldon, "Introduction," xiv–xx.

88. Mungello, *Great Encounter*, 138.

89. See I. Vossius, *Castigationes ad scriptum Horni*; and Hornius, *Dissertatio de vera aetate mundi*. For a discussion of the debate and its relevance to the reception of Chinese philosophy in the Netherlands, see T. Weststeijn, "Spinoza Sinicus," 538–41.

90. Outram, *Enlightenment*, 67–68, 77.

91. Popkin, *History of Scepticism*, 294–97; Labrousse, *Hétérodoxie et rigorisme*, 50, 256, 313, 596.

92. Israel, "Pierre Bayle's Correspondence," 488.

93. Israel, *Dutch Republic*, 931; Mijnhardt, "Dutch Enlightenment," 199.

94. Van Bunge, "Presence of Bayle," 197–99, 202–11; Verbeek, "Dutch Cartesians," 29–31.

95. Charnley, *Bayle*, 15.

96. Charnley, *Bayle*, 34, 47, 49, 61, 68, 69, 71, 73, 76, 80, 82, 91.

97. Bayle, *Pensées diverses*, 50.

98. Charnley, *Bayle*, 116–17, 119.

99. Charnley, *Bayle*, 47–49.

100. Bayle, *Dictionary*, 1:316.

101. Bayle, *Dictionary*, 1:309.

102. Charnley, *Bayle*, 35–37.

103. Bayle, *Dictionary*, 1:315–17.

104. He relied on VOC embassy reports to highlight the importance the Qing emperors assigned to astrological observations. Bayle, *Pensées diverses*, 50.

105. "Mais qu'avons nous à faire de nous écarter dans le Pays des Infidelles abrutis d'une infinite d' erreurs chymeriques, & de remonter au tems du vieux Paganisme, où il n'est pas étrange que l'Astrologie ait regné, puis que la superstition y étoit si prodigieuse. . . . Il ne faut pas aller si loin pour trouver ce que nous cherchons car n'a-t-on pas veu nôtre Occident parmi les lumieres du Christianisme tout infatué d' Horoscopes pendant plusieurs siecles?" Bayle, *Pensées diverses*, 52–53.

106. Bayle, *Dictionary*, 2:176.

107. Bayle, *Dictionary*, 3:275–76.

108. Charnley, *Bayle*, 60.

109. Charnley, *Bayle*, 61.

110. Bayle, *Dictionary*, 3:87, 90 (quote).

111. Bayle, *Dictionary*, 1:168.

112. Bayle, *Pensées diverses*, 188–89.

113. "Maintenant il ne faut plus s' étonner que les Chrêtiens soient dans le meme provision puis qu' ils sont la posterité des Payens, & qu' à l'Idolatire prés, ils donnent dans les mêmes soiblesses que les Payens." Bayle, *Pensées diverses*, 227.

114. Bayle, *Pensées diverses*, 334.

115. Relandus, *De religione Mohammedica libri duo*, unpaginated preface.

116. Relandus, *De religione Mohammedica libri duo*, unpaginated preface.

117. Relandus, *De religione Mohammedica libri duo*, unpaginated preface. See also a Dutch version in van Amersfoort and van Asselt, *Liever Turks dan Paaps?*, 113.

118. Bevilacqua, *Republic of Arabic Letters*, 84. See also de Bruijn, "Iranian Studies," 170–71; Vrolijk, "Arabic Studies," 28.

119. Hunt, Jacob, and Mijnhardt, *Book That Changed Europe*, 249, 254, 261–64.

120. Hunt, Jacob, and Mijnhardt, *Book That Changed Europe*, 262.

121. "Certe si Romana ecclesia nulla exercetur idolatria, a qua jure idolatria dici mereantur hodierni pontificii, evidentem concluditur, nullam in toto Christianismo per orbem terrarum disperso, nec in ullo Europae angulo idolatriam et praxim eius reperiri extare: imo quod majus est, illam nullibi existere aut exerceri quam apud ethnicos in Asia, Africa, and America: cum nec Turcae, nec Judaei, nec ulla sectarum, quae se a Romanae ecclesiae communione separunt, externae idolatriae, et cultus imaginum accusari possint." Heidanus, *De origine erroris*, 361.

122. "Ferner wenn wir die Deistenheyden Juden und Mahometaner berden wollen die Christiche Religion vor allen anderen anzunehmen so frage ich ob wir dieses nicht mit Beweissen-Grunden vom Urheber Christlicher Religion und dessen auch der Religion selbst Eienschafften und Wurchtungen durch vernufftigen Schluss mussen zu wegen bringen?" Wiszowaty, *Vernünfftige religion*, 20; see also unpaginated preface, 38.

123. "Geen grooter saad van Atheisterye is 'er gesayd, terwyl het licht des Evangliums, ende de kennisse des waren Gods en Godsdienst, noch niet, als een heldre sonne, met sijne stralen, waren doorgebroken, als de contineel gepretendeerde en vermeerde mirakelen en orakelen der heydensche Goden en Godinnen." Van Dale, *Verhandeling*, 392; see also 10, 403.

124. Bekker, *World Bewitch'd*, 30.

125. Israel, *Dutch Republic*, 928.

126. Wielema, *March of the Libertines*, 79.

127. Van der Wall, "Religious Context," 46.

128. Israel, *Dutch Republic*, 925–26.

129. Heidanus, *De origine erroris*, 136.

130. Heidanus, *De origine erroris*, 155.

131. "Ik den genen minst voldoen sal, die Des Cartes gronden gansch verwerpen, of te breed belimmeren." Bekker, *De betoverde weereld*, unpaginated preface.

132. Bekker, *De betoverde weereld*, 28.

133. Bekker, *De betoverde weereld*, 31, 35.

134. Bekker, *De betoverde weereld*, 37.

135. Bekker, *De betoverde weereld*, 22–23.

136. See (unpaginated) table of contents in Bekker, *World Bewitch'd*.

137. Bekker, *De betoverde weereld*, 23, 27, 30, 42, 43, 47.

138. "In't eerste ga ik dus te werk. Eerst hebbende den Leser ingeleid tot het geheele werk waer toe het eerste hoofstuk dient; so soek ik door de gansche weereld heen waar dit gevoelen sijnen oorsprong uitgenomen heeft: en om dat wel te weten sta ik rijden nochte plaatsen over. . . . Dit alles soek ik naeerst in de oudeen daar na in niewe boeken van allerleye volkeren godsdienst en gevoelen: die ik echter so als nu de weereld is in heidenen Joden Mahometanen en Kristenen onderscheiden wil." Bekker, *De betoverde weereld*, unpaginated preface.

139. "Want de geheele weereld by menschen bewoond word uit hedendaagsche ondervindinge niet better dan in drie grote Eilanden verdeeld. . . . van Europa pas half so

groot als een van d'andere twee zijn d'inwoonders aan de noorkant meest noch al in't heidendom. In Asien magh vast het tiende deel van Kristenen bewoond zijn; al 't andere sal misschien wel voor een derdendeel onder de wett van Mahomet staan; so dat verre de grootste helft noch't eenemael heidensch is. Africa in 't noorden van Mahmetanenin 't oosten beneffens die ook halve kristenen bewoond moet noch wel op twee derdeelen heidensch zijn. De nieuwe weereld . . . light noch geheel in 't heidendom; ende weet weinig van kristenen anders dan die daar uit Europa komen." Bekker, *De betoverde weereld,* 21.

140. Bekker, *De betoverde weereld,* 59, 71–72.

141. Bekker, *De betoverde weereld,* unpaginated preface.

142. "By de hedendaagsche Heidenen zijn diergelijke leeringen en seden ook te sien"; "So en kan ik niet anders oordeelen of het is aan't elf de vooroordeel dat ik hier voor ontrent den so genaamden Duiveldienst heb aangemerrckt toe te schrijven datmen enige menschen toveraars en toveressen." Bekker, *De betoverde weereld,* 21, 34.

143. Bekker, *De betoverde weereld,* 22–24.

144. Bekker, *De betoverde weereld,* 30–34.

145. "Sulx doende bevinden wy dat de volkeren in gevoelens en dienstplegingen ontrent hunne Goden en Geesten aan d'eene syde seer verscheiden; en aan d'andere nochtans wonderlijk eendraghtig zijn." Bekker, *De betoverde weereld,* 49.

146. Bekker, *De betoverde weereld,* 50.

147. Bekker, *De betoverde weereld,* 52–53.

148. Bekker, *De betoverde weereld,* 58, 62.

149. Bekker, *De betoverde weereld,* 63–65.

150. Bekker, *De betoverde weereld,* 69–77.

151. Israel, *Dutch Republic,* 929–30.

152. ". . . Godts duydelijke en menigvulde verklaringen van de goede en quaade Engelen en haar verschijningen en werkingen na buyten, ontrent goede en quaade menschen, niet alleen godloozelijk en godlasterlijk derven tegen spreeken, maar ook de klaare en van all Christenen aangenoomene zin der zelver Schrifts getuigenissen bespotten, en te spot-stellen voor al de wereldt, als of het maar een Heydensch gevoelen was, en als of zy alle betovert waren, die het zo opnamen als eenvoudige en naakte waarheidt." Koelman, *Cartesiaansche philosophie,* unpaginated preface.

153. Koelman, *Cartesiaansche philosophie,* 7, 121, 124–27.

154. [Van der Waeyen], *Balthazar Bekkers,* 56–57. The anonymous author claims to have been a student of van der Waeyen's. Internal references and scholarly consensus affirm van der Waeyen's authorship.

155. Van Goor, *Kooplieden, predikanten,* 114–21.

156. 1401 OSA, nr. 1335, "Acta South Holland Synod," [1685]; see also 1401 OSA, nr. 1335, "Acta South Holland Synod," May 9, 1684.

157. Mooij, *Bouwstoffen protestantsche kerk,* 3:656 (October 15, 1685).

158. 1401 OSA, nr. 1335, "Johannes Ruiterus to South Holland Synod," October 29, 1684.

159. Mooij, *Bouwstoffen protestantsche kerk,* 3:658–61 (October 30, 1685).

160. 1401 OSA, nr. 1335, "Johannes Ruiterus to Heeren Bewinthebberen Oost Indische Compagnie," July 1684.
161. Van Troostenburg de Bruijn, *Oost-Indische predikanten*, 374.
162. 1401 OSA, nr. 1335, "Acta South Holland Synod," [1685].
163. Županov and Fabre, "Rites Controversies," 13–14.

CONCLUSION

1. Jongeneel, *Nederlandse zendingsgeschiedenis*, 151; Vandenbosch, *Dutch East Indies*, 53–56.
2. Jongeneel, *Nederlandse zendingsgeschiedenis*, 154–59; Boneschansker, *Nederlandsch Zendeling Genootschap*, 15–16, 22–23.
3. Franciscus, *Faith of Our Fathers*, 4; Taylor, *Social World of Batavia*, 22; Joosse, "*Scoone dingen sijn swaere dingen*," 58–59; Kruijf, *Geschiedenis*, 9.
4. Van Rooden, *Religieuze regimes*, 132–35.
5. Axtell, *Invasion Within*, 131–78, 271–74.
6. "Caspar Wiltens to Amsterdam Classis," *OHZ* V:51 (May 31, 1615).

BIBLIOGRAPHY

PRIMARY SOURCES

ARCHIVAL SOURCES

Arsip Nasional Republik Indonesia (Jakarta) and Archief van de Kerkeraad van de Nederduits Gereformeerde Gemeente te Batavia (cited as ANRI)

nrs. 5–18, Notulen Akteboeken, 1700–1796
nr. 156, Makassar aankomende brieven, 1674–1737
nr. 158, Makassar aankomende brieven, 1739–1761, 1772–1784, 1799
nrs. 162–164, Ingekomen stukken van diverse comptoiren, 1621–1851

Koninklijk Instituut voor Taal-, Land- en Volkenkunde (Leiden)
(Royal Netherlands Institute of Southeast Asian and Caribbean Studies)
(cited as KITLV)

H80, Kercken ordeninge gestelt voor de gemeente van Batavia/Anthonio van Diemen (1593–1645)
H216, Verzameling kerkelijke stukken, meest brieven, van de Bataviaasche kerkeraad aan de Classis van Amsterdam, 1670–1733

Nationaal Archief (The Hague) (cited as NA)

1.04.02 Archief van de Verenigde Oostindische Compagnie (cited as VOC), 1602–1795

nr. 11160, Minuut-missiven van de Classis Walcheren aan de kerkeraden in Indie, en kopie-missiven vande kerekraden aan de classis, 1690–1722
nr. 11162, Stukken bestemd voor de classis Walcheren betreffende het geschil tussen ds. Le Boucq en leden van de kerkeraad in Batavia over het toedienen van de doop

met of zonder belijdenis aan pas bekeerde inheemsen en de bijwoning van het avondmaal van deze bekeerden, 1730–1736

nr. 4712, Kopie en minuut missive van gecommitteerde bewindhebbers aan gouverneur-general en raden en de hoofden in Ceylon, Malabar, en Kaap de Goede Hoop, over de oprichting van een seminarie in de Republiek ten dienst van de Hervormde Kerk in Indie, 1792

nr. 4778, Kopie-translaten van tractaten gesloten door de VOC en haar voorgangers met Aziatische vorsten, 1608–1622

1.11.01.01 Aanwinsten Eerste Afdeling

nr. 1373, Resoluties van de Gereformeerde kerk te Malakka, 1655–1695

Het Utrechts Archief (cited as UA)

1401 Oud Synodaal Archief van de Nederlandse Hervormde Kerk

nrs. 1325–1362

52-1 Provinciale Kerkvergadering van Utrecht.

nr. 212, Acta van de classicale vergaderinge van Pernambuco, Brazilië, 1636–1644

Stadsarchief Amsterdam (cited as SA)
379, Classis Amsterdam van de Nederlandse Hervormde Kerk

nr. 158, Amsterdam
nr. 163, Amsterdam
nr. 164, Amsterdam
nr. 165, Amsterdam
nr. 166, Amsterdam
nr. 167, Amsterdam
nr. 168, Amsterdam
nr. 169, Amsterdam
nr. 170, Amsterdam
nr. 184, East Indies
nr. 185, East Indies
nr. 186, East Indies
nr. 187, East Indies
nr. 188, East Indies
nr. 189, East Indies
nr. 191, Formosa
nr. 192, Catechismus door ds. Robertus Junius
nr. 201, Ceylon

nr. 202, Ceylon

nr. 203, Ceylon

nr. 204, Ceylon

nr. 206, Cape of Good Hope

nr. 207, Cape of Good Hope

nr. 212, Brazil

Zeeuws Archief (Middelburg) (cited as ZA)
Archief van de Classis Middelburg, 28.1 Nederlandse Hervormde Kerk,
Classis Walcheren/Classis Middelburg. 1.2.7 Zorg voor de Oostindische
en Westinidische kerken.

nrs. 65–67, Acta van de vergaderingen der gedeputeerden tot de Oostindische kerken, 1620–1804

nrs. 68–69, Correspondentie tussen de gedeputeerden tot de Oostindische kerkzaken en besturen en personen in Nederland, Indië, Colombo, en andere koloniën

nrs. 70, Register van ingekomen en uitgegane stukken van de gedeputeerden tot de Oostindische kerkzaken, 1723–1803

nr. 73, Ingekomen en minute van uitgegane stukken van de gedeputeerden tot de Westindische kerken, 1623–1641

PUBLISHED PRIMARY SOURCES

Aglionby, William. *The present state of the United-Provinces of the Low Countries.* London: John Starkey, 1671.

Amersfoort, J. van, and W. J. van Asselt, eds. *Liever Turks dan Paaps? De visies van Johannes Coccejus, Gisbertus Voetius en Adrianus Relandus op de Islam.* Zoetermeer: Boekencentrum, 1997.

Arasaratnam, S., ed. *Francois Valentijn's description of Ceylon (Oud en nieuw Oost-Indien, 1726).* London: Hakluyt Society, 1978.

Bakhuizen van den Brink, J. N., ed. *De Nederlandse belijdenisgeschriften, vergelijkende teksten samengesteld.* Amsterdam: Uitgeversmaatschappij Holland, 1940.

Baldaeus, Philip. *A true and exact description of the east India coasts of Malabar and Coromandel with their adjacent kingdoms and provinces and of the empire of Ceylon and of the idolatry of the pagans in the East Indies.* London: The Black Swan, 1703.

Baldaeus, Philippus. *Naauwkeurige beschryvinge van Malabar en Choromandel.* Amsterdam: Janssonius van Waesberge, 1672.

———. *Nauwkeurige en waarachtige ontdekking en wederlegginge van de afgoderij der Oost-Indische heydenen der zelver aangrenzende ryken, en het machtige eyland Ceylon nevens en omstandige en grondich doorzochte ontdekking en wederlegginge van de afgoderye der Oost-Indische heydenen.* Amsterdam: Johannem Janssonium, 1672.

Barlaeus, Caspar. *Nederlandsch Brazilië onder het bewind van Johan Mauritx Grave van Nassau, 1637–1644: historisch, geographisch, ethnographisch.* Edited by S. P. L. Honoré Naber. 1647. Reprint, The Hague: Martinus Nijhoff, 1923.

Bayle, Pierre. *An historical and critical dictionary, selected and abridged.* 4 vols. London: Hunt and Clark, 1826.

———. *Pensées diverses écrites à un docteur de Sorbonne, à l'occasion de la comète qui parus au mois de Décembre 1680.* Rotterdam: Reinier Leers, 1683.

Bekker, Balthasar. *De betoverde weereld: zynde een grondig ondersoek van't gemeen gevoelen aangaande de geesten, derselver aart en vermogen, bewind en bedryf: also ook 't gene de menschen door derslever kraght en gemeenschap doen.* Amsterdam: Daniel van den Dalen, 1691.

———. *The world bewitch'd.* N.p.: R. Baldwin, 1695.

Blussé, J. L., M. E. van Opstall, Ts'ao Yung-ho, et al., eds. *De dagregisters van het kasteel Zeelandia, Taiwan 1629–1662.* Vol. 1, *1629–1641.* The Hague: Martinus Nijhoff, 1986.

Boetzelaer van Asperen en Dubbeldam, C. W. Th. Baron van. "Correspondentie van Ds. Adriaan Jacobszoon Hulsebos." *Nederlands Archief voor Kerkgeschiedenis* 33 (1941–1942): 93–161.

Campbell, William, ed. *Formosa under the Dutch: described from contemporary records.* London: Kegan Paul, 1903.

Carolinus, Godefridus. *Het hedendaagsche heidendom: of beschrijving vanden godtsdienst der heidenen.* Amsterdam: Johannes Ravesteyn, 1661.

Caron, François. *Beschrijvinghe van het machtigh coninchrijck Japan.* Amsterdam: I. Hargers, 1648.

Charpentier, Joel, ed. *The Livro seita dos Indios Orientais (Brit. mus. ms. Sloane 1820) of Father Jacobo Fenicio, SJ.* Uppsala: Almqvist & Wiksell, 1933.

Chijs, J. A. van der, ed. *Nederlandsch-Indisch plakaatboek, 1602–1811.* 17 vols. The Hague: Martinus Nijhoff, 1885–1900.

Child, Josiah. *A new discourse of trade.* London: J. Hodges, 1751.

Cocceius, Johannes. *Rede over de godsdienst der Turken gehouden omstreeks het jaar 1625 te Bremen en vertaald (uit het Grieks) door John Creighton* [*Oratio de religione Turcarum, scripta Bremae circa annum Christi MDCXXV Johanne Creyghtonon interrete*]. In *Liever Turks dan Paaps? De visies van Johannes Cocceejus, Gisbertus Voetius en Adrianus Relandus op de Islam,* edited by J. van Amersfoort and W. J. van Asselt, 37–57 (Dutch text), 128–39 (Latin text). Zoetermeer: Boekencentrum, 1997.

———. *Summa theologicae ex scripturis repetita.* Geneva: Ioann. Herm. Widerhold, 1665.

Corpus Diplomaticum Neerlando Indicum verzameling van politieke contracten en verdere verdragen door de Nederlanders in het Oosten gesloten, van privilegebrieven aan hen verleend, enz., vol. 1 (1596–1650). In *Bijdragen tot de Taal-, Land- en Volkenkunde van Nederlandsch-Indië,* edited by J. E. Heeres and F. W. Stapel. The Hague: M. Nijhoff, 1907.

Dale, Antonius van. *Verhandeling van de oude orakelen der heydenen.* Amsterdam: Andries van Damone, 1718.

Dam, Pieter van. *Beschrijvinge van de Oostindische Compagnie 1639–1701, vierde boek: Het ecclesiasticq.* Edited by C. W. Th. Baron van Boetzelaer van Asperen en Dubbeldam. The Hague: Martinus Nijhoff, 1954.

Danckaerts, Sebastiaen. *Historisch ende Grondich Verhael vanden standt des Christendoms int quartier van Amboina.* The Hague: Aert Meuris, 1621.

Descartes, René. *Discourse de la méthode.* 1923. Reprint, Cambridge: Cambridge University Press, 2013.

Goens, Rijklof van. *Javaensche reyse, gedaen van Batavia over Samarangh na de koninck-lijcke hoofd-plaets Mataram, door de heere N.N. in den jare 1656.* Dordrecht: V. Caimax, 1666.

Grothe, J. A., ed. *Archief voor de Geschiedenis der Oude Hollandsche Zending. II. Aanteekeningen uit verschillende Synodale en Classicale Acta.* Utrecht: C. van Bentum, 1885.

———. *Archief voor de Geschiedenis der Oude Hollandsche Zending. V. Molukken, 1603–1624.* Utrecht: C. van Bentum, 1890.

———. *Archief voor de Geschiedenis der Oude Hollandsche Zending. VI. Molukken, 1625–1638.* Utrecht: C. van Bentum, 1890–1891.

Grotius, Hugo. *Annotationes in Novum Testamentum.* Groningen: J. Zuidema, 1826–1834.

———. *Annotationes in Vetus & Novum Testamentum.* Edited by Samuel Moody. London: Jos. Smith, Will. Mears, Jos. Pote, and N. Moody, 1727.

———. *Annotationes in Vetus Testamentum.* Hall: Jo. Jac. Curt, 1775–1776.

———. *Baptizatorum puerorum institutio.* London: Johannes Dawson, 1647.

———. *Bewijs van den waren godsdienst.* N.p.: n.p., 1622.

———. *Christus patiens.* Munich: Joan. Hertsroy & Corn. Leysser, 1627.

———. *De imperio summarum potestatum Circa Sacra.* 2 vols. Edited by Harm-Jan van Dam. Leiden: Brill, 2001.

———. *De ivre belli ac pacis libri tres. In quibus jus naturæ & gentium: item iuris publici præcipua explicantur.* Paris: Nicolavm Bvon, 1625.

———. *De jure praedae commentarius. Commentary on the Law of Prize and Booty.* 2 vols. Edited by Gwladys L. Williams and Walter H. Zeydel. Oxford: Clarendon Press, 1950.

———. *De veritate religionis Christianae.* Leiden: Ioannis Maire, 1640.

Haafner, Jacob. *Onderzoek naar het nut der zendelingen en zendelings-genootschappen.* Haarlem: Joh. Enschede en Zoonen en J. van Walré, 1807.

Heidanus, Abraham. *De origine erroris libri octo.* Amsterdam: Johannem à Someren, 1678.

Heurnius, Justus. *De legatione evangelica ad Indos capessenda admonitio.* Leiden: Elsevier, 1618.

Hoornbeeck, Johannes. *De conversione indorum & gentilium libri duo.* Amsterdam: Johannem Janssonium à Waesberge, 1669.

———. *Summa controversarium religionis cum infidelibus, haereticis, schismaticis.* Utrecht: Johannis à Waesberge, 1653.

Hornius, Georgii. *Dissertatio de vera aetate mundi.* Leiden: Elsevier, 1659.

———. *Kerkelycke historie van scheppinge des werelts to 't jaer des heeren 1666.* Amsterdam: Baltes Boeckholft, 1685.

Instructions from the Governor-General and Council of India to the Governor of Ceylon,
1656–1665. Translated by Sophia Pieters. Colombo: H. C. Cottle, 1908.

Koelman, Jacobus. *Het vergift van de cartesiaansche philosophie grondig ontdekt en meest*
historischer wijze, uit de schriften van des Cartes zelfs, en van andere schrijvers, so voor
als tegen hem, getrouwelijk aangeweezen. Opgestelt, tot een grondt van de wederlegging
van Bekkers Betooverde Wereldt. Amsterdam: Johannes Boekholt, 1692.

Koschorke, Klaus, and S. A. W. Mottau, eds. *The Dutch Reformed Church in colonial Cey-*
lon (18th century): minutes of the consistory of the Dutch Reformed Church in Colombo
held at the Wolvendaal Church, Colombo (1735–1797). Wiesbaden: Harrassowitz, 2011.

Laet, Johannes de. *Beschrijvinghe des West-Indien.* 2nd ed. Leiden: Elsevier, 1630.

———. *Kort Verhael wt de voorgaende boecken ghetrocken vande dienste ende nuttigheden*
die desen stadt heeft ghenooten by de West-Indische Compagnie; ende de schaden die de
selve den koningh van Spagnien heeft ghedaen sints haer begin tot het eynde vanden
Jaeren 1636 in *Historie ofte Iaerlijck Verhael van de Verrichtinghen der Geoctroyeerde*
West-Indische Compagnie, zedert haer begin, tot het eynde van 't jaer sesthien-hondert
ses-en-dertich; begrepen in derthien boecken, ende met verscheyden koperen platen ver-
ciert. Leiden: Bonaventuer & Abraham Elsevier, 1644.

Lery, Jean de. *History of a voyage to the land of Brazil* (1578). Translated by Janet Whatley.
Berkeley: University of California Press, 1993.

Loots, Ineke, and Joke Spaans, eds. *Johannes Hoornbeeck (1617–1666), On the conversion*
of indians and heathens. An annotated translation of De conversion indorum et gentil-
ium (1669). Leiden: Brill, 2018.

Mather, Increase (Acrescentio Mathero). *De successu Evangelii apud indos occidentales*
in Novâ-Angliâ: epistola ad cl. virum d. Johannem Leusdenum. Utrecht: Wilhelmum
Broedeleth, 1699.

Montanus, Arnoldus. *De wonderen van't oosten.* Rotterdam: Andries van Hogenhugsen,
1651.

Mooij, J. *Bouwstoffen voor de geschiedenis der protestantsche kerk in Nederlandsch-Indië.*
3 vols. Batavia: Weltevreden, 1927–1931.

Moreland, W. H., and P. Geyl, trans. *The remonstrantie of Francisco Pelsaert.* Cambridge:
W. Heffen and Sons, 1925.

Niemeijer, H. E., and Th. van den End, eds. *Bronnen betreffende kerk en school in de gou-*
vernementen Ambon, Ternate en Banda ten tijde van de Verenigde Oost-Indische Com-
pagnie, 1605–1791. 4 vols./6 parts. The Hague: Huygens ING KNAW, 2015.

Oomius, Simon. *Het geopende en wederleyde Muhammedisdom of Turckdom.* Amsterdam:
Willem van Beaumont, 1663.

Parker, Grant, ed. and trans. *The Agony of Asar: A Thesis on Slavery by the Former Slave,*
Jacobus Elisa Johannes Capitein, 1717–1747. Princeton, NJ: Markus Wiener, 2001.

Pol, Bauke van der, ed. *Mallabaarse brieven: De brieven van de Friese predikant Jacobus*
Canter Visscher (1717–1723). Zutphen: Walburg Pers, 2008.

Polyander à Kerckhoven, Johannes, Andre Rivet, Antonius Walaeus, and Antoine Thysius. *Synopsis purioris theologiae, disputationibus, qinquaginate duabus comprehensa*
ac conscripta. Leiden: Elsevier, 1642.

Rainoldus, Johannis. *De Romanae Ecclesiae idololatria*. Geneva: Jacob, Stoer, 1596.

Relandus, Adrianus. *De religione Mohammedica libri duo*. Utrecht: Gulielmi Broedelet, 1717.

Rogerius, Abrahamus. *Het open-deure tot het verborgen heydendom*. Leiden: Francois Hackes, 1651.

Schroeder, H. J., OP, ed. and trans. *The Canons and Decrees of the Council of Trent*. Rockford, IL: Tan Books, 1978.

Spoelstra, C., ed. *Bouwstoffen voor de geschiedenis der Nederduitsch-Gereformeerde kerken in Zuid-Afrika*. Vol. 1, *Brieven van de Kaapsche kerken hoofdzakelijke aan de classis Amsterdam [1655–1804]*. Amsterdam: Hollandsch-Afrikaansche Uitgevers Maatschappij Jacques Dusseau & Co., 1906.

Teellinck, Willem. *Davids wapen-tuygh ende loose der vromer krijgslieden*. Middelburg: Hans van der Hellen, 1622.

Twist, Johan van. *Generale beschrijvinghe van Indien*. Amsterdam: Joost Hartgerts, 1648.

Udemans, Godefridus. *Geestelick compas*. Dordrecht: Francoys Boels, 1637.

———. *'T geestelyck roer van't coopmans schip*. Dordrecht: Francoys Boels, 1640.

Ursinius, Zacharias. *Schat-boek der verklaringen over den Nederlandschen catechismus*. 2 vols. Edited by David Paraeus, edited and translated by Festus Hommius. 3rd ed. Gorinchem: Nicolaas Goetzee, 1736.

Uythagius, Cornelius. *Anti-Christus Mahometes*. Amsterdam: Joannem Ravesteynum, 1666.

Valentijn, Francois. *Oud en nieuw Oost-Indien*. 5 vols/8 parts. Dordrecht: J. van Braam, 1724–1726. Reprint, Franeker: Van Wijnen, 2004.

Viret, Pierre. *De la vraye et fausse religion touchant les voeus & les sermens licites & illicites: & notamment touchant les voeus de perpetuelle continence, & les voeus d'anatheme & d'execration, & les sacrifices d'hosties humaines, & de l'excommunication en toutes religion*. Geneva: Jean Rivery, 1560.

Voetius, Gisbertus. *Appendicula de precatione ad orientem* in *Selectarum disputationum pars tertia*. Utrecht: Joannes à Waesberge, 1659.

———. *De atheismo*. In *Selectarum disputationum theologicarum, pars prima*, 114–225. Utrecht: Joannes à Waesberge, 1648.

———. *De gentilismo et vocatione gentium*. In *Selectarum disputationum theologicarum, pars secunda*, 579–648. Utrecht: Joannes à Waesberge, 1655.

———. *De Judaismo*. In *Selectarum disputationum theologicarum, pars secunda*, 77–124. Utrecht: Joannes à Waesberge, 1655.

———. *De Muhammedismo*. In *Liever Turks dan Paaps? De visies van Johannes Cocceejus, Gisbertus Voetius en Adrianus Relandus op de Islam*, edited by J. van Amersfoort and W. J. van Asselt, 59–101 (Dutch text), 140–55 (Latin text). Zoetermeer: Boekencentrum, 1997.

———. *De Muhammedismo*. In *Selectarum disputationum theologicarum, pars secunda*, 659–83. Utrecht: Joannes à Waesberge, 1655.

———. *De plantatoribus ecclesiarum*. In *Selectarum disputationum theologicarum, pars secunda*, 552–78. Utrecht: Joannes à Waesberge, 1655.

——. *De praejudiciis verae religionis.* In *Selectarum disputationum theologicarum, pars secunda,* 539–51. Utrecht: Joannes à Waesberge, 1655.

——. *Politicae ecclesiasticae pars tertia & ultima.* Amsterdam: Johannem Jansonium à Waesberge, 1676.

Vossius, Gerardus. *De theologia gentili et physiologia Christiana liber I & II.* Frankfurt: Casparis Waechtleri, 1668.

——. *De theologia gentili et physiologia Christiana liber III & IV.* Frankfurt: Casparis Waechtleri, 1668.

Vossius, Isaacus. *Castigationes ad scriptum Georgii Horni de aetate mundi.* The Hague: Adriani Vlacq, 1659.

[Waeyen, Johannes van der.] *Balthazar Bekkers, en insonderheyd sijner voedsterlingen onkunde, onbescheidenheyd en dwalengen.* Franeker: Hans Gyzelaar, 1696.

Wagenaar, L. J., and Hovy, L., ed. *Ceylonees plakkaatboek: plakkaten en andere wetten uitgevaardigd door het Nederlandse bestuur op Ceylon.* Vol. 1. Hilversum: Verloren, 1991.

Walaeus, Antonius. *Loci communes s. theologiae.* In *Opera omnia,* vol. 1. Leiden: Adriani Wyngaerden, 1647.

Wiszowaty, Andrzey. *Die vernünfftige Religion.* Amsterdam: N.p., 1703.

SECONDARY SOURCES

Abulafia, Anna Sapir. *Christians and Jews in the Twelfth-Century Renaissance.* New York: Routledge, 1995.

Alam, Muzaffar, and Sanjay Subrahmanyam. *Writing the Mughal World: Studies in Culture and Politics.* New York: Columbia University Press, 2011.

Andaya, Barbara Watson. *The Flaming Womb: Repositioning Women in Early Modern Southeast Asia.* Honolulu: University of Hawai'i Press, 2008.

Andel, H. A. van. *De zendingsleer van Gisbertus Voetius.* Kampen: J. H. Kok, 1912.

Andrade, Tonio. *How Taiwan Became Chinese: Spanish, Dutch, and Han Colonization in the Seventeenth Century.* New York: Columbia University Press, 2008.

Antov, Nikolay. *The Ottoman "Wild West": The Balkan Frontier in the Fifteenth and Sixteenth Centuries.* Cambridge: Cambridge University Press, 2017.

Antunes, Catia, Erik Odegard, and Joris van den Tol. "The Networks of Dutch Brazil: Rise, Entanglement, and Fall of a Colonial Dream." In *Exploring the Dutch Empire: Agents, Networks, and Institutions, 1600–2000,* edited by Catia Antunes and Jos Gommans, 77–94. London: Bloomsbury, 2015.

Arasaratnam, S. *Ceylon.* Englewood Cliffs, NJ: Prentice-Hall, 1964.

——. "Protestants: The First Phase 1650–1880." In *Ceylon and the Dutch, 1600–1800: External Influences and Internal Change in Early Modern Sri Lanka,* 13–28. Aldershot: Variorum, 1996.

——. "Reverend Philippus Baldaeus: His Pastoral Work in Ceylon, 1656–1665." In *Ceylon and the Dutch, 1600–1800: External Influences and Internal Change in Early Modern Sri Lanka,* 27–37. Aldershot: Variorum, 1996.

Armitage, David. *The Ideological Origins of the British Empire*. Cambridge, MA: Harvard University Press, 2000.

Arnade, Peter. *Beggars, Iconoclasts, and Patriots: The Political Culture of the Dutch Revolt*. Ithaca, NY: Cornell University Press, 2008.

Asselt, W. J. van. "Amicitia Dei as Ultimate Reality: An Outline of the Covenant Theology of Johannes Cocceius (1603–1669)." *Ultimate Reality and Meaning* 21, no. 1 (1998): 35–47.

———. *Coccejus*. Kampen: De Groot Goudriaan, 2008.

———. *The Federal Theology of Johannes Cocceius (1603–1669)*. Translated by Richard A. Blacketer. Leiden: Brill, 2001.

———. "Motieven en perspectiven in de theologie van Johannes Cocceius." *Kerk en theologie* 41 (1990): 227–36.

———. "Structural Elements in the Eschatology of Johannes Cocceius." *Calvin Theological Journal* 35, no. 1 (2000): 76–104.

———. *Voetius*. Kampen: De Groot Goudriaan, 2007.

Asselt, William J. van, and Paul H. A. M. Abels. "The Seventeenth Century." In *The Handbook of Dutch Church History*, edited by Herman J. Selderhuis, 259–360. Göttingen: Vandenhoeck & Ruprecht, 2014.

Axtell, James. *The Invasion Within: The Contest of Cultures in Colonial North America*. New York: Oxford University Press, 1985.

Baer, Marc David. *Honored by the Glory of Islam: Conversion and Conquest in Ottoman Europe*. Oxford: Oxford University Press, 2007.

Barend-van Haeften, Marijke, and Bert Paasman. *De Kaap: Goede Hoop halverwege naar Indië. Bloemlezing van kaapteksten uit de companiestijd*. Hilversum: Verloren, 2003.

Berkhof, Louis. *Systematic Theology*. 4th ed. Grand Rapids, MI: Wm. B. Eerdmans, 1969.

Bertrand, Romain. *L'Histoire à partes égales: Récits d' une rencontre Orient-Occident (XVIe–XVIIe siècles)*. Paris: Éditions de Seuil, 2011.

Betancourt, Juan Fernando Cobo. "Colonialism in the Periphery: Spanish Linguistic Policy in New Granada, c. 1574–1625." *Colonial Latin America Review* 23, no. 2 (2014): 118–42.

Bethencourt, Francisco. *The Inquisition: A Global History, 1478–1834*. Cambridge: Cambridge University Press, 2009.

Bevilacqua, Alexander. *The Republic of Arabic Letters: Islam and the European Enlightenment*. Cambridge, MA: Harvard University Press, 2018.

Biewenga, Ad. *De Kaap de Goede Hoop: Een Nederlandse bestigingskolonie, 1680–1730*. Amsterdam: B. Bakker, Prometheus, 1999.

Blussé, Leonard. *Strange Company: Chinese Settlers, Mestizo Women, and the Dutch in VOC Batavia*. Dordrecht: Foris, 1986.

———. *Visible Cities: Canton, Nagasaki, and Batavia and the Coming of the Americans*. Cambridge, MA: Harvard University Press, 2008.

Blussé, Leonard, and Ernst van Veen. *Rivalry and Conflict: European Traders and Asian Trading Networks in the 16th and 17th Centuries*. Leiden: CNWS, 2005.

Boetzelaer van Asperen en Dubbeldam, C. W. Th. Baron van. *De protestantsche kerk in Nederlandsch-Indië: Haar ontwikkeling van 1620–1939.* 's-Gravenhage: Nijhoff, 1947.

Boneschansker, J. *Het Nederlandsch Zendeling Genootschap in zijn eerste periode: Een studie over opwekking in de Bataafse en Franse tijd.* Leeuwaarden: G. Dykstra, 1987.

Bono, James J. *The Word of God and the Languages of Man: Interpreting Nature in Early Modern Science and Medicine.* Madison: University of Wisconsin Press, 1995.

Borschberg, Peter. *Hugo Grotius, the Portuguese, and Free Trade in the East Indies.* Singapore: NUS Press, 2011.

———. "Hugo Grotius's Theory of Trans-Oceanic Trade Regulation: Revisiting Mare Liberum (1609)." *Itinerario* 29, no. 3 (2005): 31–53.

———. *The Singapore and Melaka Straits: Violence, Security, and Diplomacy in the 17th Century.* Singapore: NUS Press, 2010.

Bosma, Ulbe, and Remco Raben. *Being "Dutch" in the Indies: A History of Creolisation and Empire.* Translated by Wendie Shaffer. Singapore: NUS Press; Athens: Ohio University Press, 2008.

Boxer, C. R. *The Dutch in Brazil, 1624–1654.* Oxford: Clarendon Press, 1957.

———. *The Dutch Seaborne Empire 1600–1800.* London: Penguin, 1965.

Breman, Jan. *Mobilizing Labour for the Global Coffee Market: Profits from an Unfree Work Regime in Colonial Java.* Amsterdam: Amsterdam University Press, 2015.

Brug, Peter Harmen van den. *Malaria en malaise: De VOC in Batavia in de achttiende eeuw.* Amsterdam: Bataafsche Leeuw, 1994.

Bruijn, J. T. P. de. "Iranian Studies in the Netherlands." *Iranian Studies* 20, nos. 2–4 (1987): 161–77.

Bruin, J. R., F. S. Gaastra, and Ivo Schöffer. *Dutch Asiatic Shipping in the 17th and 18th Centuries: Outward-Bound Voyages from the Netherlands to Asia and the Cape (1595–1794).* The Hague: Martinus Nijhoff, 1979.

Bunge, Wiep van. "The Presence of Bayle in the Dutch Republic." In *Pierre Bayle 1647–1706, le philosophe de Rotterdam: Philosophy, Religion, and Reception, Selected Papers of the Tercentenary Conference Held at Rotterdam, 7–8 December 2006,* edited by Wiep van Bunge and Hans Bots, 197–216. Leiden: Brill, 2008.

Burke, Peter. *Cultural Hybridity.* Cambridge: Polity Press, 2009.

———. *Languages and Communities in Early Modern Europe.* Cambridge: Cambridge University Press, 2004.

———. *Towards a Social History of Early Modern Dutch.* Amsterdam: Amsterdam University Press, 2005.

Burke, Peter, and R. Po-chia Hsia, eds. *Cultural Translation in Early Modern Europe.* Cambridge: Cambridge University Press, 2007.

Burnet, Ian. *East Indies.* Kenthurst, NSW: Rosenberg, 2013.

Callenbach, Jacobus Richardus. *Justus Heurnius: Eene bijdrage tot de geschiedenis des Christendoms in Nederlandsch Oost-Indië.* Nijkerk: C. C. Callenbach, 1897.

Cañizares-Esguerra, Jorge. *Puritan Conquistadors: Iberianizing the Atlantic, 1550–1700.* Stanford, CA: Stanford University Press, 2006.

Carson, Penelope. *The East India Company and Religion, 1698–1858*. Woodbridge: Boydell Press, 2012.

Charnley, Joy. *Pierre Bayle: Reader of Travel Literature*. New York: Peter Lang, 1998.

Chaudhuri, K. N. *Trade and Civilisation in the Indian Ocean: An Economic History from the Rise of Islam to 1750*. Cambridge: Cambridge University Press, 1985.

——. *The Trading World of Asia and the English East India Company, 1660–1760*. Cambridge: Cambridge University Press, 2010.

Chiu, Hsin-hui. *The Colonial "Civilizing Process" in Dutch Formosa, 1624–1662*. Leiden: Brill, 2008.

Clossey, Luke. "Merchants, Migrants, Missionaries, and Globalization in the Early-Modern Pacific." *Journal of Global History* 1, no. 1 (2006): 41–58.

——. *Salvation and Globalization in the Early Jesuit Missions*. Cambridge: Cambridge University Press, 2008.

Clulow, Adam. *Amboyna, 1623: Fear and Conspiracy on the Edge of Empire*. New York: Columbia University Press, 2019.

——. *The Company and the Shogun: The Dutch Encounter with Tokugawa Japan*. New York: Columbia University Press, 2014.

Cohen, Paul. "Mediating Linguistic Difference in the Early Modern French Atlantic World: Linguistic Diversity in Old and New France." Working paper, International Seminar on the History of the Atlantic World, 1500–1825, Harvard University, March 2003, 1–52.

Collins, James T. *Malay, World Language: A Short History*. Kuala Lumpur: Dewan Bahasa dan Pustaka, 1998.

Cook, Harold. *Matters of Exchange: Commerce, Medicine, and Science in the Dutch Golden Age*. New Haven, CT: Yale University Press, 2007.

Dale, Stephen F. *The Muslim Empires of the Ottomans, Safavids, and Mughals*. Cambridge: Cambridge University Press, 2009.

Davidson, James W. *The Island of Formosa Past and Present*. New York: Macmillan, 1903.

Ditchfield, Simon. "Decentering the Catholic Reformation: Papacy and Peoples in the Early Modern World." *Archiv für Reformationsgeschichte/Archive for Reformation History* 101 (2010): 186–208.

——. "Translating Christianity in an Age of Reformations." *Studies in Church History* 53 (2017): 164–95.

——. "What Did Natural History Have to Do with Salvation? José de Acosta SJ (1540–1600) in the Americas." In *God's Bounty? The Churches and the Natural World*, edited by P. Clarke and T. Claydon, 144–68. Rochester, NY: Boydell, 2010.

Dumonceaux, Pierre. "Conversion, convertir: Étude comparative d'après les lexographies du XVII siècle." In *Conversion au XVIIe siècle. Actes du XIIe colloque de Marseille*, edited by Roger Duchene, 7–17. Marseilles: Centre méridionale de rencontres du XVII siècle, 1983.

Durston, Alan. *Pastoral Quechua: The History of Christian Translation in Colonial Peru, 1550–1650*. Notre Dame, IN: Notre Dame University Press, 2007.

Elliott, J. H. *Empires of the Atlantic World: Britain and Spain in America, 1492–1830.* New Haven, CT: Yale University Press, 2006.

———. *The Old World and the New: 1492–1650.* Cambridge: Cambridge University Press, 1992.

Elphick, Richard, and Robert Shell. "Intergroup Relations, Khoikhoi, Settlers, Slaves, and Free Blacks, 1652–1795." In *The Shaping of South African Society, 1652–1840,* edited by Richard Elphick and Hermann Giliomee, 184–239. Middletown, CT: Wesleyan University Press, 2014.

Emmer, P. C. *The Dutch in the Atlantic Economy, 1580–1880: Trade, Slavery, Emancipation.* Farnham: Ashgate, 1998.

Erikson, Emily. *Between Monopoly and Free Trade: The English East India Company, 1600–1757.* Princeton, NJ: Princeton University Press, 2014.

Errington, Joseph. "Colonial Linguistics." *Annual Review of Anthropology* 30 (2001): 19–39.

———. "Indonesian's Development: On the State of a Language of State." In *Language Ideologies: Practice and Theory,* edited by Bambi Schieffelin, Kathryn A. Woolard, and Paul V. Kroskity, 271–84. New York: Oxford University Press, 1996.

Evenhuis, R. B. *Ook dat was Amsterdam.* 2 vols. Amsterdam: W. ten Have N.V., 1967.

Ewing, Michael C. "Colloquial Indonesian." In *The Austronesian Languages of Asia and Madagascar,* edited by Alexander Adelaar and Nikolaus P. Himmelmann, 227–58. New York: Routledge, 2005.

Fisher, Linford D. "Native Americans, Conversion, and Colonial Practice in New England, 1640–1730." *Harvard Theological Review* 102, no. 1 (2009): 101–24.

Franciscus, S. D. *Faith of Our Fathers: History of the Dutch Reformed Church in Sri Lanka (Ceylon).* Colombo: Pragna, 1983.

Freund, William M. "The Cape under the Transitional Governments, 1795–1814." In *The Shaping of South African Society, 1652–1840,* edited by Richard Elphick and Hermann Giliomee, 324–57. Middletown, CT: Wesleyan University Press, 2014.

Frijhoff, Willem, and Marijke Spies. *Dutch Culture in European Perspective.* Vol. 1, *1650: Hard-Won Unity.* Translated by Myra Heerspink Scholz. Basingstoke: Palgrave Macmillan; Assen: Van Gorcum, 2004.

Furber, Holden. *Rival Empires of Trade in the Orient, 1600–1800.* Minneapolis: University of Minnesota Press, 1976.

Gaastra, F. S. *De geschiedenis van de VOC.* Haarlem: Fibula-Van Dishoeck, 1982.

Games, Alison. *Inventing the English Massacre: Amboyna in History and Memory.* Oxford: Oxford University Press, 2020.

Geertz, Clifford. *The Religion of Java.* Chicago: University of Chicago Press, 1976.

Gelderen, Martin van. *The Political Thought of the Dutch Revolt 1555–1590.* Cambridge: Cambridge University Press, 1992.

Gerstner, Jonathan Neil. *The Thousand Generation Covenant: Dutch Reformed Covenant Theology and Group Identity in Colonial South Africa, 1652–1814.* Leiden: Brill, 1991.

Gilbert, Claire M. *In Good Faith: Arabic Translation and Translators in Early Modern Spain.* Philadelphia: University of Pennsylvania Press, 2020.

Ginsel, Willy Abraham. *De Gereformeerde Kerk op Formosa, of de lotgevallen eener handels-kerk onder de Oost-Indische Compagnie, 1627–1662.* Leiden: P. J. Mulder & Zoon, 1931.

Gommans, Jos. "Continuity and Change in the Indian Ocean Basin." In *The Cambridge World History,* vol. 6, *The Construction of a Global World, 1400–1800 CE,* pt. 1, *Foundations,* edited by Jerry H. Bentley, Sanjay Subrahmanyam, and Merry E. Wiesner-Hanks, 182–209. Cambridge: Cambridge University Press, 2015.

Goor, Jurrien van. *Jan Kompenie as Schoolmaster: Dutch Education in Ceylon, 1690–1795.* Groningen: Wolters-Noordhoff, 1978.

———. *Jan Pieterszoon Coen (1587–1629): Koopman-koning in Azië.* Amsterdam: Boom, 2015.

———. *Kooplieden, predikanten en bestuurders overzee: Beeldvorming en plaatsbepaling in een andere wereld.* Utrecht: HES Uitgevers, 1982.

Gose, Peter. "Converting the Ancestors: Indirect Rule, Colonial Settlement Consolidation, and the Struggle over Burial in Colonial Peru, 1532–1614." In *Conversion: Old Worlds and New,* edited by Kenneth Mills and Anthony Grafton, 140–74. Rochester, NY: University of Rochester Press, 2003.

Goudriaan, Aza. *Reformed Orthodoxy and Philosophy, 1625–1750: Gisbertus Voetius, Petrus van Mastricht, and Anthonius Driessen.* Leiden: Brill, 2006.

Greenblatt, Stephen. *Marvelous Possessions: The Wonder of the New World.* Chicago: University of Chicago Press, 1991.

Greer, Allan. "Conversion and Identity: Iroquois Christianity in Seventeenth-Century New France." In *Conversion: Old Worlds and New,* edited by Kenneth Mills and Anthony Grafton, 175–98. Rochester, NY: University of Rochester Press, 2003.

Greer, Allan, and Kenneth Mills. "A Catholic Atlantic." In *The Atlantic in Global History, 1500–2000,* edited by J. Cañizares-Esguerra and E. R. Seeman, 3–19. Upper Saddle River, NJ: Pearson/Prentice Hall, 2007.

Gregerson, Linda, and Susan Juster. *Empires of God: Religious Encounters in the Early Modern Atlantic.* Philadelphia: University of Pennsylvania Press, 2011.

Grell, Ole Peter, and Andrew Cunningham, eds. *Health Care and Poor Relief in Protestant Europe, 1500–1700.* New York: Routledge, 1997.

Groeneboer, Kees. *Gateway to the West: The Dutch Language in Colonial Indonesia, 1600–1950—A History of Language Policy.* Amsterdam: Amsterdam University Press, 1999.

Groesen, Michiel van. "Introduction." In *The Expansion of Tolerance: Religion in Dutch Brazil (1624–1654),* edited by Jonathan Israel and Stuart B. Schwartz, 6–12. Amsterdam: Amsterdam University Press, 2007.

———. *Representations of the Overseas World in the De Bry Collection of Voyages, 1590–1634.* Leiden: Brill, 2008.

Guelke, Leonard. "Freehold Farmers and Frontier Settlers, 1657–1780." In *The Shaping of South African Society, 1652–1840,* edited by Richard Elphick and Hermann Giliomee, 66–108. Middletown, CT: Wesleyan University Press, 2014.

Günergun, Feza. "Ottoman Encounters with European Science: Sixteenth- and Seventeenth-Century Translations into Turkish." In *Cultural Translation in Early Modern Europe,* edited by Peter Burke and R. Po-chia Hsia, 192–211. Cambridge: Cambridge University Press, 2007.

Haefeli, Evan. *New Netherland and the Dutch Origins of American Religious Liberty.* Philadelphia: University of Pennsylvania Press, 2012.

Hägerdal, Hans. *Lords of the Land, Lords of the Sea: Conflict and Adaption in Early Colonial Timor, 1600–1800.* Leiden: KITLV Press, 2012.

Hamilton, Alastair. "From a 'Closet at Utrecht' Adriaan Reland and Islam." *Nederlands Archief voor Kerkgeschiedenis* 78, no. 2 (1998): 243–50.

———. "The Study of Islam in Early Modern Europe." *Archiv für Religionsgeschichte* 3 (2001): 169–82.

Hanks, William F. *Converting Words: Maya in the Age of the Cross.* Berkeley: University of California Press, 2010.

Harris, Stephen J. "Mapping Jesuit Science: The Role of Travel in the Geography of Knowledge." In *The Jesuits: Cultures, Sciences, and the Arts, 1540–1773,* edited by John W. O'Malley, SJ, Gauvin Alexander Bailey, Steven J. Harris, and T. Frank Kennedy, SJ, 212–40. Toronto: University of Toronto Press, 2000.

Hassig, Ross. *Mexico and the Spanish Conquest.* 2nd ed. Norman: University of Oklahoma Press, 2006.

Hayton, Bill. *The South China Sea: The Struggle for Power in Asia.* New Haven, CT: Yale University Press, 2014.

Heering, J. P. *Hugo Grotius as Apologist for the Christian Religion: A Study of His Work "De veritate religionis Christiane" (1640).* Translated by J. C. Crayson. Leiden: Brill, 2004.

———. "Hugo Grotius' De Veritate Religionis Christianae." In *Hugo Grotius Theologian: Essays in Honour of G. H. M. Posthumus Meyjes,* edited by Henk J. M. Nellen and Edwin Rabbie, 41–52. Leiden: Brill, 1994.

Heslinga, E. S. van Eyck van. *Van compagnie naar koopvaardij: Scheepvaartverbinding van de Bataafse Republiek met de koloniën in Azië, 1795–1806.* Amsterdam: Bataafsche Leeuw, 1988.

Heylen, Ann. "Dutch Language Policy and Early Formosan Literacy (1624–1662)." In *Missionary Approaches and Linguistics in Mainland China and Taiwan,* edited by Weiying Ku, 199–251. Leuven: Leuven University Press.

Hondius, Dienke. "Access to the Netherlands of Enslaved and Free Black Africans: Exploring Legal and Social Historical Practices in the Sixteenth–Nineteenth Centuries." In *Free Soil in the Atlantic World,* edited by Sue Peabody and Keila Grinberg, 372–95. New York: Routledge, 2015.

Hostetler, Laura. *The Qing Colonial Enterprise: Ethnography and Cartography in Early Modern China.* Chicago: University of Chicago Press, 2001.

Hovdhaugen, Even. "Missionary Grammars: An Attempt at Defining a Field of Research." In *. . . and the Word was God: Missionary Linguistics and Missionary Grammar,* 9–22. Münster: Nodus, 1996.

Hsia, R. Po-chia. *A Jesuit in the Forbidden City: Matteo Ricci 1552–1610.* New York: Oxford University Press, 2010.

———. "Translating Christianity: Counter-Reformation Europe and the Catholic Mission in China, 1580–1780." In *Conversion: Old Worlds and New,* edited by Kenneth

Mills and Anthony Grafton, 87–108. Rochester, NY: University of Rochester Press, 2003.

——. *The World of Catholic Renewal 1540–1770*. New York: Cambridge University Press, 1998.

Hudson, D. Dennis. *Protestant Origins in India: Tamil Evangelical Christians, 1706–1835*. Grand Rapids, MI: Eerdmans, 2000.

Hunt, Lynn, Margaret C. Jacob, and Wijnand Mijnhardt. *The Book That Changed Europe: Picart & Bernard's Religious Ceremonies of the World*. Cambridge, MA: Harvard University Press, 2010.

Hussin, Nordin. *Trade and Society in the Straits of Melaka: Dutch Melaka and British Penang, 1780–1830*. Copenhagen and Singapore: NIAS and NUS Presses, 2007.

Inventory Classis van Amsterdam van de Nederlandse Hervormde Kerk 1885–1951(–1971). Stadsarchief Amsterdam.

Irwin, Robert. *For Lust of Knowing: The Orientalists and Their Enemies*. London: Penguin, 2006.

Israel, Jonathan I. *Dutch Primacy in World Trade, 1585–1740*. Oxford: Clarendon Press, 1989.

——. *The Dutch Republic: Its Rise, Greatness, and Fall, 1477–1806*. Oxford: Clarendon Press, 1995.

——. "Pierre Bayle's Correspondence and Its Significance for the History of Ideas." *Journal of the History of Ideas* 80, no. 3 (2019): 479–500.

——. "Religious Toleration in Dutch Brazil (1624–1654)." In *The Expansion of Tolerance: Religion in Dutch Brazil (1624–1654)*, edited by Jonathan Israel and Stuart B. Schwartz, 13–34. Amsterdam: Amsterdam University Press, 2007.

Ittersum, Martine Julia van. "The Long Goodbye: Hugo Grotius' Justification of Dutch Expansion Overseas, 1615–1645." *History of European Ideas* 36, no. 4 (2010): 386–411.

——. *Profit and Principle: Hugo Grotius, Natural Rights Theories, and the Rise of Dutch Power in the East Indies (1595–1615)*. Leiden: Brill, 2006.

Jacobs, Jaap. "Jonas Michaelius (1584-c. 1638): The Making of the First Minister." In *Transatlantic Pieties: Dutch Clergy in Colonial America*, edited by Leon van den Broeke, Hans Krabbendam, and Dirk Mouw, 1–36. Grand Rapids, MI: Eerdmans, 2012.

Jacobs, Jaap. *New Netherland: A Dutch Colony in Seventeenth-Century America*. Leiden: Brill, 2005.

Johnson, Carina L. *Cultural Hierarchy in Sixteenth-Century Europe: The Ottomans and Mexicans*. Cambridge: Cambridge University Press, 2011.

——. "Idolatrous Cultures and the Practice of Religion." *Journal of the History of Ideas* 67, no. 4 (2006): 597–622.

Jongeneel, Jan A. B. *Nederlandse zendingsgeschiedenis*. Vol. 1, *Ontmoeting van Protestantse Christenen met andere godsdiensten en geloven (1601–1917)*. Zoetermeer: Boekencentrum Academic, 2015.

——. "Voetius' zendingstheologie, de eerste comprehensieve Protestantse zendingstheologie." In *De onbekende Voetius: voordrachten wetenschappelijk symposium Utrecht 3 maart 1989*, edited by J. van Oort, 117–47. Kampen: Kok, 1989.

Joosse, L. J. "Kerk en zendingsbevel." In *Het Indisch Sion: De Gereformeerde kerk onder de Verenigde Oost-Indische Compagnie*, edited by G. J. Schutte, 25–42. Hilversum: Verloren, 2002.

——. *"Scoone dingen sijn swaere dingen": Een onderzoek naar de motieven en activiteiten in de Nederlanden tot verbreiding van de Gereformeerde religie gedurende de eerste helft van de zeventiende eeuw*. Leiden: J. J. Groen en Zoon, 1992.

Kaplan, Benjamin J. *Calvinists and Libertines: Confession and Community in Utrecht, 1578–1620*. Oxford: Clarendon Press, 1995.

——. "Dutch Particularism and the Quest for Holy Uniformity." *Archiv für Reformationsgeschichte/Archive for Reformation History* 82 (1991): 239–56.

Keene, Edward. *Beyond the Anarchical Society: Grotius, Colonialism, and Order in World Politics*. Cambridge: Cambridge University Press, 2002.

Keuning, J. *Petrus Plancius: Theoloog en geograaf*. Amsterdam: P. N. van Kampen en Zoon, 1946.

Kidd, Colin. *The Forging of Races: Race and Scripture in the Protestant Atlantic World, 1600–2000*. Cambridge: Cambridge University Press, 2006.

Kilpatrick, William Heard. *The Dutch Schools of New Netherland and Colonial New York*. Washington, DC: Government Printing Office, 1912.

Klokke, Marijke J. "Hinduism and Buddhism in Indonesia." In *Worshiping Siva and Buddha: The Temple Art of East Java*, edited by Ann R. Kinney, 17–27. Honolulu: University of Hawai'i Press, 2003.

Klooster, Wim. *The Dutch Moment: War, Trade, and Settlement in the Seventeenth-Century Atlantic World*. Ithaca, NY: Cornell University Press, 2016.

Koekkoek, René, Anne-Isabelle Richard, and Arthur Weststeijn. "Visions of Dutch Empire: Towards a Long-Term Global Perspective." *BMGN, the Low Countries Historical Review* 132, no. 2 (2017): 79–96.

Kok, J. A. de. *Nederland op de breuklijn Rome-Reformatie: Numerieke aspecten van Protestantisering en Katholieke herleving in de noordelijke Nederlanden, 1580–1880*. Assen: Van Gorcum & Co., 1964.

Koot, Christian J. *Empire at the Periphery: British Colonists, Anglo-Dutch Trade, and the Development of the British Atlantic, 1621–1713*. New York: New York University Press, 2011.

Krstic, Tijana. *Contested Conversions to Islam: Narratives of Religious Change in the Early Modern Ottoman Empire*. Stanford, CA: Stanford University Press, 2011.

Kruijf, Ernst Frederik. *Geschiedenis van het Nederlandsche Zendelinggenootschap en zijne zendingsposten*. Groningen: J. P. Wolters, 1894.

Kruijtzer, Gijs. "European Migration in the Dutch Sphere." In *Dutch Colonialism, Migration and Cultural Heritage*, edited by Geert Oostindie, 97–154. Leiden: KITLV Press, 2008.

——. *Xenophobia in Seventeenth Century India*. Leiden: Leiden University Press, 2009.

Kuepers, J. J. A. M. *The Dutch Reformed Church in Formosa, 1627–1662: Mission in a Colonial Context*. Immensee: Nouvelle Revue de science missionaire, 1978.

Labrousse, Elisabeth. *Pierre Bayle*. Vol. 2, *Hétérodoxie et rigorisme*. The Hague: Martinus Nijhoff, 1964.

Lach, Donald. *Asia in the Making of Europe.* Vol. 1, books 1–4. Chicago: University of Chicago Press, 1965–1968.

Lach, Donald F., and Edwin J. van Kley. *Asia in the Making of Europe.* Vol. 3, *Century of Advance.* Chicago: University of Chicago Press, 1993.

Lamping, A. J. "Het Nederlandsch Zendeling Genootschap, oprichting en beginjaren." *Rotterdams Jaarboek,* 1997, 235–56.

Laplanche, Francois. "Grotius et les religions du paganisme dans les *Annotationes in Vetus Testamentum.*" In *Hugo Grotius Theologian: Essays in Honour of G. H. M. Posthumus Meyjes,* edited by Henk J. M. Nellen and Edwin Rabbie, 53–64. Leiden: Brill, 1994.

Lee, M. Kittiya. "Language and Conquest: Tupi-Guarani Expansion in the European Colonization of Brazil and Amazonia." In *Iberian Imperialism and Language Evolution in Latin America,* edited by Salikoko S. Mufwene, 143–67. Chicago: University of Chicago Press, 2014.

Levitin, Dimitri. "From Sacred History to the History of Religion: Paganism, Judaism, and Christianity in European Historiography from Reformation to 'Enlightenment.'" *Historical Journal* 55 (2012): 1117–60.

Levtzion, Nehemia. "Toward a Comparative Study of Islamization." In *Conversion to Islam,* edited by Nehemia Levtzion, 1–23. New York: Holmes & Meier, 1979.

Lieburg, F. A. van. "Het personeel van de Indische kerk: Een kwantitatieve benadering." In *Het Indisch Sion: De Gereformeerde Kerk onder de Verenigde Oost-Indische Compagnie,* edited by G. J. Schutte, 65–100. Hilversum: Verloren, 2002.

Lockhart, James. *The Nahuas after the Conquest: A Social and Cultural History of the Indians of Central Mexico, Sixteenth through Eighteenth Centuries.* Stanford, CA: Stanford University Press, 1992.

Luria, Keith P. "Rituals of Conversion: Catholics and Protestants in Seventeenth-Century Poitou." In *Culture and Identity in Early Modern Europe (1500–1800): Essays in Honor of Natalie Zemon Davis,* edited by Barbara Diefendorf and Carla Hesse, 65–81. Ann Arbor: University of Michigan Press, 1993.

MacCormack, Sabine. "Gods, Demons, and Idols in the Andes." *Journal of the History of Ideas* 67, no. 4 (2006): 623–47.

Mak, Geert. *Een kleine geschiedenis van Amsterdam.* Amsterdam: Uitgeverij Atlas, 1994.

Malalgoda, Kitsiri. *Buddhism in Sinhalese Society, 1750–1900: A Study of Religious Revival and Change.* Berkeley: University of California Press, 1976.

Malcolm, Noel. *Useful Enemies: Islam and the Ottoman Empire in Western Political Thought, 1450–1750.* Oxford: Oxford University Press, 2019.

Malherbe, Vertrees C. "Illegitimacy and Family Formation in Colonial Cape Town to c. 1850." *Journal of Social History* 39, no. 4 (2006): 1153–76.

Marcocci, Giuseppe. *A consciência de um império: Portugal e o seu mundo (Sécs. XV–XVII).* Coimbra: Imprensa da Universidade de Coimbra, 2012.

Mauldon, Margaret. "Introduction." In *Montesquieu Persian Letters,* edited by Margaret Mauldon, vii–xxxi. Oxford: Oxford University Press, 2008.

McGilvray, Dennis B. *Crucible of Conflict: The Tamil and Muslim Society on the East Coast of Sri Lanka.* Durham, NC: Duke University Press, 2008.

Meserve, Margaret. *Empires of Islam in Renaissance Historical Thought*. Cambridge, MA: Harvard University Press, 2008.

Meuwese, Mark. *Brothers in Arms, Partners in Trade: Dutch-Indigenous Alliances in the Atlantic World, 1595–1674*. Leiden: Brill, 2012.

———. "Disciplinary Institutions in the Atlantic World: Consistories." In *Judging Faith, Punishing Sin: Inquisitions and Consistories in the Early Modern World*, edited by Charles H. Parker and Gretchen Starr-Lebeau, 253–65. Cambridge: Cambridge University Press, 2017.

Miert, Dirk van. *The Emancipation of Biblical Philology in the Dutch Republic, 1590–1670*. Oxford: Oxford University Press, 2018.

Mijnhardt, W. W. "The Dutch Enlightenment: Humanism, Nationalism, and Decline." In *The Dutch Republic in the Eighteenth Century: Decline, Enlightenment, and Revolution*, edited by M. C. Jacob and W. W. Mijnhardt, 197–223. Ithaca, NY: Cornell University Press, 1992.

Mitter, Partha. *Much Maligned Monsters: A History of European Reactions to Indian Art*. Chicago: University of Chicago Press, 1992.

Morrison, Karl F. *Understanding Conversion*. Charlottesville: University Press of Virginia, 1992.

Mulsow, Martin. "Antiquarianism and Idolatry: The Historia of Religions in the Seventeenth Century." In *Historia: Empiricism and Erudition in Early Modern Europe*, edited by Gianna Pomata and Nancy G. Siraisi, 181–210. Cambridge, MA: MIT Press, 2005.

———. "Socinianism, Islam, and the Radical Uses of Arabic Scholarship." *Al-Qantara* 31, no. 2 (2010): 549–86.

Mungello, D. E. *The Great Encounter of China with the West, 1500–1800*. 4th ed. Lanham, MD: Rowman & Littlefield Publishers, 2013.

Nagtegaal, Luc. *Riding the Dutch Tiger: The Dutch East Indies Company and the Northeast Coast of Java 1680–1743*. Translated by Beverley Jackson. Leiden: KITLV Press, 1996.

Neill, Stephen. *A History of Christianity in India: The Beginnings to 1707 A.D.* Cambridge: Cambridge University Press, 1984.

Niemeijer, Hendrik. E. "Als een Lelye onder de doornen: Kerk, kolonisatie, en christianisering op de Banda-eilanden, 1616–1635." *Documentatieblad voor de geschiedenis van de Nederlandse Zending en Overzeese kerken* 1, no. 2 (1994): 2–24.

———. *Batavia: Een koloniale sameleving in de 17de eeuw*. Amsterdam: Balans, 2005.

———. *Calvinisme en koloniale stadscultuur, Batavia 1619–1725*. Amsterdam: Academisch Proefschrift, Vrije Universiteit, 1996.

———. "Dividing the Islands: The Dutch Spice Monopoly and Religious Change in 17th Century Maluku." In *The Propagation of Islam in the Indonesian-Malay Archipelago*, edited by Alijah Jordan, 251–82. Kuala Lumpur: Malaysian Social Research Institute, 2001.

———. "The First Protestant Churches on Java's Northeast Coast: A Church Report from Rev. J. W. Swemmelaar, Semarang 1756." *Documentatieblad voor de geschiedenis van de Nederlandse Zending en Overzeese kerken* 5 (1998): 53–73.

———. "Orang Nasrani: Protestants Ambon in de zeventiende eeuw." In *Het Indisch Sion: De Gereformeerde kerk onder de Verenigde Oost-Indische Compagnie*, edited by G. J. Schutte, 127–45. Hilversum: Verloren, 2002.

Nierstrasz, Chris. *In the Shadow of the Company: The Dutch East India Company and Its Servants in the Period of Its Decline, 1740–1796*. Leiden: Brill, 2012.

Noak, Bettina. "Glossaries and Knowledge-Transfer: Andreas Wissowatius and Abraham Rogerius." In *Dynamics of Neo-Latin and the Vernacular: Language and Poetics, Translation and Transfer*, edited by Tom Deneire, 251–65. Leiden: Brill, 2014.

Nongbri, Brent. *Before Religion: A History of a Modern Concept*. New Haven, CT: Yale University Press, 2013.

Noorlander, D. L. "'For the Maintenance of True Religion': Calvinism and the Directors of the Dutch West India Company." *Sixteenth Century Journal* 44, no. 1 (2013): 73–95.

———. *Heaven's Wrath: The Protestant Reformation and the Dutch West India Company in the Atlantic World*. Ithaca, NY: Cornell University Press, 2019.

Ostler, Nicholas. *Empires of the Word: A Language History of the World*. New York: Harper Collins, 2005.

Outram, Dorinda. *The Enlightenment*. Cambridge: Cambridge University Press, 1995.

Pagden, Anthony. *The Fall of Natural Man: The American Indian and the Origins of Comparative Ethnology*. Cambridge: Cambridge University Press, 1992.

———. *Lords of All the World: Ideologies of Empire in Spain, Britain, and France, c. 1500–c. 1800*. New Haven, CT: Yale University Press, 1995.

Parker, Charles H. "Converting Souls across Cultural Borders: Dutch Calvinism and Early Modern Missionary Enterprises." *Journal of Global History* 8, no. 1 (2013): 50–71.

———. "Diseased Bodies, Defiled Souls: Corporality and Religious Difference in the Reformation." *Renaissance Quarterly* 67, no. 4 (2014): 1265–97.

———. *Faith on the Margins: Catholics and Catholicism in the Dutch Golden Age*. Cambridge, MA: Harvard University Press, 2008.

———. "The Moral Agency and Moral Autonomy of Church Folk in Post-Reformation Delft, 1580–1620." *Journal of Ecclesiastical History* 48, no. 1 (1997): 44–70.

———. *The Reformation of Community: Social Welfare and Calvinist Charity in Holland, 1572–1620*. Cambridge: Cambridge University Press, 1998.

———. "Reformed Protestantism." In *The Cambridge Companion to the Dutch Golden Age*, edited by Helmer J. Helmers and Geert H. Janssen, 189–207. Cambridge: Cambridge University Press, 2018.

———. "To the Attentive, Nonpartisan Reader: The Appeal to History and National Identity in the Religious Disputes of the Seventeenth-Century Netherlands." *Sixteenth Century Journal* 28, no. 1 (1997): 57–78.

Pearson, M. N. "Conversions in South-East Asia: Evidence from the Portuguese Records," *Portuguese Studies* 6 (1990): 53–70.

Pomeranz, Kenneth. *The Great Divergence: China, Europe, and the Making of the World Economy*. Princeton, NJ: Princeton University Press, 2000.

Popkin, Richard H. "The Crisis of Polytheism: The Answers of Vossius, Cudworth, and Newton." In *Essays on the Context, Nature, and Influence of Isaac Newton's Theology,* edited by James E. Farce and Richard H. Popkin, 9–26. Dordrecht: Kluwer Academic Publishers, 1990.

——. *The History of Scepticism from Savanorola to Bayle.* Oxford: Oxford University Press, 2003.

——. "Polytheism, Deism, and Newton." In *Essays on the Context, Nature, and Influence of Isaac Newton's Theology,* edited by James E. Farce and Richard H. Popkin, 27–42. Dordrecht: Kluwer Academic Publishers, 1990.

Postma, Johannes Menne. *The Dutch in the Atlantic Slave Trade, 1600–1815.* Cambridge: Cambridge University Press, 1990.

Prak, Maarten. *The Dutch Republic in the Seventeenth Century: The Golden Age.* Translated by Diane Webb. Cambridge: Cambridge University Press, 2005.

Prakash, Om. *The Dutch East India Company and the Economy of Bengal, 1630–1720.* Princeton, NJ: Princeton University Press, 1985.

Prosperi, Adriano. "'Otras Indias': Missionari della controriforma tra contadini e selveggi." In *Americe e apocalisse e altri saggi,* 65–87. Pisa: Istituti editoriali e poligrafici internazionali, 1999.

Rademaker, C. S. M. *Gerardus Joannes Vossius (1577–1649).* Zwolle: W. E. J. Tjeenk Willink, 1967.

Rafael, Vicente L. *Contracting Colonialism: Translation and Christian Conversion in Tagalog Society under Early Spanish Rule.* Ithaca, NY: Cornell University Press, 1988.

Raghavan, M. D. *India in Ceylonese History, Society, and Culture.* New Delhi: Indian Council for Cultural Relations, 1969.

Reid, Anthony. "Early Southeast Categorizations of Europeans." In *Implicit Understandings: Observing, Reporting, and Reflecting on the Encounters between Europeans and Other Peoples in the Early Modern Era,* edited by Stuart B. Schwartz, 268–94. Cambridge: Cambridge University Press, 1994.

——. "The Islamization of Southeast Asia." In *Historia: Essays in Commemoration of the 25th Anniversary of the Department of History, University of Malaya,* edited by Muhammad Abu Bakar et al., 13–33. Kuala Lumpur: Malaysian Historical Society, 1984.

Restall, Matthew. *Seven Myths of the Spanish Conquest.* Oxford: Oxford University Press, 2003.

Ricci, Ronit. *Banishment and Belonging: Exile and Diaspora in Sarandib, Lanka, and Ceylon.* Cambridge: Cambridge University Press, 2019.

Richards, John F. *The Mughal Empire.* Cambridge: Cambridge University Press, 1995.

Ricklefs, M. C. *A History of Modern Indonesia since c. 1200.* 4th ed. London: Palgrave Macmillan, 2008.

——. *Mystic Synthesis in Java: A History of Islamization from the Fourteenth to the Early Nineteenth Centuries.* Norwalk, CT: Eastbridge Books, 2006.

——. *War, Culture, and Economy in Java, 1677–1726: Asian and European Imperialism in the Early Kartasura Period.* Sydney: Allen & Unwin, 1993.

Riemersma, Jelle C. *Religious Factors in Early Dutch Capitalism 1550–1650.* The Hague: Mouton, 1967.

Rogier, L. J. *Geschiedenis van het Katholicisme in Noord-Nederland in de 16e en de 17e eeuw.* 3 vols. Amsterdam: Urbi et Orbi, 1945–1947.

Rooden, Peter van. *Religieuze regimes: Over godsdienst en maatschappij in Nederland, 1570–1990.* Amsterdam: Bert Bakker, 1996.

Rossi, Paolo. *The Dark Abyss of Time: The History of the Earth and the History of Nations from Hooke to Vico.* Translated by Lydia G. Cochrane. Chicago: University of Chicago Press, 1984.

Rubiés, Joan-Pau. "Ethnography and Cultural Translation in the Early Modern Missions." *Studies in Church History* 53 (2017): 272–310.

———. *Travel and Ethnology in the Renaissance: South India through European Eyes, 1250–1625.* Cambridge: Cambridge University Press, 2000.

Rublack, Ulinka, ed. *Protestant Empires: Globalizing the Reformations.* Cambridge: Cambridge University Press, 2020.

Ruymbeke, Bertrand van, and Randy J. Sparks, eds. *Memory and Identity: The Huguenots in France and the Atlantic Diaspora.* Columbia: University of South Carolina Press, 2003.

Safier, Neil. "Beyond Brazilian Nature: The Editorial Itineraries of Marcgraef and Piso's *Historia Naturalis Brasiliae.*" In *The Legacy of Dutch Brazil,* edited by Michiel van Groesen, 168–86. Cambridge: Cambridge University Press, 2014.

Safley, Thomas Max, ed. *The Reformation of Charity: The Secular and the Religious in Early Modern Poor Relief.* Leiden: Brill, 2003.

Şahin, Kaya. *Empire and Power in the Reign of Süleyman: Narrating the Sixteenth-Century Ottoman World.* Cambridge: Cambridge University Press, 2013.

Schalkwijk, Frans Leonard. *The Reformed Church in Dutch Brazil (1630–1654).* Zoetermeer: Boekencentrum, 1998.

Schama, Simon. *The Embarrassment of Riches: An Interpretation of Dutch Culture in the Golden Age.* Berkeley: University of California Press, 1988.

———. *Patriots and Liberators: Revolution in the Netherlands 1780–1813.* New York: Vintage Books, 1977.

Schmidt, Benjamin. *Innocence Abroad: The Dutch Imagination and the New World, 1570–1670.* Cambridge: Cambridge University Press, 2001.

———. *Inventing Exoticism: Geography, Globalism, and Europe's Early Modern World.* Philadelphia: University of Pennsylvania Press, 2015.

Schneckenburger, M. *Vorlesungen über die Lehrbegriffe der kleineren protestantischen Kirchenparteien.* Edited by K. B. Hundeshagen. Frankfurt: H. L. Brönner, 1863.

Schrikker, Alicia. *Dutch and British Colonial Intervention in Sri Lanka 1780–1815: Expansion and Reform.* Leiden: Brill, 2007.

Schuringa, Gregory D. "Embracing *Leer* and *Leven:* The Theology of Simon Oomius in the Context of *Nadere Reformatie* Orthodoxy." PhD diss., Calvin Theological Seminary, 2003.

Schutte, Gerrit J. "Between Amsterdam and Batavia: Cape Society and the Calvinist Church under the Dutch East India Company." *Kronos* 25 (1989/1990): 17–49.

———. "Company and Colonists at the Cape, 1652–1795." In *The Shaping of South African Society, 1652–1840*, edited by Richard Elphick and Hermann Giliomee, 283–323. Middletown, CT: Wesleyan University Press, 2014.

———. "Een hutje in den wijngaard: Gereformeerd Ceylon." In *Het Indisch Sion: De Gereformeerde kerk onder de Verenigde Oost-Indische Compagnie*, edited by G. J. Schutte, 176–83. Hilversum: Verloren, 2002.

Schwartz, Stuart B. *All Can Be Saved: Religious Tolerance and Salvation in the Iberian Atlantic World*. New Haven, CT: Yale University Press, 2008.

Seboek, T. A. *Current Trends in Linguistics: Linguistics in South West Asia and North Africa*. The Hague: Mouton, 1970.

Selwyn, Jennifer D. *A Paradise Inhabited by Devils: The Jesuits' Civilizing Mission in Early Modern Naples*. Aldershot: Ashgate, 2004.

Sheehan, Jonathan. "The Altars of the Idols: Religion, Sacrifice, and the Early Modern Polity." *Journal of the History of Ideas* 67, no. 4 (2006): 649–74.

———. "Introduction: Thinking about Idols in Early Modern Europe." *Journal of the History of Ideas* 67, no. 4 (2006): 561–69.

Shimada, Ryuto. *The Intra-Asian Trade in Japanese Copper by the Dutch East India Company in the Eighteenth Century*. Leiden: Brill, 2006.

Sneddon, James N. *The Indonesian Language: Its History and Role in Modern Society*. Sydney: University of New South Wales Press, 2003.

Somaratne, G. P. V., and G. P. V. Somaratna. "The History of the Sinhala Bible." *Journal of the Royal Asiatic Society of Sri Lanka*, n.s., 34 (1989/1990): 41–64.

Spaans, Joke. "Introduction." In *Johannes Hoornbeeck (1617–1666), On the Conversion of Indians and Heathens: An Annotated Translation of De conversion Indorum et gentilium (1669)*, edited by Ineke Loots and Joke Spaans, 1–34. Leiden: Brill, 2018.

Spaans, Joke, and Jetze Touber. "Introduction." In *Enlightened Religion: From Confessional Churches to Polite Piety in the Dutch Republic*, edited by Joke Spaans and Jetze Touber, 1–18. Leiden: Brill, 2019.

Spicer, Andrew. "Dutch Churches in Asia." In *Parish Churches in the Early Modern World*, edited by Andrew Spicer, 321–60. Aldershot: Ashgate, 2016.

Spierling, Karen. *Infant Baptism in Reformation Geneva: The Shaping of a Community, 1536–1564*. New York: Routledge, 2016.

Steenbrink, Karel. *Dutch Colonialism and Indonesian Islam: Conflicts and Contacts, 1596–1950*. 2nd ed. Translated by Jan Steenbrink and Henry Jansen. New York: Rodopi BV, 2006.

Steenbrink, Karel A., and Jan S. Aritonang. "The Arrival of Protestantism and the Consolidation of Christianity in the Moluccas 1605–1800." In *The History of Christianity in Indonesia*, edited by K. A. Steenbrink and J. S. Aritonang, 99–133. Leiden: Brill, 2008.

———, eds. *A History of Christianity in Indonesia*. Leiden: Brill, 2008.

Steensgaard, Niels. *The Asian Trade Revolution of the Seventeenth Century: The East India Companies and the Decline of the Caravan Trade*. Chicago: University of Chicago Press, 1974.

Strasser, Ulrike, and Heidi Tinsman. "It's a Man's World? World History Meets History of Masculinity, in Latin American Studies for Instance." *Journal of World History* 21, no. 1 (2010): 75–96.

Stroumsa, Guy G. *A New Science: The Discovery of Religion in the Age of Reason.* Cambridge, MA: Harvard University Press, 2010.

Subrahmanyam, Sanjay. "Connected Histories: Notes towards a Reconfiguration of Early Modern Eurasia." *Modern Asian Studies* 31, no. 3 (1997): 735–62.

———. "Forcing the Doors of Heathendom: Ethnography, Violence, and the Dutch East India Company." In *Between the Middle Ages and Modernity: Individual and Community in the Early Modern World,* edited by Charles H. Parker and Jerry H. Bentley, 131–54. Lanham, MD: Rowman & Littlefield, 2007.

———. *The Portuguese Empire in Asia: A Political and Economic History, 1500–1700.* New York: Wiley, 2012.

Sutherland, Heather. "On the Edge of Asia: Maritime Trade in East Indonesia, Early Seventeenth to Mid-Twentieth Century." In *Commodities, Ports, and Asian Maritime Trade since 1750,* edited by Ulbe Bosma and Anthony Webster, 59–78. London: Palgrave Macmillan, 2015.

Swellengrebel, J. L. *In Leijdeckers voetspoor: Anderhalve eeuw bijbelvertaling en taalkunde in de Indonesische talen 1820–1900.* The Hague: Martinus Nijhoff, 1974.

Taylor, Jean Gelman. *The Social World of Batavia: Europeans and Eurasians in Dutch Asia.* 2nd ed. Madison: University of Wisconsin Press, 2009.

Terjanian, Anoush Fraser. *Commerce and Its Discontents in Eighteenth-Century French Political Thought.* Cambridge: Cambridge University Press, 2012.

Thianto, Yudha. *The Way to Heaven: Catechisms and Sermons in the Establishment of the Dutch Reformed Church in the East Indies.* Eugene, OR: Wipf & Stock, 2014.

Thornton, John. "The Development of an African Catholic Church in the Kingdom of Kongo, 1491–1750." *Journal of African History* 25, no. 2 (1984): 147–67.

Tielhof, Milja van. *The "Mother of all Trades": The Baltic Grain Trade in Amsterdam from the Late 16th to the Early 19th Century.* Leiden: Brill, 2002.

Touber, Jetze. *Spinoza and Biblical Philology in the Dutch Republic, 1660–1710.* Oxford: Oxford University Press, 2018.

Tracy, James D. "Dutch and English Trade to the East: The Indian Ocean and the Levant, to about 1700." In *The Cambridge World History,* vol. 6, *The Construction of a Global World, 1400–1800 CE,* pt. 2, *Patterns of Change,* edited by Jerry H. Bentley, Sanjay Subrahmanyam, and Merry E. Wiesner-Hanks, 240–62. Cambridge: Cambridge University Press, 2015.

———. *The Founding of the Dutch Republic: War, Finance, and Politics in Holland, 1572–1588.* Oxford: Oxford University Press, 2008.

———. "Introduction." In *The Political Economy of Merchant Empires: State Power and World Trade, 1350–1750,* edited by James D. Tracy, 1–21. Cambridge: Cambridge University Press, 1997.

Troostenburg de Bruijn, C. A. L. van. *Het biographisch woordenboek van Oost-Indische predikanten.* Nijmegen: P. I. L. Milborn, 1893.

Vandenbosch, Amry. *Dutch East Indies*. Berkeley: University of California Press, 1941.

Vélez, Karin. *The Miraculous Flying House of Loreto: Spreading Catholicism in the Early Modern World*. Princeton, NJ: Princeton University Press, 2019.

——. "A Sign That We Are Related to You: The Transatlantic Gifts of the Hurons of the Jesuit Mission of Lorette, 1650–1750." *French Colonial History* 12 (2011): 31–44.

Verbeek, Theo. "Dutch Cartesians in Bayle's Dictionary." In *Pierre Bayle (1647–1706), le philosophe de Rotterdam: Philosophy, Religion, and Reception, Selected Papers of the Tercentenary Conference Held at Rotterdam, 7–8 December 2006*, edited by Wiep van Bunge and Hans Bots, 21–34. Leiden: Brill, 2008.

Vermij, Rienk. "Ruzie over de antichrist: Cornelis Uythage (ca. 1640–1686) als geleerde querulant." *Studium: Tijdschrift voor Wetenschaps- en Universiteitsgeschiedenis* 7, no. 4 (2014): 209–22.

Vink, Markus P. M. *Encounters on the Opposite Coast: The Dutch East India Company and the Nayaka State of Madurai in the Seventeenth Century*. Leiden: Brill, 2016.

——. "Freedom and Slavery: The Dutch Republic, the VOC World, and the Debate over the 'World's Oldest Trade.'" *South African Historical Journal* 59, no. 1 (2007): 19–46.

——. "A Work of Compassion: Dutch Slavery and Slave Trade in the Indian Ocean in the Seventeenth Century." In *Contingent Lives: Social Identity and Material Culture in the VOC World*, edited by Nigel Worden, 463–99. Rondebosch: University of Cape Town, 2007.

——. "'The World's Oldest Trade': Dutch Slavery and Slave Trade in the Indian Ocean in the Seventeenth Century." *Journal of World History* 14, no. 2 (2003): 131–77.

Visser, Piet. "Mennonites and Doopsgezinden in the Netherlands, 1535–1700." In *A Companion to Anabaptism and Spiritualism, 1521–1700*, edited by John D. Roth and James M. Stayer, 299–347. Leiden: Brill, 2007.

Vries, Jan de, and Ad van der Woude. *The First Modern Economy: Success, Failure, and Perseverance of the Dutch Economy, 1500–1815*. Cambridge: Cambridge University Press, 1997.

Vrolijk, Arnoud. "Arabic Studies in the Netherlands and the Prerequisite of Social Impact—A Survey." In *The Teaching and Learning of Arabic in Early Modern Europe*, edited by Jan Loop, Alastair Hamilton, and Charles Burnett, 13–32. Leiden: Brill 2017.

Wagenaar, Lodewijk. *Galle, VOC-vestiging in Ceylon: Beschrijving van een koloniale samenleving aan de vooravand van de Singhalese opstand tegen het Nederlandse gezag, 1760*. Amsterdam: De Bataafse Leeuw, 1994.

Wall, Ernestine van der. "Mystical Millenarianism in the Early Modern Dutch Republic." In *Millenarianism and Messianism in Early Modern European Culture*, vol. 4, *Continental Millenarians: Protestants, Catholics, Heretics*, edited by John Christian Laursen and Richard H. Popkin, 37–48. Dordrecht: Springer, 2001.

——. "The Religious Context of the Early Dutch Enlightenment: Moral Religion and Society." In *The Early Enlightenment in the Dutch Republic, 1650–1750*, edited by Wiep van Bunge, 39–60. Leiden: Brill, 2003.

Wallerstein, Immanuel. *The Modern World-System I: Capitalist Agriculture and the Origins of the European World-Economy in the Sixteenth Century.* Berkeley: University of California Press, 2011.

Wandel, Lee Palmer. *The Reformation: Towards a New History.* Cambridge: Cambridge University Press, 2011.

Ward, Kerry. *Networks of Empire: Forced Migration in the Dutch East India Company.* Cambridge: Cambridge University Press, 2009.

Welie, Rik van. "Patterns of Slave Trading and Slavery in the Dutch Colonial World, 1596–1863." In *Dutch Colonialism, Migration, and Cultural Heritage,* edited by Geert Oostindie, 155–259. Leiden, KITVL Press, 2008.

Weststeijn, Arthur. "Colonies of Concord: Religious Escapism and Experimentation in Dutch Overseas Expansion, ca. 1650–1700." In *Enlightened Religion: From Confessional Churches to Polite Piety in the Dutch Republic,* edited by Joke Spaans and Jetze Touber, 104–30. Leiden: Brill, 2019.

———. *Commercial Republicanism in the Dutch Golden Age: The Political Thought of Johan and Pieter de la Court.* Leiden: Brill, 2012.

———. "'Love Alone Is Not Enough': Treaties in Seventeenth-Century Dutch Colonial Expansion." In *Empire by Treaty: Negotiating European Expansion, 1600–1900,* edited by Saliha Belmessous, 19–44. Oxford: Oxford University Press, 2015.

———. "Republican Empire: Colonialism, Commerce, and Corruption in the Dutch Golden Age." *Renaissance Studies* 26, no. 4 (2012): 491–509.

———. "The VOC as a Company State: Debating Seventeenth-Century Dutch Colonial Expansion." *Itinerario* 38, no. 1 (2014): 13–34.

Weststeijn, Thijs. "Een wereldse kunst." Paper presented at the Uitgesproken bij de aanvaarding van de leeropdracht 'Kunstgeschiedenis voor 1800,' University of Utrecht, September 25, 2017.

———. "Spinoza Sinicus: An Asian Paragraph in the History of the Radical Enlightenment." *Journal of the History of Ideas* 68, no. 4 (2007): 537–61.

Wickramasuriya, Sarathchandra. "The Beginnings of the Sinhalese Printing Press." In *Senarat Paranavitana Commemoration Volume,* edited by Leelananda Prematilleke, Karthigesu Indrapala, and J. E. Lohuizen-De Leeuw, 287–300. Leiden: Brill, 1997.

Wielema, Michiel. *The March of the Libertines: Spinozists and the Dutch Reformed Church (1660–1750).* Hilversum: Verloren, 2004.

Wilson, Eric. "The VOC, Corporate Sovereignty, and the Republican Sub-Text of *De jure praedae.*" In *Property, Piracy, and Punishment: Hugo Grotius on War and Booty in De jure praedae,* edited by Hans Blom, 310–40. Leiden: Brill, 2009.

Wong, R. Bin. "The Search for European Differences and Domination in the Early Modern World: A View from Asia." *American Historical Review* 107, no. 2 (2002): 447–69.

Županov, Ines G. "Twisting a Pagan Tongue: Portuguese and Tamil in Sixteenth-Century Jesuit Translations." In *Conversion: Old Worlds and New,* edited by Kenneth Mills and Anthony Grafton, 109–39. Rochester, NY: University of Rochester Press, 2003.

Županov, Ines G., and Pierre Antoine Fabre. "The Rites Controversies in the Early Modern World: An Introduction." In *The Rites Controversies in the Early Modern World*, edited by Ines G. Županov and Pierre Antoine Fabre, 1–26. Leiden: Brill, 2018.

Zürcher, Erik. "Jesuit Accommodation and the Chinese Cultural Imperative." In *The Chinese Rites Controversy: Its History and Meaning*, edited by D. E. Mungello, 31–64. Nettetal: Steyler Verlag, 1994.

INDEX